The Bicentennial History
of the Archdiocese of
New York

1808-2008

by Thomas J. Shelley

Dedicated to the

People, Priests, and Prelates

of the Archdiocese of New York

Past, Present and Future

Editions du Signe

Publisher

Éditions du Signe
B.P. 94 – 67038 Strasbourg – Cedex 2 – France
Tel (+33) 388 789 191
Fax (+33) 388 789 199
info@editionsdusigne.fr

Publishing Director
Christian Riehl

Director of Publication
Joëlle Bernhard

Design and Layout
Sylvie Tusinsky

Maps
OM Design

Photography
John Glover

Photoengraving
Atelier du Signe - 106945

© Éditions du Signe 2007
ISBN: 978-2-7468-1945-0

Table of Contents

List of the Principal Maps

Abbreviations

ACHR	*American Catholic Historical Researches*
AAB	Archives of the Archdiocese of Baltimore
AANY	Archives of the Archdiocese of New York
AAStL	Archives of the Archdiocese of St. Louis
ACUA	Archives of the Catholic University of America
ADR	Archives of the Diocese of Rochester
AICR	Archives of the Irish College, Rome
APF	Archives of the Sacred Congregation for the Propagation of the Faith
ARDC	Archives of the Religious of the Divine Compassion, White Plains
ASJC	Archives of St. Joseph's Church, New York City
ASJSD	Archives of St. Joseph's Seminary, Dunwoodie
AUND	Archives of the University of Notre Dame
AUTS	Archives of Union Theological Seminary, New York City
BN	Bibliothèque Nationale, Paris
CH	*Church History*
CHR	*Catholic Historical Review*
CNY	*Catholic New York*
Col. Doc.	*Documents Relating to the Colonial History of New York*
DACH	*Documents of American Catholic History*
DHGE	*Dictionnaire d'Histoire et de Géographie Ecclésiastiques*
EACH	*Encyclopedia of American Catholic History*
ERSNY	*Ecclesiastical Records of the State of New York*
HR&S	*Historical Records and Studies*
JCP	*John Carroll Papers*
LC	Library of Congress
N-YHS	New-York Historical Society
NYPL	New York Public Library
RACHSP	*Records of the American Catholic Historical Society of Philadelphia*
RHE	*Revue d'Histoire Ecclésiastique*
SAB	Sulpician Archives of Baltimore
SAP	Sulpician Archives of Paris
USCH	*U.S. Catholic Historian*

Acknowledgements

First of all, I wish to thank Edward Cardinal Egan, the Archbishop of New York, not only for asking me to write the Bicentennial History of the Archdiocese of New York, but also for giving me access to the archives of the Archdiocese of New York, which were indispensable for accomplishing this project. I also wish to thank Father Joseph M. McShane, S.J., the President of Fordham University, for granting me a faculty fellowship which was an invaluable help in affording me time for research and writing.

I am indebted to all the pastors who responded to Cardinal Egan's appeal to provide me with copies of the published histories of their parish. I am especially grateful to Msgr. William J. Belford, Msgr. Patrick J. Boyle, Msgr. John J. Brinn, Msgr. John J. Budwick, Father Victor J. Buebendorf, Father Matthew Fernan, Father Arthur Mastrolia, Father Peter K. Meehan, Father Robert M. Panek, Msgr. William V. Reynolds, Msgr. Edward F. Straub, Msgr. George P. Thompson, Msgr. George J. Valastro, and Msgr. William E. Williams for answering my questions about the church in their parish or their vicariates.

Every church historian since St. Luke has depended on the work of his predecessors, and I am fortunate to be able to stand on the shoulders of three New York priests who have traveled this road before me, John Talbot Smith, Florence D. Cohalan, and Hemry Browne. The diocesan histories of Talbot Smith and Florence Cohalan are goldmines of information and especially useful for their authors' acute perception of their contemporaries. Henry Browne's parish histories are noteworthy not only for their content, but also for their methodology.

Historians are at the mercy of archivists to preserve and make available to them the raw material of their craft. I have received generous cooperation from Father John Bowen, S.S., the former archivist of the American Sulpicians; M. Irénée Noye, P.S.S., the archivist of Saint Sulpice, Paris; Father Frederick O'Brien, S.J., the archivist of the New York Province of the Society of Jesus; Ms. Patrice Kane, the archivist of Fordham University; Ms. Ellen Pierce, the director of the Maryknoll Archives; Father John Lynch, C.S.P., the archivist of the Paulist Fathers; Brother Luke Salm, F.S.C., the archivist of the Christian Brothers, Manhattan College; Sister Mary Louise Salm, S.F.P., the archivist of the Franciscan Sisters of the Poor; Sister Rita King, S.C. the archivist of the Sisters of Charity, and Sister Jean Iannone, S.C., the assistant archivist of the Sisters of Charity; Sister Catherine Cleary, P.B.V.M., the president of the Presentation Sisters of New Windsor; and Sister Ellen Marie Robarge, R.S.M., the archiviste of the Sisters of Mercy.

I have been able to draw upon the rich resources of the Archbishop Corrigan Memorial Library at St. Joseph's Seminary, Dunwoodie, thanks to the generosity of the director, Sister Monica Wood, S.C., and her able assistants, Sister Kathleen McCann, R.D.C., Sister Kathleen Walsh, S.C., Mrs. Barbara Carey and Mrs. Joanne Crino. I also owe a big debt to Father Jacques Bruyère, S.J., the director of the Centre Kateri, Kahnawaké, Quebec; Father Aldo J. Tos, the pastor emeritus of St. Joseph's Church, New York. City; Father Robert J. DeJulio, the pastor of the Church of Our Lady of Perpetual Help, Pelham Manor, New York; Sister Maria Goretti, F.H.M., Congregational

Minister of the Franciscan Handmaids of the Most Pure Heart of Mary, New York City: Sister Ann-Marie Kirmsie, O.P., of Fordham University and Brother Jeremiah Myriam Shryock, C.F.R.

An unexpected treasure trove in rhe archives of the Archdiocese of New York is an extensive collection of old-fashioned photostatic plates of documents pertaining to the Archdiocese of New York in the archives of the Sacred Congregation for the Propagation of the Faith and the Irish College in Rome. I presume that they are the fruit of the researches of either Peter Guilday or Henry Browne or both, who collected the materials for biographies of Archbishop John Hughes that unfortunately were never written.

I am especially grateful to Father Anthony D. Andreassi, C.O., of the Oratory Church of St. Boniface, Brooklyn; Father John A. Boehning, the pastor of the Church of St. Thomas More, Manhattan; and Father Thomas A. Lynch, the pastor of the Church of Our Lady of the Angels, Bronx, for reading all or part of the manuscript and making many valuable suggestions. As always Father John T. Monaghan of Cardinal Spellman High School not only read the manuscript but also gave me the benefit of his wise counsel and constant encouragement.

I also wish to thank my publisher, M. Christian Riehl, to express my deep appreciation to Mme Joelle Bernhard, the director of publications of Editions du Signe, for supervising the layout and design of the book at every stage of its production.

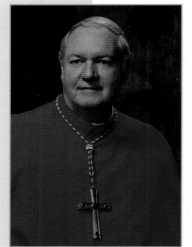

Dear Friends in Christ,

The Bicentennial of the Archdiocese of New York is an occasion of both pride and humility. Certainly, we have reason to be proud of the multitude of parishes, schools, charitable agencies, and other institutions of faith and holiness that have come into being in the Archdiocese and contributed mightily to the welfare of Catholics and others as well in the cities, towns and villages we are privileged to serve. Certainly too, we have reason to be humble. For we recognize that all that has been achieved is ultimately a gift from God. Nothing has been accomplished, or could be accomplished, without His grace and His guidance. Msgr. Thomas J. Shelley's "The Bicentennial History of the Archdiocese of New York" brings all of this to mind. His vivid and insightful telling of the story of the Catholic Church in New York amazes the reader with the wonders that have been achieved. Still, it reminds us that in all that we do, we depend utterly upon the loving providence of the Triune God. Keeping both of these perspectives before us will greatly enhance the pleasure of reading his splendid volume. When people from every corner of the world flocked to this country, they had no idea what to expect. They had uprooted themselves from their native lands where conditions, if not favorable, were at least familiar; and after what was usually a difficult passage, they found themselves in a land that held promise for the future but was often both frightening and hostile. Where would they live? How would they adjust to a new language, new customs and new people? How would they earn a living for themselves and their loved ones? How would they continue to worship their God?

As Msgr. Shelley's history makes clear, it was the parish that provided Catholic immigrants with answers to most of these questions. The parish was the place where they could practice their faith and gain spiritual strength. It was the safe haven where they could gather and adjust to a strange, new world. The Mass, the sacraments, the clergy who came with them, spoke their language, and understood their needs, and the unique sense of community that the parish engendered all gave the newcomers a much-needed sense of security and belonging. Moreover, as populations shifted with the passage of years, the parish continued to be a very special blessing for Catholics, enabling generation after generation to hear the Word of God and live it with courage and self-confidence in an everchanging and ever-challenging world. All of this Msgr. Shelley documents and illustrates with power and poignancy.

"The Bicentennial History of the Archdiocese of New York" focuses as well on three other key institutions of Catholic life that have served immigrants and all of the Catholic faithful over the past 200 years. New arrivals soon understood the value of education and wanted their children to have the best possible schooling so as to make their way in a daunting milieu. They insisted that that education offer the finest in academic training, of course, but also the best in spiritual and moral formation. Hence, with great courage and immense generosity, they created a Catholic school system that is admired across the nation and, indeed, throughout the world. In our own day, Catholic parents continue to sustain Catholic schools in the Archdiocese of New York with an ever-increasing appreciation of their educational excellence and the inestimable value of the religious instruction and guidance they give their students. As a result, as Msgr. Shelley explains, the Archdiocese rejoices in an expanding Catholic school system, which is the largest and certainly among the most outstanding in the land.

No less impressive have been the charitable works of the Church in New York throughout its 200-year history. The vast network of Catholic Charities agencies and programs that are in operation today originated with the refusal of the Catholic community from its earliest years to stand apart while others were suffering in want. Many of those who came to these shores to find a new life were desperately poor and in need of help even to survive. By the grace of the Lord, Catholic clergy, religious and laity came forward in great numbers to assist them with professional skill and total devotion, as they continue to do in our time for thousands upon thousands in need, both newcomers and others as well. In Catholic Charities undertakings and parish operations too, they feed the hungry, clothe the naked, shelter the homeless, care for widows and orphans, aid the mentally and emotionally afflicted, visit the imprisoned, welcome the stranger, and, in brief, fulfill with heroic self-sacrifice the injunction of our God that we hear and respond to the cry of the poor. Msgr. Shelley narrates all of this with charm and in remarkable detail.

Similarly in health care, the People of God of the Archdiocese of New York have much of which to be proud. They established hospitals, nursing homes, clinics and nursing schools to provide the aged and infirm with the best of medical attention; and they continue all of this in our time, guided and inspired by the Gospel of an all-loving Savior. "The Bicentennial History of the Archdiocese of New York" recounts the stories of these undertakings in each era and in each sector of the Lord's vineyard in which we have been called to serve. It is an exciting and compelling tale.

In this extraordinary book, we are inevitably and especially impressed by the saints and heroes who have played key roles in the drama of our Archdiocese. No less moving, however, are the accounts of the clergy, religious and laity who without fanfare or even notice made, and continue to make, the Church here in New York the wondrous community of faith that is it. As we enter our third century, we thank the Lord for all of them and commit ourselves to carrying their work forward with vigor and dedication. May the reading of this splendid volume strengthen and deepen that commitment

Sincerely in Christ,

Most Reverend Edward Egan
Archbishop of New York

1

Death Comes
for the Archbishop

John Carroll, 1736-1815

In the late fall and early winter of 1815 an old man was dying in Baltimore. He did not appear to be suffering from any specific malady that the medical science of that day could diagnose. He was not in physical pain or mental distress. As far as anyone could tell, after seventy-nine years, he was simply dying of old age. He was John Carroll, archbishop of Baltimore and patriarch of the Catholic Church in the United States.

In 1815 John Carroll had been the leader of the American Catholic community for over thirty years, first as the "Superior of the Mission in the thirteen United States," then as the first bishop of Baltimore, and after 1808 as the archbishop of Baltimore. He could take pride in the fact that he had placed the Catholic Church on a firm foundation in the new Republic.

Back in 1808 the Holy See had relieved him of some of his responsibilities by creating new dioceses in Boston, New York, Philadelphia and Bardstown, Kentucky. Six years later, however, the Church in New York had yet to receive its own spiritual leader. New York's first bishop, Richard Luke Concanen, an Irish Dominican living in Rome, never got closer to his diocese than Naples where he died in 1810. For the next five years the pope was a prisoner of Napoleon in France and refused to appoint any new bishops.

In the spring of 1815, however, John Carroll heard rumors that the pontiff, now back in Rome, had appointed a new bishop for New York, another Roman-based Irish Dominican named John Connolly. He received confirmation of the rumors in the summer of 1815 from Archbishop John Troy of Dublin (still another Dominican). The old archbishop of Baltimore waited impatiently for word of Connolly's arrival so that he could hand over to him responsibility for New York.

Bishop Connolly never informed Carroll of his appointment nor made any effort to communicate with him directly. "We cannot account for Bishop Connolly not yet being arrived," Carroll complained to Archbishop Troy. "His diocese is suffering for him; & for its sake it is to be wished that he may come accompanied by a number of zealous, capable and edifying clergymen." In October Carroll heard that Bishop Connolly had gotten as far as Liège (where Carroll himself had been ordained a priest fifty-four years earlier). At that point the trail went dry[1].

Archbishop Carroll was not the only one who wondered what had happened to Bishop Connolly. Two hundred miles to the north in New York City, *The Shamrock,* the local Irish newspaper noted that one ship, the *Sally,* was long overdue from Dublin. "Some apprehensions are entertained for the safety of the ship," the editor wrote. "Among the passengers was the Rt. Rev. Dr. Connol[l]y, the bishop of the Catholic Church in this state."[2]

Meanwhile in Baltimore John Carroll's health took a sudden turn for the worse. On November 22 he made his last will and testament, and on the following day he received the sacrament of the sick, or extreme unction, as it was called at that time. The next day, November 24, the good ship *Sally* finally sailed into New York harbor after a voyage from Dublin that had lasted sixty-seven days[3]. When John Connolly stepped ashore, New York finally had a resident bishop. However, he came alone. There was no sign of the "zealous, capable and edifying clergymen" whom Carroll hoped he would bring with him.

John Carroll died in Baltimore on December 3, 1815. It is not known whether he ever learned that Bishop Connolly had finally reached New York nine days before his death. Whether he did or did not, John Carroll never wavered in his concern for the Church of New York to the very end of his life.

---

1 - Carroll to Troy, [April-?]1815; Carroll to Plowden, June 25-July 24, October 15, 1815; *JCP,* III, 312, 341, 368.

2 - *The Shamrock,* November 25, 1815.

3 - *The Shamrock,* December 2, 1815.

2

Foundations and Loose Stones

Site of Old Fort La Présentation near present-day Ogdensburg.
Credit: *Harper's New Monthly Magazine*, November 1863.

Few bishops have faced such overwhelming odds as John Connolly. The church historian Peter Guilday wrote that "it may well be doubted if in the history of the Catholic Church in the United States any other bishop began his episcopal life under such disheartening conditions."[1] He had at his disposal three churches and six or seven priests to care for a diocese of about 15,000 Catholics that comprised the whole state of New York and the northern half of New Jersey, an area of 55,000 square miles. Today this same area contains two archdioceses and nine dioceses with over 2,000 churches and 6,000 priests for a Catholic population in excess of ten million.

However, John Connolly was not quite starting from scratch in 1815. Others had come before him and had laid foundations on which he could build, although in many instances the foundations were so fragile or frayed that they more nearly resembled loose stones.

The First New Yorkers

The first Europeans had arrived in New York more than two centuries before Bishop Connolly. One was Henry Hudson, the English navigator sailing in the service of the Dutch, who entered New York harbor in September 1609 and guided his little craft, the *Halve Maen* ("Half Moon") up the river that now bears his name. It was a three-masted

Henry Hudson

vessel, eighty-five feet long with a crew of sixteen, half Dutch and half English. They sailed north past the Palisades, the Tappan Zee, Bear Mountain, and West Point as far north as the site of Albany where Hudson invited some Indians aboard and treated them to brandy. Since the river had become narrower and shallower at this point, Hudson turned around and headed back to the Atlantic, disappointed that he had not discovered the elusive Northwest Passage, which was the purpose of his journey.

A few months before Hudson sailed north from New York harbor in 1609, Samuel de Champlain, who had founded the tiny French settlement at Quebec the previous year, headed south from Canada, traveling deep into New York by canoe and on foot. He discovered the long slender lake in northeastern New York that he named after himself. The French leader and his Indian allies deliberately provoked a battle with the Iroquois near the present site of Crown Point. The bow-and-arrow of the Indians proved no match for European firearms. With one blast of his arquebus, Champlain killed two Iroquois chiefs and mortally wounded a third. So began

the encounter between Native Americans and Europeans on New York soil in the summer of 1609, with Henry Hudson serving brandy and Samuel de Champlain firing bullets.

For the next century-and-a-half the Dutch and (after 1664) the English vied with the French for the control of upstate New York. Caught in the middle of the contest between the two European powers was the

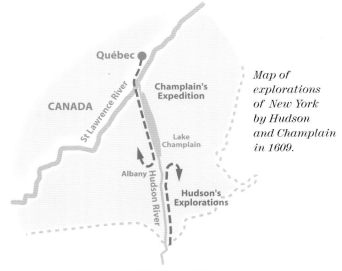

Map of explorations of New York by Hudson and Champlain in 1609.

Iroquois Confederacy, the formidable League of the Five Nations, the Mohawk, Onondaga, Oneida, Cayuga and Seneca. Some twenty-thousand strong, their influence extended from Lake Champlain to the Genesee River and from Lake Ontario to the Susquehanna River. Their presence prevented English expansion into the Mohawk Valley west of Schenectady almost to the eve of the Revolutionary War.

---

1 - Peter Guilday, "Trusteeism in New York, 1815-1821," *HR&S* 18 (1928): 49.

The Iroquois were the vital middlemen in the lucrative fur trade with the Indians of the Middle West that the French conducted from Montreal and the Dutch from Fort Orange (which the English renamed Albany). *Vellen, pelterijen, maertens, vossen* ("Skins, pelts, martins, foxes") were the words used in the report published in Amsterdam to advertise the economic potential of Hudson's voyage.[2] To preserve their own access to the fur trade the French built a string of forts in the Champlain Valley and on the southern shore of Lake Ontario, seeking allies among the Indians to compensate for the scarcity of French settlers.

The lakes and forests of upstate New York became the scene of bloody conflicts between the French and the English such as the surprise raid on Schenectady in February 1690 when the French and their Indian allies massacred some sixty people and carried off others as captives to Canada. The colonial wars with the French kept alive the fear and loathing of Catholicism that the English brought with them from their homeland. It began to subside only with the English capture of Quebec City in 1759, which brought an end to French dreams of an empire in North America.

The fur trade was not the only incentive that brought Europeans to New York. Among the French there was a small group of idealistic Jesuit missionaries who came to North America to convert the Native Americans to Christianity. The exploits of the Society of Jesus, which extended from Acadia to Wisconsin and from Ontario to the Mississippi Valley, are one of the epic stories in the annals of colonial North America. Fortunately the Jesuit saga found a master narrative historian in Francis Parkman,

Map of the extent of Iroquois Confederacy.

the nineteenth-century Boston Brahmin who overcame his innate prejudices to write a compelling tribute to them. Another nineteenth-century Yankee historian, George Bancroft, was so impressed with the scope of their endeavors that he wrote with pardonable exaggeration that in the history of French Canada "not a cape was turned nor a river entered but a Jesuit led the way."

Between 1642 and 1649 no fewer than eight of these Jesuit missionaries died as martyrs, all but one of them at the hands of the Iroquois. Five were martyred in Canada and three in New York. Although the first priest to set foot in New York was probably Father Joseph de la Roche Daillon, a Franciscan Recollect who visited the Indians of the Niagara peninsula in 1626, the story of Catholicism in New York begins with the three Jesuit martyrs in the Mohawk Valley in the 1640s.[3]

Jesuits Along the Mohawk

One of the three, Isaac Jogues, was a priest, and the other two, René Goupil and Jean De La Lande, were *donnés*, laymen who had volunteered to assist the Jesuit missionaries. The first to die was René Goupil. He and Isaac Jogues were captured by a hunting party of Mohawks,

2 - Russell Shorto, *The Island at the Center of the World* (New York: Vintage Books, 2004), 34.
3 - John Gilmary Shea, *The Catholic Church in Colonial Days* (New York: J.G. Shea, 1886), 224.

who dragged them through the forests to their village of Ossernenon (present-day Auriesville) where they confined and tortured them. Goupil was axed to death there on September 29, 1642, for blessing a child with the sign of the cross.

Isaac Jogues remained in captivity for thirteen months and baptized seventy Indians, all of them at the point of death. He escaped with the help of the Dutch, who concealed him for six weeks, part of the time in the fetid hold of a ship in the Hudson River. According to John Megapolensis, the minister of the Dutch Reformed Church at Rensselaerswyck, who befriended Jogues, "his left thumb and several fingers on both hands had been cut off, either wholly or in part, and the nails of the remaining fingers had been chewed off." The Dutch commander at Fort Orange, Arendt van Corlear, placated the Indians by paying a handsome ransom for Jogues and then got him out of harm's way by sending him down the Hudson River to New Amsterdam.[4]

St. Isaac Jogues, S.J.,
Credit: *Archdiocese of New York*

Isaac Jogues was the first Catholic priest to set foot on "the island of Manhattes," as he called the little Dutch settlement that would become New York City. He spent a month there in the fall of 1643. The governor, William Kieft, treated him kindly, but did not permit him to celebrate Mass. A keen observer, Jogues noticed that the inhabitants, who he thought numbered between 400 and 500, had already begin to spread north along the Hudson River. He was told that eighteen different languages were spoken in the colony. The Dutch Reformed Church was the only legally recognized religion, but Lutherans, English Puritans, Anabaptists, and even Catholics enjoyed de facto toleration.

One man came up to Jogues, fell at his feet, kissed his hands and exclaimed, "Martyr, martyr of Jesus Christ." Jogues discovered that he was a Polish Lutheran and regretted that he could not overcome the language barrier to speak with him. In one house he was surprised to see on the mantelpiece statues of the Blessed Virgin and St. Aloysius Gonzaga. The owner explained that his wife was a Portuguese Catholic. Jogues found only one other Catholic in New Amsterdam, an Irish Catholic recently arrived from Virginia, who asked to go to confession to him. Finally in November the governor arranged for Jogues's passage on a ship to Europe that left him stranded in England, but from there he made his way home to France where he arrived on Christmas morning in 1643.[5]

Back in France, Jogues was given a hero's welcome and was received even by the Queen. He could have spent the rest of his life in the comfort of his native land, surrounded with honors. Instead, after receiving special permission from the pope to celebrate Mass with his mangled fingers, Jogues returned to Canada. He made two trips to New York in 1646, first in the summer as part of a French diplomatic mission to the Mohawks. Passing by Lake George on the eve of the feast of Corpus Christi, Jogues named it the Lake of the Blessed Sacrament. At Ossernenon the French emissaries were well treated by the Indians and returned safely to Quebec.

---

4 - Megapolensis and S. Drisius to the Classis of Amsterdam, September 28, 1658, *ERSNY,* I, 436-439.

5 - Jerome Lalement, S.J., "Relation of 1647." in *The Jesuit Relations and Allied Documents,* ed. Reuben Thwaites (Cleveland, 1898), 31: 97-99.

In the fall of that same year, at his own request, Jogues set out once more for the Mohawk country, but this time as a missionary, accompanied by a *donné*, John de La Lande. In the meantime a pestilence had broken out among the Indians, and they blamed it on the presence of a box that Jogues had left behind at Ossernenon. On October 18, 1646, he was murdered with a blow from a tomahawk. The next day Jean de la Lande suffered the same fate. The Indians brought Jogues's missal, breviary and clothes to Megapolensis, who expressed shock that they had killed this innocent missionary.[6]

In 1644, the year after the Dutch rescued Jogues from the Mohawks, they did the same for another Jesuit missionary, Joseph Bressani, who also came to them with maimed and bloody fingers. "We clothed him, placed him under the care of our surgeon, and he almost daily fed at my table," Megapolensis told the officials of the Dutch Reformed Church in Amsterdam. Like Jogues, Bressani was sent back to Europe by the Dutch and then returned to Canada. In 1653 the Dutch at Fort Orange (now renamed Beaverwyck) were equally kind to still another French Jesuit, Joseph Poncet, who had been captured by the Mohawks. In an intolerant age marked by bitter religious strife, the charitable treatment of these French Catholic missionaries by the Dutch Protestants stands out as a rare exception.

In 1649 the blackrobes withdrew temporarily from New York to Canada. In the following decades their missionary efforts among the Iroquois depended on the Indian policy of the French officials in Canada, which alternated between efforts to conciliate the Iroquois or to defeat them militarily. The 1670s were the peak period of the Jesuit missions in New York with at least ten blackrobes at work among all five nations of the Iroquois Confederacy. The Christian Huron captives of the Iroquois remained the core of the Christian Indian population, but perhaps as many as a quarter of the Iroquois themselves also became Christians.

However, in the 1680s the English made a determined effort to win the allegiance of the Iroquois at the expense of the French. Ironically one of the architects of this policy was Thomas Dongan, the Irish Catholic governor of New York. English success and bumbling efforts by the French officials in Canada led to the decline of French influence and the end of the Jesuit missions. By 1709 the last of the blackrobes had left New York, bringing to a close more than a half-century of missionary activity.[7]

Blessed Kateri Tekakwitha

One reason for the limited success of the Jesuit missionaries was the culture shock that conversion involved for Native Americans, who often founded themselves isolated from the other members of their family and people. Although the Jesuits, unlike the Franciscan Recollects, made a serious effort to accommodate Christianity to the native culture, they drew the line at tolerating traditional Iroquois practices like polygamy, dream divination and ritual cannibalism. Perhaps the best illustration of this culture shock is to be found in the life of one of the most famous of all the Indian converts to Christianity, Kateri Tekakwitha. The daughter of an Algonquin mother and a Mohawk Iroquois father, Kateri was born in 1656 in Ossernenon, the Mohawk village where René Goupil, Isaac Jogues and Jean de La Lande had been martyred a decade earlier.

---

6 - The standard biography of Jogues remains Francis X. Talbot, S.J., *Saint Among Savages* (New York: Harper and Brothers, 1935), which draws extensively on the *Jesuit Relations*.

7 - Christopher Vecsey, *The Paths of Kateri's Kin* (Notre Dame: University of Notre Dame Press, 1997), 77-86. A total of eighteen Jesuit priests labored in New York between 1642 and 1709 as well as the two *donnés* who were martyred with Isaac Jogues. For a brief biographical sketch of each, see Thomas J. Campbell, S.J., *Pioneer Priests of North America* (New York: America Press, 1913).

*The oldest picture of
Blessed Kateri Tekakwitha, 1656-1680.*
Credit: *St Francis Xavier Mission, Kahnawake, Canada.*

In 1675 Kateri met a French Jesuit missionary, Father Jacques de Lamberville, in Gandaouagué or Caughnawaga, present-day Fonda, where she was living at that time. He instructed her in the Christian faith and baptized her on Easter Sunday of the following year when she took the Christian name of Kateri or Catherine after St. Catherine of Siena. However, she found it so difficult to live a Christian life among her pagan relatives that within a year of her baptism she fled north to Canada. She walked for two hundred miles until she reached the safety of St. Peter's Mission in the self-governing Christian Indian village of Kahnawake on the south shore of the St. Lawrence River near the city of Montreal.

Surrounded by her fellow Christian Indians, Kateri was now able to practice her religion in peace. Her piety was so impressive that she was allowed to make her first Communion within a year of her conversion, a very unusual practice with Native American converts. Kateri devoted the last three years of her life to acts of charity, prayer, fasting, and other devotional practices. Her penances became so severe, such as walking barefoot on the ice in winter, eating ground glass, or holding a red hot coal between her toes, that her Jesuit spiritual directors grew alarmed and urged her to mitigate them. As Christopher Vecsey has suggested, Kateri and other Christian Indians at Kahnawake were practicing a kind of "syncretistic asceticism." "They wore hairshirts, kept fasts, exposed themselves to the cold, and performed other acts of self-abnegation. They did these things as good Iroquois would," he explained, "hardening themselves against pain, torture and starvation. They now engaged in such asceticism as Christians, combining the native and Christian ethos of self-sacrifice." [8]

In the years after her death at the age of twenty-four on April 17, 1680, Kateri became an object of veneration for Christian Iroquois as well as for French-Canadians. Two contemporary French Jesuit missionaries in Canada, Claude Chauchetière and Pierre Cholenec, were instrumental in promoting her fame both in Europe and the New World. Within thirty years of her death a German Jesuit missionary in the American Southwest was publicizing her sanctity, and in 1724 a biography was published in Mexico City. Native Americans admired her and venerated her as the "Lily of the Mohawks."

However, devotion to Kateri Tekakwitha became widespread in the United States and Canada only in the late nineteenth century. At the third plenary council of Baltimore in 1884 the U.S.

---

8 - Vecsey, *Paths of Kateri's Kin*, 97-98.

bishops approved a petition for her beatification (although the formal cause for her canonization was not introduced in Rome until 1932). Only in the late nineteenth century did it become common to refer to her as Kateri rather than Catherine as way of emphasizing her Native American identity.[9]

On June 22, 1980, Pope John Paul II beatified Kateri, the first Native American to receive this honor. Ironically devotion to her today appears to be stronger among Native American Catholics in the western and southwestern United States than in upstate New York or eastern Canada. The Tekakwitha Conference, the leading national Catholic Native American organization, actively supports the cause of her canonization as a symbol of Native American identity and unity. Her feast day is observed on July 14 in the United States and on April 17 in Canada.

The North Country Missions

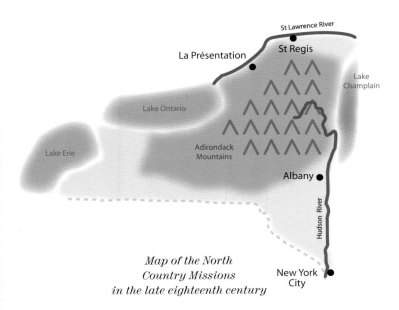

Map of the North Country Missions in the late eighteenth century

Francis Parkman called the Jesuit missionary efforts among the Iroquois a "glorious failure" because relatively few of them became Catholics. Those who did embrace the Catholic faith usually followed the example of Kateri Tekakwitha and moved north to Canada where they settled in the Christian missions along the St. Lawrence River. In the Mohawk Valley and in western New York nothing remained of the Jesuits' effort to establish the Catholic faith among the Iroquois. When European settlers reintroduced the Catholic faith in the early nineteenth century, they had to build on entirely new foundations. However, two Indian missions established by the French in northern New York in the mid-eighteenth century provided a tenuous link between the colonial period and nineteenth-century Catholicism.

One mission was established in 1749 on the south shore of the St. Lawrence River at the mouth of the Oswegatchie River by the Abbé François Picquet, a French Sulpician. He called it La Présentation because the date of his arrival was November 21, 1749, the feast of the Presentation of the Blessed Virgin Mary, the patronal feast of the Sulpicians . Within a few years, it was a thriving Christian Iroquois town of four hundred families. Bishop Henri de Pontbriand of Quebec visited the mission for Confirmation in May 1752, the first time that the sacrament was administered within the present boundaries of New York State.

An avid French patriot as well as a dedicated missionary, Picquet hoped that La Présentation would attract French-Canadian settlers and also serve as a French military bastion against the British. A person not given to self-doubt, he boasted in 1752: "I have succeeded

---

9 - "If you take the French sound of 'Catherine' and try to pronounce it with an Iroquois accent, you end up with something that might well be rendered 'Kateri' by an English speaker." Allan Greer, *Mohawk Saint: Catherine Tekakwitha and the Jesuits* (New York: Oxford University Press, 2005), 193-205.

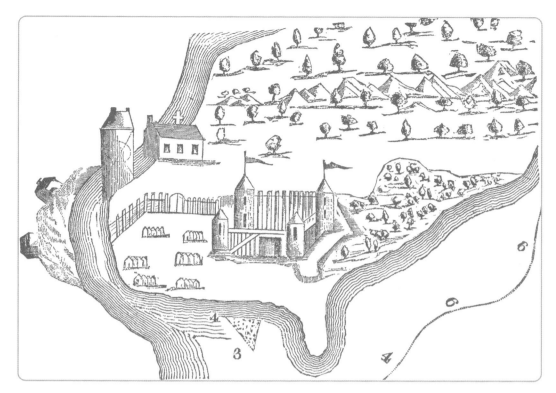

Sketch of Old Fort La Présentation with Abbé Piquet's chapel.
Credit: John Gilmary Shea, *The Catholic Church in Colonial Days*, 616

in establishing within three years one of the most flourishing missions in Canada. I am now in a position to extend the empire of Jesus Christ and of the King, my two good masters, to the extremity of the New World . . . and do more than England or France could do with several millions and all their troops."[10]

Picquet himself volunteered as a military chaplain in the French and Indian War and saw action in western Pennsylvania and in the Champlain Valley. In 1759, a scant ten years after its establishment, the British captured La Présentation and renamed it Fort Oswegatchie. Picquet returned to France the following year, and the Indians were scattered to other missions in Canada. Two dozen Indian families remained in the vicinity of La Présentation until 1807 when they were evicted. Ten years later the village of Ogdensburg was incorporated near the site of the Abbé Picquet's ill-fated and short-lived mission of La Présentation. In the 1880s John Gilmary Shea

noted that the cornerstone of the Abbé Picquet's stone chapel had been recovered and placed on display in Ogdensburg.[11]

The other mission had a happier fate. It was founded by a Jesuit missionary, Father Antoine Gordon, in 1754 at the mouth of the St. Regis River. Although Gordon was a member of the Lyons province of the Society of Jesus, it is not clear whether he was French, Irish or Scottish. Whatever his nationality, he can lay claim to the fact that he founded the last Jesuit mission in New France. It was originally intended for the Catholic Iroquois at the overcrowded St. Peter's Mission at Kahnawake, which had been renamed St. Francis Xavier Mission. Over the years the St. Regis Mission cared not only for the Kahnawake Indians, but also for other Christian Indians, as well as for French-Canadians and for Loyalist Scottish Highlanders from the Mohawk Valley who settled across the St. Lawrence River in Ontario during the American Revolution.

10 - Martin Becker, *A History of Catholic Life in the Diocese of Albany, 1609-1864* (New York: U.S. Catholic Historical Society, 1975), 23-25
11 - *Shea, Catholic Church in Colonial Days*, 618.

In the early nineteenth century Irish immigrants also came to the mission for Mass from nearby Hogansburg, Massena and Malone.

One of the most remarkable pastors at St. Regis was not a Frenchman at all, but Father Roderick MacDonnell, a Scottish priest who died at the mission in 1806 at the age of fifty after twenty-one years of service to his diverse congregation.[12] A man of great physical strength, Father MacDonnell was very popular with the Indians. After his death, they threatened to go to war with the Scots unless they returned his body to them because they wanted to bury him under the little stone church that he had built for them. The church was located in Canada, which caused complications for Americans, who had to cross the border for Sunday Mass. The problem was not completely resolved until 1834 when St. Patrick's Church was built in Hogansburg.[13]

The St. Regis Mission, often known now by the aboriginal Mohawk name of Akwesasne, survives to this day straddling the border between Canada and New York under the spiritual jurisdiction of three dioceses in the United States and Canada, Ogdensburg, Valleyfield and Alexandria-Cornwall. It remains the only continuous institutional link between the Catholic Church in colonial New York and the present day. As late as the 1930s it retained its Indian cultural identity to such a degree that an English-speaking priest said that seventy percent of the Indians "could not sufficiently grasp the truths of our religion in a foreign tongue."

From the mid-1930s to the mid-1960s the pastor of St. Francis Mission was a Mohawk Jesuit, Father Michael Kahrienton Jacobs. In recent years the resurgence of Iroquois nationalism has spurred the growth of the

Old church at St. Regis, which is known today by the Iroquois name of Akwesasne. Credit: *Harper's New Monthly Magazine,* November 1863

12- A native of Glengarry in the Western Highlands of Scotland and a graduate of the Scots College in Valladolid, MacDonnell received permission from the British government in 1785 to go to Canada as a missionary to the Indians and the Glengarry Scots in Upper Canada (Ontario). Ewen J. MacDonald, "Father Roderick MacDonnell, Missionary at St. Regis and the Glengarry Catholics," *CHR 19* (1933): 265-274.

13 - Becker, *Catholic Life in Albany,* 56-57.

Longhouse religious movement, which has weakened the ties of some of the Native Americans to the Catholic Church. In 1989 the pastor of St. Francis Xavier Mission reported that seventy-five percent of the 8,000 Indians still considered themselves Catholics, but only a few hundred attended Sunday Mass.[14]

Thomas Dongan

Peter Stuyvesant

A Catholic Moment in Colonial New York

On August 26, 1664, an English fleet appeared at the entrance to New York harbor. Hopelessly outnumbered and outgunned, the Dutch garrison in New Amsterdam surrendered on September 8, much to the frustration of Peter Stuyvesant, the pugnacious governor. New Amsterdam became New York and Beaverwyck became Albany. The political change would have made little difference to Catholics, who remained as scarce in New York as they had been in New Netherland, except for the fact that the new English proprietor of the colony was James, the Duke of York.

The younger brother of King Charles II, James was well disposed toward Catholics, and he himself became a Catholic sometime in the 1670s. In 1685 he succeeded his brother on the English throne as James II. His reign lasted only three years until the so-called Glorious Revolution of 1688 toppled him from power and drove him into exile in France. Both as proprietor and as king, however, James was responsible for a brief interlude when New York was one of the few places in the entire English-speaking world where Catholics could practice their faith in freedom.

In September 1682 James appointed a new governor, Thomas Dongan, who arrived in the colony on August 28 of the following year. Dongan found that New York lagged behind the New England colonies both in population and wealth despite its natural advantages as the gateway to the interior of the continent. Over the course of the next five years Dongan did his best to remedy the situation.

By any objective standard Dongan must rank as one of the most effective English colonial governors of New York despite the fact that he was not English at all but an Irish Catholic. Born in Castletown, County Kildare, in 1634, he was one of the "wild geese" who fled his native land in the wake of the Cromwellian invasion and served in an Irish regiment in the French army where he rose to rank of colonel by 1674. Called back to England by Charles II, Dongan spent two years as lieutenant governor of Tangier. In New York he made no secret of his own religious convictions, but he also demonstrated a thorough commitment to religious toleration.[15]

One result of the General Assembly that he summoned to meet on October 17, 1683, was a Charter of Liberties and Privileges that the Assembly passed on October 30 and Dongan

---

14 - Vecsey, *Kateri's Kin,* 109-123.

15 - Dongan's father, John, was a member of the Irish Parliament, and his mother, Mary Talbot, was the sister of Archbishop Talbot of Dublin and Richard Talbot, Earl of Tyrconnell and Lord Lieutenant of Ireland under James II. John H. Kennedy, *Thomas Dongan, Governor of New York,1682-1688* (Washington, D.C.: The Catholic University of America Press, 1930), 15.

New York City in 1667 shortly after its capture from the Dutch. Credit: *Archdiocese of New York*

published the following day. It guaranteed freedom of worship to all who "professe ffaith in God by Jesus Christ." Charles II refused to confirm the Charter, and James formally "disallowed" it in 1686 after he became king, squelching any further attempts at representative government in New York. Charles seems to have taken particular offense at the reference to the authority of the people in the Charter. However, the provisions regarding religious toleration were left untouched. When James became king in 1685, he not only ordered Dongan to maintain them, but also to broaden them to include "all persons of what Religion soever." Upon Dongan's request, the crown permitted a group of French Huguenot refugees to settle in New York.[16]

Dongan brought with him to New York an English Jesuit, Thomas Harvey, who celebrated the first Mass in New York City one Sunday in 1683 with Dongan in attendance. Dongan also set up a Catholic chapel within the precincts of Fort James. Two other English Jesuits, Henry Harrison and Charles Gage, arrived in New York soon after. With Dongan's encouragement they opened a Latin school in 1687 in a building at what is now the corner of Broadway and Wall Street. The provincial of the English Jesuits, John Warner, foresaw a bright future for the Society of Jesus in New York. "In that colony is a respectable city," he informed the General in Rome on February 26, 1683, "fit for the foundation of a college, if faculties are given, to which college

16 - *The Colonial Laws of New York* (Albany: James B. Lyon, 1894), I, 111-116. *Col. Doc.*, III, 357-358, 373, 419-420, 426-427. The king's council informed Dongan, "The words The People . . . are not used in any other Constitution in America, but only the words General Assembly." *Col. Doc.*, III, 358.

those who are now scattered throughout Maryland may betake themselves and make excursions from thence into Maryland." [17]

Catholics were a tiny segment of the population, no more than five percent at most. Like most visitors to the colony, Dongan noted the religious diversity of the inhabitants. "Here bee not many of the Church of England," he informed the home government in London in 1684, "few Roman Catholicks; abundance of Quakers preachers men and Women especially; Singing Quakers; Ranting Quakers; Sabbatarians; anti-Sabbatarians; some Anabaptists; some Independants; some Jews; in short of all sorts of opinions there are some, and the most part, of none at all. [18]

Dongan saw no conflict between his political responsibilities and his religious convictions. He vigorously asserted English claims to upstate New York, demanding that the French recognize the St. Lawrence River and Lake Ontario as the boundary between Canada and New York. The key to gaining effective control of central and western New York was to win the allegiance of the Iroquois, whom Dongan described as "the most warlike people in America." Dongan was convinced that the French were using the Jesuit missionaries as "a stalking horse" to establish their political domination of upstate New York. [19]

His solution was to bring English Jesuits to New York to replace the French Jesuits. He even hoped to lure Christian Iroquois back from the Christian missions in Canada by setting aside land for them near Schenectady and promising to provide them with a church and priest. [20] For most of Dongan's five years as governor his counterpart in Canada was the Marquis de Denonville. Their correspondence began with an exchange of pleasantries but it ended in bitter recriminations with the Frenchman often on the receiving end of Dongan's caustic Irish wit. Denonville initially tried to win Dongan's goodwill by alluding to his service in the French army. In reply, Dongan coolly informed him that Louis XIV still owed him 25,000 *livres* in back pay and asked him to collect it for him. Dongan rejected point blank Denonville's claim that the activities of the French Jesuits gave France a legitimate title to upstate New York. Dongan mentioned that he heard that that "the King of China never goes anywhere without two Jesuits with him" "I wonder you make not the like pretence to that Kingdome," he added tongue in cheek. [21]

In August 1688 Thomas Dongan suffered the same fate as many other loyal servants of the notoriously ungrateful Stuarts. James II dismissed him as governor and replaced him with Sir Edmund Andros, whom he commissioned to amalgamate New Jersey, New York and New England into a super colony, the Dominion of New England. He also instructed Andros to "permit a liberty of conscience to all persons." [22] Dongan retired to his estate at Lake Success on Long Island. Three months later the Glorious Revolution in England swept James from the throne. When the news reached New York early in the following year, Jacob Leisler led a populist revolt which unleashed a panic fear of popery that has been likened to the popular hysteria against witches in contemporary Salem. Dongan fled for his life, first to Massachusetts, and finally to London where he arrived in 1691. Although he inherited the title of Earl of Limerick in 1698, he fought a fruitless battle to regain his confiscated family lands in Ireland and died in England on December 14, 1715.

---

17 - Foley, *Records of the English Province of the Society of Jesus,* VII, 343.

18 - *Col Doc.,* III, 415; Jason Duncan, " 'A Most Democratic Class': New York Catholics and the Early American Republic," Ph.D. diss., University of Iowa, 1999," 22.

19 - Dongan to Lord President of the Council, February 19, 1687, Col. Doc., III, 453, 511.

20 - *Col Doc.,* III, 394.

21 - *Col Doc.,* III, 456-458, 460-461, 465, 472-475.

22 - *Col Doc.,* 546.

The Citadel at Quebec City, the center of the French Empire in North America

No Priest Land

With the breakdown of the royal government in New York following the Glorious Revolution, Leisler and his followers ruled the colony for the better part of the next two years. They dismissed Catholic officials, closed the chapel and Latin school, and forced the Jesuits to flee for their life. When the new royal governor, Henry Sloughter, arrived in New York in March of 1691, he promptly arrested Leisler and seven of his confederates, not because of their persecution of Catholics, but because they were perceived as a threat to the propertied classes. Leisler and his son-in-law Jacob Milbourne were hanged on May 16, 1691, but their execution did not put an end to the harassment of Catholics. In fact, three days before the execution, the government amended the religious toleration provisions of the Charter of 1683 to exclude "any person of the Romish Religion," which was in keeping with the instructions that Sloughter had brought with him from England.[23]

In 1691 William III ordered the enforcement of the Test Act in New York, which required all office holders to abjure their belief in transubstantiation and the veneration of the Blessed Virgin Mary and the saints. Five years later the mayor of New York City reported that he could find no more than ten men in New York City who were Catholics.[24] In 1700 the new governor, Richard Coote, Lord Bellomont, was determined to make that situation permanent. At his behest the Provincial Assembly passed an Act Against Jesuits and Popish Priests with the penalty of life imprisonment for any Catholic priest who set foot in the colony. Further provisions of the law

---

23 - *Col Doc.,* III, 689; Duncan, " 'A Most Democratic Class,' " 44.
24 - *ERSNY,* II, 1012-1013; *ACHR* 5 (1888): 93.

entailed the death penalty for any priest who escaped and returned as well as heavy fines for lay people who sheltered priests. The law remained in force for eighty years, as long as New York remained an English colony.[25]

For the most of the eighteenth century the history of Catholics in New York is a blank. Despite the absence of Catholics, however, fear of Popery remained very much alive. This became abundantly clear in 1741 when a series of mysterious fires in New York City led to rumors of an impending slave rebellion. James Oglethorpe, the governor of Georgia, added to the apprehensions of New Yorkers when he urged colonial officials to beware of Spanish priests who had been sent to the English colonies to burn down their cities.

The Hudson Highlands near Newburgh.
Credit: *Harper's New Monthly Magazine,* January 1858

In the ensuing panic African Americans and Catholics were linked together as co-conspirators in the popular imagination. Daniel Horsmanden, the judge who presided at the trial of the alleged perpetrators, made the same connection, noting ominously that the first fires had started on the evening of St. Patrick's Day. An effort was made to link the fires to four British soldiers in the local garrison who happened to be named Ryan, Connolly, Kelly, and Murphy. They were exonerated for lack of witnesses, but others were not as fortunate. Before the hysteria subsided, seventeen African Americans and four whites were hanged, and thirteen African Americans were burned to death. Among the victims was John Ury, an innocent Anglican clergyman who was mistaken for a Catholic priest. Apparently he was the only one ever executed under the Anti-Priest Law of 1700.[26]

If Catholics did not actually become extinct in New York in the middle of the eighteenth century, they certainly became an endangered species, who survived as isolated individuals, not as members of an organized community. Perhaps there were others like John Leary, the owner of a livery stable on Cortland Street. He attended services at Trinity Church on Sunday, but went to Philadelphia once a year to fulfill his Easter duty. He became a parishioner of St. Peter's Church, New York City's first Catholic church, when it was opened in 1786. William Mooney is another example of an Irish Catholic who attended Trinity Church until the erection of St. Peter's and then became a parishioner there. An upholsterer with a shop on William Street, he is best remembered as the founder of the Society of Tammany or Columbian Order.[27]

25 - *Colonial Laws of New York*, I, 429-430.

26 - "The Trial of John Ury," *ACHR* 16 (1899): 1-53. The most recent study of the events of 1741 is Jill Lepore, *New York Burning* (New York: Knopf, 2005).

27 - Michael J. O'Brien, *In Old New York: The Irish Dead in Trinity and St. Paul's Churchyards* (New York: The American Irish Historical Society, 1928), 10-13.

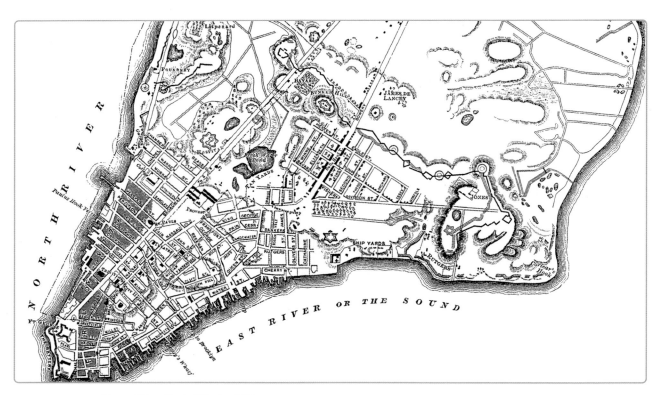

Map of New York City in 1782

The Coming of the Revolution

There is a tradition that in the late 1770s Catholics met secretly in New York City to attend Mass celebrated by Father Ferdinand Steinmeyer, a German-born Jesuit better known as Father Farmer, who made trips from Pennsylvania for that purpose. However, there is no solid evidence that Father Farmer visited New York prior to the Revolution. The earliest reference that he makes to a visit to New York was in October 1781 when he baptized fourteen children in Fishkill. By that time Fishkill was in the hands of the American rebels. As long as New York City and its environs remained under British control, it remained No Priest Land[28].

Catholics in New York had little reason to expect any improvement in their condition as long as they continued to live under British rule. As late as 1771, when William Tryon, the last royal governor was dispatched to New York, his instructions included an order "to permit a liberty of conscience to all persons, except Papists."[29] On the other hand, as the Thirteen Colonies moved closer to armed insurrection against Great Britain in the mid-1770s, American Catholics had little reason to expect that they would receive more favorable treatment from the Patriots, if they were successful in overturning British rule. Most Americans shared the same ingrained suspicion of Catholics as their English cousins. Neither the Loyalists nor the Patriots showed the

28 - William Harper Bennett, *Catholic Footsteps in Old New York* (New York: U.S. Catholic Historical Society, 1909), 249; John F. Quinn, S.J., "Father Ferdinand Farmer," *HR&S* 6:2 (1913): 238.

29 - *Journals of the Provincial Congress, Convention, Committee of Safety and Council of Safety of the State of New York, 1775-1776-1777* (Albany: Thurlow Weed, 1842), I, 542.

slightest disposition to welcome Catholic support or to offer them any concessions. As a result, wrote Charles Metzger, as the coming of the Revolution forced Americans to take sides for or against the Patriot cause, "no other religious community found the choice so difficult."[30]

The Patriots' hostility to Catholics was intensified when the British parliament passed the Quebec Act in 1774. That legislation awarded the vast area beyond the Appalachian Mountains to Canada and gave religious toleration to the French-Canadian Catholics. In New York the reaction to the Quebec Act was as hostile as in the rest of the colonies. Young Alexander Hamilton, still a student at King's College (today's Columbia University), published an anonymous pamphlet in 1774 in which he exclaimed, "Does it not make your blood run cold to think that an English parliament should pass an Act for the establishment of arbitrary power and Popery in such an extensive country?" "If they had any regard for the freedom and happiness of mankind, they would never have done it," he declared.[31]

Philip Livingston, another young Patriot about to represent New York in the Continental Congress, raised the same alarm. He deplored the Quebec Act because he claimed that it established in that colony "the most horrible religious tyranny that my mind is capable of conceiving." He probably expressed the feelings of many of his fellow New Yorkers, whether they were Patriots or Loyalists, Christians or Deists, when he drew a sharp distinction between

Alexander Hamilton

Protestantism and Catholicism. "Protestantism is the tender child of freedom and science," he wrote. "How then can it exist in the bold bosom of ignorant despotism?"[32]

On the eve of the Revolution anti-Catholic sentiment in New York was not confined to the political and intellectual elite. It found popular expression in the local General Committee of Association, which presented a protest to Lieutenant Governor Cadwallader Colden in May 1775 against the establishment of popery in Canada. However, the New York Patriots tried to play the same double game with the French-Canadians as the Continental Congress. Less than a month after this protest the members of the First New York Provincial Congress invited the French-Canadians to join them in a common alliance against Great Britain. In an address written by Philip Livingston, the quondan critic of the Quebec Act, they assured the French-Canadians: "We consider you as our friends, and we feel for you the affection of brothers." The Canadians were as skeptical about this overture from New York as they were about the similar appeal from the Continental Congress a year earlier.[33]

Catholics as Patriots

Despite the outburst of anti-Catholic feeling occasioned by the Quebec Act, Catholics overwhelmingly supported the Revolution. In Maryland, the colonial heartland of American Catholicism, Charles Carroll of Carrolltown, the

30 - Charles H. Metzger, S.J., *Catholics and the American Revolution* (Chicago: Loyola University Press, 1962), 275.

31 - Alexander Hamilton, *A Full Vindication of the Measures of the Congress from the Calumnies of their Enemies* (New York: James Rivington, 1774), 16.

32 - Philip Livingston, *The Other Side of the Question* (New York: James Rivington, 1774), 23-24.

33 - General Committee of Association of the City and County of New York to Cadwallader Colden, May 11, 1775, *American Archives*, 4th series, II, 534; "Address of the Provincial Congress at New York to the Inhabitants of the Province of Quebec", June 2, 1775, *ACHR*, 9 (1892): 11.

wealthiest man in the thirteen colonies (according to John Adams), signed the Declaration of Independence, while his cousins Daniel and Father John Carroll threw their support to the Patriot cause. In Philadelphia, the first urban Catholic center in America, wealthy businessmen like Stephen Moylan, George Meade and Thomas FitzSimons, did the same. John Barry, a sea captain, became the first American to capture a British warship.

Pierre Gibault, a French-Canadian diocesan priest, helped George Rogers Clark, to secure the vast trans-Appalachian West for the Americans. In 1776, at the request of the Continental Congress, John and Charles Carroll accompanied Benjamin Franklin and Samuel Chase on a mission to Montreal in a vain attempt to obtain French-Canadian support for the revolution. They stopped briefly in New York City and witnessed the city preparing for a British invasion. This diplomatic mission to Canada, the first in the nation's history, was a failure. With the hostile American reaction to the Quebec Act fresh in their memory, the French-Canadians, led by Bishop Jean-Olivier Briand of Quebec, once again rebuffed the American overtures. As far as Catholic support of the Revolution was concerned, however, a far most significant development occurred two years later when France entered the conflict as the ally of the Americans, and Spain followed suit the next year.

As a result of the participation of American Catholics in the war effort, and the French and Spanish alliance, there was a massive change in attitude toward Catholics among Patriots throughout the colonies. George Washington forbade the celebration of Pope's Day by the army on November 5 because of its traditional anti-Catholic festivities. Members of Congress attended services at St. Mary's Church in Philadelphia as a body on four different occasions, two of them requiem Masses for French and Spanish diplomats. A scrupulous Benjamin Rush politely declined the invitation to one of the requiem Masses on the grounds that his presence would be "incompatible with the principles of a Protestant."

Catholics in New York City gained little immediate benefit from this new spirit of toleration because the British invaded and occupied the city in September 1776. The British armada that appeared off Sandy Hook consisted of over 400 ships with 1,200 cannon. On board were 32,000 troops and 4,000 seamen, the greatest military force ever gathered in the colonies and the largest overseas expedition ever mounted by Great Britain up to that date. "I could not believe my eyes," said an American lookout on Staten Island. "I declare that I thought all London was afloat."[34]

In a series of battles for control of New York City between September and November 1776 the Americans suffered heavy casualties---over 600 dead and 4,000 prisoners---as well as the loss of much of their equipment and supplies. General Washington was lucky to escape across the Hudson with the remnants of the Continental army. Meanwhile, New York City became a mecca for Loyalists from upstate and the neighboring colonies. The anti-Catholic laws remained in effect, including the Anti-Priest Law of 1700, as Father Henry de la Motte, a captured French Catholic navy chaplain, discovered to his cost. He had been released on parole in the city and was asked by some Catholics to celebrate Mass for them. Father de la Motte asked permission from the British authorities, who turned down his request. He either misunderstood the answer or ignored it and was clapped in jail for violating the law.

34 - Edwin G. Burrows and Mike Wallace, Gotham: *A History of New York City to 1898* (New York: Oxford University Press, 1999), 230, 234-235.

As the Patriots warmed up to Catholics, especially after the conclusion of the French alliance, the British and their Tory allies tried to exploit it to their own advantage by fomenting anti-Catholic sentiment. In British-occupied New York City the Tory press had a field day heaping ridicule on the volte face of the rebels. James Rivington's *Royal Gazette* accused them of hypocrisy for claiming that they had taken up arms against "our gracious King" to prevent him from introducing popery to America when they had now formed a solemn league and covenant with the French king for that very purpose.

The *Gazette* predicted that a rebel victory would lead to the destruction of the Protestant Church in America and its re-placement by the Popish Church. Another writer blamed the war on the Presbyterians who had been frustrated in their attempt to suppress the Church of England in the colonies and had now joined forces with the papists to accomplish what they had been unable to do alone.[35]

John Gilmary Shea

For those who found the byzantine logic of that argument too difficult to follow, James Rivington offered a nightmarish glimpse of how America would fare if the rebels won the war and allowed their popish allies to establish the Catholic Church. The *Royal Gazette* claimed that Spanish ships were ready to sail to America loaded with

> 50 tons of holy water for the use of the soldiers, 400 casks of consecrated oil for extreme unction; 10,000 cuts of various saints with brief accounts of the miracles worked by

their reliques and at their shrines; 20,000 hair shirts, cowls and scourges and hempen girdles for the use of the religious orders to be established immediately; 3,000 wheels, hooks, pincers, knives, shackles and fire brands for the use of the Inquisition in converting heretics; 10,000 copies of a treatise called *Wholesome Revelries or the Necessity of Extirpating Heretics;* 1,000 bales of indulgences; 20,000 copies of the Pope's Bull of Absolution of the French and Spanish armies for the massacres, burning of hospitals, butchering of infants, rapes and other crimes and cruelties committed in the reduction of Great Britain.[36]

John Gilmary Shea, the pioneer American Catholic historian, once claimed in a flight of fancy that every American Catholic without exception supported the revolution. "The Catholics spontaneously, universally, and energetically gave their adhesion to the cause of America," he boasted. "There were no Catholic Tories." It was an exaggeration that Shea must have known was inaccurate, but it indicated how desperate American Catholics were to demonstrate their patriotism a century ago. In fact the British enjoyed some limited success when they attempted to recruit Irish Catholic soldiers in both Philadelphia and New York City.[37]

The British scored their greatest success in upstate New York where several hundred Highland Scottish Catholics remained staunch Loyalists. Recent arrivals in America, the Scots were refugees from rack-renting landlords. They had been required to take an oath of allegiance to King George III before leaving their homeland.

---

35 - *Royal Gazette,* June 20, 1778, October 7, 1778.

26 - *Royal Gazette,* January 29, 1780.

37 - Martin I.J. Grffin, "Catholic Loylalists of the Revolution," *ACHR 6* (1889): 77-88.

They had settled in the Mohawk Valley under the patronage of Sir William Johnson, an Irish-born Tory land speculator, Indian agent and self-promoter who owned a half-million acres of New York real estate.

At the outset of the Revolution, the Scots were disarmed by Patriot troops dispatched from Albany. Together with their Irish chaplain, Father John MacKenna, the Scots fled to Canada where they settled in Ontario across the St. Lawrence River from the St. Regis Indian Mission. Some of them joined the British army in Canada and participated in Colonel Barry St. Leger's invasion of New York and attack on Fort Stanwix in 1777.[38]

Papists as Quasi-Citizens

While New York City remained firmly under British control until the end of the war, the Patriot leaders outside the city set about the task of devising a post-war government for the state.

The framers of the Constitution of 1777 included some of New York's leading families, many of them connected by ties of blood or marriage, like Robert Livingston, Philip Livingston, Gouverneur Morris, Philip Schulyer, Alexander Hamilton and George Clinton.

Unfortunately for New York Catholics the state's Founding Fathers also included John Jay whose hatred of popery amounted to an obsession. He was at the beginning of a long and successful political career that would lead to his selection as the first chief justice of the U.S. Supreme Court. Jay once confided to a friend that he wished "to erect a wall of brass around the country for the exclusion of Catholics."[39]

The thirty-year old Jay got the opportunity to do so as the principal author of the first draft of the state constitution. His antipathy to Catholics can be traced to the persecution that his Huguenot ancestors experienced in France after the revocation of the Edict of Nantes. That resentment was not at all assuaged by the fact that his grandfather, a refugee from the bigotry of Louis XIV, found a safe haven in New York thanks to the tolerance of Thomas Dongan and King James II.

The State Constitution of 1777 declared that the Convention, "in the name and by the authority of the good people of this State, ordain, determine and declare that the free exercise and enjoyment of religious profession and worship, without discrimination or preference, shall forever hereafter be allowed within this State to all mankind." John Jay was not pleased with this blanket declaration of religious liberty. He wanted it amended to read "except the professors of the religion of the Church of Rome." The Convention rejected Jay's amendment by a vote of 19 to 10 on March 20, 1777.[40]

However, the resourceful Mr. Jay was not yet finished. Foiled in his attempt to deny religious toleration to Catholics, he now attempted to restrict their civil rights by requiring all office holders to take an oath to abjure all foreign jurisdictions, ecclesiastical as well political. This maneuver also failed because the state constitution did not prescribe any official oath for office holders. Jay then turned his attention to the naturalization of immigrants, and here he was successful in making it impossible for conscientious foreign-born Catholics to attain the full rights of citizenship.

---

38 - Richard K. McMaster, S.J., "Parish in Arms: A Study of Father John MacKenna and the Mohawk Valley Loyalists, 1773-1778," *HR&S 45* (1957): 107-126.

39 - Max M. Mintz, *Gouverneur Morris and the American Revolution* (Norman: Oklahoma University Press, 1970), 75.

40 - *Journals of the Provincial Congress,* I, 185-186, 544-545, 549.

At his instigation an amendment was added to the state constitution requiring all immigrants who wished to become citizens to take an oath to "abjure and renounce all allegiance and subjection to all or every foreign king, prince, potentate and state, in all matters ecclesiastical as well as civil." The Convention approved it by a vote of 24 to 9. In case there was any doubt that this legislation was directed at Catholics, Jay wished to add a rider (which was rejected) specifically excluding from its provisions the "innocent connections" of the Dutch and all non-Episcopalian congregations in New York with their mother churches in Europe.[41]

John Jay

and State, in all matters ecclesiastical as well as civil, and that I will bear faith and true allegiance to the State of New York.[42]

The law remained in effect for the next thirty years as a pointed reminder to Catholics that most of their fellow New Yorkers were reluctant to extend the full benefits of citizenship to them. Jason Duncan summed up the situation neatly. "It was convenient for New York to grant religious liberty to Catholics in the abstract," he wrote, "and then erect legal barriers to discourage Catholics from entering the state and deny full citizenship to those Catholics already living there."[43]

The state naturalization law remained on the books for a dozen years and was never repealed. It lapsed in 1789 when the new constitution gave the federal government jurisdiction over naturalization. However, just as this law with its invidious anti-Catholic oath was about to expire, the state legislature imposed an even more severe restriction on the political rights of Catholics. John Jay must have been delighted in 1788 when the state legislature imposed an oath for all elected and appointed officials. The wording was virtually identical with the terminology that Jay had devised for the state naturalization statute:

> I do solemnly without any mental reservation or equivocation whatsoever, swear and declare that I renounce and abjure all allegiance and subjection to all and every foreign King, prince

The Fruits of Victory

Despite its bias against Catholics, the constitution of 1777 was an impressive achievement, but it would have remained a dead letter if the Patriots had not won the War of Independence, and a Patriot victory was far from assured in 1777. "Seldom has a government been established in the face of more forlorn circumstances," wrote one historian.[44] Nowhere in the thirteen colonies was the fighting more severe or more extensive than in New York. Almost one-third of all the battles of the Revolutionary War were fought on New York soil. New York probably had a higher percentage of Loyalists than any other colony. Not only did the British continue to occupy New York City

41 - Ibid., I, 853, 549.

42 - *Laws of the State of New York*, II, 637-638.

43 - Duncan, " 'A Most Democratic Class,' " 91-95

44 - James A. Frost, in David M. Ellis, James A. Frost, Harold C. Syrett, and Harry J. Carman, *A History of New York State* (Ithaca: Cornell University Press, 1967), 114.

throughout the war, but in the frontier regions of upstate New York a combination of British regulars, Loyalists and their Indian allies carried out a campaign of guerrilla warfare, terrorizing Patriots and depriving American troops of much-needed supplies.

The last major battle in New York resulted in an American victory near Johnstown in the Mohawk Valley on October 25, 1781. It was completely overshadowed by a far more significant military event that occurred a week earlier at Yorktown in Virginia, when the British commander, General Charles Cornwallis, surrendered to the American and French armies. It was the beginning of the end of hostilities. The British surrender at Yorktown led to a new ministry in Great Britain the following year and eventually to the peace of Paris on September 3, 1783, when the British recognized the independence of the United States.

The British evacuated New York City on November 25. On the same day General Washington led the continental army into the city, a little over seven years since his hasty retreat. The rather shabby looking American troops inched their way down Broadway, careful not to collide with the last remnants of the smartly dressed British garrison who were being evacuated from the Battery. In a final act of petty spite, the departing British troops greased the flagpole in Fort George. However, a determined American sailor wearing cleats climbed to the top of the flagpole, pulled down the Union Jack, and replaced it with the Stars and Stripes to the accompaniment of a thirteen-gun salute.[45]

The Royal Navy leaving New York on November 25, 1783.
The Stars-and-Stripes has already been raised over the Battery

45 - Burrows and Wallace, *Gotham*, 260.

The Battery in the early nineteenth century.
Credit: *Harper's New Monthly Magazine*, July 1861

New York's tiny Catholic community had good reason to celebrate the Patriot victory. If their legal status was less than perfect, they now at least enjoyed greater religious freedom than at any time in a century. Moreover, New York was not unique in barring Catholics from public office while simultaneously giving them religious toleration. All but five states did the same, the exceptions being Rhode Island, Virginia, Maryland, Delaware and Pennsylvania.

Although the British military presence ended when the redcoats sailed out of New York harbor in November 1783, the whole corpus of English colonial laws remained in effect, including the Anti-Priest Law of 1700. In 1784, however, the state legislature repealed the law. It seemed like an afterthought on their part, one line tacked on to the bottom of a bill dismantling the quasi-establishment of the Episcopal Church in New York, Richmond, Queens and Westchester counties.[46]

It made little difference to the grateful Catholic community whether it was an afterthought or not. The repeal of the law made it legal for a priest to set foot in New York and aroused hopes among the Catholics that it would soon be possible for them to organize a community centered around the celebration of the Eucharist. In the following year a group of lay people in New York City took the initiative to make that hope a reality.

46 - *Laws of the State of New York, 1777-1784* (Albany: Weed Parsons and Company, 1886), I, 661-662.

3

Catholics in the New Republic

New York City in 1787 four years after the British evacuation. Credit: *Archdiocese of New York.*

No one appreciated the changed status of Catholics in America after the Revolution more than John Carroll, who was beginning to emerge as the leading figure among the Catholic clergy. Writing to Rome in November 1783, as the British were evacuating their last troops from New York, he informed the authorities there that "our religious system has undergone a revolution, if possible, more extraordinary than our political one." He minimized the political disabilities that Catholics still suffered in states like New York and emphasized instead the solid gains that the American Revolution had brought to the American Catholic community and the bright hopes for the future. "This is a blessing and an advantage which it is our duty to preserve and improve with the utmost prudence," he added.

By prudence Carroll meant that American Catholics would have to demonstrate tact in reconciling their civil allegiance to the new Republic with their fidelity to the spiritual authority of the bishop of Rome. Carroll's immediate concern was that American Catholics were technically still subject to the spiritual jurisdiction of an Englishman, the vicar apostolic of the London District. Carroll feared that this English connection would be a red flag to Americans flushed with their recent victory over the mother country. He recommended the appointment of an American cleric to head the Church in the United States. A year later Rome not only took his advice, but conferred the job on him.[1]

The department of the Roman Curia that made this decision was the Sacred Congregation for the Propagation of the Faith, which was responsible for the Church in all missionary areas. The officials of the Propaganda (as the Roman congregation was commonly called) agreed with the American clergy that it was premature and risky to appoint a bishop in the United States for fear of provoking an anti-Catholic backlash. Therefore, on June 9, 1784, they selected John Carroll to be the "Superior of the Mission in the thirteen United States of North America."[2]

As Superior of the Mission, John Carroll's jurisdiction covered the whole country from the Atlantic Ocean to the Mississippi River, and from Maine to Georgia. However, his authority over this vast area was more theoretical than real. He estimated that the total number of Catholics was no more than 25,000, about one percent of the population, most of whom lived in Pennsylvania or Maryland. As for New York, he had heard that there were at least 1,500 Catholics there (an estimate that most historians consider too high), and he regretted that he was unable to send them any spiritual assistance.[3]

For the next five years John Carroll was to direct the affairs of the infant Catholic Church in the new Republic as the Superior of the Mission. As the leader of a free church in a free state, Carroll had no road map to follow because nowhere else in the world did the Catholic Church enjoy the freedom from state interference that it possessed in the United States. He discharged his duties intelligently and conscientiously. In several places, however, he encountered serious opposition from clergy or laity, or sometimes from both. He quickly discovered that he was handicapped in dealing with these crises because he was only a priest and not a bishop. This was to be especially true in New York.

New York City
after the Revolution

In 1783 New York City showed the scars of seven years of British military occupation as well as two major fires, which destroyed Trinity Church and 500 houses, a quarter of the city's dwellings. Many of the Loyalists left with the British army, reducing the size of the population to about half of the pre-war figure of 20,000. Many of churches had been badly damaged, since the British military authorities had converted them into barracks, hospitals or stables The whole interior of the Middle Dutch Church was demolished when it was turned into a riding academy, and three Presbyterian churches had been left in ruins.

---

1 - Carroll to Cardinal Vitaliano Borromeo, November 10, 1783, *JCP*, I, 80-81. The vicar apostolic of the London District, Bishop James Talbot, was as eager to be rid of the Americans as John Carroll was to be rid of him. A staunch Tory, he refused to give faculties to two American priests returning to their homeland in 1783. James Hennesey, S.J., *American Catholics* (New York: Oxford University Press, 1981), 69-70.

2 - The proper canonical term was Prefect Apostolic, but Carroll never received that title.

3 - Carroll to Cardinal Lorenzo Antonelli, March 1, 1785, *DACH*, I, 147-150.

One eyewitness, William A. Duer, recalled that the burnt out district extended up both sides of Broadway from the Battery to Rector Street, and no effort had been made to clear the rubble. St. Paul's Chapel had been saved from the flames, but the shell of Trinity Church looked like a skeleton. North of St. Paul's there were no paved streets, only open fields and empty lots. To the west there was an unbroken view of the Hudson River, and to the east the grim Bridewell, Poorhouse, Gaol and Gallows. There were virtually no trees left standing, most of them having been chopped down for firewood by desperate residents during the Revolutionary War.

Robert Livingstone.

Trinity Church after it was rebuilt in 1788.

In 1783 New York City made a remarkably peaceful transition from British to American rule unmarred by any violence against the remaining Loyalists. "We have been in town for five days without the slightest disturbance," Robert Livingston wrote to John Jay on November 29, "the shops [of the Loyalists] were opened the day after we came in... The race of Tories will not after all be totally extinct in America." Even James Rivington, the publisher of the Royal Gazette and one of the most hated men in New York, survived the change of regime handily and simply renamed his newspaper *Rivington's New-York Gazette and Universal Advertiser.*[4] To the delight of the Patriots, Rivington's rechristened newspaper failed within a month and he eventually found himself in debtors' prison.

St. Peter's Church

It is impossible to say how many Catholics there were in the city in 1783. Although John Carroll heard that there were at least 1,500, the first resident pastor put the figure at 200. Most of them were Irish, but only about twenty appear to have been practicing Catholics. The majority of them were poor people, but at least a few were quite well off, especially Dominick Lynch, a native of Galway whose family had long-standing commercial ties with Spain. Lynch opened a branch of his father's business in Bruges in what was then the Austrian Netherlands and amassed a considerable fortune before coming to America in 1785.

Together with another wealthy Catholic immigrant, Thomas Stoughton, with whom he had formed a partnership in Bruges, Lynch established a store at 26 Greenwich Street that featured imported luxury items like Sherry wines from Cadiz and Malaga raisins, almonds, oranges and lemons. Although Lynch and Stoughton had

4 - I.N. Phelps Stokes, *The Iconography of Manhattan Island* (New York: Robert H. Dodd, 1926), 1036, 1172, 1175, 1180. *The Correspondence and Public Papers of John Jay* (New York: G.P. Putnam's Sons, 1891), III, 98.

a falling out and dissolved their partnership, they both remained active parishioners and trustees of New York's first Catholic Church for many years. Stoughton was also the Spanish consul in New York until his death in 1826.

Lynch was an especially prominent figure in the New York Catholic community. He came to America as a wealthy man and became even wealthier in New York. He was one of the purchasers of the DeLancey estates (confiscated because of the family's Loyalist sympathies), and lived in a townhouse on Broadway adjacent to the residence of the Spanish minister and George Washington. He also built a country home in Clason's Point overlooking Long Island Sound and practically founded the upstate city of Rome, which was originally called Lynchville. He was also one of four laymen who together with John Carroll sent George Washington a formal address of congratulations from the Catholic community of the United States upon his election as President.[5]

While Dominick Lynch was exceptional, Cornelius Heeney was another native of Ireland who prospered in New York. They were the first two Catholics admitted to the Friendly Sons of St. Patrick, which had been founded in New York City by Irish Protestants. Unlike Lynch and Stoughton, Heeney came to America penniless, but he made a fortune in the fur business and in his later years resided on a seventeen-acre estate in Brooklyn Heights. A lifelong bachelor, he was exceptionally generous to Catholic causes,

Plaque of Cornelius Heeney erected by the Brooklyn Benevolent Society.
Credit: Diocese of Brooklyn

especially St. Peter's Church.[6] Catholics also benefited from the fact that New York City was the national capital in 1789. The presence of the French and Spanish ministers in the city and the social events that they sponsored at their embassies gave the fledgling Catholic community a prestige that it otherwise would not have had.

As far as organized Catholic life was concerned, Father Ferdinand Steinmeyer, better known as "Father Farmer," the German-born former Jesuit priest from Pennsylvania, occasionally visited New York to celebrate Mass. At first he used a rented hall, but later a Portuguese businessman, José Roiz Silva, made his house available. Moreover, there was usually a Catholic chaplain attached to the French and Spanish embassies. In 1785, Barbe Marbois, the chargé d'affaires at the French embassy thought that the establishment of a chapel in the French Embassy would "give Catholics of that city all the spiritual aid that they can desire." Despite the French diplomat's good intentions, however, New York Catholics wanted something more than a chapel in a foreign embassy. They wanted their own parish church and a resident pastor. In the five months between October 1784 and February 1785 their dream began to come true.

New York's Catholics got a pastor before they got a church. He was Charles Whelan, an Irish Capuchin who had served as a chaplain in the French navy during the Revolutionary War. Captured by the British in 1782 and interned in

5 - Richard H. Clarke, "Dominick Lynch," *ACHR 5* (1888): 73-78. *New York Directory for 1786* (New York: Trow City Directory, 1886), 91.

6 - Thomas F. Meehan, "Some Pioneer Catholic Laymen in New York: Dominick Lynch and Cornelius Heeney," *HR&S 4* (1906): 285-301; "A Self-Effaced Philanthropist: Cornelius Heeney," *CHR 4:1* (1918): 3-17.

Jamaica for thirteen months, Whelan was released at the end of the war and arrived in New York City in October 1784.[7] Now that they had a priest, the next step for New York's Catholics was to build a church. On February 3, 1785, twenty-two laymen asked the French consul, Hector St. John Crèvecoeur, to help them obtain a site for a church from the municipal government. Except for De Silva and one or two others, the petitioners were all Irish. Crèvecoeur was an odd person for them to seek out as an intermediary, since he seems to have been more a Deist than a Catholic, but he responded generously, as did the mayor James Duane. As a result of the mayor's intervention, the Corporation of Trinity Church agreed to the transfer of several lots at the corner of Church and Barclay Streets from their leaseholders to the Catholics of New York.

Before the Catholics could take title to the lots, however, they had to form a legal entity in accord with the state law of April 16, 1784, governing the incorporation of church organizations. Therefore, on June 10, 1785, they formed a corporation that they called "The Roman Catholic Church in the City of New York." The four trustees of the parish corporation were Crèvecoeur, José Roiz Silva, James Stewart and Henry Duffin. They then issued a public appeal to "all well disposed Christians in the City of New York" to raise the money to buy the property from Trinity Church. At the head of the appeal were the names of

Governor George Clinton

Mayor James Duane

Governor George Clinton and Mayor James Duane, both of whom were of Irish Protestant ancestry.

The appeal brought in enough money for the congregation to proceed with the laying of the cornerstone of St. Peter's Church on October 5, 1785. Significantly it was Don Diego de Gardoqui, not Father Whelan, who presided at the ceremony. The church was dedicated on November 4, 1786, although the interior was still unfinished.

Born Amid Strife and Confusion

Meanwhile, the Catholic community became enmeshed in an internal power struggle that may seem like a tempest in a teapot in view of the small numbers involved, but in fact it involved vitally important issues for the future of the Catholic Church in the United States. At stake was the question of authority in the Church, more specifically the respective roles of the pastor and the lay trustees in the governance of St. Peter's Church.

The crisis began in the spring of 1785 when Father Whelan alienated a number of his parishioners because of his unpolished manners and his disappointing performance in the pulpit.

Tensions were aggravated in the fall of 1785 with the arrival of another priest, a second Irish Capuchin, Andrew

---

7 - Whelan said that in Jamaica he administered the sacraments to over 4,000 sick and dying fellow prisoners of war. J.M. Lenhart. O.F.M. Cap., "Contribution to the Life of the Reverend Charles Whelan," *RACHSP 37* (1926): 242-249.

The original
St. Peter's Church,
dedicated on
November 4, 1786.

The present
St. Peter's Church,
dedicated
on February 25, 1838,
as it appeared before
September 11, 2001,
with the twin towers
of the World Trade
Center in the
background.

Nugent, who was twelve years Whelan's senior and a better preacher. The two friars took a dislike to one another, and the congregation split into two factions, each backing one of the priests. At Mass on Sunday, December 18, two partisans of Nugent seized the collection.

Carroll tried to effect a reconciliation between Whelan and Nugent, and urged them to work together as co-pastors. At the same time Carroll realized that the troubles in New York involved more than a clash of personalities. He identified the deeper ecclesiological issues involved and confronted them directly when he rejected the claims of the lay trustees to appoint and dismiss the pastor. He told Dominick Lynch and Thomas Stoughton:

> If ever the principles there laid down should become predominant, the unity and Catholicity of our Church would be at an end; & and it would be formed into distinct and independent Societies, nearly in the same manner, as the Congregational Presbyterians of your neighboring New England States.

While rejecting the claims of the trustees to appoint and dismiss the pastor, Carroll did not object to the system of lay trusteeism as such. He was familiar with the system in Maryland where it usually worked well. In responding to the tug of war between clergy and laity in New York, Carroll was groping for a via media between clerical absolutism and ecclesiastical democracy that would offer the laity of the new Republic an appropriate role in a hierarchical Church. "Whenever parishes are established," Carroll assured Lynch and Stoughton, "a proper regard, and such as is suitable to our Governments, will be had to the rights of the Congregation in the mode of election & presentation [of pastors]: and even now I shall ever pay to their wishes every deference consistent with the general welfare of Religion."[8]

Despite the strife and confusion attending its early years, however, St. Peter's made steady progress as New York City's one and only Catholic church for thirty years. Although most of the parishioners of St. Peter's were Irish, it was an ethnically diversified congregation from the very beginning. In 1785 Father Whelan reported that the pastor needed to know the six languages that were commonly spoken by the members of the congregation, namely, English, French, Dutch [i.e, German], Spanish, Portuguese and also Irish. Despite the presence of wealthy individuals like Dominick Lynch, Whelan described the bulk of his parishioners as not only poor, but very poor.[9]

The domestic situation improved temporarily at St. Peter's when Whelan resigned in disgust and left New York in February 1786, eventually to work as a missionary in Kentucky.[10] His departure cleared the way for Carroll to appoint Nugent as his successor, but Nugent soon wore out his welcome with many members of the congregation, who then demanded that John Carroll remove him as pastor. Carroll came to New York in October 1787 to conduct his own investigation. He discovered that Nugent had been suspended by the archbishop of Dublin for sexual misconduct even though he came to America with several letters of recommendation, including one from his own religious superior. Carroll had previously formed a rather favorable opinion of Nugent, but he now came to the conclusion that Nugent was "a most infamous

8 - Carroll to Nugent, January 17, 1786; Carroll to Charles Whelan, January 18, 1796; Carroll to Dominick Lynch and Thomas Stoughton, January 24, 1786, *JCP*, I, 200-206. Thomas W. Spalding, *The Premier See: A History of the Archdiocese of Baltimore, 1789-1989* (Baltimore: The Johns Hopkins University Press, 1989), 28.

9 - Norbert H. Miller, O.F.M., Cap. "Pioneer Capuchin Missionaries in the United States (1784-1816)," *HR&S* 21 (1932: 182, 185.

10 - Whelan left Kentucky in 1790 after a quarrel over money with his parishioners, worked in upstate New York and Delaware, and died at Old Bohemia, the Jesuit mission on the eastern shore of Maryland, on March 21, 1806. He was about sixty-five years old. Miller, "Pioneer Capuchin Missionaries,"196-201.

The sanctuary of St. Peter's Church today

fellow." He removed him as the pastor of St. Peter's, suspended him from the priesthood, and replaced him with Father William O'Brien, an Irish Dominican.[11]

Before Father O'Brien could settle in as the new pastor of St. Peter's, he had to overcome the active opposition of Nugent, who mounted a counterattack with the assistance of some parishioners who were still loyal to him. On two successive Sundays they forcibly took possession of St. Peter's Church, preventing John Carroll from celebrating Mass, embarrassing him in the presence of many non-Catholics, and forcing him to go the chapel in the Spanish embassy for Mass. Father O'Brien recovered control of his parish church only after the trustees successfully appealed to the civil authorities to recognize them as the legitimate owners of St. Peter's.

Legally barred from using St. Peter's Church, Nugent continued to celebrate Mass for his followers in a private house despite his suspension by John Carroll. He thus has the dubious distinction of creating the first schism in the history of the American Catholic Church. He seems to have become an embarrassment even to some of his former admirers, one of whom was James Shea, the father of the historian John Gilmary Shea. At the request of James Shea, in January 1790, the trustees of St. Peter's voted to provide Nugent with enough money to allow him to return to France. The money was well spent. In contrast to the contentious Nugent, Father O'Brien remained as pastor for the next twenty years, finally bring peace to a parish that was "born amidst strife and confusion," in the words of Leo Ryan, the historian of the parish.[12]

---

11 - Carroll to Antonelli, March 18, 1788, *JCP,* I, 283.

12 - Patrick Carey, *People, Priests, and Prelates: Ecclesiastical Democracy and the Tensions of Trusteeism* (Notre Dame: University of Notre Dame Press, 1987), 16, On returning to France, Nugent discovered that the revolutionary regime had suppressed the mendicant orders. Ever resourceful, he survived the Reign of Terror and died on September 8, 1795, at the age of fifty-five. Miller, "Pioneer Capuchin Missionaries," 196.

John Carroll:
Bishop of Baltimore
(1789-1808)

John Carroll returned to Maryland from New York convinced that the Catholic Church in the United States needed a bishop to deal with situations like the Nugent affair. By this time most of the priests agreed with him. Although they had been adamantly opposed to the appointment of a bishop only four years earlier, they changed their mind when they witnessed the difficulties that Carroll experienced in attempting to deal with pastoral problems not only in New York, but also in Boston and Philadelphia. Another reason was that they did not believe that there would be any hue and cry over the appointment of a Catholic bishop. The Episcopalians had already come to the same conclusion.

In the spring of 1788, therefore, a committee of three priests acting on behalf of the rest of them, sent a petition to Pope Pius VI asking the Holy See to provide the American Church with a bishop. They also requested that, "at least for the first time," the priests should have the right to elect their bishop. John Carroll was one of the three members of the committee and was probably the author of the petition. They made specific mention of the difficulties in New York, and Carroll followed up the petition a week later with his own letter to

Cardinal Lorenzo Antonelli, the prefect of the Propaganda. "The time has come," he told Antonelli, "for the appointing of a bishop over the Church of America, because his very title and dignity may be effective in coercing those of intractable disposition."[13]

The Holy See proved to be amenable to both requests and left it to the American clergy to decide whether they wanted to have vicar apostolic (a missionary bishop directly subject to the Holy See) or a full-fledged diocesan bishop. When the priests met at the Whitemarsh plantation in May 1789 to consider the Roman response, they rejected the suggestion of a vicar apostolic, which John Carroll once called "a refined Roman political contrivance." Instead they opted for a diocesan bishop and decided that he should reside in Baltimore.

As for the candidate, on May 18, they voted overwhelmingly for John Carroll by a margin of twenty-four to two with three abstentions. Pope Pius VI confirmed the election of John Carroll on November 6, 1789, with the brief *Ex hac apostolicae,* appointing him the bishop of Baltimore and formally establishing the American hierarchy. Carroll's response did not sound like that of an ambitious man. "The event was such as deprived me of all expectations of rest or pleasure henceforward," he confided to Plowden," and fills me with terror with respect to eternity."[14]

John Carroll traveled to England for his episcopal ordination, which took place on the feast of the Assumption of Mary, August 15, 1790, in the private chapel of Lulworth Castle in Dorsetshire. The ordaining prelate was Bishop Charles Walmesley, the Benedictine vicar apostolic of the Western District. The ceremony had to take place in a private chapel because until the following year English law prohibited Catholics from having public chapels.

---

13 - Petition of Clergy to Pius VI, March 12, 1788, in Guilday, *Carroll,* 347-348; Carroll to Antonelli, March 18, 1788, *JCP,* I, 282-287.
14 - Carroll to Plowden, May 1789, Guilday, *Carroll,* 355.

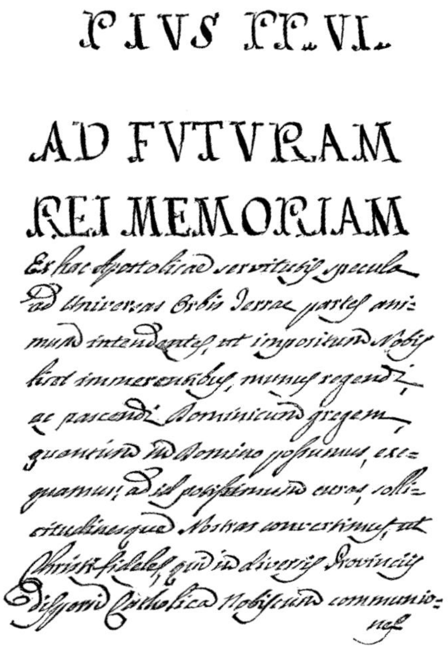

PIVS PP. VI.

AD FVTVRAM

REI MEMORIAM

Ex hac Apostolicae servitutis specula
ad universas Orbis Terrae partes ani-
mum intendentes, ut impositum Nobis
licet immerentibus, munus regendi,
ac pascendi Dominicum gregem,
quantum in Domino possumus, exe-
quamur; ad id perficiendum curas, solli-
citudinesque Nostras convertimus, ut
Christifideles, qui in diversis Provinciis
dispersi Catholicae Nobiscum communio-
ne

The pontifical brief Ex hac apostolicae *of November 6, 1789, established the Diocese of Baltimore and appointed John Carroll the first Bishop*

As Bishop of Baltimore John Carroll had more authority than he did as Superior of the Mission, but he was still expected to administer a diocese that included the whole United States. In fact the burden got heavier in 1805 when he was given responsibility for the vast area of the Louisiana Territory that the United States had acquired from France two years earlier. In theory his jurisdiction new stretched as far west as the Rocky Mountains.

Scandal in Gotham

Closer to home, Carroll could take comfort from the fact that New York was relatively quiet and St. Peter's Church seemed to be thriving. The Irish comprised almost three-quarters of the congregation (73 percent), followed by the French, both from France and Saint Domingue (14 percent), the Germans (5 percent), the African Americans (3 percent), and lesser numbers of Spanish, Portuguese, Italians, English, and native-born Americans. Socially if not economically, the French may have been better off than the other ethnic groups, since many were well educated political refugees, like Jean-Jacques Bérard, a plantation owner from Saint Domingue. He fled from the island to New York in 1787, bringing with him several of his slaves, one of whom was Pierre Toussaint.

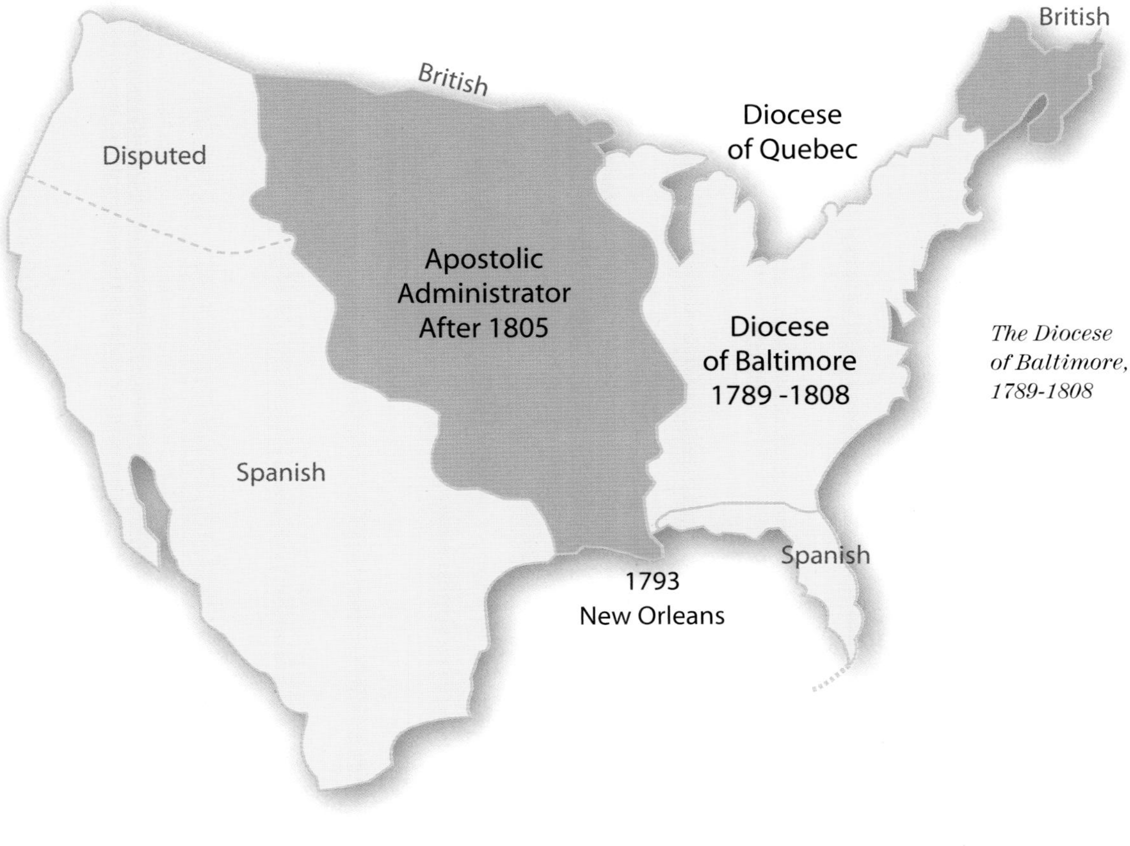

The Diocese of Baltimore, 1789-1808

The increase in the percentage of poor parishioners in St. Peter's parish is evident from the data about their occupations and the neighborhoods where they lived. There was a decline in the percentage of tradesmen, while the percentage of unskilled workers, mainly cartmen and laborers, increased from 4 percent to 23 percent. Since St. Peter's was New York's only Catholic church until 1815, it attracted parishioners from all over the city, but there was a marked decline in the percentage of those who lived in the wealthier wards and a considerable increase in the percentage of those who lived in the poorer wards.[15]

In 1807, after twenty relatively peaceful years with Father William O'Brien as pastor, the whole situation began to unravel once again when Bishop Carroll removed O'Brien and suspended him for unspecified "irregular conduct." Shortly thereafter, Carroll also removed and suspended the two assistant priests, Matthew O'Brien and Patrick Kelly. He told Kelly bluntly: "The sooner you quit N.Y., the better for you, the other clergymen, & generally for the welfare of the Church." To make matters worse, on the heels of these scandals, the trustees asked for the removal of William O'Brien's successor as pastor, Father Louis Sibourd, a French Sulpician, not because of misconduct, but because he spoke English so poorly.[16]

The new crisis in New York came at a most unfortunate moment for Carroll. He was in the process of negotiating with Rome over the division of his vast diocese of Baltimore and the creation of four new dioceses to be located in Boston, Philadelphia, New York, and Bardstown, Kentucky. He was pleased that the officials of the Propaganda readily agreed to the division of his diocese and accepted his candidates for Boston, Philadelphia and Bardstown, all of whom were experienced missionaries in America.

However, in view of the clerical scandals at St. Peter's Church, Carroll had no suitable candidate to suggest for New York. He told Richard Luke Concanen, an Irish Dominican in Rome who sometimes served as his Roman agent, "You may be surprised that no mention is made on this occasion of your and my good old friend, Dr. William O'Brien of New York. I am sorry to say that without wronging my conscience I could not recommend him."[17] In the absence of a suitable local candidate, Carroll asked Rome to leave the diocese of New York vacant temporarily and to place it under the care of the bishop of Boston.

In this instance Carroll's advice was rejected. The cardinals of the Propaganda wanted New York filled immediately along with the other three new American dioceses. Therefore they themselves selected the first bishop of New York. Their choice was Richard Luke Concanen, Carroll's Roman correspondent, who had lived in the Eternal City for the previous forty-three years.

Bishop Richard Luke Concanen, O.P.

John Carroll was unhappy with the selection of Concanen to head the Church in New York, but Concanen may have been even more unhappy than Carroll. When he was privately informed that he had been nominated for New York on March 4, 1808, he called it an "unfortunate appointment." Many people have agreed with him ever since, but perhaps not always for the right reasons.

15 - Anne Hartfield, "Profile of a Pluralistic Parish: St. Peter's Roman Catholic Church, New York City, 1785-1815," *Journal of American Ethnic History* 12:3 (1993): 30-33, 35, 38-40.

16 - Concanen to Maréchal, November 30, 1809, Hughes, *Concanen*, 130; Carroll to Kelly, January 15, 1808; Carroll to Cornelius Heeney, February 13, 1808, *JCP*, III, 37-38, 45.

17 - Carroll to Concanen, June 17, 1807, in Vincent Hughes, O.P., *The Rt. Rev. Richard Luke Concanen, O.P., First Bishop of New York (1747-1810)* (Freiburg: Studia Freiburgensia, 1926), 89. Whatever O'Brien's offense was, he lived in New York until his death in 1816, but never functioned again as a priest. In 1810 the trustees of St. Peter's Church voted to give him a pension of $500 per annum, the same amount as a pastor's salary. Ryan, *Old St. Peter's*, 87-88.

The problem was not ignorance of America on the part of Concanen. He was as well informed as anyone in Rome about the state of the Catholic Church in the United States. The problem was his age and precarious health. Cardinal Michael di Pietro, the prefect of the Propaganda, came to the Dominican monastery where Concanen lived to break the news to him personally. He found Concanen in bed, so ill that he himself thought he was going to die. He was too weak even to stand to greet the cardinal. Writing later to Archbishop Troy of Dublin, Concanen said: "You must undoubtedly be astonished… to hear that instead of now being in my grave, as my most severe and

Richard Luke Concanen, O.P,
First Bishop of New York,
1808-1810.
Credit: *Archdiocese of New York*

On April 8, 1808, Pope Pius VII created four new American dioceses -- Bardstown, Boston, New York, Philadelphia --and made Baltimore a metropolitan see with John Carroll the first Archbishop

long illness then threatened, I am appointed Bishop of New York in North America."

Concanen "strenuously" recommended that the appointment should go instead to John Connolly, a slightly younger Irish Dominican confrere, but he finally accepted the post when he was told that it was the express wish of the Holy Father. "Obedience to the Church has alone made me change an easy, quiet and comfortable way of life for a disastrous one," he told Troy with deep resignation and somewhat muted optimism.[18] A week later Concanen's health was still so doubtful that, unknown to him, Cardinal di Pietro hedged his bets by obtaining a rescript from the pope dated April 1 to replace him with Connolly if necessary. However, Concanen made a speedy recovery and a few weeks later Pope Pius VII formally appointed him the first bishop of New York.[19]

U.S CHURCH IN 1808
Canada

DIOCESE OF BOSTON

DIOCESE OF NEW YORK
DIOCESE OF PHILADELPHIA

ARCHDIOCESE OF BALTIMORE

DIOCESE OF BARDSTOWN

SPANISH FLORIDA

U.S. Church in 1808 after the division
of the Diocese of Baltimore

---

18 - Concanen to Troy, March 25, 1808, cit. in Victor O'Daniel, O.P., "Concanen's Election to the See of New York (1808-10)," *CHR 2* (1916-1917): 22-23.

19 - APF, Acta de 1814, Congregazione dei 19 Settembre 1814, fol. 45v., copy in AANY.

Concanen was born in the little town of Kilbegnet in County Roscommon on December 27, 1747, and was baptized the next day by a Dominican friar. At the age of seventeen, he left Ireland forever to join the Irish province of the Order of Preachers at their college of the Holy Cross in Louvain where he made his religious profession on September 14, 1765. He was ordained a priest in Rome on December 22, 1770. By 1808 Concanen already had a distinguished career behind him as a theologian, receiving the coveted Dominican degree of Master of Sacred Theology in 1783. He also had the advantage of considerable administrative experience both as sub-prior and prior of San Clemente, the monastery of the Irish Dominicans in Rome. He also served as an assistant to two Masters General of the Dominican Order at the monastery of the Minerva, their headquarters in Rome.

Before establishing the four new American dioceses in 1808, the cardinals of the Propaganda consulted Concanen several times because of their apprehensions about the possibly negative reaction of the American government. He reassured them that their fears were groundless. Concanen informed the Propaganda that the constitution of the United States "guaranteed to all the inhabitants of the globe the free exercise of worship and the profession of faith without distinction or preference."

Nevertheless, the Propaganda still hesitated to establish the American dioceses and once again turned to Concanen for advice. He was annoyed to be asked a question that he thought he had already answered. Concanen's response reveals how well he had mastered the delicate art of dealing with fastidious clerical bureaucrats

The Tontine Coffee House on Wall Street in 1797. Credit: *Archdiocese of New York*

during the course of his forty-three years in Rome. Appealing to their *amour propre*, he warned the cardinals of the Propaganda that their failure to establish these new dioceses now would call into question the wisdom of their own congregation, which had been urging Carroll to do since 1802.

Concanen's clarification of the religious situation in the United States in 1808 indicates an extraordinarily keen understanding of American political institutions for an eighteenth-century Catholic cleric living in Rome where churchmen tended to view all revolutions through the prism of the worst excesses of the French Revolution. Concanen made a sharp distinction between the European revolutions that he himself had experienced and the situation in the United States. "The fundamental laws of the American government," Concanen explained, "not only assure toleration but also encouragement and protection for all religions without preference for any in particular…" He traced this tradition back to the Second Continental Congress of 1776, which had numbered among its members Charles Carroll. If Concanen had expressed such views a century later, he would have been labeled an "Americanist" in Rome.[20]

Waiting for Godot

Ordained a bishop in Rome on April 24, 1808, Concanen was delegated to bring with him to America the bulls of appointment for the three other bishops-elect. He was also entrusted with bringing Carroll the pallium, the band of white wool that an archbishop wears over his shoulders at liturgical functions as a symbol of his metropolitan authority and his unity with the Bishop of Rome. On a more mundane note, Carroll asked Concanen for a dozen pair of purple silk stockings, which led Concanen to wonder if he needed so many because he wore them all the time. He also wondered whether he would be expected to do the same.

Almost at once Concanen discovered that he would have a major problem in getting from Rome to America because of the naval war between France and England. He went first to the port of Livorno (Leghorn, as the English called it) where there was an American ship in the harbor. The French refused to allow it to depart because of the embargo that Napoleon had imposed on continental ports as part of his strategy to cripple England economically.

Dejected after waiting for four months in Livorno, Concanen returned to Rome where for the second time in a decade he witnessed the occupation of the city by the French and the exile of the pope to France.[21]

His own Dominican confrères in Rome, including John Connolly, gave him little consolation or material support. "[They] wish me to depart," he told Archbishop Troy, "lest they should be obliged to maintain me." The prefect of the Propaganda ordered the community of San Clemente to pay for Concanen's room and board at the Minerva. By this time there was no love lost between Concanen and Connolly, the Dominican friars who had lived together at San Clemente for ten years and who were the first two bishops of New York.

Connolly thought that Concanen was a penny-pincher who feigned poverty because he was reluctant to part with any of his own money. "He has money enough of his own to take him not only to New York, but to New Holland [Australia]," Connolly told John Carroll. Despite their vow of

---

20 - Cit. in Hughes, *Concanen*, 197-200. Concanen mistakenly identified Charles Carroll as the brother rather than as the cousin of John Carroll.

21 - AAB, Concanen to Carroll, Leghorn, July 26, 1808, copy in AANY.

poverty, eighteenth-century Irish Dominicans were allowed to possess a certain amount of money because of the impossibility of maintaining their community life in Ireland. In 1805, when Connolly was the bursar of San Clemente, he and the prior were sometimes obliged to lay out their own money to keep the monastery afloat. They found Concanen unwilling to lend them anything without security and interest, and he was still demanding an annual payment of 40 *scudi* for the 800 *scudi* that he had given San Clemente in 1797.

On the other hand, Concanen regarded Connolly as an inept financial manager of San Clemente, although he had courageously prevented its confiscation during the radical Roman Republic of 1798-1799. When Concanen added a codicil to his will in 1810, he specified that certain money should go to San Clemente only if someone other than John Connolly was in charge of it. His poor opinion of Connolly's administrative abilities went back at least to 1802, well before he "strenuously'" recommended him for the diocese of New York.[22]

After eighteen months of enforced idleness in Rome, Concanen decided to try to get to America from France. "I look upon the plan to be desperate," he said, "yet I believe that I must adopt it, if I get the passports." He also decided to wait until he got to France to buy Carroll's purple silk stockings because he was told that they were cheaper in France than in Rome.

In March 1810 Concanen was about to set out from Rome for France, but he heard that there were two ships scheduled to leave for America from Naples, and he headed to that city instead. In fact only one ship was allowed to leave, the *Frances,* which was to sail for Salem, Massachusetts, on June 17. At first the captain of the *Frances* refused to take Concanen as a passenger, but he relented at the insistence of the two American consuls in Naples.

It was not likely to be a pleasant voyage with 260 people crammed on board. Many were American seamen whose own ships had been confiscated by the French in Naples. At the last moment, however, just when everything seemed ready for Concanen's departure for America, the port authorities claimed that his passport was not in order and refused to allow him to leave.[23] He died two days later, on June 19, and was buried in an unmarked tomb in the Domincan Church of San Domenico Maggiore in Naples.[24] John Carroll never got his dozen pair of purple silk stockings, at least not from Concanen.

Meanwhile, the Church in New York, wracked by a series of clerical scandals, had to wait another five years before it received its first bishop.

Father Anthony Kohlmann, S.J.

The person who came to the rescue of the Church in New York in 1808 was Anthony Kohlmann, S.J. Kohlmann's Jesuit superior, Robert Molyneux, released him for service in New York City after John Carroll pleaded that he needed "a priest of the most respectable character" to handle "dreadful" and "grievous" scandals in that city.[25] Carroll sent Kohlmann to New York before he heard of the establishment of the new diocese and then kept him on when Bishop Concanen asked him to appoint a vicar general to administer the diocese in his absence.

22 - AAB, Connolly to Carroll, April 12, 1810, copy in AANY. Leonard P. Boyle, O.P., *San Clemente Miscellany I: The Community of SS. Sisto e Clemente in Rome, 1677-1977* (Rome: Apud S. Clementum, 1977), 77-83.

23 - Concanen to Maréchal, June 15, 1810, Hughes, *Concanen,* 137-141.

24 - On July 9, 1978, Cardinal Cooke dedicated a memorial tablet to mark the site of Bishop Concanen's burial. Florence D. Cohalan, *A Popular History of the Archdiocese of New York* (Yonkers: U.S. Catholic Historical Society, 1983), 24.

25 - Carroll to Robert Molyneux, February 25, 1807, *JCP,* III, 10.

Father Kohlmann was to remain in charge of the Church in New York for the next six years through the two years of Concanen's episcopate and most of the long interregnum that followed his death. A native of Kayserberg near Colmar in Alsace where he was born on July 13, 1771, Kohlmann was fluent in German, French and English.

Father Anthony Kohlmann, S.J.
Credit: *Georgetown University Library*

Kohlmann was in New York by October or November 1808. He did not come alone. He brought with him Father Benedict Fenwick, the descendant of an old Maryland Catholic family, and four Jesuit scholastics or seminarians. The reason for bringing the seminarians to New York was that Kohlmann intended not only to take charge of St. Peter's Church, but also to establish a Catholic college as soon as he could. He estimated that there were about 14,000 Catholics in New York City. Most were Irish, but there were

Father Benedict Fenwick, S.J.

also hundreds of French and Germans, and Kohlmann used his linguistic gifts to provide them with sermons every Sunday in all three languages.

The trustees of St. Peter's gave him a warm reception and allocated $800 to renovate the rectory. Their generosity surprised Kohlmann in view of the fact that the recent clerical scandals in the parish had led to the loss of many parishioners and, in Kohlmann's words, had brought the parish "very near its ruin." He offered an explanation for the scandals that would have occurred only to a nineteenth-century Jesuit.

"Almighty God seems to have permitted this," he confided to one of his confreres in somewhat shaky English, "to furnish the Society with an opportunity of diffusing the good odour of it & of disposing the minds to favour its establishment."[26]

Shortly after his arrival in New York, Father Kohlmann realized that one church building was no longer sufficient to care for the pastoral needs of New York's Catholics, and he moved quickly to rectify the situation. Less than a year after his arrival in New York, on October 8, 1809, he laid the cornerstone of New York's second Catholic Church, St. Patrick's, which was to be the cathedral of the newly established diocese. Located at Mott and Prince Streets, it was on the northern edge of the city surrounded by open meadows and woodlands. Kohlmann appealed to every Catholic to contribute at least twenty-five cents a month to the building fund, but he got the same tepid response that John Carroll did when he began work on the nation's first Catholic cathedral in Baltimore a few years earlier. The money came in slowly, and New York's first cathedral was not completed until 1815.

In the meantime, Kohlmann set to work in establishing a Catholic college in New York, which he called the New York Literary Institute. It began as a day school in a rented building on Mulberry Street opposite the first St. Patrick's Cathedral and found a permanent home in 1810 at the southeast corner of Fifth Avenue and 50th Street, four miles north of the city limits.

---

26 - Kohlmann to Strickland, November 7, 1808, "Unpublished Letters of Father Anthony Kohlmann, S.J.," *HR&S*. 1:1 (1899): 71.

The New York Literary Institute

In its new location the Literary Institute became a traditional Jesuit boarding school. Kohlmann remained in the city as pastor of St. Peter's while Fenwick ran the school. By 1813 the enrollment had grown to thirty-five or forty boarders, including a number of non-Catholics and the future prospects seemed bright. However, the Jesuit superior in America, Father John Grassi, ordered the Literary Institute closed that year because he needed the Jesuit scholastics to staff Georgetown College. He ignored Kohlmann's protest that the future of the Society was to be in New York, not in Washington, which he predicted would "always be a poor beggarly place." Kohlmann blamed the decision on the three Neale brothers, old Maryland Jesuits with considerable influence in the Society, but Grassi was also under intense pressure from another old Maryland (former) Jesuit, John Carroll, who wanted Georgetown College kept open, because he was the one who had founded it.[27]

The Confessional Case

The same year that the Literary Institute was closed, Kohlmann became involved in a celebrated court case involving the seal of the confessional. Kohlmann had acted as an intermediary for the return of stolen goods to a Catholic merchant named James Keating. He refused to divulge to a grand jury the name of the person who gave him the goods because it was based on knowledge he obtained through the confessional. "I shall become a traitor to my church, to my sacred ministry, and to my God," said Kohlmann. The district attorney was willing to drop the case, but the trustees of St. Peter's Church realized the implications of the case and wished to establish a legal precedent that would assure the inviolability of the seal of confession in civil law.

---

27 - Francis X. Curran, S.J., *The Return of the Jesuits* (Chicago: Loyola University Press, 1966), 37, 42.

The result was a collusive lawsuit. On April 19, 1813, the trustees respectfully asked the district attorney to challenge Kohlmann's refusal to answer in the Court of General Session. He did so reluctantly in June 1813. The case was heard before a large crowd in the new City Hall. District Attorney Gardiner explained that he was only pursuing this case because he had received a very earnest request to do so from the Roman Catholic Church.

Since the Catholics wanted Father Kohlmann to be prosecuted, Gardiner did his best to oblige, arguing that neither the state constitution nor the common law re-cognized the privileged nature of confessional knowledge. He also pointed out that the state constitution of 1777 outlawed preferential treatment for any religious group. He argued that Catholics were demanding preferential treatment for confessional secrets, since a Protestant minister could be obliged to reveal anything confessed to him by a layman.

Mayor DeWitt Clinton

Kohlmann's two attorneys were both Protestants, City Recorder Richard Riker, and William Sampson, an Irish Anglican and one of the most respected figures in New York's Irish community. He has been described as "America's first civil rights lawyer, preceding Clarence Darrow by almost a century."[28] Sampson pointed out that not even in eighteenth-century Ireland was a Catholic priest ever compelled to violate the secrecy of the confessional.

Riker challenged both of the district attorney's arguments. He claimed that the common law protected Father Kohlmann because no one could be compelled to answer a question that would lead to his disgrace, which would inevitably happen to Kohlmann if he were to violate the secrecy of the confessional. Moreover, Riker cleverly argued that, if the state constitution assured Catholics the full benefit of religious freedom, including the right to administer the sacraments according to their own norms, that right must include the protection of the secrecy of confession.

The court consisted of four judges headed by Mayor DeWitt Clinton. They voted unanimously in favor of Kohlmann on June 14, 1813. Clinton delivered the verdict of the court. "If he tells the truth he violates his ecclesiastical oath," the judges said. "If he prevaricates he violates his judicial oath." Therefore the justices decided: "The only course is for the court to declare that he shall not testify or act at all."[29]

The judges were obviously impressed with the argument of Richard Riker. "Secrecy is of the essence of penance," they wrote. "The sinner will not confess, nor will the priest receive his confession, if the veil of secrecy is removed. To decide that the minister shall promulgate what he receives in confession is to declare that there shall be no penance, and this important branch of the Roman Catholic religion would be thus annihilated."[30]

28 - William J. Walsh, "Religion, Ethnicity, and History," in Bayor and Meagher, *New York Irish*, 56.

29 - Ryan, *Old St. Peter's*, 111-115.

30 - William Sampson, *The Catholic Question in America* (New York: Edward Gillespie, 1813), 7, 13-14, 30, 42, 45, 103, 111. Sampson's book was published with a 128-page appendix, *A True Exposition of the Doctrine of the Catholic Church Touching the Sacrament of Penance with the Grounds on Which This Doctrine Is Founded,* probably written by Kohlmann.

The case had more than local significance. At least one legal expert gives the trustees of St. Peter's Church credit for winning "the first victory for free religious exercise in American constitutional law." In his opinion, "the event ranks as perhaps the earliest recorded instance of impact litigation in American constitutional history--a test case in which an insular minority deliberately sought to appropriate the power of the courts to transform the political structure of American society." [31]

Bishop John Cheverus of Boston, who presided of the dedication of St. Patrick's Cathedral

The First St. Patrick's Cathedral

In 1814 Kohlmann was ordered to return to Maryland to take charge of the Jesuit novices, leaving Fenwick as pastor of St. Peter's and responsible for the completion of St. Patrick's which had been delayed by the lack of money. On Ascension Day, May 4, 1815, Bishop John Cheverus of Boston dedicated New York's first cathedral in the presence of the mayor, former Mayor DeWitt Clinton, and the Board of Alderman. When Bishop Joseph Octave Plessis of Quebec visited New York City later that year, he noted that the new cathedral lacked a steeple or a sacristy (both had been deliberately omitted to save money), but he was impressed with the size of the building and the decorations of the interior. By the late spring of 1815, New York's Catholics had a functioning cathedral, but they would have to wait another six months before they had a bishop to go with it.

St. Patrick's Old Cathedral, dedicated in May 4, 1815

---

31 - Walsh, "Religion, Ethnicity, and History," 53, 55.

*Rear View of St.Patrick's
Old Cathedral
on Mulberry Street.
Little has changed in
almost 200 years*

St. Patrick's Old Cathedral

Bishop John Connolly, O. P.

Meanwhile in Rome, after the death of Concanen, Msgr. Quarantotti, the pro-prefect of the Propaganda, wrote to the pope, who was a prisoner of Napoleon at Savona in France, and asked if he wished to implement the rescript of April 1, 1808, appointing John Connolly bishop of New York instead of Concanen. The pope replied on August 12, 1810, that he did not consider it opportune to appoint Connolly, and there the matter rested for the time being.[32] During the next four years, while Pius VII remained a prisoner of Napoleon in France, he refused to make any episcopal appointments until he had regained his freedom.

Meanwhile, after the pope's return to Rome in 1814, one of his highest priorities was to fill vacant dioceses like New York. Aware that Connolly had been recommended for New York four years earlier by the Propaganda, the cardinals of the congregation unanimously nominated him at a meeting on September 19, 1814. The pope approved their choice, and New York's new bishop was formally appointed on October 4, 1814. He received episcopal ordination on November 6, 1814, in the large church that is now the chapel of the Pontifical University of St. Thomas Aqunas.[33]

Connolly was a native of County Meath where he was born around 1747. Like Richard Concanen and many other young Irishmen of his generation who wished to follow a vocation to the religious life, he entered the Irish province of the Order of Preachers in Louvain. Ordained in Malines on September 24, 1774, he moved to San Clemente in Rome three years later and succeeded Concanen as prior in 1787.

During the French-sponsored Roman Republic in 1798-1799, Connolly remained on his own at San Clemente for sixteen months in a successful effort to prevent the anticlerical government from confiscating the property. He later boasted: "By attending the venerable basilica of St. Clement's gratis during the French government here, I have saved it and the convent from ruin though I was thrice ordered to go to Paris for having contemptuously refused to swear allegiance to Napoleon."[34]

John Connolly, O.P.,
Second Bishop of New York.
Credit: *Archdiocese of New York*

As we have seen, in the summer of 1815 Archbishop Troy informed Carroll that the rumors of Connolly's appointment were true, and he sent him the formal notice from Archbishop Lorenzo Litta, the prefect of the Propaganda. The news did not please John Carroll anymore than he had been pleased with the appointment of Concanen in 1808. He was disappointed both with the new bishop and especially with the process by which he had been selected.

"Mr. Connolly is appointed," Carroll complained to his old English friend Charles Plowden, "with whom none of us are acquainted; nor has anyone in this country been consulted. I wish that this may not become a very dangerous precedent," he added, "fruitful of mischief by

32 - APF, Acta de Anno 1814, Congregazione dei 19 Settembre 1814, folio 45v., copy in AANY.

33 - Victor O'Daniel, O.P., *The Dominican Province of Saint Joseph* (New York: National Headquarters of the Holy Name Society, n.d.), 118-119. O'Daniel mistakenly gives November 4 as the date of Connolly's appointment.

Winter Scene in Brooklyn in 1810. Credit: *Harper's New Monthly Magazine,* August 1862

drawing censure upon our religion, & false opinion of the servility of our principles." Carroll had special reason to be angry over Connolly's appointment because in 1809 Bishop Concanen had assured him that this sort of thing would not happen. "On this subject," Concanen told Carroll, "permit me to add, and assure your Grace, that no appointment, no arrangement of any importance, regarding the Churches of the United States, will be adopted by the Holy See without your previous advice and consent. This I have taken special care to have determined on…"[35]

John Connolly left Rome in March 1815 and interrupted his journey in Liège at the request of a friend, John Arnold Barrett, the vicar capitular of that diocese, which had been without a bishop for almost fourteen years. Connolly spent several weeks there confirming young and old alike. His pastoral activities in Liège nearly led to his undoing. At the same time that Connolly left Rome, Napoleon escaped from confinement on the island of Elba to begin the Hundred Days. He landed in southern France on March 1, made a triumphal march to Paris and launched an invasion of Belgium.

Bishop Connolly may have wondered if he was destined to share the fate of Bishop Concanen and become the second bishop of New York to be kept from his diocese by Napoleon. However, as the English, Dutch and Prussians assembled their armies for the battle that was to be fought at Waterloo on June 18, Connolly slipped quietly out of Belgium, reached England in June, and then made his way to Ireland. In September he set sail from Dublin for America. All told his trip from Rome to his diocese took him eight months. No wonder John Carroll grew impatient.[36]

34 - Boyle, *San Clemente Miscellany* I, 68.

35 - Carroll to Plowden, June 25-July 24, 1815, *JCP,* III, 338; Concanen to Carroll, August 9, 1809, O'Daniel, "Concanen's Election," 36.

36 - APF, Lettere della S. Congregazione, Vol. 296, Propaganda to Carroll, July 1, 1815, copy in AANY; O'Daniel, *Dominican Province of St. Joseph,* 119-120.

4

New York Catholics

View of New York harbor in 1816 from Governor's Island. It is the scene that Bishop Connolly would have observed as the Sally *sailed up the East River.* Credit: *Archdiocese of New York*

The New York that Bishop Connolly saw in 1815 as the *Sally* sailed up the East River was a city of about 95,000 people, most of whom lived south of Houston Street. Visually it must have been a disappointment to someone who was long familiar with the grandeur of Rome and who had gotten a glimpse of the elegance of Georgian Dublin prior to his departure for America. The only noteworthy public building was the new City Hall, completed three years earlier at the astronomical cost of $500,000. The entrance pointed south in the direction of the center of the population, and the city fathers had trimmed costs by using inexpensive brownstone on the northern façade where few people would notice.[1]

---

1 - Eric Homberger, *The Historical Atlas of New York City* (New York: Henry Holt and Company, 1994), 59.

The physical layout of the future metropolis had been determined four years earlier when the state-appointed Streets Commission devised a map that divided Manhattan into a rigid grid of twelve north-south avenues intersected every 200 feet by east-west streets. From Houston Street to 155th Street they carved up the city into some 2,000 long narrow blocks that made no concessions to the natural geographical features of the island and ruthlessly obliterated hills, meadows, fields, swamps, ponds, and streams in the name of progress. In the words of two savvy local historians, the Commissioners' Plan represented the triumph of technique over topography.[2]

The New York Irish

Although New York Catholics formed a multi-ethnic community from the beginning, the great majority of them were Irish. In the nineteenth century New York City became the capital of Irish-Catholic America with an Irish population larger than that of Dublin. It was the city where most of the immigrant ships from Ireland docked, the gathering place of exiled Irish nationalists, the nerve center of Irish-American efforts to assist the cause of Irish freedom, and the site of the most important archdiocese in North America.[3]

Even when the percentage of the Irish in the overall Catholic population of New York began to decline in the early twentieth century, leadership in the archdiocese remained firmly in Irish-American hands. Only one of the eleven bishops and archbishops of New York in the course of the past two hundred years was not Irish-born or of Irish ancestry. That was John Dubois, and he died in 1842. The experiment was not repeated.

There has been an Irish presence in New York City as far back as the seventeenth century, but contrary to the image of the New York Irish

City Hall Park in 1827. Credit: *Archdiocese of New York*

2 - Burrows and Wallace, *Gotham*, 421.

3 - George Potter, *To the Golden Door: The Story of the Irish in Ireland and America* (Westport, Ct.: Greenwood Press, 1960), 180.

that emerged in the later nineteenth century, not all of them were Catholic and not all of them were poor.

Kerby Miller estimated that between 400,000 and 650,000 Irish emigrated to North America before 1815. During the following thirty years almost twice as many came as in the previous two centuries, between 800,000 and 1,000,000. Prior to the 1830s, however, these Irish immigrants were overwhelmingly Protestant, mainly Presbyterians fleeing from overpopulation in Ulster.[4]

NEW YORK'S IRISH AND GERMAN WARDS
in the early nineteenth century

GERMAN WARDS
IRISH WARDS

Only in the early 1830s did Catholics begin to outnumber Protestants among the Irish immigrants to the United States. The Catholics tended to be poorer than the Protestants, although not totally destitute because the cost of a transatlantic voyage was well beyond the means of the poorest elements in Irish society. One indication of the increasing poverty of the Irish immigrants in the 1830s was the fact that many more came to America now as single men and women rather than as families. This poverty was also reflected in their occupations. In 1836 almost sixty percent of the Irish immigrants arriving in New York City were either laborers or servants compared with thirty-eight percent ten years earlier.[5]

Perhaps as many as 100,000 Irish Catholics emigrated to North America in the colonial period, but they left little trace. As Kerby Miller has also pointed out, Irish Protestant emigration was "a mass movement, a social exodus," while Irish Catholic emigration was "largely a trickle of footloose individuals" and "most Irish Catholic emigrants lived short, brutish lives in colonial America toiling in obscure poverty for harsh taskmasters." In 1785 John Carroll estimated that there were no more than 25,000 Catholics in the United States (and not all of them were Irish), perhaps a quarter of the number of Irish Catholics who came North America during the previous two centuries. Many died young while others, deprived of their own churches and priests, joined one of the various Protestant churches.[6]

Orange and Green

Two of the oldest Irish organizations in New York City were non-sectarian, the Friendly Sons of St. Patrick (founded in 1784) and the Hibernian

4 - Kerby A. Miller, *Emigrants and Exiles: Ireland and the Irish Exodus to North America* (New York: Oxford University Press, 1985), 137, 169-170.

5 - Ibid., 198.

6 - Ibid., 146; *DACH,* I, 148. Affluence could be as big a cause of "leakage" from the Catholic Church as poverty. Most of the thirteen children of Dominck Lynch married non-Catholics and raised their children as Protestants.

Provident Society of New York (founded in 1802)[7]. So was New York's first Irish newspaper, *The Shamrock*. During the first few decades of the nineteenth century the three leading figures in New York City's Irish community were Thomas Addis Emmet, William Sampson and William MacNeaven. All three were political exiles, deported by the British because of their leadership role in the revolt of the United Irishmen in 1798.

Like his more famous brother Robert, Thomas Addis Emmet was a Protestant as was Sampson, and MacNeaven was a Catholic, but their patriotism transcended their religious differences. Together they organized the Association of the Friends of Ireland in New York to raise funds for Daniel O'Connell's efforts to gain Catholic Emancipation in Ireland. Like the United Irishmen in Ireland in 1798, they used their influence in New York City to promote peace and harmony between their Protestant and Catholic countrymen.

In Ireland the tenuous alliance of Protestants and Catholics promoted by the United Irishmen broke down in the 1820s with the revival of the Orange Lodges, an aggressive Protestant campaign to proselytize the Irish Catholics, and the increasing identification of Irish nationalism with Catholicism. The consensus also broke down in New York City under the impact of the increasing number of poor Irish Catholic immigrants. On July 12, 1824, Orangemen celebrated the anniversary of the battle of the Boyne with a parade down Sixth Avenue in Greenwich Village. Accompanied by fifes and drums, they taunted Catholic bystanders with cries of, "Come forward, you damned croppies." In the ensuing riot, thirty-three Catholics were arrested for disturbing the

Intersection of Canal and Walker Streets in the early nineteenth century. Credit: *Archdiocese of New York*

7- The only qualification for membership in the Hibernian Provident Society was that "no Irishman who has willingly aided in continuing the dominion of Great Britain over Ireland shall be admitted." *Constitution of the Hibernian Provident Society of New-York* (New-York: Denniston and Cheatham, 1802), 6.

May 1st was Moving Day in New York City when the leases expired and the streets were filled with poor people moving their possessions from one tenement house to another. Credit: *Harper's New Monthly Magazine,* May 1856

peace. Both Emmet and Sampson came to their aid and secured their acquittal.[8] Commenting on the conduct of the Orangemen, Sampson said sadly, "In this land of freedom we have not been accustomed heretofore to witness such a celebration."[9]

While the Greenwich Village riot of 1824 marked the beginning of open conflict between Irish Protestants and Irish Catholics in New York City, an even more serious riot ten years later sealed their mutual antagonism. The Congressional elections in the fall of that year touched off four days of rioting in the largely Irish Catholic Sixth Ward, which signaled the division of the New York Irish not only along religious lines but also along economic and class lines as well. Thereafter middle-class Irish Protestants tended to vote for the Whigs, while the poorer Irish Catholics backed the Jeffersonian Democrats.

Running as a Whig candidate in the Sixth Ward, William Sampson went down to defeat. Even better off Catholics like Patrick Casserly, the founder of a classical academy, severed his ties with the "illiberal, intolerant and persecuting Whigs." Another sign of the polarization within New York's Irish community was the evolution of the Friendly Sons of St. Patrick into an Irish Catholic society by the 1840s, although they still toasted the Queen at their St. Patrick's Day festivities.[10]

Poverty and Prejudice

In 1834 Bishop Dubois estimated that there were 30,000 Irish Catholics in New York City, one-seventh of the total population. A decade later, on the eve of the Great Famine in 1845, there were an estimated 70,000 Irish-born residents of New York City, which was more than half of the foreign-

---

8 - Walter J. Walsh, "Religion, Ethnicity and History," in Bayor and Meagher, eds., *The New York Irish,* 64-69; Paul A.Gilje, *The Road to Mobocracy* (Chapel Hill: University of North Carolina Press, 1987), 138-142.

9 - *The Trial of John Moore and Others for Assault and Battery, New York City, 1824, in American State Trials,* ed. John D. Lawson (St. Louis: Thomas Law Book Company, 1921), XIII, 190.

10 - Walsh, "Religion, Ethnicity and History," 66-68; Potter, *To the Golden Door,* 262; *Truth Teller,* April 1, 1843.

born population and almost one-fifth of the total population. Not all of them were Catholic, but the percentage of Catholics continued to increase every year thereafter. Twenty years later in 1865 it is estimated that one of every four New Yorkers was born in Ireland, and the great majority of them were Catholic.[11]

While Irish clerics were staking out their claim to the leadership of the American Catholic Church, the rank and file of their countrymen and countrywomen found that working and living conditions in early nineteenth-century New York City could often be cruel and dehumanizing. In 1827 an English visitor noticed that the Irish filled "the lowest stations of the hard-working class" and were subjected to the same discrimination as in England or Scotland. "If any peculiar atrocity is committed in the land," he added, "friend Pat is immediately suspected." Patrick Casserly made the same observation five years later. "If a swindler, thief, robber or murderer, no matter what his color or country, commit any nefarious or abominable act throughout the Union," he said, "he is instantly set down as a native of Ireland."[12]

Many Irishmen found work as laborers in shipyards, construction sites and on the docks. Laborer was a catchall term that admitted of various gradations. In the shipyards Irish workers complained that they rarely had access to the better-paying jobs. Likewise on the docks they did the back-breaking work of longshoremen but were hardly ever promoted to stevedores who

supervised the work. In the construction industry, however, many Irish helpers and hod carriers had the opportunity to rise to the level of skilled artisans as masons, plasterers and carpenters.

Some Irishmen found employment as waiters and private coachmen where they competed with African Americans for jobs. Others were involved in local transportation either as carters, draymen, teamsters, omnibus and stage coach drivers, or as conductors, signalmen and brakemen on the railroads, or as boatmen, watermen and ferrymen in New York harbor. Still others were to be found as farm workers on Long Island and the Hudson Valley and as quarrymen, blasters and rockmen in nearby quarries.

A familiar figure was the Irishman or Irishwoman who ran the corner grocery store and who might make a modest profit working a fourteen-hour day by selling customers a penny's worth of sugar or a dram of gin.[13]

For single Irish women domestic service was often an attractive occupation because the free room and board gave them the opportunity to save money. However, Irish women experienced the same discrimination in employment as Irish men. In 1843 a newspaper advertisement specified a position available for "a clean respectable Protestant girl to do the house work of a small family. Neither Irish nor Catholics need apply." Nevertheless, three years later, three-quarters of the foreign-born maids, cooks, housekeepers, nurses, charwomen, and

A typical want ad from the New York Sun *in 1843.*

---

11 - *New-York Weekly Register and Catholic Diary,* February 1, 1834; Ira Rosenwaike, *Population History of New York City* (Syracuse: Syracuse University Press, 1972), 41.

12 - *Tour through Parts of the United States and Canada* (London: Longman, Rees, Orme, Brown & Green, 1828), 16; Potter, *To the Golden Door,* 167.

13 - Carol Groneman Pernicone, "The 'Bloody Ould Sixth': A Social Analysis of a New York City Working-Class Community in the Mid-Nineteenth Century," Ph.D. diss., University of Rochester, 1973, 112.

A defense of Irish servant girls in the New York Catholic press.

laundresses in New York City were Irish. Those women who could not find work as domestics often turned to the sewing trades where they worked as seamstresses, dressmakers, shirt and collar makers, milliners, embroiders, and artificial flower makers. On the bottom of the economic ladder were Irish women selling fruit and vegetables on the city's street corners.[14]

The Bloody Ould Sixth Ward

If working conditions were grim and debilitating, housing conditions were often worse. Poor Irish immigrants were concentrated in the Fourth, Fifth and Sixth Wards where ramshackle tenements, overcrowding, lack of basic sanitation, crime and disease made life extremely difficult. John Griscom, a medical doctor who investigated the housing conditions in the slums in the 1840s, placed much of the blame on sub-landlords, who would rent a building and subdivide it into as many cubicles as they could for maximum profit. In the two-room apartments the bedrooms usually had no windows or other ventilation. Conditions were even worse in the cellars that were frequently flooded and overrun with vermin.[15]

If the Sixth Ward was the most overcrowded neighborhood in antebellum New York, Five Points, the intersection of Anthony, Orange and Cross Streets, was the most densely populated area in the Sixth Ward, perhaps even in the world. For years it was a tourist attraction made famous by Charles Dickens who visited it in 1841. In the 1840s and 1850s enterprising landlords replaced the two-story wooden rookeries with four and five-story brick tenements. However, this did little to improve the quality of life of the tenants because the landlords squeezed many more people into these wretched buildings.[16]

14 - *New York Sun,* March 9, 1843; Robert Ernst, *Immigrant Life in New York City, 1825-1863* (Syracuse: Syracuse University Press, 1994), 66-71.

15 - John H. Griscom, M.D., *The Sanitary Condition of the Laboring Population of New York* (New York: Harper and Brothers, 1845), 6-9.

16 - For an evocative re-creation of the sounds and sights and especially the smells of Five Points ("an olfactory nightmare"), see Tyler Anbinder, *Five Points* (New York: Plume, 2001). A seven-story tenement built in the 1820s still stands at 65 Mott Street. Ibid., 81.

The notorious Five Points in 1827. Credit: *Archdiocese of New York*

As late as 1857 three-quarters of the city's 500 miles of streets lacked sewers with the result, as Robert Ernst expressed it, that "life in the slums was a continual struggle with illness and death." The immigrants often lost the battle. The Sixth Ward was notorious for periodic outbreaks of typhoid, typhus and cholera as well as for the high incidence of tuber-culosis, a disease that John Hughes once called "the natural death of the Irish immigrant." In a desperate effort to escape from the slums of lower Manhattan some immigrants moved north of the city proper and established shanty colonies on vacant land.

The proliferation of grog shops in the Irish wards shocked many native-born Americans who regarded it as evidence of moral degradation and a major cause of Irish poverty. One Protestant temperance preacher wondered if St. Patrick's Cathedral was to blame for the number of gin-

shops on Mott Street. In mock horror he rejected the suggestion. "No, no," he protested, "to suppose that these shops are sustained by the worshippers of St. Patrick's when going to or returning from church, would be very unkind, and perhaps very unjust."[17]

The Five Points in 1859. Credit: *Archdiocese of New York*

17 - Griscom, *Sanitary Condition*, 35

*In 1852 Brenan's grog shop shared quarters in the Old Brewery
with the Five Points Mission of the Methodist Episcopal Church.*

On the eve of the Civil War there was no doubt that the New York Catholic community was overwhelmingly Irish. No fewer than twenty-two of the city's thirty-one parishes were territorial parishes, which meant in effect that they were Irish parishes.

Kleindeutschland

The second-largest ethnic group among New York City Catholics was the Germans. As German-American Catholics they were a minority three times over, first in the general population, then in the local Catholic community, and finally within New York's German-American community. In the early nineteenth century German immigrants were concentrated on the Lower East Side of Manhattan, in the area that was known as Kleindeutschland or Little Germany, and that later became the center of Eastern European Jewish settlement.

Kleindeutschland comprised some 250 city blocks bounded by 14th Street on the north, Division Street on the south, the Bowery on the west and the East River. Avenue B was the main commercial strip while Avenue A was dotted with beer gardens, oyster saloons, grocery stores and butcher shops. Many German theatres and social clubs were clustered near the Bowery and Canal Street. According to one estimate, at mid-century, New York's Kleindeutschland was the third largest German-speaking city in the world, surpassed only by Vienna and Berlin. By 1875 the population of the four wards that made up the neighborhood (the 10, 11, 13 and 17 Wards) was almost two-thirds German. By that date German immigrants and their descendents may have accounted for almost one-third of the population of New York City.[18]

Perhaps one-third of the population of Kleindeutschland was Catholic, reflecting the fact

18 - Stanley Nadel, *Little Germany: Ethnicity, Religion, and Class in New York City, 1845-80* (Urbana and Chicago: University of Illinois Press, 1990), 32, 36, 41-42.

that about eighty percent of the pre-Civil War German immigrants came from Bavaria and the Rhineland, traditionally Catholic areas of Germany. The other two-thirds of New York's German population were divided among Lutherans, members of the Reformed churches, Jews, socialists, and freethinkers. The latter were aggressively sectarian in their secularism and even founded their own network of "churches" and "parochial" schools.

German immigrants tended to be somewhat better off economically than the Irish and came to dominate certain trades and industries as tailors, shoemakers, cabinetmakers, bakers, butchers, cigar makers and especially as brewers, the most successful of whom formed the elite in the German community. It has often been claimed that, in contrast to the Irish, the Germans emigrated to America as families rather than as single individuals. Recent studies suggest that this contrast needs to be nuanced. Many of the residents of Kleindeutschland were probably single or young married couples without children while "single" Irish immigrants often brought the rest of their family to America after they had made enough money to do so.[19]

Both Irish and German immigrants suffered from the absence of zoning regulations in their neighborhoods, which meant that factories, stables, coal and lumber yards and even slaughterhouses shared the same block with residential buildings. In the 1860s the family of Samuel Gompers found a four-room apartment at Houston and Attorney Streets in the Eleventh Ward where the father made cigars at home with the help of his thirteen-year old son. The younger Gompers left an often-quoted description of the neighborhood:

> Our house was just opposite a slaughter house. All day long we could see the animals being driven into the slaughter-pens and could hear the turmoil and the cries of the animals. The neighborhood was filled with the penetrating, sickening odor. The suffering of the animals and the nauseating odor made it physically impossible for me to eat meat for many months.
> Back of our house was a brewery which was in continuous operation and this necessitated the practice of living-in for the brewery workers. Conditions were dreadful in the breweries of those days and I became very familiar with them from our back door.[20]

A Squatters' Settlement
between 1st and 2nd Avenues
near 36th Street in 1858.
Credit: *Archdiocese of New York*

---

19 - Ibid., 26, 32, 63, 91-99; Pernicone, " 'Bloody Ould Sixth,' " 53-59.

20 - Samuel Gompers, *Seventy Years of Life and Labor: An Autobiography* (New York: E.P. Dutton & Company, 1925), 24.

Mere Irish and Damned Dutch

Native-born American Protestants liked to make invidious comparisons between Irish Catholic and German Protestant immigrants. "They [the Germans] are the opposite of the Irish," reported the Association for Improving the Condition of the Poor in 1860, "being generally a self-reliant, sober, frugal, thrifty people. . . . They often move in families, sometimes by villages, accompanied by their minister and doctor. . . . They can work for less wages than Americans and live where an Irishman would starve. As they limit their wants to their necessities, and rarely spend all they earn, they generally become prosperous, money-making citizens."[21]

A contemporary English visitor gave a less flattering portrait of New York's Germans. He said that native-born Americans showed equal contempt for the "mere Irish" and the "damned Dutch." According to him, the clannishness of the Germans was a particular irritant. "They keep up all their old national habits, customs, amusements, associations as tenaciously and more heartily than the Irish adhere to theirs." The German propensity to indulge in their favorite beverage on Sunday afternoons at their "lager-bier saloons, winter-gardens, summer-gardens, and volk-gartens" shocked pious teetotaling American Protestants as much as the prevalence of grog shops in the Irish wards. Evidently too the German dedication to the Protestant work ethic was not universally admired. According to this same English observer, many New Yorkers regarded the Germans as "so bent on money-getting that for its sake they will live sordidly and follow any occupation, however vile and repulsive." Skilled workmen were said to be especially resentful of the Germans because of their willingness to work for lower wages than they themselves would accept.[22]

Estimates of the size of New York's German-Catholic community in the mid-nineteenth century vary from 28,000 to 70,000. Whatever their exact numbers, the Catholics were the best-organized and dominant religious group in Kleindeutschland. In addition to the common problems that all immigrants encountered, however, German-American Catholics also had to defend themselves from attacks by Protestants, freethinkers and socialists within New York's German-speaking community.

German New Yorkers enjoying their favorite beverage at Jones's Wood, a popular picnic area on the East River. Credit: *Harper's New Monthly Magazine,* July 1861

21 - New York Association for Improving the Condition of the Poor, *Seventeenth Annual Report,* 1860, 50-51.

22 - D[avid] W. Mitchell, *Ten Years in the United States* (London: Smith, Elder and Company, 1862), 151, 158.

As far back as 1808, German Catholics who were worshipping at St. Peter's Church asked Bishop John Carroll for their own parish in New York. Five laymen signed a petition requesting "a pastor who is capable of undertaking the spiritual care of our souls in the German language, which is our Mother Tongue." They explained that "many of us do not know any English at all and those who have some knowledge of it are not well enough versed in the English language as to attend Divine Service with any utility to themselves."[23]

For the next few years Father Anthony Kohlmann was able to provide for the pastoral needs of the New York's German Catholics at St. Peter's. After his departure in 1814, however, it took almost another two decades before the hopes of New York's German Catholics were realized with the establishment of St. Nicholas Church, the first national parish in the diocese of New York. The key figure in founding St. Nicholas was an Austrian-born priest, Father Joseph Raffeiner, who arrived by chance in New York City in 1833.[24]

Father Joseph Raffeiner

Father Raffeiner was forty-eight years old in 1833 with a full life behind him as a physician and army surgeon in his native Austria. He was forty years old when he was ordained a priest and volunteered to go to America eight years later as a missionary to German Catholic immigrants in the Midwest. He was on his way to Cincinnati when he stopped in New York in 1833. Bishop John Dubois explained to him the urgent need for a German-speaking priest in New York and persuaded him to remain in his diocese. In subsequent years Raffeiner crisscrossed New York State as the vicar general for the Germans seeking out German Catholics and founding several dozen parishes for them. Shortly after his arrival in America, he wrote back to a bishop in Germany:

More than 60,000 German immigrants live in the Diocese of New York, and wherever I go I find them without priests and without churches, deprived of Christian instruction and the sacraments. What else can be expected under such conditions than that the priceless heritage these people brought with them from the Fatherland gradually disappears; and what a wonderful work it would be, if the dying flame of the religion of so many thousands of these immigrants could be brought to life again, a work which, with the Grace of God, could be accomplished within a few years by a few more priests.[25]

Father Johann Stephan Raffeiner (1785-1861), pioneer German Catholic priest in New York.
Credit: *Diocese of Brooklyn*

Father Raffeiner's first order of business was to find a permanent spiritual home for the German Catholics in New York City. He celebrated Mass first in a rented carpenter's shop on Delancey Street in 1833 and then in a former Baptist church at the corner of Delancey and Pitt Streets that he rented for eighty dollars a year. The following year Raffeiner brought four lots from John Jacob Astor on 2nd Street between First Avenue and Avenue A. The cornerstone of St. Nicholas Church was blessed on Easter Monday in 1835 and it was dedicated a year later on Easter Sunday. The congregation was so desperate for space that they used the unfinished church even before its dedication.

23 - Petition of the German Catholics of New York for a Pastor, 1808, *ACHR 9* (1892): 63.

24 - Thomas F. Meehan, "Very Rev. Johann Stephan Raffeiner, V.G.," *HR&S 9* (1916): 161-175.

25 - *St. Nicholas Church in Second Street* (New York: St. Nicholas Church, 1933), 30.

On June 26, 1836, the new church was the scene of a First Mass celebrated by Father John Neumann. A native of Bohemia, where he was born on March 28, 1811, John Neumann arrived in New York as a deacon on June 2, 1836, and offered his services to Bishop Dubois as a priest of his diocese. Bishop Dubois readily accepted the offer and ordained him a priest three weeks later. Two days after his First Mass at St. Nicholas he was dispatched upstate to care for German-speaking Catholics in the Buffalo area. Neumann later joined the Redemptorist Fathers, and in 1852 became the fourth bishop of Philadelphia where he died on January 5, 1860. He was canonized by Pope Paul VI on June 19, 1977.

Statue of St. John Neuma *at St. John Neumann Hall* *Residence.* Credit: Chris Sheri *Catholic New York*

St. Nicholas Church on East 2nd Street: New York's first German Church

St. John Neumann, Fourth Bishop of Philadelphia, 1852-1860. Credit: Chris Sheridan, *Catholic New York*

Meanwhile, in New York City, Father Raffeiner resigned as the pastor of St. Nicholas Church in 1840 because of bitter and interminable disputes with the lay trustees of the parish. After his unpleasant experience at St. Nicholas, he was happy to move across the East River to Williamsburg where he established Most Holy Trinity Church, the first of eight German parishes that he was instrumental in starting in Brooklyn. At St. Nicholas several others pastors followed Father Raffeiner in quick succession until Bishop Hughes asked the Redemptorists to take charge of the parish.

"I know that it is contrary to your practice to take charge of churches where there are trustees," Bishop Hughes wrote to the Redemptorist superior, "but for the sake of religion and the poor and pious German people, I hope you will make this an exception."[26] The Redemptorists acceded to Hughes' request and assigned the tough-minded Father Gabriel Rumpler as pastor. However, he was no more successful in dealing with the trustees than his predecessors. Like the Holy Roman Emperor Joseph II, the trustees even dictated the number of candles he could light at High Mass. (It was only in 1908 that the trustees finally surrendered control of the parish to the archdiocese.)

26 - AANY, Hughes to Alexander Czvitkovicz, C.Ss.R., August 16, 1842, copy.

In 1844 Rumpler resigned and with the permission of John Hughes built a new German Church, Most Holy Redeemer, only two blocks away, on East 3rd Street. It soon replaced St. Nicholas as the premier Catholic church in Kleindeutschland, especially after the dedication of the present huge stone church on November 28, 1852, with its 250-foot bell tower dominating the skyline of the neighborhood.

The Germans were the first non-English speaking Catholic ethnic group in New York, and they were the first to disappear into the American melting pot, a process that was accelerated with almost indecent haste by the outbreak of anti-German hysteria during World War I. The evolution of St. Nicholas Church illustrates the stages of assimilation. The parish history published to commemorate the fiftieth anniversary in 1883 was entirely in German; the history published to commemorate the hundredth anniversary in 1933 was entirely in English. The parish itself was suppressed in 1960s and the church building was demolished.

Two centuries after the pioneer German Catholics asked Bishop John Carroll for their own parish in New York, the sole reminder of the once vibrant German-language Catholic community in Manhattan was a monthly Mass celebrated in German at St. Joseph's Church on East 87th Street in Yorkville.

The Church of the Most Holy Redeemer today.

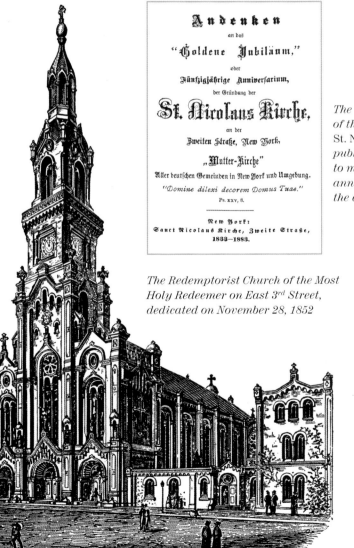

The title page of the History of St. Nicholas Church *published in 1883 to mark the fiftieth anniversary of the church*

The Redemptorist Church of the Most Holy Redeemer on East 3rd Street, dedicated on November 28, 1852

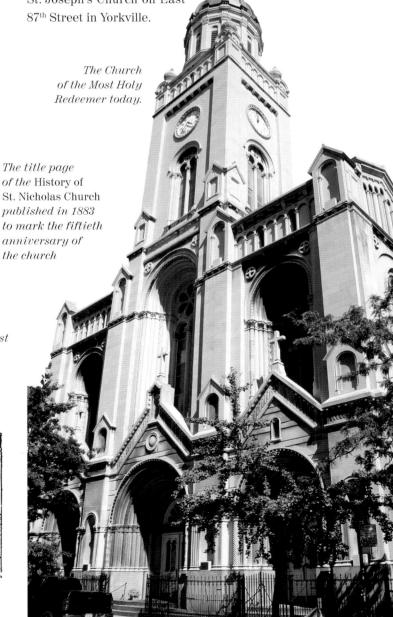

The French-Speaking Catholics

French immigration to the United States has been a mere trickle compared to that of virtually every other European country. It is estimated that no more than one percent of the French ever settled permanently in the United States. The topic has scarcely been studied, one historian suggested, because Americans regard it as unimportant and the French consider it too painful to contemplate. The 14,000 Huguenots who emigrated to America in the colonial period were virulently anti-Catholic, none more so than one of their most prominent descendants in New York, John Jay. The French Revolution brought another wave of 10,000 French exiles to America, who came not only from France but also from Saint Domingue (Haiti). Many found a temporary refuge in New York.

In the 1790s there may have been as many as 3,000 or 4,000 French-speaking immigrants in New York City, and they added a lively new dimension to Manhattan's streets.

> The city thronged with people of all shades of color from the French colonies and took on the appearance of a great cosmopolitan hotel. *La mode française* disrupted old ways of living; French boarding houses sprang up on every street; Creoles from Haiti proudly flounced through the streets clad richly in West Indian materials; "coal black Negresses," in flowing white dresses and colorful turbans made of muchoir de madras, strolled with white or mixed Creoles, adding to the picturesqueness of the scene. These people formed a lively contrast to the dour native Americans and émigrés from old France.[27]

Many of the émigrés returned to France after 1800, and ten years later a visitor noted the small number of French-speaking people whom he encountered in New York. Nonetheless, the French-speaking Catholic community wanted their own parish, and they got it in 1841 with the establishment of the Church of St. Vincent de Paul, originally located on Canal Street and relocated to West 23rd Street in 1856.

As late as 1890 there were only 9,910 French-born residents in New York City. They supported three Protestant churches as well as the Church of St. Vincent de Paul. Many of them lived in rundown buildings in the area south of Washington Square Park known as the French Quarter. A reporter who visited the bakeries and restaurants in the neighborhood was struck by the poverty of the French-speaking people whom he met. The French Catholic community in New York City also included a few prominent families like the Hoguets, Binsses, Bouviers, Delmonicos and Couderts. Nonetheless, lack of financial support from French Catholics was a constant complaint from the Fathers of Mercy, a small French religious community who staffed St. Vincent de Paul Church almost from the beginning. No less an authority than John Dubois, New York's only French bishop, contrasted the stinginess of his fellow countrymen with the generosity of the Irish.[28]

Venerable Pierre Toussaint

The most notable French-speaking Catholic layman in nineteenth-century New York was not an émigré nobleman, but Pierre Toussaint, a slave who was born in Saint Domingue in 1766, and who came to New York in 1787. Like his master, Jean-Jacques Bérard, a plantation owner who was fleeing from the revolution on the island, the twenty-one year old Toussaint expected that his stay in New York would be brief. Instead he was to remain in New York City for the next sixty-six years.

27 - Rosenwaike, *Population History,* 14-25; Roy Ottley and William J. Weatherly, *The Negro in New York: An Informal Social History* (New York: New York Public Library, 1967), 47-48.

28 - Rosenwaike, *Population History,* 67; "The French Quarter of New York," *Scribner's Monthly* 19:1 (November 1879), in *Gaslight New York Revisited,* ed. Frank Oppel (New York: Castle, 1989), 135-143. "Bishop Dubois on New York in 1836," *HR&S 10* (1917): 126.

The revolution in Saint Domingue ruined Bérard financially, but Toussaint, supported him and later his widow from his own earnings as a hairdresser. Shortly before her death, Mme Bérard went to the French consulate where she signed a document on July 2, 1807, giving Toussaint his freedom.[29] Toussaint prospered as a hairdresser and included among his customers some of the city's leading socialites such as the Schuylers, Hamiltons and Livingstons. He was sufficiently well off to purchase the freedom of his sister Rosalie and his future wife, Rose Marie Juliette Noël, whom he married in St. Peter's Church on August 5, 1811. He also was a stockholder in the North River Bank and owned his own home at 144 Franklin Street.

A devout Catholic and pewholder at St. Peter's Church, he attended the six o'clock Mass there every morning for sixty-six years. Toussaint was known for his generosity to needy individuals and to institutions like the Catholic Orphan Asylum. His charity was not limited to almsgiving. He was much in demand as a "watcher," someone who would remain with fever victims until they died or recovered. Although he and his wife were childless, they made it a practice to take into their home destitute black youngsters and to teach them a trade until they were old enough to fend for themselves. When Toussaint considered moving to Paris in 1819, an old friend from Saint Domingue and New York, Jean Sorbieu, urged him to remain in New York because his charity was so much need in that city.[30]

Despite his relative wealth, Toussaint was not spared the racial prejudice that all African Americans experienced in New York at that time. The easiest way for him to travel to his customers who were scattered around the city would have been by means of the public horse cars, but

Venerable Pierre Toussaint (1766-1853).
Credit: *Archdiocese of New York*

Receipt issued to Pierre Toussaint in 1822 for the payment of pew rent to St. Peter's Church.
Credit: *Archdiocese of New York*

Received, New-York, *february 18* 182 2
from *M.* Peter Toussaint ~~part pew~~ holder of pew
No. 25 F in St. Peter's Church, the sum of *fourteen dollars*
in full to 1 of May next, *James Mill*, Sexton.
Dlls. *14*

African Americans were barred from using them until 1854, the year after his death. Even in church he was not immune from racial bias. In the summer of 1842 he was insulted in St. Patrick's Cathedral by a white usher who objected to his presence in the congregation. Louis Binsee, the French-speaking president of the board of trustees, sent Toussaint an apology, but even his apology revealed the unconscious racism that prevailed among the best-intentioned white New Yorkers. "If God by His will has created you and your wife with black skin," Binsee told him, "by His grace He has also made your heart and soul as white as snow."[31]

Toussaint played no role in the abolitionist movement, which is not surprising in view of the anti-Catholic attitude of many abolitionists. More puzzling was his silence about slavery at a time when it was becoming the dominant moral issue in America. The explanation is that he was a man of peace who feared violent social change, a legacy of his own experience of the early stages of the Haitian revolution. *"Madame, ils n'ont jamais vu couler le sang comme moi* [They never saw blood flow as I did]," he explained to a woman who asked him why he did not take a more

29 - NYPL, Pierre Toussaint Papers, Extrait des Minutes de la Chancellerie du commisariat de France à New-York, No. 633, July 2, 1802.

30 - [Hannah Sawyer Lee], *Memoir of Pierre Toussaint, Born a Slave in St. Domingo* (Boston: Crosby, Nichols and Company, 1854), 71, 82, 86; NYPL, Pierre Toussaint Papers, Sorbieu to Toussaint, January 27, 1819.

31 - NYPL, Pierre Toussaint Papers, Binsse to Toussaint, August 24, 1842.

St. Elizabeth Ann Bayle
Seton as a young woman
as the founder of the Sist
of Charity.

aggressive stand against slavery.[32] In 1989 John Cardinal O'Connor introduced the cause of his canonization in Rome, exhumed his body and placed it in the crypt under the high altar of St. Patrick's Cathedral. He was declared Venerable in 1997.[33]

The Converts

On March 14, 1805, St. Peter's Church was the scene of an event that was to have a major impact on the Church in New York and on the whole American Catholic Church. On that day Father Matthew O'Brien received Elizabeth Ann Bayley Seton into the Catholic Church. The daughter of Dr. Richard Bayley, a distinguished physician, and the widow of William Seton, a businessman, she entered the Catholic Church despite the opposition of many of her Episcopalian relatives.

As a young widow with five children to support, Elizabeth Seton found herself in difficult financial straits. She opened a school and later a boarding home for young children, but both projects failed. In 1808 she moved to Baltimore where she established a school for girls. The following year she moved again, this time to Emmitsburg, Maryland, where she made her religious vows on March 29 in the presence of Archbishop Carroll. Later that year several other women joined her, leading to the beginning of regular community life on July 29, 1809, which is regarded as foundational date of the Sisters of Charity of St. Joseph. Archbishop Carroll gave final approval to the rule of the new community on January 17, 1812.

Mother Seton died of tuberculosis at Emmitsburg on January 4, 1821. By that date her sisters had already opened orphanages in Philadelphia (1814) and New York (1817). In 1850 the Sisters of Charity of Emmitsburg affiliated with the Daughters of Charity in France and were known thereafter as the Daughters of Charity. Five other communities of the Sisters of Charity in the United States and Canada trace their origins to Mother Seton and her little community at Emmitsburg, including the Sisters of Charity of St. Vincent de Paul of New York. The communities of Mother Seton's sisters spread throughout the country, establishing or staffing thousands of schools, hospitals, orphanages and other institutions. Mother Seton herself was declared Venerable on December 18, 1959, beatified on March 17, 1963, and canonized on September 14, 1975, the first native-born American to be declared a saint.

St. Peter's Church was the scene of another remarkable event in February 1817 when Father Benedict Fenwick received into the Church Virgil Barber, an Episcopalian clergyman in upstate New York, together with his wife and their five children. Subsequently Barber and his wife separated, and he became a Jesuit priest and she became a Visitation nun. All of their children either became priests or entered religious life as well. Moreover, Barber's parents, his sister and brother-in-law, and their eight children all followed him into the Catholic Church.

32 - Lee, *Memoir,* 85-86.

33 - Arthur Jones believes that Toussaint was born in 1781 and that he did not come to the United States until 1797. Arthur Jones, *Pierre Toussaint: A Biography* (New York: Doubleday, 2003. See also Thomas J. Shelley, "Black and Catholic in Nineteenth-Century New York City: The Case of Pierre Toussaint," *RACHSP* 102 (1991): 1-18.

Elizabeth Seton and the Barbers were the first of a long line of Episcopalians and other Protestants who either entered the Catholic Church in New York or made their home there. Bishop Dubois said that there were between 300 and 600 adult converts every year. In 1840 the Rev. Mr. Maximilian Oertel, a Lutheran minister in New York City, became a Catholic. Another convert clergyman was a relative of Elizabeth Ann Seton, James Roosevelt Bayley. Ordained an Episcopalian clergyman in 1840, Bayley was the rector of St. Andrew's Church in Harlem. He became a Catholic in Rome in 1842 and was ordained a priest of the diocese of New York two years later. A trusted advisor to Archbishop Hughes, Bayley was named the first bishop of Newark in 1853 and became the archbishop of Baltimore in 1872.

Bayley was only one of several Episcopalian clergymen who entered the Catholic Church in the 1840s and 1850s as the result of the Oxford Movement whose spiritual center in America was located at General Theological Seminary in New York City. Several prominent alumni of that institution became Catholic priests, including William Everett and Thomas Preston, who was to serve as chancellor and vicar general of the archdiocese of New York under three archbishops. Another convert was John Murray Forbes, who returned to the Episcopal Church after several years as pastor of St. Ann's Church.[34]

On his first visitation of the diocese in 1839 Bishop Hughes discovered a community of eighteen Catholics, all converts, near Syracuse. Their leader was a Colonel Dodge, who had set up a private chapel in his residence where a priest occasionally celebrated Mass for them. "There they have their altar," Bishop Hughes reported, "adorned and decorated in the richest manner that the resources of the country would allow.

Father William Everett

Archbishop James Roosevelt Bayley

Silver candlesticks, a very neat ivory crucifix, white fine linen, and beautiful fresh flowers at the foot of a small picture of the Blessed Virgin, constituted its decorations when I had the pleasure of visiting this excellent family last summer."[35]

Two of the leading American Catholic intellectuals in the nineteenth century, Orestes Brownson and Isaac Hecker, were converts with strong ties to New York. Brownson soon moved across the river to New Jersey to escape from John Hughes' jurisdiction. Hecker remained in New York City where he founded the Society of Missionary Priests of St. Paul the Apostle, better known as the Paulist Fathers, the first male religious community to be established in the United States. Like Hecker, the first Paulists were all converts, Augustine Hewitt, George Deshon and Francis Baker.

Orestes Brownson

Father Isaac Hecker. C.S.P.

34 - See Robert Kent Wilson, "The Oxford Movement and the Church of New York." M.A. thesis, St. Joseph's Seminary, Dunwoodie, 1990.
35 - Hassard, *Hughes,* 202.

James McMaster, the acerbic journalist, and Levi Silliman Ives, the former Episcopal bishop of North Carolina, both discovered a spiritual home in the New York Catholic community. Both Ives and another convert, Henry J. Anderson, a former professor of astronomy at Columbia University, served as president of the St. Vincent de Paul Society.

James A. McMaster

were troublesome characters whose bishops were happy to speed them on their way to America. As a result the general quality of the clergy left much to be desired, not only in New York, but elsewhere in the United States as well. "Soon do I begin to experience the sad effects of taking up with volunteer clergymen emigrants to America," John Carroll wrote in 1787.

Dr. Levi Silliman Ives

Rose Hawthorne Lathrop, founder of the Dominican Sisters for the Relief of Incurable Cancer

Mother Veronica Starr, founder of the Religious of Divine Compassion

A decade later Anthony Kohlmann may have been reflecting more than Jesuit hauteur when he told a confrere that he did not want diocesan priests associated with Jesuits in staffing the cathedral in New York. Nonetheless, Kohlmann was well aware that one of the most disruptive priests in New York was a fellow Jesuit, the Belgian-born Peter Malou. Bishop Dubois publicly complained about immigrant priests who came uninvited to New York. "With a few exceptions," he declared candidly in a pastoral letter, "they are men of inferior capacity and doubtful character, and on that account obtain a ready consent from their ecclesiastical superiors."[36]

Converts were prominent in leadership roles among women religious. Elizabeth Boyle, Mary Jerome Ely, Alice Madeleine Thorpe, Rose Hawthorne Lathrop and Veronica Starr were all converts who either founded or headed communities of women religious in New York. The long line of prominent converts stretched well into the twenty century with Dorothy Day, Catherine de Hueck Doherty and Thomas Merton.

The Diocesan Clergy

The lack of native vocations to the priesthood forced American bishops to rely heavily on foreign-born priests. The results were mixed. While some of the foreign recruits were capable and zealous men, others

Not one of the first six pastors of St. Peter's Church was a diocesan priest and only one of them was a native-born American, Edward Fenwick, who was pastor from 1815 to 1817. Not until 1881 did the parish have a second American-born pastor, James H. McGean. Although foreign-born priests were indispensable and some like the Cuban-born Felix Varela and the Irish-

---

36 - Carroll to Plowden, November 7, 1787, *JCP*, I, 265; Kohlmann to William Strickland, April 14, 1809, in Ryan, *Old St. Peter's*, 103; Dubois, *New-York Weekly Register and Catholic Diary*, February 23, 1834.

BISHOPRIC OF NEW-YORK.

Rt. Rev'd. Dr. John Connolly, *Bishop.*

THE bishopric of New-York, comprehends the whole state of New-York, together with the northern parts of Jersey. The residence of the Bishop is in New-York. This city contains two Catholic Churches, viz: the Cathedral (St. Patrick's) and St. Peters.

The Cathedral is a superb edifice, 120 feet long by 80 feet wide, finished in a superior manner in the inside, and is capable of holding 6000 people. The exterior, as to the ornamental part, is yet unfinished. The style of the building is Gothic; and from its great extent and solidity, must have cost upwards of 90,000 dollars. No church in the United States, (the Cathedral in Baltimore excepted) can compare with it.

St. Peter's, which is the first Catholic Church erected in New-York, is a neat, convenient, and handsome building. It was erected about 20 years ago, at which time the number of Catholics did not exceed three hundred. At present they number upwards of twenty thousand. They are mostly natives of Ireland and France.

There are in this city two extensive Catholic charity schools, conducted upon a judicious plan, and supported partly by the funds of the state, and partly by moneys raised twice a year by the two congregations. Independently of these two establishments, the Emittsburg sisters of charity have a branch here of their pious institution, exclusively for the benefit of female orphan children, whom they board, clothe and educate. Their house fronts the side of the Cathedral, and is in one of the most healthy situa-'tions in New-York.

In Albany there is likewise a Catholic church—a neat and compact building. It was erected about 14 years ago, and is attended by a growing congregation. The clergyman officiating in this church, visits occasionally Troy, Lansingbugh, Johnstown and Schenectady.

In Utica, a large and beautiful church has lately been erected and consecrated, which reflects great honour on the Catholics residing there. Their number is not great; neither are they generally wealthy —their zeal however *for the house of God, and the place where his glory dwelleth,* has enabled them to surmount every obstacle to the exercise of their piety. From the multitude flocking annually to this flourishing village, no doubt can be entertained but this will shortly become one of the most numerous, and respectable congregations in the diocess.

In Rome, (15 miles distant from Utica,) there is as yet no Catholic church, but a beautiful lot is reserved, by the liberality of Dominick Lynch, Esq. on which one will be erected, as soon as the number of Catholics settling there will render its erection necessary. The situation of this little town is healthy and beautiful.

In Auburn, an agreeable little town, still farther distant in the state, there is likewise a Catholic church, recently erected.

In New-Jersey, in the town of Patterson, there is also one, which is regularly attended by a clergyman.

In Carthage, near the Black River, a small and neat church has been lately erected.

THE FOLLOWING ARE THE CATHOLIC CLERGYMEN OFFICIATING IN THIS DIOCESS.

NEW-YORK.

Rt. Rev'd. Dr. John Connolly, } St. Patrick's Cathe-
Rev. Michael O'Gorman,   } dral.
Rev'd. Charles French, } St. Peter's.
Rev'd. John Power,   }
Rev'd Mr. Bolger, *Patterson.*
Rev'd. Michael Carroll, *Albany and vicinity.*
Rev'd. John Farnan, *Utica and vicinity.*
Rev'd. Patrick Kelly, *Auburn, Rochester, and other districts in the Western parts of this state.*
Rev'd. Philip Larissy *attends regularly at Staten-Island, and different other congregations along the Hudson River.*

The Laity's Directory to the Church Service for the Year of Our Lord, M, DCCC, XXII, revised and corrected by the Rev. John Power of St. Peter's Church (New York: William H. Creagh, 1822), pp. 104-106

born John Power were widely esteemed, the lack of an American-born and American-trained clergy was a severe handicap for the Church in the United States.

It is not surprising, therefore, that every bishop of New York, beginning with Bishop Concanen, recognized the need for a diocesan seminary to provide for the pastoral needs of the diocese. It would take several decades, however, before American-born priests appeared in any numbers in New York. John Talbot Smith, writing from personal experience, mentioned that even in the late nineteenth century non-Catholics in New York City routinely referred to all Catholic priests as either Irish or Dutch, i.e, German. [37]

Even in John Carroll's day, New York made unique demands on diocesan priests. In 1796 Carroll refused to appoint one Michael Burke as an assistant at St. Peter's Church. "Between ourselves," Carroll confided to the pastor of St. Peter's, "He does not come up to my ideas of the person fit to be your vicar. N[ew] York is a city of too much consequence not to demand superior abilities…" New York's third bishop, John Dubois, came to the same conclusion. "This diocese differs from all others in this respect," he explained to Bishop John Purcell of Cincinnati, that "men of weak abilities" even though "zealous and pious," will not be effective pastors in New York. "If our priests are wanting in elocution," he wrote, "the comparison turns to the disadvantage of our Holy Faith. The Protestants deride us and the Catholics are ashamed." He also pointed out to Purcell that the laity in New York were better educated than ever before and expected their priests to be as well educated as they were.[38]

37 - Smith, *Catholic Church in New York,I,* 297.
38 - Carroll to William O'Brien, July 5, 1796, *JCP,* II, 184; AUND, Dubois to Purcell, December 9, 1831; January 31, 1832, copies in AANY.

However, Bishop Dubois was so desperate for priests in the 1830s that he did not live up to his own high standards. In 1836 he tried to persuade Bishop Francis Patrick Kenrick of Philadelphia to come to New York as his coadjutor. Kenrick declined the offer and revealed to the prefect of the Propaganda that Dubois had taken into his diocese a number of priests whom he had expelled from Philadelphia. I do not think that they would be happy to see me come to New York," he explained.[39]

The shortcomings of the New York diocesan clergy cannot be blamed entirely on the foreign-born clergy. One of the first American-born diocesan priests in New York was Ambrose Manahan, who was also one of the first New York priests to earn a doctorate in theology in Rome. He seemed well qualified to fulfill Bishop Dubois' profile of the kind of clergy who were needed in the diocese. However, he proved to be impossibly overbearing in any position of responsibility. John Hughes removed him as president of St. John's College after a few months.

Manahan was no more successful in his next assignment as pastor of St. Joseph's Church in Greenwich Village. When Bishop Hughes dismissed him from that post, he sent him the following memorable letter:

> Not wishing to have the pain of inflicting any public censure on your character, I advise you to resign, to ask [for] your exeat, in the almost extinguished hope that on a new scene where your future character will be determined by your future conduct, you may disappoint the melancholy anticipations that the past is too well calculated to inspire.

Hughes signed the letter, "Your afflicted friend in Christ."[40]

Downtown New York in the Winter of 1828: Provost (now Franklin) Street and Chapel (now Church) Street.
Credit: *Fordham University Archives*

39 - APF, Amer. Centr., Vol. 11, 474, Kenrick to Cardinal Prefect, February 22, 1836. Kenrick wrote that he had deprived the priests of faculties because of *crimina*.
40 - AANY, A-5, Hughes to Manahan, September 4, 1845.

Despite their personal failures and foibles, many New York priests endeared themselves to their parishioners because they risked their life to bring the sacraments to the sick and dying during the periodic outbreaks of cholera and other contagious diseases that were a common occurrence in New York City. By mid-century, wrote Jay Dolan, this was the heroic standard to which all priests were expected to aspire. For Archbishop John Hughes a priest could find no more glorious end than by contracting a fatal disease while bringing the sacraments to the sick and dying.[41]

During the yellow fever epidemic of 1805, John Hardie, the secretary of the Board of Health, mentioned that three priests from St. Peter's Church "were incessant in administering spiritual consolation to the sick of their congregation, nor did they, in the discharge of this duty, avoid the most filthy cellars, or most infected places…"[42] The priests at St. Peter's were the ones who first set this high standard of care for the sick by the clergy in New York.

During the scandals that engulfed the parish in 1807, Bishop Carroll initially hesitated to remove one of the curates, Father Matthew O'Brien, because of the care that he had shown for the sick at great danger to himself. The trustees showed the same compassion to Father William O'Brien, the pastor whom Carroll removed and suspended from the priesthood in 1807. Although O'Brien was never permitted to function again as a priest, the trustees gave him a generous pension in 1810, $500 per annum, the same salary as a pastor. They had a long and grateful memory. When O'Brien died in 1816, they placed a memorial tablet in the church recalling his devotion to duty during the yellow fever epidemics of 1795 and 1798.[43]

Not all New York priests were so fortunate. Father William Hussey, a curate at Immaculate Conception Church on East 14th Street, died on February 7, 1865, from typhoid fever that he contracted on a sick call. Newly ordained, he was only twenty-three years old.[44]

Lay Trustees

Another significant feature of Catholicism in early nineteenth-century New York was the important role played by the lay trustees, at least until Bishop John Hughes broke their power in the 1840s. A decade earlier, at the First Provincial Council of Baltimore in 1829, the U.S. bishops had effectively outlawed the system when they decreed that all church property was to held in the name of the bishop. The decision stemmed from the fact that in some parishes the system had led to serious quarrels between clergy and laity, and on occasion even to schism.

New York parishes experienced their full share of such controversies, beginnng at St. Peter's in 1787, when the Irish Capuchin Father Andrew Nugent and his supporters defied the authority of John Carroll. An earlier generation of American Catholic church historians like John Gilmary Shea and Peter Guilday severely criticized the lay trustees for seeking to devise a "republican" form of church government that threatened to subvert the hierarchical structure of the Catholic Church. They blamed the trustees for seeking to introduce American notions of political democracy into the Catholic Church or slavishly following the example of Protestant parish organizations. John Talbot Smith, writing a century ago, castigated the pewholders who elected the trustees. "[They] very often professed the faith with their mouths, but lived the lives of pagans," he wrote. "Many of them were filled with heretical notions and admired ultra-Protestant customs…"[45]

41 - Jay P Dolan, *The Immigrant Church: New York's Irish and German Catholics, 1815-1865* (Baltimore: The Johns Hopkins University Press, 1975), 64.

42 - James Hardie, *An Account of the Malignant Fever, Which Prevailed in the City of New York; during the Autumn of 1805* (New York: Southwick and Hardcastle, 1805), 181.

43 - Carroll to Cornelius Heeney, February 18, 1808, *JCP,* III, 45; Ryan, *Old St. Peter's,* 88. To his death O'Brien continued to reside in the same house where he had lived as pastor, 57 Warren Street.

44 - AANY, Burtsell Diary, February 8, 1865.

45 - Smith, *Catholic Church in New York,* I, 65.

Today church historians like Patrick Carey and David O'Brien take a more benign view of lay trusteeism. Carey, the leading authority, regards trusteeism as a legitimate if sometimes messy effort to adapt European customs of church government such as lay patronage to the American scene rather than the result of American political influence or Protestant example. The basic problem, as he sees it, is that "the trustees' understanding of the church as the People of God clashed with the bishops' understanding of the church as a supernatural mystery with a divinely established episcopal structure." Although Carey does not believe that these two approaches were inherently contradictory (and John Carroll tried to reconcile them), he traces the conflict between the laity and the clergy to the fact that "neither side had the theological concepts to bring the two emphases together in a satisfactorily coherent way."[46]

At least in New York the lay trustees were for the most part devout Catholics, not anticlerical rabble rousers, and they sometimes had good reason to challenge the priests with whom they came in conflict. If the bishops of New York complained about their clergy and suspended them with unusual frequency, it is not surprising that the laity should have had many of the same grievances. There is no doubt that in some instances the trustees were arrogant and overbearing, but it would be inaccurate to conclude they devoted all their waking hours to

formulating a republican ecclesiology to match their Jacksonian political convictions. They were much too busy with the more mundane task of trying to raise enough money to keep their parish financially solvent, often at their own expense.

In his analysis of the lay trustees in selected parishes in early nineteenth-century New York City, Jay Dolan made the unsurprising discovery that they generally belonged to a higher economic and bracket than the rest of the parishioners. That would appear to have been true also at St. Peter's from the very beginning of the parish. The occupation of eight of the nine trustees elected in 1789 can be identified. In addition to Dominick Lynch and Thomas Stoughton (whose wealth placed them in a special category), three others were merchants, José Roiz Silva, Charles Naylor and George Barnwell. William Mooney was an upholsterer, Andrew Morris was a chandler and John Sullivan a grocer.[47]

Two trustees of St. Peter's were the first of a long line of Catholics to hold public office in New York. The first was Andrew Morris, who became the assistant alderman of the wealthy First Ward in 1802. Four years later another trustee of St. Peter's, Francis Cooper, (who was of German, not Irish ancestry), was elected to the State Assembly. His election precipitated a minor political crisis because he refused to take the oath required of all office holders repudiating allegiance to all foreign jurisdictions, "ecclesiastical as well as civil."

---

46 - Carey, *People, Priests and Prelates*, 281.

47 - Dolan, *Immigrant Church*, 52; Bennett, *Catholic Footsteps*, 391-397.

The Catholics held a meeting on January 6,1806, protesting that the oath was a violation of their religious liberty because it interfered with their spiritual allegiance to the pope. They also pointed out that no other state had imposed a religious test for public office. They drew up a petition with 1,300 signatures asking the state legislature to repeal the law. Both houses of the legislature agreed, despite some opposition in the Assembly, and they repealed the last remaining legal disability on Catholics in the state. On February 7, 1806, Francis Cooper became the first Catholic to take his seat in the Assembly. Significantly it was not the pastor, Father William O'Brien, but the trustees, who informed John Carroll of the Catholic victory. [48]

Although it would be anther fifty years before Irish Catholics politicians gained control of Tammany Hall, the local Democratic organization, as early as the 1830s there were complaints about the inordinate political influence of Catholics in the city. During the cholera epidemic of 1832, which claimed over 3,500 lives in three months, many Catholics were buried in the cathedral graveyard in special cholera graves, which were dug deep enough to hold four coffins. John Pintard, a wealthy banker, complained that it was a health menace. "Were it a Protestant burial place," he said, "it would be interdicted, but so many of our Corporation depend on Irish votes at elections that the nuisance passes unheeded by."[49]

Diversity of many kinds has been a distinguishing characteristic of the New York Catholic community from the very beginning. As Bishop Connolly quickly discovered, New York Catholics were mainly Irish, but they also included French and Germans with a sprinkling of other nationalities as well. Most were cradle Catholics, but there was also a continuing stream of converts. Overwhelmingly white, the Catholic community numbered at least a few African Americans like Pierre Toussaint and several hundred Native Americans in the far northern areas of the diocese. It was a community that became poorer as a result of immigration, but it always contained a few wealthy individuals like Dominick Lynch and Cornelius Heeney. It was also a community where clergy and laity not infrequently clashed over their respective roles. In 1815, seven years after the establishment of the diocese, the greatest need of New York Catholics was a spiritual leader who could pull together these disparate elements and give unity and direction to a rapidly growing heterogeneous community.

Harlem Plains in 1821. Credit: *Archdiocese of New York*

48 - *ACHR* 11 (1894): 182-184.

49 - *Letters of John Pintard to His Daughter, Elisa Noel Davidson, 1816-1833* (New York: New-York Historical Society, 1941), IV, 78.

5

A Diocese Adrift

View of New York from New Jersey in 1828. Credit: *Fordham University Archives*

In 1815 the diocese of New York was a missionary diocese that would have taxed the physical strength and spiritual resources of the most energetic and zealous young bishop.   John Connolly was in his late sixties, a total stranger to America, and had no pastoral experience whatsoever. It is no wonder that John Carroll hoped that at least he would bring with him "zealous, capable and edifying clergymen" to assist him. Instead, he arrived alone in New York City on November 24, 1815, to face almost insuperable odds.

The immense size of the diocese together with the scattered Catholic population, the poverty of most of the laity and the scarcity of priests, would have been enough to discourage any bishop. He had three churches, two in New York City and one in Albany, and six or seven priests (two of whom were not capable of preaching in English), to care for a Catholic population of between 12,000 and 15,000 in New York City and an unknown number of Catholics upstate and in northern New Jersey. He also had to contend with a faction-ridden Catholic community that often put him at odds with significant segments of the laity and clergy.

The dearth of clergy actually got worse after his arrival. Two of the Jesuits, Benedict Fenwick and Maximilian Rantzau, were recalled from New York to Maryland by their superior. A third Jesuit, the eccentric and irascible Peter Malou was more of a liability than an asset. He was suspended by Connolly and resigned from the Society of Jesus a few years later. A fourth priest, Thomas Carbry, an Irish Dominican who had been a student of Connolly in Rome, soon left for Virginia where he was caught up in a scheme abetted by Connolly to make him a bishop. That left Connolly with Malou and two Irish priests, Michael Carroll and Michael O'Gorman, a twenty-three year old graduate of St. Kieran's College, Kilkenny, whom Connolly appears to have ordained in Ireland as New York's first diocesan priest and who reached New York in April 1816. Paul McQuade, the pastor of St. Mary's Church in Albany, returned to Canada in 1817.[1]

Bishop Connolly arrived in New York with a cold that he caught at sea. After forty years in Rome he was not prepared for the harsh New York winter, which left him ill for several months. Nine months later he sent a somber report to the Propaganda. "My daily burdens are truly greater than my strength," he wrote, "owing to my not having more than three priests to help me in this city, where among Catholics, there are at least twelve thousand Irish Catholics, my countrymen. I am forced also to fulfill the duties of curate or subcurate for the three priests. I hope that the Lord will give me strength to go on for some years more." One of Connolly's biggest concerns was the scarcity of priests. "American Catholics have absolutely no inclination to become ecclesiastics," he told the Roman authorities, "and those few priests that come here from Europe, not knowing the English language, can be of little help to us [until] after they have spent some years residence in this country."[2] The latter comment is strange in view of the fact that most of the foreign priests in New York were Irish like himself.

New York's first resident bishop was remembered as a short, well-groomed man, who was unpretentious and approachable to the members of his own flock. Unlike John Carroll in Baltimore or Jean Cheverus in Boston, however, Connolly never participated in civic affairs or social activities with non-Catholics. As he mentioned himself, he functioned more as a parish priest than as a bishop in his own cathedral, regularly hearing confessions and bringing Communion to the sick in their homes.

St. Patrick's Old Cathedral.

1 - John Gilmary Shea, *History of the Catholic Church in the United States* (New York: John G. Shea, 1890), 176-178; *The Shamrock,* April 13, 1816.

2 - APF, scritt. rifer., Congressi: amer. cent., section III, folio 500rv, n. 228, Connolly to the Prefect of the Propaganda, September 1, 1816.

On Sunday he always celebrated high Mass without a miter or crozier because of the lack of attendants. He never wore his religious habit in public. His street dress was similar to that of a Protestant minister, a dark suit with a white cravat rather than a clerical collar, which was the standard attire for Catholic priests in America until later in the century.[3]

Upstate New York and Northern New Jersey

The second oldest Catholic church in New York State, St. Mary's Church in Albany, dates from 1797, the same year that Albany became the state capital and eleven years before the foundation of the diocese. As in the case of St. Peter's Church in New York City, the initiative for the founding of St. Mary's came from the laity, since there was no resident priest in the city. The Albany Common Council obligingly donated a plot of land for a Catholic church on Pine Street between Barrack (now Chapel) and Lodge Streets. On October 6, 1796, nine laymen formed a corporation to erect a church and elected Thomas Barry, a prosperous merchant, president of the corporation. To raise the necessary funds, they appealed for help from as far away as Canada. On September 13, 1797, Barry laid the cornerstone of the little brick church. It was about fifty feet square and in use by the following year whenever the Catholics of Albany were fortunate enough to find a priest to celebrate Mass for them.[4]

Most of the original trustees were Irish, the major exceptions being James Robichaud, a French-Canadian, and Louis Le Couteulx de Chaumont, an exiled French aristocrat. The first pastor was a Yankee, Father John Thayer, an angular Boston-born convert from the Congregational Church who never stayed long anywhere and who soon left Albany in search of greener

The City of Albany in 1828

3 - James Roosevelt Bayley, *A Brief Sketch of the Early History of the Catholic Church on the Island of New York* (New York: The Catholic Publication Society, 1870), 84-86.

4 - Sally Light, *Canals and Crossroads: An Illustrated History of the Albany, New York, Roman Catholic Diocese* (Albany: Albany Catholic Press Association, 1997), 36-38.

pastures. For the next twenty years St. Mary's was the only Catholic Church between New York City and the Great Lakes. It ranks as the mother church of Catholicism in upstate New York not only because of the date of its founding, but also because several parishioners were instrumental in establishing some of the first Catholic churches in central and western New York.

One of them was John C. Devereux, a native of County Wexford, who moved to Utica in 1802, where his brother Nicholas joined him four years later. They did well in business, banking and politics, and on January 25, 1819, they organized a corporation to start St. John's Church in that city with the help of seven other lay people from as far away as Auburn and Rochester. They called their corporation "The First Catholic Church in the Western District of the State of New York." The Devereuxs subscribed $1,125 and others gave between $1.00 and $50.00.

The wife of Nicholas Devereux, who was not a Catholic, was impressed with the number of Catholics who came to the first Mass in Utica, which was celebrated in a school building in 1819. "I was very much surprised to find so many Catholics in this part of the country," Mrs. Devereux wrote to her mother. "Some came fifty miles and some two days journey to partake of the sacrament. This will show you how much attached they are to their religion. The [Erie] canal has brought many Catholics to this place."[5]

The celebrant of the Mass in Utica in 1819 was probably Father Michael O'Gorman, the pastor of St. Mary's Church in Albany. He regularly celebrated Mass for the construction workers on the Erie Canal and their families, traveling as far west as Auburn which he may have visited as early as 1816. Around 1820

Bishop Connolly appointed the first resident pastor in Utica, Father John Farnan (or Farnum), a tall loquacious heavy-set native of County Cavan, and on August 19, 1821, the bishop dedicated St. John's Church.[6]

St. Mary's Church, Albany, which dates from 1797.

Father Farnan was responsible not only for Utica, but for all of Western New York, including Carthage in Jefferson County, where in 1818, a French land developer, James Le Ray de Chaumont, was instrumental in building a Catholic church. Le Ray solicited funds from the French-Canadian and Irish residents of the area for the erection of a small frame building forty feet long and thirty feet wide. Some responded with money, others with promises of labor, merchandise, grain, whiskey and, in one case, "shaving knifes, 2 pairs of mittens and 1 saw." Bishop Connolly blessed the little building dedicated to St. James in 1820, although it was not completed until four years later.[7]

The year 1820 also witnessed the beginning of organized Catholic life in Rochester when on July 12 Father Farnan met with six Irish immigrants, most of them farmers from nearby Paddy Hill, to form a corporation that they called

5 - David O'Brien, *Faith and Friendship: Catholicism in the Diocese of Syracuse, 1886-1986* (Syracuse: Diocese of Syracuse, 1987), 31.

6 - Robert F. McNamara, *The Diocese of Rochester in America, 1868-1993*, 2nd edn. (Rochester: Roman Catholic Diocese of Rochester, 1998), 31-34.

7 - Thomas C. Middleton, O.S.A., "An Early Catholic Settlement," *RACHSP* 10 (1899): 17-51.

"The Third Roman Catholic Church in the Western District." On April 29, 1822, they purchased a lot in Rochester for $200. By the end of the following year St. Patrick's Church was nearly finished. It was a small stone building, thirty-eight by forty-two feet, with large Gothic windows.

The Catholics in Auburn were not as fortunate as their neighbors in Utica or Rochester. In the summer of 1820 the ubiquitous Father Farnan met with a group of local Catholics who selected five of their number to form "The Fourth Catholic Church of Western New York." For the nominal sum of five dollars they got property for a church and cemetery with the proviso that they would have to build a church on the site within five years. Auburn's Catholics began construction of a church, but they were unable to complete it and the property reverted to its original owners. Not until 1834 did Auburn get its first Catholic Church.[8]

In addition to John Devereux, another parishioner of St. Mary 's Church in Albany who moved west was Louis Le Couteulx. He settled permanently in Buffalo in 1824 where he became a prominent figure in business and politics. As late as that date there was still no Catholic church building or priest in the city. However, in 1828, Father Stephen Badin, a French-born missionary spent six weeks in Buffalo as the guest of Louis Le Couteulx and persuaded him to donate land for a church. On January 5, 1829, Le Couteulx followed Badin's advice and donated the land on the corner of Main and Edwards Streets where Buffalo's first Catholic church was to be built in 1830. Originally called Lamb of God Church, it was soon renamed St. Louis Church. Before he died in 1840, Le Couteulx also donated land for Immaculate Conception Church in Buffalo.[9]

In northern New Jersey Catholics were cared for by circuit-riding priests from Philadelphia like the famous Father Farmer and later Father Philip Lariscy (or Larissy), one of the Irish Augustinian friars in that city who was fluent in Irish as well as in English. The textile mills of Paterson attracted a number of Irish settlers to the area and they received their first resident pastor in 1820 when Bishop Connolly assigned the newly ordained Father Richard Bulger to them. He has the distinction of being the first diocesan priest ordained in the diocese. The following year thirteen Catholic families in Paterson bought a plot of land at the corner of Mill and Congress (now Market) Streets where they erected a little frame church, thirty feet by twenty-five feet, that they incorporated as "The Catholic Chapel of St. John."[10]

DIOCESE OF NEW YORK IN 1838

CARTHAGE
St. PATRICK
1820

ROCHESTER
St. PATRICK
1823

ROME
St. PETER
1837

BUFFALO
LAMB OF GOD
St. LOUIS
1830

ERIE CANAL

GENEVA
St. FRANCIS DE SALES
1835

AUBURN
HOLY FAMILY
1834

SENECA FALLS
St. PATRICK
1831

UMCA
St. JOHN
1821

TROY

ALBANY
St. MARY
1797

SAUGERTIES
St. MARY OF THE SNOW
1833

POUGHKEEPSIE
St. PETER
1837

NEWBURGH
St. PATRICK
1838

COLD SPRING
OUR LADY OF LORETTO
1834

PATERSON
St. JOHN
THE BAPTIST
1821

BROOKLYN
St. JAMES
1822

NEW YORK CITY
St. PETER 1785
St. PATRICK 1815
St. MARY 1826

St. JOSEPH 1829
St. NICHOLAS 1833
St. PAUL 1834

St. JAMES 1836
TRANSFIGURATION 1836

8 - McNamara, *Diocese of Rochester*, 33-34.

9 - J. David Valaik, et al., *Celebrating God's Life in Us: The Catholic Diocese of Buffalo, 1847-1997* (Buffalo: Diocese of Buffalo, 1997), 20-21.

10 - Raymond J. Kupke, Living Stones: *A History of the Catholic Church in the Diocese of Paterson* (Paterson: Diocese of Paterson, 1987), 42-44.

Louis Le Couteulx de Chaumont, benefactor of the church in Albany and Buffalo.
Credit: *Diocese of Buffalo*

The Port of Buffalo in 1812.
Credit: *Harper's New Monthly Magazine,* July 1861

Brooklyn and Long Island

While the construction of the Erie Canal was bringing thousands of Irish Catholic immigrants to upstate New York, another important Catholic community was taking shape in Brooklyn. Without a church of their own at first, the scattered Catholics of Brooklyn traveled across the East River by ferryboat on Sunday morning to Mass in Manhattan at either St. Peter's Church or St. Patrick's Cathedral. One of them was young John McCloskey, who was to succeed John Hughes as the archbishop of New York in 1864 and to became the first American Cardinal in 1875.

On New Year's Day in 1822 Peter Turner, an Irish immigrant who worked in the Brooklyn Navy Yard, decided that it was time for the Catholics in the village of Brooklyn to have their own parish church. He circulated a petition among his fellow Catholics calling for an association to establish a Catholic church in Brooklyn. "We want our children instructed in the principles of our Holy Religion," the petition read, "we want more convenience in hearing the word of God ourselves. In fact we want a church, a pastor, and a place for interment--- all of which we have every reason to expect by forming ourselves into a well regulated society."[11]

The result of Peter Turner's efforts was the establishment of St. James Church, the first Catholic parish in Brooklyn. On April 25, 1822, Bishop Connolly took the ferry across the East River to bless the ground for the new church at the corner of Chapel and Jay Streets. A little more than a year later, on August 28, 1823, he returned to dedicate the new building. At the time the total population of the village of Brooklyn was less than 11,000.

St. James Church, today St. James Pro-Cathedral, in Brooklyn in the 1840s

---

11 - John K. Sharp, *History of the Diocese of Brooklyn, 1853-1953* (New York: Fordham University Press, 1954), I, 39.

Mass was celebrated on Sunday by priests from Manhattan like John Power, Richard Bulger, Michael O'Gorman or John Shanahan, until the appointment of the first resident pastor, John Farnan, the former pastor of St. John's Church in Utica. Despite Farnan's pioneer work upstate, Bishop Connolly had suspended him in 1823 after he quarreled with the trustees over his salary and refused to reinstate him. John Power, the administrator of the diocese after Connolly's death, gave Farnan a second chance by appointing him pastor of St. James in April 1825.

Farnan lasted four years in Brooklyn until he was again suspended, this time by Bishop Dubois, for public drunkeness. Farnan then bolted, started his own church five blocks from St. James, and allied himself with some of the most notorious anti-Catholic bigots among the Protestant clergy. Notices were posted in the Catholic press warning Catholics to beware of him. Years later, poor and forgotten, Farnan was reconciled to the Church by Bishop John Hughes, who allowed him to function as a priest in the diocese of Detroit where he died in 1849.[12]

Just as St. Mary's Church in Albany was the mother church of Catholicism in upstate New York, St. James was the mother church of Catholics not only in Brooklyn but also throughout the rest of Long Island. Before long Catholics were to be found in Williamsburg, Flatbush, and Flushing where they clamored for their own parish churches. The coming of the railroad had the same result for Catholics on Long Island that the Erie Canal did upstate, spreading the Catholic population to the very tip of the island. The Long Island Rail Road Company, one of the oldest in the nation, began laying track east from Brooklyn in 1834, reached Hicksville in 1837 and Greenport on the North Fork in 1844. Eventually the branch lines of the railroad blanketed Long Island. Wherever there was a railroad station, there was eventually a Catholic church caring for the needs of the local Catholic community.

The Erie Canal

Much of the growth of the Catholic population in upstate New York during Bishop Connolly's ten-year episcopate was due to the construction of the Erie Canal. In 1817, when Governor DeWitt Clinton persuaded the state legislature to spend seven million dollars to build a canal between Buffalo and Albany in order to connect Lake Erie with the Hudson River, critics laughed at the idea and called it "Clinton's Folly." They were quickly proven wrong. The canal carried so much cargo and so many passengers that, within ten years of its completion in 1825, it paid for itself.

The single largest public works project in the United States up to that date, the canal was a tribute to the skill of the self-taught American engineers who planned and constructed it. One proud New Yorker bragged that "it beggars to insignificance all similar undertakings in the old world, and which in point of extent is the largest

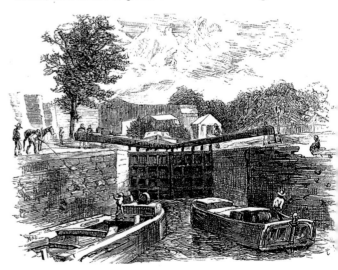

Lock at the eastern entrance to the Erie Canal at Troy
Credit: *Harper's New Monthly Magazine*, December 1873.

12 - Ibid., 48-54.

13 - James Hardie, *The Description of the City of New York* (New York: Samuel Marks, 1827), 135.

line of continued labour in the world after the wall of China."[13] When completed, the canal was 363 miles long and forty feet wide, but only four feet deep. It required 18 stone aqueducts to carry the canal over rivers and 83 locks (each 90 feet long) to lift or lower the canal boats 568 feet from the level of the Hudson River to the level of Lake Erie. Motive power was supplied by horses, who pulled the canal boats from an adjacent towpath at the speed of one-and-a-half miles per hour.

It would be difficult to exaggerate the effect of the canal in transforming New York into the Empire State. It opened the upstate counties and even the Midwest to settlement and development. It gave farmers throughout those regions a cheap and convenient way to ship their grain and flour to the Atlantic seaboard, and it enabled many new immigrants to flee the crowded cities of the seaboard for the interior of the country.

Both the building and the completion of the Erie Canal had a major impact on the Catholic Church in New York State. Especially after 1821, as many as a quarter of the laborers who dug the canal were Irish immigrants who were recruited for the work in New York City. They earned one dollar a day. Many settled in the towns and cities along the route of the canal. Thanks to the practice of the canal commissioners of awarding contracts to local bidders for small segments of the work, the more fortunate Irish laborers were able to become contractors and subcontractors themselves, forming the nucleus of an Irish-American middle class. They were well positioned to take advantage of the next phase of the early nineteenth-century transportation revolution, the building of the railroads.

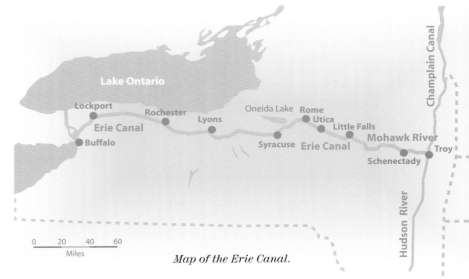

Map of the Erie Canal.

According to one estimate by 1825 almost 50,000 Irish Catholics had settled along the route of the canal between Buffalo and Albany and along the branch canals, establishing or greatly enlarging the Catholic communities in those localities. They pleaded with Bishop Connolly for a priest as they collected the money to erect the first Catholic churches west of Albany. As Thomas D'Arcy McGee put it, the Irish laborers were not only building a canal; they "were working on the foundations of three episcopal sees [Albany, Rochester and Buffalo], and opening the interior of the State to the empire of religion as well as of commerce."[14]

The Rise of the Port of New York

The Erie Canal was especially a boon for New York City, confirming its reputation as the premier East Coast port. By 1825 the Port of New York was already handling half of the country's imports and a third of its exports. With the completion of the Erie Canal, the growth of New York City broke all previous records. By 1830 the population of the city was 200,000. During the next thirty years it quadrupled, and by 1860 New York City contained more people than Baltimore, Philadelphia and Boston combined.

As Robert Albion pointed out in his classic study of the Port of New York, the prosperity of

---

14 - Potter, *To the Golden Door*, 184-186.

The busy East River docks in the early nineteenth century. Credit: *Harper's New Monthly Magazine*, July 1861

the city was not due solely to the Erie Canal since imports always exceeded exports. New York City became so important economically that for many years the import duties collected at the New York Custom House practically financed the federal government. In 1818, for example, the import duties "were enough to finance the whole running expenses of the national government, except the interest on the debt."[15]

Not only did New York City outstrip all of its maritime rivals in the years before the Civil War, but it also became the largest manufacturing center in the United States. The researches of Sean Wilentz indicate that "by the 1840s [it] was probably the fastest-growing industrial area in the world." Between 1800 and 1850 the rate of growth was 750%, higher than that of Manchester or Liverpool or, in Wilentz's expressive phrase, "higher than all of the jerry-built catastrophes of Dickensian lore."[16]

In the 1820s the newcomers who were flooding into New York City as a result of its maritime and industrial prosperity were mainly Protestants from rural New England and upstate New York, supplemented by a substantial number

of Protestant immigrants from the British Isles and Ireland. In 1825, the year of Bishop Connolly's death, New York was still an overwhelmingly Protestant city with only two Catholic churches. In the 1830s the religious demographics of the city would begin to change dramatically because of shifts in the pattern of European immigration. In that decade, for the first time, the city would begin to experience a rising tide of Irish and German Catholic immigrants. Even in the 1820s, however, Bishop Connolly was hard pressed to keep pace with the growth of the Catholic population.

City Hall illuminated in 1825 to celebrate the completion of the Erie Canal. Credit: *Archdiocese of New York*

Catholics in Protestant Gotham

New York's first Catholic charitable institution, the Roman Catholic Orphan Asylum, reflected Catholic efforts to protect their interests in a predominantly Protestant and often hostile environment. The care of orphans was a major concern within the Catholic community in an era when many parents died young, leaving their children to be cared for in public or private institutions where they were frequently raised as Protestants. That was the complaint that Catholics in New York City made against the New York Orphan Asylum, the city's only child-caring institution. As a result they organized the Roman

---

15 - Robert Albion, *The Rise of New York Port,1815-1860* (New York: Scribner's, 1939), reprint 1984, 94-95, 224.

16 - Sean Wilentz, *Chants Democratic: New York City and the Rise of the American Working Class, 1788-1850* (New York: Oxford University Press, 1984), 107-109.

Catholic Benevolent Society. The leaders of the society included prominent Catholics like Francis Cooper, Cornelius Heeney, and other dedicated laymen, a dimension that needs to be remembered when judging their role in the disputes with the bishop over trusteeism.

The Roman Catholic Benevolent Society purchased a frame building on Prince Street near the cathedral for the purpose of starting a Catholic orphan asylum. The building was popularly known as the Dead House from its service during the Revolution as a rudimentary military hospital, and the blood-stained floors attested to its history. Having secured a building for an orphanage, the laymen and Bishop Connolly asked Mother Seton to send Sisters of Charity from Emmitsburg to take charge of the institution as she had already done in Philadelphia. She readily obliged, sending three sisters to her native city. The superior was Rose White, one of her closest collaborators, assisted by Cecilia O'Conway and Felicité Brady.

It was the first permanent foundation of a congregation of men or women religious in the diocese of New York.[17] It was also the beginning of an association between the Sisters of Charity and the diocese that would pay handsome dividends to the Catholic community of New York over the next two centuries through the multiplicity of charitable and educational activities sponsored by the sisters. Five years after assuming the direction of the orphan asylum, the Sisters of Charity also took charge of St. Patrick's Free School, the oldest parochial school in continuous existence in the diocese. It is housed today in the three-story brick building at the corner of Mott

---

17 - Earlier foundations by Irish Ursulines and French Trappists did not endure, and both returned to their native land in 1815.

and Prince Streets that was erected in 1826 as the new home of the Catholic Orphan Asylum. The principal benefactor was Cornelius Heeney, who donated $18,000.[18]

The new home of the Roman Catholic Orphan Asylum at Mott and Prince Streets, erected in 1826. Today it houses the parochial school of St. Patrick's Old Cathedral

In 1822 Bishop Connolly was still struggling to meet the needs of his diocese. He had only eight priests, three in New York City, one in New Jersey, and four upstate. Local vocations to the priesthood were non-existent and it was difficult to create a stable presbyterate from the medley of foreign priests who wandered in and out of the diocese. A case in point was Father Paul McQuade, who was ordained in Canada in 1808. He was the pastor of St. Mary's Church in Albany when Bishop Connolly came to the diocese. He left for New Brunswick in 1817, was in Newfoundland the following year, and turned up in Boston in 1821.

In 1824 Bishop Connolly finally heeded the advice of the Propaganda and asked for a coadjutor bishop. His choice was Father Michael O'Gorman, the young priest who had come from Ireland in 1816 serving first as pastor in Albany, then as an itinerant missionary along the Erie Canal, and finally as a curate in the cathedral. The Propaganda rejected Connolly's request for O'Gorman on a technicality and told him to resubmit it as part of a terna (a list of three names). At that point the niceties of canon law did not make much difference to Father O'Gorman. He died on November 24, 1824, at the age of thirty-two, after eight years of service as New York's first diocesan priest. It must remain a matter of conjecture how successful he might have been as New York's third bishop.[19] Eight days after O'Gorman's death, the bishop lost another young priest, Richard Bulger. Like O'Gorman, Bulger was also a native of Kilkenny and an alumnus of St. Kieran's College. He had been ordained four years.

Bishop Connolly himself survived these two young priests by only two months. He collapsed while officiating at a burial shortly after Christmas and died at his residence on February 6, 1825. He was waked for two days at St. Peter's Church where the funeral Mass was also celebrated. His body was then carried in procession to the cathedral where he was buried near the altar and later re-interred in one of the basement vaults. Despite his best efforts, Connolly left his successor as many problems as he found in 1815. In some respects the situation was even worse because of the growth of the Catholic population.

"He had ruled the diocese over ten years, faithfully if not with success" was the dispassionate if not overly generous verdict of John Talbot Smith on John Connolly's episcopate. "Every character has its limitations."[20] Connolly

18 - Sister Marie de Lourdes Walsh, S.C., *The Sisters of Charity of New York, 1809-1959* (New York: Fordham University Press, 1960), 40-59.

19 - O'Gorman received a glowing recommendation from the Irish bishop who had been his seminary rector, but Archbishop Maréchal, who had little regard for Irish-born priests, informed the Propaganda that O'Gorman was an unpolished country bumpkin who was "totally lacking in the qualities needed in a bishop… and spoke and wrote the English language in a barbarous manner." Peter Guilday, *The Life and Times of John England* (New York: The America Press, 1927), I, 434.

20 - Smith, *Catholic Church in New York*, I, 68.

was an exemplary priest and pastor, but he lacked the physical strength and administrative ability to organize a chaotic new diocese with the slender resources of men and money available to him. John England, the most capable of the early nineteenth-century American bishops, described Connolly as a "man [who] was a saint in his convent, a good clergyman in any place, but [one who] knew nothing of an American mission and could never be brought to know it."[21]

French Interlude: Bishop John Dubois

The first two bishops of New York were foreigners who had no pastoral experience prior to their appointment as bishop. New York's third bishop, John Dubois, was different. He had spent thirty-five years in America as a parish priest, educator and religious superior, before coming to New York. Born in Paris, France, on August 24, 1764, he was ordained in that city on September 22, 1787, and fled to the United States in 1791 to escape the religious persecution of the French Revolution. For fourteen years he was the pastor of Frederick, Maryland, founded Mount St. Mary's Seminary and College in nearby Emmitsburg in 1808, and served as the first ecclesiastical superior of Mother Seton's Sisters of Charity from 1811.

Two decades of unchallenged authority over seminarians and sisters were not necessarily the best preparation for dealing with the independent-minded New York clergy and laity. However, Dubois' biggest handicap was his French birth. He incurred the resentment of many of the New York Irish, who wanted one of

John Dubois, Third Bishop of New York, 1826-1842. Credit: *Archdiocese of New York*

their own countryman as bishop, and who were convinced that French-born bishops in the United States were intent on stacking the American hierarchy with fellow Frenchmen at the expense of the Irish. There was some basis for this Celtic paranoia. In addition to Archbishop Maréchal in Baltimore, the first bishops of Boston, Bardstown, Mobile and Vincennes were all French. Louis Dubourg became the bishop of Louisiana in 1815, and another Frenchman nearly became the second bishop of Philadelphia.

A further complication for Dubois was the long vacancy in the diocese between the death of Bishop Connolly on February 6, 1825, and his own installation in New York on November 1, 1826. During the twenty-month interval the diocese was administered by Father John Power, the popular young Irish-born pastor of St. Peter's. Two days before his death, Bishop Connolly had named him vicar general, and in the event of his death, administrator of the diocese.

Father Power was the favored candidate of the local Irish community to be the next bishop of New York. During his tenure as administrator he proved to be far more successful than Bishop Connolly in dealing with the clergy and the trustees of St. Peter's. He restored the faculties of several priests whom Connolly had suspended, including Peter Malou, and he strengthened the local presbyterate by accepting into the diocese Thomas Levins, a former Jesuit, and Felix Varela, an exiled Cuban patriot. The range of his activities suggests how resourceful he might have

Father John Power, pastor of St. Peter's Church and administrator of the diocese, 1825-1826

---

21 - AICR, England to M. O'Connor, February 25, 1835, copy in AANY.

been as a bishop. He raised the funds to complete the new building for the Catholic Orphan Asylum, supported the establishment of a Catholic newspaper, the *Truth Teller*, and gave New York City its third Catholic parish when he bought an old Presbyterian church on Sheriff Street and reopened it in May 1826 as the Church of St. Mary. The longer that Dr. Power remained as administrator, the more he appeared to be the ideal person to bring peace and harmony to the faction-ridden diocese. It was a thought that also occurred to Father Power.

The seal of Bishop Dubois.
Not only did he place a shamrock
in his episcopal coat of arms, but
he also took as his motto the motto
of the United States,
E Pluribus Unum, *"One from Many".*

Once installed as the new bishop of New York, Dubois tried to dissipate some of the opposition to him in his first pastoral letter. He denied that Archbishop Maréchal had engineered his appointment to New York and claimed the right to be considered an American, not a foreigner, after thirty-five years of residence in the United States. He pointed out that the apostles were not natives of the countries they evangelized, and even more provocatively mentioned that St. Patrick was not a native of Ireland, but of Gaul (like himself).

The bishop got to the heart of the matter by asking: "Who are those who object to our foreign birth? Are they not in the same sense foreigners themselves, for the question was not why an American had not been appointed, but why it was not an Irishman?" Dubois appealed to the patriotism of his flock. "[Did] we not cease to be Irishmen, Frenchmen and Germans as soon as by our oath of allegiance, we had shaken off all foreign political ties to become children of the great American family?" he asked "Whence then this national jealousy?" For good measure he even extended a peace offering to the New York

Irish by placing a shamrock in his coat of arms.[22]

The *Truth Teller* omitted to publish his pastoral letter, and some claimed that he spoke English so poorly that they could not understand him in the pulpit. Power said that at Mass on Sunday "hundreds leave the church and go to the rum shops while he is speaking."[23] During his sixteen years as the spiritual leader of New York's Catholics, Dubois had to face all of the problems that Bishop Connolly did, and an additional one that Connolly did not have to contend with, the growth of a militant Nativist reaction to Catholic immigrants.

Despite his age (he was sixty-three in 1827), Dubois was a peripatetic bishop who often left New York City to visit the rest of his diocese, which still included the whole state of New York and half of New Jersey. On a pastoral visitation in 1829 he traveled as far west as Buffalo and as far north as the Canadian border, logging 3,000 miles by steamboat, canal barge and stagecoach. He traveled alone in order to save money. Wherever he went, he was surprised to discover more Catholics than he had anticipated. "Seven hundred are found where I understood there were but fifty or sixty;" he said, "eleven hundred where I was told to look for two hundred." He calculated that he heard over 2,000 confessions on his visitation of the diocese.

In Buffalo 800 people attended a Mass that Bishop Dubois celebrated in the court house, and then walked in procession to the site where the bishop blessed the ground for the erection of Lamb of God Church. The Germans were the largest ethnic group in the Catholic community,

22 - Guilday, *England*, 446-448.
23 - Power to Conwell, January 30, 1829, ibid., I, 447.

and four elderly men led the procession reciting the rosary aloud in German while the rest of the people responded in French, English and German.

At the St. Regis Indian reservation the bishop tried to mediate a dispute between the Canadian and American Indians. The latter wanted the Stars-and-Stripes flown along with the Union Jack outside the chapel even though it was on British soil. He urged them to remain united, using the old example of a bundle of sticks that are easily broken when separated but impossible to break when fastened together. A dozen young Indians served his Mass in surplices made from blankets while the choir sang Indian hymns that reminded him of Gregorian chant.

In New York City he estimated that the Catholic population was 35,000 out of a total population of 202, 589. He added a fourth church in 1827, Christ Church on Ann Street, thanks to Father Felix Varela, who raised $19,000 from wealthy Spanish residents to purchase it from the Episcopalians.[24] In contrast to the four Catholic churches, there were more than seventy Protestant churches in New York City. Dubois not only wanted more churches, but he wanted beautifully decorated churches to impress non-Catholics with the splendor of the Catholic liturgy.

Faith and Practice

New York Catholicism was by no means a cultural wasteland. Although a thirty-minute Low Mass was the common practice, St. Patrick's Cathedral, St. Peter's and St. Mary's all had a tradition of good music that attracted many non-Catholics on special occasions like Easter and charity concerts. George Templeton Strong, an Episcopalian of High Church instincts and an indefatigable diarist, was so impressed with a

service in St. Peter's Church in April 1838 that he recorded in his diary: "I never heard anything equal for richness and softness and grandeur the magnificent body of sound that the full band with kettle drums or the sub-bass of the organ produced." He was equally impressed after attending Christmas Mass at St. Peter's two years later. Snob that he was, however, he could not refrain from adding" "It's a shame that [St. Paul's Episcopal] Church can't or don't [sic] have such music as is thrown away on those rowdies at St. Peter's."[25] John Pintard, another Episcopalian, shared Strong's favorable impression of the music in the Catholic churches. He regretted missing the benefit concert for the Catholic Orphan Asylum in St. Patrick's Cathedral in February 1830. "I should have been gratified to hear the superb music usual on those occasions which attracts great numbers of other denominations," he said.[26]

One of Bishop Dubois' pet projects was to lengthen the cathedral by forty feet and embellish the interior, but he hesitated to do so until he had paid off the debt of $24,000. The cathedral did not even have a complete set of vestments, and on solemn occasions he had to make do with one miter and a wooden crozier. Like all the New York Catholic churches, the cathedral was unheated, which explained why attendance at the early morning Masses fell off precipitously during the winter when the temperature sometimes dropped to ten degrees below zero.[27]

For Dubois the biggest need was not vestments or chalices or even more churches, but more "spiritual helpers," that is, more priests. "What then may be done to remedy this painful want?" he asked. He did not expect the supply of Irish priests to continue indefinitely. "There is no other means than the founding of a seminary

---

24 - Joseph and Helen McCadden, *Father Varela, Torch Bearer from Cuba* (New York: U.S. Catholic Historical Society, 1969), 77.

25 - Strong, April 26, 1839, December 25, 1841, *The Diary of George Templeton Strong, 1820-1875*, eds. Allan Nevins and Milton Halsey Thomas (New York: Macmillan, 1952), I, 102, 171.

26 - Pintard, June 11, 1830, *Letters of John Pintard*, III, 152-153.

27 - *New-York Weekly Register and Catholic Diary*, February 1, 1834.

where we may train up a national clergy," he concluded. "This then is the object dearest to my heart," he told the Society for the Propagation of the Faith, the French missionary aid society, to which he appealed for money in the spring of 1830.[28]

Knowing that he could not raise the funds he needed in New York, Bishop Dubois had left for Europe on September 29, 1829, and only returned to his diocese two years later, on November 20, 1831. He visited Ireland, Rome, Lyons and Paris. In France he had the characteristic bad luck to experience another French Revolution, the July Revolution of 1830, that toppled King Charles X from the throne and unleashed a wave of anti-clerical violence because the Church had been closely associated with the unpopular Bourbon king.

DeTocqueville in New York

While Bishop Dubois was in France, two French visitors arrived in New York City, Alexis de Tocqueville and his friend Gustave de Beaumont. They attended Mass in a large church, probably the cathedral, which they said was full of worshippers. Disappointed to find Bishop Dubois away in Europe, they had an interview with Father John Power, who spoke French fluently. He informed them that the Catholics were already the single largest denomination in the city even though they had only five churches compared to a much larger number of Protestant churches. He added that the increase in the number of Catholics was due to conversions as well as immigration. "What struck me most in Mr. Power's conversation," Tocqueville recorded in his diary, "[is] that he appears to have no prejudice against republican institutions [and] that he regards education as favorable to morality and religion."

After a few weeks in New York City, Tocqueville wrote home to a friend that "the religious state of this people is perhaps the most curious thing to examine here." He attended services in several Protestant churches and remarked on the lack of doctrinal content in the sermons. He found the Catholics poor but zealous and praised the local clergy for their devotion to

The Staten Island Ferry and the U.S. Barge Office at the foot of Whitehall Street in 1831. Credit: *Archdiocese of New York*

28 - John Dubois, "The Diocese of New York in 1830," *HR&S* 5:2 (1907): 216-230.

The Junction of Broadway and the Bowery in 1831.
Credit: *Archdiocese of New York*

Churches and Priests

their people. "They are not businessmen of religion like the Protestant ministers," he observed. As for Power's claim about the number of converts, Tocqueville attributed it to the desire for an authoritative religion and the beauty of the Catholic liturgy. He noted too that most of the converts to Catholicism came from the lower classes while the better-educated Protestants were attracted to Unitarianism.

The young French aristocrat also noticed how Catholicism flourished in the free soil of America, but he observed that Catholics kept aloof from contact with members of other religious denominations. He wondered how committed they really were to the principle of religious toleration. "I am not sure," he wrote, "that they would not persecute if they found themselves the strongest." It was a latent fear that many American Protestants would continue to harbor until Vatican Council II, when the Catholic Church committed itself unambiguously to the principle of freedom of conscience.[29]

Tocqueville's reference to five Catholic churches is something of a puzzle because there were only four Catholic churches in New York City in 1831, St. Peter's, St. Patrick's Cathedral, St. Mary's and Christ Church. New York's fifth church, St. Joseph's Church in Greenwich Village dates from 1829, but the church was not completed until 1834.

In addition to the 35,000 Catholics in New York City, Bishop Dubois estimated that in the rest of the diocese in 1830 there were at least 150,00 Catholics at a time when the population of New York State was 2,112,000. Six years later he thought that there were 200,000 Catholics in the whole diocese, including 20,000 in New Jersey.[30] Charles Herbermann, who studied the statistics carefully, came to the conclusion that it was impossible to come up with even an approximate number of Catholics. Whatever their exact number, by 1836, there were thirty-three churches and four chapels in the whole diocese. Dubois said that he needed twelve more churches in the city alone where more than half the people stood

---

29 - George William Pierson, *Tocqueville and Beaumont in America* (New York: Oxford University Press), 69, 137-138, 153-157.

30 - The U.S. bishops finally determined the ecclesiastical map of New Jersey at the Second Provincial Council of Baltimore in 1833. They assigned Bergen, Sussex, Essex, Morris, Somerset, Middlesex and Monmouth counties to the diocese of New York, and Hunterdon, Warren, Burlington, Gloucester, Salem, Cumberland and Cape May counties to the diocese of Philadelphia. Mansi, *Amplissimae Collectionis Conciliorum* (Paris, 1907): 39:310.

in the doorway to hear Mass because there was no room for them inside. Upstate more than fifty private homes were used for Mass due to the lack of churches.

The bishop was edified by the faith of the people. "The zeal of all my Catholics exceeds belief," he wrote in 1836. There were between 8,000 and 10,000 infant baptisms every year and 300 to 400 adult converts. Many Catholics were unable to attend Mass for months or even years because they had to work on Sunday morning. There were long lines for confession throughout the year on Saturday evening and Sunday morning with some people waiting for hours and others being turned away. He and two other priests at the cathedral heard 300 confessions every week, but only 100 people received Holy Communion at the three Masses on Sunday morning, which Dubois considered an exceptionally high figure.

To care for his scattered flock Dubois had a total of thirty-eight priests, three or four times as many as he found on his arrival in 1826. Of that number, thirty-three were Irish, three were German and two were Canadian.[31] However, the quality of many of the new recruits left much to be desired. Thomas Levins, the rector of the cathedral and a graduate of Stonyhurst College in England, claimed that "many of the carters in the streets… know more theology than the priests who ascend the pulpit to instruct them."

He told Paul Cullen, the rector of the Irish College in Rome, that many priests could not write a sentence grammatically. "Unless their knowledge of moral theology came by inspi-

Father William Beecham the "Pope of Rome."

ration," he added, "I am ignorant of its source, for the language of casuistry is to them an unknown tongue." Levins was hardly an unbiased witness, since he was feuding with Dubois at the time, but both Francis Patrick Kenrick and John Hughes made similar comments about the low intellectual and moral caliber of the New York clergy in the 1830s.[32]

Despite the increase in the ranks of the clergy, it was still common for upstate priests like Father William Beecham to cover wide areas. Beecham was yet another convert from the Protestant Church of Ireland. He came to New York and was ordained by Bishop Dubois in 1836. Two years later the bishop sent him to Rome, New York, where he founded St. Peter's Church and remained as pastor for the next thirty-eight years. From his base in Rome, Father Beecham traveled on horseback through eight counties in central New York, preaching the Gospel, celebrating Mass, and administering the sacraments from the St. Lawrence River to the Pennsylvania border. Thirteen years after the opening of the Erie Canal, half of his parishioners were canal workers who had no fixed residence. Beecham himself became such a familiar figure that he was popularly known as the "Pope of Rome."[33]

One of the most positive developments during the troubled years of Dubois' episcopacy was the growth of the Sisters of Charity from their modest beginning with three sisters at the Catholic Orphan Asylum in 1817. By 1839 there were five Catholic orphan asylums in the diocese, two in New York City, and one each in Brooklyn,

31 - "Bishop Dubois on New York in 1836," *HR&S* 10 (1917): 124-129; Charles G. Herbermann, "The Rt. Rev. John Dubois, Third Bishop of New York," *HR&S* 1 (1900): 304, 348-355;

32 - AICR Levins to Cullen, n.d. [1835-?]; APF, Amer. Centr., Vol. 11, 474, Kenrick to the Cardinal Prefect of the Propaganda, February 22, 1836; AUND, Hughes to Purcell, February 24, 1838, copies in AANY.

33 - AANY, Beecham to Hughes, September 13, 1838; O'Brien, *Faith and Friendship*, 36-37.

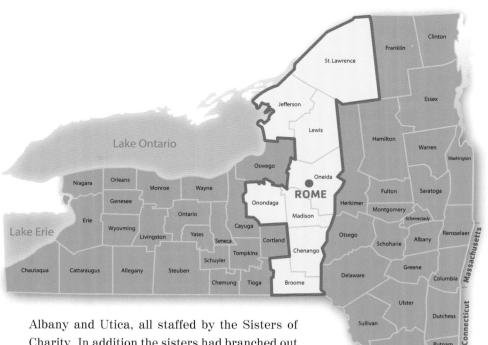

Albany and Utica, all staffed by the Sisters of Charity. In addition the sisters had branched out into education. They conducted two academies in New York City and one in Albany as well as two free schools in New York City.

New York's First Seminary

One of the principal reasons for Bishop Dubois' two-year trip to Europe in 1829-1831 was to raise enough money to build a seminary, which he regarded as the key to solving the shortage and poor quality of the priests in the diocese. On April 13, 1832, less than five months after his return from Europe, he bought a 162-acre farm in Upper Nyack and on May 29, 1833, he blessed the cornerstone of the new building and began construction. He had chosen a picturesque location thirty miles from New York City at the widest part of the Hudson River. The property ran up from the river in a series of gently rolling slopes to the top of a mountain a mile or so inland, affording a splendid view of the Tappan Zee and the heavily forested east bank of the river.

As one might expect, Dubois' model for the Nyack seminary was the first seminary that he had founded, Mount St. Mary's in Emmitsburg. As at the Mount, he planned to have both a college

and seminary so that the tuition of the lay students could support the seminary and the seminarians could teach in the college. However, his efforts to complete the project over the next four years became a nightmarish illustration of all of tensions and divisions in the diocese. The neighbors in Upper Nyack were mostly Dutch and Huguenot farmers who were anti-Catholic and resented the new institution in their midst.

The trustees of the cathedral gave Dubois no help because they had no confidence in his financial ability. His own vicar general, John Power, reported him to Rome for wasting the money of the Propaganda and schemed to have himself put in charge of the project.[34] Then there was the poverty of the Catholic immigrants, who arrived every year in New York by the thousands, Dubois informed Rome, "in search of bread." Finally, the latent Irish-French conflict bubbled to the surface again. Dubois complained that some Irish immigrants were so "infected with nationalistic prejudices that they wanted to

---

34 - Power to Paul Cullen, September 15, 1833, *RACHSP* 8 (1897): 463-465.

*Warren Landing or Haverstraw in 1828, a few miles north of the site
of Bishop Dubois' ill-fated seminary in Upper Nyack.* Credit: *Fordham University Archives*

change the Catholic church into an Irish church." He noted bitterly that some of his own priests, including Thomas Levins, the rector of the cathedral, "were trying to persuade this blind population that I am the enemy of Ireland because I am the enemy of abuses." Levins claimed that Dubois was the one who was condoning clerical abuses.[35]

Twice Bishop Dubois ran out of money in his attempt to build a seminary, but twice he started over again. In the meantime, he opened the seminary for a year in a farmhouse on the property in Upper Nyack with a faculty of two priests and five students. Then, as the new building neared completion in April 1837, it was totally destroyed by fire. The cause was a careless workman cooking eggs for his lunch near a pile of wood shavings. Local tradition preserves

the story that the crowd that gathered to watch the conflagration made no secret of their glee and sent up a loud cheer when the roof fell in. Dubois said that the fire "swallowed up in two hours $25,000." There was no insurance, and he did not have the money needed for rebuilding. For the third and last time he abandoned the project.[36]

At this juncture the ever faithful and ever generous Cornelius Heeney came to the rescue, or, at least, he tried to come to the bishop's rescue. He offered the bishop land for a seminary on his seventeen-acre estate in Brooklyn Heights, and some of the stone from the Nyack seminary was actually transported to Brooklyn. However, the deal fell through when Heeney insisted on retaining title to the building until it was completed. Dubois refused to accept the condition, and Heeney withdrew his offer.[37]

---

35 - APF, Amer. Centr., 11 (1835), fol. 485rv-487, Dubois to Cardinal Prefect, March 13, 1835, copy in AANY; AICR, Levins to Cullen, n.d., copy in AANY.

36 - AASL, Dubois to Bishop Joseph Rosati, April 18, 1837.

37 - AUND, Hughes to Bishop John Purcell, February 24, 1838; Herbermann, "Bishop Dubois," 323-324.

The Nativists

Anti-Catholicism was a staple feature of political and religious life in the Thirteen Colonies, but it practically disappeared in the wake of the American Revolution to the surprise and delight of American Catholics. One reason for the change was American Catholic support for the Revolution and the assistance furnished to the Patriot cause by Catholic France and Spain. The impact of the Enlightenment, however detrimental it may have been to religious practice, also helped to foster a spirit of toleration that was broad enough to include Catholics.

The small size of the Catholic population, which amounted to only 25,000 in a population of 2,500,000, was also a factor in allaying traditional English Protestant fears of Catholicism. Moreover, the lay leaders of the American Catholic community, whether they were wealthy Maryland planters like Charles Carroll or prosperous New York businessmen like Dominick Lynch, were thoroughly assimilated individuals who mixed easily with the most favored elements in American society. The same was true of the spiritual leaders of the Catholic community. John Carroll was a polished eighteenth-century gentleman with a European education that few Americans could match. Jean Cheverus, the first bishop of Boston, was an exiled French aristocrat who charmed the local Brahmins not only with his lineage and impeccably good manners, but also with his transparently authentic spirituality.

This era of good feelings began to change in the 1830s. The reason was simple: immigration. In that decade Catholics began to emigrate to the United States in greater numbers than ever before. Most were Irish, but many were German. Not only did Catholics come to America in ever increasing numbers, but they also tended to be poor and to congregate in the major port cities of the Northeast like Boston, Philadelphia, Baltimore, and especially New York.

This wave of Catholic immigrants provoked a backlash from native-born Americans who felt threatened for several reasons. One reason was economic, the fear that immigrants were depriving native-born Americans of work or depressing their wages. Another reason was religious. The influx of European Catholics coincided with the Second Great Awakening, a major religious revival among American Protestants that was spearheaded by evangelical denominations like the Baptists, Methodists, Presbyterians and Disciples of Christ. The fundamentalist biblical theology of these denominations, who regarded the Roman Church as the Whore of Babylon and the Pope as the anti-Christ, made them particularly apprehensive as they witnessed an ever increasing number of Catholic immigrants descending upon American shores.

The combination of economic and religious factors made lower class American Protestants especially susceptible to anti-immigrant propaganda. The Nativist crusade to defend American values from subversive foreigners occurred in several waves in the three decades before the Civil War. It began in the 1830s with a small but vociferous group of fundamentalist Protestant preachers who made a career of promoting anti-Catholic prejudice. They concentrated on two aspects of Catholic practice that were strange and threatening to many Americans and could easily be distorted to appear in the most unfavorable light because they were shrouded in secrecy. They were the confessional and the convent. Protestant polemicists tried to link both with sexual misconduct on the part of the clergy.

The Protestant Crusade

New York City was the center of what Ray Allen Billington called the Protestant Crusade, and two of the most prominent local leaders were George Bourne and William Craig Brownlee, both of whom were Protestant clergymen. Brownlee was particularly vituperative, "that arch-hypocrite and unblushing calumniator," the *Truth Teller* called him. Bourne founded a weekly newspaper called *The Protestant* that first appeared on January 2, 1830. "*The Protestant* is established in the city of New-York," Bourne announced," and is designed to expose the errors, superstitions and idolatries of Popery."[38]

During the course of the next few years *The Protestant* went through several changes of names and editors (including Brownlee), but its basic thrust remained the same, to frighten Protestants about the growth of popery in their midst. There were alarmist reports about the activities of the Jesuits and Massmen (i.e., priests), and the arrival of "black nuns" and "gray nuns" from Canada to open "gratuitous" schools for proselytizing Protestant children. Bourne and his friends were so gullible that they gladly published four articles about the growth of Popery in Pennsylvania submitted by a reader in Philadelphia who called himself "Cranmer."

"The Papists are worming their way into every nook and corner of our country," Cranmer warned. "Why are Protestants asleep?... Let the trumpet be sounded." Bourne expressed deep satisfaction with the writings of this "genuine Protestant." After three more articles the author revealed that it was a hoax in a letter to the *Truth Teller* signed "A Catholic." It soon became known that he was Father John Hughes, the pastor of

St. John's Church in Philadelphia. He taunted Bourne with his readiness to publish his "broad, palpable and grinning lies." "[I]t is remarkable," Hughes wrote, "that the greater the slander, the greater the eulogium that was bestowed on me by the editor, and the better Protestant he said that I was." Bourne refused to admit that he had been hoodwinked and steadfastly maintained the authenticity of the Cranmer articles.[39]

In addition to publishing *The Protestant*, Bourne, Brownlee and like-minded colleagues started the New York Protestant Association in January 1832 to coordinate their activities against the spread of Popery. They held public meetings and sponsored debates with Catholic priests. John Power, Felix Varela and Thomas Levins accepted the challenge and defended the Church in these debates, but Bishop Dubois ordered them to stop because of the disorderly conduct of the crowds that attended them. The pugnacious Brownlee even produced a pamphlet to prove that "St. Patrick was neither a papist nor a Roman Catholic [because] he came from a land where popery was utterly unknown."[40]

New York Catholics had to endure more than harsh words. On November 9, 1831, St. Mary's Church on Sheriff Street was burned to the ground. The frame building was pillaged and set on fire in three places in the middle of the night. The arsonists even stuffed the bell so that parishioners could not summon help. On a happier note, in the aftermath of the fire, the trustees of the First Universalist Church at the corner of Grand and Pitt Streets made their church available to Catholics for three Masses every Sunday morning until they could rebuild St. Mary's Church.[41]

---

38 - *The Protestant,* February 20, 1830.

39 - *The Protestant,* February 27, March 20, June 12, June 26, July 10, August 14, 1830; *Truth Teller,* July 3, 1830.

40 - *William Craig Brownlee, The Religion of the Ancient Britons and Irish: No Popery and the Immortal St. Patrick Vindicated from the False Charge of Having Been a Roman Catholic* (New-York: New-York Protestant Press, 1855), 20.

41 - *Truth Teller,* November 12, 1831.

Maria Monk

New York City was not the only center of anti-Catholic agitation. In Boston a similar fear of Catholic immigrants led to the burning of the Ursuline convent in suburban Charlestown on the night of August 11, 1834, by a mob shouting "No Popery." A dozen nuns and sixty students had to flee for their lives in the middle of the night.[42] The burning of the Charlestown convent marked a new stage in the development of the Protestant Crusade. It spawned a whole cottage industry of stories about escaped nuns and the horrors of convent life. The books were eagerly consumed by a credulous public that was ready to believe the worst about Catholics. The classic example of this genre of anti-Catholic literature was *The Awful Disclosures of the Hôtel Dieu Nunnery of Montreal,* which was published in New York City in 1836. Billington called it "by far the single most influential work of American nativistic propganda in the period preceding the Civil War."[43]

The notorious Maria Monk dressed as a "Black Nun" with the child whom she claimed was fathered by a priest in a convent in Montreal.
Credit: *Library of Congress*

The book purported to be the account of a nun who had escaped from a convent in Montreal where young women were imprisoned in basement dungeons, where they were exploited sexually by priests, and their illegitimate children were strangled and buried in the cellar. In reality Maria Monk was a mentally disturbed young woman who had been confined in a custodial institution in Montreal. Her disclosures of convent life were a total fabrication that was written by a Protestant minister in New York City, the aptly named J.J. [John Jay] Slocum, who claimed that she had dictated the contents to him. He and his collaborators profited handsomely from the book while Maria Monk received virtually nothing and died penniless in a jail in New York City in 1849 after her arrest for picking pockets in a Sixth Ward brothel. Harper Brothers was eager to cash in on the profits by publishing the book, but reluctant to sully the family name by publishing it under their own imprint. They solved their moral and financial dilemma by setting up a dummy firm in the name of two employees, Howe and Bates.

Awful Disclosures attempted to tap into every latent Protestant suspicion of Catholics, but it did so in such a ham-handed way that many American Protestants reacted to it with skepticism and derision. "I never saw a Bible in the convent from the day I entered as a novice," Maria Monk claimed. When she takes her religious vows, she is laid out in a coffin with a black cloth covering her body. One of the penances she is obliged to

AWFUL DISCLOSURES

OF

MARIA MONK,

AS EXHIBITED IN A NARRATIVE OF HER SUFFERINGS DURING A RESIDENCE OF FIVE YEARS AS A NOVICE, AND TWO YEARS AS A BLACK NUN, IN THE HOTEL DIEU NUNNERY AT MONTREAL.

" Come out of her, my people, that ye be not partakers of her sins, and that ye receive not of her plagues."---*Rev.* xviii. 4.

NEW-YORK:
PUBLISHED BY HOWE & BATES,
NO. 68 CHATHAM-ST.
1836.

[Facsimile]

The title page of Maria Monk's tale of convent life in Montreal.

---

42 - The most recent study is Nancy Lusignan Shultz, *Fire and Roses: The Burning of the Charlestown Convent, 1834* (New York: The Free Press, 2000).

43 - Ray Allen Billington, "Maria Monk and her Influence," *CHR* 22 (1936): 283.

perform is to drink the water that Mother Superior has used to wash her feet. There is an unintentionally hilarious description of the murder of a disobedient young nun, who is tied to a bed and covered with a mattress while a priest and a half-dozen nuns jump up and down on mattress for twenty minutes until she is suffocated.[44]

Not content with publishing *Awful Disclosures,* Maria Monk's handlers put her on the lecture circuit where she appeared dressed in a fake religious habit clutching her illegitimate baby. The money made from this road show inspired another entrepreneur in Philadelphia, Samuel B.

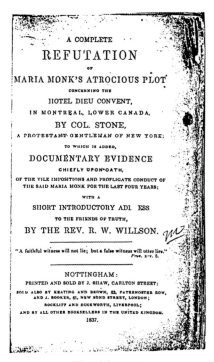

The title page of Colonel William Stone's exposé of Maria Monk's fabrication

Smith, to produce his own "escaped nun" from the same convent in Montreal as Maria Monk. She went by the name of Sister St. Francis Patrick. In one touching scene the two bogus nuns met on stage and wept as they embraced one another.

Maria Monk attracted a following, but Sister St. Francis Patrick was one escaped nun too many and aroused suspicions that it was all a hoax. Colonel William L. Stone, the editor of the New York *Commercial Advertiser* and a militant Protestant who was well known for his antipathy to Catholicism, went to Montreal where he conducted a thorough investigation of the Hôtel Dieu convent and concluded that Maria Monk's story was a tissue of lies. "Maria Monk is an arrant imposter," said Stone, "and her book in all its essential features is a tissue of lies."[45]

Nonetheless, the book continued to sell like hot-cakes, since it offered readers the opportunity to satisfy their prurient interest under the guise of defending the virtue of American women from the rapacious designs of Romish priests. By contemporary standards it would hardly qualify as even soft-core pornography, since it relied largely on the power of suggestion rather than graphic descriptions to make its point. For example, with regard to the abuse of the confessional, a frequent theme of the book, Maria Monk wrote: "I cannot persuade myself to speak plainly on such a subject as I must offend the virtuous ear."[46] Some 300,000 copies were in print by the Civil War, which led Billington to characterize it as the *Uncle Tom's Cabin* of the Nativist movement.

Another outspoken foe of Popery in New York City in the 1830s was Samuel F.B. Morse, who is better known as the inventor of the telegraph. A native of New England, he claimed that his dislike of Catholicism stemmed from an incident in Rome when a soldier knocked his hat off because he failed to doff it while watching a street procession. Morse's contribution to the Protestant Crusade in New York City was *Foreign Conspiracy against the Liberties of the United States* which originally appeared in the *New-York Observer* under the pseudonym Brutus. Morse claimed that the Pope was intent of seizing control

44 - *Awful Disclosures of Maria Monk* (New York: Howe & Bates, 1836), 55, 99, 117-118.

45 - William L. Stone, *Maria Monk and the Nunnery of the Hotel Dieu* (New York: Howe and Bates, 1836), 33.

46 - *Awful Disclosures,* 125.

of the Midwest through Catholic immigrants. The ostensible proof was the financial assistance that German Catholic priests in America received from the Leopoldinen Stiftung, the Austrian missionary aid society, whose headquarters were in Vienna where Prince Clemens von Metternich presided over the reactionary politics of the Holy Alliance. Morse warned Americans about an unholy alliance of the pope and Metternich designed to fasten upon the United States "the chains of papal bondage."[47]

The Coadjutor

Bishop Dubois had few happy days during his sixteen years in New York. As the difficulties mounted, he may have regretted that he did not remain in Paris during the Revolution and take his chances with the Jacobins. The Irish never forgave him for being a Frenchman, or more accurately, for not being an Irishman, no matter how hard he tried to placate them. However, dissatisfaction with Dubois was based on more than ethnic prejudice. Both John Power and Thomas Levins, the vicar general and the rector of the cathedral respectively, criticized him harshly as an incompetent administrator. As early as 1828 Power came to the conclusion that "the screws are loose in his head." From distant Charleston, South Carolina, Dubois' fellow bishop, John England kept up a steady drum beat of complaints to Rome, describing the diocese as "a volcano

John England, First Bishop of Charleston, 1820-1842

about to erupt" in the hope of replacing Dubois with his friend John Power.[48]

The local presbyterate was a source of unending concern and anxiety. For someone who was a former seminary rector, Dubois sometimes showed surprisingly poor judgment of people. For example, he hastily ordained a German-speaking seminarian named James Tervouren whom he had met on his trip to Europe. Tervouren promptly stole several hundred dollars from Dubois and absconded back to Europe with it. Twice Dubois suspended Levins for insubordination. When Levins delivered an address on St. Patrick in the cathedral on March 17, 1828, he pointedly dedicated it to Bishop Conwell, Bishop England and the "Irish Clergy of the Catholic Church in the United States."

Blinded perhaps by his own ambition, Power saw little possibility that Dubois would ever win acceptance in New York. "This Catholic community in every sense is Irish," he informed Bishop Conwell. "There are French here, but where is their faith? Even on their deathbeds they seldom seek the aid of a priest. Hence, I say, French priests are useless in this mission..."[49] Among the New York clergy, the only person who seems to have befriended Dubois was Felix Varela. Dubois made him co-vicar general with Power as a way of curbing the latter's authority.

47 - *Foreign Conspiracy against the Liberties of the United States* (New-York: Leavitt, Lord and Company, 1835), 38-39.

48 - APF, Scritture, Riferite Nei Congressi, Amer Cent., Vol. 6, fol. 1035, Power to My dear James, Vol. 12; England to the Propaganda, February 26, 1837, copies in AANY.

49 - Thomas Levins, *A Discourse Delivered on the 17th of March 1828 in St. Patrick's Cathedral, New-York* (New-York: The Truth Teller, 1828); Power to Conwell, January 14, 1829, cit. in Richard Shaw, *John Dubois: Founding Father* (Yonkers: U.S. Catholic Historical Society, 1983), 126.

Bishop Dubois had the same difficulties as Bishop Connolly with the trustees of the cathedral, who sided with Levins in his disputes with Dubois. At one point the trustees continued to pay Levins' salary while he was suspended but refused to pay the salary of his successor. They also threatened to discontinue Dubois' salary unless he gave them a pastor of their own choice. In a memorable confrontation Dubois told them: "Well, gentlemen, you may vote the salary or not, just as seems good to you. I do not need much. I can live in the basement or in the garret, but whether I come up from the basement or down from the garret, I will still be your bishop."[50]

As Bishop Dubois approached his fiftieth anniversary as a priest, he gave serious thought to requesting a coadjutor. One person whom he definitely did not want for understandable reasons was John Power. His first choice was John Timon, an American-born Vincentian priest of Irish descent whom he had never met. When that proposal did not work out, Dubois suggested Francis Patrick Kenrick, the coadjutor bishop of Philadelphia. Kenrick had spent the previous seven years jousting with his madcap ordinary, the ninety-two year old Henry Conwell, who once sold all of Kenrick's furniture while he was away on a pastoral visitation. Kenrick wanted to get out of Philadelphia, but not to come to New York where he feared his situation would be even worse, a "thorny crown," as he put it.[51]

Kenrick asked the Propaganda to divide the large diocese of Philadelphia by creating a new see in Pittsburgh for the western part of the state of Pennsylvania. He wanted to go to Pittsburgh and have John Hughes, the pastor of St. John's Church in Philadelphia, succeed him as the coadjutor to Bishop Conwell. The Propaganda approved the plan in January 1836, but Pope

Henry Conwell,
Second Bishop
of Philadelphia,
1820-1842

*Francis Patrick Kenrick,
coadjutor
to Bishop Conwell,
1830-1842,
Bishop of Philadelphia,
1842-1851,
Archbishop of Baltimore,
1851-1863*

Gregory XVI deferred action because he wished to give the U.S. bishops the opportunity to consider the proposal to divide the diocese of Philadelphia at their next provincial council, which took place in Baltimore in April 1837.

Bishop Dubois did not attend the provincial council but sent Father Varela as his representative. The bishops decided to leave the diocese of Philadelphia intact for the time being, which meant that Kenrick was destined to spend five more years as Henry Conwell's episcopal keeper (he died at the age of 97). As for New York, Dubois had suggested two other names in addition to Kenrick, Father Samuel Mulledy, S.J., a former president of Georgetown College, and John Hughes. The bishops placed Hughes' name first on the terna that they sent to Rome. Their decision was unanimous except for one dissenting voice, John England, who was still angling to get New York for John Power. The Holy See accepted the recommendation of the American bishops,

50 - Bayley, *History of the Catholic Church,* 112.

51 - AICR, Kenrick to Cullen February 14, 1837, copy in AANY.

and the pope appointed John Hughes titular bishop of Basileopolis and coadjutor to Bishop Dubois on August 8, 1837. John Carroll would have been pleased with the process, if not with the nominee.

Hughes did not receive word of his appointment until November 3. His episcopal ordination took place on January 7, 1838, in St. Patrick's Cathedral, the first time that the cathedral had been the scene of such a ceremony. The ordaining prelate was Bishop Dubois, assisted by Bishop Kenrick of Philadelphia and Bishop Fenwick of Boston, and the preacher was Father Samuel Mulledy, S.J. At the last moment Hughes had to send to Philadelphia for suitable vestments and a cope. Although it was the dead of winter, the windows were left open so that the crowds outside could catch a glimpse of the ceremonies. While the laity turned out in record numbers, few New York priests were present in silent protest that their favorite, John Power, had not been selected for the post.

One of the few New York priests present was John McCloskey. Twenty-six years later to the very day, as the preacher at John Hughes' funeral, he eulogized his departed friend and mentor from the pulpit of the same cathedral. Hughes' coffin rested in the sanctuary in almost exactly the same spot where he had received episcopal orders. Although no one is under oath when he delivers a eulogy, McCloskey's funeral oration gave a vivid picture of the impression that John Hughes made on his first public appearance in New York.

John Hugues, ordained titular bishop of Basileopolis and coadjutor to Bishop Dubois in St. Patrick's Old Cathedral on January 7, 1838

I well remember that grand and imposing scene, said McCloskey, contrasting so mournfully with that which is now before me. I remember how all eyes were fixed, how all eyes were strained to get a glimpse of their newly consecrated bishop; and as they saw that dignified and manly counte-nance, as they beheld those features beaming with the light of intellect, bearing already upon them the impress of that force of character which peculiarly marked him throughout his life, that firmness of resolution, that unalterable and unbending will, and yet blending at the same time that great benignity and suavity of expression---when they marked the quiet composure and self-possession of every look and every gesture of his whole gait and demeanor---all hearts were drawn and warmed towards him.[52]

Bishop Dubois and his new coadjutor knew one another well, perhaps too well. They had first met in 1819 when Hughes applied for admission to Mount St. Mary's Seminary in Emmitsburg, Maryland, where Dubois was the rector. Dubois refused to admit the young Irishman because of his deficient educational background and assigned him to a year of remedial studies while he worked as gardener and overseer of slaves. It was a slight that the sensitive and egotistical Hughes never forgot.

When Hughes expressed his apprehensions to Dubois about his role as coadjutor, the old

---

52 - *Complete Works of the Most Rev. John Hughes,* ed. Lawrence Kehoe (New York: Lawrence Kehoe, 1866), I, 18-19.

bishop assured him that he would not have the same difficulties with him that Kenrick had experienced with Conwell in Philadelphia. "You surely could not suppose a moment that I would encroach upon the rights and privileges attached to that sacred office," he told him, "and I have too great an opinion of your merit and affection for me to suppose that you would encroach upon mine." [53]

Dubois' optimistic forecast was put to the test within a month of Hughes' episcopal ordination. Dubois suffered the first of a series of strokes that left him progressively impaired both physically and mentally. On June 1, 1839, Rome relieved John Dubois of his authority as bishop and made John Hughes the administrator of the diocese. Archbishop Samuel Eccleston came from Baltimore to break the news to Dubois personally. At first he reacted badly, asking to know what crime he had committed to deserve such treatment. He soon calmed down and resigned himself to the situation. "He obeyed the bit," Dubois wrote about himself, "but not till he had covered it with foam."

John Dubois lingered for another three years. He continued to live in the same house as John Hughes on Mulberry Street across from the cathedral, but they rarely spoke to one another, and Dubois always referred to him as "Mr. Hughes." He died at his residence in New York on December 20, 1842. The preacher at the funeral three days later was John Hughes, who mentioned that he was a last-minute substitute for Bishop Benedict Fenwick of Boston, who was unable to be present.

John Hughes was hardly ever at a loss for words on any subject and rarely preached from a prepared text. On this occasion, however, he scarcely mentioned the deceased prelate at all and devoted most of his sermon to a justification of the Catholic practice of praying for the dead. His lame excuse was that Bishop Dubois had no need for a eulogy, since his memory was enshrined in the hearts of the priests, the Sisters of Charity, the orphans, and the assembled mourners. It was not John Hughes' finest hour. [54]

Broadway and Grand Street around 1818.

53 - AANY, Dubois to Hughes, November 6, 1837, copy.

54 - *New York Herald,* December 24, 1842.

6

Bishop and Chief

When John Hughes arrived in New York in 1838, there were many farms and open fields north of 14th Street. Above the intersection of Broadway and Eighth Avenue in 1861. Credit: *Archdiocese of New York*

*Bishop and Chief:
Archbishop John Hughes*

John Hughes automatically became the fourth bishop of New York upon the death of John Dubois on December 20, 1842. He had been in effective charge of the diocese since becoming the apostolic administrator in 1839. He went on to become the first archbishop of New York in 1850, and died at his residence at Madison Avenue and East 36th Street on January 3, 1864. The twenty-five years that he was the spiritual leader of New York Catholics were the most significant quarter-century in the history of the diocese. For better or for worse, no bishop or archbishop of New York before or since has had as profound an impact on New York Catholicism as John Hughes. He inherited a rudderless ship with a mutinous crew and bequeathed to his successor the largest, wealthiest and most important archdiocese in North America. The fact that he was able to do this despite his well-deserved reputation as a poor administrator and worse financial manager (he could not even manage his own checkbook) suggests the thought that the transformation of the diocese was not due solely to the talents of John Hughes.

After surveying the sad state of the diocese in 1838, he confided to his friend Bishop John Purcell, "I feel that I have been appointed in punishment for my sins." Reflecting on his experience twenty years later, he painted a vivid if slightly inaccurate picture for another friend of what he found upon his arrival in New York:

> There were then about 46 churches and as many priests for the Catholics scattered over this immense surface. There were no really Catholic schools in existence, except two, kept by the Sisters of Charity who had charge of orphan children at the cathedral and St. Peter's. One or two other churches had schools under a hired male teacher for the instruction of poor boys. There were no religious communities in the diocese---the Sisters of Charity having been obtained from Emmitsburg as missionaries and liable to be recalled at any moment. There was no provision made for the Catholic education of youth or the training of ecclesiastics to meet the increasing wants of the people. The churches were too few and these [were] in debt to an amount greater than they would have brought at public auction. The people were too poor and for a long time the increase of their numbers only added to their poverty as emigrants arrived in our port from Europe penniless and destitute.[1]

John Hughes was only forty years old when he was made coadjutor to Bishop Dubois in 1837. It was an era in the American Church when it was customary to appoint young bishops because of the rigorous physical demands of the episcopal office. John England was thirty-four when he was appointed the bishop of Charleston in 1820, and Francis Patrick Kenrick was thirty-three when he was made coadjutor to Bishop Henry Conwell in 1830. As Bishop Hughes took up his new responsibilities in New York, he not only had the advantage of youth and boundless energy, but also enormous confidence in his own ability and an intense desire to succeed.

John Joseph Hughes was born on the feast of St. John the Baptist, June 24, 1797, in Annaloghan, County Tyrone, the son of a tenant farmer. Although his father eked out a modest living from the land, young John Hughes had plenty of experience of the poverty and prejudice that were the common lot of Catholics in eighteenth-century Ireland, especially in the heavily Protestant part of Tyrone where he grew up. He never disguised his humble origins and said later in life, "They told me when I was a boy that for five days I was on a social and civil equality with the most favored subjects of the British Empire. These five days would be the interval between my birth and my baptism." He also recalled the scene at the burial of his little sister Mary. When the funeral procession approached the cemetery, the priest stopped at the entrance because he was forbidden by the penal laws from setting foot in it. He blessed a handful of dirt and handed it to a layman to throw over the coffin after it had been lowered into the grave.[2]

John Hughes emigrated to America in 1817. Since he had little formal education, his employment possibilities were limited, and he worked for two years as a manual laborer, stone cutter and gardener. As was mentioned already, when he applied for admission to Mount St. Mary's Seminary in Emmitsburg in 1819, the rector, John Dubois, required a year of remedial

---

1 - AUND, Hughes to Purcell, February 24, 1838; AANY, Hughes to Abbot Bernard Smith, July 9, 1858. The latter letter was edited by Henry Browne and published as "The Archdiocese of New York A Century Ago: A Memoir of Archbishop Hughes, 1838-1858," *HR&S* 39-40 (1952): 129-187.

2 - Hassard, *John Hughes,* 17-18.

work before he admitted him to the regular seminary course. Ordained a priest of the diocese of Philadelphia by Bishop Conwell on October 15, 1826, he spent the next twelve years in Philadelphia, the first six as a curate in St. Joseph's Church, and then as pastor of St. John's Church which he founded in 1832. He also acquired a reputation as a capable defender of Catholicism against Nativist attacks as a result of a series of exchanges in print and on stage with the Reverend John Breckenridge, a prominent Presbyterian minister.

The youthful new bishop presented a stark contrast to his two predecessors both of whom were in their sixties when they became the bishop of New York. A strikingly handsome man, John Hughes was about five feet nine inches tall, with a large head, sharp gray eyes, a Roman nose, a firm-set jaw, brown hair and a resonant voice with just the slightest trace of a soft Irish accent. He became prematurely bald in his forties and wore a wig thereafter. Extremely sensitive about any slight, real or perceived, he enjoyed a joke but not at his own expense. Invariably polite to high and low alike, he could wither an unwary conversation partner with an intimidating look. He also had a fierce temper. "It needed a brave man to face him when he was displeased," said his lay secretary, John Hassard. "His rebukes were terrible. He had the power of expressing scorn to a greater degree than any other man I ever saw."[3]

Hughes quickly discovered that there was an urgent need to develop the infrastructure of the diocese to meet the demands of a rapidly growing Catholic population. However, as he set about the task of building more churches and educational and charitable institutions, and finding the priests and religious to staff them, he became involved in three public controversies that made him a nationally famous figure within six years. In the words of one of his biographers, Henry Browne,

by 1844 John Hughes was the best known, if not necessarily the best loved Catholic prelate in the United States. The first of the three controversies was lay trustreeism, an intramural Catholic issue that was closely watched by a hostile public eager to depict it as an example of clerical oppression of the laity.

The End of Lay Trusteeism in New York

In Philadelphia Father John Hughes witnessed some of the worst excesses of the system of lay trusteeism at St. Mary's Church where the hapless Bishop Conwell lost control of his own cathedral to a combination of aggressive lay trustees and a series of expatriate Irish clerical adventurers. In New York the situation varied from parish to parish depending largely on the ability of the pastor to command the respect of the laity. John Hughes came to New York convinced that the system itself was pernicious regardless of the personalities involved because it involved the attempt of the laity to use the civil law to usurp the authority that rightfully belonged to the clergy. A test case presented itself early in 1839 when Hughes was still only the coadjutor to Bishop Dubois.

Bishop Dubois had long been at loggerheads with Father Thomas Levins, the rector of the cathedral. When he suspended Levins for the second time, the trustees of the cathedral sided with Levins and hired him to run the parish school, which also included responsibility for the Sunday school. The conflict escalated on Sunday, February 10, 1839, when the trustees authorized Levins to summon the police and to remove from the Sunday school a lay catechist whom Bishop Dubois had appointed. Dubois was unable to handle the situation and allowed Hughes to act in his name. For Hughes it was a perfect illustration of his contention that lay trusteeism subordinated

3 - Ibid., 324-328.

canon law to civil law, since, he said, the civil law invoked by the trustees "gives them the same right to send a constable into the sanctuary to remove a priest from the altar."[4]

Hughes demanded an apology from the trustees of the cathedral. When he failed to get it, he appealed from the trustees to the pew-holders who had elected them and scheduled a public meeting for Sunday, February 24. That afternoon a large crowd showed up. It included all but one of the 200 pew-holders of the cathedral parish as well as 400 to 500 Catholics from other parishes, including a number of trustees who had a special interest in the outcome of the meeting. "New York has become a bye-word of reproach to the Catholic name throughout the land," Hughes told them. Getting right to the point, he depicted the issue between Bishop Dubois and the trustees as a matter of divine law versus human law.

John Hughes knew how to appeal to an Irish-American audience. Rather than explain the technical details of canon law, he went straight for the jugular and compared the trustees to the British authorities in Ireland. He told Archbishop Samuel Eccleston of Baltimore the next day, "I recalled to them the glory of their fathers in Ireland battling for three hundred years against the abused civil power of the British government." Pulling out all the stops he admonished them that "the sainted spirits" of their ancestors were

looking down on them from heaven "ready to disavow and disown them if… they allowed pygmies among themselves to filch away the rights of the Church which their glorious ancestors would not yield but with their lives to the persecuting giant of the British Empire." According to Hughes, as he warmed to his theme, many in the audience wept like children. And he added (after listening to his own rhetoric), "I was not far from it myself."[5]

The interior of St. Patrick's Old Cathedral, the scene of Bishop Hughes' meeting with the pew holders on February 24, 1839. The interior of the cathedral was completely remodeled after the fire of 1866. Credit: *Yvon Meyer*

4 - Quoted by Hassard, *Archbishop Hughes,* 192.
5 - AAB, Hughes to Eccleston, February 25, 1839.

It was sheer demagoguery, but the young bishop's words went down like treacle with the pew-holders. "The whole assembly was his," said Hassard, "he could do with it what he wanted." What he wanted and what he got from them was a resolution disavowing any action that would "hinder or prevent our bishop from the full, free and entire exercise of the rights, powers and duties which God has appointed as inherent in his office." With the passage of that resolution, the power of the trustees at the cathedral was broken, and both the trustees and Hughes knew it. He gloated to Archbishop Eccleston: "We killed the trustees, as I told you, but they could not believe that they were dead---it came so sudden. So that now, although they still grieve, they have not strength enough to give even a decent kick." He was so pleased with the outcome that he told Bishop Joseph Rosati of St. Louis, "It is a revolution, and I trust a happy one in its consequence for religion."[6]

Archbishop Samuel Eccleston of Baltimore. A convert to the Catholic Church, he was appointed the fifth archbishop of Baltimore in 1834 at the age of thirty-three

Although the confrontation on February 24, 1839, involved only the trustees of the cathedral, Hughes' victory was the beginning of the end of trusteeism throughout the diocese. He gave the coup de grace to the whole system three years later at the first diocesan synod, which met at St. John's College, Fordham, in 1842. At Hughes' direction the synod enacted legislation that severely limited the authority of the trustees over church property and parish finances and required them to obtain the pastor's approval for virtually all of their decisions. Having rendered the system harmless, he made no effort to eliminate trustees in the parishes where they already existed. In fact he commented that his critics "may still be further surprised to learn that many trustees of churches have tendered their trust into my hands and that I have declined to receive it."[7]

One of the first parishes to experience the change was St. Joseph's Church in Greenwich Village, where opposition from the trustees had driven out two pastors and led Bishop Dubois to place an interdict on the parish only a few years earlier. In a remarkable turnabout the trustees elected the pastor, Father John McCloskey, the president of the board on February 17, 1843. They called upon him at the rectory, escorted him to the meeting room, and installed him in the president's chair. Two years later most of the trustees resigned and the board simply expired for lack of a quorum. After the financial panic of 1837, many trustees found it increasingly difficult to keep their churches solvent and they filed for bankruptcy in four parishes, St. Peter's, St. James, Transfiguration and St. Paul's in Harlem. Hughes bought them at auction and secured title to them in his own name.[8]

By the mid-1840s lay trusteeism was dead in the diocese of New York, except for a few German parishes, most notably St. Nicholas Church in New York City and St. Louis Church in Buffalo. As a result the laity lost even an advisory role in the administration of their parishes. The big winner in New York was not the parish clergy, but the bishop, who arrogated more and more authority to himself. Bishop Hughes had attacked trusteeism on the grounds that it violated canon law. However, he showed little regard for canon law when it threatened to fetter his own authority. When two Irish-born priests complained that he

6 - AAB, Hughes to Eccleston, March 10, 1839; AASL, Hughes to Rosati, May 7, 1839.
7 - "Bishop Hughes' Apology for his Pastoral Letter," November 1842, in *Complete Works of John Hughes*, I, 334.
8 - ASJC, Minutes of the Meetings of the Board of Trustees, February 17, 1843; February 6, 1845; Dolan, *Immigrant Church,* 49-50.

had violated their rights in canon law, he replied that he would teach them "[County] Monaghan canon law" and "send them back to the bogs whence they came."[9]

Episcopal autocracy could be as subversive of normal church governance, to say nothing of Christian charity, as lay trusteeism, especially in the hands of a born autocrat like John Hughes. "I had to stand up among these people as their bishop and chief," he declared, "to knead them up into one dough…" He seemed genuinely surprised that some priests favored trusteeism because it shielded them from what they called "episcopal tyranny." It would never have dawned on John Hughes that there was any other role for the clergy and laity of his diocese except unquestioning obedience to him.[10]

Catholics and Public Education in New York City

Lay trusteeism was essentially an internal quarrel within the Catholic community, although some Protestants regarded Bishop Hughes' victory over the trustees as an ominous sign of the shift of power within the Catholic community from the laity to the clergy. However, the second major controversy in which Bishop Hughes became involved was the highly sensitive issue of public education. In the early nineteenth century educational reform was a vital concern to Americans, who eagerly embraced Horace Mann's notion of the "common school" as a means of providing free education to all children regardless of their social, ethnic or religious background.

An integral feature of the common school was the inculcation of ethical values through the reading of the "received" version (i.e., the King James version) of the Bible, the recitation of prayers at the beginning of the school day, and the acceptance of the core religious beliefs that all American Christians were thought to share. The result was that the common schools were permeated with a kind of least-common-denominator Protestantism that avoided mention of the specific doctrines of any particular church in the interests of wider religious harmony. The common school was nineteenth-century America's closest approximation to an established church, and it engendered the same kind of intense emotional loyalty. The leveling and unifying influence of the common school was a source of civic pride, and the non-sectarian religious instruction that it provided satisfied many American Protestants who were increasingly inclined to regard their churches as various denominations of the one Christian Church.

The religion of the common schools was based on the premise that all Christian accepted this denominational principle, and that any Christians who objected to it were to be regarded as narrow-minded bigots. This was the basic difference between Protestants and Catholics in their attitude to religion in the common school. Catholics most assuredly did not consider themselves to be just one more denomination of the Christian Church. As one of the trustees of the Public School Society of New York City noted with frustration in 1840, "[The Catholics] do not class themselves among 'sectarians' or 'denominations of Christians' but claim to be emphatically 'The Church.' "[11]

All of the Catholic objections to the common schools stemmed from their convictions about the uniquely authoritative nature of their Church. In cities like New York where Catholics were a fifth of the population, their rejection of the "received" religion of the common schools threatened to wreck the convenient arrangement whereby Protestant America educated its children in a

9 - AANY, Burtsell Diary, July 26, 1865

10 - Henry A. Brann, *Most Reverend John Hughes, First Archbishop of New York* (New York: Privately Printed, 1912), 132. Hughes, *Memoir*, 139.

11 - N-YHS, Minutes of the Meetings of the Board of Trustees of the Public School Society of New York, August 27, 1840.

reassuring religious environment at public expense. The fact that the threat came from a despised group of immigrants made the situation all the more annoying. The fact that the political clout of these immigrants was constantly increasing made the situation all the more alarming.

The Public School Society

Since 1825 public education in New York City had been in the hands of the Public School Society, a private charitable organization designated by the Common Council to be the sole recipient of the educational funds allocated by the state legislature for the city's public schools. Catholics chafed under the monopoly enjoyed by the Public School Society, which introduced into the schools the non-denominational Christianity that was a standard feature of the common schools elsewhere in the United States. Moreover, Catholics claimed that the atmosphere in such schools was often biased against them. Hassard commented tartly that "instead of teaching religion without sectarianism, they almost may be said to have taught sectarianism without religion."[12]

Catholics objected to the mandatory reading of the King James version of the Bible and the use of textbooks that they regarded as offensive to Catholic beliefs and practices. Their complaint about Bible reading "without note or commentary" was not due simply to the fact that the schools used the standard Protestant version of the Bible. They believed that it was inculcating in their children the Protestant principle of the private inter-pretation of the Scriptures without the guidance of the magisterium of the Catholic Church.

Robert C. Cornell, the President of the Public School Society of New York in the 1840s

Governor William H. Seward

Bishop Hughes estimated that half of the city's Catholic children were receiving no education at all because their parents would not send them to the public schools and there was no room for them in the over-crowded Catholic schools. Charles Stuart, the deputy superintendent of schools for New York City, basically confirmed Hughes' statistics. In 1842 he reported that, of 65,000 children in New York City, 42,000 were enrolled in the schools of the Public School Society. That left 23,000 children to be accounted for. Stuart estimated that 4,000 of them were in Catholic or other religious schools, and the rest received no education at all. Stuart also said: "I have also recently visited several of the schools connected with the Catholic churches and found them crowded to overflowing... In many instances schools were so full that every bench and seat was occupied; the scholars being so closely packed together that they had hardly room to move."[13]

Catholics were not the only New Yorkers who deplored this situation. Governor William H. Seward mentioned it in his address to the state legislature on January 7, 1840:

The children of foreigners, found in great numbers in our cities and towns... are too often deprived of the advantages of our system of public education in consequence of prejudices arising from differences of language or religion... I do not hesitate, there-fore, to recommend the establishment of schools in which they may be instructed by teachers speaking the same language and professing the same faith... [14]

12 - Hassard, *Hughes*, 226.

13 - *Truth Teller*, July 2, 1842.

14 - *The Works of William Seward*, ed. George E. Baker (New York: J.S. Redfield, 1853), II, 215.

Not unreasonably Catholics interpreted this statement as an invitation to ask for public funds for their own schools. It was an unexpected offer from a Whig governor, since the Whigs' main constituency was the native-born Protestants. While Seward's statement could be construed as an astute political move to win the immigrant vote, and critics were quick to accuse him of pandering to Catholics, the governor seems to have been motivated primarily by a genuine concern for the education of the children of immigrants. A visit that he made to Ireland in 1833 where he witnessed the oppression of Irish Catholics made a deep impression on him.[15]

Whatever Seward's motive may have been, Father Joseph Schneller, the pastor St. Mary's Church in Albany, who had close ties to several members of the legislature, told the diocesan authorities that the time was ripe to request public funding of Catholic schools. It was not an unprecedented request. Religious schools in New York City received public funds from 1813 until 1825 when the state legislature changed the law after complaints that the Bethel Baptist Church had misused the money. In the absence of Bishop Hughes, who was on a nine-month visit to Europe, ecclesiastical jurisdiction in the diocese devolved on John Power and Felix Varela, the two vicars general. However, for the next six months it was especially laymen like Thomas O'Connor, George Pardow, Hugh Sweeney, Andrew Carrigan and Peter Duffy who assumed the leadership of the campaign for public funds for Catholic schools. In effect that meant a campaign to deprive the Public School Society of its monopoly over public education in New York City.

During the spring and summer of 1840 the Catholics held regular meetings every two weeks. They sometimes became so boisterous and so blatantly political that some of the clergy ceased to attend them. William Denman, the influential editor of the *Truth Teller*, was typical of many of the ardently Democratic New York Irish Catholics. He was suspicious of any Whig bearing gifts, even if he happened to be the governor of the state. "They have often complimented us as the spawn of garrets and cellars," Denman once noted. Father Felix Varela, the editor of the *New York Catholic Register*, accused Denman of inconsistency in advocating equal treatment for Catholic children in theory but trying to block the most practical way to achieve it because of his loyalty to the Democratic Party.[16]

The Great School Controversy: Round One

Round One of the Great School Controversy occurred in the spring of 1840. The eight Catholic churches in New York City that operated free schools petitioned the Board of Assistant Aldermen of the Common Council for a proportionate share of the school fund that the state legislature allotted to the city each year.[17] As Vincent Lannie observed, the arguments used by the Catholics and their opponents have a remarkably contemporary ring, indicating how little has changed in the position of both sides in the past 150 years. The Catholic churches submitted written petitions to the Board of Assistant Aldermen as did the Public School Society and several Protestant congregations. Both sides also sent representatives to a public hearing on March 12.

15 - Vincent P. Lannie, "Archbishop John Hughes and the Common School Controversy, 1840-1842," Ph.D. diss., Teachers College, Columbia University, 1963, 62-65. I have relied heavily on Lannie's splendid dissertation for this whole chapter. For a contrary point of view, which regards Seward's proposal as a political ploy worked out beforehand with the Catholics, see John V. Pratt, "Governor Seward and the New York City School Controversy, 1840-1842," *New York History* 42:4 (1961): 351-364.

16 - *Truth Teller*, November 2, 1844; Lannie, "Hughes and the Common School Controversy," 128.

17 - The churches were St. Patrick's Cathedral, St. Peter's, St. Mary's, St. James, St. Joseph's, Transfiguration, St. John's and St. Nicholas. The bicameral Common Council consisted of a Board of Aldermen and a Board of Assistant Aldermen.

The Catholics contended that they were entitled to a fair share of the school taxes that they paid into the general fund for the maintenance of their own schools because they could not in good conscience send their children to schools where their religion was censured and ridiculed. The Public School Society countered that the Catholic request was both unconstitutional and inexpedient. They claimed that it was unconstitutional because it would tax the whole community to support schools where sectarian dogmas were taught, and inexpedient because it would lead to a mad scramble for funds from other denominations and result in the destruction of the Public School Society.

The Board of Assistant Aldermen rejected the Catholic petition with only one dissenting vote, and so Round One of the Great School Controversy ended with a decisive victory for the Public School Society and their many allies and supporters. The trustees of the society boasted that "no decision of the city government ever met with a more general or cordial response in the public mind." Nevertheless, they sensed that their monopoly of public education in New York city was in jeopardy. At the May meeting of the trustees, it was reported that the Catholic petition was the gravest threat that the society had experienced in many years, and that, if the Catholics ultimately prevailed, it would result in "the total prostration of the public schools of our city."[18]

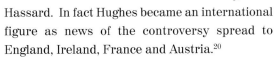

The Seal of the Public School Society of New York

The Return of Achilles

Despite their initial defeat, the Catholics continued to hold their bi-weekly meetings. One was scheduled for July 20, two days after Bishop Hughes returned from Europe. "On my return," said Hughes, "I found my diocese, and especially the city of New York in a ferment." Hughes showed up at the meeting on July 20, urged the Catholics to continue the struggle, and assumed command of the Catholic forces.[19]

John Hughes' battle with the Public School Society lasted for twenty-one months, from July 1840 until April 1842. It absorbed so much of his time and energy that his friends noticed the toll it took on his health and even his appearance. Even more than his fight with the trustees, this was the issue that really made Hughes a national figure even though he was still only the coadjutor bishop of New York. "Certainly from 1840 to 1844 he was one of the best abused men in the country," said Hassard. In fact Hughes became an international figure as news of the controversy spread to England, Ireland, France and Austria.[20]

It is no wonder that many Protestants perceived Hughes as a menace to America. In the 1840s the Protestant Crusade took on broader dimensions as its focus shifted from titillating stories about escaped nuns or the dangers of the confessional to the threat that Catholics posed to the common school and the reading of the Bible in the classroom. Fear of Catholicism was no

---

18 - *Documents of the Board of Aldermen of the City of New York* (New York: Bryant and Boggs, 1840) 7: 306; N-YHS, Minutes of the Meetings of the Board of Trustees of the Public School Society of New York, May 1, 1840.

19 - Hughes, "Memoir," 149.

20 - Hassard, *Archbishop Hughes,* 247.

longer confined to a handful of professional bigots, but became widespread in most mainstream Protestant churches. The defense of the common school and the Bible became a rallying cry for millions of Protestants who would never have picked up a copy of the *Awful Disclosures* of Maria Monk. As concerned Protestants tried to identify the leader of the Catholic threat to America, the most visible candidate was Bishop John Hughes, who rather relished the role that was ascribed to him in the city that was the capital of Protestant America in the mid-nineteenth century.

After his return from Europe on July 18 Bishop Hughes attended every meeting of the Catholics who were involved in the school controversy. He dominated these meetings by rallying, haranguing, encouraging and cajoling the audience to persevere in their cause. Like the monster rallies that Daniel O'Connell's Loyal National Repeal Association was sponsoring in Ireland, these bi-weekly meetings helped to forge a sense of Catholic solidarity and to give Catholics a taste of their potential political power in a city long dominated by a Protestant elite. Unlike Daniel O'Connell, of course, Hughes was a bishop, not a politician, but his militant opposition to the Public School Society inevitably led him into deep involvement in city and state politics. No American Catholic bishop had ever assumed such a role before. A lawyer for the Public School Society pointedly contrasted the feisty behavior of New York's upstart Irish immigrant bishop with the aristocratic reserve of Bishop John Cheverus of Boston who, he said, "achieved a widespread reputation by mere acts of private benevolence."[21]

Hughes thought the situation required more than acts of private benevolence. At the next meeting in the school-room (i.e., the basement) of St. James Church on July 27, he proposed the formation of a steering committee to coordinate the Catholic efforts. Thomas O'Connor, the chairman, appointed the bishop to head the committee and selected eight members, all veterans of the struggle, James McKeon, Hugh Sweeney, James White, James Kelley, Gregory Dillon, B. O'Connor, John McLaughlin and himself. At the next scheduled meeting they produced a pamphlet written by Hughes, *An Address of the Roman Catholics to the Fellow Citizens of the City and State of New York,* which received unanimous approval from those in attendance.

Like Daniel O'Connell and contemporary liberal Catholics in Europe, Hughes asserted that Catholics in New York were not seeking special privileges for their church, but recognition of their civil rights as American citizens. "We do not wish to diminish [your rights]," he wrote, "but to secure and enjoy our own." He thought that it was reasonable to suppose that, when the state legislature voted to fund public education in New York, it intended to so without infringing on the civil and religious rights of the citizens. Although the legislators had satisfied most Protestants in New York City, they had not satisfied Catholics, who now sought redress for their grievances as taxpaying citizens. In what would become a standard Catholic argument for the next 150 years, Hughes complained that Catholics were subject to double taxation. They were compelled to support public schools that they abhorred while also financing their own schools, which was a heavy burden for a poor immigrant community.

If Hughes' main purpose was to appeal to the general public, another purpose was to rally and unify the politically divided Catholic forces. To do so he employed the same tactics that he had used against the trustees of the cathedral. He compared the Public School Society to the Protestant Church of Ireland. "We are the sons of martyrs in the cause of religious freedom," he

---

21 - William Oland Bourne, *History of the Public School Society of the City of New York* (New York: William Wood and Company, 1870), 230.

reminded his fellow Irish immigrants. In Ireland, he said, a poor Irish Catholic "was compelled to support a church hostile to his religion, and here he is compelled to support schools where his religion fares but little better, and to support his own school besides." "What do we contend for?" he asked. "We contend for liberty of conscience and freedom of education."[22]

Round Two: The Catholic Counterattack

Round Two of the Great School Controversy began on September 7, 1840, at the usual biweekly meeting of the Catholics in St. James church basement. Hughes got an enthusiastic response to his proposal to form a committee of five to prepare a second petition to the Common Council. At his suggestion two Democrats were selected and two Whigs, Thomas O'Connor, Hugh Sweeney, James McKeon and James Kelley. He himself was the fifth member. The petition was read at the meeting on September 21 and presented to the Board of Aldermen that very evening. The Catholics reiterated their allegations about sectarianism in the public schools ("although others may call it only religion") and their demand for public funding of their own schools. They promised not to teach religion during the regular school hours and offered to allow non-Catholics, even the members of the Public School Society, to supervise the disbursement of the funds.[23]

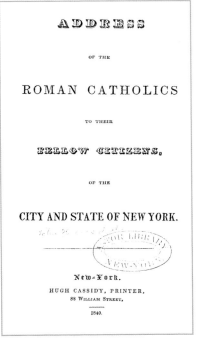

ADDRESS

OF THE

ROMAN CATHOLICS

TO THEIR

FELLOW CITIZENS,

OF THE

CITY AND STATE OF NEW YORK.

New-York.
HUGH CASSIDY, PRINTER,
83 WILLIAM STREET.
1840.

Title page of Bishop Hughes' pamphlet in 1840

The Public School Society lost no time in filing a counter petition or remonstrance. They kept it brief because they believed that the Board of Assistant Aldermen had already refuted and rejected most of the Catholic claims in its decision of April 27. They did complain, however, that the Catholics had used garbled and misleading excerpts from earlier annual reports of the Society to advance their case. They also complained that the Catholic leaders refused to cooperate with their efforts to eliminate any offensive materials from the textbooks or library books used in the public schools.[24]

Here they were on solid ground. Neither Hughes nor Varela nor Power followed through on offers from the Society to purge its books of anti-Catholic references, and so the Society decided to do so on its own. Hughes had no confidence in the sincerity of the offer and did not want to see Catholics depicted as public censors. Moreover, it was a clever tactic for the Public School Society to make textbooks the principal cause of disagreement between them and the Catholics, and then to appear as the aggrieved party when the Catholics did not respond to their offers to expurgate these books. The textbooks were never the major issue. It was the monopoly of public education exercised by a private Protestant organization in New York City. The Catholics would not rest content until they had broken this monopoly and secured equal status for their own schools.

---

22 - *Address of the Roman Catholics to their Fellow Citizens of the City and State of New York* (New-York: Hugh Cassidy, 1840), 3-4. 10-11, 13.

23 - *Documents of the Board of Aldermen of the City of New York* 7 (1840): 296-297.

24 - Ibid., 308-309. The remonstrance of the Public School Society was sweetness and light compared to that of the Methodist Episcopal Church, which accused Catholics of teaching that it was lawful to murder heretics. Ibid.,339.

James Gordon Bennett, the editor of the *New York Herald,* who was usually an unrelenting critic of Hughes, thought that the attempt of the Public School Society to purge its textbooks to please the Catholics was ludicrous. Next will come the Jews with their complaints, he predicted tongue in cheek, and then the Socinians, and then a half-dozen other denominations, and finally the infidels. "They will insist on the whole of the balance of the book being expunged so that nothing but blank or blackened pages will remain for the child's instruction." He predicted that Catholics would not be satisfied with something negative, but wanted something positive. "Let them then have their fair proportion of the fund and educate their children to their heart's content," he urged. "Things will never be settled till this is done. It is all they want, and it is not an unreasonable request."[25]

Daniel in the Lions' Den

When the Catholics submitted their second petition to the Common Council on September 21, they also asked for the opportunity to argue their case before the Council. After initially rejecting this unusual request, the Board of Aldermen reversed itself and granted their wish. This decision set the stage for the most famous incident in this long controversy---Hughes' appearance before the full Common Council. On two successive days, October 29 and 30, 1840, the bishop spoke for eight-and-a-half hours presenting and defending the Catholic case to the municipal authorities. The Catholics agreed that he should be their sole spokesman in the interest of presenting a united front. The Public School Society was represented by two experienced lawyers, Theodore Sedgwick and Hiram Ketchum.

The Rev. Dr. Thomas Bond appeared on behalf of the Methodist Episcopal Church and four other Protestant ministers also spoke in opposition to the Catholic petition.

The proceedings began in a crowded council chamber at City Hall on Thursday, October 29, at 4:00 p.m. Bishop Hughes appeared alone without the benefit of legal counsel. Catholics regarded him as Daniel in the lions' den. An Irish immigrant with only a patchwork seminary education, as James Gordon Bennett liked to remind him, he was confronting the Wasp political establishment and two prominent lawyers as he challenged the prerogatives of one of the city's most respected Protestant organizations in front of a hostile audience. Interestingly both sides presumed that New York was still a Christian city, part of Christendom, as Theodore Sedgwick phrased it, where they could appeal unself-consciously to "the teachings of Our Savior."

Hughes spoke first. He identified himself as the "first pastor" of a community that comprised one-fifth of the population and included one-third of the poor children of the city. He began with a tedious point-by-point rebuttal of the remonstrances of the Public School Society and the Methodist Episcopal Church. Due perhaps to his lack of legal training (which he acknowledged), he did not come to grips effectively with the all-important constitutional question of whether the Common Council had the authority to subsidize religious schools[26]. He also repeated his now familiar claim that Catholic parents refused to send their children to the public schools because they fostered both "infidelity" (i.e., Deism) and Protestant sectarianism. He became more eloquent, if not

---

25 - *New York Herald,* October 23, 1840.

26 - The constitutional issue revolved around the interpretation of the law of November 19, 1824 (which took effect on May 15, 1825), that amended the law of March 12, 1813. The previous legislation authorized the Commissioners of School Monies to distribute the state school fund to the Free School Society in the City of New York (the predecessor of the Public School Society) as well as to "incorporated religious societies in the city as supported or should establish charity schools." After the Bethel Baptist Church misused the money, the state legislature passed the act of 1824, specifying that the school fund should go to "institutions and schools." Hughes contended that the legislature did not intend to exclude religious schools, while the Public School Society claimed that it did when it dropped the reference to "incorporated religious societies.".

City Hall, the scene of Bishop Hughes' appereance before the Common Council and his confrontation with the lawyers of the Public School Society on October 29 and 30, 1842

more persuasive, as he proceeded, emphasizing that the basic issue was not money, but the power of one private organization to shape the minds of tens of thousands of children.[27]

Theodore Sedgwick, one of the two lawyers for the Public School Society, rehearsed the history of public education in the state and presented a carefully reasoned legal brief outlining the reasons why he believed that it would be illegal for the city to subside religious schools. He claimed that the law of 1824 clearly prohibited the city from using the school fund for such purposes. If the Catholics wished to change the law, he suggested that they should go to Albany, not to City Hall. It was advice that they were soon to accept.

More than any other speaker Sedgwick cut through the confusion over terminology and took issue with Hughes' argument that the public schools were fostering both agnosticism and Protestant sectarianism. "The State intends to give a 'secular' or moral, but not a religious education," he said. "The State does not intend to give a sectarian education, and that is precisely what, if I apprehend correctly, the reverend gentleman does intend to give." He wondered how the public schools could be accused of simultaneously training children to be both unbelievers and Protestants. "A child cannot well grow up a Protestant and an infidel at the same time," he observed. He seemed to be particularly stung by Hughes' references to the monopoly enjoyed by Public School Society, which was the heart of the Catholic case. On a more positive note he expressed the hope that the vexatious issue of Bible reading in the public schools could be resolved by taking excerpts from both the King James version and the Douay-Rheims version used by English-speaking Catholics.[28]

Sedgwick was polite but firm in his defense of the Public School Society and Hughes regarded him as a challenging but fair opponent. The second speaker for the Society, Hiram Ketchum, was altogether different. He was well known for his bulldog style in the courtroom. A longtime trustee of the Society, Ketchum's disdain for Hughes and his Church was apparent from his

27 - Bourne, *History of the Public School Society*, 202-224.
28 - Ibid., 224-239.

opening remarks when he launched into a personal attack on him. He repeatedly referred to the bishop as "the mitred gentleman" and accused him of staging public political spectacles where he stirred up the passions of his flock. Like Sedgwick, Ketchum denied that the public schools could be called irreligious because he maintained that they taught the basic precepts of morality on which all Christians were agreed.

His Nativist prejudice came to the surface, however, when he rejected out of hand Sedgwick's suggestion about using both the Protestant and Catholic versions of the Bible in the public schools. A similar proposal in Ireland had been submitted to the pope for his approval by some of the bishops. Ketchum bellowed that he would allow no foreign potentate to ban the Protestant Bible from American classrooms and warned that the pope might also want to ban the reading of the Declaration of Independence or the Constitution. Hughes smiled in derision as Ketchum worked himself into a lather and made a fool of himself.[29]

The hearings resumed the next day with addresses by five Protestant ministers. One Presbyterian clergyman, Dr. Gardiner Springer, denounced Hughes for demanding money from "a community of Protestant citizens." He concluded his diatribe with the comment that, if there were no alternative between infidelity and the dogmas of the Catholic Church, he would choose to be an infidel tomorrow. John Hughes had the last word, speaking for three-and-a-half hours. He reserved his choicest remarks for Ketchum, sarcastically thanking him for his amusing performance on the previous day. Ketchum glared at Hughes through-out his talk, which was his calculated way of unnerving an adversary in the courtroom. This tactic did not work with Hughes, who ridiculed Ketchum's theatrics. "I really expected every

moment," said Hughes, "he would forget himself and say, 'The prisoner at the bar.' " At one point, when Ketchum interrupted Hughes to ask on what authority he had explained a certain point of Catholic doctrine, he replied with characteristic bravado, "I am authority myself in matters of my religion. Surely, sir, I am not here to betray it…"

In conclusion Hughes quoted some of the hostile remarks made in the course of the two days and tried to use them as illustrations of the prejudice that Catholic children experienced everyday in the schools of the Public School Society. He appealed to the aldermen to imagine that they were in the position of the Catholic parents whom he represented. Being John Hughes, however, the bishop could not resist a final sally at the religion of the common schools, which did his cause no good. "They say the [Catholic] objection to the present schools is that there [the children] are made Protestants. No, sir, it is because they are made *Nothingarians,* for we cannot tell what they are."[30]

The aldermen appointed a committee to consider the Catholic petition and the counter petitions. On January 11, 1841, the committee issued its report. They praised the Society as "a monument of disinterestedness and public spirit" and blamed their failure to work out a compromise on the intransigence of the Catholics. They conceded that Catholics had the right to operate their own schools, but denied that they had any valid claim to public aid because it would force taxpayers to support a religion that they disapproved. The Board of Aldermen accepted the report by a vote of fifteen to one.[31] Round Two of the Great School Controversy resulted once again in a crushing defeat for the Catholics. The scene now shifted from City Hall to the state capitol in Albany for Round Three.

---

29 - Ibid., 239-249. Catholics were not the only ones who found Ketchum's courtroom demeanor offensive. George Templeton Strong once referred to him as "that foolish fat bag of unfragrant fatulence." *Diary,* I, 250, cit. in Lannie, "Archbishop Hughes and the Common School Controversy," 326, n.55.

30 - Ibid., 277-313.

31 - *Documents of the Board of Aldermen of the City of New York 7* (1840): 559-568.

Round Three: Hardball Politics

On February 11, 1841, exactly one month after the Common Council rejected the Catholic petition, Bishop Hughes addressed an enthusiastic meeting of Catholics who were eager to carry on the fight. When they cheered his appearance at the rostrum, he told them to quiet down because Hiram Ketchum might think that it was a political rally. "We come here denied of our rights, but not conquered," he told the audience. He urged them to appeal to a "higher power," the state legislature. The bishop's remarks that evening led to the formation of a committee that collected 7,000 signatures for a petition to the state legislature that was entrusted to Gulian Verplanck, a Whig senator from New York City, who was sympathetic to the Catholic demands.[32]

Father Constantine Pise, a friend of Verplanck, explained the reasons for the Catholic petition:

> These children of foreigners are Americans--and it behooves the Legislature, it seems to me, to take care lest they should be suffered to be deprived of the only sure support of their morals---education with religion. To the common schools they will not resort. Their parents, for the most part ignorant and taken up with their laborious occupations, do not see the necessity or have not the time to insist on their going to school. Our own schools are full to overflowing---and cannot contain the fiftieth part of the children to be taught. Under these circumstances, it was thought advisable to petition the Common Council to allow us a portion of the Fund under whatever supervision or regulations they might justly require---with the hope that the children of foreign Catholics could in this manner be trained up in the convictions of religion, and with a knowledge of their duties as citizens and children of this our glorious Republic.
> The Common Council having, after a very useless debate among several clergymen of different sects, which degenerated into a mere controversy about dogmas, rejected our petition, an appeal is now made to the wisdom of the state legislature.[33]

Father Constantine Pise, New York pastor and former chaplain to the U.S. Senate

After Verplanck submitted the petition on March 29, 1841, the State Senate referred it to the secretary of state, John C. Spencer, who also happened to be *ex officio* the state superintendent of common schools. A month later, on April 26, Spencer issued his report, which was a major victory for the Catholics. He recommended that the monopoly of the Public School Society in New York City, which he called an anomaly, should be terminated in favor of locally elected school boards, which was the norm in the rest of the state.[34]

Decentralization of the New York City public schools on the model recommended in the Spencer Report would have been a bonanza for Catholics. Since the Catholic population was concentrated in the poorer neighborhoods of the city like the Sixth Ward, locally elected school boards in such neighborhoods would likely have favored the kind of religious instruction that would have been acceptable to Catholic parents. If the Catholics were delighted with the Spencer Report, the Public School Society was alarmed because it was the first legal setback that they had suffered since the Catholics had challenged their monopoly. They dispatched a delegation to Albany that included Hiram Ketchum, who presented the Society's case before a Senate committee. He concentrated on the religious provisions of the Spencer Report, warning that they would lead to the tyranny of the majority over the minority in the city wards, forcing Catholics and Protestants to support one another's religion in the common schools. He could not have stated his case more clearly when he said: "I affirm that the religion taught in the

32 - Kehoe, *Works of John Hughes*, I, 242-246.

33 - N-YHS, Verplanck Papers, Pise to Verplanck, March 23, 1841.

34 - Bourne, *History of Public School Society*, 356-373.

Castle Garden at the Battery. Built as a fort, it was a popular music hall in John Hughes' time and served as the city's immigration center from 1855 to 1892 when it was replaced by Ellis Island. Credit: *Archdiocese of New York*

public schools is precisely that quantity of religion that we have a right to teach. It would be inconsistent with public sentiment to teach less; it would be illegal to teach more."[35]

A bill embodying the main features of the Spencer Report was introduced in the Senate on May 11 and was promoted vigorously by Senator

Carroll Hall, a former Universalist church that the Catholics purchased for a meeting hall. It later became St. Andrew's Church.

Verplanck. Both Whig and Democratic politicians recognized that it was a highly sensitive issue that could affect their political career. On May 25, by a vote of 11 to 10, the senators voted to table the bill until the legislature reconvened in the new year. Their decision to postpone a vote on the bill meant the Third Round of the Great School Controversy ended in a temporary stalemate as the politicians awaited the outcome of the November elections.

The Carroll Hall Ticket

In New York City, where the seats of two senators and thirteen assemblymen were at stake, the school question was the paramount issue in the election. Predictably all fifteen Whig candidates were pledged to maintain the status quo, which meant the continuation of the monopoly of the Public School Society. The Democratic candidates seemed to be leaning in the same direction, which would have left the Catholics without anyone for whom to vote at the polls. Hughes reacted by

35 - Ibid., 389-390.

plunging even more deeply into the political fray. While stoutly maintaining that he was not a politician, he organized his own political party. It originated at a meeting of New York Catholics in Carroll Hall on October 29, just six days before the election. It was one of the largest Catholic gatherings since the school agitation had begun almost two years earlier. Hughes presented the crowd with his own slate of fifteen candidates, the Carroll Hall Ticket. Only five candidates were actually running on the Carroll Hall Ticket. The other ten were regular Democratic candidates whom he endorsed because he thought they were favorable to the Catholic cause.

That evening Hughes delivered a rousing campaign speech that was to have reverberations for years to come. As he read off the names of the candidates, the audience roared their approval. Once he realized that he had the audience with him, he engaged them in a spirited dialogue like a veteran politician. "You have often voted for others, and they did not vote for you," Hughes told them, "but now you are determined to uphold with your own votes your own rights." The applause lasted for several minutes. When it died down, he asked, "Will you adhere to the nominations made?" That brought loud cries of "we will, we will." "Will you be united?" he asked. That brought more cheers. "Will none of you flinch?" At that point the audience rose to their feet in pandemonium, cheering, shouting their approval, clapping their hands, waving hats, handkerchiefs and (according to one report, probably untrue) shillelaghs. Hiram Ketchum's reaction is not recorded, but sitting inconspicuously in the gallery that evening, soaking in the scene before him, was Thurlow Weed, Governor Seward's mentor, and one of the most astute politicians in the state.[36]

The next morning, as the newspapers spread the news of Hughes' speech, it brought angry cries that this time he had gone too far. The

Nativists reacted by imitating the Catholics and organizing their own Union Party under the aegis of William Brownlee (of Maria Monk fame) and Samuel Morse. To Hughes' chagrin, all of the Democratic candidates repudiated the Catholic endorsement, but that did not prevent the Whigs from questioning their sincerity. At the same time the Democrats claimed that the Carroll Hall Ticket was a Whig plot concocted by Bishop Hughes and Governor Seward. In the confusion three candidates actually found themselves endorsed by both the Catholics and the Nativists. They were the "tight-rope candidates," Horace Greeley quipped.

The November 1841 elections resulted in a landslide victory for the Democrats throughout the state that gave them control of both houses of the legislature. However, in New York City, the most significant result was that the only Democrats who were defeated were four of the five candidates who had failed to receive Catholic endorsement. Bishop Hughes had made his point. The Democrats should not take the Catholic vote for granted. It was a lesson they were not likely to forget it when they returned to Albany in January for the next legislative session.

Round Four:
Decision in Albany

Round Four of the Great School Controversy began with Governor Seward's address to the legislature in which he essentially endorsed the findings and recommendations of the Spencer Report. Once again the Catholics submitted a petition, this time with over 12,000 names. They entrusted it to a New York City assemblyman, William Maclay, a Democrat and the son of a Baptist minister, who presented it to the Assembly. The Assembly promptly referred it to the Committee on Colleges, Academies and Common Schools, which happened to be headed

---

36 - Kehoe, *Complete Works of John Hughes*, I, 275-281; Lannie, Archbishop Hughes and the Common School Controversy," 442-446.

by Maclay. Within three weeks Maclay reported back to the Assembly with a bill very similar to John Spencer's proposal to extend the system of local school boards to the city of New York.[37]

In the meantime, Maclay consulted Seward, Thurlow Weed, Horace Greeley and Bishop Hughes about the content of the bill. When the news leaked out about Hughes' involvement, it required some fancy doubletalk on his part to deny the allegation without actually lying about it. Maclay was able to brush aside a last-minute attempt to amend the bill to include a prohibition of sectarian religious teaching, and the Assembly approved the bill on March 21, 1842 by a margin of 65 to 16 with 47 abstentions. All but one of the New York City Democratic delegation voted for the bill after fighting to defeat it for two years.[38]

In the Senate, where the Democrats had only a two-vote majority, it was expected that the Maclay bill would encounter tougher opposition. As a concession to the Whigs, the Democrats added an amendment prohibiting sectarian religious teaching in the common schools. Even with this amendment, however, the bill's fate was in doubt. In order to strengthen the backbone of the Democrats, the Catholics resorted to the same tactics that they had employed the previous November. They nominated their own candidates for mayor and for four members of the Common Council in the municipal elections that were scheduled for April 12 in New York City. On April 8 the Senate passed the Maclay bill by thirteen to twelve on a straight party vote. Not one Whig supported it. Governor Seward signed the bill the next day, bringing to a close Round Four of the Great School Controversy that had begun in January 1840.[39] Two days later the Catholics withdrew their candidates in the municipal election.

Victory and Defeat

More than any other issue, the Great School Controversy made John Hughes famous or infamous depending on one's point of view. His reputation spread well beyond the confines of New York State, giving him a prominence that neither Bishop Connolly nor Bishop Dubois had ever attained. By any standard it was an amazing performance. The pugnacious Irish immigrant bishop defeated the wealthy and prestigious Public School Society and ended its monopoly of public education in New York City. He achieved this victory in the face of bitter opposition from alarmed Protestants by uniting the Catholic immigrants under his leadership and turning them into a potent political force. It was no mean achievement for him to persuade a reluctant Democratic party to implement the educational reforms of a Whig governor who was unable to get his own party to support him. Throughout the long struggle Hughes' sole motivation was unquestionably his concern for the spiritual welfare of the poor Catholic children of the city.

However, his victory was not complete by any means, and he knew it. The overthrow of the monopoly of the Public School Society was only one part of his program. They attributed the defeat "of their noble institution to the blighting influence of party strife and sectarian animosity."[40] The other part of Hughes' program was to obtain public funding for his own Catholic schools. In this regard he went down to resounding defeat. The alluring prospects raised by the Spencer Report that the common schools in the Catholic neighborhoods of New York City might become de facto Catholic schools went up in smoke when the Senate amended the Maclay bill to exclude any sectarian religious instruction in the common schools.[41]

37 - Bourne, *History of the Public School Society*, 501--506,519

38 - Lannie, "Archbishop Hughes and the Common School Controversy," 514-517, 529-530.

39 - *Laws of the State of New York* (Albany: Thurlow Weed, 1842), 184-189.

40 - N-YHS, Minutes of the Meetings of the Board of Trustees of the Public School Society of New York, May 6, 1842. The Public School Society continued to exist until 1853 when it was voluntarily disbanded.

41 - The amendment read: "No school above mentioned, or which shall be organized under this Act, in which any religious sectarian doctrine or tenet shall be taught, inculcated or practiced, shall receive any portion of the school moneys to be distributed by this Act." *Laws of the State of New York*, 187.

The city's public schools retained a residual Protestant character for several decades after the demise of the Public School Society. The first superintendent of the city's schools under the new system was Colonel William L. Stone, an ardent admirer of the Public School Society. The *Truth Teller* labeled him "the most inveterate enemy of the education of Catholic children that can be found in our city." Stone even tried to deprive the Sisters of Charity of the stipends they received for teaching in the schools of the two Catholic orphan asylums, although he claimed to be doing so with "unaffected reluctance."[42] However, as the Protestant influence gradually declined and the public schools became increasingly secular, Hughes railed against them as centers of Godless education. Unintentionally he had made a major contribution to that development by his opposition to sectarian education.

After the Great School Controversy of 1840-1842, Hughes avoided any further involvement in public education. He made no effort to work with the new system of locally elected schools boards because the law excluded the kind of religious instruction that he thought was essential to sound education. Instead, he concentrated on building his own system of Catholic schools. Only a few years later, in 1850, he announced in a pastoral letter that "the time is almost come when it will be necessary to build the school-house first and the church afterwards."[43] As a result of this policy of building his own network of Catholic schools, which the American Catholic bishops extended to the whole country at the Third Plenary Council of Baltimore in 1884, many have regarded him as the father of the parochial school system. "If this be true," commented Lannie, "then it is paradoxical that the father of American Catholic education

Spuyten Duyvil Creek between Manhattan and the Bronx in the early nineteenth century.
Credit: *Archdiocese of New York*

---

42 - *Truth Teller,* May 20, 1843; *Report of William L. Stone to the Board of Education of the City and County of New-York* (New-York: William Osborne, 1843), 10.

43 - Kehoe, *Works of John Hughes,* II, 715.

should unwittingly have become a leading light in the ultimate secularization of the American public school."[44]

Still another consequence of the publicity surrounding the Great School Controversy in New York was an intensification of Protestant fears that Catholics were intent on destroying the common schools, driving the Bible from the classroom and seeking public money to establish a rival system of sectarian education. These fears played into the hands of the Nativists who found a much larger audience than ever before for their warnings about the dangers of Catholic immigration. It served as the background to the third issue which made John Hughes nationally famous, his spirited defense of Catholic interests against the Nativists, which came to a head when they threatened to stage a major demonstration in New York City on May 9, 1844.

John Hughes and the Nativists

The Nativist movement continued to attract more and more sympathizers throughout the 1840s especially in the port cities of the East Coast where tension between native-born Americans and Catholic immigrants was most acute. In Philadelphia mutual animosity erupted into three days of rioting in the Kensington section of the city in May 1844, leading to the death of thirteen people, the destruction of two Catholic churches and widespread damage to Catholic property. The immediate cause of the rioting was rumors, whipped up in the Protestant pulpit and press, that the Catholics were attempting to ban the Bible from the public schools. In an effort to placate the rioters and to assist the civil authorities in restoring law and order, Bishop Kenrick left the city for three days and suspended the celebration of Mass in Philadelphia's Catholic churches. John Hughes, who as a young priest had ample experience of anti-Catholic prejudice in the City of Brotherly Love, thought that Kenrick's decision was a mistake. "They should have defended their churches,' he said, "since the authorities could not or would not do it for them."

In New York City local Nativist leaders followed the events in Philadelphia with great interest. On May 7, during the height of the disturbances in Philadelphia, they announced plans for a large public demonstration two days later in City Hall Park, the favored site for political rallies. The Nativists also made known that a delegation from Philadelphia would attend the demonstration with a tattered American flag that had supposedly been desecrated by the Catholic rioters. The demonstration was likely to be a deliberately provocative event that might touch off the same kind of violence that had occurred in Philadelphia.

Realizing the implications of the situation, Bishop Hughes responded decisively on two different levels, demonstrating both firmness and flexibility. He urged Catholics not to attend the rally on May 9 so that they could not be accused of inciting a riot. At the same time he assured them that, if attacked, they had the right to use every means to defend their property. He himself posted armed guards around the city's Catholic churches. While Hughes tried to restrain his own people and protect his churches, he went to City Hall and urged the mayor, Robert H. Morris, to ban the Nativist demonstration. "Are you afraid," asked the mayor, "that some of your churches may be burned?" "No, sir," replied Hughes, "but I am afraid that some of *yours* will be burned. We can protect our own. I come to warn you for your own good."[45]

44 - Lannie, "Archbishop Hughes and the Common School Controversy," 571.

45 - Hassard, *Hughes*, 278.

City Hall Park where the Nativists threatened to hold a rally in May 1844.

When Morris asked Hughes what he wanted him to do, he urged him to reinforce the police with a detachment of soldiers and to warn the mayor-elect, James Harper, who had just been elected with Nativist support, to use his influence with his political allies to call off the demonstration. Whatever the reason for their decision, the Nativists canceled their demonstration at the last minute, averting the kind of violence that had just occurred in Philadelphia. John Hughes was not shy about publicly claiming the credit for averting a bloodbath.

Writing in the *Freeman's Journal* in the immediate aftermath of the crisis, he congratulated the Catholics of New York for their admirable self-control in the face of insulting provocations. "But, at the same time," he added

> it is not to be disguised that, if aggression had been carried farther than insult, and any act of violence had been committed by the inflamed rabble who made up the train of the "Native American" processions, the carnage that would have ensued is now utterly beyond calculation. There is not a Church of the city, which was not protected with an average force

of one to two thousand men---cool, collected, armed to the teeth, and with a firm determination, after taking as many lives as they could in defence of their property, to give up, if necessary, their own lives for the same cause.[46]

Hughes made clear that he would give his people the same advice in the future if they were again confronted by threats of Nativist violence. He would urge them first to be patient and to trust the laws of the country for justice and protection. However, he added, "when in violation of those laws, their property or persons are assailed by violence, we think them justified in defending these by every means which the Providence of God has put within their reach."

It is difficult to know how seriously to take Hughes' claim that he single-handedly saved New York City from a Nativist riot. The bishop's reflections hardly reflected the spirit of the Sermon on the Mount, but, more to the point, it is not clear how accurate they were. If he really posted as many as 1,000 to 2,000 armed guards around each Catholic church, it would mean that

46 - *Freeman's Journal*, May 11, 1844.

he was able to raise and arm a private militia of 10,000 to 20,000 men within a couple of days. It is inconceivable that such a force would have escaped public notice, but there is no mention of it in the secular press. The critics who constantly criticized Hughes for donning the mantle of a politician would hardly have remained silent at the prospect of Hughes as a military commander. Mayor James Harper, in his address to the Common Council a week later, made no mention of it. Hughes also declared that "if a single Catholic church were burned in New York, the city would become a second Moscow," but it is not clear where or to whom he made that remark.

Nevertheless, despite the retrospective episcopal hyperbole, Ray Allen Billington, the respected historian of American Nativism, gave Hughes high marks for the way that he handled the situation. Billington believed that, if the Nativists had proceeded with their plans for a rally in City Hall Park, it might very well have led to widespread violence and arson. "Bishop Hughes deserves credit for saving New York from a period of mob rule such as that which had racked Philadelphia," Billington wrote.[47]

John Hughes and the Press

Colonel William Stone, the editor of the Commercial Advertiser

There were two journalists whom Hughes especially blamed for fomenting Nativist prejudice against Catholics and attempting to deprive them of what he considered their just rights. They were Colonel William Stone, the co-proprietor and editor of the *Commercial Advertiser,* and James Gordon Bennett, the publisher and editor of the *Herald.* His anger at them, held in check during the Great School Controversy, exploded in the spring of 1844 immediately after the cancellation of the Nativist rally. Eight years earlier Stone had earned the gratitude of Catholics for exposing Maria Monk as a fraud, but he had long expressed dismay at the growth of the Catholic population and he had been a relentless critic of Hughes, calling him a Jesuit and a political priest. He would never let Hughes forget the famous speech he gave at Carroll Hall on October 29, 1841, on the eve of the November elections. "The thundering sound of the shillelahs [sic]," he told Hughes," as you called upon them not to flinch in the coming political contest would have acidulated the milk of human kindness." Stone would not even give Hughes credit for averting violence in New York City in May 1844. Instead he twisted Hughes' words to mean that he the power to plunge the city into chaos, if he wished to do so.[48]

Although Stone liked to distance himself from professional bigots like Dr. Brownlee, he had much in common with them, even stooping to using pejorative adjectives like Papist and Romish. James Gordon Bennett, on the other hand, was an adversary of an altogether different type. Born into an old Scottish Catholic family in Banffshire, he spent four years in a seminary in Aberdeen before coming to America. A pioneer in the field of popular journalism, Bennett turned the *Herald* into the largest and most successful newspaper in the United States. Although he claimed to be a Catholic, albeit an "enlightened Catholic," and initially expressed sympathy for Hughes' position in the school controversy, he became the bishop's most vitriolic opponent. The *Herald* was the first newspaper to break the story of Hughes' Carroll Hall speech and its graphic account caused a sensation. [49]

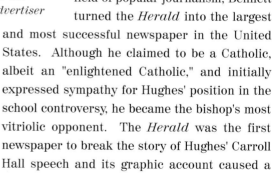

---

47 - Billington, *Protestant Crusade,* 232.

48 - New York *Commercial Advertiser,* June 6, 1844.

49 - New York *Herald,* November 1, 1841.

Bennett not only criticized Hughes for meddling in politics but also attacked him personally with a venom that was exceptional even by the rough-and-tumble standards of nineteenth-century journalism. He lambasted Hughes as an ignorant cabbage farmer who had risen to the office of bishop by clerical intrigue and then surrounded himself with a coterie of flatterers. Moreover, Bennett tried to drive a wedge between Hughes and his senior clergy like John Power and Constantine Pise and called upon New York Catholics to petition the pope to remove him from office. In his wilder moments he even advocated the formation of an independent American Catholic Church free from papal control, and he pledged a thousand dollars to get it started.[50]

To the end of his days Hughes could never bring himself to admit the accusations of Stone and Bennett that he had involved himself in partisan politics. "I never was, I never will be a politician," he protested to Mayor James Harper despite abundant evidence to the contrary. Even he had to concede, however, that the Carroll Hall speech of October 29, 1841 could hardly qualify as a homily. "If this was a political speech," he grudgingly admitted, "then have I made one political speech in my life."

Unlike Colonel Stone, Bennett had attacked Hughes personally. Hughes responded in kind with a ferocity that would have been exceptional in a politician, much less a bishop. "I regard him as decidedly the most dangerous man to the peace and safety of a community that I have ever known," he warned the mayor in an open letter. He added for good measure: "If he were even more depraved or less despised, he would not be so

A LETTER

ON

THE MORAL CAUSES

THAT HAVE PRODUCED

THE EVIL SPIRIT OF THE TIMES;

ADDRESSED TO

THE HONORABLE JAMES HARPER,

MAYOR OF NEW-YORK.

INCLUDING

A VINDICATION OF THE AUTHOR

FROM THE

INFAMOUS CHARGES MADE AGAINST HIM BY JAS. GORDON BENNETT
WILLIAM L. STONE, AND OTHERS.

BY THE RIGHT REV. DR. HUGHES,
BISHOP OF NEW YORK.

New-York:
J. WINCHESTER, NEW WORLD PRESS,
XXX ANN STREET.

*Bishop Hughes' Open Letter
to Mayor James Harper in 1844*

dangerous; but being without any fixed principle of good, he occupies that ambiguous position which renders him too contemptible for notice, yet not sufficiently so to be below the power of mischief."[51]

John Hughes the Americanist

Although none of Hughes' critics bothered to notice, throughout all his long controversy with the Nativists, Hughes never flinched (to use one of his favorite words) in his commitment the principles of American democracy, including religious freedom for every denomination.

50 - *New York Herald,* November 6, 17, December 4, 1841.
51 - Kehoe, *Complete Works of John Hughes*, I, 456-457.

Bennett and Stone attempted to identify Hughes with the reactionary and intolerant policies of Pope Gregory XVI, the author of the encyclical *Mirari Vos* in 1832, which was a sweeping condemnation of contemporary liberalism. Their fire was misdirected. Although Hughes never publicly criticized the encyclical, his total silence about it indicates that he did not believe that it had any direct application in the United States.

However questionable Hughes' tactics may have been at times, he treasured the American system of democratic government. He gloried in the fact that he was an American citizen and wanted to assure immigrants the same rights that were enjoyed by native-born Americans. "My feelings and habits and thoughts have been so much identified with all that is American," he wrote in 1844, "that I had almost forgotten I was a foreigner until recent circumstances have brought it too painfully to my attention."[52] John Hughes was part of that long line of American bishops stretching back to John Carroll who, unlike many of their counterparts in nineteenth-century Europe, regarded political and religious freedom as the friend, not the enemy of their church.

By 1844 John Hughes was the most famous Catholic prelate in the United States due to his highly visible role during the previous six years in combating lay trusteeism, the Public School Society and Nativism in his own diocese. It is indicative of his national stature that four years later, when President James Buchanan wanted Catholic military chaplains to serve in the Mexican War, he appealed to John Hughes for assistance rather than to the archbishop of Baltimore. Not for another century would any archbishop of New York enjoy the same national prominence as John Hughes.

However, Bishop Hughes' primary responsibility was not to represent the Catholic Church on the national scene, but to develop the physical and spiritual resources of his large diocese. It was a daunting challenge even for someone with the enormous self-confidence of John Hughes.

52 - Ibid., 452.

7

The Construction of a Diocese

The High Bridge across the Harlem River at 173rd Street. The oldest major bridge in New York City, it was built between 1837 and 1848 to bring Croton water to Manhattan. Credit: *Archdiocese of New York*

Thirty-four years after the creation of the diocese of New York, John Hughes summoned the first diocesan synod. The delay is a fair indication of how little spade work had been done to organize the diocese to that date. By contrast, John Carroll convened a synod for the diocese of Baltimore within a year of his return from England after his episcopal ordination. That synod of Baltimore in 1791, the first in American Catholic history, and the subsequent provincial councils of Baltimore after 1829, laid down many of the rules and regulations that were to govern the American Catholic community for the next century, including the much of the legislation of New York's first diocesan synod.

The Synod of 1842

The New York synod met at St. John's College, Fordham, on August 21, 1842. It began with an eight-day retreat preached by Father John Timon, C.M., the future bishop of Buffalo, followed by a three-day synod. In summoning the clergy to the synod, Bishop Hughes took note of the fact that the missionary nature of the diocese had often made it difficult, if not impossible, to observe exactly all the prescriptions of canon law. "The time, however, has now arrived," the bishop told his priests, "when it is believed that these irregularities, resulting from the necessity of circumstances, may be diminished, if not entirely removed."[1]

Some of the priests attending the synod knew that they would be absent from their parishes for two or three successive Sundays, and Hughes told them to take care of the sick before they left. "We hope that nothing less than the weightiest reason will prevent any of the clergy from attending," he said sternly. By this time the New York priests had taken the measure of the bishop and had become acquainted with his fierce temper. As a result all but six of the seventy-two priests in the diocese were present at Rose Hill when the synod opened. They came from as far away as Buffalo, Watertown, Oswego, Odgensburg, Sandy Hill and French Creek. It was probably the first time that many of them had the opportunity to meet one another, since they were natives of a half-dozen different countries and had been educated in at least as many different seminaries. John Hughes kept a careful record of attendance and even appointed Joseph Schneller, the pastor of St. Mary's in Albany, to be the "prefect of discipline" at the synod as if it were a gathering of obstreperous high school boys.

Some of the priests who participated in the synod were veteran pastors who had made outstanding contributions to the diocese like John Power, Felix Varela, and John Raffeiner. Others were promising young men at the beginning of their clerical careers like David Bacon, Andrew Byrne, John Loughlin, John McCloskey, Bernard O'Reilly and William Quarter, all of whom were to become bishops within the next decade. The roster of the clergy included William Beecham, the "Pope of Rome," whose parish once included eight upstate counties, Alessandro Muppiatti, a former Carthusian monk, who was New York's first Italian-born diocesan priest, and Michael McCarron, a New York City pastor who was known as the Archdeacon. It was a heterogeneous group that included such characters as the hapless Ambrose Manahan (the secretary of the synod), "Mad Phil" O'Reilly, the pioneer priest in the Hudson Valley, and James Shanahan, who joined the Gold Rush to California where he ministered to the miners in their camps even after going blind and returned to New York to die as a curate in St. Peter's Church in Barclay Street in 1870 at the age of seventy. Perhaps John Hughes had good reason to make a no-nonsense German the prefect of discipline at his synod.

The synod passed thirty-three diocesan statutes, some of them of the most elementary kind, such as the requirement that within three months every church with a resident pastor should have a baptismal font and confessional. Baptisms were no longer to take place at home except in case of emergency. Four day's notice was required for weddings. Priests were not to be absent from their parish on Sunday without the permission of the bishop, and they were ordered to wear a cassock at Mass under penalty of suspension. Funerals were to take place in

---

1 - Hughes to Rev. and Dear Sir, July 28, 1842, in Kehoe, *Complete Works of John Hughes,* I, 313-314.

church and funeral orations were to be discouraged. Some of the most important synodal legislation pertained to finances. No church property was to be held in the pastor's name and the trustees were forbidden to spend any parish money without the permission of the pastor. With the exception of ordinary expenses, neither the pastor nor the trustees could spend more than $100 without the permission of the bishop.[2]

The New Metropolis

While John Hughes was engaged in laying down the ground rules for his diocese, his see city, which contained the great bulk of the Catholic population, was undergoing a transformation that was to have a profound impact on the diocese of New York. During the next quarter century not only did the population of the city more than double from 312,710 in 1840 to over 800,000 in 1865, but there was also a major shift in the distribution of the population. When New York's new coadjutor bishop arrived on the scene in 1838, only 33,000 people lived north of 14th Street, and one-third of them listed their occupation as agriculture in the census two years later. Between 1845 and 1860, however, as the population pushed north from the crowded wards of lower Manhattan, they created a new city of 290,000 people above 14th Street, almost as many people as the population of the whole city fifteen years earlier.

In 1860 the population of New York City was larger than that of twenty of the thirty-three states. By 1858, the year that John Hughes blessed the cornerstone for New York's new Catholic cathedral, urban development had reached 50th Street on the West Side and 36th Street on the East Side. Lower Fifth Avenue was the favorite location for the mansions of wealthy businessmen like August Belmont and James Lenox while prosperous middle-class New Yorkers filled the stately but monotonous rows of brownstones that sprouted everywhere on the side streets above 14th Street. One unfortunate aspect of the building boom was the neglect of green space. There was not a single park or square to be found in the four square miles between Madison Square and 57th Street.[3]

The "New Metropolis" was the name that the historian Edward Spann gave to this booming city that was now America's undisputed leader in commerce, manufacturing and finance. Spann astutely called attention to the fact that New York City at mid-century was also the capital of Protestant America. The Public School Society may have become a spent force after its encounter with John Hughes, but New York City was home to the American Bible Society, the Home Missionary Society, the American Temperance Union and other powerful national Protestant organizations. As Spann notes, the leaders of these benevolent associations made no secret of their belief that "Roman Catholicism was alien and inferior." The same was true of the leaders of two of the most important private charitable organizations in the city, the Association for Improving the Condition of the Poor and the Children's Aid Society.[4]

Croton Water

The New Metropolis could never have sustained a population of 800,000 squeezed into an area of twenty-two square miles without two vital public improvements. One was a reliable source of clean water, and the other was an adequate system of public transportation. New

2 - *Synodis Diocesana Neo-Eboracensis Prima* (New York: George Mitchell, 1842), passim. There is a handy summary in Smith, *Catholic Church in New York*, I, 210-211.

3 - Edward K. Spann, *The New Metropolis: New York City, 1840-1857* (New York: Columbia University Press, 1981), 103-105,121.

4 - Ibid., 273, 277.

Yorkers relied upon private wells and springs for water and on backyard privies and cesspools for sanitation with the predictable result that they suffered from periodic outbreaks of disease like the cholera epidemics of 1849 and 1854. In John Hughes' day New York was a dirty, fetid, unhealthy city. It became increasingly unhealthy in the middle decades of the nineteenth century, especially for children. Less than one-half of the infants born in the city in the 1850s survived to the age of six. The overall mortality rates for the rest of the population were only marginally better. In the year 1840 one of every forty New Yorkers died, but by 1857 it was one of every twenty-seven New Yorkers. In some years in the 1850s deaths exceeded births. The city health commissioner stated that the city's population would actually have declined except for the constant stream of immigrants.

Closeup of construction
of the High Bridge across the Harlem River.
Credit: *Archdiocese of New York*

October 14, 1842, should have been a banner day in the history of public health in New York City, when thousands turned out for the celebration of the opening of the Croton Aqueduct. A marvel of nineteenth-century engineering, the gravity-fed system could deliver thirty million gallons of pure water every day to the Distributing Reservoir at Fifth Avenue and 42nd Street from a dam in Westchester County forty miles away. However, Croton Water was slow to realize its potential to make New York a safer and cleaner city for economic reasons. Many landlords refused to hook up to the system because of the high installation costs and the yearly Water Rent of $10. As a result ten years later two-thirds of the city's dwellings still had no running water. Even more incredibly, in 1856 there were only 1,631 baths and 10,384 water closets in the entire city for a population of over 600,000. In 1859 three-quarters of the paved streets still had no sewers.[5]

5 - Ibid., 117-120, 128, 133

Public Transportation

Public health remained a major issue in New York City throughout the nineteenth century, and so did public transportation. New York was once a compact "walking city" where most residents, especially those of the working class, lived within a short distance of their place of employment. They walked to work, shops, schools, taverns, churches and places of amusement. As the city grew in size, however, it became imperative to provide cheap and reliable public transportation for the general public. By the early 1830s New Yorkers were already complaining about the congested streets, and John Pintard was certainly not the only one who found it was dangerous to cross Broadway because of the heavy traffic. While New Yorkers had a dense network of ferries to take them to Brooklyn, Williamsburg, Hoboken and Jersey City, efficient public transportation lagged behind within the city itself.[6]

For years the main means of travel within Manhattan was the omnibus, a distinctively box-shaped stage coach with a rear entrance that held a dozen passengers. Almost 700 of them were in operation in the early 1850s, offering 100,000 passengers a day a bumpy ride on the city's cobblestone streets. They impressed the tourists, but were less appreciated by native New Yorkers. "The omnibuses of this city should hereafter be styled nuisances or perhaps more appropriately 'packing boxes,' " wrote the editor of the *Truth Teller* in 1836. "The drivers of them are generally reckless and impudent, as ready in uttering abusive language to passengers as they are careless in endangering lives." George Templeton Strong made the mistake of taking the Greenwich Street omnibus home from church one Christmas Day. "The driver was drunk," he said, "and the progress of the vehicle was like that of a hippopotamus through one of the quagmires of Africa."[7]

Omnibuses on Broadway and Park Row in front of City Hall Park. Credit: *Archdiocese of New York*

6 - Pintard, March 1, 1833, *Letters of John Pintard,* IV, 130.

7 - Spann, *New Metropolis,* 285; *Truth Teller,* August 27, 1836; Strong, *Diary,* December 26, 1848, cit. in Juliana Gilheany, "Subjects of History: English, Scottish and Welsh Immigrants in New York City, 1820-1860," Ph.D. dissertation, New York University, 1989, 192.

The Loew Bridge at Broadway and Fulton Street with St. Paul's Chapel in the background.
Credit: *Archdiocese of New York*

The big innovation in public transportation came with the transition from the omnibus to horse-drawn streetcars. As far back as November 1832 the New York and Harlem Railroad was operating horse cars on its rails from Prince Street near City Hall to 23rd Street. However, the big breakthrough in mass transit came in 1851 and 1852, when the Common Council finally overcame the opposition of the omnibus operators and granted charters for the construction of horse car lines on Second, Third, Sixth, Eighth and Ninth Avenues (but not on Broadway where the omnibus operators retained their monopoly). The horse-drawn streetcars cars provided a smoother and faster ride to and from work than the omnibuses for thousands of New Yorkers, who could now choose to live many miles north of the downtown business district. The horse cars remained the backbone of the city's transportation system until later in the century when they were supplanted by electric streetcars and elevated railways. The five-cent fare that the Common Council established in the 1850s became a sacrosanct institution that no politician dared to question for the next century.[8]

The implications of these changes for the diocese of New York were obvious. As the city grew in size and area, the Catholic Church was compelled to keep pace by establishing additional parishes in the new residential neighborhoods that were beginning to appear in midtown and upper Manhattan. When Bishop Hughes became the apostolic administrator of the diocese in 1839, he had about forty churches and fifty priests to care for the whole state of New York and northern New Jersey. Eight of the churches were in Manhattan, and, except for St. Paul's in the village of Harlem, all were located below 14th Street. In upstate New York only Albany, Rochester and

---

8 - Spann, *New Metropolis,* 293. Joseph Warren Greene, Jr., "New York City's First Railroad: The New York and Harlem, 1832-1867," *New-York Historical Society Quarterly Bulletin 9* (1926): 107-109.

Buffalo could boast of more than one Catholic church. In many other places the church buildings were still under construction and had not yet been dedicated. Important cities like Schenectady, Saratoga and Plattsburg had no church at all. In those localities Catholics thought they were fortunate if a circuit-riding missionary priest visited them once or twice a month to celebrate Mass for them in a private residence.[9]

In New York City between 1840 and 1865 the Catholic population mushroomed from 80,000 or 90,000 to 300,000 or 400,000, which meant that Catholics constituted almost half of the population. Most of the newcomers were Irish immigrants fleeing from the Great Famine in their homeland. According to Bishop Hughes, at the height of the famine in the late 1840s, these refugees arrived at the rate of 1,000 or 2,000 each day. "The utter destitution in which they reached these shores," he added, "is almost inconceivable." At the same time there was an increased number of German-speaking Catholics for whom the diocese needed to provide churches and schools. According to one calculation, during the next quarter-century Bishop Hughes added sixty-one new parishes, twenty-four of them in Manhattan and the other thirty-seven on Staten Island and in the seven upstate counties that now comprise the archdiocese of New York. Seven of the new city churches were German national parishes, one was French, and the others were Irish in fact, if not in name. By 1863 there were thirty-two Catholic churches in New York City where forty years earlier there had been only two churches.[10]

Horse cars in Chatham Square in 1858. Credit: *Archdiocese of New York*

9 - *The Metropolitan Catholic Almanac and Laity's Directory for the Year of Our Lord 1839* (Baltimore: Fielding Lucas, Jr., 1839), 106-109.
10 - Dolan, *Immigrant Church,* 12-19, Cohalan, *Popular History,* 75.

The Church in the Old City

Despite the growth of the "new city" north of 14th Street, the majority of New York's Catholics continued to live in the poorer and more congested areas of lower Manhattan whose total population also continued to increase. There were already seven Catholic churches south of 14th Street in 1840. Bishop Hughes added seven more churches at a time when twenty-two Protestant congregations were busy relocating their churches from lower Manhattan to better neighborhoods uptown.[11]

CATHOLIC CHURCHES
in New York City in 1865

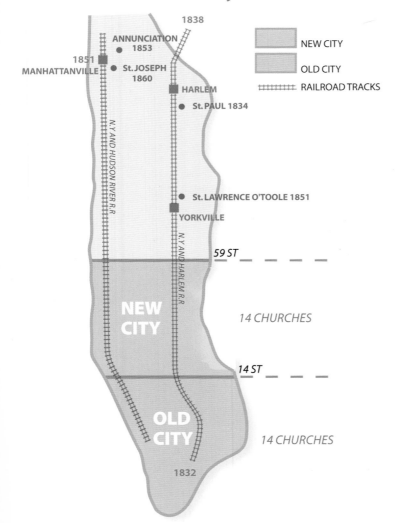

In 1839 all seven Catholic churches in lower Manhattan had large and growing congregations. The oldest of them all, St. Peter's, was now far too small for the number of parishioners. "It has literally grown old in the service and is entirely inadequate to accommodate its overflowing congregation," reported the *Truth Teller* in 1836. That same year, when a portion of the church ceiling collapsed, it was decided to replace the building rather than to repair it. The new stone structure was built in the Greek revival style and was dedicated by New York's new coadjutor, Bishop Hughes, on February 25, 1838. It featured an imposing classical façade and won favorable comment from even the usually censorious George Templeton Strong, who called it approvingly an "Iconic temple."[12]

The cost, however, was a staggering $134,945, which resulted in bankruptcy six years later. Not until November 1849 was the diocese able to regain title to the church, seven months after the death of John Power whose physical and mental health had deteriorated under the strain. An unfortunate side effect of the erection of the new St. Peter's Church was the obliteration of New York's oldest Catholic cemetery, which had surrounded the original church. The bodies were re-interred in the cathedral graveyard, but, as John Gilmary Shea remarked, it meant that the oldest Catholic tombstones in New York City were now those of the pre-Revolutionary Irish buried in Trinity churchyard.

---

11 - For the growth of the parish infrastructure in New York City under Archbishop Hughes, I have relied heavily upon John Gilmary Shea, ed., *The Catholic Churches of New York City* (New York: Lawrence Goulding, 1878).

12 - Strong, *Diary*, I, 81.

CATHOLIC CHURCHES
in the "Old City" and in the "New City" in 1865

St. PAUL THE APOSTLE

59TH STREET

ASSUMPTION

6TH AVE

St. JOHN
THE EVANGELIST

St. BONIFACE

HOLY CROSS

42 STREET

St. MICHAEL

St. GABRIEL

New City

St. FRANCIS ASSISI

3RD AVE

St. JOHN THE BAPTIST

St. COLUMBA

St. STEPHEN

St. VINCENT DE PAUL

St. FRANCIS XAVIER

IMMACULATE
CONCEPTION

● GERMAN CHURCHES
● FRENCH CHURCHES

14TH STREET

St. JOSEPH

St. ANN

St. BRIGID

9TH AVE

BOWERY

BROADWAY

MOST HOLY REDEEMER

Old City

NATIVITY

St. NICHOLAS

HOUSTON ST.

St. PATRICK'S
OLD CATHEDRAL

St. MARY

GRAND ST.

St. ALPHONSUS

St. TERESA

CANAL ST.

TRANSFIGURATION

DIVISION ST

St. JAMES

St. ANDREW

St. PETER

The new St. Peter's Church

St. Peter's was not the only church that was too small for its congregation. Between 1838 and 1842 St. Patrick's Cathedral was remodeled and enlarged with the addition of a bigger sacristy. St. Mary's Church on Grand Street, the only Catholic church in the densely populated Lower East Side, was also too small for the large congregation that filled the church for five Masses every Sunday morning. Between 1864 and 1871 the interior was extended and remodeled, a new façade was built, and the twin towers were added.

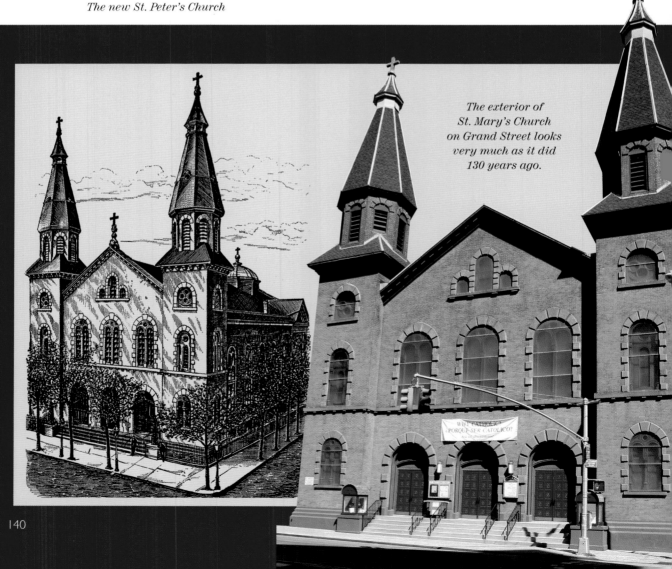

The exterior of St. Mary's Church on Grand Street looks very much as it did 130 years ago.

Crucifixion Scene: St. Mary's Church.
Credit: *Yvon Meyer*

On the West Side St. Joseph's Church on Sixth Avenue was dedicated by Bishop Dubois on March 16, 1834, just as Greenwich Village was ceasing to be a bona fide suburban village. The northernmost of New York's early Catholic churches, it is the oldest unaltered church structure in the diocese. Its original boundaries extended from Canal Street to West 34th Street and from Broadway to the Hudson River. The parish included the Ninth or American Ward, where native-born Americans continued to predominate long after the neighboring wards had filled up with immigrants.[13]

As was mentioned already, in 1835 the German Church of St. Nicholas had found a permanent home on East 2nd Street where the lay trustees persisted in making life difficult for a series of pastors and successfully resisted even the efforts of John Hughes to curb their authority.

Father Felix Varela,
1788-1853.
Credit: John Gilmary Shea,
History of the Catholic Church
in the United States

The last two downtown churches, St. James on James Street and Transfiguration on Mott Street, were both offshoots of Christ Church, the former Episcopalian church on Ann Street that Father Felix Varela had bought in 1827 and converted into a Catholic church of the same name. When Christ Church was declared unsafe in 1833, the congregation moved to temporary quarters first on William Street and later on Ann Street, and then purchased property in 1835 for a new church on James Street. Whether by design or accident it was called St. James Church. Bishop Dubois blessed the building in September of the following year. It soon became the center of a Catholic community of 25,000 regular parishioners in addition to a floating population of 3,000 Catholic seamen from all parts of the world who came to Mass on Sunday from the ships berthed at nearby East River docks.

St. Joseph's Church in Greenwich Village as it appeared shortly after its completion and today

13 - On St. Joseph's Church, see Thomas J. Shelley, *Greenwich Village Catholics: St. Joseph's Church and the Evolution of an Urban Faith Community, 1829-2002* (Washington, D.C.: The Catholic University of America Press, 2003).

When Christ Church was declared unsafe in 1833, many of the parishioners objected to attending Mass at St. James Church because it was too far away. To accommodate them, Father Varela purchased the Scottish Reformed Presbyterian Church on Chambers Street, which had once been a bastion of strict Caledonian Calvinism. He renamed it the Church of the Transfiguration. Dedicated by Bishop Dubois on March 31, 1836, it contained within its boundaries both City Hall and the notorious Five Points. Father Varela, immensely popular with his Irish parishioners, remained as pastor until ill health forced him to move to Florida in 1850. Three years later the small church was sold and another larger Episcopalian church at the corner of Mott and Cross Streets was purchased as its replacement. Bishop Hughes dedicated it on May 14, 1853. Like all the other Catholic churches in lower Manhattan, it had a huge congregation.

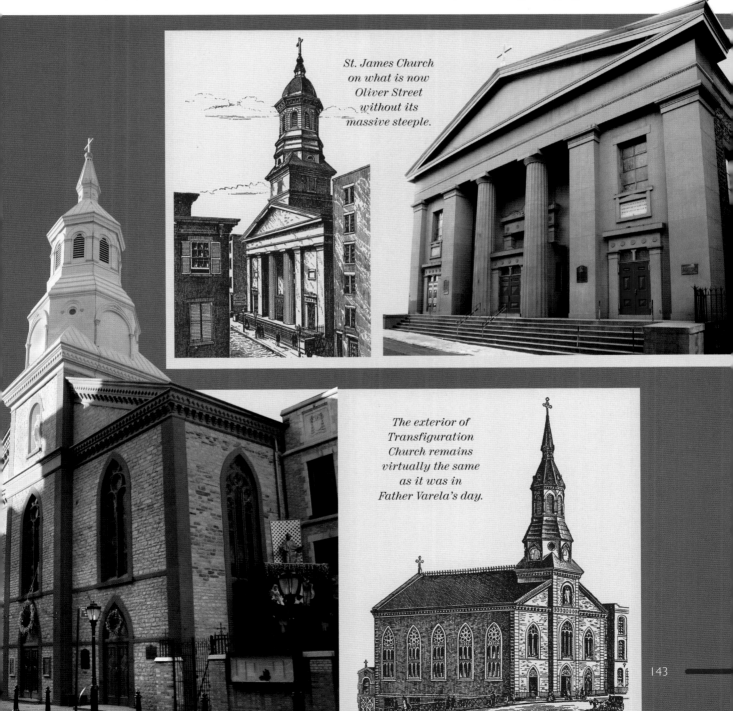

St. James Church on what is now Oliver Street without its massive steeple.

The exterior of Transfiguration Church remains virtually the same as it was in Father Varela's day.

New Churches in the Old City

Despite the best efforts to enlarge the existing Catholic churches in Lower Manhattan, it was obvious that more churches were needed. No one recognized this more clearly than the local pastors. In several instances they gave up their own flourishing parishes to establish new ones in the same neighborhood. The process began in 1842, when Father Andrew Byrne, the pastor of St. James Church, was instrumental in founding St. Andrew's Church and the Church of the Nativity. Both of them were housed in former Protestant churches. John Gilmary Shea remarked that there always seemed to be a Protestant church for sale in New York City.

Two years after founding these two parishes, Father Byrne was appointed the first bishop of Little Rock, Arkansas. He received episcopal ordination from the hands of John Hughes in St. Patrick's Cathedral on March 10, 1844, together with Father William Quarter, the pastor of St. Mary's, who had been appointed the first bishop of Chicago, and Father John McCloskey, who had been made coadjutor to Bishop Hughes.

As was mentioned already, that same year Bishop Hughes tried to break the stranglehold of the lay trustees over St. Nicholas Church by inviting the German-speaking Redemptorist Fathers to the diocese. After the first Redemptorist pastor, Father Gabriel Rumpler, C.Ss.R., tried in vain to dislodge the trustees at St. Nicholas, he founded the Church of the Most

Andrew Byrne, the First Bishop of Little Rock, 1844-1862.
Credit: John Gilmary Shea, *History of the Catholic Church in the United States*

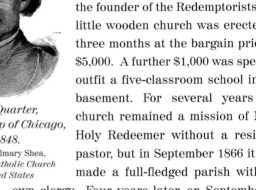

William Quarter, the First Bishop of Chicago, 1844-1848.
Credit: John Gilmary Shea, *History of the Catholic Church in the United States*

Holy Redeemer on East 3rd Street with Hughes' approval and support. A temporary frame church with two galleries was constructed in the space of seven weeks and was dedicated by the new coadjutor, Bishop John McCloskey, on April 8, 1844. The construction was so spindly that one observer thought that it resembled a rope house rather than a church. Eight years later, on November 28, 1852, John Hughes dedicated the present cathedral-like structure. Its commanding presence soon overshadowed St. Nicholas Church both literally and figuratively and became the center of German Catholic life in *Kleindeutschland*.

Father Rumpler gave New York's German Catholic community another church in 1847 when he established St. Alphonsus Church on Thompson Street just north of Canal Street. Named after St. Alphonsus Ligouri, the founder of the Redemptorists, the little wooden church was erected in three months at the bargain price of $5,000. A further $1,000 was spent to outfit a five-classroom school in the basement. For several years the church remained a mission of Most Holy Redeemer without a resident pastor, but in September 1866 it was made a full-fledged parish with its own clergy. Four years later, on September 4, 1870, Archbishop John McCloskey blessed the cornerstone of a new stone-and-brick church that ran through the block from Thompson Street to South Fifth Avenue (present-day West Broadway). The new church, with a seating capacity of 1,800 and an elaborate altar imported from Munich, cost $275,000 or fifty-five times as much as the original church two decades earlier.[14]

14 - Francis X. Murphy, C.Ss.R., *The Centennial History of St. Alphonsus Parish* (New York: St. Alphonsus Church, 1947), 18; Smith, *Church in New York,* I, 201.

The original Church of St. Andrew at Duane Street and City Hall Place. A former Universalist Church, it was purchased for $5,400 in 1841

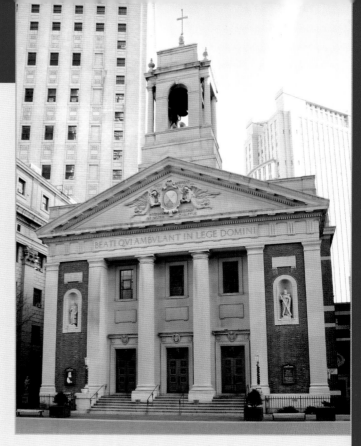

The second St. Andrew's Church, dedicated by Archbishop Spellman on November 20, 1939. It is located on the site of Cardinal Hayes' birthplace.

The original Church of the Nativity, a former Presbyterian Church on Second Avenue.

The Church of the Nativity was replaced with a nondescript modernistic structure in the 1960s and consolidated with St. Teresa's Church in 2007

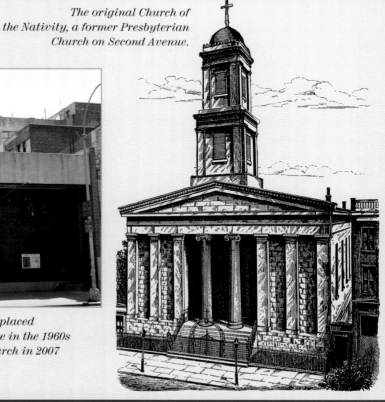

The second St. Alphonsus Church, now demolished, was located on South Fifth Avenue (today's West Broadway) just north of Canal Street

St. Ann's Church on East 12th Street, New York's first carriage trade parish, later the Armenian Catholic Cathedral, and now demolished

The Tower of the Church of the Most Holy Redeemer.
Credit: *Yvon Meyer*

The interior of the Church of the Most Holy Redeemer.
Credit: *Yvon Meyer*

Three other parishes were established in Lower Manhattan before the Civil War, all on the East Side. St. Brigid's Church dates from 1848 when another local pastor, Father Richard Kein of the Church of the Nativity, recognized that an additional parish was needed closer to the East River. The site fronted directly on Tompkins Square, providing a vista for St. Brigid's that no other Catholic church in the city could match. Kein's achievement was all the more impressive because money was extremely scarce among New York's Irish Catholics in 1848 since relief efforts on behalf of the Famine victims had severely depleted their financial resources.

St. Brigid's Church on Avenue B at Tompkins Square Park. In 2007 it was slated to be merged with St. Emeric's Church with a new chapel to be established.

St. Ann's was another of the new downtown churches. Founded in 1852, its original location was a former Protestant church on Astor Place. The first pastor was Father John Murray Forbes, a convert Episcopalian clergyman who returned to the Episcopal Church in 1859. Three years later the parish was confided to another former Episcopalian clergyman, Father Thomas Preston, the chancellor of the diocese and later vicar general, who remained pastor until his death in 1891. In 1870 Preston broke ground for a new French-style Gothic church on East 12th Street between Third and Fourth Avenue that Archbishop McCloskey dedicated on January 1, 1871. Thomas Preston's reputation as a preacher and the high quality of the choir helped to make St. Ann's the most fashionable Catholic parish in Manhattan. On special occasions, when Monsignor Preston was the featured preacher, the carriages of wealthy Catholics lined East 12th Street from Second Avenue to Fifth Avenue, waiting for the service to end.

One may wonder, however, how many of the Catholics who frequented St. Ann's Church in the fashionable Fifteenth Ward could claim the same social status as the tony congregations of nearby Grace Church on Broadway or the Church of the Ascension and the First Presbyterian Church on Lower Fifth Avenue. Lorenzo Delmonico paid $575 for a pew in St. Ann's; in 1872 Cornelius Vanderbilt paid $1,509 for a pew in the new St. Bartholomew's Episcopal Church at Madison Avenue and 44th Street. In fact, despite St. Ann's reputation as a bon ton parish (to use the clerical argot of the day), Preston left the parish practically bankrupt at his death with a staggering debt of over $91,000. It was little solace to his successor that the parishioners fondly remembered Monsignor Preston as a kindly pastor who never asked them for money. [15]

15 - Eric Homberger, *Mrs. Astor's New York* (New Haven: Yale University Press, 2002), 114; Henry J. Browne, *St. Ann's on East Twelfth Street* (New York: Church of St. Ann, 1952), 2-16, 29.

The last of the pre-Civil War Catholic churches in Lower Manhattan was St. Teresa's Church on Rutgers Street. In this case the founder was Father James Boyce, an assistant at St Mary's Church for nine years, who saw the need for an additional Catholic Church on the Lower East Side between St. Mary's and St. James. In 1863 the Rutgers Presbyterian Church, which was located almost midway between the two Catholic churches, was put up for sale. Father Boyce took advantage of the opportunity and raised enough money to buy the church.

The dedication of St. Teresa's on June 21, 1863, was an historic event because it was the last time that John Hughes presided at such a function. Too feeble to celebrate the Solemn High Mass and too weak even to stand, the old archbishop delivered his last sermon at the dedication of a church seated in the sanctuary of St. Teresa's. His theme was not the new church, but the horrific Civil War in which the nation was then engaged. He urged the congregation and all those who would worship at St. Teresa's to pray and to pray earnestly for the end of hostilities and the return of peace.

The Church in the New City

For more than twenty years the pastoral responsibilities of the cathedral clergy included all of Manhattan north of Houston Street, a rural area where they could respond to sick calls only on horseback.. To rectify the situation, Bishop Dubois established St. Paul's Church in Harlem in 1834, a full three years before the New York and Harlem Railroad reached the remote hamlet, which dated from Dutch days. The bishop blessed the cornerstone of the small stone church on East 117th Street between Third and Fourth (today Park) Avenues on June 29, 1835. The first pastor was Father Michael Curran who had previously served as a pastor in the mountains of central Pennsylvania.

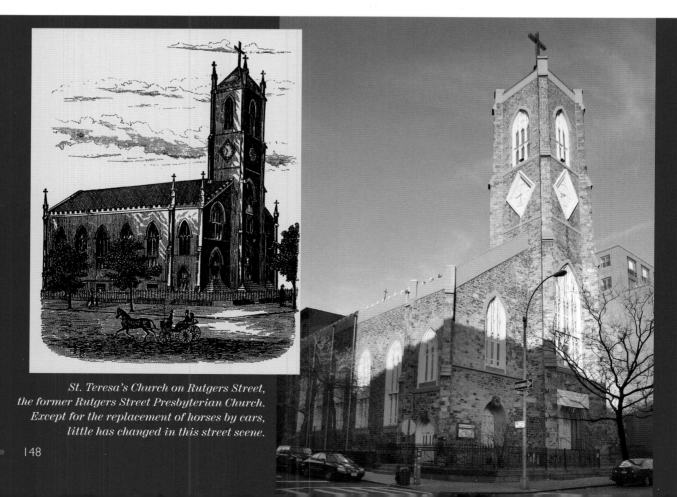

St. Teresa's Church on Rutgers Street, the former Rutgers Street Presbyterian Church. Except for the replacement of horses by cars, little has changed in this street scene.

View of Harlem from Central Park in 1869. Credit: *Archdiocese of New York*

Father Curran's parish included not only upper Manhattan, but also much of southern Westchester and Astoria. Writing in 1856, the Irish journalist Thomas D'Arcy McGee paid tribute to him as the pioneer priest of that area.

> Where there are now twenty flourishing parishes with resident priests, wrote McGee, there was then not one. Mass was celebrated in private homes, in rented halls and in barns. A numerous dispersed population were to be cared for and called in. Mr. Curran's popular manner, his old-fashioned frankness, his knowledge of the Irish tongue again enabled him to be of the highest service.[16]

If anything, McGee underestimated the changes that had taken place since Father Curran had first come to Harlem. Between 1840 and 1860 seventeen new parishes were opened in midtown and upper Manhattan alone.

The first was the Church of St. John the Baptist, the second German parish in the diocese. It began as a little wooden church on 31st Street and Seventh Avenue and led a tenuous existence for the first thirty years. The lay trustees, like their fellow countrymen across town at St. Nicholas Church, were so overbearing that they drove out several pastors. In desperation Archbishop McCloskey appealed to the Capuchins to take charge of the parish.

The first Capuchin pastor, Father Bonventura Frey, was a native of Switzerland and one of the first two Americans to enter the Capuchins. He appealed both to the ethnic and civic pride of the parishioners, expressing astonishment that German Catholics in the great city of New York would be content with a decrepit little church that was worse than any he had seen as a missionary in the most desolate areas of the Wild West.

---

16 - Shea, *Catholic Churches of New York*, 566.

The original St. Paul's Church on East 117th Street.

St. Paul's Church on East 117th Street. Archbishop McCloskey blessed the basement church on July 9, 1871. The church is administered by the priests of the Institute of the Incarnate Word

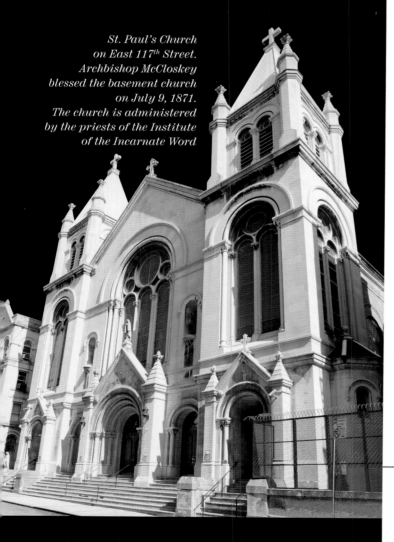

His magic worked. Within two years this talented friar ended thirty years of squabbling and revitalized the parish. He broke ground for a new church on Pentecost Sunday, June 4, 1871, and sent out fellow friars all over the city begging for donations. The result was a large stone Gothic church on West 30th Street that was 165 feet long and 67 feet wide with a nave 70 feet high. It was completed within a year at the cost of $175,000.

A second St. John's Church was founded in 1840, this one dedicated to St. John the Evangelist, across town at Fifth Avenue and 50th Street. The parish boundaries were extensive, to say the least, running from the Hudson River to the East River, from 30th Street to 86th Street on the East Side and from 40th Street to 86th Street on the West Side. Mass was first celebrated at the southeast corner of Fifth Avenue and 50th Street in the mansion had once been the home of the Jesuits' New York Literary Institute and had served briefly thereafter as a monastery for exiled French Trappists. The first resident pastor, Father John Maginnis, erected a small frame church at the northeast corner of Fifth Avenue and 50th Street, now the site of St. Patrick's Cathedral.

The pastor from 1850 to 1879 was Father James J. McMahon who became a legend in his own lifetime. He was the wealthiest priest in New York, perhaps in the United States. Born in Dublin in 1814, McMahon used his family patrimony to speculate in New York City real estate. He was spectacularly successful. When he retired in 1891 to live on the campus of the Catholic University of America, he gave the university real estate valued at $515,000. He explained to puzzled newspaper reporters, "I never ran after the real estate. It ran after me."[17]

17 - George A. Kelly, *The Parish as seen from the Church of St. John the Evangelist* (New York: St. John's University, 1973), 28-30, 49-51.

The first Church of St. John the Evangelist at 50th Street and Fifth Avenue

Father James J. McMahon, pastor of the St. John the Evangelist Church, 1850-1879

CHURCH OF ST. JOHN THE EVANGELIST

The Church of the St. John the Evangelist on the ground floor of the New York Catholic Center.

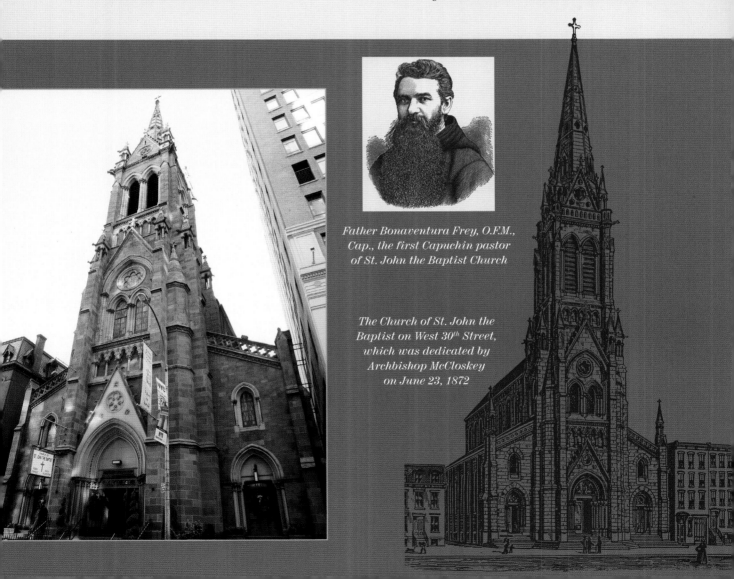

Father Bonaventura Frey, O.F.M., Cap., the first Capuchin pastor of St. John the Baptist Church

The Church of St. John the Baptist on West 30th Street, which was dedicated by Archbishop McCloskey on June 23, 1872

The site of the parish was moved several times, and in 1887 the fourth church in fifty years was erected at 55th Street and First Avenue. It was a richly decorated Gothic edifice that John Talbot Smith described as a mini-cathedral. It was demolished in 1969 to make way for the Catholic Center that included a new St. John's Church on the ground floor.

New York's first and only French parish was founded in 1841. Unlike so many national parishes in the United States, the impetus did not come from the local ethnic Catholic community, but from a visiting French bishop, Charles-Auguste de Forbin-Janson, who gave a retreat to French-speaking Catholics in St. Peter's Church on April 10, 1841. Echoing complaints of Bishop Dubois and many New York priests about the religious indifference of the French Catholics, he chided them on their failure to establish a French parish.

> In this great city of New York, he said, where Catholics of Irish and German ancestry have hesitated at no sacrifice to secure churches and priests of their own nationality, how is it possible that the French, so famous for the faith of their fathers, should have remained indifferent? They are lacking in interest both for their own salvation for that of their countrymen. In truth, how can they hope to maintain their traditions on a foreign soil without the strong ties of religion? Such a church is most strongly desired by Bishop Hughes, who expects great things from his diocese from it.[18]

The bishop's words had the desired effect. The next day a group of French Catholics formed a committee for the purpose of building a French church and elected John LaFarge the treasurer. They moved quickly and on May 2 bought property on Canal Street just east of Broadway where the Episcopal Church of the Annunciation had stood until it was destroyed by fire. Ground

was broken on October 11, 1841, in a ceremony presided over by the French consul-general. On August 21, 1842, Bishop Hughes blessed the new church, which was dedicated to St. Vincent de Paul. Three months later a permanent pastor was appointed, Father Annet Lafont, a member of the Fathers of Mercy, who had been working as a missionary in the American South.

For the next thirty-two years Father Lafont was the spiritual leader of New York's small French Catholic community. He got little financial support from most of them, but he was able to supplement the meager parish income with generous donations from the Society for the Propagation of the Faith in France (25,000 francs the first year) and from Bishop Forbin-Janson, who gave $6,000. Despite his straightened financial circumstances, Father Lafont managed to begin the St. Ann's Society for New York's African American Catholics, most of whom were French-speaking immigrants from Haiti and the French West Indies. He also established a French orphan asylum, brought the Brothers of the Christian Schools from France to New York, and promoted the work of the St. Vincent de Paul Society, the great French Catholic charitable organization.

In the 1850s it was decided to move St. Vincent de Paul Church farther north. Property was bought on West 23rd Street near Sixth Avenue, and Bishop Hughes blessed the cornerstone of the new church on June 14, 1857. He used the occasion to deliver an eloquent defense of the notion of a national parish.

> While all are blended in one community of belief by the term Catholic, said the archbishop, still every nation and tongue prefers to hear the word of God in that language which has first sounded in the ears of childhood and infancy. Hence it is that we have French churches---not that they are

---

18 - Henry Binsse, "The Church of St. Vincent de Paul," *HR&S* 12 (1918): 102-114; Shea, *Catholic Churches of New York*, 710.

The Church of St. Vincent de Paul on West 23rd Street en principe *and in reality. in 2007 New York's only French church was slated to be combined with the Church of St. Columba with a new chapel to be established.*

French other than in the sense that I have just mentioned---so also we have German churches, and would to God we could have churches devoted to every language of the nations where Catholicity could be made known.

The archbishop's words did little to open the purse strings of his listeners. Money came in so slowly that a full eleven years elapsed before the new Church of St. Vincent de Paul was finally dedicated by Archbishop McCloskey on May 9, 1868.

East Side, West Side

In the mid-nineteenth century the West Side of Manhattan developed more quickly than the East Side, and the demographic differences were reflected in the disparity of Catholic parishes, with almost twice as many new parishes being

founded on the West Side as on the East Side. In addition to St. John the Baptist and St. Vincent de Paul, nine other parishes were established between 1844 and 1860 between West 31st Street and West 125th street.

St. Francis of Assisi was the first. It was a German parish that was founded in 1844 as a direct result of turmoil over lay trusteeism at St. John the Baptist. Although the first two pastors were Franciscans, it was only twenty years later that the Franciscans permanently assumed the direction of the parish. As Catholics became more numerous in Chelsea, they petitioned the bishop for their own church, since the closest territorial parish was St. Joseph's in Greenwich Village. In 1845 Bishop Hughes established the Church of St. Columba for them on West 25th Street near Ninth Avenue.

One of the oldest Catholic churches in New York City, St. Columba was dedicated by Coadjutor Bishop John McCloskey on October 12, 1845

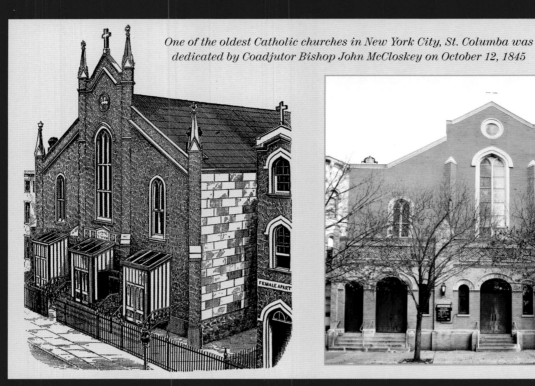

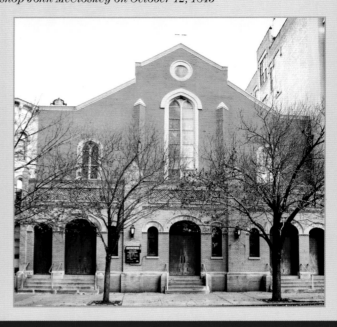

The original Church of St. Francis of Assisi, 1844-1892

The second Church of St. Francis of Assisi, which was dedicated by Archbishop Corrigan on July 17, 1892.

The next addition to the Catholic churches on the West Side of the New City was the first Jesuit Church in New York City. It began in 1847 as the Church of the Holy Name of Jesus in a former Protestant church on Elizabeth Street. It lasted a scant six months before it was destroyed by fire. However, the Jesuits did not give up and two years later, on September 24, 1850, they laid the cornerstone for their Church of St. Francis Xavier on West 16th Street between Fifth and Sixth Avenues. As the parish grew, so did the need for a larger church. The Jesuits purchased additional property on West 16th Street and, on May 5, 1878, they broke ground for the present Baroque church that was designed by Patrick Keely to accommodate 2,500 worshippers.

Holy Cross Church on West 42nd Street dates from 1854. The construction was so shoddy that it had to be replaced with a new church in 1870. The increase in the German population on the West Side led to the establishment of two additional parishes for them. The Church of the Assumption of the Blessed Virgin Mary was started in 1858 and found a permanent home the following year on West 49th Street between Ninth and Tenth Avenues. German Catholics in Manhattanville originally worshipped in the chapel of the Academy of the Sacred Heart, but in 1860 they built St. Joseph's Church on West 125th Street and Ninth Avenue.

For almost twenty years the only Catholic church in Manhattan north of 50th Street was St. Paul's in Harlem. However, in 1852 Archbishop Hughes commissioned Father Arthur J. Donnelly to establish a new parish for the area north of 100th Street and west of Eighth Avenue. It was the first of three parishes that Donnelly would begin in the space of

The interior of the Church of St. Francis Xavier. Credit: *Yvon Meyer*

The Church of St. Francis Xavier on West 16th Street

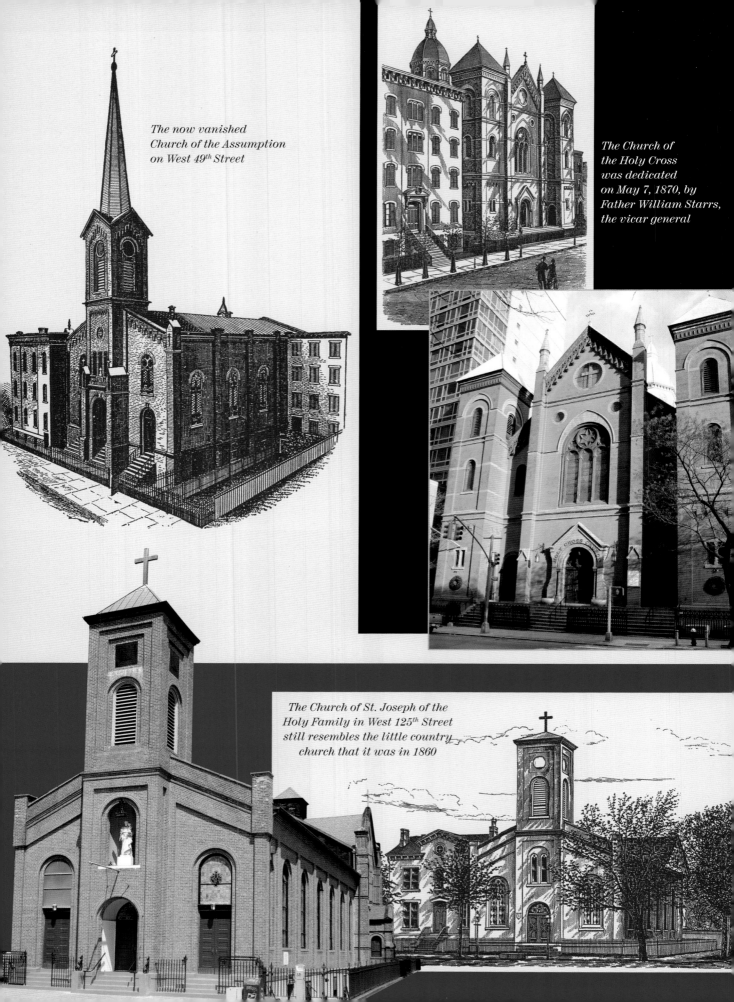

The now vanished Church of the Assumption on West 49th Street

The Church of the Holy Cross was dedicated on May 7, 1870, by Father William Starrs, the vicar general

The Church of St. Joseph of the Holy Family in West 125th Street still resembles the little country church that it was in 1860

five years. A native of County Kildare, Donnelly had been ordained only three weeks earlier at the age of thirty-two. Before entering St. Joseph's Seminary at Fordham, Donnelly had spent ten years in the dry goods business (eight of them at Lord and Taylor) and Hughes had a high opinion of his business abilities. Since the Christian Brothers were interested in establishing a college in

Monsignor Arthur J. Donnelly, V.G.

the same area as the new parish, they collaborated with Father Donnelly in purchasing two square blocks between Broadway and 11th Avenue between West 131st Street and West 133rd Street. Father Donnelly retained the corner of Broadway and West 131st Street for his Church of the Annunciation while the brothers used the rest of the property for the campus of Manhattan College. By the winter of 1854 the brick Gothic church was ready to be dedicated.

A year later Hughes appointed Donnelly the procurator or business manager of St. Joseph's Seminary at Fordham with the additional responsibility of transforming the seminary chapel into the parish church of Our Lady of Mercy for the Catholics in the area. Two years after that the archbishop appointed Donnelly to establish his third parish in five years, St. Michael's on the West Side of Manhattan midway between St. Columba on West 25th Street and Holy Cross on West 42nd Street, an area that was rapidly filling up with Irish immigrants. The parish boundaries ran from West 28th Street to West 38th Street, and from Sixth Avenue to the Hudson River. Father Donnelly bought land for a church on West 31st Street between Ninth and Tenth Avenues, but the Depression of 1857 forced him to delay his building plans.

The first Church of the Annunciation at Broadway and 131st Street

The Church of the Annunciation on Convent Avenue at 131st Street, dedicated by the Archbishop Farley on December 15, 1907. Since 1977 it has been administered by the Calasanian (Piarist) Fathers.

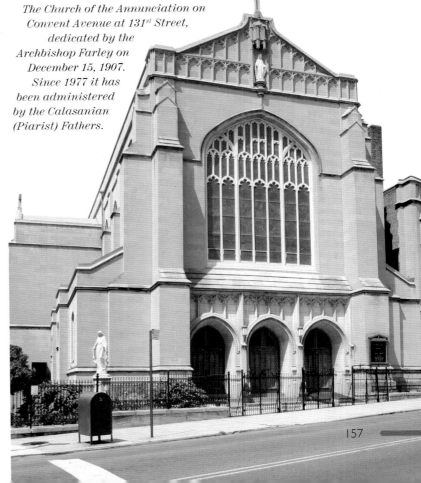

The original Church of Our Lady of Mercy, now the University Church of Fordham University

The Church of Our Lady Mercy on Marion Avenu constructed in the Spani mission style in 1908

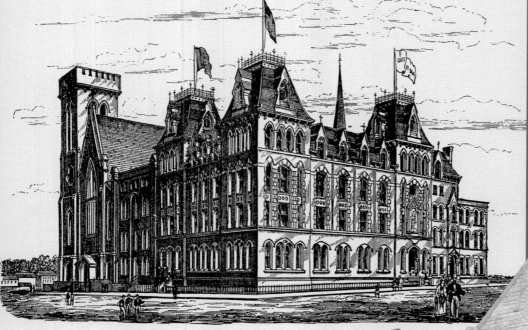

*Father Donnelly's Plant:
the first St. Michael's Church, rectory, school
and convent on the west side of 9th Avenue between
31st and 32nd Streets*

*St. Michael's Church on 34th Street between 9th
and 10th Avenues. it was built between 1906 and
1907 by the Pennsylvania Railroad together with
a new school, rectory and convent at a cost of over
$1,000,000, when the railroad acquired the site
of the original plant for Pennsylvania Station.*

Archbishop Hughes did not live to see the finished church, which was dedicated three months after his death. No sooner was the church completed, however, than it became apparent that it was inadequate for the size of the congregation. In 1868 Donnelly extended the church the full width of the block from 31st to 32nd Street, a distance of 200 feet. He also began two parochial schools, one for boys and one for girls, which were in operation by 1870. By that time St. Michael's could boast of one of the largest parish plants in the diocese valued at over $400,000. Due perhaps to the fact that he was a late vocation, Donnelly organized a special class at St. Michael's for boys who expressed an interest in the priesthood. He got 100 applications and accepted twenty-five of them, eight of whom were eventually ordained.

One of the last West Side churches established in the New Metropolis during the administration of John Hughes was the Church of St. Paul the Apostle, the mother church of Father Isaac Hecker's Missionary Society of St. Paul the Apostle, better known as the Paulist Fathers. The cornerstone of the Church of St. Paul the Apostle that John Hughes blessed on June 19, 1859, was a modest structure that was twice enlarged and replaced later with a monumental building that was second in size to Hughes' new cathedral.

At mid-century the real estate developers found the East Side of Manhattan less attractive terrain than the West Side and population growth in that part of the city lagged accordingly. However, New York Catholics, who were largely poor immigrants seeking affordable housing, continued to make their home in the less expensive neighborhoods of the East Side. One result was the establishment of one of nineteenth-century New York's most famous parishes, the Church of St. Stephen.

The Church of St. Stephen on East 28th Street, one of the largest parishes in the archdiocese in the later nineteenth century

The founding pastor was Father Jeremiah W. Cummings whom Bishop Hughes appointed in November 1848 to erect a church and organize a parochial school. A native of Washington, D.C., where he was born in 1814, and an alumnus of Bishop Dubois' seminary in Nyack, Cummings was one of the first New York priests to earn a doctorate from the college of the Propaganda Fide in Rome and was well known as a writer and lecturer. Like so many other founding pastors, Cummings decided to erect a temporary church first and then build a permanent structure later as more money became available. The first church was ready within a year and was dedicated by Bishop Hughes on December 23, 1849. However, the site on Madison Avenue at the corner of East 27th Street, proved to be impractical because of its proximity to the depot of the New York and Harlem Railroad.

For his permanent church Cummings purchased property between East 28th Street and East 29th Street near Lexington Avenue and erected one of the most impressive Catholic churches in New York City, which was dedicated by John Hughes on May 21, 1854. The architect was James Renwick, who was later to design the new St. Patrick's Cathedral; Patrick Keely designed the three marble altars; and above the high altar was a Crucifixion scene by Brumidi. Among the prominent parishioners was Orestes Brownson, a close friend of Dr. Cummings who was a frequent contributor to *Brownson's Quarterly Review.*

Father Jeremiah Cummings, the founding pastor of St. Stephen's Church

As in the case of St. Michael's Church on the West Side, the congregation soon outgrew the church. "This parish is one of the largest in New York," Cummings informed Hughes in1858. "It is fair to suppose that about ten thousand people attend some service in the church every Sunday." In addition Cummings and his curate were responsible for the Catholic patients in Bellevue Hospital, a thousand-bed institution.[19] St. Stephen's was soon extended the full width of the block to West 29th Street. The expansion was begun by Dr. Cummings in 1865 and completed the following year by his successor, Dr. Edward McGlynn, another graduate of the Propaganda Fide college in Rome, who was to become one of the most famous and controversial New York priests later in the century.

Although the New York and Harlem Railroad reached Yorkville by 1834, the Catholic population remained small and scattered. In 1851, however, Archbishop Hughes sent Father E.J. O'Reilly to organize the first parish on the East Side between St. Paul's in Harlem and St. John the Evangelist on East 50th Street. Father O'Reilly bought property on East 84th Street between Fourth and Fifth Avenues where first a temporary chapel and then a brick church was erected. The boundaries extended from the East River to the Hudson River until the establishment of the Church of St. Paul the Apostle on the West Side in 1858

In the 1860s Yorkville had not yet become a German neighborhood, but there was already a small German population at Dutch Hill in the East

---

19 - AANY, A-12, Cummings to Hughes, March 29, 1858.

Second Avenue looking north from 42ⁿᵈ Street in 1861. Credit: *Archdiocese of New York*

Forties. A group of Catholic families collected $792.88 and borrowed more money to purchase three lots for a church which they named in honor of St. Boniface, the Anglo-Saxon missionary monk who is the patron saint of Germany. Archbishop Hughes blessed the building on October 17, 1858. The first pastor, Father Matthew Nicot, was a German-speaking native of Lorriane, who came to the United States in 1857 and served for a time as an assistant to Father Lafont at the Church of St. Vincent de Paul. During his long tenure as pastor St. Boniface remained remarkably peaceful, escaping the internal divisions that plagued several of the other German parishes in New York.

The Church of the Immaculate Conception on East 14ᵗʰ Street owed its origin to the rapid increase of the Catholic population in that part of the city and got its name due to the proclamation of the dogma of the Immaculate Conception of Mary by Pope Pius IX on December 8, 1854. John Hughes was present in St. Peter's Basilica for the solemn ceremonies, only four or five feet away from the pope, he claimed. "Just at that moment," he said, "I resolved on my return to New York to erect a church to commemorate the event." The cornerstone was blessed, appropriately enough, on December 8, 1855, and the church was dedicated three years later.

The now demolished St. Boniface Church at Second Avenue and 47ᵗʰ Street

Father Matthew Nicot, the founding pastor of St. Boniface Church

St. Gabriel's Church was the last of the churches in the New City established by John Hughes. He created the parish in 1859 to provide a church for the growing Catholic population on the East Side between St. John the Evangelist on East 50th Street and St. Stephen's on East 28th Street. It was unique among early New York parishes because the site of the church on East 37th Street between First and Second Avenues was the gift of a single individual, Henry J. Anderson, a convert to the Catholic faith who was a professor of astronomy at Columbia College and member of Columbia's board of trustees.

Father William Clowry, the founder of St. Gabriel's Church

The first pastor, Father William Clowry, had served a rather demanding apprenticeship under Dr. Cummings at St. Stephen's. Unlike Cummings, who outraged John Hughes when he closed his basement school and deposited the children in the nearest public school, Clowry took to heart John Hughes' injunction about the priority of a parochial school over a church. In 1859 he erected a school building with a chapel that served as the location for three Sunday Masses until the church was completed six years later.

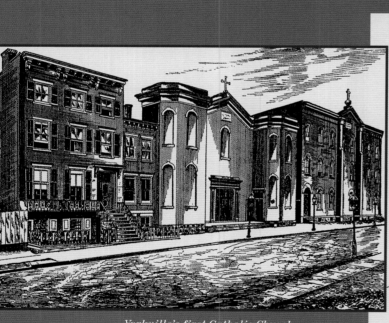

Yorkville's first Catholic Church, St. Lawrence O'Toole, on East 84th Street between Fourth (Park) and Fifth Avenues

St. Gabriel's Church on East 37th Street between First and Second Avenues. It was sold and demolished in 1939 to make way for the construction of the Queens Midtown Tunnel. The last Mass was celebrated in the church on January 15, 1939.

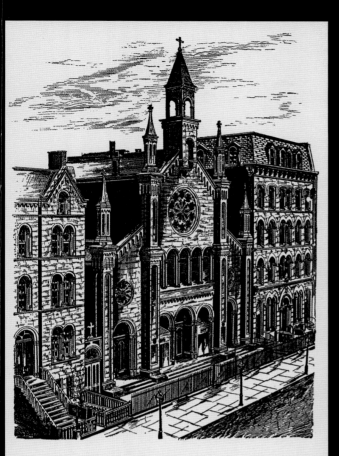

The first Church of the Immaculate Conception located on the north side of 14th Street between Avenue A and Avenue B. At the blessing of the cornerstone on December 8, 1855, John Hughes said that it was the ninety-ninth church that he had blessed within the confines of the original diocese of New York

The Church of the Immaculate Conception on the south side of 14th Street east of First Avenue. A former chapel of Grace Church, it was acquired by the archdiocese in 1943 when the construction of Stuyvesant Town forced the closing of the original church. The last Mass was celebrated in the old church on August 20, 1945.

There were thirty-two parish churches in New York City by 1864. The first, St. Peter's, dated from 1785, but it had taken another thirty years before a second Catholic church (St. Patrick's Old Cathedral) was opened. Only six more churches were added during the next quarter century. Beginning in 1840, however, the pace of church building accelerated. Between that date and 1864, the number of Catholic churches in Manhattan quadrupled. The exponential change reflected not only the rapid growth of the Catholic population, but also the determination of John Hughes to give every Catholic in New York City a proper place to celebrate the Eucharist and receive the sacraments of the Church.

The Hudson Valley

John Hughes established twenty-four new parishes in New York City, but it is difficult to say exactly how many parishes he established outside the city. In 1839 there was only one Catholic parish on Staten Island, but the first St. Peter's church was not built until four years later. There were only four Catholic churches north of Manhattan within the confines of the seven counties in the present-day archdiocese of New York. Located in Cold Spring, Poughkeepsie, Newburgh, and Saugerties, the last two churches were still unfinished. All of them had been established by Bishop Dubois in the 1830s, and all

were located in the Hudson Valley, which was the cradle of Catholicism in the upper counties of the archdiocese.

The pioneer priest in the mid-Hudson Valley was Father Philip J.M. O'Reilly, a native of County Cavan, who functioned as a circuit-riding missionary in the 1830s celebrating Mass in private homes throughout the area. A former Irish Dominican who was educated in Italy, Reilly was received into the diocese by Bishop Dubois in 1830. A large, powerfully built man with a passion for military history, "Mad Phil" (even Archbishop Corrigan called him that) was regarded as notably eccentric even in a diocese with a high incidence of eccentric clerics. Whatever, his personal foibles, however, in 1833 he laid the cornerstone of the first Catholic churches in Putnam and Ulster counties, both of them dedicated to the Blessed Virgin, Our Lady of Loretto in Cold Spring and St. Mary of the Snow in Saugerties.

Irish immigrants had been attracted to both communities by opportunities for jobs in the local industries. In Saugerties they found work in the iron and paper mills on Esopus Creek and in the bluestone quarries in the mountains west of the village. At their peak the quarries employed 2,000 men and furnished New York City with many of its sidewalks and curbstones. In Cold Spring the principal industry was the West Point Foundry, established by an Act of Congress in 1818, to supply cannon and other military ordnance for the army and navy. At the height of its operations the foundry included eighteen buildings spread over 150 acres with 800 to 1,000 employees.

Fortunately for the Catholics in Cold Spring, the owner of the West Point Foundry, Gouverneur Kemble, who was a Protestant, donated land a Catholic church and contributed to its construction. Probably built in the summer of 1833, it was dedicated by Bishop Dubois on September 21, 1834, as the Church of Our Lady of

The Church of Our Lady of Loretto in Cold Spring, dedicated by Bishop Dubois on September 21, 1834. It was sold by the archdiocese during the administration of Cardinal Cooke. The oldest Catholic church in the Hudson Valley is now a museum.
Credit: *Catholic New York:* Chris Sheridan

The announcement of the dedication of the Church of Our Lady of Loretto in the diocesan newspaper

NEW-YORK WEEKLY REGISTER
AND
CATHOLIC DIARY.

" ALL THINGS WHATSOEVER YOU WOULD THAT MEN SHOULD DO UNTO YOU, DO YOU ALSO TO THEM."

Volume III.]   SATURDAY, NOVEMBER 15, 1834.   [Number 7.

CHURCH OF OUR LADY OF COLD SPRING.
(Drawn by Weir—engraved by Adams.)

We herewith present our readers with a sketch by our friend Weir, of the Catholic chapel of "Our Lady of Cold Spring," one of the most classical and beautiful little churches we have ever seen. The building is of brick, coloured with a composition which gives it the character and appearance of a light, yellowish-brown stone; and the portico, which is of the Tuscan order, of the most correct proportions. Its situation, opposite West Point, on a high rock overhanging the Hudson, and surrounded by majestic mountains, is extremely well chosen; and the traveller, sailing up and down the river, cannot but be struck with its romantic beauty.

It was our fortune to be present at the consecration of this little temple, a few weeks since,* by the Right. Rev. Bishop Dubois, assisted by the Rev. Messrs. Power, Varela, and O'Reilly.

Loretto. The dedication was a civic as well as a religious event with the music provided by the band from the U.S. Military Academy at nearby West Point. Gouverneur Kemble's generosity to his Catholic employees did not go unobserved by Nativist bigots who denounced him for "aiding and abetting the Papist idolatry of the Mass." The brownish-yellow brick church that he helped to build resembled a Greek temple and featured a portico with four columns. Situated on a bluff close to the water's edge framed by the mountains of the Hudson Highlands, it was clearly visible from the river. "The traveler, sailing up and down the river, cannot but be struck by its romantic beauty," wrote one enthusiastic newspaper reporter.[20]

The Catholics in Saugerties were not nearly as fortunate as those in Cold Spring. Lacking a local benefactor like Kemble, they were hard pressed to complete and furnish their stone church with their own limited resources. The walls were finished in the fall of 1833, but construction then ground to a halt when the congregation ran out of money. Two years later the church was just an empty shell without a roof, doors, windows or

The present Church of Our Lady of Loretto, dedicated by Archbishop John Farley on October 20, 1907

20 - John A. Grace, "The first 150 Years," *Our Lady of Loretto Church 1834-1984* (Cold Spring: Our Lady of Loretto Church, 1984), 35-47; *Truth Teller,* November 15, 1834.

even a floor. Bishop Dubois authorized Father O'Reilly to make an appeal to the Catholic of the whole diocese, which he did through the pages of the *Truth Teller*. "Is there an Irishman to whom he will apply," asked the editor, "who will deny a few shillings for the completion of such an object?"[21] It was not finished until 1852.

In Poughkeepsie it appears that Mass was celebrated in private residences as early as 1831 by itinerant missionary priests like Father O'Reilly. The following year, on October 14, 1832, twenty local Catholics organized a Catholic Association for the purpose of establishing a parish in Poughkeepsie that would serve them and the Catholics of the surrounding area. They made no progress until three years later when John Delafield donated land on Mill Street to the diocese on the condition that a church would be built on the location within two years. The Catholic Association took advantage of the opportunity and raised enough money for the erection of St. Peter's Church, the first Catholic church in Dutchess County, which was blessed by Bishop Dubois on November 24, 1837. The first pastor was Father John Maginnis, who was also given responsibility for Rondout and Saugerties as well as for the rest of Dutchess County.[22]

The ubiquitous Father O'Reilly was active in Newburgh from 1830, celebrating Mass in private homes, but it was not until 1836 that Father Patrick Duffy was appointed as the first resident pastor. In 1838 property was purchased for a church, and construction of St. Patrick's Church began the following year. By 1841 sufficient progress had been made to celebrate Mass in the unfinished building, which was not formally dedicated until 1849. It was a small structure,

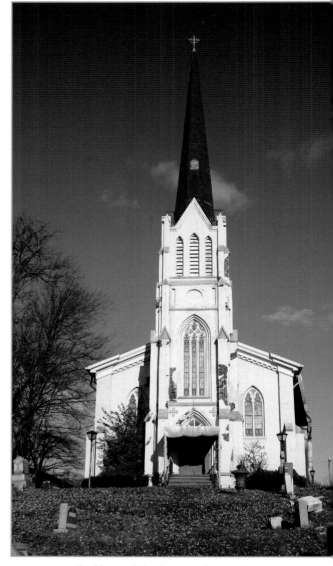

*St. Mary of the Snow in Saugerties,
which was begun in 1833 but not completed until 1852*

90 feet long by 55 feet wide, that was adequate for a congregation of 200. By 1860, however, the number of parishioners had grown to 2,000, and St. Patrick's second pastor, Father Edward J. O'Reilly, enlarged and altered the church and also added a 135-foot steeple. [23]

21 - *Truth Teller,* July 26, 1834, October 10, 1835.

22 - *St. Peter's 150th Anniversary* (Poughkeepsie: St. Peter's Church, 1987) unpaginated.

23 - *St. Patrick's Church 150th Anniversary* (Newburgh: St. Patrick's Church, 1986), unpaginated.

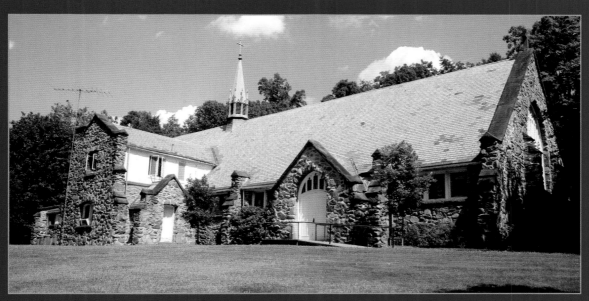

The successor to St. Peter's Church, Poughkeepsie, which was moved to Hyde Park in 1965

By 1842 there were still only two priests at work in the mid-Hudson Valley, Father Patrick Duffy in Newburgh and Father John Smith in Poughkeepsie. Father Philip O'Reilly had been moved to St. John's Church in Paterson, New Jersey, and Father John Maginnis had been sent to establish St. John the Evangelist Church in Manhattan. From his unfinished church in Newburgh, Father Duffy also took care of Our Lady of Loretto in Cold Spring and a mission in West Point. Father Smith celebrated Mass twice a month in St. Peter's Church in Poughkeepsie and once a month in Saugerties and Rondout.[24]

Rural Catholics and their Pastors

The Irish and German Catholic immigrants who settled in the upstate counties of the archdiocese rarely became farmers, except for some German and Irish immigrants in Sullivan County. Few of them had the capital to buy a farm, or in the case of the Irish, the skill to work it. The Irish were among the least efficient farmers in Europe. Moreover, after eking out a living growing potatoes on a quarter-acre plot in Ireland, rural life in America had few attractions for most Irish immigrants.

Some of those who settled upstate sought employment in local quarries or brickyards. Others found backbreaking jobs as manual laborers on major engineering projects like the Delaware and Hudson Canal or the Croton Dam and Aqueduct. Still others worked on the construction gangs that built the railroads. By 1851 New York City could boast of four trunk line railroads, more than any other East coast city, the New York and Harlem, the New York and Hudson River, the New York and New Haven, and the New York and Erie, although the Erie never got closer to New York than Jersey City.

The D & H Canal and the railroads brought new industries to the upstate counties like the cement plants in Rosendale or the railroad shops in Port Jervis or the tanneries in Ellenville or the coal yards in Port Ewen. Almost all of the new parishes established north of the city in the mid-nineteenth century owed their origin directly or indirectly to communities of immigrant Catholics whose livelihood depended on the canal or the railroads and the industries they served.

At the time of John Hughes' death in 1864, instead of the five country parishes that he

24 - *The Metropolitan Catholic Almanac and Laity's Directory for the Year of our Lord 1842* (Baltimore: Fielding Lucas, 1842), 148-151.

to determine when a mission church became a full-fledged parish church for a variety of reasons. Diocesan records are incomplete, the listings in the *Catholic Almanac* are often inaccurate, local traditions are not always reliable, and sometimes the same priest was the pastor of more than one parish. Some parishes date their history from the appointment of the first pastor while others date it from the beginning or completion of their first parish church.

In 1848 Father Edward J. O'Reilly was made the pastor of new parishes in Port Chester and New Rochelle. He remained in Port Chester for a year and then moved to New Rochelle. In 1864, Father Francis Caro, an Italian Franciscan, was pastor of both Our Lady of Loretto in Cold Spring and St. Thomas Church in Buttermilk Falls (Highland Falls) across the river in Orange County. St. Joseph's Church in Rhinecliff dates from 1862. It established the mission church of the Good Shepherd in Rhinebeck in 1903, which became a separate parish in 1955. Today St. Joseph's is a mission of Good Shepherd.

A mission might find itself attached successively to several different parishes as the original mother parish was subdivided. This was the case with the mission of St. Denis in Sylvan Lake before it became a parish in 1899. St. George's Church in Jeffersonville in Sullivan County was a parish with a resident pastor for five years in the 1860s and then ceased to have a resident pastor for over a century. Since 1982 it has shared the same pastor with St. Francis of Assisi Church in Youngsville. St. Patrick's in Millerton in northeastern corner of Dutchess County has been a mission since 1864 and is older than eighty percent of the parish churches in the archdiocese.

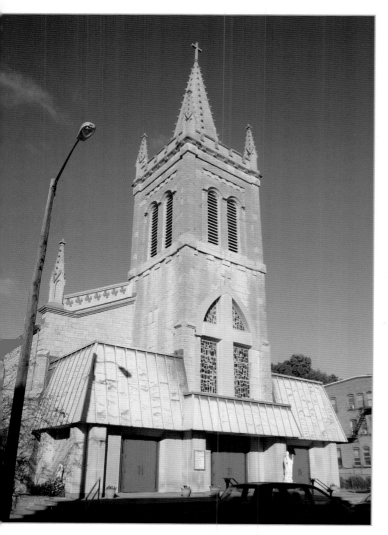

St. Patrick's Church, Newburgh, which was constructed between 1839 and 1849

inherited in 1839, there were about thirty-seven country parishes, including three parishes on Staten Island, and several dozen missions without a resident pastor.[25] A mission might be a small chapel without a resident pastor or even a private residence where a priest celebrated Mass occasionally on Sunday. It is sometimes difficult

---

25 - Florence Cohalan gives the figure of 37 new rural parishes, but it is not clear on what basis he made that tabulation. Cohalan, *Popular History,* 75.

If rural Catholics often experienced severe privations because of their living and working conditions, so did their pastors. When Archbishop Hughes sent Father Caro to the unfinished church in Buttermilk Falls in the fall of 1859, he assured him that the parishioners were able and willing to support him. If they failed to do so, however, the archbishop told him: "I shall take upon myself to see that you shall not be exposed to any suffering for want of support, at least during the coming winter."[26] At St. Mary's Church in Ellenville in 1864, the pastor, Father Daniel Mugan, had twelve missions to take care of, including Monticello and Liberty. A later pastor begged Archbishop Corrigan not to deprive him of the mission in Liberty because he could not support the parish without it.[27]

In the 1880s a Redemptorist priest named Edward Weigel described for his superior his experiences in giving a parish mission at St. Mary's in Ellenville. Although the congregation numbered only 120, they refused to attend Mass at St. Andrew's, the German church on the same street. Upon arrival in Ellenville Father Weigel discovered that he was expected to celebrate Mass on Palm Sunday at the mission in Wurtsboro, twelve miles away. He went there late on Saturday afternoon, a two-hour ride through mountains still covered with snow even though it was April. In Wurtsboro Father Weigel heard confessions, celebrated the Stations of the Cross and Benediction and stayed overnight at a little hotel. The next morning he again heard confessions, celebrated the 8:00 a.m. Mass, blessed palms, baptized two babies, "churched" a women and invested two others with the scapular and then left for Ellenville. "We had a fast horse," he wrote

It was a beautiful morning; everything grand except the roads. All the way I was subjected to a shower of mud pellets, which was fun for the horse, but not for me. My coat looked like a speckled trout and was as variegated as Joseph's coat. We reached [Ellenville} in time for the 11:00 a.m. Mass. I was as much of a curiosity as if I had been advertised as a side show of Barnum's circus.

Back in Elleville Father Weigel realized that the housekeeper was tipsy, and it was not until 2:00 p.m. that he got any breakfast. One consoling feature of his week in Ellenville was that he could always visit his Redemptorist confrere at St. Andrew's rectory down the street for a glass of beer in the evening.[28]

Father Weigel spent one week in Ellenville. Some pastors spent most of their ministry in the country, like Father Joseph Roesch, who was the pastor of St. Mary's in Obernburg for twenty-five years. Father Vincent Arcese was the pastor of St. Thomas Aquinas in Forestburg for forty-six years. Other country pastors found the strain too great and resigned within a short time, sometimes with their health permanently destroyed. Still other pastors (both in the city and country) were clerical birds of passage whose origins were as mysterious as those of Melchisedek and who disappeared with as little trace. Sometimes only their last name is known from the list of priests published in the annual *Catholic Almanac*. In 1890s, when Archbishop Michael Corrigan attempted to chronicle the work of the pioneer clergy of the archdiocese, he could often find little information about priests who had served in New York only forty years earlier.

26 - AANY, A-2, Hughes to Caro, November 28, 1859.

27 - AANY, J.H. Hayes to Charles McDonnell, March 16, 1889.

28 - AANY, Edward Weigel to Father Rector, April 2, 4, 1887.

8

The Archdiocese of New York

View of New York City from New Jersey in 1869. Credit: *Archdiocese of New York*

In the six years between 1847 and 1853 the diocese of New York experienced three major changes that permanently affected its geographical boundaries and ecclesiastical status. The first change occurred on April 23, 1847, when Pope Pius IX established the dioceses of Albany and Buffalo in upstate New York.[1] The second major change occurred on July 19, 1850, when the Holy Father elevated the diocese of New York to the status of an archdiocese with suffragan sees in Albany, Buffalo, Hartford and Boston, and named John Hughes the first archbishop of New York. Finally, on July 29, 1853, two other new dioceses were established, one in Newark for all of New Jersey and the other in Brooklyn for all of Long Island.[2]

---

1 - As the Catholic population multiplied in upstate New York, still more dioceses were needed. Accordingly in 1868 the eastern half of the diocese of Buffalo was made the separate diocese of Rochester. The large diocese of Albany was twice divided. In 1872 the North Country got its own bishop when a diocese was established in Ogdensburg. The last of the new upstate dioceses was Syracuse, which was created for central New York in 1886

2 - In 1957, with the creation of the diocese of Rockville Centre for Nassau and Suffolk counties, the diocese of Brooklyn was reduced to Kings and Queens counties. The diocese of Newark (elevated to an archdiocese on December 10, 1937) has been subdivided into the dioceses of Trenton (1881), Camden (1937), Paterson (1937) and Metuchen (1981).

The establishment of the archdiocese of New York in 1850, and the creation of four new dioceses, was a recognition of the massive growth of the Catholic population in the nation's largest city. As a result of these changes, by 1853 the archdiocese of New York was only about one-tenth the size of the original diocese of New York in 1808. However, by the 1860s the archdiocese had a Catholic population of between 300,000 and 400,000, twice the size of the Catholic population in the whole state in 1840, and over 300 times the size of the Catholic population of the original diocese in 1808.

By 1853 the archdiocese of New York had assumed its present territorial boundaries. To this day it remains unique among major American archdioceses because its boundaries have remained unchanged for over 150 years, except for a minor border adjustment with the diocese of Albany in 1861. In 1853, in addition to New York City, which was coterminous with Manhattan, the new archdiocese included Westchester, Putnam, Dutchess, Rockland,

Pope Pius IX (1846-1878), who made the diocese of New York an archdiocese on July 19, 1850, and established five other dioceses in New York State: Albany and Buffalo (1847), Brooklyn (1853), Rochester (1868) and Ogdensburg (1872).
Credit: Clarke, *Catholic Church*

Orange, Ulster and Sullivan counties north of the city line as well as Richmond County (Staten Island). When Greater New York City was created in 1898, three of the five boroughs or counties that made up the enlarged metropolis were part of the archdiocese, Manhattan, Staten Island and the newly established borough of the Bronx. Brooklyn and Queens remained part of the diocese of Brooklyn.

Westchester, Putnam and Dutchess Counties

At the end of the Civil War more than a third of the upstate parishes were located in Westchester County, including four in the southern part, an area that would later become Bronx County. The first of the four future Bronx parishes was St. Raymond's, established in the Town of Westchester in 1842 by Father Felix Vilanis, an Italian-born diocesan priest had been the first rector of St. Joseph's Seminary at Fordham two years earlier. He began the construction of a red brick church on West Farms Road (now East Tremont Avenue) that was completed in 1845. Father Vilanis and his immediate successors at St. Raymond's were not only responsible for their own parish, but also for a far-flung string of missions that included Throgs Neck, Williamsbridge, City Island, Mount Vernon, Tuckahoe, New Rochelle, Port Chester, Yonkers, Ossining and Verplanck.

The original St. Raymond's Church, the first Catholic Church in the future Bronx, erected between 1842 and 1845. Credit: *St. Raymond's Church*

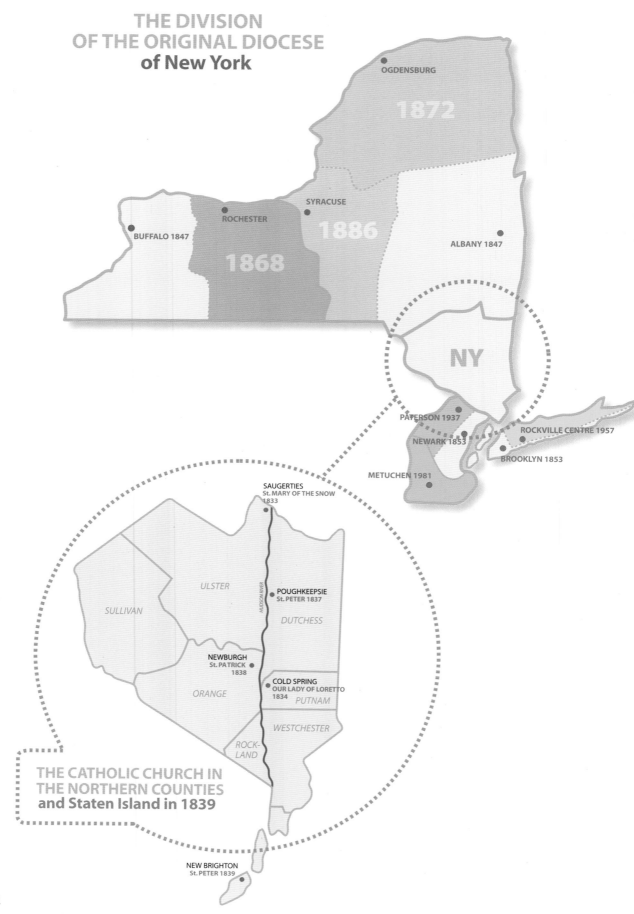

THE DIVISION
OF THE ORIGINAL DIOCESE
of New York

OGDENSBURG

1872

ROCHESTER

SYRACUSE

BUFFALO 1847

1886

ALBANY 1847

1868

NY

PATERSON 1937

NEWARK 1853

ROCKVILLE CENTRE 1957

BROOKLYN 1853

METUCHEN 1981

SAUGERTIES
St. MARY OF THE SNOW
1833

ULSTER

HUDSON RIVER

POUGHKEEPSIE
St. PETER 1837

SULLIVAN

DUTCHESS

NEWBURGH
St. PATRICK
1838

COLD SPRING
OUR LADY OF LORETTO
1834

ORANGE

PUTNAM

WESTCHESTER

ROCK-
LAND

THE CATHOLIC CHURCH IN
THE NORTHERN COUNTIES
and Staten Island in 1839

NEW BRIGHTON
St. PETER 1839

menia - Immaculate Conception 1866

eacon (Matteawan) – St. Joachim 1860

lauvelt (Blauveltsville) – St. Catherine 1869

uttermilk Falls (Highland Falls)
St. Thomas 1859

ld Spring – Our Lady of Loretto 1834

obbs Ferry – Sacred Heart 1862

roton Falls (Owensville) – St. Joseph 1845

llenville – St. Mary c.1850

llenville - St. Mary of the Assumption c.1850

ordham – Our Lady of Mercy 1855

ingston (Rondout) – St. Mary 1842

ingston (Rondout) – St. Peter 1858

ingston – St. Joseph 1869

oshen – St. John the Evangelist 1849

averstraw – St. Peter 1848

effersonville – St. George 1843

elrose – Immaculate Conception 1853

iddletown – St. Joseph 1865

orrisania – St. Augustine 1855

ew Brighton – St. Peter 1839

ew Rochelle – Blessed Sacrament
(St. Matthew) 1848

ewburgh – St. Patrick 1838

yack – St. Ann 1870

bernburg – St. Mary 1854

ssining (Sing Sing) – St. Augustine 1853

eekskill – Assumption 1859

iermont – St. John 1852

ort Chester (Saw Pit) – Our Lady of Mercy
848

ort Jervis (Deerpark) – Immaculate
onception 1851

oughkeepsie - St. Peter 1837

hinecliff – St. Joseph 1862

osebank (Clifton) St. Mary 1852

osendale – St. Peter 1855

ossville – St. Joseph 1855

augerties – St Mary of the Snow – Diocese of
lbany

uffern – Sacred Heart (St. Rose of Lima)
868

leepy Hollow (North Tarrytown) – St. Teresa
853

erplanck (Verplanck's Point) – St. Patrick
843

Vappingers Falls (Channingsville) – St. Mary
850

Varwick – St. Stephen 1865

Vest Hurley – St. John 1860

Vestchester – St. Raymond 1842

White Plains – St. John the Evangelist 1868

onkers – Immaculate Conception 1848

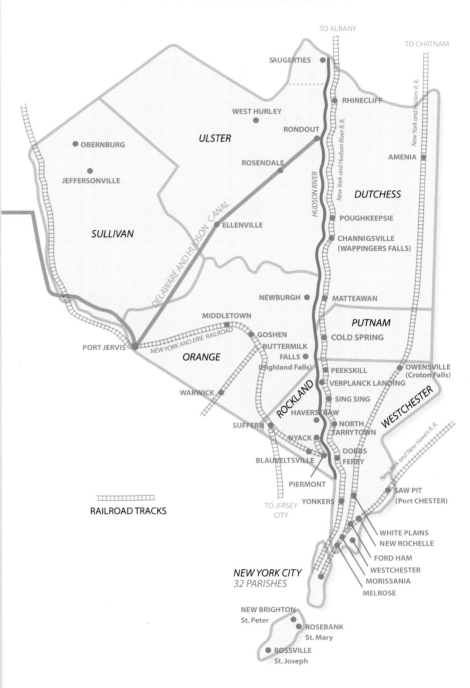

COUNTRY PARISHES OF
THE ARCHDIOCESE
of New York circa 1870

In the later nineteenth century St. Raymond's became one of the most important parishes in the Bronx. After 1866 it included within its boundaries the Catholic Protectory, one of the largest child-caring facilities in the country, which occupied the present site of Parkchester. Ten years later Father Michael McEvoy began the largest Catholic cemetery in the Bronx when he bought a tract of land called the Underhill Farm. Monsignor Edward McKenna, the pastor from 1888 to 1931, built the present church, one of the first in the archdiocese to be constructed in the Byzantine style. It was dedicated by Archbishop Corrigan on October 23, 1898.

Monsignor Edward McKenna, the pastor of St. Raymond's Church, 1888-1931.
Credit: *St. Raymond's Church*

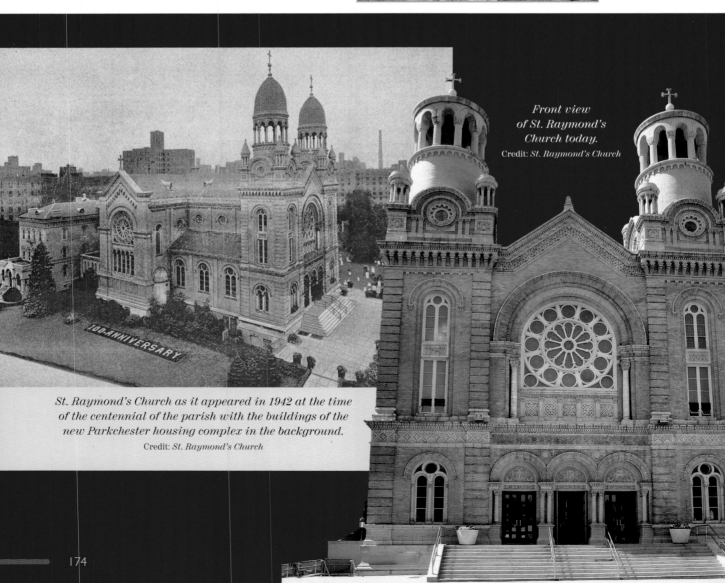

Front view of St. Raymond's Church today.
Credit: *St. Raymond's Church*

St. Raymond's Church as it appeared in 1942 at the time of the centennial of the parish with the buildings of the new Parkchester housing complex in the background.
Credit: *St. Raymond's Church*

The second of the future Bronx churches was the Church of the Immaculate Conception in Melrose, started by Father Joseph Stumpe and given to the Redemptorists in 1886. The third was St. Augustine's on 170th Street near Franklin Avenue in Morrisania, which dates from 1855, although construction of the church began only three years later. In 1855 the future Bronx got its fourth parish when Archbishop Hughes told Father Arthur Donnelly to make the chapel at St. John's College, Fordham, the parish church of Our Lady of Mercy.

No fewer than six of John Hughes' new Westchester parishes were located in commu-

Father Joseph Stumpe, the German-born diocesan priest who founded the Church of the Immaculate Conception in Melrose

nities on the Hudson River. The first, St. Patrick's in Verplanck's Point, as it was then called, is the oldest parish in Westchester County. It dates from 1843 when Verplanck was still very much a river town, six years before the coming of the railroad. The first Catholics were Irish immigrants who worked in the local brickyards. The first pastor was the same Father Felix Vilanis who had founded St. Raymond's Church in the Town of Westchester the previous year.[3]

The first Church of the Immaculate Conception on East 151st Street

The second Church of the Immaculate Conception on East 150st Street between Melrose and Cortland Avenues, erected in 1888, two years after the Redemptorists took charge of the parish

3 - *St. Patrick's Church,1843-1993* (Verplanck: St. Patrick's Church, 1993), unpaginated.

American Gothic, Clerical Style. Msgr. Charles Corley, the pastor of the Church of the Immaculate Conception Church, Yonkers, who built the present church in 1892, flanked by Father Andrew O'Reilly and Father Thomas McLaughlin.
Credit: *Church of the Immaculate Conception*

The first Church of Our Lady of Mercy, Fordham, now the University Church of Fordham University

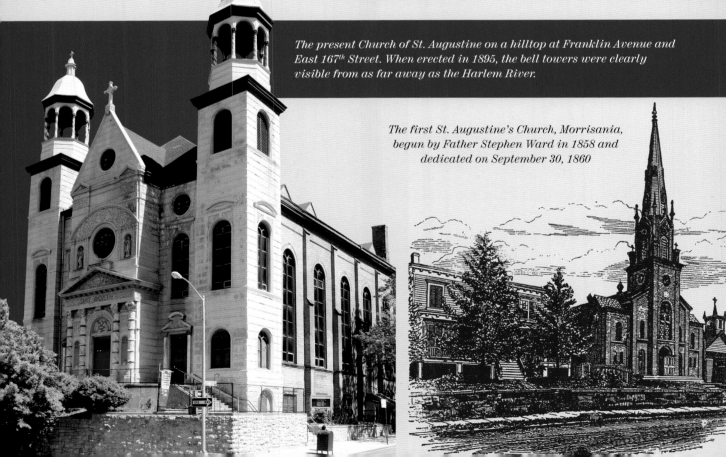

The present Church of St. Augustine on a hilltop at Franklin Avenue and East 167th Street. When erected in 1895, the bell towers were clearly visible from as far away as the Harlem River.

The first St. Augustine's Church, Morrisania, begun by Father Stephen Ward in 1858 and dedicated on September 30, 1860

St. Mary's Church in Yonkers owes its very existence to the New York and Hudson River Railroad. It was established in 1848 as the Church of the Immaculate Conception to care for the Irish laborers who had come to Yonkers the previous year to build the railroad through the city. Previously diocesan priests and later Jesuits had traveled from St. John College in Fordham to celebrate Sunday Mass in private homes and rented quarters. One of the Jesuits, Father John Ryan, began the construction of St. Mary's Church in July 1848. That Christmas Mass was celebrated for the first time in the little church "which had boards instead of glass in the windows, some backless benches that were made in the church, two iron stoves, bare brick walls, a roof but not a ceiling, and a $1,000 mortgage."[4]

The first St. Patrick's Church in Verplanck, built in 1843, probably with local brick and donated labor. It was destroyed by fire on February 3, 1980.

The new St. Patrick's Church, built in 1983, which incorporated the brick bell tower of the original church.

Artist's sketch of the first Church of the Immaculate Conception, Yonkers, which was erected in 1848.
Credit: *Church of the Immaculate Conception*

The Romanesque Church of the Immaculate Conception, constructed in 1892, with its 160-foot tower that dominated downtown Yonkers.

- Florence D. Cohalan, *History of the Parish of the Immaculate Conception, Yonkers, N.Y.,* (Yonkers: Church of the Immaculate Conception, 1948), unpaginated.

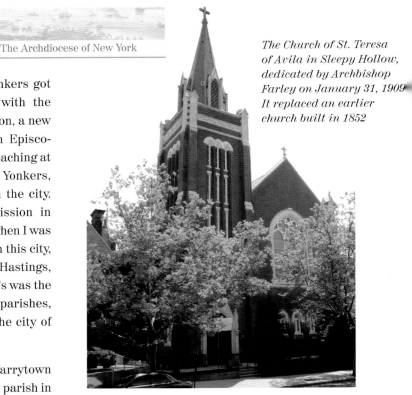

The Church of St. Teresa of Avila in Sleepy Hollow, dedicated by Archbishop Farley on January 31, 1909. It replaced an earlier church built in 1852

In June 1851 the Catholics of Yonkers got their first resident diocesan pastor with the appointment of Father Thomas S. Preston, a new ordained priest who was formerly an Episcopalian clergyman. Many years later, preaching at the dedication of a new church in Yonkers, Preston reflected on his early days in the city. "I recall vividly to mind my first mission in Yonkers thirty-six years ago," he said, "when I was the pastor of the only Catholic church in this city, and acted in the capacity of pastor for Hastings, Dobbs Ferry and Tarrytown."[5] St. Mary's was the mother church not only of these three parishes, but also of twenty-three churches in the city of Yonkers alone.

St. Teresa's Church in North Tarrytown (Sleepy Hollow) became an independent parish in 1853 as did St. Augustine's Church in Sing Sing (Ossining). In both localities the growth of the Catholic community can be traced to the Irish immigrants who were employed in building the Croton Dam and Aqueduct two decades earlier. Father James Cummiskey, the former pastor of

St. Joseph Church in Greenwich Village, who had been hounded out of the parish by the trustees, celebrated Mass for the construction workers and their families in a wooden shed in Sing Sing and in other camps along the route of the aqueduct between Sing Sing and Yonkers. He gave his address in 1842 as "Sing Sing and Water Works, New York."

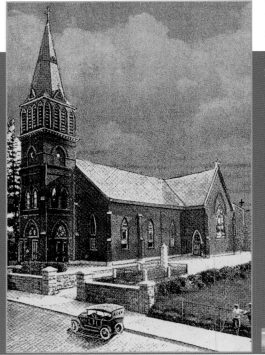

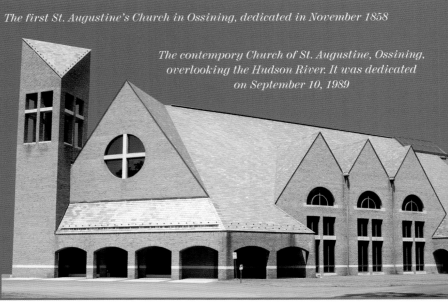

The first St. Augustine's Church in Ossining, dedicated in November 1858

The contempory Church of St. Augustine, Ossining, overlooking the Hudson River. It was dedicated on September 10, 1989

5 - Yonkers *Gazette*, February 25, 4, 1848. The basic source for the history of the Catholic Church in Yonkers is Thomas C. Cornell, "Catholic Beginnings in Yonkers," *HR&S 36* (1947): 68-96. It is based on the unpublished account written in 1888 by Judge Francis X. Donoghue, in whose childhood home the priests from Fordham often celebrated Mass before the erection of St. Mary's Church. See also Daniel F. Tanzone, ed., *175th Anniversary of the Church of New York* (Yonkers: Yonkers Area Conference, 1983).

View of the Hudson River at Sing Sing (Ossining) in 1828.
Credit: *Fordham University Archives*

The boisterous hard-drinking Irish construction gangs were hardly a welcome presence in the sedate Westchester communities along the Hudson. Although some residents of Sing Sing expressed admiration at seeing these same men kneeling outdoors at Mass on Sunday because they could not fit into Father Cummiskey's little shed, others blamed them for theft and vandalism. One wealthy landowner sent a bill to the aqueduct commissioners for $3,012 for damages to his property. He told them, "I can assure you that it is no pleasant thing to have [their] huts or shantees as they are called stuck up within a few yards of my dwelling with people of the lowest and filthiest of mankind, children nearly naked before your eyes, and that of your family." In Sleepy Hollow Washington Irving complained sarcastically that "a colony of Patlanders have been encamped about this place all winter [forming] a kind of Patsylvania in the midst of a 'wiltherness.' "[6]

The Aqueduct Bridge at Sing Sing

Two other Hudson River towns in Westchester County got their own parishes in the waning years of John Hughes' administration. The Church of the Assumption in Peekskill, which began life as a mission of St. Patrick's in Verplanck Point, became a separate parish in 1859. Peekskill got one of its greatest civic boosters with the arrival of Father James T.

6 - Cit. in Gerard T. Koeppel, *Water for Gotham: A History* (Princeton: Princeton University Press, 2000), 208, 250.

Curran as the new pastor in October 1891. Convinced that the little city was destined to become a major metropolis, in 1905 he began to build a four-story building called the Guardian which contained a sixteen-classroom school, 1,100-seat theatre, recreation hall, dining room, roof garden, bowling alleys and squash courts. Unfortunately there was no church and the Guardian saddled the little parish with a debt that amounted to the enormous sum of $396,000 in 1914.[7]

first resident pastor. Four years later he erected Sacred Heart Church, which was a combination of church, carriage house and stable.

On the Sound Shore of Westchester County the two oldest Catholic communities were in New Rochelle and Saw Pit or Saw Pit Landing (today's Port Chester). The New York and New Haven Railroad connected them with New York City and with southern New England in 1848, spurring the same kind of development that the arrival of the

The Guardian, Father Curran's Church of the Assumption in Peekskill, dedicated by Archbishop Farley on October 31, 1909

The Church of the Sacred Heart, Dobbs ferry, dedicated by Archbishop Farley on February 16, 1896. It replaced an earlier church built in 1866.

In Dobbs Ferry the pioneer priest was the nomadic Father Cummiskey, who celebrated Mass in a shed on a dock in 1837 or 1838. For the next quarter century Dobbs Ferry remained a mission. It finally became a parish on November 26, 1862, when Father David O'Connor was appointed the

railroad did elsewhere in the diocese. As far back as the late 1830s Catholics in New Rochelle and Port Chester were visited by circuit-riding missionary priests like the hard-working Father Cummiskey and Father Michael Curran, the pastor of St. Paul's in Harlem.

---

7 - Florence D. Cohalan, *The Church of the Assumption,* 1859-1959 (Peekskill: Church of the Assumption, 1959), unpaginated.

Catholic institutional life in southern Westchester can be traced to the establishment of St. Raymond's Church in the present-day Bronx in 1842. Shortly thereafter St. Raymond's founded permanent missions in both New Rochelle and Port Chester. The key figure in both places was Father Matthew Higgins, a young Irish priest who was the pastor of St. Raymond's from 1845 to 1848. He purchased a hall for the celebration of Mass in Port Chester and in 1848 began construction of St. Matthew's Church in New Rochelle. Unfortunately he did not live to see it finished. Plagued by ill health, that same year he returned to Ireland where he died in 1851.

From 1848 to 1853 New Rochelle and Port Chester shared the same pastor, Father Edward J. O'Reilly, who was appointed the pastor on the day of his ordination. During those five years Father O'Reilly enlarged St. Matthew's Church in New Rochelle and erected the first Church of Our Lady of Mercy in Port Chester. He also built St. John's mission church in White Plains in 1848. On the same Sunday in June 1852 Archbishop Hughes blessed the churches in Port Chester and White Plains. When Father O'Reilly was transferred to St. Patrick's Church in Newburgh in 1853, both New Rochelle and Port Chester got a resident pastor, Father Thomas McLoughlin in New Rochelle and a few months later Father Martin Dowling in Port Chester.

Father Edward J. O'Reilly, a native of Savannah, Georgia, who was appointed the pastor of Port Chester and New Rochelle on the day of his ordination, September 23, 1848. In 1853 he was transferred to St. Patrick's Church, Newburgh, where he remained until 1867 when he was appointed pastor of St. Mary's, Grand Street, where he died in 1881

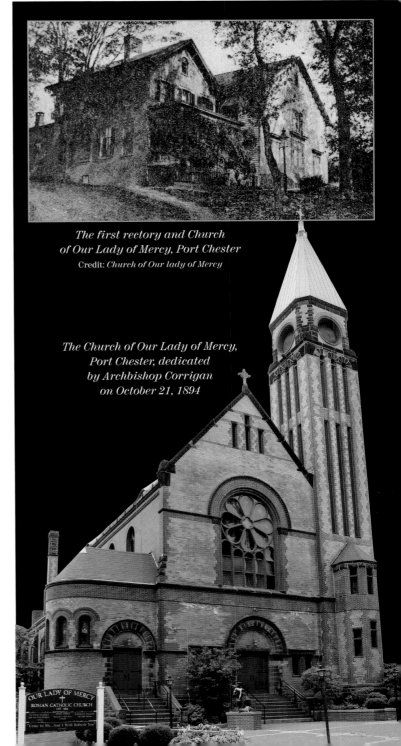

The first rectory and Church of Our Lady of Mercy, Port Chester
Credit: *Church of Our lady of Mercy*

The Church of Our Lady of Mercy, Port Chester, dedicated by Archbishop Corrigan on October 21, 1894

St. Matthew's Church, New Rochelle, erected in 1848 as a mission chapel by Father Matthew Higgins, the pastor of St. Raymond's Church.
Credit: *Blessed Sacrament Church*

However, the pioneer days of the Church in southern Westchester were not over. Between them, the two pastors were also responsible for missions in Mamaroneck, Tuckahoe, White Plains, City Island, Pelhamdale, Harrison, and Rye. In Port Chester Father Dowling had faculties from the bishop of Hartford to care for the Catholics in Greenwich and the neighboring towns in Connecticut. On a typical Sunday in New Rochelle Father McLoughlin left the rectory at 6:00 a.m. in his horse-drawn wagon to drive to one of the mission churches and returned in time for the 10:30 a.m. Mass in St. Matthew's. He remained as pastor for forty-nine years. When he built a new and larger church

Father Thomas McLoughlin, the pastor of St. Matthew/Blessed Sacrament Church, New Rochelle, 1853-1902.
Credit: *Church of the Immaculate Conception, Tuckahoe*

in 1874, he changed the name to the Church of the Blessed Sacrament Church and paid off the debt in 1883 with a handsome donation from Mrs. Adrian Iselin. When that church was hit by lighting and burned to the ground, he built the present church in 1897. At his death in 1902 there were a dozen parishes in the area that he had once served alone.[8]

White Plains remained a mission for twenty years, first of New Rochelle and then of Port Chester, until 1868, when Father John McEvoy was appointed the first pastor. The Catholics continued to use the little Church of St. John the Evangelist erected by Father Edward O'Reilly in 1852 until 1892 when the present church was opened. It was debt free at its completion, thanks to the generosity of Mrs. Nathalie Reynal, and consecrated by Archbishop Corrigan on June 9, 1892.[9]

Farther north in Westchester County, St. Joseph's Church was established in Croton Falls (then called Owenville or Owensville) in 1845 to serve the Irish immigrants who had come to work on the construction of the first Croton Dam and then settled in the neighboring communities. Two years later the New York and Harlem Railroad reached the hamlet, and in 1849 St. Joseph's Church was built adjacent to the railroad depot. Jesuit priests from Fordham traveled north on the railroad to celebrate Mass on Sunday until 1859 when Father Charles Slevin was given charge of the whole Harlem Valley. That year he built a church in Dover Plains named after St. Charles Borromeo, but he appears to have resided in Croton Falls.[10]

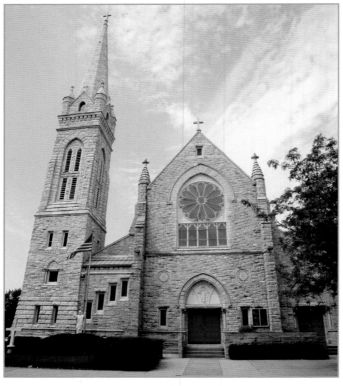

The second Church of the Blessed Scrament, New Rochelle, erected by Father Thomas McLoughlin in 1897.

8 - *1848-1998 Blessed Sacrament Parish, New Rochelle, New York* (New Rochelle: Blessed Sacrament Church, 1998), unpaginated; Edward P. Brogan, *The One Hundredth Anniversary of Our Lady of Mercy Parish*, Port Chester, New York, 1854-1954 (Port Chester: Our Lady of Mercy Church, 1954), 12-18.

9 - *The Story of St. John the Evangelist Church* (Custombook, 1978), 9-12.

10- *St. Joseph's Church, 150th Anniversary, 1845-1995* (Croton Falls: St. Joseph's Church, 1995) 23-25.

*The first Church of St. John the Evangelist
in White Plains, dedicated in 1852.*
Credit: *Church of St. John the Evangelist*

*The Church of St. John
the Evangelist in the 1920s.*
Credit: *Church of St. John the Evangelist*

*The Church of St. John
the Evangelist, White
Plains, consecrated by
Archbishop Corrigan
on June 9, 1892.*

Father John Orsenigo, a native of Italy who succeeded Father Slevin as the pastor of Croton Falls in 1864, continued this itinerant missionary work, traveling as far north as Amenia where he celebrated Mass occasionally in the railroad station and in private homes in the vicinity. In 1866 Amenia became a separate parish, when Father Patrick Tandy was appointed the first resident pastor of the Church of the Immaculate Conception. These two Harlem Valley parishes at Croton Falls and Amenia, located thirty-three miles apart on the New York and Harlem Railroad, became the twin anchors for a network of mission churches, in northern Westchester, Putnam and Dutchess counties that stretched as far east as the border with Connecticut and Massachusetts. Croton Falls was responsible for the "out-missions" in Mahopac, Brewster, Katonah,

*Father Patrick Tandy,
first pastor of
the Church of the
Immaculate
Conception, Amenia*

Patterson and Towners, while Amenia took care of Dover Plains, Pawling, Millerton, Millbrook and Beekman (Sylvan Lake).

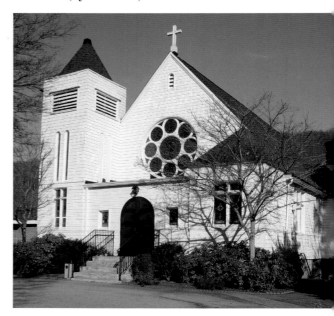

*St. Joseph's Church, Croton Falls, dedicated
by Archbishop Corrigan on November 11, 1894. It replac
an earlier church built in 1849 which burned to the grou
in 1893 when sparks from a wood-burning locomotive
started a grass fire that engulfed the church*

The Croton Dam in 1842

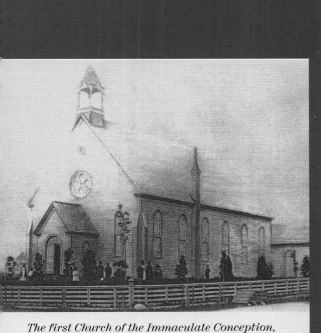

The first Church of the Immaculate Conception, Amenia, built between 1866 and 1868

Three additional parishes were founded in the western part of Dutchess County along the Hudson. The first was St. Mary's in Channingsville (Wappingers Falls), which dates from 1850 (one year after the arrival of the New York and Hudson River Railroad), when Father George Brophy was assigned as the first resident pastor. Two of Father Brophy's missions were in Fishkill Landing and Matteawan. In Matteawan Mass was celebrated first in a school and later in a renovated barn that served as a temporary church. It was replaced with a permanent church in the late 1850s and became a separate parish on October 7, 1860, with the appointment of Father James Coyle as the first resident pastor. When the church was dedicated by Archbishop Hughes on August 18, 1861, the name was changed from St. Mary to St. Joachim.[11]

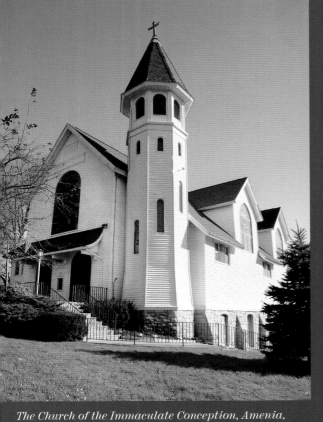

The Church of the Immaculate Conception, Amenia, dedicated by Archbishop Corrigan on February 12, 1888

St. Mary's Church, Wappingers Fall. the cornerstone was blessed by Cardinal McCloskey on September 27, 1877. The church was restored and rededicated by Bishop Dominick Lagonegro on October 5, 2002

---

11 - In 1913 Matteawan and Fishkill Landing combined to form the city of Beacon. Edward D. Archer, *The Warmth of a Church: A Brief History of St. Joachim's Roman Catholic Parish in Beacon*, New York (Beacon, 1998), 6-7.

*St. Joachim's Church, Beacon, dedicated
by Archbishop John Hughes on August 18, 1861, enlarged
and rededicated by Cardinal McCloskey on June 26, 1881,
renovated again in 1905 and 1963.*

*St. Joseph's Church, Rhinecliff, dedicated by
Archbishop Hughes on March 19, 1863.
It is now a mission of its former mission,
the Church of the Good Shepherd, Rhinebeck.*

The last of the Dutchess County parishes founded by Archbishop Hughes was St. Joseph's in Rhinecliff, which he established in 1862. The first pastor, Father Michael Scully, was a native of Kerry and an alumnus of the Irish College in Paris. His parish comprised all of northern Dutchess County with missions in Hyde Park, Staatsburg, Barrytown and Tivoli. He died ten years later at the age of thirty-eight.[12]

West of the Hudson

Much of the growth of the Catholic Church in the interior of the four counties west of the Hudson River can be traced to the building of two major transportation arteries, the Delaware and Hudson Canal and the New York and Erie Railroad.

The canal came first. It was a 108-mile engineering wonder with 108 locks, more locks than the Erie Canal, which was four times as long. Constructed between 1823 and 1828 under private auspices with a state subsidy, the canal was designed to bring highly-prized anthracite coal from the Pennsylvania coal fields to the lucrative New York City market. The canal ran east from Honesdale, Pennsylvania, to the Delaware River, then turned south and paralleled the river to Port Jervis. At that point the canal left the river and cut northwesterly across Orange and Ulster counties to Rondout where the coal was shipped down the Hudson to New York City. Villages along the route such as Port Jervis, Ellenville and Rosendale owed the existence of their first Catholic communities to the Irish and German immigrants who constructed the canal and settled in the area.

---

12 - Florence D. Cohalan, *Regina Coeli Centennial* (Hyde Park: Regina Coeli Church, 1964), n.p.

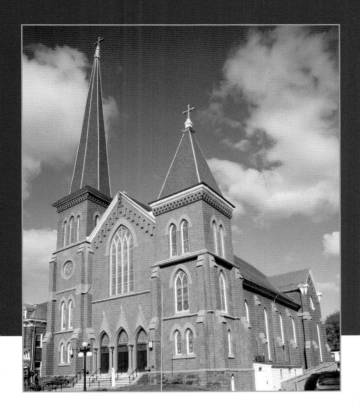

The ruins of the first Church of the Immaculate Conception, Port Jervis, which was destroyed by fire on Christmas Eve 1868

The Church of the Immaculate Conception, Port Jervis. The cornerstone was blessed on July 5, 1869.

Father John Raufeisen, the pioneer German priest in Sullivan and Ulster Counties, who was the pastor of St. Peter's Church, Rondout, from 1861 until 1876.
Credit:
St. Peter's Church, Kingston

Port Jervis had been a sleepy little village called Deerpark until the canal gave it a tenuous link to the Atlantic and a pretentious new name. The arrival of the New York and Erie Railroad on the last day of the year in 1847 added to the importance of Port Jervis as a transportation hub. Four year later, the Church of the Immaculate Conception, which had been a mission of St. Patrick's in Newburgh since 1841, became a parish with the appointment of Father Edward S. Briady (or Briody) as the resident pastor. The church was dedicated by Archbishop Hughes on November 18, 1855, but it was destroyed in a disastrous fire on Christmas Eve in 1868 five months after the arrival of a new pastor, Father James A. Nilan. Work began on a new church the next year following the blessing of the cornerstone on July 5, 1869. The architect was I. G. Perry of Binghamton, who later designed the Capitol in Albany. At a cost of $60,000 he gave the Catholics of Port Jervis a spacious church with two steeples, one 200 feet tall, that dominated the city.[13]

The Catholic presence in Ellenville dates from the early 1850s when Irish Catholics bought a former Protestant church, moved it to Main Street and called it St. Mary's. However, around the same time the German Catholics in Ellenville organized their own parish under the leadership of Father John Raufeisen. They also called their church St. Mary (St. Mary of the Assumption), but the confusion between two churches of the same name was avoided because people referred to them as either the Irish or the German Church. In 1881, when Father Andrew Sauer, began work on a new German church, he changed the name from St. Mary to St. Andrew. In October 1956 the two parishes were merged after a major flood swept St. Mary's Church into the canal. Within a year of the merger a mission was begun in Kerhonkson, using the fire house for Sunday Mass, until June 17, 1962, when Our Lady of Lourdes Church was dedicated. In 2006 the Church of St. Mary and St. Andrew was one of the largest in area in the archdiocese, comprising about 600 square miles.[14]

13 - *The Parish of the Immaculate Conception* (Port Jervis: Church of the Immaculate Conception, 2001),unpaginated.

14 - John A. Unverzagt, "A Brief History of Our Parish," *The Glory of Ellenville*, ed. Anthony Puduchery (Ellenville: Church of St. Mary and St. Andrew, n.d.), 10-12.

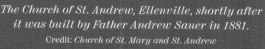

The Church of St. Mary and St. Andrew, Ellenville, which incorporates both the former territorial parish of St. Mary and the German church of St. Andrew.

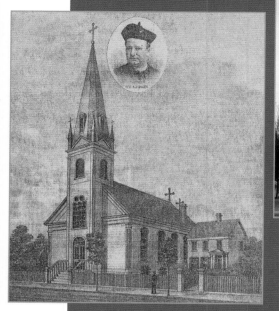

The Church of St. Andrew, Ellenville, shortly after it was built by Father Andrew Sauer in 1881.
Credit: *Church of St. Mary and St. Andrew*

Church in 1855, one of the largest Catholic churches in Ulster County. An elderly parishioner described the origins of the parish for Archbishop Farley. "Sixty years ago," he said,

my father and a great many more immigrants like himself left their native land to come to America to make a home for themselves in the land of liberty. When they reached New York, they inquired where they could get work. About that time Rosendale Cement was discovered in Ulster County, and there was a demand for men at Rosendale, so a few of the immigrants walked from New York City to Rosendale to get work at the mills which were being erected at that time. Their wages was [sic] about $.75 per day [and] the hours was [sic] from sunrise to sunset. There was at that time no church nearer to them than the Rondout Church in the City of Kingston, so they had to walk to Kingston once a month to hear Mass.

Rosendale was another Ulster County community that prospered from the Delaware and Hudson Canal. The canal engineers discovered that the rock from nearby quarries produced better cement than the product they were using. For fifty years thereafter Rosendale was a major center for the manufacture of cement. The Irish and German Catholics established St. Peter's

The work in the quarries was extremely dangerous, and one pastor warned Archbishop Corrigan not to leave Rosendale without a resident pastor. "As a rule," he explained, "when explosions occur, men are either instantly killed or they live only a little while."[15]

Our Lady of Lourdes Church, Kerhonkson, a mission of the Church of St. Mary and St. Andrew, Ellenville, dedicated by Bishop John Maguire on June 17, 1962

15 - AANY, Jacob Huben to Farley, September 14, 1903; John J. Gleason to Corrigan, August 27, 1892.

St. Peter's Church, Rosendale, overlooking the Rondout Valley. It replaced an earlier church and was first used for Mass on Christmas Day 1876.

committee to purchase land for their own church which they called St. Peter's. By 1858 they had a basement church in operation and, on April 15, 1860, Archbishop Hughes dedicated the finished church and proceeded down the street to St. Mary's Church where he confirmed 850 people. The following year Father Johannes Raufeisen moved from Ellenville to St. Peter's where he built a new church in 1872 and remained as pastor until his retirement four years later. In the meantime "Upper Kingston" got its own parish with the establishment of St. Joseph's Church, which was dedicated on July 27, 1869.[16]

Even more than Ellenville or Rosendale, Rondout grew rich as the eastern terminus of the Delaware and Hudson Canal. Sometimes as many as fifty or sixty canal boats were backed up waiting to pass through the locks while Rondout Creek was crowded with schooners, steamboats and tugs. The rich built their mansard-roofed mansions on the heights overlooking the town while on the slopes below the workers' houses were packed tightly together without water or sewers while chickens and pigs ran wild in the front yards. One pious Protestant gentleman hoped to improve the morals, if not the manners, of the bargemen by placing a Bible in every canal boat.

St. Mary's mission in Rondout became a parish 1842, and Rondout got a second parish when the German-speaking parishioners complained that they could not understand the sermons in St. Mary's. In 1856 they formed a

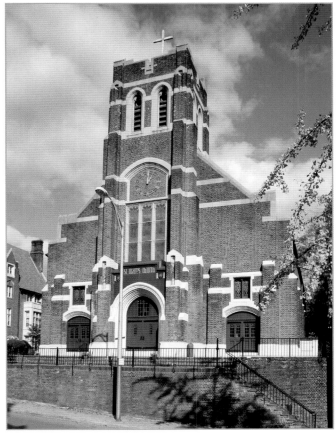

St. Mary's Church, Kingston, which dates from 1846. It was blessed on July 8, 1849, renovated by Dr. Burtsell and consecrated by Archbishop Corrigan on September 6, 1896. In 1932 the exterior was veneered with brick and limestone.

---

16 - *Centennial of St. Peter's Parish, Kingston, New York, 1858-1968* (Kingston: St. Peter's Church, 1968), 27-31; *St. Joseph's Church, Kingston, New York* (Kingston: St. Joseph's Church, 1969), 6-8.

St. Peter's Church, founded by German Catholics in Rondout and dedicated by Archbishop Hughes on April 15, 1860.

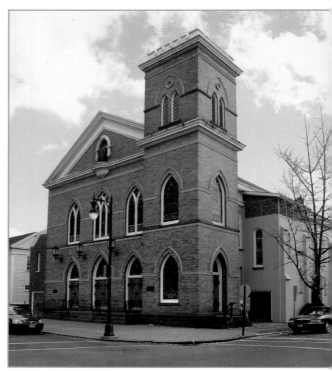

St. Joseph's Church, the first Catholic church in Upper Kingston, dedicated on July 27, 1869. The brick front was added in 1898.

Farther north, after the establishment of the new diocese of Albany in 1847, Our Lady of the Snow in Saugerties became part of the diocese of Albany. For the next quarter-century Saugerties and Shandaken were missions of the parish in Hudson, New York. In the mountains west of Kingston and Saugerties quarries continued to flourish and with them the formation of small communities of tough and muscular Irish quarrymen. By 1874 St. Mary of the Snow---now back in the archdiocese of New York---had two missions to care for them and their families, St. John the Evangelist at Fish Creek or Clow Quarries, which dates from 1848, and St. Patrick's in Quarryville, which was started in 1874.

Like Our Lady of the Snow in Saugerties, St. Mary's Church in Rondout also provided pastoral care for the quarrymen and their families in mountain hamlets like Stony Hollow, Jockey Hill and Flagg Quarries. St. John's Church

in West Hurley traces its origin to 1860 when Father James Coyle, the pastor of St. Mary's in Rondout, began to use a school house in Jockey Hill for the occasional celebration of Mass. In 1865 Father Stephen Mackin was appointed the pastor of Jockey Hill and Stony Hollow, but went home to Ireland for an extended visit. In his absence in 1869 Father Coyle built St. John's Church in Stony Hollow, the settlement that had the largest number of Catholics. Upon his return from Ireland, Father Mackin became the first resident pastor of a parish that included most of northwestern Ulster County with missions at Boiceville, Shandaken and Phoenicia.

In 1875 St. John's Church was relocated to Bristol Hill. The church burnt down in 1896, but was quickly rebuilt. The population of the parish declined as the quarries petered out and the construction of the Ashokan Reservoir submerged the old village of West Hurley. However, after

Father M. Julien Ginet, M.S., the French-born La Salette priest who was the first pastor of St. Francis de Sales. He was both the architect and contractor of the church, which he built and furnished for $9,000.

The second St. John's Church in Bristol Hill, constructed in 1896.

The fourth St. John's Church, West Hurley-Woodstock, dedicated by Cardinal Cooke on April 5, 1975.

World War II the parish got a new lease on life because of the construction of the IBM plant in Kingston. As the number of parishioners increased, it was decided to relocate the church to a more convenient location midway between West Hurley and Woodstock. A new St. John's Church and new parish center were dedicated by Cardinal Cooke on April 5, 1975.[17]

Much of the interior of Ulster County remained missionary territory well into the twentieth century. Phoenicia was made a separate parish in 1902, and entrusted to the La Salette Fathers, a small French religious community, but two years later the pastor of St. Francis de Sales Church had only 200 parishioners in Phoenicia and his missions in Allaben and Pine Hill. He was boarding in a hotel because there was no money to buy a house for a rectory. Conditions were even worse in St. Ann's Church in Sawkill, which became a parish in 1905, where the only industry was the bluestone quarries. In 1911 the pastor told Archbishop Farley that there were only 175 wage earners in the parish, "some eking out a weekly pittance of six and seven dollars." A few years later there were only 112 parishioners left, the pastor was owed $1,000 in back salary, and he was appealing to priest friends for second-hand vestments. There was a rectory in Sawkill, but it was so dilapidated that a local physician declared it unfit for human habitation. When the pastor announced a fund-raising drive to replace it with a more modern residence, Cardinal Hayes sent him a check for $100.[18]

St. Francis de Sales Church, Phoenicia, dedicated by Bishop Thomas Cusack on August 21, 1904.

17 - *Celebrating 125 Years of Service* (West Hurley-Woodstock: St. John's Parish Center, 1985), 10-15.

18 - AANY, Father Ginet, M.S. to Joseph Mooney, January 30, 1904; Edward O'Sullivan to Farley, January 9, 1911, January 10, 1906; George Vaeth to Hayes, July 5, 1919; Hayes to Vaeth, July 15, 1919.

The first St. Augustine's Chapel in the old village of West Shokan, built in 1893. It served a a mission of St. John's Church, West Hurley, until the old village was submerged by the Ashokan Reservoir.

The present St. Augustine's mission chapel, built in 1952 to meet the needs of parishioners in the new village of West Shokan.

The chapel of Our Lady of Lourdes in Allaben, now closed, formerly a mission of St. Francis de Sales in Phoenicia.

The chapel of Our Lady of La Salette in Boiceville, now closed, formerly a mission of St. Francis de Sales in Phoenicia.

Like the Delaware and Hudson Canal, the New York and Erie Railroad played a major role in the development of the Catholic Church in the western parts of the archdiocese. Chartered in 1832, nineteen years elapsed before it was completed between Piermont on the Hudson River and Dunkirk on Lake Erie. With 447 miles of track, it briefly claimed to be the longest railroad in the world. The claim, while accurate, seemed pretentious in view of the fact the railroad's two termini were both located in obscure hamlets, giving rise to the jibe that it ran from Nowhere-in Particular to Nowhere-at-All. At Piermont, twenty miles north of New York City, a 4,000 foot pier was built out into the Hudson River. It was selected as the eastern terminus of the railroad for no better reason than that it was the home of the railroad's first president.

From Piermont the Erie's rails stretched across Rockland and Orange counties in an northwest arc to Port Jervis and then north along the Delaware River on the border between Sullivan County and Pennsylvania. The Irish came to Piermont with the railroad and provided most of the laborers who built the right of way for the princely wage of seventy-five cents a day. They built a small brick church in Piermont named in honor of St. John that was first used for the celebration of Mass on New Year's Day in 1852. They got their first resident pastor six months later with the appointment of Father John Quinn on July 1, 1852. The population of Piermont peaked in 1860 with 2,426 residents, a figure that would not be reached again for over a century, and a new church was opened on August 13, 1861. Unfortunately for Piermont, the next year the Erie acquired a connection to Jersey City, its natural destination, and Piermont slipped back into a state of picturesque sylvan repose until the opening of the Tappan Zee Bridge in 1955.[19]

The second St. John's Church, Piermont, which was built in 1861.

The modern St. John's Church, Piermont, erected in 1964.

Father John Quinn, pastor of St. John's Church, Piermont, 1852-1875. His parish originally comprised all of Rockland County south of Haverstraw, including Nyack, Spring Valley, Suffern, Monsey, and Chester and Greenwood Lake in Orange County.

19 - *The Story of a Hundred Years, 1852-1952* (Piermont: St. John's Church, 1952), 9-11; Edward Hungerford, *Men of Erie* (New York: Random House, 1946), 17-18, 111, 130.

In 1841 the Erie Railroad reached Goshen where there was already a small Catholic community that was visited first by a priest from Jersey City and later by the pastor of St. Patrick's Church in Newburgh. Although the Church of St. John the Evangelist in Goshen claims to date from 1837, it had no resident pastor until the appointment of Father Stephen Ward on July 17, 1849. In the later nineteenth century St. John's Church in Goshen was to become the mother church, directly or indirectly, of a half-dozen new parishes in central Orange County. The process began in 1865 when the out-missions in Warwick and Middletown became independent parishes.[20]

The railroad came to Warwick in 1862. The first St. Stephen's Church was a former Methodist church that apparently was purchased by St. John's Church when Warwick was still an out-mission of Goshen. An antique structure with a potbelly stove in the center aisle, it served the Catholics of Warwick until 1903 when they erected an imposing fieldstone church at a cost of $10,500. It was dedicated by Archbishop Farley

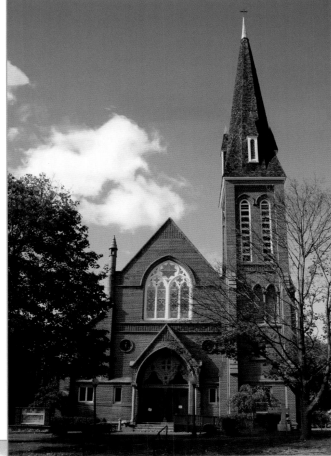

The Church of St. John the Evangelist, Goshen, dedicated by Archbishop Corrigan on September 2, 1885

on September 27, 1903. Meanwhile, in June 1887, St. Stephen's acquired a former Presbyterian church in Florida and opened it as the mission church of St. Edward. By the 1990s the congregation in Warwick had grown far too large for the church. A building campaign was launched to replace it, and the present St. Stephen's Church was dedicated by Cardinal O'Connor on May 10, 1992.[21]

The Church of St. Stephen, the First Martyr, dedicated by Cardinal O'Connor on May 10, 1992

---

20 - *St. Catherine of Alexandria Church* (Blauvelt: Church of St. Catherine, 1993), 7; J. Keogan, *History of St. John's Parish, Goshen, Orange County, New York* (1889), unpaginated; T.J.V. Cullen, *St. John the Evangelist: A House for Worship in Goshen, N.Y.,* (Jeffersonville: The Sullivan County Record, 1962), 53.

21 - *St. Stephen's Church* (Warwick: St. Stephen's Church, 1965), unpaginated.

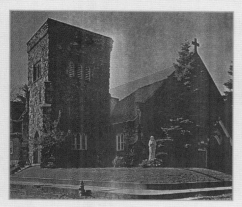

The second St. Stephen's Church, Warwick, dedicated by Archbishop Farley in 1903.
Credit: St. Stephen's Church

The Church of St. Edward, Florida, a mission of St. Stephen Church, Warwick, founded in 1887 and scheduled to be closed in 2007.

In Middletown the roots of the Catholic community go back at least to 1859 when a group of laymen organized the Saint Joseph Society for the purpose of building a church. They delayed construction until the end of the Civil War, but in 1865 they asked Archbishop McCloskey for a priest. He sent them Father Andrew O'Reilly, and on October 2, 1867, the archbishop came to Middletown to dedicate the first St. Joseph's Church, a small frame building that cost $7,000. It was replaced with the present church in 1880.[22]

Father Andrew O'Reilly, the first pastor of St. Joseph's Church, Middletown.

A branch line of the Erie brought the railroad to Haverstraw where the riverfront was lined with brickyards all the way to Grassy Point. The brickyards had attracted a number of Irish workers who founded St. Peter's Church. The first Mass was celebrated in Haverstraw on November 14, 1847, a year before the church was erected. Another branch line brought the Erie to Nyack. In 1865 the local Catholic community built a small mission chapel where Father John Quinn celebrated Mass once a month. Shortly thereafter they replaced it with a church named in honor of St. Ann which Father Quinn used for Mass for the first time on New Year's Day in 1870. That same year St. Ann's became a separate parish, although it continued to share the same pastor with St. John's Church in Piermont until 1885.[23]

Father Peter Prendergast, the pastor of St. Joseph's Church, Middletown, 1875-1888. A native of County Tipperary, he was one of seven brothers who became priests, one of whom was Archbishop Edmond Prendergast of Philadelphia.

The first St. Joseph's Church in Middletown, dedicated by Archbishop McCloskey on October 2, 1867

St. Joseph's Church in Middletown, dedicated by Bishop Patrick Lynch of Charleston on May 9, 1880

22 - *St. Joseph's Church Centennial Journal* (Middletown: St. Joseph's Church 1980), unpaginated.

23 - *St. Ann's Church, Nyack*, New York (Custombook, 1969), 4-9.

The invitation to the consecration of St. Peter's Church, Haverstraw, on October 22, 1899.

The Church of St. Peter, Haverstraw, constructed in the late 1860s and consecrated by Archbishop Corrigan on October 22, 1899.

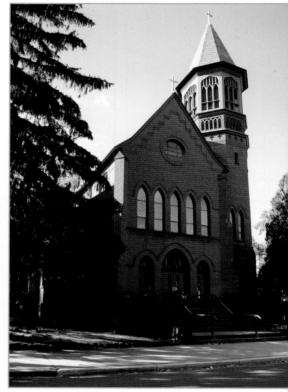

St. Ann's Church, Nyack, consecrated by Archbishop Corrigan on June 16, 1895. It was debt free at its opening thanks to the generosity of a wealthy parishioner, Marquise Helena de San Marzano.

In Blauvelt (or Blauveltsville, as it was commonly called) there was another Catholic community composed largely of German immigrants who had moved to Rockland County from *Kleindeutschland* in New York City. They preserved close ties with the clergy of St. Nicholas Church on East 2nd Street who occasionally celebrated Mass for them in private homes. A group of laymen headed by George M. Leidiger, were responsible for establishing the Church of St. Catherine of Alexandria in Blauveltsville, which was dedicated on January 17, 1869, although the first resident pastor was not appointed until the following year. The parish remained largely German well into the twentieth century. The first non-German pastor was not appointed until 1917.[24]

In Suffern at the western end of Rockland County Mass was first celebrated in a private home in 1865 by Father John Quinn, who traveled from Piermont four times a year, until St. Rose of Lima Church was established in 1868. George Suffern, the grandson of the founder of the village, donated the land where the first pastor, Father John Brogan, erected a small frame church that same year. At the turn of the century Thomas Fortune Ryan and his wife, Ida Barry Fortune, bought large tracts of land in the area and built a mansion on Montebello Road. They donated much of their property to religious communities and in 1903 built the present church in Suffern, which was renamed the Church of the Sacred Heart at the request of Mrs. Ryan.[25]

24 - *Saint Catherine of Alexandria*, 7-11.

25 - *Sacred Heart Church, Suffern, New York, 1868-1968* (Suffern: Church of the Sacred Heart, 1968), unpaginated.

Farther north in rural Sullivan County devout German Catholic farmers were responsible for the creation of the first Catholic church in that county. In the 1840s Solomon Royce, a real estate developer, actively recruited German farmers to settle in western Sullivan County. As the German immigrants stepped ashore from the ships at Castle Garden, they were given handbills in German advertising the rich farm lands that were available for them in Sullivan County. However, when they got there, what awaited them was not fertile fields but dense forests that they had to clear before they could even put a plow in the ground.

George M. Leidiger, one of the German Catholic immigrants who was responsible for the founding of St. Catherine's Church in Blauvelt in 1869.
Credit: *St. Catherine's Church*

Many of the German immigrants were Catholics from Bavaria who were visited by Father Raufeisen from Ellenville four times a year. He celebrated the first Mass in the county in 1843 near Jeffersonville in the home of Joseph Seibert, one of the lay leaders of the Catholic community. Seibert's house was so small that many who attended Mass had to stand outdoors even in the rain and snow. That same year another layman, Francis Breiner, donated land for a church and asked every parishioner to contribute lumber and labor to build it. They responded readily, and the result was the first Catholic church in Sullivan County. It was an unheated makeshift chapel, located two miles from Jeffersonville and dedicated to St. George, but often called "Breiner's Church."[26]

The Church of St. Catherine of Alexandria, Blauvelt, dedicated by Cardinal Cooke on October 6, 1968.

The Church of the Sacred Heart, Suffern, the gift of Mr. and Mrs. Thomas Fortune Ryan, in 1903.

A sketch of the Seibert Log Cabin where Mass was first celebrated in Sullivan County in 1843.
Credit: *Church of St. George and St. Francis, Jeffersonville.*

The Church of St. George and St. Francis, Jeffersonville, erected in 1914.

26 - Charles S. Hick, "Historical Sketch of St. George's Catholic Church, Jeffersonville, N.Y.," *Souvenir of the One Hundredth Anniversary of St. George's Church, Jeffersonville, N.Y.* (Jeffersonville: St. George's Church, 1943), 3-10.

Ten miles from Jeffersonville on winding dirt roads, there was another German Catholic farming community in Sullivan County at Obernburg which was named after the village in Bavaria from which many of the settlers came. Unhappy with the lack of a resident priest, they asked Archbishop Hughes for their own pastor. In 1854 Father Raffeiner responded on behalf of the archbishop and sent them Father Joseph Roesch, a thirty-year old Austrian priest. In the course of the next twenty-five years, Father Roesch founded St. Mary's Church in Obernburg as well as a tiny parochial school. His parish boundaries ran from Beaverkill to Narrowsburg and from Liberty to French Woods in Delaware County in the diocese of Albany. The parish records indicate that he baptized between 70 and 100 infants each year. His salary, originally $100 a year, was increased to $200, one-third of the standard pastor's salary in the diocese.

In Obernburg Father Roesch inherited a small chapel that had cost only $133.42 to build but still had a debt of $32.00. He replaced it in 1861 with a new church seating 150 people. The previous year a new church was also built in Jeffersonville, which was Father Roesch's responsibility, except for the years between 1863 and 1868, when it had a resident pastor, Father George J. Vaith. When Archbishop John McCloskey visited Jeffersonville on June 22, 1865, he blessed the new church and administered Confirmation to 105 people.

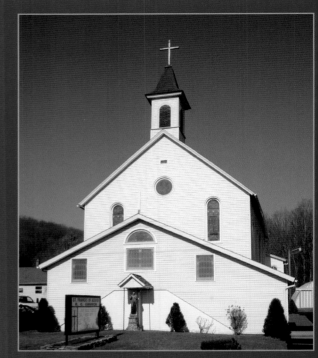

St. Francis of Assisi Church in Youngsville, which began as a mission of St. Georges's Church in Jeffersonville in 1909. The front of the church was extended and enclosed in 1980.

St. Francis Xavier Church in Narrowsburg, which began as a mission of St. Mary's in Obernburg in 1862.

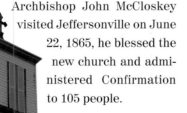

St. Mary's Church, Obernburg, which dates from 1861, in the little farming community named after the village in Bavaria from which many of the first settlers came.

In 1892 Archbishop Corrigan asked the Franciscan friars to take charge of Obernburg and Jeffersonville as well as St. Francis Xavier mission in Narrowsburg. The friars, who were well supplied with German-speaking priests as a result of Bismarck's persecution of the Catholic Church in Germany, readily agreed. It was the beginning of a pastoral ministry in western Sullivan County that has lasted for more than a century. By the 1950s from their seminary in Callicoon the Franciscans staffed three parishes and eight missions in Sullivan County.[27]

Obernburg remained a predominantly German-speaking Catholic community until the turn of the twentieth century. Father Bonaventure Jahn, O.F.M., the pastor from 1900 to 1907, refused to introduce English-language homilies because many of the parishioners had only a limited command of English. "By and by things will change here in the mountains," he said, "but for the present it would be at least imprudent to force the people to listen to English sermons of which many understand very little." A layman made the same comment about the congregation of the mission in Narrowsburg, asking Archbishop Corrigan for a German priest. In Obernburg, the first "Irish" pastor, Father Godfrey Doyle, O.F.M., was not appointed until 1934.[28]

By contrast St. George's Church in Jeffersonville had a mixed congregation of both German and Irish parishioners, many of whom worked in the local tanneries. In 1908 a mission of St. George's Church was established in Youngsville. A small frame church named in honor of St. Francis of Assisi was blessed by auxiliary bishop Thomas Cusack on October 13, 1909. In 1982 Cardinal John O'Connor changed the status of St. Francis of Assisi from mission to parish, although it continued to share the same pastor as St. George's Church. Today the parish is known officially as the Church of St. George and St. Francis.[29]

Staten Island

At the southern end of the diocese Staten Island got its first Catholic parish when St. Peter's Church in New Brighton was incorporated on September 24, 1839. The village had recently become a popular summer resort for wealthy residents of Manhattan. Today the mother church of thirty-seven parishes on Staten Isand, St. Peter's was the sole parish on the island for more than a decade. The first pastor, Father Ildefonso Medrano, a political refugee from Spain, was also the pastor

Sailing off Staten Island in the 1850s. Credit: *Archdiocese of New York*

27 - AANY, Celsus R. Wheeler, O.F.M., to John J. Maguire, August 1, 1958.

28 - AANY, Chares Koeferl to Corrigan, September 24, 1890. Doyle was really Irish, a native of Dublin. *St. Mary's Church 1854-2004* (Obernburg: St. Mary's Church, 2004), 1-8, 12-15.

29 - Ildefonso J. Gillogly, O.F.M., *Souvenir of the Thirtieth Anniversary of St. Francis of Assisi Church, Youngsville, N.Y.* (Youngsville: St. Francis Church, 1939).

in Perth Amboy, New Jersey. The congregation probably consisted of no more than 100 people who gathered for Mass in a former gun factory on Richmond Terrace. Due to the poverty of the Catholic community it took five years to build a small brick church that was first used on March 25, 1844, and was dedicated by Bishop Hughes on September 7, 1845.

Father Medrano and his successors at St. Peter's had one of the most dangerous pastoral assignments in the diocese because their duties included visiting the Quarantine Hospital. Located in Tompkinsville, the Quarantine was often filled with as many as 850 or 900 patients, many of them Catholics, who had been removed from incoming vessels because they were suffering from contagious diseases like "ship fever" (typhus). The Quarantine was particularly crowded with Catholics during the late 1840s and early 1850s and became the final destination of many victims of the Great Famine in Ireland. Father Patrick Murphy, the pastor of St. Peter's, died from "ship fever" on February 11, 1848, at the age of twenty-nine after visiting patients in the hospital.[30]

Not only the Quarantine Hospital, but Tomkinsville itself was pest hole of disease, as two local historians vividly described it. "Quarantined ships anchored in front of the hospital and the shore was constantly strewn with filth of every kind. The men working on infected ships, and those employed about the sick, were all the time in and out of the village and associating with the people everywhere. The consequence was that whatever contagious disease was in the quarantine soon found its way outside." In 1858 the exasperated residents of Tomkinsville took matters into their own hands and burned the hospital buildings to the ground.[31]

Father Patrick Murphy's successor as pastor of St. Peter's was his older brother, Father Mark Murphy. He began the expansion of the Church on Staten Island when he established missions in Rossville in 1848 and Port Richmond in 1853. In Rossville work began on St. Joseph's Church in 1848 and it was dedicated in1851, but it was not completed until January 1853. It was a modest-sized building, only 42 feet by 64 feet, built in a simple style that was called disparagingly Carpenter Gothic. It remained a mission of St. Peter's until 1852 and today is the oldest Catholic church building on Staten Island.

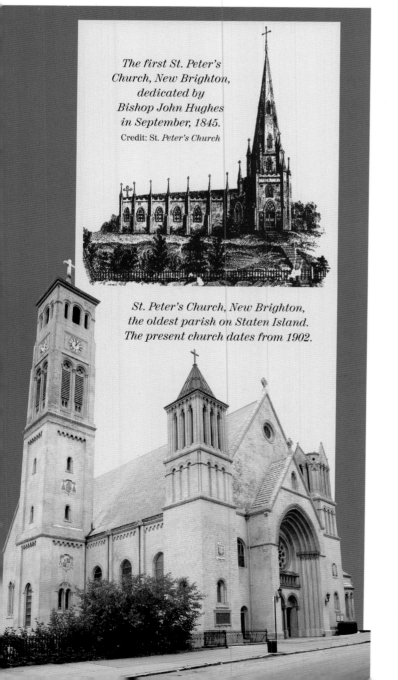

The first St. Peter's Church, New Brighton, dedicated by Bishop John Hughes in September, 1845.
Credit: St. Peter's Church

St. Peter's Church, New Brighton, the oldest parish on Staten Island. The present church dates from 1902.

30 - Cohalan, *Popular History,* 60.

31 - Charles W. Leng and William T. Davis, *Staten Island and Its People, 1609-1929* (New York: Lewis Publishing Company, 1930), I, 263

The Quarantine buildings in Tomkinsville in 1858 shortly before they were burned to the ground by local residents. Credit: *Archdiocese of New York*

That same year Staten Island got its second parish when John Hughes responded to a petition from a group of lay people for a church in Clifton (today's Rosebank). He sent them Father John Lewis, a native of France, who stepped off the ferry in Clifton on October 2, 1852, and lost no time in starting work on a small church. He broke ground for St. Mary's Church on November 4 and had it ready for the celebration of Midnight Mass at Christmas. The building also included a parochial school on the second floor, which consisted of a grand total of two classrooms, one for the boys and one

Father John Lewis, pastor of St. Mary's Church, Rosebank, 1852-1887.
Credit: *St. Mary's Church.*

for the girls. Father Lewis remained as pastor for the next thirty-five years. He built the present St. Mary's Church, which Archbishop Hughes dedicated on July 28, 1858, and opened the first free-standing parochial school on Staten Island in 1865. He also took over responsibility for St. Joseph's mission in Rossville from 1852 to 1855. The line of demarcation between St. Peter's and St. Mary's was the Richmond Turnpike (today's Victory Boulevard).[32]

Staten Island's third parish dates from November 22, 1855, when Father Francis Caro, an Italian Franciscan, was appointed the pastor of St. Joseph's in Rossville, where he remained for two-and-a-half years before moving on to other assignments upstate. Rossville owed its brief prominence to the Staten Island oystermen who collected their catch in Rossville and shipped it to market in New York City by ferry. It was never an affluent parish, and a half-century later the annual income was little more than $450.[33] Rossville relieved St. Peter's of the responsibility for the mission of St. Mary of the Assumption in Port Richmond until 1877 when St. Mary's became a separate parish. In the meantime, in 1862, Father John Barry, the third pastor of Rossville, began building a mission church in Richmond, the present St. Patrick's Church, which became an independent parish in 1884.

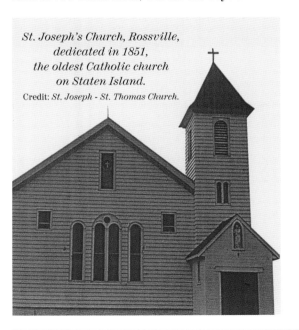

St. Joseph's Church, Rossville, dedicated in 1851, the oldest Catholic church on Staten Island.
Credit: *St. Joseph - St. Thomas Church.*

32 - Julia I. Martin, *The Ties That Bind: St. Mary's Roman Catholic Church, Rosebank, Staten Island* (Rosebank: St. Mary's Church, 2002), 6-14.

33 - AANY, Bernard McCrossan to Preston, March 17, 1901.

View of South Beach from Richmond Avenue in 1878. Credit: *Harper's New Monthly Magazine,* September, 1878

St. Mary's Church, Rosebank, built by Father John Lewis and dedicated by Archbishop Hughes on July 28, 1858.

The Church of St. Thomas the Apostle, Pleasant Plains, a mission of St. Joseph's Church, Rossville, opened in 1938 and destroyed by fire in 1983. Credit: *St. Joseph - St. Thomas Church*

The Church of St. Mary of the Assumption, Port Richmo[...] dedicated on May 4, 1884

In the twentieth century another pastor of St. Joseph's in Rossville, Father Thomas S. McGrath, opened a mission church in Pleasant Plains, St. Thomas the Apostle. It was first used for Midnight Mass in 1938. In a poor parish hard hit by the Depression, Father McGrath minimized expenses by using Belgian stone blocks that the WPA had discarded when they ripped up the old streetcar tracks. However, on March 20, 1983, a fire completely destroyed St. Thomas Church. The present church was begun in 1996 by Msgr. Peter G. Finn and dedicated by Cardinal O'Connor on March 28, 1998, giving St. Joseph-St. Thomas Parish the oldest and newest Catholic churches on Staten Island.[34]

In the nineteenth century population growth on Staten Island lagged behind the rest of the region. There were only 25,492 residents in 1860 despite the fact that the Staten Island Railway was in operation by that year from Clifton to Tottenville. In 1871 a committee of the state legislature blamed the slow development on poor ferry service and the popular belief that the island was infected with malaria. The situation began to improve in the 1880s and 1890s when the railroad was doubled-tracked, two branch lines were constructed, and the main line was extended to St. George where there was a direct connection with the Manhattan ferries.

---

34 - AANY, Florence Cohalan, unpublished history of St. Patrick's Church, Richmond, 1963. Julia I. Martin, *One Parish, Two Temples, St. Joseph-St. Thomas* (Rossville: St. Joseph-St. Thomas Church, 2001), 11-13, 31-33, 42, 46.

A Cathedral of Suitable Magnificence

John Hughes' most enduring physical monument is the cathedral that he gave his diocese. The new St. Patrick's Cathedral was meant to be a declaration in stone of the importance of the Catholic community in New

aying the foundations of St. Patrick's Cathedral.
Credit: *Archdiocese of New York*

York and also an expression of the civic pride of New York's Catholics. We intend "to erect a cathedral in the city of New York that may be worthy of our increasing numbers, intelligence and wealth as a religious community," the archbishop announced, and "a public architectural monument of the present and prospective greatness of this metropolis of the American continent."

The site between Fourth and Fifth Avenues from 50th Street to 51st Street, had been bought by the joint trustees of St. Peter's Church and Old St. Patrick's Cathedral for a cemetery in 1828, but the ground proved to be unsuitable for burials because it consisted of almost sold rock. In 1852 the trustees of the cathedral became the sole owners of the property when they bought out the trustees of St. Peter's Church. The following year Hughes began to discuss his plans with the James Renwick, the architect who had designed Grace Episcopal Church in 1843. Hughes also wanted William Rodrigue, his brother-in-law, associated with the planning, but it seems clear that James Renwick was the real designer of the building.

Rare view of the construction of St. Patrick's Cathedral before the addition of the Lady Chapel. Credit: *Archdiocese of New York*

*The interior of
St. Patrick's Cathedral
from the choir loft.*

*St. Patrick's Cathedral
as it appeared in 2007*

The original plans called for an even bigger building than the one that was erected. Other features of Renwick's plan were not eliminated from the blueprints, but were never constructed such as a 135-foot spire at the intersection of the nave and transept, twenty-four massive flying buttresses and a stone ceiling. The "temporary" plaster ceiling remains in place to this day.

The blessing of the cornerstone took place on August 15, 1858, before a large crowd of some 100,000 people, not all of them Catholics. A few weeks earlier, on July 14, 1858, Hughes sent a letter to about 140 wealthy Catholics asking each of them to subscribe $1,000 to the building fund. He reported at the blessing of the cornerstone that over 100 people had responded favorably to his request. Hughes originally thought that the cathedral could be completed within five years. The work on the foundation proceeded quickly during the first two years, but then the archbishop suspended construction on August 15, 1860, after he had spent all of the $73,000 that had been collected. Not all of the $1,000 subscribers made good on their pledge.[35]

John Hughes did not live to see the completion of his new cathedral, which was dedicated by his protégé and successor, John Cardinal McCloskey, on May 25, 1879. Nonetheless, it is really John Hughes' cathedral because he was the one who conceived it, planned it, raised the initial funds and began the construction despite the criticism that the project was too expensive and the site was too far from the center of the city. It remains to this day a tribute to the vision and determination of New York's most celebrated Catholic leader.[36]

New York Catholics and the Civil War

When the Confederate guns opened fire on Fort Sumter in Charleston harbor early in the morning of April 12, 1861, they unleashed a bloody Civil War that was to last for four years. Even before the outbreak of hostilities, however, it appeared that the election of President Abraham Lincoln the previous November was likely to strain the bonds between New York City and Washington to the breaking point. The city was a Democratic stronghold where many influential businessmen feared that Lincoln's resistance to Southern demands would jeopardize their profitable commercial ties with the South. At one point Mayor Fernando Wood even floated the idea that the city should consider seceding from the state to protect its economic interests. However, as one Southern state after another announced its secession, New Yorkers rallied behind President Lincoln. On February 20, 1861, a huge crowd that may have numbered as many as 250,000 people gathered in Union Square to demonstrate their commitment to the preservation of the Union.

During the course of the war, the Empire State contributed more than a half-million men to the Union army, more than any other state. Like most wars, the Civil War was "a rich man's war and a poor man's fight." While the average soldier was paid thirteen dollars a month and some 50,000 New Yorkers died on the battlefields, several hundred fortunate New Yorkers became millionaires and made huge profits from wartime contracts or even from trading with the enemy. In the opinion of two knowledgeable historians of the city, "New York's upper classes made money in

---

35 - Thomas G. Young, *A New World Rising: The Story of St. Patrick's Cathedral* (New York: Something More Publications, 2006), 23-26.

36 - Margaret Carthy, O.S.U., *A Cathedral of Suitable Magnificence* (Wilmington, De.: Michael Glazier, 1984), 25-35.

quantities never before seen or even imagined." According to them in 1863 the richest one percent of New Yorkers accounted for about sixty-one percent of the city's wealth.[37]

One New York military unit that saw action in numerous Civil War engagements was the "Fighting Sixty-Ninth" Regiment, led by the Irish-born Colonel Michael Corcoran. The ranks of the Sixty-Ninth Regiment were filled largely with Irish-Americans from New York City. In October 1860 Corcoran and the regiment had endeared themselves to New York's Irish Catholics when they refused to turn out for the civic reception in honor of the Prince of Wales (the future Edward VII). On April 23, 1861, Archbishop Hughes blessed the regiment at St. Patrick's Old Cathedral before they marched off to take part in the first battle of Bull Run. Later that year Thomas Francis Meagher, another Irish political exile, organized an Irish Brigade.

As the chief spiritual leader of New York's Catholics, Hughes voiced strong support for the war. He flew the Stars and Stripes from the cathedral and urged Catholics to back the war effort. In May 1861 he told General Winfield Scott, the commanding general of the United States Army, "I cannot do much for war. But I am willing to do all in my power for humanity and the alleviation of the horrors of war." He offered Scott the services of a dozen chaplains and 50 to 100 women religious, either Sisters of Charity or Sisters of Mercy "like those who toiled in the Crimea." He assured Scott that, if his offer were accepted, the priests and religious "will have their bags packed and be on the road within two hours.[38]

One of the priests who volunteered to serve as a chaplain with the Sixty-Ninth Regiment was Father Thomas Mooney, the pastor of St. Brigid's Church in Manhattan. His patriotism outstripped his judgment on one occasion when he solemnly baptized a cannon. In an accompanying homily, he noted that babies sometimes cried at baptism when they got water in their eyes. However, "on this occasion," Mooney observed, "this noble son of a great father has his mouth wide open, evidently indicating that he is anxious to speak, which I have no doubt he will soon do, in a thundering voice, to the joy of his friends and the terror of his enemies." When Hughes heard of the incident, he immediately recalled Mooney to New York. "Your inauguration of a ceremony unknown to the Church, viz., the blessing of a cannon, was sufficiently bad," Hughes told him, "but your remarks on that occasion are infinitely worse."[39]

Like most Northern Catholics, Hughes supported the war as a struggle to preserve the Union, but not as a crusade against slavery. Privately he warned Secretary of War Simon Cameron in October 1861 that, if Catholics were asked "to fight for the abolition of slavery, then indeed, they will turn away in disgust from the discharge of what would otherwise be a patriotic duty." He thought that President Lincoln committed a major mistake when he issued the Emancipation Proclamation on January 1, 1863, freeing the slaves in the Confederate states.[40]

Hughes' lack of sympathy for the plight of African Americans reflected the attitude of most Irish-Americans. One reason for their antipathy was fear that freed slaves would compete with them for the same low-paying jobs. Another reason was that many of the leading abolitionists

---

37 - Burrows and Wallace, *Gotham*, 877.

38 - AANY, A-6, Hughes to Scott, May 7, 1861.

39 - AANY, A-5, Hughes to Mooney, July 3, 1861. Frank Moore, *The Civil War in Song and Story* (New York: Colliers, 1889), 217.

40 - Hassard, *Hughes*, 437.

The Departure of the 69th Regiment from New York after the blessing of the colors in St. Patrick's Old Cathedral by Archbishop John Hughes on April 23, 1861. Credit: *Archdiocese of New York*

were anti-Catholic bigots, who made no secret of the fact that they regarded the Catholic hierarchy of the North and the slave-owning oligarchy of the South as the two biggest threats to American democracy.

However, it is hard to avoid the conclusion that still another reason for Catholic opposition to emancipation was the deep-seated racism of many Irish-American Catholics, even wealthy Catholics who had no reason to fear black competition for their jobs. Two of the leading Catholic journalists in New York City, James Mullaly and James McMaster (who was Scottish,

Charles O'Conor, a prominent Catholic layman and an ardent defender of slavery.

not Irish), were outspoken opponents of emancipation. McMaster was even imprisoned for a brief period because of his opposition to the war. Charles O'Conor, a leading Catholic layman and Hughes' lawyer, took pride in prosecuting runway slaves under the notorious Fugitive Slave Law of 1850. He declared in a speech in December 1859: "I insist that negro slavery is not unjust. It is not unjust; it is just, wise and beneficent." Harriet Thompson, an African American Catholic in New York complained to Pope Pius IX that Hughes himself had such a strong aversion to black people that he would not allow them to come near him.[41]

41- *A Speech by Charles O'Conor at the Union Meeting at the Academy of Music, New York City, December 19, 1859;* Harriet Thompson to Pius IX, October 29, 1853, in Cyprian Davis, O.S.B., *The History of Black Catholics in the United States* (New York: Crossroad, 1990), 96.

In the fall of 1861 Archbishop Hughes went to France at the request of his old friend William Seward, now the secretary of state, to present the Union case to the Emperor Napoleon III. Hughes received a cool reception in Paris from the American ambassador who regarded him as an interloper. He finally got a brief interview with the emperor on Christmas Eve. However, Napoleon politely rejected Hughes' request that France should act as a mediator between Great Britain and the United States in their dispute over the *Trent* affair, when the American navy forcibly removed Confederate emissaries from a British ship on the high seas.

The New York Draft Riots

John Hughes' final public appearance took place during the draft riots of July 1863. The cause of the riots was a new draft law, passed by Congress the previous March that went into effect on Saturday, July 11. It favored the rich at the expense of the poor because a draftee could obtain an exemption by paying $300 or hiring a substitute to take his place. The reaction in New York City was four days of bloody riots, beginning on Monday, July 13, that left 119 people dead. Orestes Brownson estimated that nearly nine-tenths of the rioters were Irish immigrants who blamed African Americans for the war. They killed any African Americans they happened to meet in the streets and even burned the Colored Orphan Asylum to the ground.[42]

Archbishop Hughes issued two public appeals, pleading with the rioters to return to their homes. At the request of Governor Horatio Seymour, the archbishop addressed a crowd of some 5,000 people from the balcony of his house at Madison Avenue and 36th Street on July 17. Horace Greeley, who blamed the Irish Catholics for the riots, taunted Hughes by saying that the

shepherd was about to summon the wolves, "a congregation of abandoned and vicious wretches."

It was not the wolves, but the law-abiding Catholics who showed up to hear him. The archbishop was a dying man who had been unable to celebrate Mass for the previous three months. He apologized for addressing his listeners seated, but assured them that his lungs were better than his legs. In fact his voice was so weak that few were able to hear him, and his words had little effect on ending the violence. It required the intervention of 6,000 troops dispatched from General Meade's army at Gettysburg to quell the worst urban riots in American history to that date. The troops began arriving in New York City on July 15. The violence had such a searing impact that contemporary witnesses and even reputable historians many years later assumed that the death toll was in the thousands.[43]

During the height of the riots several New York priests risked their life to quell the violence. Father Arthur Donnelly, the pastor of St. Michael's Church, prevented a mob from setting fire to a Presbyterian church at the corner of Ninth Avenue and 31st Street. Many of the rioters were probably his parishioners and he dared them to set fire to his church first. In Yorkville Father William Quarter, the pastor of St. Lawrence O'Toole, pacified a crowd of several hundred people who wanted to burn down a house on Prospect Hill (today's Carnegie Hill). Father William Clowry, the pastor of St. Gabriel's Church, was less successful. He was summoned to give the last rites to Colonel Henry O'Brien, the commanding officer of the Eleventh Regiment of the New York State Volunteers. The rioters allowed the priest to anoint him, and then finished him off and dragged his body through the streets as soon as Father Clowry had left.[44]

---

42 - *Brownson's Quarterly Review*, October 1863, 386.

43 - *New York Herald*, July 17, 18, 1863.

44 - Browne, *Parish of St. Michael*, 7; *New York Herald*, July 15, 16, 1863. Greeley also blamed Hughes for the riots because he had earlier advocated conscription. Hughes replied lamely that he favored only "voluntary" conscription.

Charge of the police in front of the office of Horace Greeley's New York Tribune.
Credit: *Harper's Weekly,* August 1, 1863

Lynching an African American in Clarkson Street.
Credit: *Harper's Weekly,* August 1, 1863

Ruins of the Provost-Marshal's Office where the draft records were kept.
Credit: *Harper's Weekly,* August 1, 1863

John Hughes died six months after the draft riots, on January 3, 1864, from kidney failure and general debility. The funeral Mass took place in the cathedral on January 7, which was the twenty-sixth anniversary of his episcopal ordination in the same sanctuary. He was buried in one of the vaults beneath the cathedral and later his remains were transferred to the new cathedral that he had started but did not live to see completed.

Dragging Colonel O'Brien's body through the streets.
Credit: *Harper's Weekly,* August 1, 1863

The Legacy of John Hughes

If John Hughes is the single most important figure in the history of the Catholic Church in New York, he was also a bundle of contradictions. An Irish immigrant who gloried in his humble origins, he also created Welsh ancestors for himself to enhance his pedigree. He adamantly denied that he ever involved himself in politics even as he organized his own political party. An ardent admirer of American democracy, he voted only once in his life, for Henry Clay in the presidential election of 1832. A tenacious champion of the rights of his fellow Irish immigrants, he took little interest in the members of his flock who did not share his Celtic blood. He also had an amazing facility, not confined to him by any means, of inventing or denying reality as it suited the purposes of his rhetoric. His spiritual life is a blank for even his most sympathetic biographers.

His lifestyle was equally contradictory. Although he added a fourth floor to his residence to house his personal library of 8,000 to 10,000 volumes, he rarely read a book. Instead he stayed up late into the early hours of the morning reading newspapers, often dashing off lengthy letters to the editor when an article displeased him. In one such letter he used the personal pronoun 361 times. A stickler for ecclesiastical discipline, he lived apart from his clergy for the last decade of his life in his own residence with his sister and brother-in-law and their family. He rose late every morning, ate little during the day, shunned social occasions, and never took any exercise. At his office on Mulberry Street he quickly tired of the routine of daily business and perched himself on a stool in the adjoining office of his priest secretary, James Roosevelt Bayley, telling stories by the hour. "Most of the conversation," said Bayley, "as you may well suppose, was on one side."

The Lion in Winter:
John Hughes in his later years.
Credit: *Archdiocese of New York*

For thirty years John Hughes hardly ever committed to paper the text of a sermon or speech so that some of his best public addresses were never recorded unless someone in the audience happened to jot them down as they were delivered. In his impromptu remarks he could be extremely witty. On one occasion, when he was coming through customs in Liverpool, the customs agent charged him duty on two vials of snuff. "A tribute to Her Majesty," he said sarcastically. Hughes replied: "I would like to give her a pinch."

His devoted lay secretary, John Hassard, attributed the lack of order in his life to his haphazard education. "He had no fixed time for anything," said Hassard. "He lacked all idea of order or system. He never followed a regular plan of action and never laid out his work in advance. All his great achievements, such as the overthrow of the trustee system or the destruction of the Public School Society, originated by accident." Hughes' outstanding personal characteristic was his unbounded self-confidence. A fellow passenger on the ship that brought him back to America in the spring of 1862 commented on how "he stood among the passengers as one born to command. He seemed the owner of the vessel," said this observer, "and he looked as if he could command the very waves."[45]

John R.G. Hassard, John Hughes' lay secretary and biographer and later a distinguished music critic in New York City.

John Hughes was a controversial figure in his own lifetime, and he remains a controversial figure today as historians debate his contribution to American Catholicism. Some consider him an unfortunate choice for the first archbishop of New York because he was a strong-minded individual who rarely consulted the clergy or laity and brooked no interference from them. "In New York no one had to ask who ruled the church," said Jay Dolan. "John Hughes was boss... He ruled the Church like an Irish chieftain." Andrew Greeley deplored "his posture of pugnacious militancy vis-à-vis non-Catholics in American society." David J. O'Brien thought that Hughes' belligerence backfired because it intensified the Nativist opposition that he tried to combat, and he faulted Hughes for encouraging Catholics to retreat into their own cultural ghetto rather than participate in the civic affairs of the community.

John Tracy Ellis offered a more favorable assessment. While Ellis deplored Hughes' bluster and lack of tact, and he admitted that Hughes was "not what one would call a likeable character," he insisted on the necessity of judging him in the context of his own time. Writing in 1966, Ellis pointed out that "the Protestantism of the 1840s, or for that matter the Protestantism of the United States down almost to the present decade, was in no sense the ecumenical-minded, irenic Protestantism [that] has so radically altered its tone with regard to Catholicism in recent years..." For that reason, said Ellis, "there were times when [Hughes'] very aggressiveness was about the only approach that would serve the end that he was seeking, viz., justice for his people.[46]

John Hughes' self-definition of his role as bishop and chief gave the Church in New York both the advantages and disadvantages of episcopal autocracy. It enabled him to speak as the unchallenged leader of the New York Catholic community, which he did with determination and courage on a variety of public issues as he confronted an entrenched Protestant elite that viewed the growth of Catholicism with alarm and disdain. On the other had, his voice was so powerful that it drowned out all anthems but his own, depriving the Catholic community of the wisdom and insight that might have been derived from a more collegial and collaborative style of leadership.

45 - Hassard, *Hughes*, 333; Brann, Hughes, 175.

46 - Dolan, *Immigrant Church*, 164-165; Andrew M. Greeley, *The Catholic Experience* (Garden City: Doubleday, 1967), 124; David J. O'Brien, "American Catholicism and the Diaspora," *Cross Currents 16* (summer 1966): 307-322. ACUA, John Tracy Ellis Papers, Ellis to David O'Brien, October 8, 1966

9

The Gilded Age and the New Immigration

Wall Street in 1892, the symbol of American capitalism in the Gilded Age

During the four decades after the end of the Civil War the United States became the leading industrial power in the world. As the economy boomed, a favored few made huge fortunes in railroads, mining, manufacturing, shipping, banking, and related enterprises. The rich found it relatively easy to become even richer in a day when there was neither a minimum wage nor an income tax nor inheritance taxes. "The only hard step in building up my fortune was the first step," said John Jacob Astor. "After that it was easy." By 1890 there were over 4,000 millionaires in the nation, although few of them could match the fortunes of magnates like Cornelius Vanderbilt, Andrew Carnegie, John D. Rockefeller and J. Pierpont Morgan. Mark Twain and Charles Dudley Warner called it the Gilded Age in contrast to a genuinely Golden Age and as a critique of the *nouveaux riches* whose wealth sometimes outstripped their taste.

Nowhere in America was the impact of the Gilded Age more evident than in New York City. Between 1860 and 1900 the population of the city almost quadrupled from 813,000 to 3,473,000 with the creation in 1898 of Greater New York that included not only Manhattan, but also the Bronx, Brooklyn, Queens and Staten Island. By 1900 New York City had more people than all but six states, was twice as large as Chicago, and was home to one-quarter of the nation's millionaires. It was also the headquarters of two-thirds of America's largest corporations. In 1901 its factories produced more than one billion dollars worth of goods, products that ran the gamut from the clipper ships of the East River shipyards to Duncan Phyfe furniture to Henry Steinway's pianos to jewelry, clothes, books, even cigars. Thirsty New Yorkers could find solace in the knowledge that their city's breweries produced more of the poor man's champagne than Chicago, Milwaukee and St. Louis combined.

Commodore Cornelius Vanderbilt created the New York Central Railroad and left a fortune of over $100 million at his death in 1877.

The rear of the Cornelius Vanderbilt mansion on Fifth Avenue.
Credit: *Harper's Weekly,* September 1863

The Brooklyn Bridge from the Brooklyn side of the East River.
Credit: *Yvon Meyer*

On May 24, 1883, proud New Yorkers gathered to witness the inauguration of one of the great engineering marvels of the century, the opening of the Brooklyn Bridge, the longest suspension bridge in the world, which linked the first and third largest cities in the country. Unfortunately the inaugural date also happened to be Queen Victoria's birthday, a coincidence that was not appreciated by the city's Irish Catholics who nearly rioted to show their displeasure. Three years later New York harbor received its most famous landmark and tourist attraction, the Statue of Liberty, a gift of the French republic.

In the 1870s and 1880s New York City acquired some of its most prominent public buildings. Commodore Vanderbilt's Grand Central Station with its ninety-foot high train shed began operations in 1871. In 1874 the first Madison Square Garden was opened, and the following year Boss Tweed's courthouse was completed at a cost of $13 million. A monument to municipal corruption, it cost twice as much as the acquisition of Alaska seven years earlier. The American Museum of Natural History opened its doors on Central Park West in 1877. Three years later the Metropolitan Museum of Art moved to new quarters on the east side of Central Park on Fifth Avenue and 82nd Street, and the

Metropolitan Opera House staged its first production in 1883. On May 25, 1879, New York's Catholics made their own contribution to the city's architectural repertoire when they dedicated the new St. Patrick's Cathedral, a potent symbol of the Irish Catholic presence in New York City.

During America's Gilded Age a few people made huge fortunes but many others lived in dire poverty, a contrast that was clearly evident in New York City. Upper Fifth Avenue became known as Millionaires' Row as the Vanderbilts, Whitneys, Astors and others vied with one another in erecting ever more elaborate reproductions of Loire Valley chateaux. A few miles away, however, on the Lower East Side of Manhattan, the mansions of the wealthy gave way to squalid and unsanitary tenement houses. In that part of the city newly arrived immigrants were crowded together under such appallingly inhumane conditions that the population density reached 640,000 people per square mile, a figure unmatched even in the worst slums of Calcutta.

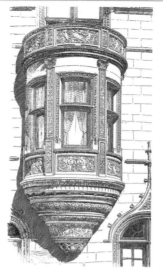

The bay window in the mansion of William K. Vanderbilt on 52nd Street.
Credit: *Harper's New Monthly Magazine,* September 1863

The New Immigration

Immigration had built the Catholic Church in New York and it continued to do so throughout the Gilded Age. The only variable was the country of origin of the immigrants. Prior to the Civil War the overwhelming majority of the Catholic immigrants had been either Irish or German. Both ethnic groups continued to come to the United States in large numbers, and for several decades after the end of the Civil War German immigration to the United States outstripped all others. Irish immigration also picked up after 1880, spurred by agrarian distress at home especially in the West of Ireland, although not on the same scale as during the Great Famine.

As late as 1890 a number of Irish bishops appealed to Archbishop Corrigan for assistance. In thanking Msgr. Preston for the help sent from New York, John Lister, the bishop of Achonry, claimed that his diocese was the poorest in Ireland. "Within my jurisdiction," he said, "there

The opening of the Brooklyn Bridge in 1883 relieved some of the overcrowding on the Fulton Street Ferry.
Credit: *Archdiocese of New York*

is not a single Catholic of means." He mentioned that the previous year 17,000 men went to England at harvest time, leaving the women and children to dig up the potatoes in the fields. "This is how the rents are earned in Sligo," he explained.[1]

The Irish continued to set the tone of New York Catholicism, if only by their sheer numbers, as newly arrived Irish immigrants reinforced the bonds between Irish-Americans and their homeland. The new Irish Catholic immigrants were likely to be better instructed in their religion and more faithful in practicing it as a result of the Devotional Revolution in Ireland. Many of the new parishes established in the archdiocese of New York during the Gilded Age were Irish in fact, if not in name. Most of the vocations to the priesthood and religious life also came from the Irish-Americans. The roster of the diocesan seminary was overwhelmingly Irish well into the twentieth century, and even religious communities like the Christian Brothers and the Redemptorists that were French or German in origin became largely Irish in composition as a result of the influx of Irish-American vocations. The Jesuits at Fordham were transformed from a French to an Irish community within two decades. The first three postulants to join Mother Cabrini's Missionary Sisters of the Sacred Heart in 1889 were Elizabeth Garvey, Loretta Desmond and Mary McDermott.[2]

The card that the St. Raphaelsverein distributed to German Immigrants to America directing them to Father Frederic Wayrich on Ellis Island and to the Leo House at 6 State Street.

Fatherland could count on the assistance of the St. Raphael's Society, the local branch of the St. Raphaelsverein, a Catholic immigrant aid society founded in Germany in 1871. Representatives of the society met the immigrants at Ellis Island, steered them clear of the swindlers and pickpockets who were waiting to fleece them when they landed at the Battery, and helped them to secure transportation to their destinations. In 1889, the St. Raphael's Society established the Leo House at 6 State Street, a shelter where German Catholic immigrants could find safe and inexpensive lodging.

In Manhattan, as the center of the German population shifted north from the Lower East Side to Yorkville, St. Joseph's Church on East 87th Street replaced the Church of the Most Holy Redeemer as the unofficial German cathedral. In a sense Most Holy Redeemer followed the German migration north. Yorkville's German Catholics first worshipped in the chapel of the German Catholic Orphan Asylum at York Avenue and 89th Street that had been established by the Redemptorists at Most Holy Redeemer and was operated by the School Sisters of Notre Dame. They got their own church in 1873 when the Jesuits at St. Lawrence O'Toole sent them Father Joseph Durthaller, S.J., to begin St. Joseph's Church.

The Waning of Kleindeutschland

German-speaking Catholics continued to constitute a sizeable proportion of the New York Catholic community throughout the Gilded Age. After 1883 newly arrived immigrants from the

In the agreement that Archbishop McCloskey made with the Jesuits, he required them always to provide a German-speaking priest for the church, which he dedicated on April 26, 1874. In 1888 the diocesan clergy took over the parish from the Jesuits. Father Anthony Lammel,

1 - AANY, C-28, Lister to Thomas Preston, January 2, 1891.

2 - Mary Louise Sullivan, M.S.C., *Mother Cabrini "Italian Immigrant of the Century"* (New York: Center for Migration Studies, 1992), 103.

the first diocesan pastor, replaced the original church with the present building, which was dedicated by Archbishop Corrigan on November 3, 1895. Designed by William Schickel, it was an imposing stone building, although not built on the same grand scale as Most Holy Redeemer.[3]

In the Bronx Melrose remained a predominantly German area until the turn of the century. There was a German corridor that extended north of Melrose along both sides of Third Avenue through Morrisania to Tremont. It was dotted

Father Joseph Durthaller, S.J., the first pastor of St. Joseph's Church, Yorkville.

with small red-brick Lutheran churches and German bakeries, butcher shops and breweries. In 1873 Archbishop McCloskey established St. Joseph's Church on Washington Avenue near 177th Street for the German Catholics in Tremont and the surrounding areas. In 1891 Archbishop Corrigan invited Benedictine monks at St. John's Abbey in Collegeville, Minnesota, to start a second German parish in Melrose, which they named in honor of their fellow Benedictine, St. Anselm, the eleventh-century Archbishop of Canterbury.

The German Catholic Orphan Asylum at the corner of East 89th Street and Avenue A (York Avenue).

3 - AANY, Memorandum of John McCloskey, February 12, 1873; *St. Joseph's Yorkville 125th Anniversary* (New York: St. Joseph's Church, 1998), 9-13.

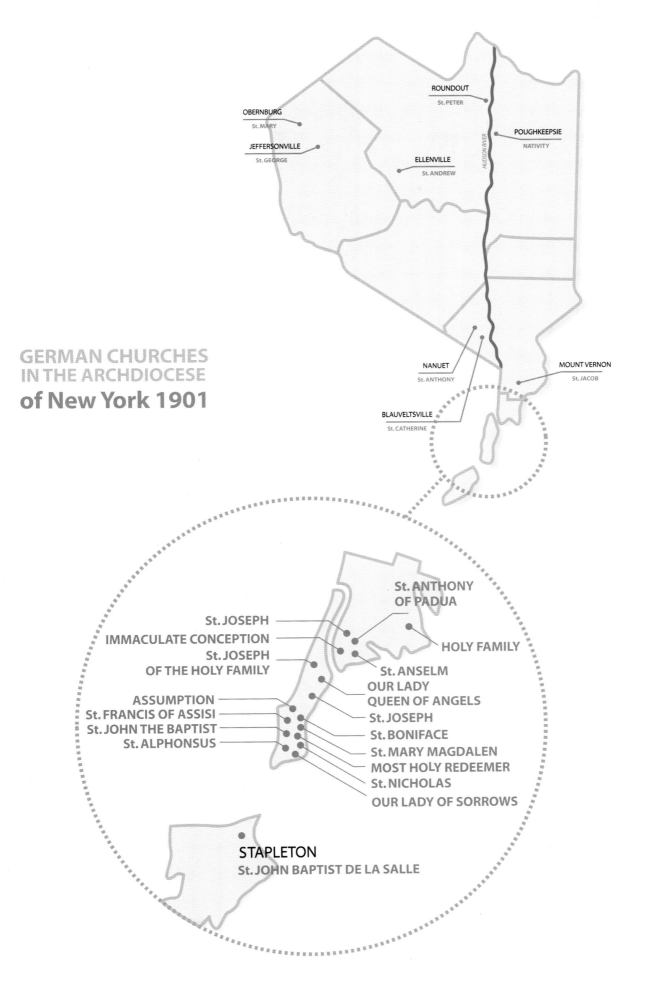

**GERMAN CHURCHES
IN THE ARCHDIOCESE
of New York 1901**

OBERNBURG
St. MARY

JEFFERSONVILLE
St. GEORGE

ROUNDOUT
St. PETER

ELLENVILLE
St. ANDREW

POUGHKEEPSIE
NATIVITY

HUDSON RIVER

NANUET
St. ANTHONY

MOUNT VERNON
St. JACOB

BLAUVELTSVILLE
St. CATHERINE

St. ANTHONY
OF PADUA

St. JOSEPH

IMMACULATE CONCEPTION

St. JOSEPH
OF THE HOLY FAMILY

HOLY FAMILY

St. ANSELM

OUR LADY
QUEEN OF ANGELS

ASSUMPTION

St. FRANCIS OF ASSISI

St. JOHN THE BAPTIST

St. ALPHONSUS

St. JOSEPH

St. BONIFACE

St. MARY MAGDALEN

MOST HOLY REDEEMER

St. NICHOLAS

OUR LADY OF SORROWS

STAPLETON
St. JOHN BAPTIST DE LA SALLE

Old prints of churches often featured steeples that were never built. St. Joseph's Church actually had an imposing steeple that added the finishing touch to the already impressive building.

The first Church of St. Joseph in Tremont, on Washington Avenue near 177th Street.

St. Joseph's Church, Tremont, built in 1902.

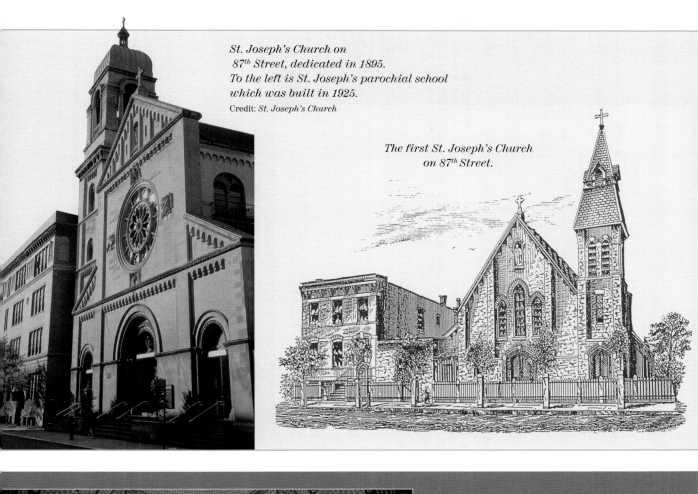

St. Joseph's Church on 87th Street, dedicated in 1895. To the left is St. Joseph's parochial school which was built in 1925.
Credit: *St. Joseph's Church*

The first St. Joseph's Church on 87th Street.

The Church of St. Anselm, erected in 1917. Founded by Benedictine monks in 1891 to serve the German Catholics of Melrose, it is now staffed by Augustinian Recollects for a largely Hispanic congregation.

The richly decorated interior of the Church of St. Anselm.

In Unionport in the East Bronx another community of German Catholics got their own parish with the founding of Holy Family Church in 1896. The petition that a group of laymen sent to Archbishop Corrigan was similar to many that he recived in those years. "The number of Catholics" they told him, "are exceedingly anxious that a church be erected here where they are so that their children might worship God as they have been taught to worship Him by their fathers." Farther north the first Catholic church was established in Mount Vernon thanks to efforts of the German Catholics who founded St. Jacob's Church in 1871. They got a permanent pastor two years later with the arrival of Father Joseph Albinger. This German national parish became largely Irish and Italian by 1910 when the name was changed to Our Lady of Victory. Since the 1960s it has ministered to the growing Portuguese community in Mount Vernon and in 2002 was entrusted to the Scalabrinian Fathers.[4]

In 1894 the German Catholic Central Verein, the most important German Catholic organization in the United States, held its annual convention in New York City in the basement of Most Holy Redeemer Church. Archbishop Corrigan got a warm reception when he defended the right of German-Americans to preserve their language. "No bishop in the United States ever appoints a German pastor but he feels sure that in due time a schoolhouse will be erected," he told the delegates. "It is said that this is done to perpetuate the language. Even if this is so," he added, "there is no harm in it. If a man uses both languages, is there any sin or shame in it?"[5]

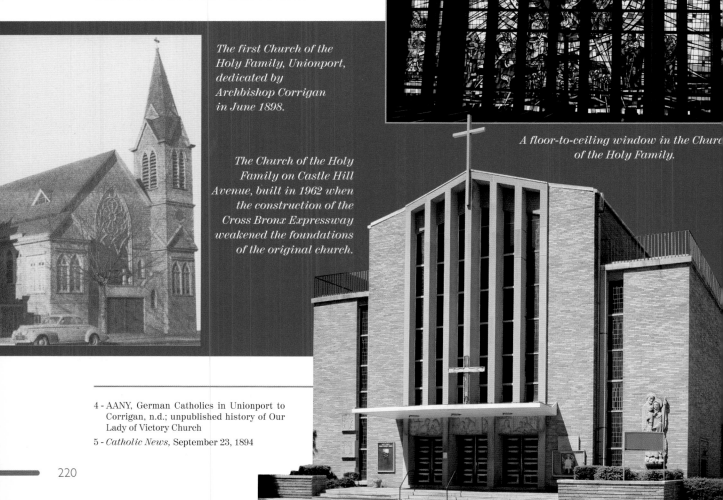

The first Church of the Holy Family, Unionport, dedicated by Archbishop Corrigan in June 1898.

The Church of the Holy Family on Castle Hill Avenue, built in 1962 when the construction of the Cross Bronx Expressway weakened the foundations of the original church.

A floor-to-ceiling window in the Church of the Holy Family.

4 - AANY, German Catholics in Unionport to Corrigan, n.d.; unpublished history of Our Lady of Victory Church
5 - *Catholic News,* September 23, 1894

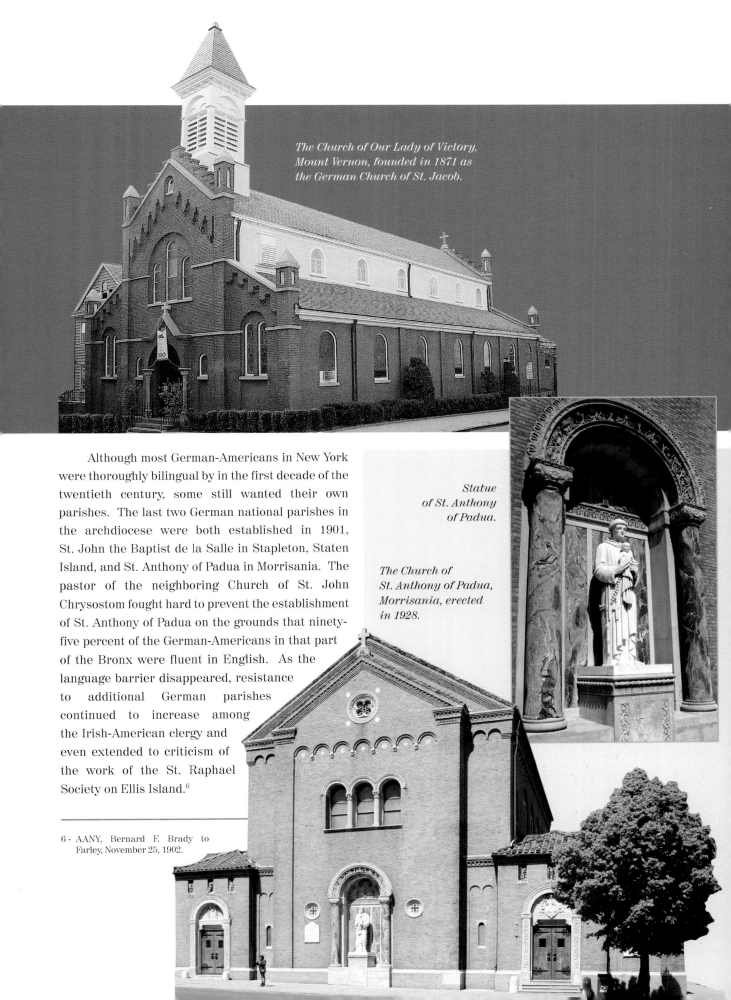

The Church of Our Lady of Victory, Mount Vernon, founded in 1871 as the German Church of St. Jacob.

Although most German-Americans in New York were thoroughly bilingual by in the first decade of the twentieth century, some still wanted their own parishes. The last two German national parishes in the archdiocese were both established in 1901, St. John the Baptist de la Salle in Stapleton, Staten Island, and St. Anthony of Padua in Morrisania. The pastor of the neighboring Church of St. John Chrysostom fought hard to prevent the establishment of St. Anthony of Padua on the grounds that ninety-five percent of the German-Americans in that part of the Bronx were fluent in English. As the language barrier disappeared, resistance to additional German parishes continued to increase among the Irish-American clergy and even extended to criticism of the work of the St. Raphael Society on Ellis Island.[6]

Statue of St. Anthony of Padua.

The Church of St. Anthony of Padua, Morrisania, erected in 1928.

6 - AANY, Bernard F. Brady to Farley, November 25, 1902.

Father Joseph Kirchofer, pastor of St. John the Baptist de la Salle, 1917-1941.

The Church of St. John Baptist de la Salle, Stapleton, founded in 1901 and scheduled to be closed in 2007.

Even as these two new parishes were founded, other German national parishes were either in decline or had ceased to be exclusively German. A young German-American curate in St. Joseph's, Yorkville, seemed to believe that he had been born out of due season. He lamented that St. Joseph's in Tremont now had an Irish-American pastor, most of the parishioners at St. Joseph's on West 125th Street were no longer German, and the Church of the Assumption on West 49th Street was in dire financial straits. With Wagnerian histrionics he warned Archbishop Corrigan of the impending *Götterdämmerung.* "If we are destined to die out" he said, "let us die at this moment, for it is a terrible thing to see death continually before our eyes and the downfall of our race, and what is more the loss of its souls."[7]

Not all pastors of German parishes shared this point of view. Father Joseph Kirchofer became pastor of St. John Baptist de la Salle in Stapleton in October 1917, six months after the United States entered World War I. He announced to his startled parishioners that he was not a German, but a native of Alsace who looked forward to an Allied victory and France's recovery of the lost provinces of Alsace and Lorraine from the Kaiser's Germany. Although he was fluent in German, Kirchofer refused to use that language in the pulpit. A notably eccentric man who remained pastor of St. John Baptist de la Salle for twenty-four years, Kirchofer maintained a mini-zoo in the basement of the church with a donkey, cow, ducks, sheep and goats so that he could stage a "living" nativity scene at Christmas.[8]

The Italians in New York

In the mid-1880s a marked change took place in the character of European immigration to the United States as the tide shifted from Northern and Western Europe to Southern and Eastern Europe. This "New Immigration," as historians call it, brought to America for the first time large numbers of Italians, Greeks, Slavs and other Eastern Europeans, including many Jews from Czarist Russia. Not all of the new immigrants were Catholic by any means, but many of them were Catholics, and their presence posed a daunting pastoral problem to the American bishops as they attempted to provide them with adequate spiritual care. The preferred response of the bishops was to continue the practice that had worked well with the earlier wave of German immigrants, the creation of national parishes for every ethnic group.

Although New York harbor was the gateway to America for the great majority of European immigrants in the late nineteenth century, the Catholic population of the archdiocese of New York never became as ethnically diversified as

7 - AANY, John Weber to Corrigan, December 6, 1895.

8 - *1900-2000: Church of St. John the Baptist de la Salle* (New York: Church of St. John Baptist de la Salle, 2000), unpaginated.

The Statue of Liberty, a gift of the French Republic, dedicated on October 28, 1886. Credit: *John A. Boehning*

that of Chicago, Milwaukee or Cleveland. Most of the millions of immigrants who poured through Ellis Island (which replaced Castle Garden as the immigration reception center in 1892) quickly scattered throughout the United States. The exception was the Italians. The great majority of them settled in New York, New Jersey, Pennsylvania and Southern New England.

In 1880 there were only 12,223 Italians in New York City. In 1900 they numbered 225,024, and ten years later their numbers had doubled to 554,449. Not since the days of the Great Famine in Ireland had so many Catholic immigrants from one country descended upon New York in such a short period of time. Many settled across the East River in the diocese of Brooklyn, but Bishop Farley's estimate of 300,000 Italians in the archdiocese of New York in 1898 seems reasonably accurate.[9] This massive influx of hundreds of thousands of Italian immigrants was the single biggest pastoral challenge faced by the Archdiocese of New York during the administrations of Archbishop Michael Corrigan (1885-1902) and John Cardinal Farley (1902-1918).

Mulberry Street in the heart of Manhattan's largest Little Italy in 1906. Credit: *Library of Congress*

9 - Mary Elizabeth Brown, "Italian Immigrants and the Catholic Church in the Archdiocese of New York, 1880-1950," Ph.D. dissertation, Columbia University, 1967, 67; AANY, Minutes of the Meetings of the Board of Archdiocesan Consultors, June 3, 1898.

The first attempt at an Italian parish in New York City dates from 1857, when Father Antonio Sanguinetti tried to establish a church dedicated to St. Anthony. He incurred the ire of John Hughes by collecting money without his permission and Hughes expelled him from the diocese. The first permanent Italian parish dates from 1866 when Italian Franciscans from St. Bonaventure's College in upstate New York responded to Archbishop McCloskey's appeal and established the Church of St. Anthony of Padua in Greenwich Village. Most of the parishioners were immigrants from northern Italy, first from Genoa, later from Piedmont and Tuscany. Not until after 1900 did southern Italians move into Greenwich Village in any appreciable numbers, and even then leadership in the community remained firmly in the hands of the northern Italians.[10]

The first Church of St. Anthony of Padua, a former Protestant church on Sullivan Street, purchased by the Franciscan friars in 1866.

By 1900 Greenwich Village contained only one of the three "Little Italies" in Manhattan. The second and largest was in Lower Manhattan, centered around Mulberry Bend in the formerly Irish Sixth Ward. The third, made famous by Robert Orsi's book, *The Madonna of 115th Street,* was located uptown in East Harlem. However, from 1866 to 1884 the Franciscans at St. Anthony of Padua in Greenwich Village were the only religious community caring for the Italians in New York. Like the German Redemptorists at St. Alphonsus Church a half-century earlier, the Italian friars quickly discovered that the Irish were more generous contributors than their own countrymen. Predictably the reaction among the parishioners was also the same as it had been at St. Alphonsus. The Italians promptly complained that they were being neglected in favor of the Irish.

Father Anacletus da Roccagorga O.S.F.

Among the early pastors of St. Anthony the outstanding figure was Father Anacletus da Roccagorga. In 1888 he replaced the original St. Anthony's Church, a former Methodist church on Sullivan Street, with the present Romanesque church at the corner of Houston and Sullivan Streets. The luck of Father Anacletus was legendary. The property on Sullivan Street that he wanted as the site for his new church was scheduled to be sold at auction on January 31, 1882. That day a blizzard left New York City paralyzed by snow drifts. Father Anacletus was the sole bidder to show up at the auction. He got the property at the price he wanted.

Despite such feats, Msgr. John Farley, who knew the archdiocese as well as anyone, expressed unhappiness with the friars' management of the Italian apostolate. He was especially concerned about aggressive Protestant pros-

---

10 - Caroline Ware, *Greenwich Village, 1920-1930* (Berkeley: University of California Press, repr. 1994), 127, 152-153.

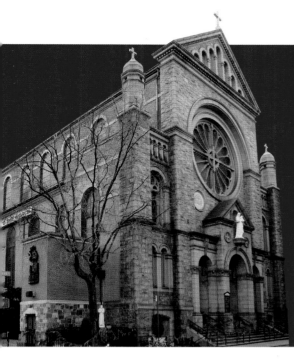

The interior
of the Church
of St. Anthony
of Padua.
Credit: *Yvon Meyer*

The Church of St. Anthony of Padua, dedicated in 1888.
When Houston Street was widened, it left St. Anthony's
with a prime corner location, perhaps a posthumous
example of the luck of Father Anacletus.

elytism among the Italians. He told Archbishop Corrigan in 1883: "Something more must be done for these poor unfortunate people: the children are being swallowed up everyday by heretics--- and the Franciscans are utterly inefficient." Corrigan agreed with Farley's criticism and reported to Rome that only one of the friars at St. Anthony's took any interest in the Italians. [11]

Archbishop Corrigan's solution was to request other religious communities such as the Pallottines, Salesians and Jesuits to send Italian-speaking priests to New York. He was especially interested in enlisting the services of the Pious Society of St. Charles (the Scalabrinians), a religious community founded by Bishop Giovanni Battista Scalabrini of Piacenza in 1887 specifically for missionary work among Italian immigrants. Bishop Scalabrini was also instrumental in founding the Italian St. Raphael Society for the protection of these immigrants. By 1892 the Scalabrinians had opened four parishes in Manhattan, Three of them, St. Joachim on Roosevelt Street, Most Precious Blood on Baxter Street, and the Church of the Resurrection on Centre Street, were located in the heart of the Little Italy in Lower Manhattan. The Church of

the Resurrection, founded in 1889, lasted only about a year and was then folded into the Church of the Most Precious Blood. The fourth parish, which proved to be the most successful, was the Church of Our Lady of Pompei in Greenwich Village.

Bishop John Baptist
Scalabrini of
Piacenza, who
founded the Pious
Society of St. Charles
for work among the
Italian immigrants

The Church of
St. Joachim on
Roosevelt Street,
1888-1958.
Credit: *Center for
Migration Studies*

---

11 - AANY, C-2, Farley to Corrigan, November 1, 1883, cit. in Stephen M. DiGiovanni, *Archbishop Corrigan and the Italian Immigrants* (Huntington, Ind.: Our Sunday Visitor Press,1994), 114-115. Farley's letter is no longer available in the archives of the Archdiocese of New York.

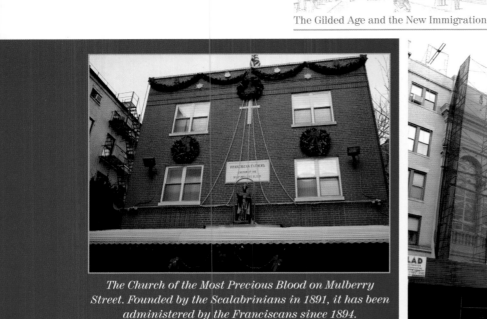

The Church of the Most Precious Blood on Mulberry Street. Founded by the Scalabrinians in 1891, it has been administered by the Franciscans since 1894.

The Church of Our Lady of Pompei at the corner of Carmine and Bleecker Streets, built in 1928.

The founding pastor of Our Lady of Pompei was Father Pietro Bandini, who came to New York in 1891 to serve as the director of the Italian St. Raphael Society. He established the headquarters of the society in a private residence at 113 Waverly Place and fitted out a chapel on the ground floor where he celebrated Mass for the first time on May 8, 1892. Father Bandini posted a sign on the door on his "microscopical chapel" announcing that admission was restricted to Italians. This precaution did not prevent the pastor of St. Joseph's Church on Sixth Avenue from denouncing him to the Chancery Office for stealing his parishioners. Our Lady of Pompei moved twice in the next six years, first to a former Protestant church on Sullivan Street and then to the former church of St. Benedict the Moor at Bleecker and Downing Streets. It finally found a permanent home in 1928 when the present church was erected at the corner of Carmine and Bleecker Streets.[12]

The Church of Our Lady of Mount Carmel on East 115th Street, the second oldest Italian church in the archdiocese, founded by the Pallotine Fathers in 1884.

The Pallottines (then called the Pious Society of Missionaries and now known as the Society of the Catholic Apostolate) were the second religious community to come to the archdiocese specifically to serve the Italians. They established two churches in East Harlem, Our Lady of Mount Carmel on 115th Street in 1884 and St. Ann's on 110th Street in 1911. The first pastor of Our Lady of Mount Carmel, Father Emiliano Kirner, and several workmen

12 - AANY, G-77, Bandini to Rev. Dear Father, August 11, 1892; Mary Elizabeth Brown, *From Italian Villages to Greenwich Village: Our Lady of Pompei, 1892-1992* (New York: Center for Migration Studies, 1992), 15-16.

St. Ann's Church on East 110th Street, founded by the Pallotine Fathers in 1911 and now staffed by the Don Orione Fathers.

were killed in 1887 when a wall of the parochial school that they were building collapsed on them. The Franciscans, in addition to staffing St. Anthony of Padua, replaced the Scalabrinians at Most Precious Blood in 1894, established St. Clare on West 36th Street in 1903, Our Lady of Pity in Melrose in 1908, and St. Sebastian on East 22nd Street in 1915. The last three churches are now closed.

In 1891 the Jesuits under Father Nicholas Russo established the Church of Our Lady of Loretto for the Sicilians in two converted tenement houses on Elizabeth Street just north of Houston Street. "The nature of the work speaks for itself," Father Russo told Archbishop Corrigan, "no human motive can induce anyone to undertake it, and therefore I feel assured that my desire of doing it cannot but please our Lord."[13] The Jesuits also established an outreach to the Italians in Nativity parish when they took over that parish from the diocesan clergy in 1917. The Salesians took charge of the Italians at St. Brigid and Epiphany in the 1890s, replaced the diocesan

clergy at Transfiguration in 1902 and opened the Church of Mary Help of Christians in 1906.

Archbishop Corrigan did not leave the pastoral care of the Italians in New York entirely in the hands of Italian religious communities. In 1889 he issued a pastoral letter in Italian welcoming the new immigrants to the archdiocese and listing the names and churches of thirty-six Italian-speaking diocesan priests who were ready to serve them. At the head of the list was St. Patrick's Cathedral and *noi stessi* ("we ourselves"). Almost all of the priests on the list were Irish-Americans who had spent their seminary years in Rome as Corrigan himself had done.[14]

The Pastoral letter of Archbishop Corrigan to the Italian Catholics of New York, January 15, 1889.
Credit: *Archives of the Archdiocese of New York.*

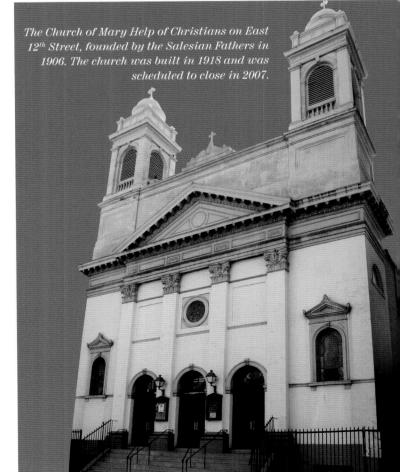

The Church of Mary Help of Christians on East 12th Street, founded by the Salesian Fathers in 1906. The church was built in 1918 and was scheduled to close in 2007.

---

13 - AANY, C-28, Russo to Corrigan, May 3, 1891.

14 - AANY,G-59, Michele Agostino Corrigan ai Cattolici Italiani dimoranti in questa Diocesi, January 15, 1889.

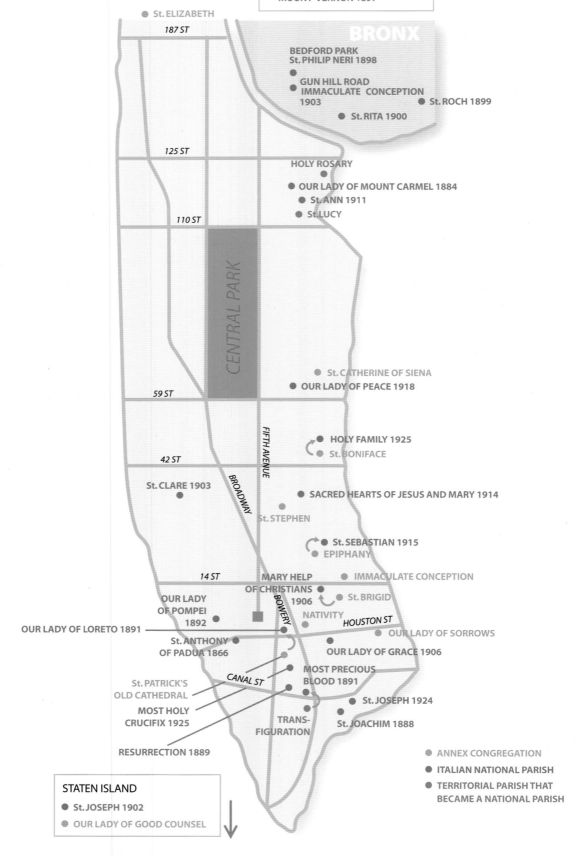

THE ITALIAN PARISHES IN THE ARCHDIOCESE
of New York

WESTCHESTER
- St. JOSEPH NEW ROCHELLE 1901
- St. ANTHONY YONKERS 1900
- OUR LADY OF MOUNT CARMEL MOUNT VERNON 1897

BRONX

St. ELIZABETH

187 ST

BEDFORD PARK
St. PHILIP NERI 1898

GUN HILL ROAD
IMMACULATE CONCEPTION
1903
St. ROCH 1899
St. RITA 1900

125 ST

HOLY ROSARY

OUR LADY OF MOUNT CARMEL 1884
St. ANN 1911
St. LUCY

110 ST

CENTRAL PARK

St. CATHERINE OF SIENA
OUR LADY OF PEACE 1918

59 ST

FIFTH AVENUE

HOLY FAMILY 1925
St. BONIFACE

42 ST

BROADWAY

St. CLARE 1903

SACRED HEARTS OF JESUS AND MARY 1914

St. STEPHEN

St. SEBASTIAN 1915
EPIPHANY

14 ST

MARY HELP
OF CHRISTIANS
1906

IMMACULATE CONCEPTION

St. BRIGID

OUR LADY
OF POMPEI
1892

BOWERY

NATIVITY

HOUSTON ST

OUR LADY OF LORETO 1891

OUR LADY OF SORROWS

St. ANTHONY
OF PADUA 1866

OUR LADY OF GRACE 1906

St. PATRICK'S
OLD CATHEDRAL

CANAL ST

MOST PRECIOUS
BLOOD 1891

MOST HOLY
CRUCIFIX 1925

St. JOSEPH 1924

TRANS-
FIGURATION

St. JOACHIM 1888

RESURRECTION 1889

- ANNEX CONGREGATION
- ITALIAN NATIONAL PARISH
- TERRITORIAL PARISH THAT BECAME A NATIONAL PARISH

STATEN ISLAND
- St. JOSEPH 1902
- OUR LADY OF GOOD COUNSEL

Italian Laity and Irish Clergy

The attitude of New York's Irish clergy to the Italian immigrants varied greatly. They tended to judge the religious commitment of the Italians by the same criteria that they used for their for own parishioners, namely, respect for the clergy, attendance at Mass on Sunday and financial support. By those criteria the Italians frequently fell short of the mark. The New York priests were especially appalled at the religious ignorance of the Southern Italians whose folk religion was often, in the words of one historian, "a fusion of Christian and pre-Christian elements, of animism, polytheism, and sorcery with the sacraments of the Catholic Church."[15] The New York priests did not blame the immigrants, but the clergy of their homeland. They wondered why a country that was awash with priests did such a poor job of instructing their people in the basic elements of their faith.

There was also a huge cultural gap between the Irish and Italian expression of their common faith. The thirty-minute inaudible Latin Mass that was common in Irish parishes, what the Paulist Walter Elliott once called "catacombical public worship," seemed like a Protestant service to many Italians. Reciprocally some of the more emotional manifestations of Southern Italian popular piety like the annual *festa* seemed little better than a pagan ritual to Irish-American pastors. "The fact is that the Catholic Church in America is to the mass of Italians almost like a new religion," said one Irish-American.[16] There were also deep cultural differences within the Italian community itself due to the persistence of provincial loyalties and local dialects. In Chicago a young priest from Tuscany was assigned to a Sicilian parish. "Is it possible that these are Italians?" he exclaimed after meeting his parishioners.

Another source of friction between the Irish clergy and the Italian laity was the anticlericalism of many of the Italian men. Much of it stemmed from the political situation in Italy where the efforts of Italian nationalists to unify the peninsula met bitter opposition from the pope who was determined to remain the temporal ruler of central Italy. In Ireland and Poland Catholicism and nationalism reinforced one another. In nineteenth-century Italy it was difficult to be both a loyal Catholic and an Italian patriot because of the so-called Roman Question. Irish-American Catholics reacted with horror every year when Italian-Americans celebrated the Italian occupation of Rome on September 20, 1870.

American Protestants, especially the Episcopalians, Baptists, Methodists and Presbyterians, made a concerted effort to proselytize the Italian immigrants, opening 326 Italian Protestant churches in the United States by 1918. In New York City alone, which was described as "the nursery of Protestant proselytism among the Italians," there were forty-four Italian Protestant churches in 1912. In 1899 the University Place Presbyterian Church established the Bethlehem Mission on Bleecker Street to offer religious services in Italian. One wealthy parishioner contributed $190,000 to rescue the Italians from popery. The following year they got six converts. Despite a massive expenditure of money and manpower the Protestants reaped a meager harvest not only in New York City but throughout the country. After forty years they claimed a total of 14,000 converts among four million Italian immigrants. The Italians may not have measured up to the Irish-American definition of a good Catholic, but that did no mean that they were about to become Protestants.[17]

---

15 - Rudolf Vecoli, "Prelates and Peasants: Italian Immigrants and the Catholic Church," *Journal of Social History 2* (1969), 228.

16 - Bernard J. Lynch, "The Italians in New York," *The Catholic World 47* (1888), 72.

17 - Dorothy Fowler, *A City Church: The First Presbyterian Church in the City of New York, 1716-1976* (New York: The First Presbyterian Church, 1981), 100. F. Aurelio Palmieri, O.S.A., "Italian Protestantism in the United States," *The Catholic World 108* (1918): 177-189. Palmieri thought that the real number of converts less than 7,000.

Italian Parishes and Annex Congregations

A particular grievance of many New York pastors was that the Italians did not support the Church as generously as did the Irish. At Transfiguration Church, Father Thomas Lynch said: "These people would hardly be able by themselves to erect and support a church in New York, but they could certainly share in the support of any church which is in a tolerably good financial condition."[18] As a result of such advice Archbishop Corrigan hesitated to multiply Italian national parishes for fear that they would not be financially viable. Instead he resorted to the tactic of creating Italian chapels or "annex congregations" in existing territorial parishes.

Unfortunately this meant in practice that the Italians were usually relegated to the basement of the "Irish" church for Sunday Mass, a practice which many of them found insensitive and demeaning. St. Brigid's listed its lower church as the Italian Church in the *Catholic Almanac*. Father John Kearney, the pastor of St. Patrick's Old Cathedral, refused to allow Father Nicholas Russo to give a mission to the Italians in the upper church in 1891 "for reasons," Russo said, "that a priest should feel ashamed to give." Even at the Pallottine Church of Our Lady of Mount Carmel in East Harlem, founded in 1884, the Italians were sent to *la chiesa inferiore* until 1919.[19]

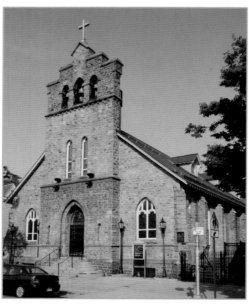

The Church of St. Philip Neri on the Grand Concourse in Bedford Park, dedicated in May 1900, two years after the founding of the parish by Father Daniel Burke.

One Irish-American curate at St. Jerome's Church in the Bronx, Father Patrick J. Mahoney, offered an explanation for the paltry financial support from the Italians. He told Archbishop Corrigan: "*Andare alla chiesa e pagare* (Go to church and pay) is something very harsh to a poor Italian. They have been brought up in Italy where they had to pay little or nothing." "If we treat the present generation generously," he added, "I believe that their children will pay nearly as well as other Catholics when they shall have been rightly instructed."[20]

When Archbishop Corrigan issued his pastoral letter to the Italians in 1889, he could mention only four Italian parishes and two annex congregations, all of them located in Manhattan. In 1903, the year after his death, there were fifteen Italian parishes and ten annex congregations. The Italians were already beginning to move out of Manhattan. By that date there were four Italian parishes in the Bronx, three in Westchester County, and one on Staten Island.

The Church of St. Philip Neri was established in the Bedford Park area of the Bronx in 1898 to care for the Italian laborers who were constructing the reservoir on the site of the former Jerome Park Racetrack. The founding pastor was Father Daniel Burke, a Roman-educated Irish-American. According to Mary Elizabeth Brown, Burke is the sole example of a non-Italian cleric starting an Italian parish in New York.

---

18 - AANY, G-33, Thomas F. Lynch, *Some Facts Concerning the Italian Congregation of the Church of the Transfiguration, Mott Street*, n.d.

19 - Mary Elizabeth Brown, *Churches, Communities and Children: Italian Immigrants in the Archdiocese of New York, 1880-1945* (New York: Center for Migration Studies, 1995), 56. Robert Orsi, *The Madonna of 115th Street* (New Haven: Yale University Press, 1985), 54.

20 - AANY, G-59, Mahoney to Corrigan, May 5, 1893.

He did it again in 1906 when he started Our Lady of Mount Carmel on 187th Street.

In 1899 Father John Milo started St. Roch's Church in the South Bronx in a former Lutheran church at 150th Street near Jackson Avenue. At his first Christmas Mass a congregation of thirty people contributed a grand total of $1.64. "The badge of poverty has always more or less clung to the parish from the beginning," noted the parish history published in 1949. Starting in the Depression year of 1930, it took the third pastor, Father Ignatius Cirelli, almost twenty years to erect the present church.[21]

St. Rita of Cascia was another Bronx Italian parish that got off to a rocky start. It began its existence in 1900 in a rented store at the corner of 148th Street and Cortland Avenue. When the first pastor, Father Charles Ferina, ran into financial difficulties, Archbishop Corrigan reminded him that St. Rita was the patron saint of impossible

Msgr. Daniel F.X. Burke, the founding pastor of the Church of St. Philip Neri, Bedford Park, Bronx.
Credit: *Church of St. Philip Neri*

causes and told him to start a novena in her honor. Later he sent more tangible assistance in the form of a check.[22]

The fourth Italian parish in the Bronx, Immaculate Conception in Wakefield, was started in 1902 by Father Giuseppe Cirringione in a rented store on White Plains Road across the street from St. Mary's Church. After Cirringione's abrupt return to Italy the following year,

The Church of St. Rita of Cascia at the corner of College Avenue and 145th Street was built by Father Ferina in 1904.

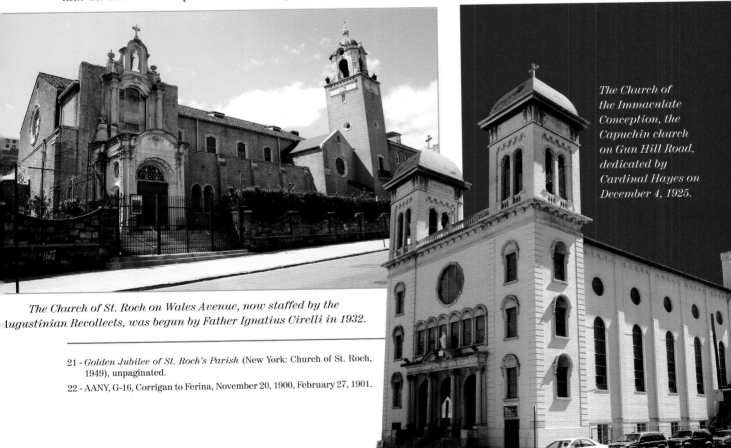

The Church of St. Roch on Wales Avenue, now staffed by the Augustinian Recollects, was begun by Father Ignatius Cirelli in 1932.

The Church of the Immaculate Conception, the Capuchin church on Gun Hill Road, dedicated by Cardinal Hayes on December 4, 1925.

21 - *Golden Jubilee of St. Roch's Parish* (New York: Church of St. Roch, 1949), unpaginated.
22 - AANY, G-16, Corrigan to Ferina, November 20, 1900, February 27, 1901.

The forlorn looking first Church of St. Joseph, New Rochelle. Credit: *St. Joseph's Church*

St. Joseph's Church, New Rochelle, which was dedicated by Archbishop Farley on January 3, 1904

The Church of Our Lady of Mount Carmel in Mount Vernon, the oldest Italian parish in Westchester County.

Archbishop Farley replaced him with Father Patrick Lennon, who built a small church on Gun Hill Road and Holland Avenue. The Italian Capuchins were asked to take charge of the parish in 1920. After a disastrous fire on December 23, 1923, the friars built a new church on the south side of Gun Hill Road that was dedicated by Cardinal Hayes on December 4, 1925.[23]

By the turn of the century there were also three Italian parishes in southern Westchester, Our Lady of Mt. Carmel in Mount Vernon (1897), St. Anthony on Willow Street in Yonkers (1900), and St. Joseph in New Rochelle (1901). Italian communities in the East Bronx, White Plains, Tuxedo Park, Newburgh and Poughkeepsie were all clamoring for a priest. The first Italian parish on Staten Island dates from 1902, when St. Joseph's was founded in Rosebank, and there was also an annex congregation at the Augustinian Church of Our Lady of Good Counsel in Tompkinsville. It was only a harbinger of things to come. In the 1920s there was to be a dramatic growth in the number of Italian parishes

23 - *Golden Jubilee of the Immaculate Conception Church* (New York: Church of the Immaculate Conception, 1974).

in both Staten Island and the Bronx and to a lesser extent in southern Westchester and the upstate counties.

St. Joseph's Church in Rosebank was the first Italian parish on Staten Island.

In Manhattan several annex congregations developed into full-fledged parishes. The Church of Mary Help of Christians on East 12th Street, established by the Salesians of Don Bosco in 1906, grew out the basement congregation in St. Brigid's Church. Two decades earlier the nucleus of the Scalabrinian Church of the Most Precious Blood was the Italian congregation that had met in the basement of Transfiguration Church. Transfiguration itself became an Italian parish and was staffed by the Salesians of Don Bosco from 1902 until 1950.

In 1891 Father Nicholas Russo started Our Lady of Loreto for the Sicilians who felt unwelcome in the basement of St. Patrick's Old Cathedral. In 1915 the Italian congregation at Epiphany established St. Sebastian's Church on East 22nd Street. Ten years later the Italians who had been worshipping at the German Church of

St. Boniface did the same and started the Church of the Holy Family on East 47th Street. The first two churches have since been closed and demolished.

In East Harlem both the Church of the Holy Rosary and St. Lucy's Church began as territorial parishes, but became Italian parishes in the 1920s and 1930s. In the case of St. Philip Neri Church in the Bronx, the process was reversed. It began as an Italian parish, but quickly became a territorial (i.e, Irish) parish. The Church of Our Lady of Grace on Stanton Street, founded in 1906, was unique among the Italian parishes in New York because it was established by Italo-Albanians who celebrated the Eucharist in the Greek rite.[24]

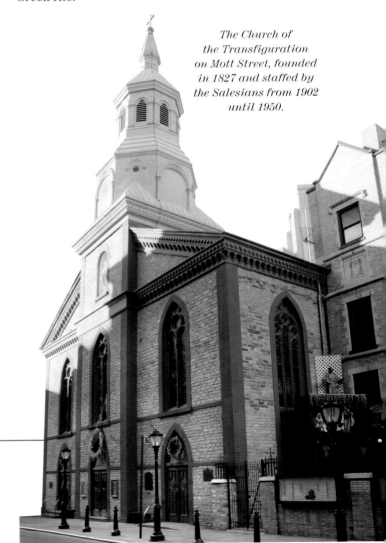

The Church of the Transfiguration on Mott Street, founded in 1827 and staffed by the Salesians from 1902 until 1950.

---

24 - Brown, Churches, *Communities and Children*, 55-56, 181-188; and Thomas F. Meehan, "Evangelizing the Italians," *The Messenger* 39 (1903): 16-17.

The last four Italian parishes in Manhattan were founded between 1914 and 1925. Two were on the East Side, Sacred Hearts of Jesus and Mary on 33rd Street (1914)[25] and Our Lady of Peace on 62nd Street (1918). The other two were in Lower Manhattan, both opened in 1925, Most Holy Crucifix on Broome Street and St. Joseph's on the corner of Catherine and Monroe Streets. Unlike the other three, which were small diocesan parishes, St. Joseph's was a large Scalabrinan parish, founded by Father Vincent Jannuzzi, the pastor of St. Joachim's, who built St. Joseph's to relieve the overcrowding in his own church. It was a four-story building that

The Church of the Most Holy Crucifix on Broome Street, today the Filipino Chapel of San Lorenzo Ruiz.

combined a church that seated 1,100 people on the first two floors and a school with eighteen classrooms on the upper two floors. Mass was first celebrated in the unfinished church on Christmas Eve in 1924 on a dirt floor amid the scaffolding and debris.[26]

The number of nominal parishioners in the Italian churches was staggering. The Scalabrinians at St. Joachim claimed 23,300 "souls" and the annex congregation at St. Patrick's Old Cathedral claimed 28,000 "souls." These figures were only estimates of the number of Italians residing within the parish, not regular church-goers. However, the sacramental statistics give a clearer picture of the pastoral demands made upon the clergy in these parishes.

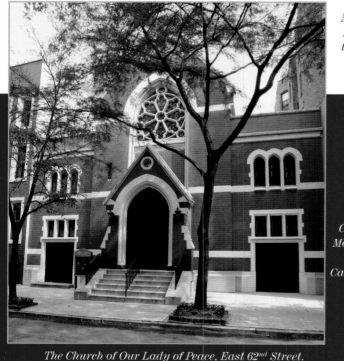

The Church of Our Lady of Peace, East 62nd Street.

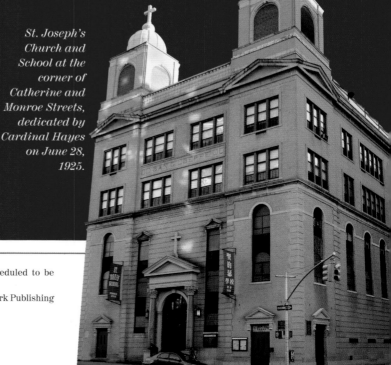

St. Joseph's Church and School at the corner of Catherine and Monroe Streets, dedicated by Cardinal Hayes on June 28, 1925.

25 - In 2007 Sacred Hearts of Jesus and Mary was scheduled to be merged with St. Stephen's Church.

26 - *50th Anniversary Saint Joseph Church* (New York: Park Publishing Company, 1977), 8-10.

In 1902 the Pallottines at Our Lady of Mount Carmel Church baptized 2,721 children, and the Jesuits at the Sicilian Church of Our Lady of Loreto on Elizabeth Street baptized 1,188 children. At the Church of the Most Precious Blood on Baxter Street the Franciscans baptized 1,914 children and witnessed 488 marriages in 1902.[27]

The most famous of the Italian immigrants in New York, if not in the United States, was Mother Francis Xavier Cabrini, who arrived in New York on March 31, 1889, with six Missionary Sisters of the Sacred Heart. She got a cool reception from Archbishop Corrigan when she met him the next day. Unknown to Corrigan, she had failed to receive his letter urging her to delay her departure from Italy until proper housing could be found for her sisters in New York. The archbishop told her to return to Italy. She replied that she had been sent by the Holy See and would remain in New York.[28]

Despite this initial misunderstanding, Corrigan soon came to appreciate the work of Mother Cabrini and her sisters. They were active in the Italian community as teachers, nurses, social workers and counselors even ministering to prisoners on death row in the prisons. Mother Cabrini was personally responsible for the founding of Columbus Hospital in 1892 after earlier efforts by the Scalabrinian Fathers to establish an Italian Catholic hospital had ended in failure. She was canonized on July 7, 1946, the

St. Francis Xavier Cabrini, 1850-1917.
Credit: *Archives of the Archdiocese of New York*

first American citizen to receive this honor, and is buried in New York City.[29]

In view of the great efforts that the archdiocese of New York had made on behalf of the Italian immigrants, Archbishop Farley was incensed in 1903 when an article appeared in *La Civiltà Cattolica,* the Roman Jesuit periodical, calling upon American Catholics to do more for the Italian immigrants. Farley wrote an uncharacteristically blunt letter to the editor, Father Salvatore Brandi, S.J., referring him to a recent article by Thomas F. Meehan in *The Messenger.*[30] In that article Farley told Brandi, "it is pointed out clearly and statistically what had been done by the late archbishop for the salvation of the Italians, under circumstances perhaps unprecedented in the history of the Church." As a parting shot, he added, "I should like to know how such a condition of things would be met in Italy, if the case were reversed." Farley's letter produced the desired results. Shortly thereafter *La Civiltà Cattolica* published a glowing account of the way that the archdiocese of New York had cared for the Italians.[31]

The Eastern Europeans

The Italians posed a daunting pastoral challenge because of their sheer numbers. In the case of the Eastern European immigrants, the difficulty was the multiplicity of the different ethnic groups, many of whom were mutually

27 - Meehan, "Evangelizing the Italians," 16-17.

28 - DiGiovanni, *Corrigan and Italian Immigrants,* 179-180.

29 - On the establishment of Columbus Hospital (today's Cabrini Medical Center), see John P. DeLora, "Corrigan, Cabrini and Columbus: The Foundation of Cabrini Medical Center, New York City," M.A. thesis, St. Joseph's Seminary, Dunwoodie, 1994.

30 - *The Messenger* 39 (1903): 16-32.

31 - AANY, I-6, Farley to Brandi, March 20, 1903; "Gli Emigranti Italiani a Nuova York," *La Civiltà Cattolica* 55 (April 4, 1904): 172-179.

antipathetic. The Poles were the single largest group of Slavic immigrants in New York, followed by lesser numbers of Slovaks, Czechs, Croatians, Slovenes, Ukrainians and Ruthenians or Carpatho-Rusyns. The latter two groups were Catholics of the Byzantine Rite who were frequently called Greek Catholics. There were also the Hungarians and Lithuanians, neither of whom were Slavic. All of these Catholic peoples had their own distinctive religious traditions that they wished to preserve in America.

Some American bishops, notably Archbishop John Ireland of St. Paul, urged Catholic immigrants to shed their foreign customs as soon as possible and become thoroughly Americanized. Catholic immigrants in New York, whether they were German or Italian or Slavic, never heard that demand from Archbishop Michael Corrigan, who sympathized with their desire to maintain their distinctive cultural and religious heritage in a strange new land.

The Poles

The first Polish church in the archdiocese of New York dates from November 1873 when a group of lay people formed the St. Stanislaus Society to erect a church of that name for the 2,000 Polish Catholics in New York City. The following year Father Adalbert Mielinszny, a Polish priest, purchased a frame building on Henry Street in Lower Manhattan. In 1876 he was succeed by Father Francis Xavier Wayman, a native of Posen in the Prussian part of partitioned Poland and a newly arrived refugee from Bismarck's *Kulturkampf.* Under Wayman's leadership the Poles moved to larger quarters two years later when they bought a box-like building at Stanton and Forsyth Streets that had once

been a Protestant church and more recently a synagogue. It was dedicated on July 14, 1878.

More than any other ethnic group in the American Catholic Church, the Poles were prone to bitter disputes between pastors and parishioners and among the parishioners themselves. St. Stanislaus Church was no exception. In the 1890s a protracted struggle by a group of dissident parishioners over the ownership of the property led to a six-year court fight that ended only when the New York State Court of Appeals settled the case in favor of the archdiocese in 1900. At one point the dissidents complained that the pastor, Father John Strzelecki, whipped out a pistol and drove them off the church premises at gunpoint. Despite his fractious congregation, Father Strzelecki was able to erect the present Church of St. Stanislaus on East 7th Street between First Avenue and Avenue A, which was dedicated by Archbishop Corrigan on May 19. 1901.[32]

Like the Irish, the Poles could be exceptionally generous to the church despite their poverty. However, the laity expected a high degree of accountability from the clergy, especially since they were usually the ones who took the initiative in establishing a Polish parish and retained a strong sense of ownership. In 1889 in the Wakefield area of the Bronx sixty-five Polish families complained that they derived no spiritual benefit from attending St. Mary's Church on White Plains Road because they did not speak English. They banded together and, with the permission of Archbishop Corrigan, bought land and erected their own church of St. Valentine in 1890 with the help of Father Hieronymous Klimecki, the pastor of St. Stanislaus.[33]

---

32 - New York Times, January 24, 24, 1894; AANY, Dennis Spellisy to Corrigan, November 21, 1900. Louis L. Makulec, *Church of St. Stanislaus Bishop and Martyr* (New York: Church of St. Stanislaus, 1954), 4-34.

33 - AANY, Petition of Polish Catholics to Corrigan, October 19, 1899. *St. Stanislaus B.M. Parish* (New York: Church of St. Stanislaus, n.d.), 16-19.

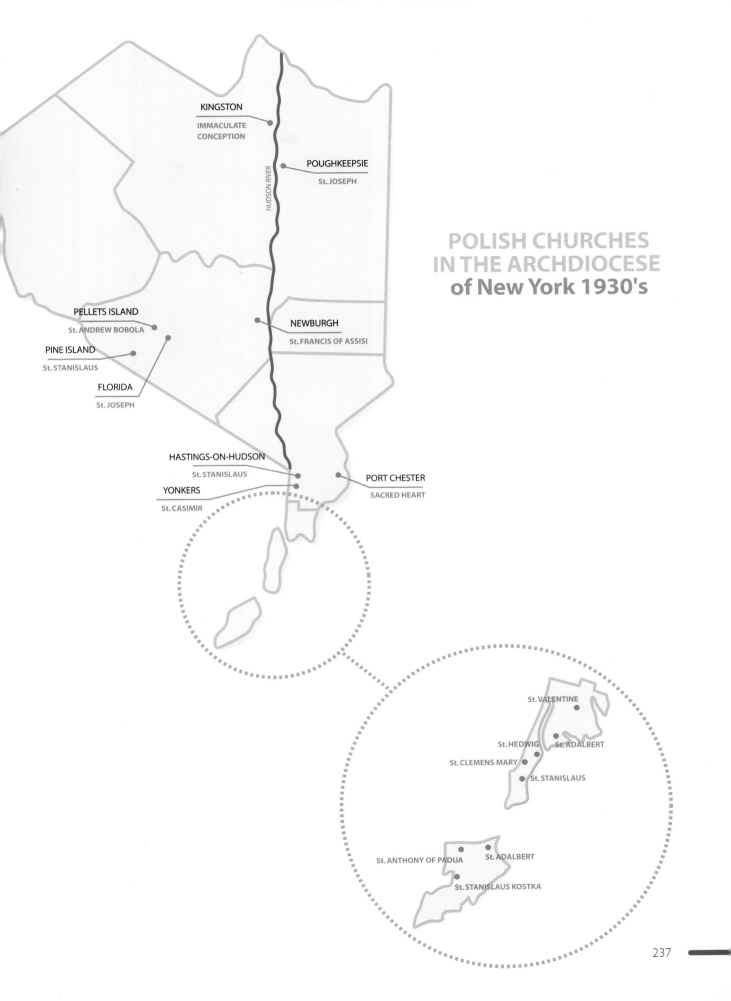

POLISH CHURCHES
IN THE ARCHDIOCESE
of New York 1930's

KINGSTON
IMMACULATE
CONCEPTION

POUGHKEEPSIE
St. JOSEPH

HUDSON RIVER

PELLETS ISLAND
St. ANDREW BOBOLA

PINE ISLAND
St. STANISLAUS

FLORIDA
St. JOSEPH

NEWBURGH
St. FRANCIS OF ASSISI

HASTINGS-ON-HUDSON
St. STANISLAUS

YONKERS
St. CASIMIR

PORT CHESTER
SACRED HEART

St. VALENTINE

St. HEDWIG   St. ADALBERT

St. CLEMENS MARY

St. STANISLAUS

St. ANTHONY OF PADUA   St. ADALBERT

St. STANISLAUS KOSTKA

The second
St. Stanislaus Church,
a former synagogue at
the corner of Stanton
and Forsyth Streets

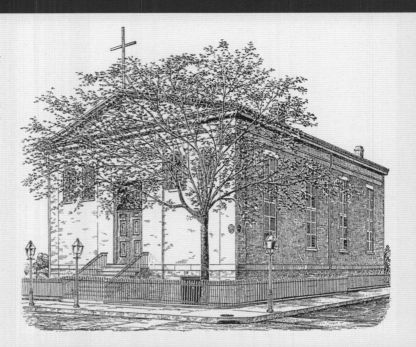

Msgr. John H.
Strzelecki,
the pastor of
St. Stanislaus Church,
1892-1918

Father Francis Xavier
Wayman,
the second pastor
of St. Stanislaus Church

The Church of St. Stanislaus,
Bishop and Martyr,
on East 7th Street, dedicated
by Archbishop Corrigan
on May 19, 1901. The church
is now administered
by the Pauline Fathers.

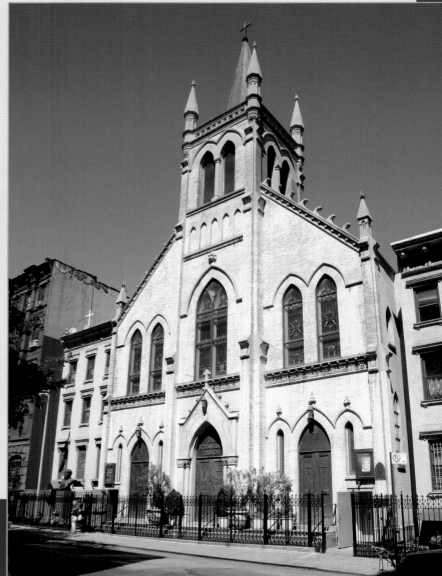

St. Stanislaus was the mother church of the first Polish parish on Staten Island, St. Adalbert, which was founded in 1902. The key figure at St. Adalbert's was Joseph Brzoziewski, the second pastor, who came to St. Adalbert in 1902 and remained for the next sixty-two years. He in turn was instrumental in starting two other Polish parishes in Staten Island, St. Anthony of Padua in Travis in 1908 and St. Stanislaus Kostka in New Brighton in 1923.[34]

St. Stanislaus Kostka Church, New Brighton, Staten Island

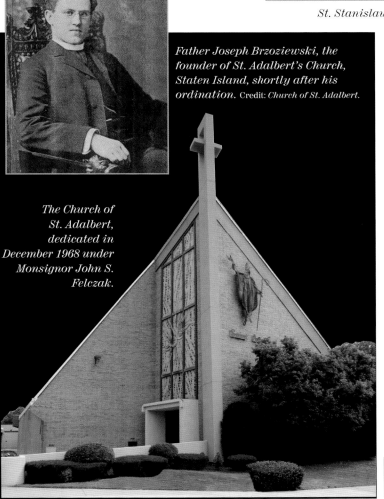

Father Joseph Brzoziewski, the founder of St. Adalbert's Church, Staten Island, shortly after his ordination. Credit: *Church of St. Adalbert.*

The Church of St. Adalbert, dedicated in December 1968 under Monsignor John S. Felczak.

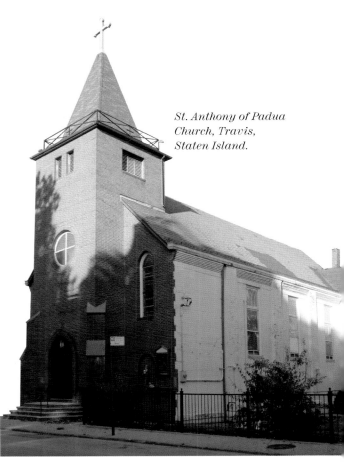

St. Anthony of Padua Church, Travis, Staten Island.

34 - *Church of St. Adalbert: 100th Anniversary* (New York: Church of St. Adalbert, 2001), unpaginated.

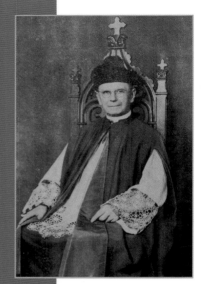

Father John C. Dworzak, the pastor of St. Valentine's Church, shortly after his arrival in America in 1894.

Monsignor Dworzak in his later years as the pastor of St. Casimir Church, Yonkers.

The Church of St. Valentine, the Bronx, which today serves New York's Indian Catholic community as St. Thomas the Apostle Syro-Malabar Catholic Church.

At St. Valentine's Dworzak was instrumental in founding both St. Adalbert's Church in Melrose (1898) and St. Casimir's Church in Yonkers (1899) where he moved four years later and became one of the leading figures in the large Polish community in that city until his death in 1951. He was particularly anxious to start a Polish parish in Yonkers for fear that the

When the personal chemistry was right, Polish pastors and parishioners formed a tight bond because the pastor of a Polish immigrant parish wore many hats. In the words of the historian James Pula, he was "a spiritual father, temporal leader, priest, teacher, legal counselor, business advisor and intermediary with the unfamiliar ways of American society." Such was the multifaceted role played by Father Joseph Dworzak in the archdiocese of New York. He was made the pastor of St. Valentine's Church in the Bronx on April 13, 1894, three days after he arrived in New York with his Roman doctorate. It was the beginning of a ministry to Polish Catholics in New York that was to last fifty-seven years.

The Church of St. Adalbert, East 156th Street, Melrose, which is now the chapel of St. Crispin's Friary of the Franciscan Friars of the Renewal.

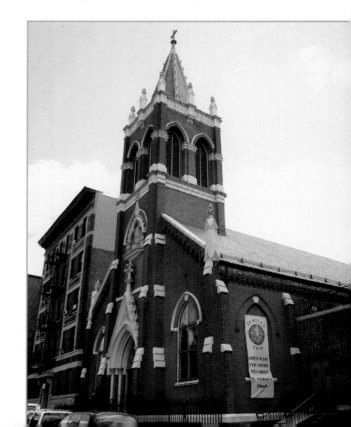

schismatic Polish National Catholic Church would beat him to the punch. He had difficulty in obtaining the property he wanted because the owners did not want it used for a Catholic Church, but he managed to circumvent them by buying it through a third party. The first Mass was celebrated in the little red brick church on Nepperhan Avenue on June 7, 1903.[35]

Dworzak established his third parish when he got permission from Archbishop Farley on September 15, 1909, to organize a Polish parish on the West Side of Manhattan. The result was the Church of St. Clemens Mary on West 40th Street. His fourth parish was St. Stanislaus in Hastings-on-Hudson, which he began in 1914 in a former Baptist church that he bought for $3,000. He remained pastor of both St. Casimir and St. Stanislaus until 1918 when a resident pastor was appointed for St. Stanislaus. He nearly established a fifth Polish parish in Tarrytown in

1917, to be called St. John Kanty, but he abandoned the project when he failed to get sufficient local support.[36]

Unlike Chicago, Detroit or Buffalo the Polish population in New York was not concentrated in one area but dispersed throughout the archdiocese. In Rondout there was a Polish community as far back as 1878. Perhaps because they were natives of the Prussian part of partitioned Poland, they worshipped with the Germans at St. Peter's Church. In 1895 a young curate at St. Peter's who spoke both German and Polish, Father Francis Fremel, took the initiative in establishing a Polish parish, which was called Immaculate Conception. The second pastor, Father Francis Fabian, built the church, which was first used for Mass on Christmas 1896 and dedicated by Archbishop Corrigan on November 21, 1897.[37]

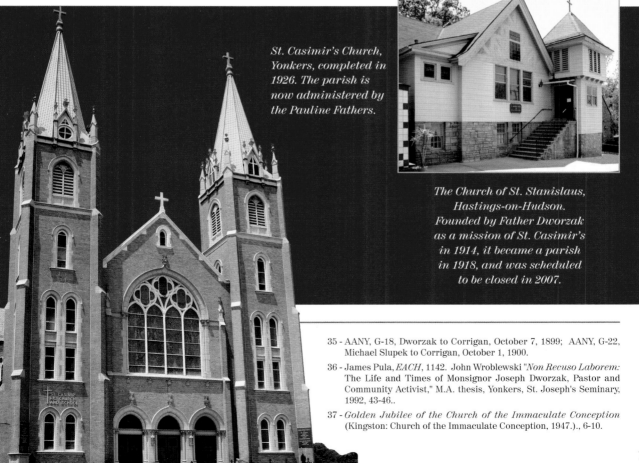

St. Casimir's Church, Yonkers, completed in 1926. The parish is now administered by the Pauline Fathers.

The Church of St. Stanislaus, Hastings-on-Hudson. Founded by Father Dworzak as a mission of St. Casimir's in 1914, it became a parish in 1918, and was scheduled to be closed in 2007.

35 - AANY, G-18, Dworzak to Corrigan, October 7, 1899; AANY, G-22, Michael Slupek to Corrigan, October 1, 1900.

36 - James Pula, *EACH*, 1142. John Wroblewski "*Non Recuso Laborem:* The Life and Times of Monsignor Joseph Dworzak, Pastor and Community Activist," M.A. thesis, Yonkers, St. Joseph's Seminary, 1992, 43-46..

37 - *Golden Jubilee of the Church of the Immaculate Conception* (Kingston: Church of the Immaculate Conception, 1947.)., 6-10.

In 1909 Father Fabian was transferred to Newburgh where he founded his second Polish parish, the Church of St. Francis of Assisi. He had a small chapel ready for use within nine months and began work on constructing a permanent church. Hard pressed for cash, he rented a barge and begged for discarded bricks in the brickyards that lined the Hudson. The church was dedicated by Bishop Thomas Cusack on September 1, 1913. By that date there was also a Polish church in Poughkeepsie, St. Joseph, which dates from 1901, and a Polish church in Port Chester, Sacred Heart, which was founded in 1917.

Not all of the Poles settled in the cities. Some moved to the Black Dirt area of Orange County between Florida and Pine Island where they succeeded in reclaiming the "drowned lands" and making them productive once again. At first they went to Mass in St. John's Church in Goshen where the pastor occasionally provided a Polish priest for confessions. In 1894 a group of laymen organized a committee to purchase land for a church in Florida. They then requested Archbishop Corrigan to send them a Polish-speaking priest, which he did in the person of Father Stanislaus J. Nowak, who celebrated the first Mass in Florida in the fire house on July 7, 1895. The church of St. Joseph was ready for use later that year and was dedicated by Archbishop Corrigan on November 20, 1895.

As the population of the Black Dirt area increased, St. Joseph's Church established St. Stanislaus mission in Pine Island in 1912. In 1924 it became a separate parish. In 1945 Father Vincent J. Raith seized the opportunity to establish another mission in Pellets Island when a former public school building in that hamlet was put up for auction. The minimum bid had been set at $3,000. Father Raith got it for $3,025. He named it in honor of St. Andrew Bobola.[38]

The Church of the Immaculate Conception, Kingston, dedicated by Archbishop Corrigan on November 21, 1897.

St. Francis of Assisi Church, Newburgh, dedicated by Bishop Thomas Cusack on September 1, 1913.

38 - *St. Joseph's Church, Florida, New York* (Custombook, 1971), 5-11.

t. Joseph's Church, Poughkeepsie, erected in 1901 and renovated in 1939. Since 2003 the parish has been administered by the Fathers of the Society of Christ for Polish Immigrants.

St. Joseph's Church, Florida, dedicated by Archbishop Corrigan on November 20, 1895.

The mission of St. Andrew Bobola, Pellets Island. The church is named after a seventeenth-century Polish Jesuit who was martyred in 1657.

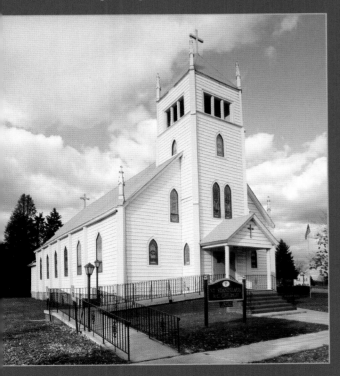

St. Stanislaus Church, Pine Island. Established as a mission of St. Joseph, Florida, in 1912, it became a parish in 1924.

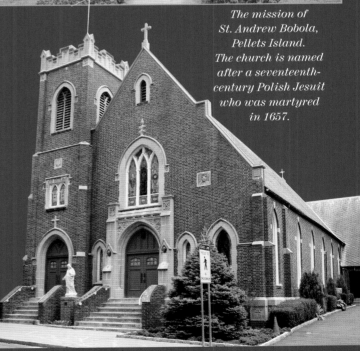

Sacred Heart Church, Port Chester, a former Baptist church acquired in 1917, renovated and consecrated in 1990. In 2007 Sunday Mass was offered in four languages: English, Spanish, Latin and in the liturgical language of St. Thomas Syro-Malabar Church of South India.

The Slovaks

Numerically the Slovaks were second only to the Poles among the Slavic Catholic immigrants to the archdiocese. Unlike the Poles, however, the Slovaks never had an independent country in modern times. For centuries they lived under Hungarian rule within the Hapsburg Empire. In the later nineteenth century the Slovaks grew increasingly restive as Hungarian domination became more oppressive and their own sense of national identity became more pronounced. This development was reflected among Slovak immigrants in America who became more nationalistic and resented the efforts of pro-Hungarian clergy (some of them subsidized by the Hungarian government) to thwart Slovak nationalist aspirations in their own parishes. For the benefit of Irish-American bishops Slovak-Americans frequently likened Hungarian control of their homeland to that of the English in Ireland.

At the first Slovak parish in New York, the Church of St. Elizabeth of Hungary on East 4th Street, which was founded in 1891, the pastor, Father Francis Dénes, tried to cater to both the pro-Hungarian ("Magyarone") and anti-Hungarian Slovaks, but he pleased neither of them. Small incidents could sometimes take on cosmic dimensions. When a later pastor of St. Elizabeth, Father John Pollýakovícs, tried to remove the word "Hungarian" from the cornerstone of the church, an angry Magyarone parishioner stole it and deposited it in a neighborhood bar. Archbishop Corrigan received so many letters of complaint from unhappy parishioners that he told one of them in 1895: "The statements made by different persons concerning St. Elizabeth's Church are so conflicting that I do not know what to believe." His solution was to allow the Slovak nationalists to withdraw from

the parish and form the Church of St. John Nepomucene in a former synagogue a few doors away on the same street. Six years later the ethnic Hungarians did the same and formed the Church of St. Stephen of Hungary on East 14th Street.[39]

As the Slovak congregations became more prosperous and moved uptown, their churches followed them. St. Elizabeth of Hungary moved to a former Lutheran church on East 83rd Street in 1917. Its rival, St. John Nepomucene, moved to East 57th Street in 1911 and later to its present location at East 66th Street and First Avenue where a handsome Romanesque church was dedicated by Cardinal Hayes on May 30, 1925. St. Stephen of Hungary joined the procession and moved to East 82nd Street in 1929.

As in the case of the Poles, it often proved difficult to find suitable clergy for the Slovaks. At both St. Elizabeth of Hungary and St. John Nepomucene, and at the Church of the Most Holy Trinity in Yonkers, which was founded in 1894, pastors came and went in rapid succession.[40] Two years later at Most Holy Trinity a group of parishioners asked Archbishop Corrigan, "Why do you punish us for our hard-earned money with German or English priests, which do as they like with us, and besides we cannot understand?" In another Slovak parish, St. Mary's in Haverstraw, there were sixteen pastors during one eight-year period. One of them, Father Edward Heinlein, stayed only six weeks.[41]

However, peace descended upon the Slovak parishes in the early twentieth century with the appointment of several capable and popular pastors, Father Stephen Krasula at St. John Nepomucene (1916-1968), Father Andrew Dzijacký at St. Elizabeth of Hungary (1925-1958),

39 - AANY, G-82, Leopold Luft to Corrigan; Corrigan to G. Paulits, August 13, 1895.

40 - On Most Holy Trinity Church, see Thomas J. Shelley, *Slovaks on the Hudson: Most Holy Trinity Church, Yonkers, and the Slovak Catholics of the Archdiocese of New York* (Washington, D.C., The Catholic University of America Press, 2002).

41 - AANY, G-42, Petition to His Grace, the Archbishop of New York, March 19, 1896; AANY, V-8, Blaznik to Joseph Dineen, October 9, 1922.

and Father Stephen Kubašek at Most Holy Trinity (1913-1950). The parish history of St. Elizabeth's published in 1941 mentions with an almost audible sigh of relief that "Father Dzijacký (whose pastorate still continues) has performed one great task: he has given the parish stability."

Both Krasula and Kubašek were foreign-born but all three were educated at St. Joseph's Seminary, which set them apart from the long line of foreign-born predecessors. As the chancellor of the archdiocese remarked in 1920 about another Slovak-American priest, Father Andrew Novajovský, "This priest is particularly useful to us in New York because he has studied and been trained in our diocesan seminary and consequently has been fairly well imbued with a proper diocesan spirit---a spirit that is invariably lacking in outsiders that are brought in here to help out."[42]

The Church of the Most Holy Trinity, Yonkers, dedicated on September 5, 1910.

The Church of St. Elizabeth of Hungary on East 83rd Street. It now serves as the Archdiocesan Center for the Deaf.

The Slovak Church of St. John Nepomucene at First Avenue and 66th Street.

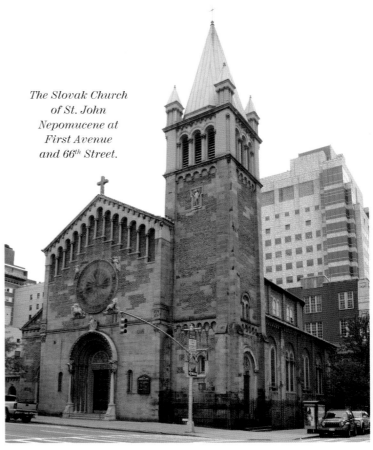

The combined Church and School of St. Stephen of Hungary on East 82nd Street.

As in Manhattan Catholics in the suburbs often built a small temporary church and replaced it with a larger one later. The original Church of the Most Holy Trinity on Walnut Street in Yonkers, dedicated on June 9, 1895.
Credit: *Church of the Most Holy Trinity.*

St. Mary's Church, Haverstraw, which was incorporated as St. Mary of the Assumption Church in October 1897 for the Slovak immigrants who worked in the local brickyards.

The last two Slovak parishes in the archdiocese were founded in the 1920s. Holy Cross Church in Sleepy Hollow was established as a mission of Most Holy Trinity in Yonkers in 1910 and became an independent parish in 1922. It was scheduled for closure in 2007. The last of the Slovak parishes was St. John the Baptist in Poughkeepsie. Unlike all the other Slovak parishes which were founded by the laity through their fraternal societies, St. John the Baptist owed its origin to an Irish-American cleric, Msgr. Joseph F. Sheahan, the pastor of St. Peter's Church and the dean of Dutchess County. He made the basement of his own church available to the Slovaks and then arranged for the purchase of a former Lutheran church on Grand Street where St. John the Baptist was founded in April 1923. The last of the Slovak parishes to be established, it was the first to decline and was closed in 2007.[43]

The initiative for founding Slavic parishes frequently came from the local branches of their national fraternal societies. Above: the members of the First Catholic Slovak Ladies Union (later Association) at the Church of the Most Holy Trinity, Yonkers, c. 1895. Credit: *Church of the Most Holy Trinity.*

The newly ordained Father Stephen Krasula, center, flanked by Msgr. Joseph Lings, V.F., the dean of Westchester and Putnam Counties, and Father John J. Kubasek, June 6, 1914. Credit: *Slovak Catholic Sokol*

Holy Cross Church in Sleepy Hollow began in 1910 as a mission of Most Holy Trinity in Yonkers, became an independent parish in 1922, and was slated to be closed in 2007.

42 - AANY, O-11, Joseph Dineen to Benedict Gillon, August 12, 1920.

43 - Shelley, *Slovaks on the Hudson,* 151-153.

The Czechs

In contrast to the Poles and Slovaks relatively few Bohemian Catholics (as the Czechs were then called) settled in New York City. Since many Czech Catholics knew German, they worshiped first at the German Church of St. Nicholas on East 2nd Street. In 1875 two Czech Catholic fraternal societies organized the Church of Sts. Cyril and Methodius on East 4th Street. In 1887 the Redemptorists took over the parish, renamed it Our Lady of Perpetual Help, and moved it to East 61st Street between First and Second Avenues where it lasted for more than a century.

The pastor, Father Frederick Henn, C.Ss.R., found that few of the Czechs were regular

The Church of St. John the Martyr,
New York's short-lived Czech church, on East 72nd Street.

churchgoers and they resented the fact that he was a German, although he claimed to speak Czech fluently. "If an angel from heaven would be among them, they would not go [to Sunday Mass]," Henn said. Without the financial support of the Irish who flocked to the church because of its convenient location, he said that the church would not have survived the first year. "The last day that I collected among the Bohemians," he added, "I visited 30 families and all I got was a mere seven cents." The Redemptorists were handicapped by the fact that their Czech province was only founded in 1901. Nevertheless, by 1904 they had a Czech-born priest at Our Lady of Perpetual Help and 400 Czech-American children attended the parochial school.[44]

Meanwhile, a diocesan priest, Father John T. Prout, founded a second Czech parish, St. John the Martyr (i.e., St. John Nepomucene) in a private residence on East 71st Street. The following year it moved to its present location, a former Presbyterian church on East 72nd Street near Second Avenue. It had a short history as a national parish. Prout was the first and last Czech-speaking pastor. Cardinal Farley removed him in 1918 and all of his successors were either Irish or Polish.[45]

In the years prior to World War I, Polish, Slovak and Czech clergy throughout the United States were often active in promoting the liberation of their homeland from foreign domination. In New York this was especially true of Msgr. Strzelecki at St. Stanislaus, Msgr. Dworzak at St. Casimir and Father Kubašek at Most Holy Trinity. Kubašek was one of the signatories to the Pittsburgh Agreement of 1918, which was one of the foundational documents in the establishment of Czechoslovakia.[46]

44 - AANY, Henn to Corrigan, September 8, 1889; I-7, W.J. Lucking, C.Ss.R., to Farley, May 2, 1904.

45 - AANY, Patrick Hayes to Patrick McGovern, September 18, 1917.

46 - On Kubašek, see Daniel F. Tanzone, "John F. Kubašek, Priest and Patriot," *Slovakia* 26 (1976): 69-75.

The Croatians and the Slovenians

Two other Latin-rite Slavic Catholics---the Croatians and the Slovenes---only came to the archdiocese in any appreciable numbers in the early twentieth century. Both were cared for by Franciscan friars of their own nationality. In the case of the more numerous of the two ethnic groups, the Croatians, the pioneer priest was Father Irenej Petricak, who was persuaded to come to the United States by a Slovenian Franciscan missionary in America, Father Kazimir Zakrajsek. Arriving in New York in 1913, Father Petricak gathered together the scattered Croatian Catholic community. With the permission of Msgr. Joseph Mooney, the vicar general, he began to offer Mass in the Italian Franciscan church of St. Clare in September 1913. Within a month the Croatians bought and renovated an abandoned Protestant church on 50th Street between Tenth and Eleventh Avenues, which they named in honor of Saints Cyril and Methodius. Msgr. Mooney blessed the church on November 15, 1913.

After World War II the influx of Croatian refugees made it imperative to find a larger church. In 1971 the arch-diocese gave permission for the

The first Church of Sts. Cyril and Methodius, a former Protestant church, on 50th Street between 10th and 11th Avenues. Credit: *Church of Sts. Cyril and Methodius*

Father Irenej Petricak, O.F.M., the pioneer Croatian priest in New York. Credit: *Church of Sts. Cyril and Methodius*

Croatians to use the Church of St. Raphael on West 41st Street which had become a chapel of Holy Innocents Church. On November 10, 1974, the last Mass was celebrated in the old church and St. Raphael's officially became the Church of St. Cyril and Methodius. Since 1916 the Slovenian Catholics in New York have also been cared for by Slovenian Franciscans at the Church of St. Cyril, which today is located in Lower Manhattan on St. Mark's Place west of First Avenue. [47]

The Church of Sts. Cyril and Methodius, the former St. Raphael's Church, on West 41st Street.

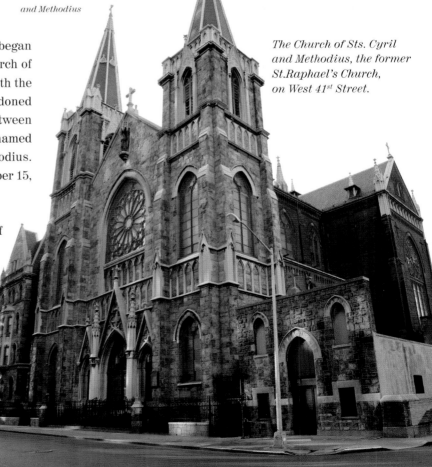

---

47 - *Croatian Catholic Church of New York*, 1913-1988 (New York: Church of Sts. Cyril and Methodius, 1988), unpaginated.

The Slovenian Catholic Church of Sts. Cyril on St. Mark's Place in Lower Manhattan.

The Greek Catholics

Of all the Catholic immigrants from Europe, those who experienced the greatest misunderstanding at the hands of their fellow Catholics were the so-called "Greek" Catholics. They were not ethnic Greeks at all, but Byzantine-rite Catholics from the eastern provinces of the Hapsburg Empire. Their ancestors were Eastern Orthodox Christians who had reunited with the Catholic Church and acknowledged the authority of the pope in the late sixteenth and early seventeenth century. The churches and the liturgy of the Greek Catholics were indistinguishable from those of Eastern Orthodox Christians. They had their own bishops and canon law, and they preserved their ancient tradition of having both a married and celibate clergy.

When the Greek Catholics first came to America in the 1880s, however, they received a frosty reception from many of their fellow Catholics, who did not think that they were real Catholics. The American bishops objected especially to the Greek

Catholic practice of a married clergy and prevailed upon the Holy See to forbid married priests to function in the United States.

When Archbishop Corrigan asked Julius Firczák, the Greek Catholic bishop of Muckachevo in Hungary for priests, he replied that the only priests he had available were married priests and regretted that they were not welcome in America. "The Catholic Church has allowed the Greek Catholic priests the privilege of marriage and the Roman Pontiff has confirmed it," he observed. "Now when they wish to make use of this privilege, it so disqualifies them that they cannot serve the Catholic cause in America." "Our people are abandoned like sheep without a shepherd," he complained. He added all too accurately, "What will be the consequences of this deplorable state of things, but many will fall into schism or Protestantism?"[48] In fact a quarter-of-a-million Greek Catholics eventually became members of the Russian Orthodox Church because of the lack of their own priests.

A typical seventeenth-century Greek Catholic Church in Eastern Europe.

48 - AANY, G-3,, Julius Firczák to Corrigan, April 20, 1893.

The first Greek Catholic church in the Archdiocese of New York was the Ruthenian Church of St. Nicholas of Myra on Ash Street on Nodine Hill in Yonkers, which dates from 1892. The first pastor was Father Eugene Szatala, a married priest whose wife was in Europe. Fortunately the dean of the clergy in Yonkers was Father Joseph Lings, the German-born pastor of St. Joseph's Church, who made an effort to understand and welcome these Greek Catholic newcomers. "Recognize them without making any conditions," he urged Archbishop Corrigan, "and you will have them body and soul."[49] Lings arranged for an interview between Father Szatala and Archbishop Corrigan, and the archbishop came to Yonkers to rededicate the church in 1894 after the trustees had handed over the property to the archdiocese.

Dean Lings soon discovered that the ethnic and cultural differences among Greek Catholics could be every bit as deep as those among his own Irish and German parishioners at St. Joseph's Church. Most of the parishioners of St. Nicholas of Myra were Ruthenians or Carpatho-Rusyns from the area south of the Carpathian Mountains that lay within the Hungarian part of the Hapsburg Empire. However, a sizeable minority came from the area north of the Carpathian Mountains which was then the Hapsburg province of Galicia and is now western Ukraine. Since Galicia was under Austrian rather than Hungarian rule, the Slavic immigrants from this region had escaped the magyarization policies of the Hungarian government and tended to be more nationalistic than their Ruthenian kinsmen.

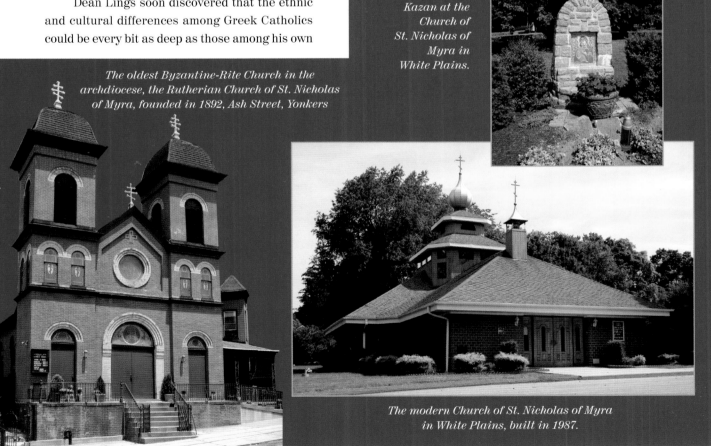

The mosaic of Our Lady of Kazan at the Church of St. Nicholas of Myra in White Plains.

The oldest Byzantine-Rite Church in the archdiocese, the Rutherian Church of St. Nicholas of Myra, founded in 1892, Ash Street, Yonkers

The modern Church of St. Nicholas of Myra in White Plains, built in 1987.

49 - AANY, G-2, Lings to Corrigan, January 21, 1893.

In 1898 the parishioners from Galicia withdrew from St. Nicholas of Myra and formed their own parish of St. Michael in Yonkers. Since they were at a stage in the development of their modern national consciousness when they were just beginning to call themselves Ukrainians, they designated their new parish as the Little Russian St. Michael Greek Catholic Church. This new parish brought Father Lings into contact with the first pastor of St. Michael's, Father Paul Tymkewych, whom Archbishop Corrigan suspended for starting the parish without his approval.

As Lings had done previously with the Ruthenians, he now acted as an intermediary between the Ukrainians in Yonkers and Arch-bishop Corrigan. As Lings became better acquainted with Tymkewych, he came to respect and admire him. Tymkewych explained his dilemma to Lings: "On the one hand they are my people and I am their priest, and on the other hand I must not break with the bishop."[50] Lings arranged for a meeting between Tymkewych and Corrigan at which the archbishop lifted his suspension and recognized him as the legitimate pastor of St. Michael's Church. Corrigan was so impressed with Lings' success in dealing with the Greek Catholics in Yonkers that in August 1897 he got the New York State bishops to appoint him to the new post of Commissary for the Greek Clergy in the Province of New York. This appointment made him responsible for evaluating the credentials of Greek Catholic priests who wished to function in the state.[51]

The sympathetic attitude of Lings and Corrigan to the Greek Catholics was a marked contrast to the attitude of many other American Catholic priests and bishops. Lings had no

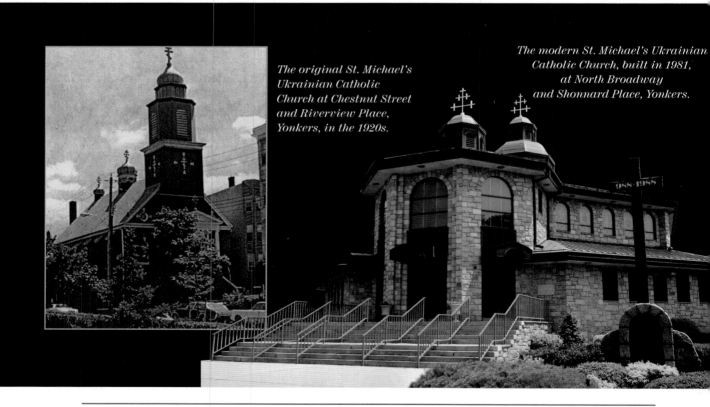

The original St. Michael's Ukrainian Catholic Church at Chestnut Street and Riverview Place, Yonkers, in the 1920s.

The modern St. Michael's Ukrainian Catholic Church, built in 1981, at North Broadway and Shonnard Place, Yonkers.

50 - AANY, G-19, Tymkewych to Lings, n.d. [March 1899].

51 - For Lings' remarkable career in Yonkers between 1867 and 1915, see Thomas J. Shelley, "Dean Lings' Church: The Success of Ethnic Catholicism in Yonkers in the 1890s," *CH* 65:1 (1996): 28-41.

problem with the Greek Catholic tradition of a married clergy. "It is certain," he told Archbishop Corrigan, "that married priests have shown themselves as effective in their church work as unmarried ones." To gain a better understanding of the Greek Catholics Lings went to Europe in the summer of 1899 and traveled to Lviv (then known as Lemberg), the spiritual center of Ukrainian Catholicism, where he was cordially received by the leaders of the Ukrainian Catholic Church and conversed with them in fluent German.[52]

Archbishop Corrigan planned a similar trip to Lviv that never materialized. Nevertheless, he made the far-sighted recommendation to Cardinal Gibbons in 1901 that the Greek Catholics in the United States should be placed under the jurisdiction of the Apostolic Delegate. He wanted to wean Greek priests in the United States from dependence on their

bishops in Europe, but he also wanted to shield them from unsympathetic American bishops. "I feel something must be done to avert schism among these people," to told Gibbons.[53] Nothing came of the proposal, however, and the Greek Catholics had to wait for relief until 1907 when the Holy See appointed the first Greek Catholic bishop in the United States, Soter Ortynsky, O.S.B.M.

The appointment of Bishop Ortynsky left many problems unresolved about the status of Greek Catholics in the United States. Ortysnky himself had little real authority in dealing with Latin-rite bishops. Moreover, he experienced the same internal divisions among his flock that had led to the founding of two separate Greek Catholic parishes in Yonkers. In 1924, eight years after Ortynsky's death, the

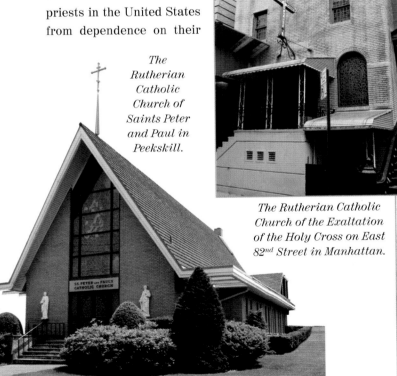

The Rutherian Catholic Church of Saints Peter and Paul in Peekskill.

The Rutherian Catholic Church of the Exaltation of the Holy Cross on East 82nd Street in Manhattan.

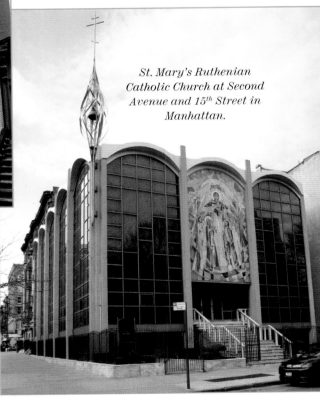

St. Mary's Ruthenian Catholic Church at Second Avenue and 15th Street in Manhattan.

52 - AANY, G-2, Lings, The Report of the Greek Church in Union with the Catholic Church in the Province of New York, n.d. [August 1898], G-19, Lings to Corrigan, July 31, 1899.

53 - AANY, G-16, Corrigan to Gibbons.

Holy See attempted to alleviate the friction among Greek Catholics by establishing two separate eparchies (dioceses), one for the Ukrainians with its headquarters in Philadelphia, the other for the Ruthenians with its headquarters in Pittsburgh. Both dioceses subsequently became metropolitan sees with several suffragan dioceses. Today the twelve Greek Catholic churches in the archdiocese of New York fall under the immediate jurisdiction of either the Ruthenian bishop of Passaic or the Ukrainian bishop of Stamford.

The oldest Greek Catholic church in the archdiocese, the Ruthenian Church of St. Nicholas of Myra in Yonkers, is now a mission of the church of the same name in White Plains. The other Ruthenian churches are the Church of the Exaltation of the Holy Cross on East 82nd Street in Manhattan, St. Mary's Church on East 15th Street, and the Church of Saints Peter and Paul in Peekskill.

There are seven Ukrainian Catholic churches in the archdiocese. In addition to the oldest, St. Michael's in Yonkers, they are St. George's on East 7th Street in Manhattan, St. Mary Protectoress on Washington Avenue in the Bronx, the Church of the Holy Trinity on Staten Island, the Church of Saints Peter and Paul in Spring Valley, St. Volodymyr in Glen Spey in Sullivan County, St. Andrew's in Hamptonburg in Orange County, and Holy Trinity in Kerhonkson in Ulster County.

The Ukrainian Catholic Church of Sts. Peter and Paul, Spring Valley. The parish was founded in 1913.

St. George's Ukrainian Catholic Church on East 7th Street, Manhattan. The parish was founded in 1905.

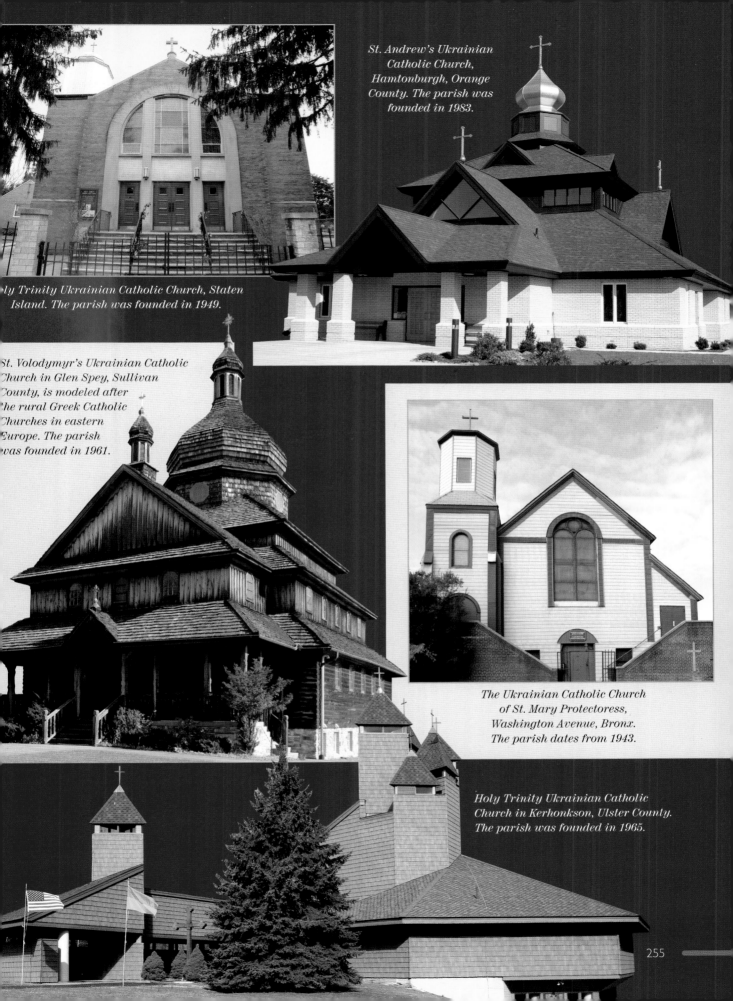

St. Andrew's Ukrainian Catholic Church, Hamtonburgh, Orange County. The parish was founded in 1983.

Holy Trinity Ukrainian Catholic Church, Staten Island. The parish was founded in 1949.

St. Volodymyr's Ukrainian Catholic Church in Glen Spey, Sullivan County, is modeled after the rural Greek Catholic Churches in eastern Europe. The parish was founded in 1961.

The Ukrainian Catholic Church of St. Mary Protectoress, Washington Avenue, Bronx. The parish dates from 1943.

Holy Trinity Ukrainian Catholic Church in Kerhonkson, Ulster County. The parish was founded in 1965.

African American Catholics

No New York Catholics found it more difficult to practice their faith than African Americans because of the widespread prejudice they encountered from white Catholics, both clergy and laity. Mention has already been made of the incident in St. Patrick's Old Cathedral when a white usher objected to the presence of the venerable Pierre Toussaint and the letter sent to Pope Pius IX in 1853 on behalf of twenty-six African Americans complaining that Archbishop Hughes "did not recognize the black race to be part of his flock."

One honorable exception to this pattern of white prejudice was Father Alphonse Lafont, the pastor of St. Vincent de Paul Church, who began a school for African American children in 1846. Father Lafont had a worthy successor in Father Thomas Farrell, the pastor of St. Joseph's Church in Greenwich Village from 1857 to 1880. Farrell was that rarest of rare birds, an Irish-American abolitionist, who flew the Stars-and-Stripes from his church during the Civil War. After the war he became a radical Republican when virtually every New York priest was a staunch supporter of Tammany Hall. [54]

On a tour of the South after the Civil War with this friend Father Sylvester Malone, a Brooklyn pastor, Farrell expressed such open sympathy for the emancipated black population that Bishop John McGill of Richmond accused him of "negrophily" as if it were a crime or sin.[55] In

Father Thomas Farrell, the pastor of St. Joseph's Church, Greenwich Village, who left $5,000 in his will to establish the first African American Church in New York.

Dr. Richard Burtsell, the first pastor of the Church of the Epiphany, who purchased a former Protestant Church on Bleecker Street that became the first Church of St. Benedict the Moor.

his will Farrell left $5,000 in Alabama state bonds for the purpose of founding a black parish in New York. Farrell's dream might never have been realized, however, except for the efforts of two young priests who were his disciples, Edward McGlynn and Richard Burtsell.

Knowing Cardinal McCloskey's lack of enthusiasm for a black church, Farrell shrewdly added a codicil to his will, specifying that, if the cardinal did not use the legacy for a black church within three years, it should go to the Colored Orphan Asylum, a non-Catholic institution. Three years elapsed without any action on the part of the archdiocese. Just as the time limit was about to expire, Edward McGlynn pleaded with McCloskey not to let slip this golden opportunity.[56]

Richard Burtsell took even more decisive action. Alerted that a former Protestant church on Bleecker Street was for sale, he offered to buy it at his own expense. He told McCloskey: "If the scheme was a success, I would be glad to turn it over to the ecclesiastical authorities. If it turned out a failure, the loss would be upon me." When McCloskey accepted the proposal, Burtsell purchased the former Third Universalist Church for the price of $40,000 and renamed it the Church of St. Benedict the Moor. It was not only the first black Catholic church in New York city, but also the first black Catholic church north of the Mason-Dixon line. The blessing of the church on November 18, 1883, was such an unusual event that it attracted a large number of curious bystanders who

---

54 - On Farrell, see Thomas J. Shelley, " 'A Good Man but Crazy on Some Points': Father Thomas Farrell and Liberal Catholicism in 19th-Century New York," *RHE* 97:1 (2002): 110-132.

55 - AANY, A-52, McGill to McCloskey, June 14, 1869.

56 - AANY, McGlynn to McCloskey, July 18, 1883.

THE CATHOLIC CHURCH
AND THE AFRICANS AMERICANS
in New York City

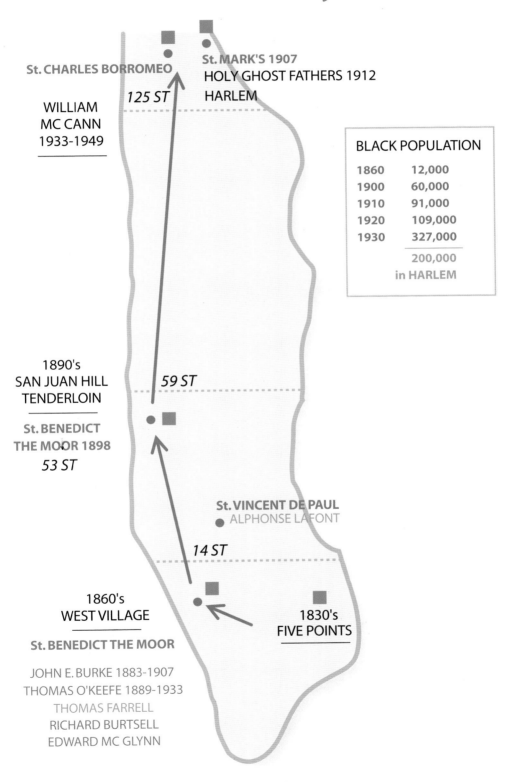

St. CHARLES BORROMEO

St. MARK'S 1907
HOLY GHOST FATHERS 1912
HARLEM

125 ST

WILLIAM
MC CANN
1933-1949

BLACK POPULATION	
1860	**12,000**
1900	**60,000**
1910	**91,000**
1920	**109,000**
1930	**327,000**
	200,000
	in HARLEM

1890's
SAN JUAN HILL
TENDERLOIN

59 ST

St. BENEDICT
THE MOOR 1898
53 ST

St. VINCENT DE PAUL
ALPHONSE LAFONT

14 ST

1860's
WEST VILLAGE

1830's
FIVE POINTS

St. BENEDICT THE MOOR

JOHN E. BURKE 1883-1907
THOMAS O'KEEFE 1889-1933
THOMAS FARRELL
RICHARD BURTSELL
EDWARD MC GLYNN

blocked traffic on Bleecker Street. The church itself was so crowded that, with the exception of the clergy, choir and reporters, admittance was restricted to African Americans.[57]

The parishioners included not only black Catholics from Manhattan, but from as far as Brooklyn, Queens and New Jersey. Most were probably working people, but at least two parishioners, Washington Parker and Robert N. Wood, were prominent in local politics and in the four Colored Catholic Congresses that were held between 1887 and 1891. Still another parishioner was Dr. John E. W. Thompson, who served as the U.S. minister to Haiti from 1885 to 1891. Not all of the worshippers at Mass on Sunday were black. Large numbers of white Catholics regularly attended Sunday Mass, which made it one of the very few racially integrated Christian churches in New York City.

Although Richard Burtsell was the founder of the church, he remained pastor of his own Church of the Epiphany. The first pastor of St. Benedict the Moor was Burtsell's curate, Father John E. Burke, who was to spend the next forty-two years working in ministry to black Catholics. In 1887 Burke prevailed upon the archdiocese to send him a curate, Father Thomas F. O'Keefe, a newly ordained priest who had been his altar boy in Epiphany Church. Like Burke, O'Keefe was to devote the rest of his life to the black apostolate and succeeded Burke as pastor in 1907 when he became the executive director of the Catholic Board for Mission Work Among the Colored People, a national orga-

An undated photo of Father John E. Burke, the first pastor of St. Benedict the Moor Church, with Father Augustus Tolton, the first African American priest ordained in the United States.
Credit: *Franciscan Sisters of Hastings-on-Hudson.*

nization established by the U.S. bishops.[58]

St. Benedict the Moor was a desperately poor parish despite contributions from white Catholics all across the city. Finances were a constant worry for Father Burke. In 1892, when Archbishop Corrigan chided him for failing to contribute to the building fund of the new seminary at Dunwoodie, Burke replied: "I have done nothing personally because I have no money." He received fewer than twenty-five Mass stipends per year and gave half of his salary to charity. "Connected with my mission," he added, "the calls for help are surprisingly constant and quickly drain my scant purse. It is simply out of the question for me to give money to the new seminary." He refused to ask his parishioners to give money to the seminary because they were so poor themselves.[59]

One of Burke's proudest accomplishments at St. Benedict the Moor was the establishment of St. Benedict's Home, an orphanage for black Catholic children whom other Catholic institutions would not accept. Originally located on MacDougal Street, St. Benedict's Home was relocated to Rye, New York, in 1890, where it was staffed by Dominican Sisters of Sparkill. The church itself was relocated to a former Protestant Church on West 53rd Street in 1898 in order to follow the uptown migration of New York's black population. However, the old church did not remain vacant long. It was quickly taken over by the Scalabrinian Fathers who renamed it the Church of Our Lady of Pompei.

57 - AANY, Burtsell, Diary, September 5, 7, 1883. *New York Times,* November 19, 1883.

58 - On the founding and the history of the parish, see Jack M. Arlotta, "Before Harlem: Black Catholics in the Archdiocese of New York and the Church of St. Benedict the Moor," *Dunwoodie Review* 16 (1992-1993): 69-108.

59 - AANY, C-29, Burke to Corrigan, June 12, 1892

Father John E. Burke (left) and Father Thomas O'Keefe (right) and the eleven Dominican Sisters of Sparkill
who staffed St. Benedict's Home in Rye, New York, in 1892.
Credit: *Dominican Sisters of Sparkill.*

St. Benedict's Home, Rye, New York, 1891-1941.

The second Church of St. Benedict the Moor on West 53rd
Street, now a mission of the Church of the Sacred Heart.

The Centenary
of the Immigrant Church

By 1908, when New York Catholics celebrated the centenary of the diocese, the Immigrant Church was alive and well. In Manhattan alone 42 of the 136 parishes were national parishes, representing eleven different ethnic groups. In addition to those already mentioned, they included the Maronites who worshipped at St. Joseph's Church on Washington Street, and the Lithuanians at the Church of Our Lady of Vilna on Broome Street.

New York got its first Spanish parish in 1902 with the establishment of the Church of Our Lady of Guadalupe on West 14th Street. It was founded by the Augustinians of the Assumption, a small French religious community with a number of Spanish-speaking priests.

The Spanish Catholic community in the archdiocese was so small, that for almost forty years Our Lady of Guadalupe advertised itself as "the parish for all Spanish-speaking people on New York." When the Augustinians expressed fears that they would not get sufficient financial support from the Spanish community, Archbishop Farley gave them advice based on his long experience in the diocese. He assured them that Irish would flock to their church and support it. That is exactly what happened.[60]

A half-century earlier the Redemptorist pastor of the German Church of St. Alphonsus had the same experience. He discovered that the Irish were more generous contributors than the Germans. When he announced plans for a new church with both an upstairs and a downstairs church, some German parishioners feared that they would be relegated to the basement. "We will not go downstairs and have the Irish over our heads," they protested. During the early years of St. Anthony of Padua, New York's first permanent Italian parish, Irish longshoremen from Greenwich Village helped to sustain the church. At the Church of St. Vincent de Paul, New York's first and only French parish, Irish marriages outnumbered those of the French by a margin of three to one during the first fifteen years. The German-born pastor of the Czech Church of Our Lady of Perpetual Help said that the church would not have survived for a year without the financial assistance of the English (i.e., Irish).[61]

The generosity of the Irish to the Church is an inescapable theme that runs throughout the history of the archdiocese in the nineteenth century. It remained constant even as the archdiocese became more ethnically diversified. German, French, Italian, Czech, African American, and other national parishes all benefited from the financial support of the Irish. No one was more aware of this than Archbishop Farley. He said in 1907: "There is no diocese in the country half as much burdened with other people's poor, illiterates and unregenerates of all states and nations as is New York, which has only one class of people (the Irish-Americans) to draw upon for the support of their own churches and schools, as well as for the maintenance of so many others."[62]

---

60 - AANY, Zachary Saint-Martin, A.A., to John J. Dunn, February 28, 1926.

61 - Dolan, *Immigrant Church,* 96; DiGiovanni, *Archbishop Corrigan and the Italian Immigrants,* 114; Faye Haun, "Immigration Stories: The Marriage Records of St. Vincent de Paul Church, New York City, 1842-1857," unpublished paper; AANY, Henn to Corrigan, September 8, 1889.

62 - ADR, Farley to McQuaid, May 5, 1907.

The first Church of Our Lady of Guadalupe on West 14th Street.

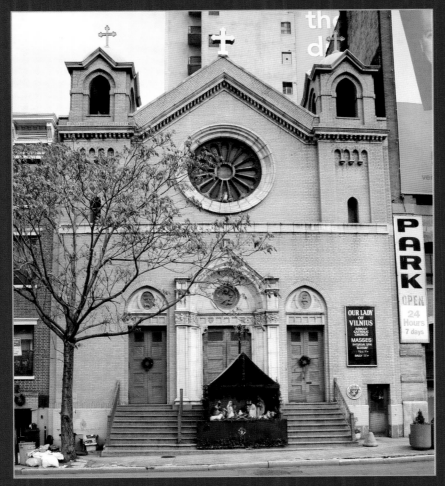

The Lithuanian Church of Our Lady of Vilna (later Our Lady of Vilnius), opened in 1905 and closed in 2007.

10

Brick and Mortar in the Railway Age

The Terrace in Central Park. Credit: *Archdiocese of New York*

During the second half of the nineteen century the Catholic population of the archdiocese probably tripled from about 350,000 to about 1,200,000.   During that same period the number of parishes in the archdiocese more than tripled from about 74 to 259, requiring a major building program to keep pace with the growth of the Catholic population. Manhattan remained the heartland of New York Catholicism with 49 new parishes added to the existing 32.

The era of the one-priest parish, which was once the norm throughout the diocese, was now only a memory in Manhattan. By the end of the nineteenth century virtually every Manhattan parish had at least two curates (as parochial vicars were then called), and the larger parishes sometimes had three curates. At St. Gabriel's Church on East 37th Street, where the pastor was auxiliary bishop John Farley, the vicar general, there were five curates, The generous staffing reflected the boom in vocations as well as the continued influx of European priests, mostly Irish and German. By 1900 there were 676 priests at work in the archdiocese, 416 diocesan priests, 227 religious order priests and 33 priests who were listed as unaffiliated.[1]

---

1 - *The Catholic Almanac* (Milwaukee: M.H. Wiltzius and Company, 1900). 114.

NEW PARISHES
in Manhattan
1865-1900

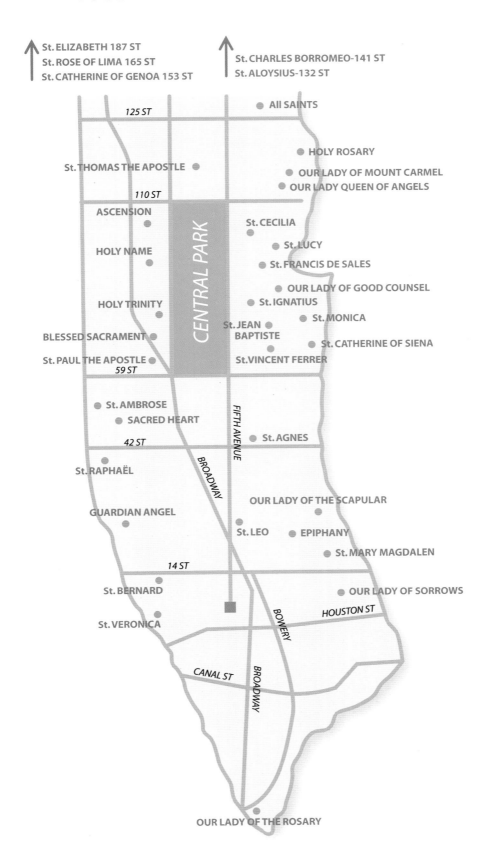

St. ELIZABETH 187 ST
St. ROSE OF LIMA 165 ST
St. CATHERINE OF GENOA 153 ST

St. CHARLES BORROMEO-141 ST
St. ALOYSIUS-132 ST

125 ST

All SAINTS

HOLY ROSARY

St. THOMAS THE APOSTLE

OUR LADY OF MOUNT CARMEL

OUR LADY QUEEN OF ANGELS

110 ST

ASCENSION

St. CECILIA

CENTRAL PARK

St. LUCY

HOLY NAME

St. FRANCIS DE SALES

OUR LADY OF GOOD COUNSEL

HOLY TRINITY

St. IGNATIUS

St. MONICA

BLESSED SACRAMENT

St. JEAN BAPTISTE

St. CATHERINE OF SIENA

St. PAUL THE APOSTLE

St. VINCENT FERRER

59 ST

St. AMBROSE

SACRED HEART

42 ST

FIFTH AVENUE

St. AGNES

St. RAPHAËL

BROADWAY

OUR LADY OF THE SCAPULAR

GUARDIAN ANGEL

St. LEO

EPIPHANY

St. MARY MAGDALEN

14 ST

St. BERNARD

OUR LADY OF SORROWS

St. VERONICA

BOWERY

HOUSTON ST

CANAL ST

BROADWAY

OUR LADY OF THE ROSARY

The Changing Face of Catholic Manhattan

Significantly almost half of the forty-nine new parishes established in Manhattan during the Gilded Age were located north of 59th Street, reflecting the northward push of the city's population. The railway age came into the heart of the city in those years with the construction of elevated railways on Second, Third, Sixth and Ninth Avenues. By 1881 New Yorkers could travel from 129th Street on the Second or Third Avenue El to South Ferry and north again on the Sixth or Ninth Avenue El to 155th Street and Eighth Avenue for five cents. The Els were to remain the backbone of the city's mass transit system for almost a half-century until they were replaced by the subways in the early twentieth century.

Real estate developers were quick to take advantage of their opportunities. They filled the vacant lots north of 59th Street with a bewildering variety of buildings to suit every need, mansions for the wealthy on Fifth Avenue, tenements for the poor in the shadow of the Els, and rows of attached high-stooped brownstones for the middle class on the side streets. The opening of the Dakota at 72nd Street and Central Park West in 1884 gave the city its first taste of a luxury apartment building.

In many new parishes in Manhattan a temporary starter church was hastily built with the intention of replacing it later with a permanent structure as the congregation increased in size and more money became available. Some of the new church buildings erected in the late nineteenth and early twentieth century were imposing architectural monuments, with richly decorated interiors, reflecting the increasing wealth and sophistication of the Catholic community and its clergy.

The Upper West Side

On the Upper West Side the first site of the Church of Blessed Sacrament in 1887 was the Havermeyer stables on West 72nd Street. It was

Blessed Sacrament parish could boast of a Gothic school building as well as a Gothic church.
Credit: *Church of the Blessed Sacrament*

The Church of the Blessed Sacrament on West 71st Street, which was modeled after the Sainte Chapell in Paris and completed in 1918.

replaced first with a red brick church and then in 1918 with the present church on West 71st Street, a French Gothic structure inspired by the Sainte Chapelle in Paris. The parish once owned the southeast corner of Broadway and 71st Street, but sold it to the Alamanc Hotel for $750,000. It left the parish with a gorgeous church hidden in the middle of the block, but paid off the debt of $600,000 on the church, school and rectory.[2]

1912.[3] It took even longer for the pastors of the Church of the Holy Name of Jesus to construct the imposing building at the corner of Amsterdam Avenue and 96th Street. The parish was founded in 1868, but Father James Galligan only erected the present church in the late 1890s. It was dedicated by Archbishop Corrigan on April 1, 1900.

Father James M. Galligan, who built the present Church of the Holy Name of Jesus.

Mass transit in New York City on a summer day in the early twentieth century. Two local trains of the Third Avenue El pass each while in the streets below open-sided streetcars met at the junction of Third Avenue and the Bowery.

Holy Trinity Church only had a hall to use for Sunday Mass when the parish was founded in 1898, which caused a number of unhappy parishioners to go elsewhere on Sunday morning. This led the first pastor, Father Joseph Bigley, to move quickly to build a church on West 82nd Street. The lower church was finished in August 1900, four months after Bigley died at the age of forty-five. His successor, Father Michael Considine, was responsible for choosing the unusual Byzantine style of architecture for the upper church which took a decade to complete and was dedicated by Cardinal Farley on May 5,

The Byzantine-style Church of the Holy Trinity on West 82nd Street, which took a dozen years to complete and was opened in 1912.

2 - *Golden Jubilee of the Church of the Blessed Sacrament* (New York: Church of the Blessed Sacrament, 1937), 15.

3 - AANY, Joseph Bigley to Corrigan, April 20, 1899; *Holy Trinity Church* (Custombook, 1973), unpaginated.,

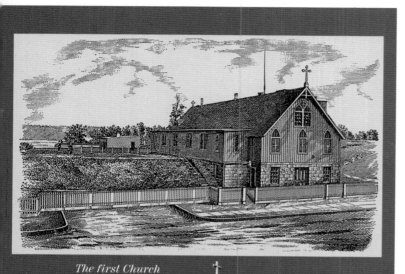

The first Church of the Holy Name of Jesus on the Boulevard (Broadway) near West 97th Street.

The Church of the Holy Name of Jesus at Amsterdam Avenue and West 96th Street dedicated in 1900. The church is now staffed by the Franciscan friars of Holy Name Province.

Impressive as these churches were, however, they were overshadowed by the Church of St. Paul the Apostle, the mother church of the Paulist Fathers. Begun in 1876 and completed in 1885, St. Paul's Church was almost 300 feet long, the largest church in the archdiocese after the cathedral, although it was said to have cost only one eighth as much to build because the stone was purchased at a bargain price from an old aqueduct. "It is the cheapest building of its kind in the country," said one knowledgeable observer.

Isaac Hecker, the founder of the Paulist Fathers, often referred to the Church of St. Paul the Apostle as a cathedral or basilica. Others called it Fortress Deshon after Father George Deshon, the Paulist priest and former army engineer who supervised the final stages of the construction. The ceiling with its depiction of the heavens was the work of another talented Paulist, the astronomer George Searle. It had a seating capacity of 2,500 with space for 2,000 more, and the lower church could accommodate an equal number of worshippers. In keeping with the missionary apostolate of the Paulists, St. Paul was essentially a preaching church. For this reason, in that pre-electronic age the pulpit was located in the center of the nave, and the front pews were reversible (like those on the new electric streetcars) so that the whole congregation could see and hear the preacher.[4]

Father Isaac Hecker, the founder of the Paulist Fathers.

4 - Joseph Scott, C.S.P., *A Century and More of Reaching Out: A Historical Sketch of the Parish of St. Paul the Apostle* (New York: Missionary Society of St. Paul the Apostle, 1983), 3-7.

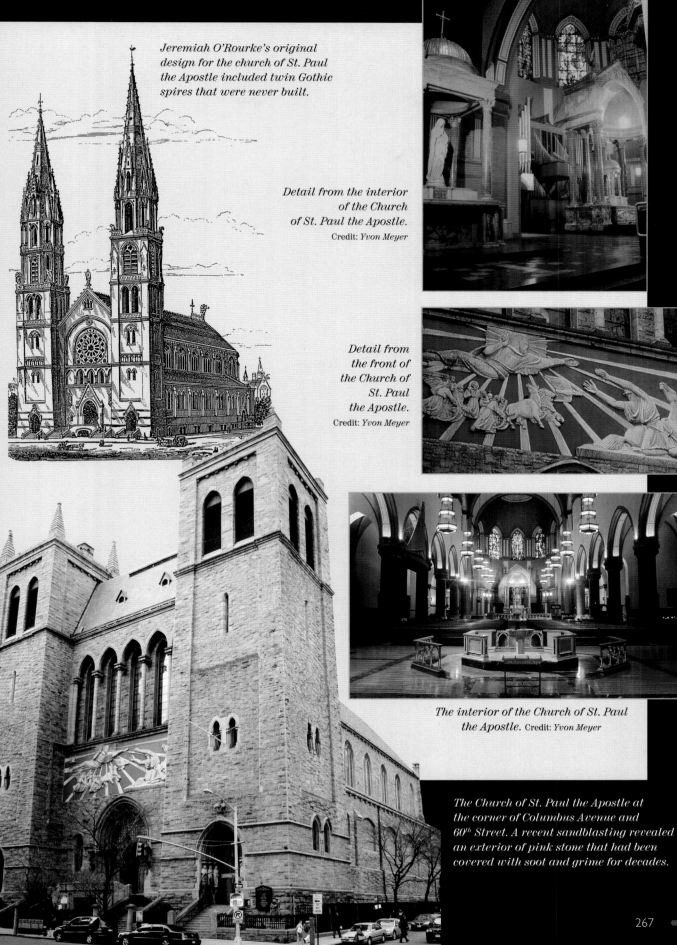

Jeremiah O'Rourke's original design for the church of St. Paul the Apostle included twin Gothic spires that were never built.

Detail from the interior of the Church of St. Paul the Apostle. Credit: *Yvon Meyer*

Detail from the front of the Church of St. Paul the Apostle. Credit: *Yvon Meyer*

The interior of the Church of St. Paul the Apostle. Credit: *Yvon Meyer*

The Church of St. Paul the Apostle at the corner of Columbus Avenue and 60th Street. A recent sandblasting revealed an exterior of pink stone that had been covered with soot and grime for decades.

267

Before the Civil War the northernmost Catholic Church on Manhattan Island was the Church of the Annunciation in Manhattanville. It lost that distinction in 1869 when the Church of St. Elizabeth was founded in Fort Washington Heights with a mission church across the Harlem River in Kingsbridge. Father Henry Brann, the pastor from 1870 to 1890, first built a church in Kingsbridge and celebrated Sunday Mass in Washington Heights in a public school until he was given property for a church at Broadway and 187th Street. The donor was a most unlikely person, James Gordon Bennett, the editor of the *New York Herald,* who had been a fierce critic of Archbishop Hughes. Bennett owned an estate in Washington Heights, and it has been suggested that the real reason for his largesse was that he wanted the servants to return from Mass in time to cook his Sunday dinner. Whatever Gordon's motives, the brick and brownstone church was dedicated by Archbishop McCloskey on January 14, 1872.[5]

The Northern Tip of Manhattan Island in 1876: Spuyten Duvil Creek with the bridge of the New York and Hudson River Railroad in the foreground and the Palisades in the background.
Credit: *Harper's New Monthly Magazine,* April 1876

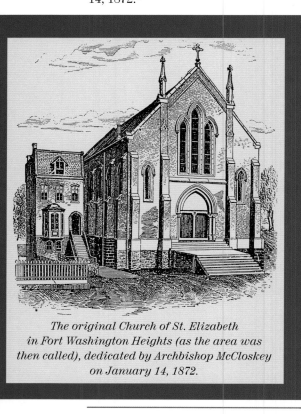

The original Church of St. Elizabeth in Fort Washington Heights (as the area was then called), dedicated by Archbishop McCloskey on January 14, 1872.

The original Church of St. Elizabeth burned down in 1925 and was replaced with modern Gothic church at 187th Street and Wadsworth Avenue that was dedicated by Cardinal Hayes on September 15, 1929.

5 - *St. Elizabeth's Church* (Custombook, 1970), 6-7.

John Gilmary Shea wondered if he would ever live to see the day when the Catholic population would cover the entire island of Manhattan from the Battery to Spuyten Duyvil. That still had not happened as late as 1899 when the pastor of St. Elizabeth, Father Thomas F. Lynch, objected vehemently at the news that the archdiocese intended to start a new parish between his own church and St. Catherine of Genoa, a parish that had been established on West 153rd Street in 1887. He said that the projected new parish would deprive him of the only part of his domain that was built up, the area between 162nd Street and 170th Street. The rest of northern Manhattan was still largely woodlands. Father Lynch was able to fend off the inevitable division of his parish, but only for two years. In 1901 the Church of St. Rose of Lima was established on West 165th Street.[6]

The Church of the Ascension on West 107th Street, built in 1897.

Another Upper West Side parish had been founded six years earlier, the Church of the Ascension on West 107th Street. In 1900 the pastor, Father Nicolas Reinhart, and one of the curates, Father August Stehle, were German, reflecting the considerable number of German-speaking Catholics in the neighborhood, although the parish itself never became a German national parish like St. Joseph's on West 125th Street.

The Church of St. Catherine of Genoa on West 153rd Street, dedicated in 1889.

The Church of St. Rose of Lima on West 165th Street, erected in 1901.

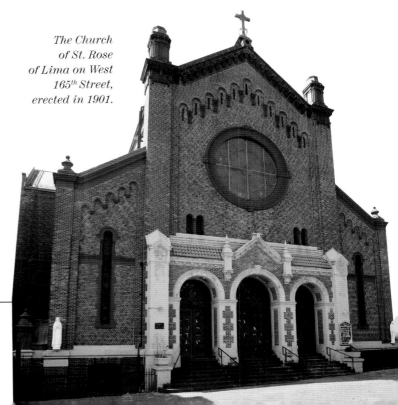

6 - AANY, Thomas F. Lynch to Corrigan, June 13, 1899.

The Upper East Side

On the Upper East Side the Church of St. Ignatius Loyola on Park Avenue, dedicated in 1898, was a classical Baroque Jesuit church. The Jesuits had been given the parish in 1866 when it was the Church of St. Lawrence O'Toole to facilitate their ministry as chaplains in the hospitals, asylums and prison on Blackwell's, Ward's and Randall's islands. As far back as 1877 the Jesuits made plans to replace the original church on East 84th Street. Father David Merrick, S.J., finished the basement of the present church in 1886, but it was not until December 11, 1898 that the upper church was completed and dedicated by Archbishop Corrigan.

The person who brought the project to completion was Father Neil McKinnon, S.J., who had become the pastor in 1893. It was said of McKinnon that he found St. Lawrence O'Toole a parish of brick and left it a parish of marble. The architect was William Schickel, a parishioner, who fulfilled his commission as a labor of love. The interior is especially noteworthy for the exquisite baptistry. The Jesuits wished to use the dedication of the new church to change the name from St. Lawrence O'Toole to St. Ignatius Loyola, the but the Roman authorities demurred and suggested a compromise. The Jesuits were allowed to call their new church St. Ignatius, but they were told to retain the original name of St. Lawrence O'Toole for the lower church.[7]

The Church of St. Ignatius Loyola at Park Avenue and East 84th Street. The original plans called for twin towers that would soar 210 feet above the pavement.

Father Neil M. McKinnon, S.J., the master builder among the pastors of St. Ignatius Loyola, who was responsible for the erection of the Park Avenue church.

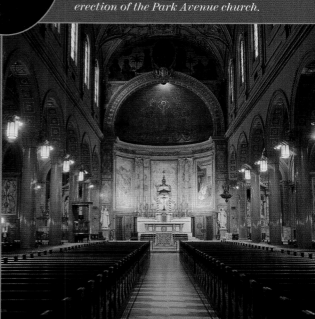

The interior of the Church of St. Ignatius Loyola.
Credit: *Yvon Meyer*

7 - *Church of St. Ignatius Loyola and St. Lawrence O'Toole* (New York: Church of St. Ignatius Loyola, 1966), 21-25. When Father McKinnon objected to supplying a chaplain for Hart's Island, Bishop John Farley insisted that the Jesuits got St. Lawrence O'Toole in return for providing chaplains for the East River Islands. "No question about it," he said. AANY, Minutes of the Meetings of the Board of Diocesan Consultors, September 6, 1899.

The Church of St. Francis De Sales on West 96th Street was built that same year in the same Baroque style as St. Ignatius Loyola, but on a smaller scale. John Talbot Smith preferred it to St. Ignatius and considered the marble façade and good lines "a delight to the artist and adorer."

The Church of St. Francis de Sales on East 96th Street. John Talbot Smith found it more impressive than the Church of St. Ignatius Loyola.

The Church of St. Jean Baptiste owes its existence to a group of devout French-Canadians in Yorkville who, like the first parishioners of Blessed Sacrament Church, began to celebrate the Eucharist in an odiferous rented loft over a stable on East 77th Street in 1882. Making the best of a bad situation, they called it the Christmas Creche. Two years later they built a small church dedicated to the patron saint of French Canada on East 76th street between Lexington and Third Avenues. The church

was staffed by a succession of French and French-Canadian priests until 1900 when Archbishop Corrigan entrusted the parish to the Blessed Sacrament Fathers, who had come to New York City from Quebec to establish a Eucharistic shrine church.

Thomas Fortune Ryan, the bene-factor of the Church of St. Jean Baptiste. Credit: *Église St. Jean Baptiste*

Fortunately for them, one of their parishioners was Thomas Fortune Ryan, a self-made multimillionaire who epitomized the opportunities of the Gilded Age for adventuresome investors like himself. Ryan was said to have been one of the ten wealthiest men in the country and the wealthiest Catholic in New York at the turn of the last century. Much of his wealth came from investments in diamond mines in the Belgian Congo and the ownership of New York City streetcar companies. Neither business was noted for enlightened employee practices.

Unable to find a seat at Mass one Sunday morning, Ryan allegedly made an offer to the pastor to build a larger church, a quixotic gesture that was eventually to cost him upwards of $600,000. The pastor, the enterprising Father Arthur Letellier, S.S.S., built the massive new Church of St. Jean Baptiste and surmounted it with a dome that soared to a height of 175 feet. Dedicated by Cardinal Farley on January 6, 1914, the focal point of the interior was the elaborate throne behind the main altar, which was designed for the perpetual exposition of the Blessed Sacrament, a devotion that was first introduced to the archdiocese by the Blessed Sacrament Fathers.[8]

8 - John A. Kamas, S.S.S., and Barbara O'Dwyer Lopez, *Eglise Saint Jean Baptiste* (New York: Eglise St. Jean Baptiste, 2001), 1-18.

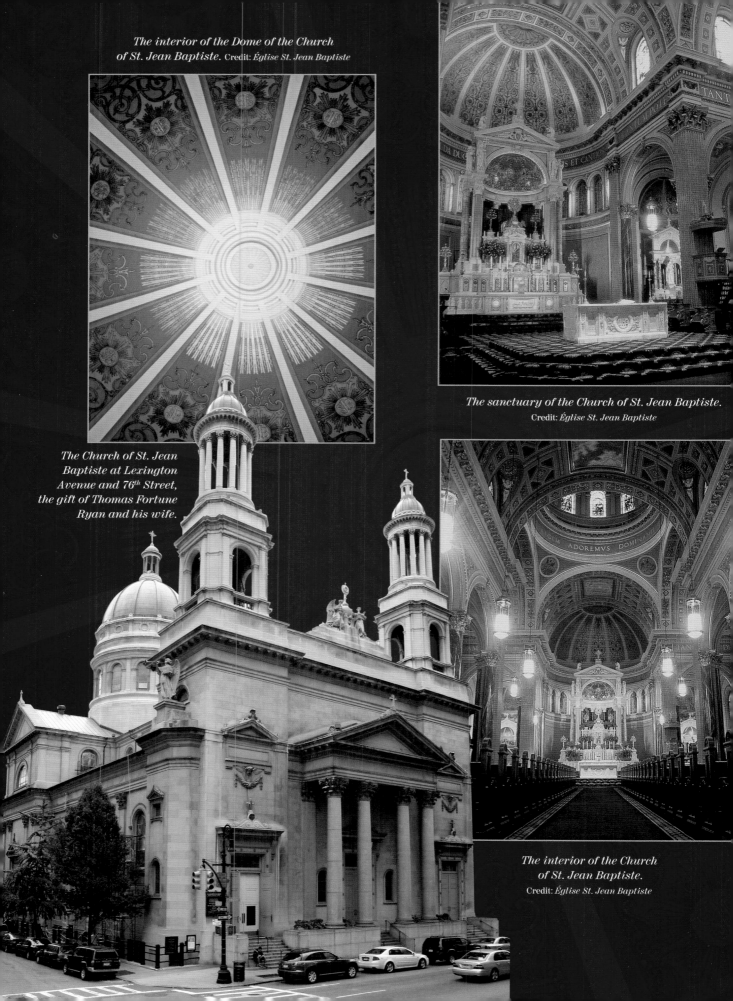

The interior of the Dome of the Church of St. Jean Baptiste. Credit: Église St. Jean Baptiste

The sanctuary of the Church of St. Jean Baptiste. Credit: Église St. Jean Baptiste

The Church of St. Jean Baptiste at Lexington Avenue and 76th Street, the gift of Thomas Fortune Ryan and his wife.

The interior of the Church of St. Jean Baptiste. Credit: Église St. Jean Baptiste

The first Dominican church of St. Vincent Ferrer was a temporary frame building at the northeast corner of Lexington Avenue and 65th Street which was built in 1867. Two years later it was replaced with a Gothic church designed by Patrick Keely. In 1893 the pastor complained that "St. Vincent Ferrer is supposed to be very large and very wealthy, but in reality it is neither large nor wealthy." He was disappointed because *only* 4,000 people came to Mass on Sunday. In 1916 the Dominican friars began work on their new Church of St. Vincent Ferrer. The most widely admired of all the new Catholic churches in New York City, it was a Gothic masterpiece that was dedicated by Cardinal Farley on May 5, 1918. The architect was Bertram G. Goodhue, who also designed St. Thomas Episcopal Church on Fifth Avenue and the Chapel at West Point. In subsequent years, as parish finances permitted, the interior of the church was embellished with sumptuous artwork and a splendid organ.[9]

While New York Catholics erected ever more impressive churches, they did not live in them, as Henry Browne dryly observed. Most New York Catholics were still poor people, immigrants or the children of immigrants who lived in tenement houses. Reflecting on his own experience growing up in St. Michael's parish in the 1920s, Browne recalled that "the culture of the tenement" meant "climbing as many as five flights of stairs perhaps several times a day. Sometimes it was to the roof to hang wet wash. It meant to be without steam heat, electric lights, inside plumbing, or even hot water, bath tub or shower, without refrigeration or closet space."[10]

The Hell Gate Ferry Slip at the Foot of 86th Street in 1860. Credit: *Archdiocese of New York*

9 - AANY, J. H. Slinger, O.P. to Corrigan, January 18, 1893; *St. Vincent Ferrer Church* (New York: Church of St. Vincent Ferrer, n.d.), 17-25.

10 - Henry J. Browne, *One Stop Above Hell's Kitchen: Sacred Heart Parish in Clinton* (New York: Church of the Sacred Heart, 1977), 33. John Tracy Ellis regarded this as the best history of any New York parish.

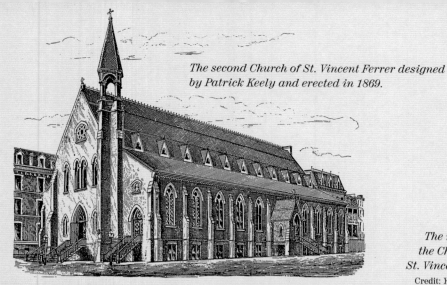

The second Church of St. Vincent Ferrer designed by Patrick Keely and erected in 1869.

Our Lady presents the rosary to St. Dominic: Church of St. Vincent Ferrer.
Credit: *Yvon Meyer*

The rear of the Church of St. Vincent Ferrer.
Credit: *Yvon Meyer*

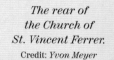

Interior of the Church of St. Vincent Ferrer.
Credit: *Yvon Meyer*

The Dominican Church of St. Vincent Ferrer at Lexington Avenue and 66th Street designed by Bertram G. Goodhue.

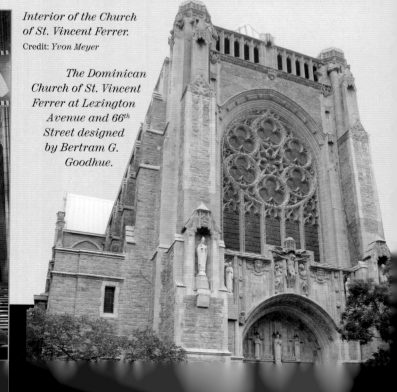

By 1900 there was a Catholic church on the Upper East Side at least every ten blocks and sometimes much closer than that. St. Cecilia's parish dates from 1873 when a small frame church was erected on East 105th Street. It was replaced with the present church in 1884. Both St. Monica's on East 79th Street and All Saints Church were founded in 1879. All Saints was still another Catholic church that was born in a stable, in this case in the unused horsecar barns at 129th Street and Third Avenue. When Father James Power finally built his church one block west at Lexington Avenue in 1893, he chose a unique design. It was a highly ornamented Gothic church, but the material that he used was red and yellow brick rather than stone. A fervent Irish patriot, Power used his pulpit every Sunday to rail against the bloody Sasenach before a captive audience.

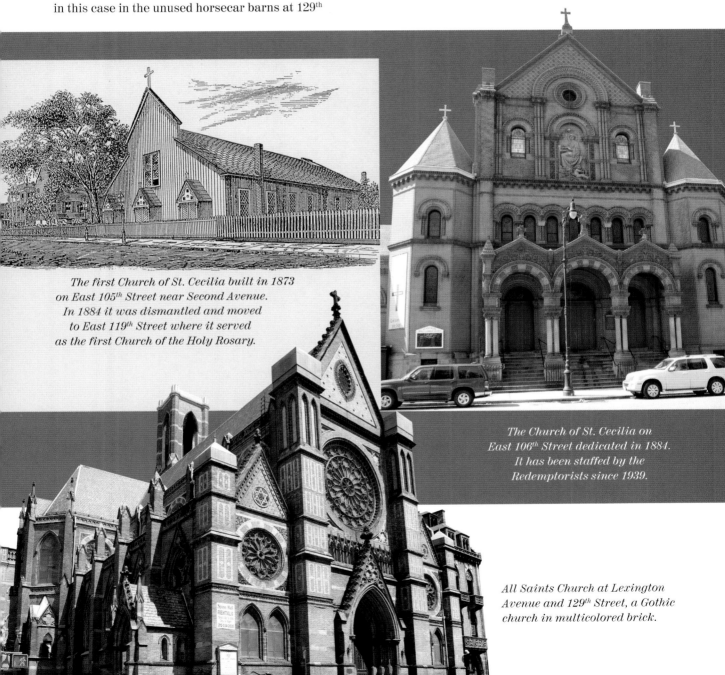

The first Church of St. Cecilia built in 1873 on East 105th Street near Second Avenue. In 1884 it was dismantled and moved to East 119th Street where it served as the first Church of the Holy Rosary.

The Church of St. Cecilia on East 106th Street dedicated in 1884. It has been staffed by the Redemptorists since 1939.

All Saints Church at Lexington Avenue and 129th Street, a Gothic church in multicolored brick.

At St. Monica's Father James Dougherty avoided still another stable for his first church, but not by much. He purchased an old feed store on 78th Street and reconstructed it as a church for 250 people in the space of six weeks at a total cost, including the land, of $7,000. In 1881 he bought the property on 79th Street where the present church is located. He laid the cornerstone later that same year and had the lower church completed by 1883. He could have purchased the corner lot but apparently decided not to do so for fear that the noise from the traffic on First Avenue would disturb church services.[11]

The establishment of the Church of Our Lady of Good Counsel on West 90st Street gave the Catholics of Yorkville their third parish in 1886. It was located across the street from the Rupert Brewery, which provided churchgoers with a fragrant aroma on the way to and from Mass. Farther south the Dominicans at St. Vincent Ferrer established a mission church on the east side of First Avenue in 1896. It quickly developed into their second New York parish, St. Catherine of Siena. The present church on East 68th Street was dedicated on May 3, 1931.

Father James J. Dougherty, LL.D., the founding pastor of the Church of St. Monica.
Credit: *Church of St. Monica*

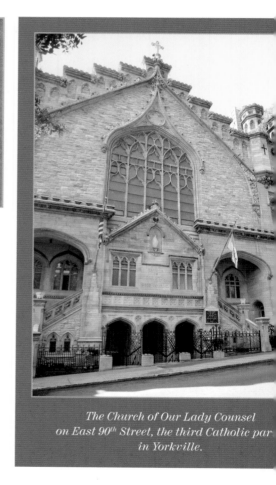

The Church of Our Lady Counsel on East 90th Street, the third Catholic par in Yorkville.

The Church of St. Monica on East 79th Street. Begun in 1881, the lower church was dedicated in 1883.

11 - George A. Kelly, *The Story of St. Monica's Parish* (New York: Monica Press, 1954), 13-17.

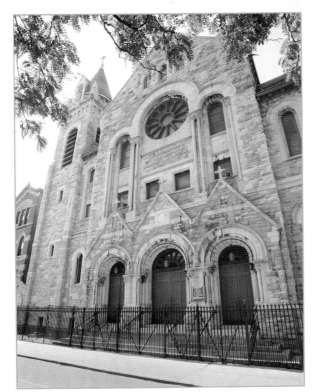

The Dominican Church of St. Catherine of Siena on East 68th Street. It was dedicated on May 3, 1931.

East and Central Harlem

As was mentioned already, East Harlem had three parishes by 1900, Holy Rosary, St. Lucy, and the Italian Church of Our Lady of Mount Carmel, in an area that was becoming increasingly Italian in its ethnic composition. The first pastor of St. Lucy was Father Edward Cronin, a Roman-educated New Yorker who was fluent in Italian. At Holy Rosary an Italian-born pastor was appointed in 1925, Father Gaetano Arcese, who was to serve as an advisor to Cardinal Hayes on the Italian parishes.

The founding pastor of Holy Rosary, Father Joseph Byron, found a unique way to provide a starter church for his parish. Fourteen blocks south, the parishioners at St. Cecilia's were moving from their little wooden church to a spanking new brick church on East 106th Street. Father Byron bought the old St. Cecilia's, dismantled it, floated it up the East River on barges and reassembled it on East 119th Street as his first church. It was replaced by the present church, which was dedicated on February 11, 1900.[12]

The Church of St. Lucy on East 104th Street, built in 1914.

---

12 - *Holy Rosary Church Diamond Jubilee* (New York: Church of the Holy Rosary, 1944), unpaginated.

As the Germans moved north from Yorkville, a German national parish was provided for them in East Harlem in 1886 at the Church of Our Lady Queen of Angels on 113th Street by the Capuchins, which was their third New York parish. It was closed in 2007.

The first parishes in Central Harlem were established in the late nineteenth century when real estate developers tried to attract prosperous middle class New Yorkers to the elegant apartment buildings that they had built on Lenox and Seventh Avenues and to the brownstones that lined the side streets. When the white middle class failed to appear in sufficiently large numbers even after the arrival of the subway in 1904, desperate landlords subdivided their half-empty buildings and rented them to African Americans, which was how Harlem became the center of New York City's largest black community.

Down to World War I, however, Central Harlem was still a predominantly white neighborhood served by St. Charles Borromeo on 141st Street, founded in 1888, and by St. Thomas the Apostle on 118th Street and St. Aloysius on 132nd Street, both founded in 1889. In the first decade of the twentieth century the pastor of St. Thomas the Apostle observed that most of the newcomers to the neighborhood were not African Americans but Jews.[13]

The Church of Our Lady Queen of Angels, founded by the Capuchins in 1886 as a German national parish on 113th Street in East Harlem. It was closed in 2007.

The Church of St. Aloysius on West 132nd Street, built in the Byzantine style in 1904. It is now staffed by the Society of Jesus.

The Church of St. Charles Borromeo on West 141st Street in Central Harlem. Opened in 1905 and severely damaged by fire in 1968, the façade of the French Gothic church was preserved when a new and smaller church was built to replace it.

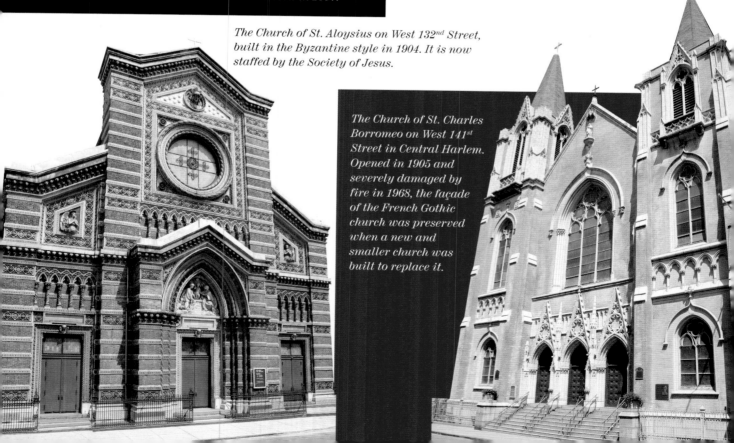

A decline in the number of parishioners led to the closing of St. Thomas the Apostle in 2005, but both St. Charles Borromeo and St. Aloysius remain vibrant African American parishes. In the 1930s and 1940s St. Charles Borromeo was the center of the Harlem Apostolate, a major effort at evangelization in the black community on the part of the archdiocese.

The first pastor of St. Charles Borromeo, Dr. Charles O'Keefe, cashed in handsomely on the real estate boom in Harlem. He bought sixteen lots in 1888 for $102,000 with borrowed money, and sold them two years later for $200,000. With the profit (and an additional outlay of $12,000), he was able to purchase property on West 141st Street and to erect a small church and rectory. The second pastor, Henry Gordon, began work in 1901 on a French Gothic church that was completed in 1905.[14]

Father James McGean, the pastor of St. Peter's Church.

Lower Manhattan in Transition

In Lower Manhattan the exodus of middle-class Protestants from the area had long been under way, and the Catholics now joined them as their economic prospects began to improve. The pastor of St. Peter's Church, Father James H. McGean, complained in 1896 that "Brooklyn and [New] Jersey have taken away our industrious middle class." He claimed that since his arrival at St. Peter's in 1882, 500 families had moved out of the parish. St. Andrew's was another downtown parish that experienced a large decline in the size of its congregation in the 1890s. "The place [is] eating itself up [financially]," the diocesan consultors were told, and one of the vicars general, Monsignor Joseph Mooney, recommended selling the property. Bishop John Farley, the other vicar general, had made the same recommendation earlier, urging the sale of several surplus downtown churches to pay the debt on the cathedral and the new seminary at Dunwoodie. It was advice that he did not choose to follow when he became the archbishop in 1902.[15]

Bowling Green in the 1890s.

---

13 - AANY, John J. Keogan to Farley, May 30, 1904.

14 - Hugh F. Corrigan, "The History of a Catholic Church in Harlem," *St. Charles Borromeo* (Custombook, 1973), 13-18 .

15 - AANY, Minutes of the Meetings of the Board of Diocesan Consultors, December 2, 1896, December 7, 1898.

Nevertheless, despite the exodus of the middle class from Lower Manhattan, Jacob Riis found that the area was still plentifully supplied with churches in 1890 when he made his famous survey. He counted 114 churches and synagogues (and 4,065 saloons) south of 14th Street.[16] Even as the two vicars general of the archdiocese were urging the closing of superfluous parishes, new ones were being added. No fewer than eighteen new parishes were started in Lower Manhattan between 1865 and 1900.

The anomaly is explained by the fact that two of them dated from 1868, when Lower Manhattan was still filling up with Irish immigrants. One was the Church of St. Bernard on West 14th Street, which straddled the boundary between Greenwich Village and Chelsea. The other was the Church of St. Rose of Lima on Cannon Street between Broome and Delancey Streets, which was founded to relieve the overcrowding in the other parishes on the Lower East Side by providing a church between St. Mary's on Grand Street and St. Brigid's on 8th Street. It was closed and demolished in the 1960s.

Fourteen other parishes were national parishes. The oldest was the Church of Our Lady of Sorrows, established by the Capuchins in 1867 for the Germans. It was the first Capuchin church in the archdiocese and the first appearance of the Capuchins in New York since the days of Father Whelan and Father Nugent at St. Peter's in the 1780s. Archbishop McCloskey was so impressed with their work at Our Lady of Sorrows that in 1870 he asked them to take charge of the troubled Church of St. John the Baptist on West 30th Street.

In addition to the Germans, the Italians, Poles, Slovaks, Hungarians, African Americans, Maronites, Lithuanians and Spanish all followed the pattern of earlier newcomers by settling in the poorest neighborhoods in the city and establishing their first parishes in Lower Manhattan. The story of the origin of those parishes has been mentioned in the previous chapter.

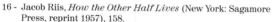

16 - Jacob Riis, *How the Other Half Lives* (New York: Sagamore Press, reprint 1957), 158.

The Church of Our Lady of Guadalupe at St. Bernard, following the amalgamation of New York City's oldest Spanish parish with St. Bernard's.

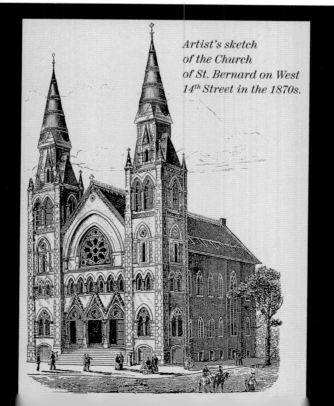

Artist's sketch of the Church of St. Bernard on West 14th Street in the 1870s.

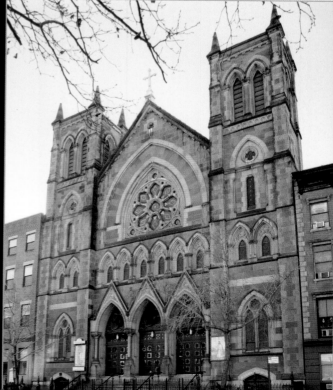

The Church of St. Rose of Lima on Cannon Street. To the left is the original church which later served as the first Church of the Sacred Heart in Highbridge. The small size of the original church explains why starter churches could be erected so quickly and so inexpensively.

The Capuchin Church of Our Lady of Sorrows in the 1860s when it was known as the Church of Our Lady of the Seven Dolors.

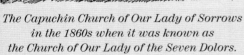

The Church of Our Lady of Sorrows on Stanton Street, dedicated by Archbishop McCloskley on September 6, 1868.

The last two territorial parishes founded in Lower Manhattan date from the mid-1880s. Our Lady of the Rosary owes its origin to Charlotte Grace O'Brien, an Irish Protestant, who wanted to provide a shelter in New York for young Irish immigrant girls. As a result of her efforts, in 1883 Cardinal McCloskey gave his blessing to the founding of the Mission of Our Lady of the Rosary for the Protection of Irish Immigrant Girls and appointed Father John J. Riordan as the director. Two years later Father Riordan located the mission at 7 State Street, a stone's throw from Castle Garden where he met the arriving immigrant ships each day. In 1887 Archbishop Corrigan made the mission a parish, much to the consternation of Father McGean who fretted about the loss of still more parishioners from St. Peter's and accused Riordan of ingratitude because earlier he had been in residence at St. Peter's.[17]

The surviving ledgers at Our Lady of the Rosary preserve the names of 60,000 young women who found shelter at the Mission over the next half century, which is probably only half of the total number. In the 1960s the archdiocese acquired an adjacent building on State Street, which had briefly been the residence of Elizabeth Bayley Seton. To commemorate her beatification in 1963, Cardinal Spellman erected a Georgian-style chapel on the site of the former mission. Of all people, Robert Moses, who destroyed more buildings than any man in the history of New York City, expressed concern at the prospect of demolishing the original building. Today it is the national shrine of St. Elizabeth Ann Seton.[18]

The last territorial parish established in Lower Manhattan was St. Veronica's on Christopher Street, which was carved out of St. Joseph's parish in Greenwich Village in 1886, to serve the Catholics of the West Village. It

The Mission of Our Lady of Rosary for the Protection of Irish Immigrant Girls at 7 State Street in the late nineteenth century.
Credit: *Archdiocese of New York*

The Church of Our Lady of the Rosary on State Street, the National Shrine of St. Elizabeth Ann Seton.

17 - AANY, Joseph R. Leahey, unpublished History of the Shrine of St. Elizabeth Ann Seton, 1975.

18 - AANY, Newbold Morris to Spellman, November 21, 1963. On the ledgers at Holy Rosary Church, see the interview with Father Peter K. *Meehan, Catholic New York,* March 2, 2006.

View of State Street fronting the Battery with Castle Garden in the background. Credit: *Archdiocese of New York*

remained the poor cousin of St. Joseph's with many families whose breadwinners were long-shoremen and teamsters. It is a fair indication of the poverty of the parish that it took thirteen years to erect a permanent church. In 1908 the principal of the parochial school reported that almost half of the fathers of the children were unemployed.[19]

When Archbishop Corrigan first proposed to establish St. Veronica's parish, Father John Salter, the pastor of St. Joseph's, voiced strenuous opposition. He insisted that the new parish would not be viable because there were hardly any Catholics in the West Village. Archbishop Corrigan did not believe him and sent Monsignor Farley to investigate. Farley did not believe Salter either, but he listened patiently to his claims about the dearth of Catholics as the two of them walked through the dark streets of the West Village on one rainy evening in November 1886.

Farley then opined that the only solution was to give St. Veronica's an even larger share of St. Joseph's parish. At this point Salter did a verbal somersault and allowed as how perhaps there were more Catholics in the West Village than he thought. "I allowed myself to be convinced of this," Farley told Corrigan with a chuckle and he left Salter thankful that he would not lose even more parishioners after Farley had called his bluff.[20]

Father John B. Salter, the pastor of St. Joseph's Church in Greenwich Village, who failed to prevent the establishment of St. Veronica's parish in 1886. Credit: *Church of the Immaculate Conception, Tuckahoe*

The Church of St. Veronica on Christopher Street, dedicated by Archbishop Farley on June 7, 1903. In 2007 it was scheduled to be merged with the Church of Our Lady of Guadalupe-St. Bernard.

19 - GHP, Mary Kingsbury Simkhovitch, Report of the Director, January 21, 1908.

20 - AANY, Farley to Corrigan, December 1, 1886.

283

Turtle Bay on the East River in 1853. Credit: *Archdiocese of New York*

The Invention of Midtown Manhattan

Midtown Manhattan did not exist even as a concept in 1865. Everything north of 14th Street was uptown, and 50th Street was considered very far uptown as late as 1858 as Archbishop Hughes discovered when critics mocked him for choosing that location for the site of the new cathedral. In the course of the Gilded Age, however, as the tide of real estate development moved inexorably north until it reached Morningside Heights and Harlem, the area between 14th Street and 59th Street acquired its own special character as a buffer zone between downtown and uptown.

Midtown Manhattan emerged in those years as a distinct geographical entity first as a residential neighborhood and later as a commercial and business center. By the mid-twentieth century the rival skyscrapers of downtown and midtown Manhattan faced one another across a concrete canyon. From the very beginning the prime real estate in Midtown Manhattan was located in the center of the island,

radiating a few blocks east and west of Fifth Avenue and Broadway. It was there that the biggest mansions, the best hotels, the smartest stores, and Grand Central Station were to be found. As one moved closer to the Hudson River or the East River, the quality of the housing stock declined with a corresponding increase in the number of tenement houses, small businesses, coal and lumber yards, stables, slaughter houses and breweries. This was the area of Midtown Manhattan where most of the Catholics lived, and the site of eight of the ten new parishes that were created during the Gilded Age to fill the gaps in the existing parochial network.

Only two churches were located in the center of what would become Midtown Manhattan, Holy Innocents and St. Leo. At Holy Innocents (which was carved out of the eastern part of St. Michael's parish in 1868), the first pastor, Father John A. Larkin, purchased the Episcopal Church of the Holy Innocents. He retained the original name, replaced it in 1870 with the present church on West 37th Street near Broadway, and added a parochial school three years later. His *bête noire,* amounting to an obsession, was the German Franciscans and Capuchins a few blocks away at St. Francis of Assisi and St. John's whom he accused of stealing his parishioners. He pleaded with Archbishop Corrigan to forbid the friars to conduct any services in English, advice which the archbishop politely declined to follow. Ironically Holy Innocents managed to survive by imitating the example of the friars and making the transition to a "business" parish which offered confession and weekday Mass for the workers and shoppers in the garment district. However, its parochial school was closed as far back as 1918 because "there were no longer any children left to attend it."[21]

Father John A. Larkin, the founding pastor of the Church of the Holy Innocents

The Church of St. Leo, established in 1880, had the best location of any midtown parish on East 28th Street between Fifth and Madison Avenues. The founding pastor was Father Thomas Ducey, a flamboyant character with a flair for self-advertisement who combined a taste for high society with progressive views on social reform. He was frequently spotted dining at Delmonico's, the best restaurant in New York City, which was only two blocks from his rectory. "Father Ducey, or as he is more generally called, Msgr. Ducey, is a unique figure in New York," reported the *New York Sun* in June 1894. "It is certain that no priest in New York has such an extended acquaintance among people of prominence."[22]

The Church of the Holy Innocents shortly after it was dedicated on February 13, 1870, by the Very Reverend William Starrs, the Vicar General of the Archdiocese.

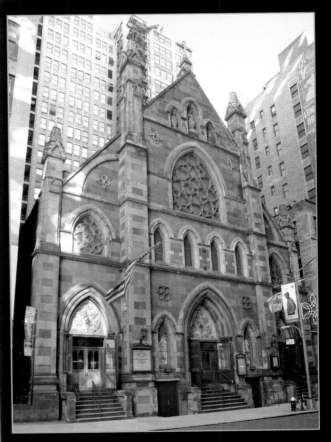

The Church of the Holy Innocents on West 37th Street near Broadway.

21 - AANY, Larkin to Corrigan, November 16, 1886.
22 - *New York Sun*, June 17, 1894.

Ducey's cultivation of wealthy New Yorkers did not prevent him from addressing a rally at the Cooper Union on behalf of the striking employees of the Pullman Company in Chicago. Ducey denounced President Grover Cleveland for sending federal troops to break the strike. He told the audience that he spoke "in the name of the Catholic religion---the religion of the masses---of which I am proud to be a priest." Earlier John Mitchell, the president of the United Mine Workers Union, invited Dicey to address a meeting of 20,000 miners in Wilkes-Barre, Pennsylvania.[23]

Like Dr. Edward McGlynn, Ducey upset Corrigan by his advocacy of political and social reform. Unlike McGlynn's conflict with Archbishop Corrigan, however, Ducey's ongoing quarrel with the archbishop had a comic opera dimension to it because it centered on whether or not Ducey had been made a monsignor. Both Corrigan and Ducey fanned the flames, Ducey by planting stories in sympathetic secular newspapers that he had been made a monsignor, and Corrigan by taking the bait and issuing indignant denials.[24]

Despite its favored location, St. Leo found it difficult to survive when the center of Midtown Manhattan became predominantly commercial. In 1885 Ducey said that he had the smallest parish in the city with only 2,000 parishioners. After the death of Ducey (still not a monsignor) in 1908, it became the chapel of St. Stephen's and then the chapel of the adjacent convent of the cloistered Sisters of Mary Reparatrix. Both the convent and St. Leo's have been demolished.

On the West Side the largest and most prosperous of the new midtown parishes was Sacred Heart on West 51th Street. It was

Grant's Tomb on Riverside Drive.

established in 1876 when that neighborhood was home to tens of thousands of Irish immigrants. Father Martin J. Brophy bought the Plymouth Baptist Church on West 51st Street between Ninth and Tenth Avenues and outfitted it as a Catholic church by June of that year. His neighbor to the South, Father Arthur Donnelly, the vicar general and the veteran pastor of St. Michael's Church, thought that Sacred Heart was one of the most promising parishes in the archdiocese, but he had little regard for the administrative abilities of Father Brophy. "It is the fertility and richness of the field and not the amount of labor and skill that has made it a financial success," he told Archbishop Corrigan.

Donnelly's harsh judgment of Brophy needs to be taken with a generous grain of salt because Brophy was a friend of Dr. Edward McGlynn, Donnelly's polar opposite among the New York clergy. In 1885 Brophy demolished the old Baptist church and replaced it with the present Church of the Sacred Heart. The parish lived up to its promise under its second pastor, Msgr. Joseph F. Mooney, who was pastor from 1890 to his death in 1926 and succeeded Arthur Donnelly as vicar general in 1892.[25]

23 - *New York Herald,* June 13, 1894, AANY, Mitchell to Ducey, September 29, 1890..

24 - AANY, G-1, Ducey to Corrigan, June 6, 1893; AANY, G-6, Corrigan to James Gordon Bennett, Jr., December 26,1894.

25 - AANY, Donnelly to Corrigan, January 14, 1890. See Browne, *"One Stop Above Hell's Kitchen," 13-17.*

The first Church of the Sacred Heart on West 51st Street between Ninth and Tenth Avenues, the former Plymouth Baptist Church.

Father Martin J. Brophy, the founding pastor of the Church of the Sacred Heart, 1876-1890.

The interior of the Church of the Sacred Heart as it looked at the time of its dedication in 1885.
Credit: *Church of the Sacred Heart*

The Church of the Sacred Heart, erected by Father Martin Brophy and dedicated by Archbishop Corrigan on May 17, 1885.

Less successful were the three other new West Side parishes, Guardian Angel, originally on 23rd Street, St. Raphael originally on 40th Street, and St. Ambrose on 54th Street. They were located on the Far West Side close to the street-level tracks of the New York Central's freight line which ran down the middle of Eleventh Avenue. Until the High Line was built in the 1930s crosstown traffic was frequently halted by long freight trains lumbering down Eleventh Avenue preceded by a rider on horseback waving a red flag. Accidents were a frequent occurrence on Eleventh Avenue, leading the residents to call it Death Avenue.

St. Ambrose was difficult to sustain even in its best years. In 1910 Father James F. Driscoll, the exiled rector of St. Joseph's Seminary, informed Archbishop Farley that "our parish really consists of two blocks." Despite this gloomy prognosis, Driscoll obediently built a parochial school. "As to the problem of maintaining the school once erected, we humbly solicit your suggestions and advice," he inquired of the archbishop. Whatever advice he got from Farley, the school lasted only twenty-five years.[26]

On the East Side the first pastor of the Church of the Epiphany on Second Avenue near 21st Street was Richard Burtsell, Dr. Burtsell, as he liked to be called because of his Roman degree. As a young curate in St. Ann's Church in East 12th Street, he persuaded Archbishop McCloskey of the need for an additional church in that part of the city. It was dedicated by Father William Starrs, the vicar general, on April 3, 1870. Burtsell was a self-taught canon lawyer who became one of the best known priests in the archdiocese in the later nineteenth century. Archbishop Corrigan banished Burtsell to Kingston because of his defense of his friend Dr. Edward McGlynn. Burtsell tried long and hard to use his canonical expertise to force Corrigan reinstate him in Epiphany, but he was unsuccessful in his quest. After John Farley became the archbishop in 1902, he was happy to leave the contentious Burtsell a hundred miles away. However, he mollified him by giving him the prize that had eluded Father Ducey. He made him a monsignor in 1907.

Macombs Dam and Bridge over the Harlem River in the 1850s.
Credit: *Archdiocese of New York.*

26 - AANY, Driscoll to Farley, March 1, 1910.

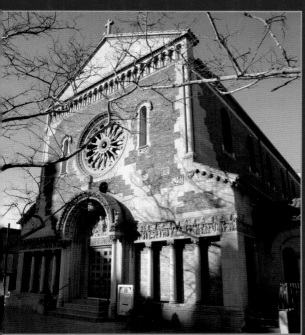

The Church of the Guardian Angel on Tenth Avenue and 21st Street.

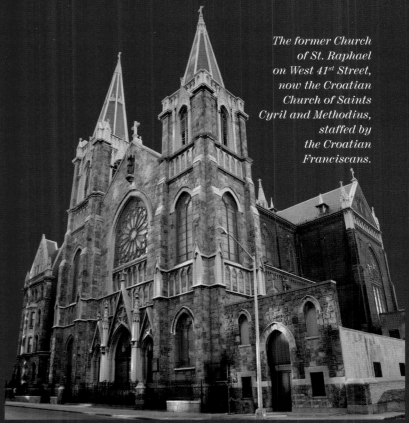

The former Church of St. Raphael on West 41st Street, now the Croatian Church of Saints Cyril and Methodius, staffed by the Croatian Franciscans.

Dr. Richard Lalor Burtsell, the founding pastor of the Church of the Epiphany.

The first Church of the Epiphany on Second Avenue near 21th Street, dedicated by Father William Starrs, the Vicar General, on April 3, 1870.

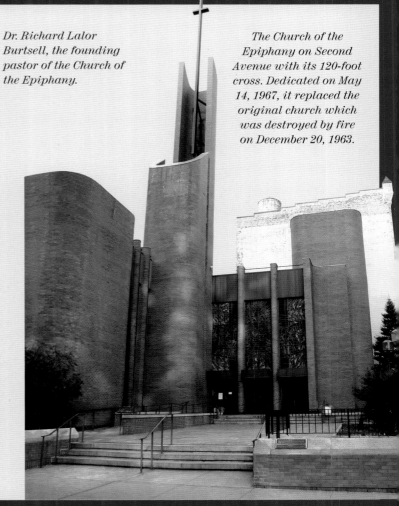

The Church of the Epiphany on Second Avenue with its 120-foot cross. Dedicated on May 14, 1967, it replaced the original church which was destroyed by fire on December 20, 1963.

St. Agnes, which was founded on East 43rd Street in 1873, was another parish that made a successful transition from a residential to a "business" parish. The Gothic church was dedicated on May 6, 1877. Its proximity to Commodore Vanderbilt's new Grand Central Station, which was opened two years earlier, provided it with a constant stream of commuters as well as long distance travelers. Unfortunately St. Agnes joined the ranks of a long line of other New York churches when it was destroyed by fire on December 10, 1992. It was rebuilt and dedicated by Cardinal O'Connor on January 17, 1999.

The Church of St. Mary Magdalen was also founded in 1873 on East 17th Street to provide the Germans with another East Side parish. It was closed and demolished in 1945 to make way for the construction of Stuyvesant Town.

For many years the church of St. Agnes celebrated its patronal feastday with a banquet. The pretentious menu for the celebration in 1896 contained nary a word in English.

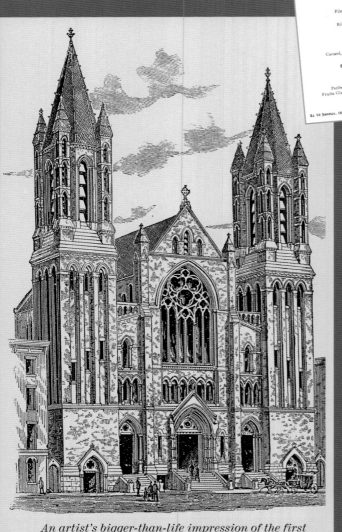

An artist's bigger-than-life impression of the first Church of St. Agnes, dedicated on May 6, 1877.

The new Church of St. Agnes, dedicated by Cardinal O'Connor on January 17, 1999.

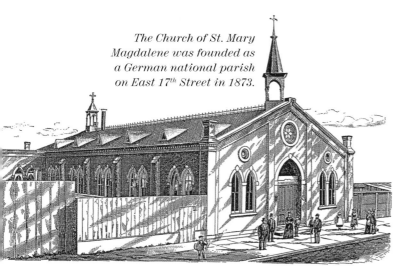

The Church of St. Mary Magdalene was founded as a German national parish on East 17th Street in 1873.

Hospital, the largest hospital in the city, where the Carmelites took over the duty of chaplains from the priests at St. Stephen's Church, who had been asking for help for over thirty years. The Carmelites maintained their hospital apostolate at Bellevue for the next 118 years, winning widespread praise for their ministry to sick and indigent New Yorkers. They continued their hospital work from St. Stephen's Church when they took over that parish and merged it with Our Lady of the Scapular. In 2007 the Carmelites were replaced at St. Stephen's by diocesan clergy.[27]

The now vanished Church of Our Lady of the Scapular on East 28th Street was the first foundation of the Irish Carmelites in New York in 1889. The parish boundaries included Bellevue

Mainland New York City: The Creation of the Bronx

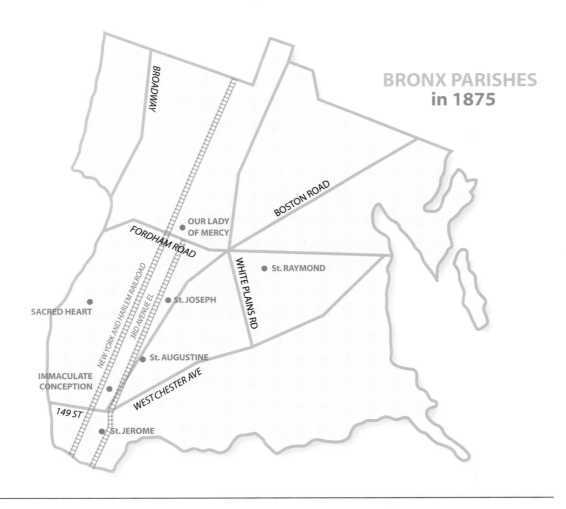

BRONX PARISHES
in 1875

27 - Alfred Isacsson, O. Carm., *The Carmelites: The Province of St. Elias* (Middletown: Vestigium Press, 2003), 5. AANY, A-11, Cummings to Hughes, March 29, 1858.

The area of the archdiocese that experienced the greatest proportionate increase in the number of parish churches during the Gilded Age was the Bronx, which did not even exist as a separate political entity in the nineteenth century. It was a collection of independent towns in southern Westchester County. With the blessing of the state legislature, the City of New York annexed this area in two stages, the area west of the Bronx River in 1874 and the rest of the future Bronx in 1895. Three years later, when Greater New York was created, the annexed areas became the Borough of the Bronx and were organized into a separate county in 1914.

In 1865 there were only four parishes in the present-day Bronx, St. Raymond's, St. Augustine, Immaculate Conception and Our Lady of Mercy. Ten years later only three additional parishes had been founded in what was still a largely rural area, St. Jerome's in Mott Haven (1869), St. Joseph's in Tremont (1873), and Sacred Heart in Highbridge (1875).

The founder of St. Jerome's was Father John J. Hughes, a thirty-five year old native of County Down, who first celebrated Mass in the parish in an abandoned market on East 136th Street. By 1871 he had constructed a school at Alexander Avenue and 137th Street and used the first floor chapel as a church. Hughes' successor, Father Patrick Tandy, came to the parish from Amenia in 1890 and built the present church at the corner of Alexander Avenue and 138th Street. It was completed in July 1900, nine months before Father Tandy's death. [28]

St. Joseph's Church, founded in 1873 for the Germans in Tremont, quickly became a prosperous territorial parish. Two years later Catholics in Highbridge got their own parish when Cardinal McCloskey appointed Father James A. Mullen the pastor of Sacred Heart Church. Newly appointed pastors had long resorted to buying abandoned Protestant churches and some had shown a predilection for stables, but Father Mullen was apparently the first pastor to buy a surplus Catholic church. He purchased the wooden chapel that had served as the first Church of St. Rose of Lima on Cannon Street in Lower Manhattan, disassembled it and moved it to Highbridge where it was dedicated by Cardinal McCloskey on October 21, 1877. As mentioned already, Father Joseph Byron did the same thing a decade later at Holy Rosary Church in East Harlem. The present Gothic Church of the Sacred Heart was built by the second pastor, Father John J. Lennon, and dedicated by Cardinal Farley on April 14, 1912. [29]

Father James A. Mullen,
the founding pastor of the Church
of the Sacred Heart, Highbridge.
Credit: *Church of the Sacred Heart.*

The first Church of the Sacred Heart, Highbridge, the former Church of St. Rose in Lower Manhattan.

---

28 - *St. Jerome's Parish: Celebration of a Century* (Custombook, 1969), 3-5.

29 - *100th Anniversary: History of Sacred Heart Parish, Bronx,* (New York: Sacred Heart Church, 1975), unpaginated.

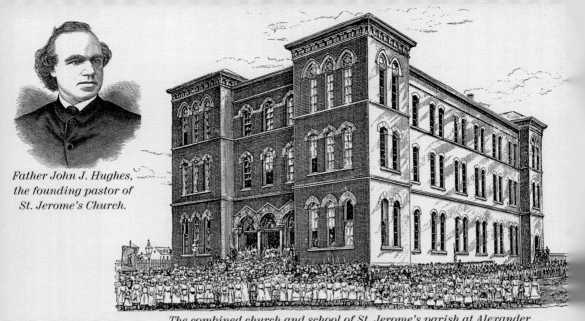

Father John J. Hughes, the founding pastor of St. Jerome's Church.

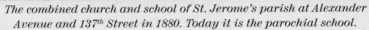

The combined church and school of St. Jerome's parish at Alexander Avenue and 137th Street in 1880. Today it is the parochial school.

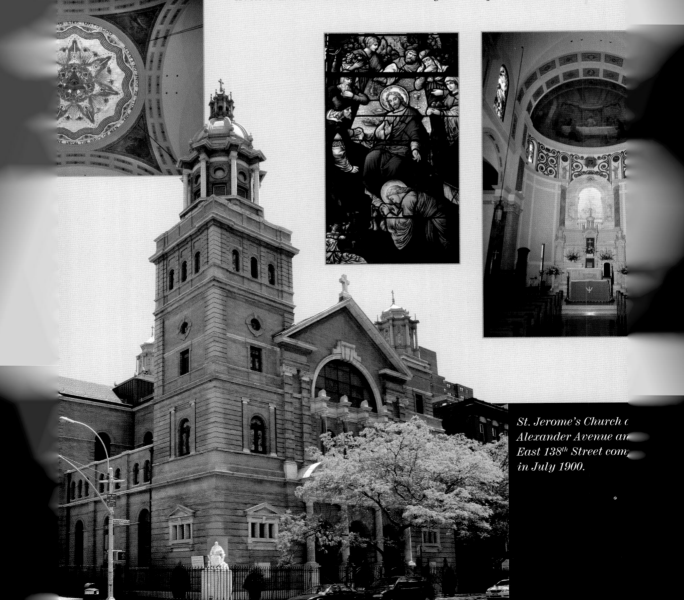

St. Jerome's Church o Alexander Avenue an East 138th Street com in July 1900.

In 1875 there were still only seven parishes in the Bronx. Between 1886 and 1899, however, the number more than tripled with the founding of seventeen new parishes. Seven of them were national parishes, German, Polish and Italian, whose origin was described in the previous chapter. Three of the new territorial parishes were founded in the South Bronx, reflecting the continuing growth of the Catholic population in that area after the extension of the Third Avenue El to the Bronx in 1886 and the creation of the Borough of the Bronx in 1898.

The crucifixion scene in the Church of the Sacred Heart.

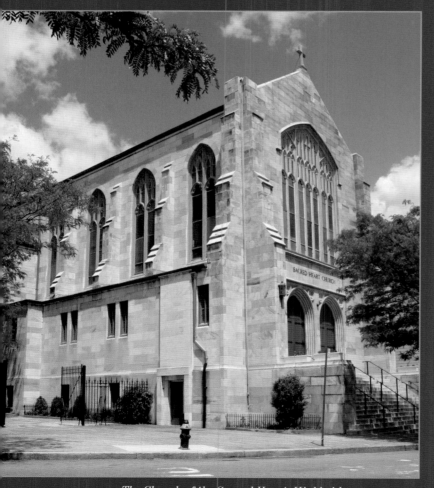

The Church of the Sacred Heart, Highbridge, dedicated by Cardinal Farley on April 14, 1912.

The interior of the Church of the Sacred Heart, in the 1950s.
Credit: *Church of the Sacred Heart.*

Mott Haven and Melrose

Mott Haven got a second Catholic parish with the founding of St. Luke's Church in 1897. Once again the first church was a converted stable, but at least this time it was a Catholic stable, donated by the widow of Denis Sadlier, the Catholic publisher. Within a year the pastor, Father John J. Boyle, built a small frame church

The combination church and school of St. Angela Merici on East 163rd Street, erected in 1923.

on 137th Street between St. Ann's and Cypress Avenues. By 1902 he had purchased property on 138th Street near Cypress Avenue and began construction of the present church. The basement church was dedicated on May 17, 1903, but the upper church was not finished until the spring of 1919.[30]

Melrose got two additional parishes at the very end of the nineteenth century, Saints Peter and Paul in 1898 and St. Angela Merici the following year. When it came time to build a permanent church in St. Angela's, the pastor opted for the plan that Father Hughes had chosen at St. Jerome's fifty years earlier. He built a school with a large auditorium that was to serve as a temporary church until a permanent church could be built. Several Bronx parishes followed the same pattern in the 1920s. Unlike St. Jerome's, however, the projected churches were never built and the school auditorium became the permanent church. By contrast the pastor of Saints Peter and Paul managed to erect both a large school and a beautiful Gothic church that was completed in the Depression year 1932.

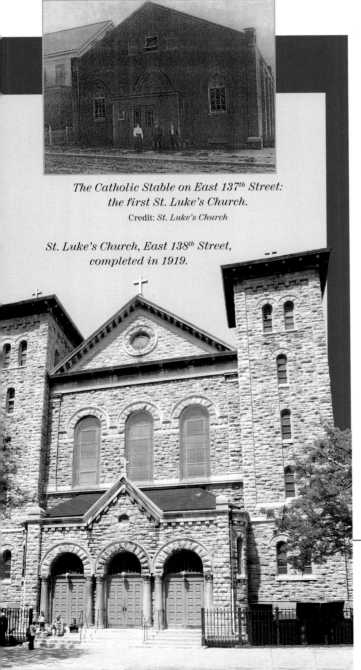

*The Catholic Stable on East 137th Street:
the first St. Luke's Church.*
Credit: *St. Luke's Church*

*St. Luke's Church, East 138th Street,
completed in 1919.*

30 - Roland Chapdelaine, *The History of St. Luke's Parish* (New York: St. Luke's Church, 1997), 1-3.

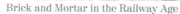

Brick and Mortar in the Railway Age

The Church of Saints Peter and Paul in Melrose, completed in the Depression year 1932.

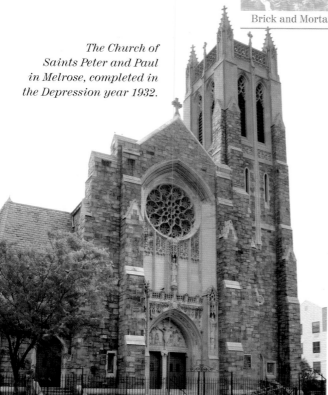

East Tremont, West Farms and Hunts Point

During the 1890s the total population of the Bronx increased from 88,000 to 139,000. One reason for the growth in population was the extension of the Third Avenue El to Fordham Road between 1886 and 1902. In 1904 the Interborough subway was extended from Harlem across 149th Street to Third Avenue and then north as an elevated line to West Farms. Together with a network of crosstown streetcar lines, the El and subway brought much of the central Bronx within relatively easy and inexpensive commuting distance of downtown Manhattan, especially after the five cent fare on the El was extended to the Bronx.

The first two parishes to be established in West Farms or East Tremont were St. Thomas Aquinas in 1890 and St. Martin of Tours in 1897. St. Thomas Aquinas began in a small brick church that was a mission of St. Augustine in Morrisania. It was a lower middle class parish where many of the men were streetcar conductors or maintenance employees of the Third Avenue Railway. Consequently money was tight, and the first few pastors deferred plans for a new church in favor of a combination school and church. In the early 1920s, however, Father John Bronsan built a splendid English Gothic church that was dedicated by Cardinal Hayes on November 22, 1925.[31]

The second parish in East Tremont, St. Martin of Tours, began in 1897 in a frame building that was replaced with a permanent church in 1904. It was never an affluent parish. During the Depression it ran a deficit because the

Father John Brosnan, the pastor of St. Thomas Aquinas, who was responsible for the erection of the new church and rectory in 1925.
Credit: *St. Thomas Aquinas Church.*

The Church of St. Thomas Aquinas, East Tremont, dedicated by Cardinal Hayes on November 22, 1925.

31 - *Church of St. Thomas Aquinas, Bronx, New York* (Custombook, 1966), unpaginated.

296

pastor could not bring himself to ask his parishioners for money when so many of breadwinners were unemployed. The church was destroyed by fire on the night of February 12, 1950, and replaced with the present church, which was dedicated by Cardinal Spellman on September 13, 1953. Hunts Point got its own parish in 1899 with the establishment of the Church of St. John Chrysostom. It comes as no surprise that the first pastor, Father Bernard Brady, first celebrated Mass in yet another stable, but he broke ground on September 16, 1900, for the present church at 167th Street and Hoe Avenue.[32]

The Church of St. Martin of Tours, dedicated by Cardinal Spellman on September 13, 1953.

BRONX PARISHES in 1900

St. MARGARET OF CORTONA
BROADWAY
St. GABRIEL
St. FRANCES OF ROME
St. MARY
St. VALENTINE
St. JOHN'S KINGSBRIDGE
St. PHILIP NERI
IMMACULATE CONCEPTION
GUN HILL ROAD
CITY ISLAND
OUR LADY OF MERCY
St. JOSEPH
TREMONT AVENUE
WHITE PLAINS RD
St. MARY STAR OF THE SEA
SACRED HEART
GRAND CONCOURSE
3RD AVENUE
St. MARTIN OF TOURS
St. AUGUSTINE
St. THOMAS AQUINAS
St. RAYMOND
St. ANGELA MERICI
St. JOHN CHRYSOSTOM
St. ANTHONY OF PADUA
Sts. PETER AND PAUL
IMMACULATE CONCEPTION
149 ST
WESTCHESTER AVENUE
St. ROCH
St. RITA OF CASCIA
St. ANSELM
St. LUKE
St. JEROME

32 - *Diamond Jubilee, St. John Chrysostom* (New York: St. John Chrysostom Church, 1974), unpaginated.

The North Bronx

The oldest parish in the northwest Bronx is St. John's Church in Kingsbridge, which began as a mission of St. Mary's Church in Yonkers and after 1869 was a mission of the newly founded St. Elizabeth's Church in Washington Heights. The following year Father Henry Brann, the pastor of St. Elizabeth's, built a small mission church in Kingsbridge that was used as the parish church after St. John's became a separate parish in 1886. The first pastor, Father Edward O'Gorman, began the erection of the present church, but only got as far as a basement church when he was transferred in 1903. Construction of the upper church was begun in 1907, and the completed church was dedicated by Archbishop Farley on May 22, 1910.[33]

In 1889, only three years after the establishment of St. John's Church, Kingsbridge, the parish of St. Margaret of Cortona was created in Riverdale for the area between St. John's and St. Mary's in Yonkers.
The first pastor, Father James K. Kiely, set up a chapel in the free school operated

St. John's Church, Kingsbridge, dedicated by Archbishop Farley on May 22, 1910.

by the Sisters of Charity on the grounds of their mother house at Mount St. Vincent. He erected a church at what is now the southeast corner of Riverdale Avenue and 260th Street that was dedicated by Archbishop Corrigan on August 16, 1892. It was hardly the bon ton parish that it was to become in later years. The first Christmas collection netted $15.24. By the early 1960s it was evident that a larger church was needed. Construction of a new church began in the summer of 1963, and it was dedicated by Cardinal Spellman on June 6, 1965.

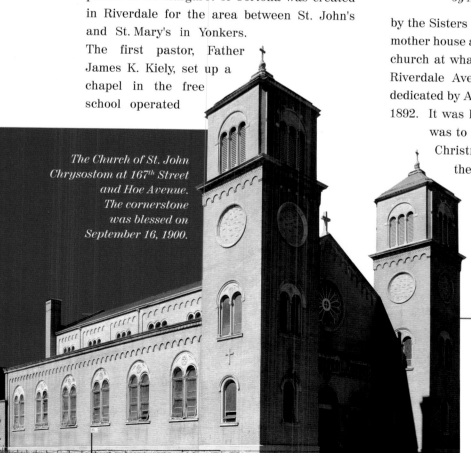

The Church of St. John Chrysostom at 167th Street and Hoe Avenue. The cornerstone was blessed on September 16, 1900.

33 - John T. Doherty, "The Story of 'The People by the Bridge,' " *St. John's, Kingsbridge, Bronx: 100 Years* (Custombook, 1986), 7-12.

In the northeast Bronx, St. Mary's Church on White Plains Road in Williamsbridge, founded as a mission of St. Raymond's, became a parish in 1886. The church was built in 1887 and served as the parish church until it was closed in 2007. It is now the Korean Church of St. John Nam. Farther north in Wakefield, the local Catholic community got its first parish in the spring of 1897 when Archbishop Corrigan selected Father Francis P. Moore to establish the Church of St. Frances of Rome. Although he was not the first new pastor to do so, he showed considerable ingenuity by using a canvas tent for the first Mass in the parish. By 1901 the tent had given way to a wooden church on Richardson Avenue.

Father Moore, the "Vicar of Wakfield," was an artist who dreamed big dreams. In 1925 he planned to construct a Byzantine basilica that would also include a school at a cost of about $2,000,000. He managed to build a basement church that was opened on the following Easter Sunday, but he got no further than that. The parishioners of St. Frances of Rome had only a basement church until Msgr. Michael McGuire erected the present building in the mid-1960s. Dedicated by Cardinal Spellman on March 12, 1967, it was built at half the price of Father Moore's ill-fated basilica of forty years earlier.[34]

City Island was as remote as many country parishes until 1873 when it was connected to the mainland by a wooden bridge. It became an out-mission of St. Raymond's at least as far back as 1886 when a mission chapel named St. Mary Star of the Sea was erected on the island. It became a parish the following year and in 1890 the little wooden chapel was destroyed by fire. It was replaced with a larger church in 1891 that lasted until it too was destroyed by fire on May 28, 1956. The present church was dedicated on May 10, 1959.

By 1900 there were twenty-five parishes in the Bronx compared to four parishes thirty-five years earlier. It left the Church well poised for the next surge in the population that followed the expansion of the IRT subway system in the borough after 1904.

The New Bridge over the Harlem River. Credit: *Archdiocese of New York*

34- *Church of St. Frances of Rome* (Custombook, 1967),unpaginated.

299

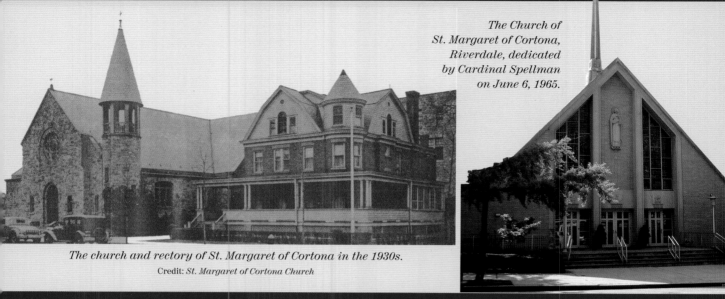

The Church of St. Margaret of Cortona, Riverdale, dedicated by Cardinal Spellman on June 6, 1965.

The church and rectory of St. Margaret of Cortona in the 1930s.
Credit: *St. Margaret of Cortona Church*

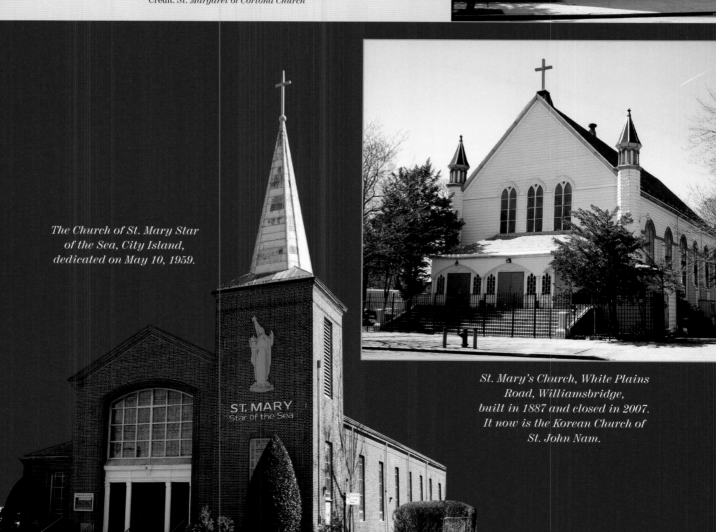

The Church of St. Mary Star of the Sea, City Island, dedicated on May 10, 1959.

St. Mary's Church, White Plains Road, Williamsbridge, built in 1887 and closed in 2007. It now is the Korean Church of St. John Nam.

The Vicar of Wakefield:
Father Francis P. Moore,
the first pastor of St. Frances
of Rome Church.
Credit: *St. Frances of Rome Church*

The Church of St. Rome, Wakefield,
dedicated by Cardinal Spellman
on March 12, 1967.

The tent that was the site of the
first Mass in St. Frances of
Rome parish on June 13, 1897.
Credit: *St. Frances of Rome Church*

Staten Island

While the Catholic population boomed in the Bronx during the last two decades of the Gilded Age, it remained relatively stagnant on Staten Island where only three new parishes were established between 1862 and 1898, Sacred Heart in West Brighton, St. Patrick in Richmond, and Immaculate Conception in Stapleton.

Like so many parishes in Staten Island, Sacred Heart in West Brighton began as a mission of St. Peter's Church. It originated in 1864 as St. Rose of Lima mission in West Brighton when that area sported the picturesque name of Factoryville. It became a parish eleven years later with the appointment of Father William Chaplin Poole, a native of Savannah, Georgia, as the first pastor. Father Poole was pastor for forty years and built the present church, which was dedicated by Archbishop Corrigan on June 17, 1899. On that occasion the name of the church was changed from St. Rose of Lima to the Sacred Heart.[35]

St. Patrick's Church in Richmond is the third oldest Catholic church on Staten Island. It was erected in 1862 by Father John Barry, the pastor of St. Joseph's, Rossville, as a mission of his parish and became a separate parish in 1884. The Church of the Immaculate Conception in Stapleton was started in 1882 by Father John Lewis as a mission of St. Mary's Church, Rosebank. Originally called Our Lady of Lourdes, it was renamed the Church of the Immaculate Conception when it became a parish in 1887 with Father Gerard Huntman as the pastor. The second pastor, Father William McClure, built the present church, which was completed in 1909.[36]

Three more parishes were created on Staten Island at the turn of the century. Our Lady Help of Christians in Tottenville was started as a mission of St. Joseph, Rossville, in 1890 and became a parish in 1898. The church was dedicated by Archbishop Corrigan on October 9, 1898. It was destroyed in a fire in 1985 and the present church was built in 1990. Our Lady of Good Counsel on Richmond Turnpike, founded in 1899, was the first Augustinian parish in the archdiocese. The original church was dedicated on September 10, 1899. The growth of the Catholic population on the island in the 1960s led to the construction of the present church, which was dedicated by Cardinal Cooke on April 26,

35 -*Church of the Sacred Heart:100th Anniversary* (Staten Island: Church of the Sacred Heart, 1975), 7-8.

36 - *History of the Parish of the Immaculate Conception* (Stapleton: Immaculate Conception Church, 1987), unpaginated.

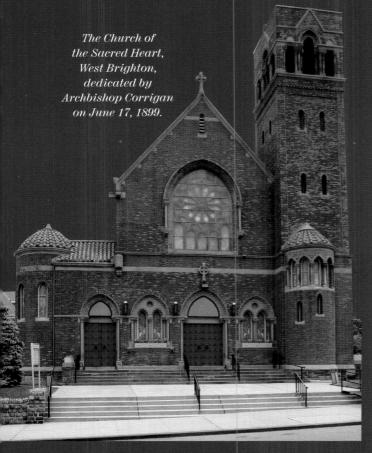

The Church of the Sacred Heart, West Brighton, dedicated by Archbishop Corrigan on June 17, 1899.

The Church of the Immaculate Conception, Stapleton, completed in 1909.

St. Patrick's Church, Richmond, around 1870.
Credit: *St. Patrick's Church.*

St. Patrick's Church, Richmond, erected in 1862 as a mission of St. Joseph's Church, Rossville.

1968. The Church of St. John Baptist de la Salle in Stapleton, opened in 1901, was the first German parish on Staten Island and one of the last two German parishes to be established in the archdiocese.

Greater New York

With the creation of Greater New York in 1898, the Bronx and Staten Island became part of the urban conglomeration of New York City, although working farms were still a common sight on Staten Island. By that date the Catholic Church had an extensive network of parishes throughout Manhattan and the Bronx, and, to a lesser extent, on Staten Island. The size, physical plant and financial resources of the parishes in these three boroughs varied greatly even in Manhattan where they ranged from quasi-cathedrals like St. Ignatius Loyola on Park Avenue to little country churches like St. Joseph of the Holy Family on West 125th Street.

However, whether these churches were large or small, made of wood or brick or stone, whether they were flush with cash or burdened with debt, they had one thing in common. They were "city parishes" and were classified as such by the diocesan authorities, the semi-official *Catholic Directory* and the clergy themselves. Most of the American-born diocesan priests were natives of New York City. For them a "city parish" meant a

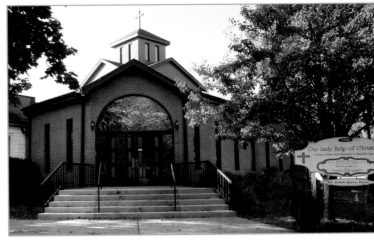

The Church of Our Lady Help of Christians, Tottenville, which was built in 1990.

parish in New York City despite the fact that there were a dozen other cities in the archdiocese, including Yonkers, which was the sixth largest city in the state in 1910. As late as the 1970s, on one occasion Cardinal Cooke responded to a request from a priest for a city parish by making him the pastor of a church in White Plains. As the disappointed priest left his office, the cardinal tried to cheer him up by saying: "Father, remember White Plains is a city."

Despite the ingrained tendency of the New York clergy to identify the whole archdiocese with New York City, by 1900 the Catholic Church was alive and well in the seven counties north of the city line where a constantly growing number of "county parishes" served the needs of the Catholic population.

Father Nicholas Murphy, O.S.A., Founding Pastor of the Church of Our Lady of Good Counsel.
Credit: *Church of Our Lady of Good Consel.*

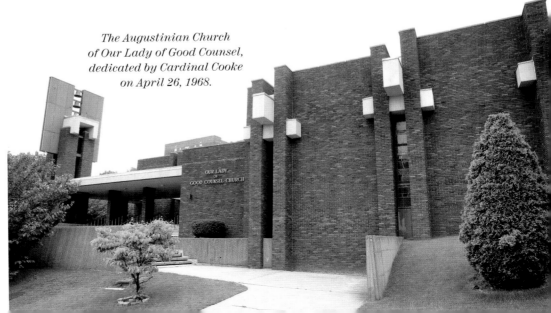

The Augustinian Church of Our Lady of Good Counsel, dedicated by Cardinal Cooke on April 26, 1968.

11

The Country Parishes

The outskirts of Ellenville in Ulster County. Credit: John A. Boehning.

I n the upstate counties of the archdiocese growth and development still followed the railroad tracks as many of the mission churches established earlier in the century evolved into independent parishes. Westchester County led the list with twenty-seven new parishes, but these statistics were deceptive because ten of the new parishes were located in two cities, Yonkers and Mount Vernon.

Yonkers

Yonkers accounted for six of them. For almost a quarter century after the founding of the Church of the Immaculate Conception (St. Mary's) in 1848, it remained the only Catholic Church in Yonkers. That came to an end in 1871 when Father Joseph Lings, a former curate at St. Mary's, established a second Yonkers parish on Ashburton Avenue and named it in honor of St. Joseph. He celebrated the first Mass in the unfinished church on November 1, 1871. One woman recalled that "it rained terribly and the rain came down through the roof and wet Father Lings. I wanted to give him my shawl to cover him." Within fifteen years the church became inadequate for the growing Catholic population. On May 16, 1886, Father Lings broke ground for the present church which was completed in 1888.

North Yonkers got its first Catholic Church in 1891 when the Capuchins (who had come to Yonkers in 1886) converted their monastery chapel into a parish church. The church and monastery were dedicated on November 15, 1891. The church was replaced with a larger one in 1917. Meanwhile the Ludlow section of Southwest Yonkers got its first Catholic parish in 1894 with the establishment of St. Peter's Church. The founding pastor, Father Anthony Malloy, a former curate at St. Joseph's, offered the first Mass in the new parish in a tent on July 29, 1894, but he pushed his luck too far. When he attempted to repeat the performance at the blessing of the cornerstone of the church, the tent collapsed under a strong wind and the worshippers had to beat a hasty retreat to a nearby school building. [1]

Monsignor Albert A. Lings,
pastor of St. Joseph's Church, Yonkers, 1871-1915,
and Dean of Westchester and Putnam Counties.
Credit: *St. Joseph's Church*

The first St. Joseph's Church, Yonkers,
which was a combination church and school built in 1871.
Credit: *St. Joseph's Church*

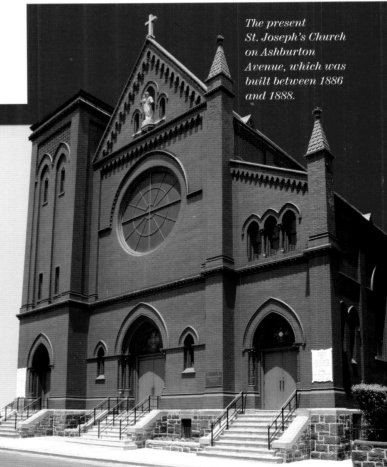

The present St. Joseph's Church on Ashburton Avenue, which was built between 1886 and 1888.

1 - AANY, G-68, Lings to Corrigan, January 10, 1897.

New Country Parishes and Out-Missions: c.1865 – c.1900

- Allaben - Our Lady of Lourdes, mission of St. Francis de Sales, Phoenicia
- Barrytown – Sacred Heart 1886
- Boiceville – Our Lady of La Salette, mission of St. Francis de Sales, Phoenicia
- Beacon (Fishkill Landing) – St. John the Evangelist 1887
- Brewster - St. Lawrence O'Toole 1877
- Bullville – St. Paul, mission of Our Lady of Mt. Carmel, Middletown
- Calicoon – Holy Cross 1875
- Clinton Corners - St. Joseph, mission of St. Joseph, Millbrook
- Congers – St. Paul 1896
- Cornwall-on-Hudson – St. Thomas of Canterbury 1870

- Croton-on-Hudson (Croton Landing) – Holy Name of Mary 1877
- DeBruce – Sacred Heart, mission of St. Aloysius, Livingston Manor
- Dover Plains – St. Charles Borromeo 1936
- Esopus – Sacred Heart, mission of Presentation of the Blessed Virgin Mary, Port Ewen
- Forestburg – St. Thomas Aquinas 1900
- Fort Montgomery – Blessed Sacrament, mission of Sacred Heart, Highland Falls
- Gardiner (Ireland Corners) – St. Charles Borromeo 1883
- Goldens Bridge – St. Michael, mission of St. Joseph, Croton Falls
- Harmon – Good Shepherd, mission of Holy Name of Mary, Croton-on-Hudson
- Harriman (Arden) – St. Anastasia (St. Mary) 1899

- Hastings-on-Hudson, St. Matthew 1892
- Hawthorne – Holy Innocents 1894
- High Falls – Our Lady Help of Christians, mission of St. Peter, Rosendale
- Highland – St. Augustine 1899
- Highland Falls – Sacred Heart 1870
- Hopewell Junction – St. Columba, mission of St. Denis, Sylvan Lake
- Hyde Park, Regina Coeli 1887
- Irvington-on-Hudson – Immaculate Conception 1873
- Larchmont – St. Augustine 1892
- Liberty – St. Peter 1897

- Livingston Manor – St. Aloysius 1899
- Long Eddy – St. Patrick, mission of Holy Cross, Calicoon
- Mamaroneck – Most Holy Trinity (St. Thomas) 1874
- Marlboro – St. Mary 1900
- Mahopac – St. John the Evangelist 1889
- Millbrook – St. Joseph 1890
- Millerton – St. Patrick, mission of Immaculate Conception, Amenia
- Milton – St. James 1874
- Mongaup Valley – St. Joseph, mission of St. Peter, Monticello
- Montgomery – Holy Name of Mary 1872
- Monticello – St. Peter 1874
- Mount Kisco – St. Francis of Assisi 1871

- Mount Vernon – Our Lady of Mount Carmel 1897
- Mount Vernon – Our Lady of Victory (St. Jacob) 1871
- Mount Vernon – Sacred Heart (St. Matthew) 1871
- Mount Vernon – St. Mary 1894
- Nanuet – St Anthony 1897
- New City – St. Augustine, mission of St. Anthony, Nanuet
- New Paltz – St. Joseph 1894
- New Rochelle – St. Gabriel 1893
- Newburgh – St. Mary 1875
- Newburgh – St. Patrick 1837

- North Salem – St. John, mission of St. Joseph, Croton Falls
- Pawling - St. John the Evangelist 1872
- Pelham – St. Catherine 1897
- Phoenicia – St. Francis de Sales, 1902
- Pocantico Hills – Church of the Magdalene 1894
- Poughkeepsie – Nativity 1863
- Poughkeepsie – St. Mary 1873
- Poughkeepsie – St. Peter 1837
- Port Ewen – Presentation of the Blessed Virgin Mary 1874

- Red Hook – mission of Sacred Heart, Barrytown
- Rhinebeck, Good Shepherd, mission of St. Joseph, Rhinecliff
- Rhinecliff – St. Joseph 1862
- Roscoe – Gate of Heaven, mission of St. Aloysius, Livingston Manor
- Roseton – Our Lady of Mercy, mission of St. Mary, Marlboro
- Rye – Resurrection 1880
- Saugerties – St. John the Evangelist 1886
- Saugerties – St. Mary of the Snow 1833
- Shrub Oak – St. John the Evangelist 1896
- Spring Valley – St. Joseph 1894

- Staatsburg – St. Paul, mission of Regina Coeli, Hyde Park
- Stony Point – Immaculate Conception 1885
- Sylvan Lake – St. Denis 1899
- Tarrytown – Transfiguration 1896
- Tivoli – St. Sylvia 1890
- Tuckahoe – Immaculate Conception 1878
- Tuxedo Park – Our Lady of Mt. Carmel 1895
- Valhalla – Holy Name of Jesus 1896
- Walkill – St. Benedict, mission of Most Precious Blood, Walden
- West Hurley – St. John 1860

- West Point – Most Holy Trinity 1899
- White Lake – St. Anne of the Lake, mission of St. Peter, Monticello
- Wurtsboro – St. Joseph 1880
- Yonkers – Immaculate Conception 1848
- Yonkers – Sacred Heart 1891
- Yonkers – St. Joseph 1871
- Yonkers – St. Peter 1894
- Yorktown Heights – St. Patrick (St. Peter) 1898

NEW COUNTRY PARISHES
1865-1900

HUDSON RIVER

ULSTER AND DELAWARE

WEST SHORE RAILROAD

ULSTER

SAUGERTIES

TIVOLI

ALLABEN

RED HOOK

PHOENICIA

BARRYTOWN

WEST HURLEY

RHINEBECK

MILLERTON

ROSCOE

BOICE VILLE

KINGSTON

RHINECLIFF

AMENIA

DEBRUCE

PORT EWEN

STRATSBURG

LIVINGSTON MANOR

CLINTON CORNERS

SULLIVAN

HIGH FALLS

ESOPUS

NEW YORK CENTRAL-HUDSON DIVISION

LONG EDDY

MILLBROOK

HANKINS

LIBERTY

NEW PALTZ

HYDE PARK

HARLEM DIVISION NEW YORK CENTRAL

CALICOON

HIGHLAND

DOVER PLAINS

WHITE LAKE

GARDINER

POUGHKEEPSIE

MILTON

MONGAUP VALLEY

MONTICELLO

WALL KILL

DUTCHESS

MARLBORO

WURTSBORO

SYLVAN LAKE

BULLVILLE

ROSETON

FORESTBURG

WALDEN

HOPE WELL JUNCTION

ONTARIO AND WESTERN RAILROAD

MONTGOMERY

BEACON

PAWLING

NEWBURGH

ORANGE

PUTNAM

CORNWALL

BREWSTER

ERIE RAILROAD

WEST POINT

PORT JERVIS

CHESTER

HIGHLAND FALLS

MAHOPAC

CROTON FALLS

FORT MONTGOMERY

WESTCHESTER

NORTH SALEM

HARRIMAN

GOLDENS BRIDGE

YORKTOWN HEIGHTS

CROTON-ON-HUDSON

Mt. KISCO

STONY POINT

HARMON

TUXEDO PARK

ROCKLAND

HAWTHORNE

CONGERS

POCANTICO HILLS

SPRING VALLEY

PUTNAM DIVISION

VALHALLA

NANUET

NEW CITY

TARRYTOWN

RYE

IRVINGTON

MAMARONECK

HASTINGS-ON-HUDSON

● PARISHES

● MISSIONS

||||||||| RAILROADS

YONKERS
{
SACRED HEART
St. JOSEPH
St. PETER

TUCKAHOE

LARCHMONT

NEW ROCHELLE

PELHAM

SACRED HEART

OUR LADY OF MT CARMEL

OUR LADY OF VICTORY

St. MARY
}
MOUNT VERNON

The Monastery Church of the Sacred Heart in North Yonkers, built in 1917.

Father Anthony Malloy, the first pastor of St. Peter's Church, Yonkers.

St. Peter's Church, Yonkers, the first Catholic church in South Yonkers.

Three national parishes rounded off the roster of Yonkers Catholic churches by 1900: St. Nicholas of Myra, the first Eastern-Rite Church in the archdiocese (1891), the Slovak Church of the Most Holy Trinity (1894), and the Polish Church of St. Casimir (1899).

Mount Vernon

Mt. Vernon had four Catholic parishes by the turn of the century. The oldest, the German Church of St. Jacob (Our Lady of Victory) dates from 1871. The roots of the first territorial parish, Sacred Heart, go back even farther, to 1849, when it originated as a mission of St. Raymond's Church in what is now the Bronx. Ten years later the small wooden mission church of St. Matthew was built at the corner of Fifth Avenue and Second Street. In 1872 it became an independent parish with the appointment of Father James Cole as the first resident pastor. At that time the name was changed from St. Matthew to Sacred Heart. In 1878 Father Cole began work on a new church that was finished in 1881.

A decade later Mount Vernon still had the appearance of a country village. "There wasn't a paved street in Mount Vernon when I came here," recalled the second pastor of Sacred Heart Church, Father Edward J. Flynn, about his arrival in 1890, two years before Mount Vernon seceded from the Town of Eastchester and incorporated itself as a city. "There were only dirt roads all about the city which had a population of only about nine or ten thousand. To go to Yonkers in those days you could take a stage which left here at ten in the morning and two in the afternoon. The fare was twenty-five cents."[2]

Madonna and Child from the Church of the Sacred Heart, Mount Vernon

The Church of the Sacred Heart, Mount Vernon, which dates from 1881.

That was the extent of the development in Mount Vernon when the little city got its third parish with the establishment of St. Mary Church in 1894. Father Charles McCabe, the first pastor, celebrated the first Mass in the parish in a makeshift chapel in a private residence on December 2, 1894. He continued to use the chapel for the next two years until the completion of St. Mary's Church, which was dedicated by Archbishop Corrigan on December 13, 1896.[3]

The following year the Franciscan friars established the Church of Our Lady of Mt. Carmel for the growing Italian population in Mount Vernon. The first pastor, Father Ubaldo Maravalle, O.F.M., celebrated the first Mass in a rented store. Three years later the basement church of the present Church of Our Lady of Mount Carmel was completed, and in 1910 the upper church was opened. At one point Our Lady of Mount Carmel also had two missions, St. Anthony and St. Francis of Assisi. In 1949 St. Anthony was closed and St. Francis of Assisi became a parish.

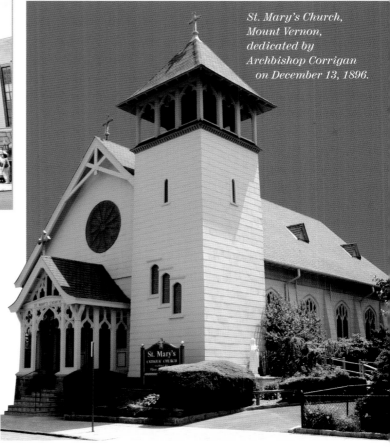

St. Mary's Church, Mount Vernon, dedicated by Archbishop Corrigan on December 13, 1896.

2 - *Centennial Journal: Sacred Heart School* (Mount Vernon: Sacred Heart Church, 1963), unpaginated.

3 - *The Spirit of St. Mary's* (Mount Vernon: St. Mary's Church, 1984), 15-19.

*The First Church of the Immaculate Conception,
Irvington-on-Hudson, a former Presbyterian Church
that served as the parish church from 1874 to 1974.*
Credit: *Church of the Immaculate Conception*

Westchester-on-Hudson

Throughout Westchester, Putnam and Dutchess counties the railroads shaped the process of church building as well as community development. Along the Hudson River where the New York Central and Hudson River Railroad hugged the east bank of the river all the way to Albany, new Westchester parishes were established in Hastings, Irvington, Tarrytown and Croton-on-Hudson.

The parish in Irvington, or Irvington-on-Hudson to use its fancier name, came first. When Archbishop McCloskey sent Father Patrick Maguire to start a new parish there in 1873, he discovered a community of fellow Irish

immigrants clustered so thickly in East Irvington that the area was called Dublin. Most were servants or laborers on the great estates that lined the river. They were so poor that they could not afford to raise the $8,000 that was needed to purchase a former Presbyterian church that was for sale. Father Maguire paid for it himself and took no salary during his first thirteen years in the parish. The Church of the Immaculate Conception was dedicated on December 8, 1874, and served as the parish church for a century. The present church was dedicated by Cardinal Cooke on November 3, 1974.[4]

Croton Landing, as Croton-on-Hudson was then called, had fewer than 500 people in 1877 when Father Patrick McGovern was appointed the first pastor, but the population increased dramatically during the construction of the new Croton Dam between 1892 and 1905. Fifty years earlier Irish immigrants had built the first Croton Dam. Most of the laborers and stonemasons who built the second Croton Dam were Italian immigrants who put down roots and settled in the vicinity. The chief contractor for the dam, Bernard Coleman, was a Catholic who built a chapel at the workers' village on the construction site. There on Easter Sunday in 1900 Mass was celebrated under unusual circumstances in the middle of a bitter labor dispute with the strikers, foremen, contractors and armed guards all in attendance.

The first Church of the Holy Name of Mary in Croton-on-Hudson was a mission chapel built between 1868 and 1874. It was replaced with a second stone church in 1898. Construction of the present English Gothic church was begun in September 1928, with the bulk of the cost defrayed by a bequest of $100,000 from Bernard Coleman. The church was dedicated by Cardinal Hayes on October 13, 1929.[5]

---

4 - *Centennial Journal* (Irvington-on -Hudson: Immaculate Conception Church, 1974), 3-10.

5 - Joseph Fiorentino and Frank Totillo, *Holy Name of Mary Parish History* (Croton-on-Hudson: Holy Name of Mary Church, n.d.). 4-10.

The first Church of the Holy Name of Mary, Croton-on-Hudson, built in 1874. Credit: *Church of the Holy Name of Mary*

The Church of the Holy Name of Mary, Croton-on-Hudson, the third parish church, dedicated by Cardinal Hayes on October 13, 1929.

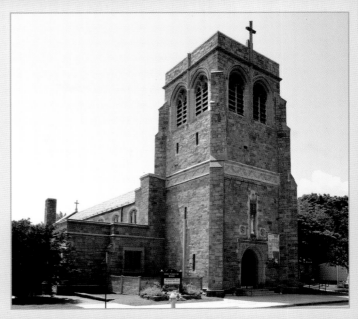

Good Sheperd Church in Harmon, a mission of the Church of the Holy Name of Mary in Croton-on-Hudson.

The Church of the Immaculate Conception, Irvington, dedicated by Cardinal Cooke on November 3, 1974.

St. Matthew's Church, Hastings-on-Hudson, erected in 1914

St. Matthew's Church in Hastings-on-Hudson began as an out-mission of St. Mary's in Yonkers in the 1850s and after 1862 it was a mission of the Church of the Sacred Heart in Dobbs Ferry. By 1870 there was a small mission church in the village where a visiting priest could celebrate Mass instead of in private homes. In 1892 Hastings officially became a parish with the appointment of Father Quinn as the first resident pastor. The second pastor, Father Thomas O'Keefe, built the present St. Matthew's Church in 1914.

Tarrytown got its own parish four years later when Archbishop Corrigan asked the Carmelites to establish a parish there. They had only come to the United States from Ireland in 1889 and started the Church of Our Lady of the Scapular on East 28th Street that same year. Tarrytown was their first foundation outside New York City. They began construction of the Church of the Transfiguration on October 24, 1897. The present church, one of the first built in the archdiocese after Vatican Council II, was completed in 1967.[6]

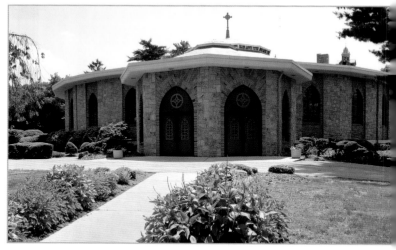

The Carmelite Church of the Transfiguration, Tarrytown, completed in 1967, two years after the close of Vatican Council II.

The sanctuary of the Church of the Transfiguration, Tarrytown, which was constructed in conformity with the liturgical changes of Vatican Council II.

6 - *Transfiguration Church, Tarrytown, New York* (Custombook, 1971),5-8.

View of the Hudson River at Tarrytown in 1828. Credit: *Fordham University Archives*

From Out-Missions to Parishes

Farther inland in the western part of Dutchess, Putnam and Westchester Counties the story of the Catholic Church in the later nineteenth century is the story of how the out-missions of Amenia, Croton Falls, New Rochelle and Port Chester gradually evolved into full fledged parishes with out-missions of their own which is due time became parishes themselves.

In Amenia, where the parish of the Immaculate Conception dates from 1866, the founding pastor, Father Patrick Tandy, had an out-mission in Millerton in the extreme northwest corner of Dutchess County. Founded in 1864, it remains a mission to this day in that rural part of the county. Father Tandy established another out-mission in Millbrook in 1870 one year after the village was founded. The mission church of St. Joseph was completed two years later and became the parish church of Millbrook in 1890 with the appointment of Father Edward Byrne as the first resident pastor.

St. Joseph's Church, Millbrook, as it appeared in 1872. Credit: *St. Joseph's Church*

St. Joseph's Church, Millbrook, erected in 1872 when it was a mission of the Church of the Immaculate Conception, Amenia

St. Patrick's Church, Millerton,
a mission of the Church of Immaculate Conception in Amenia.

St. Joseph's Church, Clinton Corners,
a mission of St. Joseph's Church, Millbrook.

Dover Plains and Pawling both have a tangled Catholic institutional history dating back to 1859 when Archbishop Hughes gave Father Charles Slevin responsibility for the whole Harlem Valley and he built a church in Dover Plains named in honor of St. Charles Borromeo. After Father Selvin's resignation in 1864, Dover Plains became an out-mission first of Croton Falls, then of Amenia, and finally of Pawling until it became a parish in 1936. In 1869 Father Tandy bought a former Methodist church in Pawling and converted it into the Church of St. John the Evangelist. Unfortunately it burned to the ground in 1872, the year that Pawling got its first resident pastor, Father Patrick Healy. Shortly thereafter Father Healy followed the example of several of his predecessors and resigned. Once again Pawling became a mission of Amenia. Only in the 1880s did it become a parish permanently.

The Church of St. Lawrence O'Toole in Brewster came into existence in 1871 as a mission of St. Joseph's in Croton Falls. The pastor, Father Lawrence McKenna, may have picked the name of the eleventh-century archbishop of Dublin for no better reason than that it was his own name. That was not an uncommon form of clerical self-advertisement in nineteenth-century New York. Its history as a parish began six years later when Father Patrick J. Healy settled in Brewster after five years of a nomadic ministry in various locations between Dover Plains and Beekman that included his unhappy experience in Pawling. The little church, dedicated on October 28, 1871, was enlarged several times and served the parish until the construction of the present English Gothic style church, which was dedicated on June 27, 1915.[7]

---

7 - Dominick J. Romano, ,"History of St. Lawrence O'Toole Paris, 1878-2003," *St. Lawrence O'Toole Parish 125th Anniversary* (Brewster: St. Lawrence O'Toole Church, 2003), unpaginated.

The Church of St. Charles Borromeo, Dover Plains.

The Church of St. John the Evangelist, Pawling.

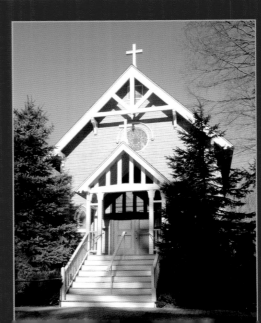

The first Church of St. Lawrence O'Toole, built in 1871 and enlarged in 1915. Credit: Church of St. Lawrence O4Toole.

The Church of St. Lawrence O'Toole, Brewster, dedicated on June 27, 19156.

St. Michael's Chapel, Golden's Bridge, a mission of St. Joseph's Church, Croton Falls.

St. John's Church, North Salem, a mission of St. Joseph's Church, Croton Falls.

315

In Mount Kisco the local Catholic community built a small church dedicated to St. Francis of Assisi in 1862 (at a cost of $2,500), but it remained a mission first of St. Augustine's, Sing Sing, and then of St. Joseph's, Croton Falls, until 1871 when Father Michael Brennan was appointed the first resident pastor. He and his successors in Mount Kisco were also responsible for out-missions in Pleasantville, Bedford Village and Katonah. The little church burned to the ground in November 1886 and was replaced with a larger church two years later. The present church, a modern Gothic structure with limestone trim, was completed in October 1930.[8]

Father John Ambrose Keogh, the first pastor of the Church of the Immaculate Conception, Tuckahoe.

Irish Catholics were attracted to Tuckahoe because of the quarries where in 1850 they could earn $8.75 per week as semi-skilled laborers. In 1853 Father Thomas McLoughlin, the pastor St. Matthew's Church in New Rochelle, established an out-mission in Tuckahoe. Three years the little wooden Church of the Immaculate

Conception was built in Waverly Square in the center of the village. In 1878 Tuckahoe became a parish with the appointment of Father John Ambrose Keogh as the first resident pastor. He had already established the parish in Cornwall eight years earlier. The pastor in the 1890s, Father John B. Salter, complained about the poverty of his parishioners, as he complained about conditions wherever he went, but a decade later his successor, Father John G. McCormick, was able to acquire a prime location on Winter Hill for a new church.

The cornerstone of the new church was blessed on November 8, 1908, and the present Church of the Immaculate Conception, a French Gothic structure constructed of local Tuckahoe marble, was dedicated by Cardinal Farley on May 18, 1912. By that date the Catholic community of Tuckahoe was no longer exclusively Irish but also included many Italians, who founded their own Church of the Assumption

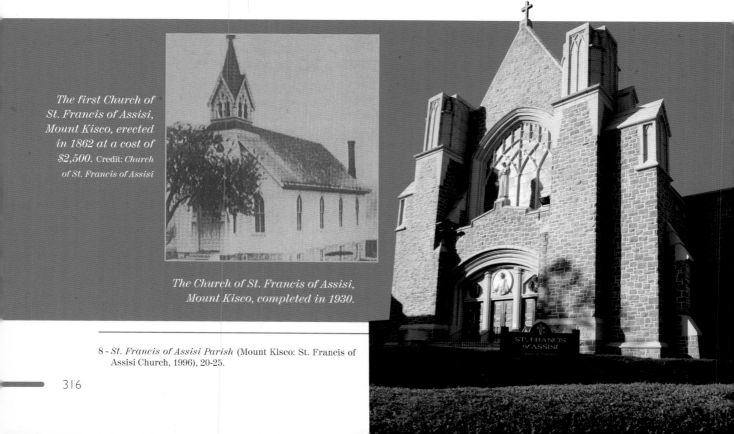

The first Church of St. Francis of Assisi, Mount Kisco, erected in 1862 at a cost of $2,500. Credit: *Church of St. Francis of Assisi*

The Church of St. Francis of Assisi, Mount Kisco, completed in 1930.

8 - *St. Francis of Assisi Parish* (Mount Kisco: St. Francis of Assisi Church, 1996), 20-25.

The Italian Church of the Assumption, Tuckahoe, now merged with the Church of the Immaculate Conception.

In Valhalla the Church of the Holy Name of Jesus was founded by the Dominicans in 1896. The first church, which could hold barely 150 people, was completed the following year. The present church was completed in 1979. In 1998 the Dominicans withdrew from the parish and were replaced with diocesan clergy.

in 1911. Like the Church of the Immaculate Conception, it was constructed of Tuckahoe marble. A noteworthy feature of the religious climate in Tuckahoe was the amicable relations between Catholics and Protestants. "God bless the Catholics and non-Catholics of Tuckahoe," Father McCormick wrote in the souvenir journal commemorating the dedication of the new church in 1912.[9]

The Church of the Holy Innocents in Pleasantville began in 1876 as an out-mission of St. Francis of Assisi Church in Mount Kisco. In 1894 it became a parish with the appointment of the first resident pastor, Father Michael Reinhart, a diocesan priest. Three years later the parish was given to French Dominicans of the Lyons Province, who served the parish until 1915 when they were replaced by American Dominicans who have staffed it to the present day. A new church was built to replace the original church which burned to the ground in 1912. By the 1980s it was inadequate for the growing congregation and a new church was built which was opened in November 1987.[10]

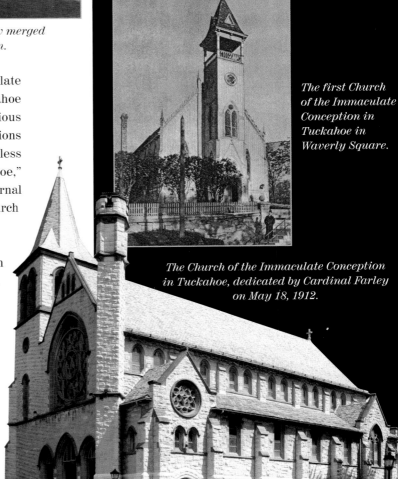

The first Church of the Immaculate Conception in Tuckahoe in Waverly Square.

The Church of the Immaculate Conception in Tuckahoe, dedicated by Cardinal Farley on May 18, 1912.

9 - Thomas A. Brennan, Jr., *Church of the Immaculate Conception, Tuckahoe, New York, 1853-2003* (Tuckahoe: Church of the Immaculate Conception, 2003), 7-25.

10 - *Holy Innocents Parish 1894-1994* (Pleasantville: Holy Innocents Church, 1994).

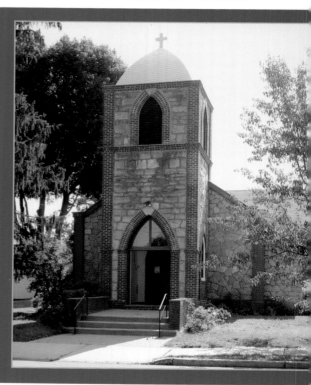

The Church of the Holy Name of Jesus, Valhalla, built in 1979.

The Church of the Holy Name of Jesus, Pleasantville, built in 1987.

The Chapel of Our Lady of Pompei, Pleasantville, completed in 1918, and since 1938 a mission of the Church of the Holy Innocents

On the Sound Shore

On the Gold Coast of Long Island Sound the connecting rail link was the New York, New Haven and Hartford Railroad. By 1900 there were three new parishes between Port Chester and New Rochelle in Mamaroneck, Rye, and Larchmont Manor as well as a second parish in New Rochelle, and a parish in Pelham midway between New Rochelle and Mount Vernon

The parish in Mamaroneck developed from one of the out-missions that Father Thomas McLoughlin visited once a month from New Rochelle. By 1866 or 1867 there was a small

mission church in Mamaroneck named after St. Thomas. It became a parish church in 1874 when Father Christopher Farrell was made the first resident pastor. He succumbed to tuberculosis within two years and was succeeded by Father Isidore Meister, who was the real founder of the parish.

Born in Alsace but educated in the United States, Meister built the present church in 1886. Archbishop Corrigan used the occasion to change the name of the church to that of the Most Holy Trinity. The dedication ceremony on May 15, 1886, must have been a tense occasion because the preacher was Dr. Edward McGlynn, who was already on a collision course with Archbishop Corrigan. Meister's choice of McGlynn may give some hint of his own ideological leanings and explain why in the course of a pastorate that lasted thirty-seven years he played an active role in local civic affairs.[11]

For Catholics in Rye the closest Catholic Church was Our Lady of Mercy in Port Chester until 1880 when Father James McEvoy was sent to establish a new parish there. He bought a house that was used as both a church and rectory until his successor, Father James Mee, built a small wooden church around 1888 that served as the parish church until 1931 when Father James E. Goggin built the present imposing Gothic church. A lavish tribute to Father Goggin, published ten years later by the parish (perhaps written by him), hailed him as "a great and eloquent preacher" and "a tireless and zealous shepherd of souls" who had built a church "that will stand for centuries." At least the last part of the tribute seems justified.[12]

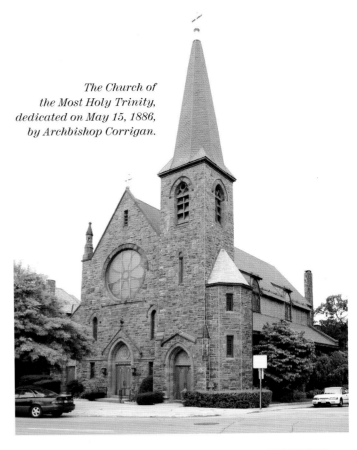

The Church of the Most Holy Trinity, dedicated on May 15, 1886, by Archbishop Corrigan.

Father James E. Goggin, who built the Church of the Resurrection in Rye.
Credit: *Church of the Resurrection.*

The Church of the Resurrection, Rye, completed in 1931.

11 - *Most Holy Trinity, 1874-1974* (Mamaroneck: Most Holy Trinity Church, 1974), 4-12
12 - *Golden Book of the Church of the Resurrection, Rye, N.Y.,* (Rye: Church of the Rsurrection, 1941), unpaginated.

Larchmont's claim to fame originated with its popularity as a summer resort when the population swelled to over 1,000 with the annual arrival of wealthy New York families with their Irish Catholic servants. Unlike many other Westchester communities, there were several wealthy Catholic families in Larchmont who took the lead in forming a new parish. One of them, Thomas J. McCahill, explained to Archbishop Corrigan that the Catholic servants found it difficult to attend Mass in either New Rochelle or Port Chester because public transportation was so expensive. "The result," he said, "was that two-thirds do not go to Mass at all."

The Larchmont Manor Company, which developed the community, donated land for a Catholic church. Several wealthy families, many of them Protestants, raised $5,000 to build a small Catholic church that was dedicated on August 21, 1892. In 1926 Father James Brady began plans to replace the now outdated building. The bill for the real estate and the construction of the new building came to almost $500,000, or one hundred times the cost of the old church. The new church was dedicated by Cardinal Hayes on May 27, 1928. By 1939 the debt was only $14,000, a fair indication of how far the Irish in Larchmont had risen on the social scale since the days when most of them could not afford the carfare to Mamaroneck.[13]

New Rochelle got a second parish in 1893 with the establishment of St. Gabriel's Church. The line of demarcation between the new parish and Blessed Sacrament Church was the New Haven railroad tracks. St. Gabriel's Church was debt free when it opened thanks to a gift of $150,000 from Mrs. Adrian Iselin, who also made generous donations to Blessed Sacrament Church and St. Joseph's Church. The church was consecrated by Archbishop Corrigan on May 29, 1893.

In New Rochelle the wealthy Iselin family was the principal benefactor of the Catholic Church. In Pelham a day laborer named Patrick Farrell filled the role of the Iselins when he donated a lot next to his house for a Catholic church. On December 8, 1896, Mass was celebrated for the first time in this mission church dedicated to St. Catherine. It remained an out-mission of St. Gabriel's in New Rochelle until December 8 of the following year when it was made a parish with Father Francis P. McNichol as the pastor. At Mass that holyday he had a congregation of one hundred people. The collection amounted to $2.87.[14]

St. Gabriel's Church, New Rochelle, consecrated by Archbishop Corrigan on May 29, 1893.

13 - Mary E. McGahan, "The First Half-Century," *St. Augustine's Parish: A Centennial History, 1892-1992* (Larchmont: St. Augustine's Church, 1992), 3-13.

14 - *St. Catherine's Centennial, 1896-1996* (Pelham: St. Catherine's Chuch, 1996), unpaginated,

The first St. Augustine's Church, Larchmont Manor, dedicated by Archbishop Corrigan on August 21, 1892.
Credit: St. Augustine's Church.

St. Augustine's Church, Larchmont, dedicated by Cardinal Hayes on May 27, 1928.

St. Catherine's Church, Pelham, originally a mission church of St. Gabriel's, New Rochelle, where Mass was celebrated for the first time on December 8, 1896.

The Putnam Division

In the heyday of the Railway Age even the lowly one-track New York and Northern Railroad (later the Putnam Division of the New York Central) could boast of two new Catholic churches along its right of way, St. John the Evangelist in Lake Mahopac and the Church of the Magdalene in Pocantico Hills.

In Mahopac the Church of St. John the Evangelist began as an out-mission of St. Joseph's in Croton Falls as far back as 1866, but it did not become a parish until 1889 when Father Patrick J. McCabe was appointed the first pastor. In 1901 the parish suffered a major setback when New York State ordered the demolition of all houses within two hundred feet of any stream that flowed into the Croton River in order to protect the New York City watershed. It meant the end of the old village of Lake Mahopac and of the Catholic church that was built there in 1869. A new church was built in 1903 and enlarged in 1930. By the 1960s the church was hopelessly inadequate for the growing congregation and was replaced with the present church, which was dedicated by Cardinal Cooke on June 7, 1970.

In 1894 Father Joseph F. Egan resigned as the pastor of St. Teresa's Church in Sleepy Hollow to start the Church of the Magdalene in Pocantico Hills. He had less than an acre of land at the same time that John D. Rockefeller, Sr., was assembling his three thousand acre estate. The little church was dedicated by Archbishop Corrigan on October 6, 1895. The stained-glass windows were the gift of James Butler and his wife whose estate at Eastview was nearby. The second pastor, Father Joseph F. Sheahan, was so pleased with the location that he said: "I do not know of another spot anywhere in the state which is so well adapted for the ideal church and churchyard. I have been so much taken by the old English name for the churchyard, "God's Acre," that I have chosen it for mine."[15]

The railroad, which ran past the front of the church, was the lifeline of the parish. Father Sheahan even got the railroad to reduce the Sunday fare to half-price for his parishioners. However,

in 1930 John D. Rockefeller, Jr., complained that cinders from the steam engines soiled the white shirts of the golfers on his nine-hole course. He persuaded the New York Central to move the right of way five miles east, which was a crippling blow to the future development of the village and the parish. One of the pastors of the Church of the Magdalene who was invited to use Mr. Rockefeller's golf course was young Father Aloysius Dineen. "On my first visit I received from him three new dimes and one new nickel," he reported to Cardinal Hayes. "Since the first game I have collected about twenty new dimes and ten new nickels."[16]

For a brief period there was a second Church of St. John the Evangelist located in Shrub Oak. Founded in 1896 by Father John J. McEvoy with territory taken from the Church of the Assumption in Peekskill, this Church of St. John the

Father Patrick H. McCabe, the first pastor of the Church of St. John the Evangelist, Mahopac. Credit: *Church of St. John the Evangelist.*

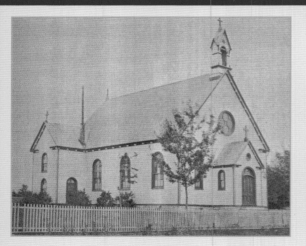

The first Church of St. John the Evangelist, Mahopac, built in 1869 as a mission church of St. Joseph's Church, Croton Falls. Credit: *Church of St. John the Evangelist.*

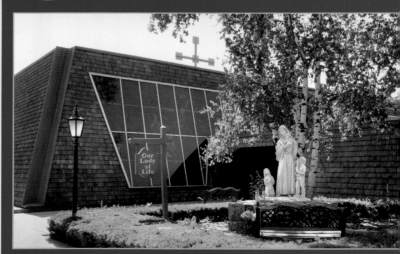

The Church of St. John the Evangelist, Mahopac, dedicated by Cardinal Cooke on June 7, 1970

15 - AANY, Sheahan to Corrigan, September 19, 1894. Bill Gilmartin, "God's Acre," unpublished history of the Church of the Magdalene.
16 - AANY, Dineen to Hayes, August 22, 1927.

The Church of the Magdalene, Pocantico Hills, dedicated by Archbishop Corrigan on October 6, 1895.

The Church of St. John the Evangelist in Shrub Oak, founded in 1896.
Credit: *Church of St. Elizabeth Ann Seton.*

Evangelist was suppressed in the early twentieth century after the pastor moved his residence from Shrub Oak to St. Peter's mission in Yorktown Heights because it was closer to the railroad. In 1915 the parish got a second church, St. George's Chapel in Mohegan Lake, a Norman Gothic gem, designed by the firm of Heins and LaFarge, the first architects of the Cathedral of St. John the Divine. It was built by Aimee LaFarge Heins as a memorial to her late husband, George Heins. For the next decade it was the principal church in the parish.

However, when Father Patrick O'Leary became the pastor in 1927, he reversed the arrangement and made St. Peter's Church in Yorktown Heights the main church. He quickly discovered that when long-time residents spoke of going to the city, they meant Peekskill. Despite the Depression, he built a new church, which was dedicated by Cardinal Hayes in 1933, who described it as "the most beautiful rural church in the archdiocese." The cardinal also changed the name of the church from St. Peter to St. Patrick, either in honor of himself or the pastor or the patron saint of the archdiocese, or perhaps

all three. Father O' Leary later built a Shrine to the North American Martyrs in Putnam Valley modeled after an Iroquois longhouse. Stung by complaints about the Irish name of the church in Yorktown Heights, he is supposed to have remarked at the dedication of the shrine: "You want an American church? There's your American church!"[17]

Dutchess County

In Dutchess County Poughkeepsie got its third parish with the establishment of St. Mary's Church in 1873. The first pastor, Father Edward McSweeny, Irish-born and Roman-educated, was the brother of Father Patrick McSweeny, the pastor of St. Peter's Church, who devised the ingenious Poughkeepsie Plan for integrating his parochial school into the public school system. Edward McSweeny bought an old Protestant church and had it ready for use by the summer of 1873. Twenty years later Father Terrence Earley replaced it with a more substantial Gothic church that served the parish until November 17, 1968, when it was destroyed by fire. The present St. Mary's Church was dedicated on May 13, 1973.

---

17 - *St. Patrick's Celebrates 100 Years* (Yorktown Heights: St. Patrick's Church, 1998), unpaginated.

St. Patrick's Church, Yorktown heights, dedicated by Cardinal O'Connor in November 1984.

The Shrine of the North American Martyrs in Putnam Valley, built by Msgr. Patrick O'Leary as a mission of St. Patrick's Church, Yorktown Heights and now a mission of St. Columbanus Church, Cortland Manor.

Old St. Mary's Church on Cannon Street, Poughkeepsie, 1873-1893. Credit: *St. Mary's Church*

Dr. Edward McSweeny, the pastor of St. Mary's Church's, Poughkeepsie, 1873-1884.
Credit: *St. Mary's Church*

St. Mary's Church, Poughkeepsie, dedicated on May 13, 1973.

The Church of St. John the Evangelist, Beacon, completed in November 1891.

The Church of St. Denis, Sylvan Lake, enlarged and rededicated on October 6, 1991.

The future city of Beacon got a second parish when the Church of St. John the Evangelist was established in Fishkill Landing in 1887. An old hall was renovated for use as a church and dedicated by Archbishop Corrigan on October 21, 1888. Eighteen months later it burned "clean to the foundation" and was replaced with the present St. John's Church, which was completed in November 1891.[18]

Farther east in Sylvan Lake the mission church of St. Denis became a separate parish in 1899. It had been founded as a mission of St. Mary's in Wappingers Falls at least as far back as 1874, perhaps even earlier. The original mission church, built in 1860, burned in 1935 and was replaced with a new church the following year. St. Denis had two out-missions, one in Clove or Clove Valley and the other in Hopewell Junction. Our Lady of Mercy Chapel in Clove was a tiny building that could hold no more than fifty people. It was built in

the mid-1880s for the benefit of the workers in the iron ore mines and was closed shortly after World War II.

By contrast St. Columba's mission in Hopewell Junction prospered because of its proximity to the railroad. The first mission church in Hopewell Junction was the former St. Sylvia's Church in Tivoli, which was dismantled and moved piecemeal to Hopewell Junction in the early twentieth century after a new church was built in Tivoli in 1902. By 1904 St. Columba's in Hopewell Junction was in operation as a mission of St. Denis. [19]

The Church of St. Columba, Hopewell Junction, dedicated in April 1989.

18 - *St. John the Evangelist Church, 1887-1977: A History* (Beacon: St. John the Evangelist Church, 1977), 8-11.

19 - John P. McHale, A History of the Church of St. Denis, unpublished paper.

Except for some of the parishes in the Catskills, St. Denis remained one of the most extensive parishes in the archdiocese comprising over 200 square miles. As the size of the Catholic population continued to grow, new facilities were built in both Sylvan Lake and Hopewell Junction. In Hopewell Junction a new church was dedicated in April 1989. In Sylvan Lake the church built in 1936 was renovated and enlarged, and rededicated on October 6, 1991.

In northern Dutchess County four of the out-missions of St. Joseph in Rhinecliff became parishes by the end of the century, Regina Coeli in Hyde Park, Sacred Heart in Barrytown, St. Sylvia in Tivoli, and Good Shepherd in Rhinebeck. In the case of the first three parishes, wealthy women played a key role in establishing them. In Hyde Park Mrs. Sylvia Livingston Drayton Kirkpatrick, a Catholic member of the Livingston clan, built a chapel in Hyde Park around 1864 that became the parish church of Regina Coeli when it was made a parish first in 1887 and permanently in 1891. After World War II the population of Hyde Park increased dramatically from little more than 3,000 in 1940 to more than 12,000 by 1960, requiring the parish to build a new church that was dedicated by Cardinal Spellman on May 8, 1966.[20]

Like Hyde Park itself Staatsburg had originally been an out-mission of Rhinecliff and later became an out-mission of Regina Coeli. St. Paul's Church in Staatsburg was dedicated on May 8, 1887.

In Barrytown the Donaldson family, especially Miss Eliza Donaldson, were the principal benefactors. They donated the land for the church, rectory and cemetery. The cornerstone of Sacred Heart Church was blessed by Msgr. Thomas Preston on October 28, 1875, and it functioned as an out-mission of St. Joseph's Church in Rhinecliff until it was made a separate parish in 1886. In the early twentieth century an out-mission was established in Red Hook where Sunday Mass was celebrated in a theater until the construction of St. Christopher's Church, which was dedicated on October 22, 1926. As the center of population shifted inland from the river to Route 9, and the Christian Brothers closed their novitiate in Barrytown, the mission church and the parish church reversed roles. Today the Church of the Sacred Heart in Barrytown is a mission of St. Christopher's Church in Red Hook.[21]

Five miles north of Barrytown in the river town of Tivoli another Catholic member of the Livingston family, Mrs. Johnston Livingston, established a chapel in 1856 for the Irish railroad workers and the servants in the great riverfront estates. It remained a mission of Barrytown until 1890 when it became an independent parish. That same year Mrs. Livingston's two daughters donated the present graystone church dedicated to St. Sylvia as a memorial to their mother. It was completed and dedicated two years later.[22]

Ironically the last of the out-missions of Rhinecliff to become a parish was Rhinebeck, which had nearly beaten Rhinecliff in the competition for the site of the original parish in 1862. In 1901 Father James D. Lennon bought the Episcopal Church of the Messiah in Rhinebeck and renamed it the Church of the Good Shepherd. It was dedicated by Archbishop Farley on March 26, 1903. As in the case of Barrytown and Red Hook, the shift in population from the river and the railroad to the highway caused the parish and the mission to exchange places. Today Rhinecliff is a mission of Rhinebeck.[23]

20 - Florence D. Cohalan, "Regina Coeli History," *Regina Coeli Centennial* (Hyde Park: Regina Coeli Church, 1964), unpaginated.

21 - Walter V. Miller, "A Parish History," *Sacred Heart, Barrytown, St. Christopher, Red Hook* (Barrytown: Sacred Heart Church, 1975), unpaginated.

22 - Margaret Guski Tomson, "A History of St. Sylvia's Parish," *St. Sylvia's Church* (Tivoli: St. Sylvia's Church, 1974), unpaginated.

23 - *Church of the Good Shepherd, Rhinebeck,* New York (Rhinebeck: Good Shepherd Church, 2001), 6-9.

Regina Coeli Church, Hyde Park, c. 1864.
Credit: Regina Coeli Church.

St. Paul's Church, Staatsburg, a mission on Regina Coeli Church in Hyde Park, dedicated on May 8, 1887.

Regina Coeli Church, Hyde Park, dedicated by Cardinal Spellman on May 8, 1966.

The Church of the Sacred Heart, Barrytown, built in 1875, now a mission of St. Christopher's Church, Red Hook.

St. Christopher's Church, Red Hook, dedicated on October 22, 1926.

*The Church of St. Sylvia, Tivoli,
completed and dedicated in 1892.*

*The Church of Good Shepherd, Rhinebeck, dedicated
by Archbishop Farley on March 26, 1903.*

The Land beyond the Tappan Zee

On the far side of the Tappan Zee, in Rockland, Orange, Ulster and Sullivan counties the growth of the Catholic community was slow but steady during the Gilded Age. Approximately one new parish was established each year between 1865 and 1900. In that horse-and-buggy era the Hudson River remained a vital commercial artery for the cities and villages located along its banks, which were also served by the West Shore Railroad after 1883.

The Left Bank of the Hudson

In northern Rockland County the influx of Irish Catholics after 1850 led to the founding of the Church of the Immaculate Conception in Tomkins Cove in 1861. It remained a mission of St. Peter's Church in Haverstraw until May 8, 1885, when it became a separate parish with the appointment of Father Joseph Brennan as the first resident pastor. Grassy Point was another river village in northern Rockland County with a substantial Catholic population by the 1880s, mainly Irish, but also some French-Canadians,

The Hudson River from the front lawn of Clermont, the ancestral home of the Livingstons in Columbia County.

who worked in the brickyards. After one particularly hazardous journey across the river to Verplanck for Sunday Mass, a group of local Catholics sat down in Clancy's Tavern to consider the state of their soul and decided to build their own church in Grassy Point. They completed it in 1889 and named it in honor of St. Joseph. At first an out-mission of St. Peter's in Haverstraw, St. Joseph's became a mission of Immaculate Conception in 1893. It was closed in 1969 and demolished in 1974. The old church in Tomkins Cove was replaced with the new Church of the Immaculate Conception in Stony Point in 1982.[24]

In Orange County new Hudson Valley parishes were founded in 1870 in Highland Falls and Cornwall. The pioneer priest in that locality was Father Francis Caro, an Italian missionary whom Archbishop Hughes sent to Buttermilk Falls to start a parish in 1864. A decade later apparently nothing remained of Father Caro's work except the name of his church, St. Thomas the Apostle, if indeed he ever had a church building. Father Terence J. Earley chose

Father Terence J. Earley

that same name for the parish that he established in Highland Falls in 1870. By 1875 he had built a church and renamed it the Church of the Sacred Heart. His parishioners were farmers, miners from the Forest of Dean, the families of enlisted men at West Point, and later railroad workers on the West Shore Railroad, mostly Irish but some Italians. In 1925 the mission chapel of the Blessed Sacrament was begun in Fort Montgomery, an area that had become a popular summer resort after the opening of the Bear Mountain Bridge the previous year.[25]

Father Earley and his successors at Highland Falls were also responsible for providing Mass for the cadets at West Point. In 1896 Father Cornelius G. O'Keefe, who like previous pastors had been celebrating Mass at the Academy in a small building between a stable and a coal yard, decided that it was time for the Catholic cadets to have their own chapel at the Academy. His efforts provoked a national controversy as Protestant ministers across the country lined up in opposition.

Artist's sketch of the brickyards in Stony Point.
Credit: Immaculate Conception Church

24 - *One Hundred Years of Worship: The Parish of the Immaculate Conception* (Custombook, 1985), 5-7

25 - Kathleen Daly and Angela D'Arps, *Ninety Years in the Highlands* (Highland Falls: Church of the Sacred Heart, 1960), 7-34.

The Church of the Immaculate Conception, Stony Point, erected in 1982.

The S.S. Peter Stuyvesant *docked at Bear Mountain State Park in the 1950s with the Bear Mountain Bridge in the background.*
Credit: John A. Boehning

Blessed Sacrament Church in Fort Montgomery, a mission of the Church of the Sacred Heart, Highland Falls, begun in 1930.

The Church of the Sacred Heart, Highland Falls, built by Father Terence J. Earley in 1875.

Msgr. Cornelius O'Keefe,
the pastor of the Church
of the Sacred Heart,
Highland Falls, who
led the fight for
the establishment of
the Catholic chapel
on the grounds of the U.S.
Military Academy
At West Point.

The nub of the controversy was the fact that the Catholic chapel was to be the first Catholic church erected on government property, although not at government expense. Opponents claimed it was a violation of the separation of church and state and they waged a vigorous campaign to stop it. Father O'Keefe's petition received the approval of the Secretary of War, Daniel Lamont, in March 1897. However, Joseph McKenna, the Attorney General in the McKinley administration and a Catholic, got cold feet, nullified the permission and ruled that only Congress could authorize the construction of a Catholic church on the grounds of the Academy.

Archbishop Corrigan weighed into the controversy with an uncustomary feistiness that was reminiscent of John Hughes. He asked Secretary of War Russell Alger, "Why may we not advance with our fellow-citizens, and secure a place of worship in harmony with our increase in number, wealth and social standing?" He reminded Alger that 50,000 Catholic Republicans in New York State and hundreds of thousands more across the country would not be pleased with a refusal.[26] After a spirited debate in the House of Representatives, Congress gave approval for the church on July 8, 1898, and the federal government issued a license to build it on April 28, 1899. Construction began that same month.

Designed by Heins and LaFarge in the Norman Gothic style, the Church of the Most Holy Trinity was built with stone quarried on the grounds of the Academy. It was dedicated on June 10, 1900, by Bishop Farley in the presence of Elihu Root, the Secretary of War, and

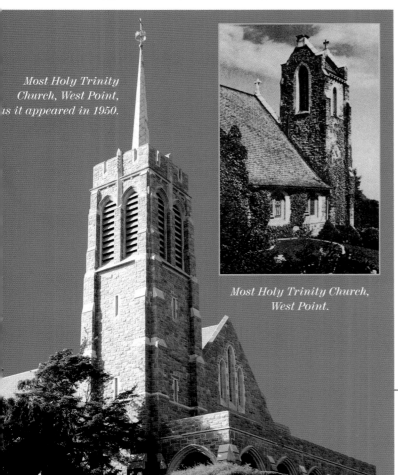

Most Holy Trinity
Church, West Point,
as it appeared in 1950.

Most Holy Trinity Church,
West Point.

26 - AANY, C-16, Corrigan to Alger, February 24, 1898,

over one hundred army officers. The preacher was Father George Deshon, the Paulist priest who was a graduate of the Academy in 1843 and a classmate of U.S. Grant. Most Holy Trinity remained a mission church of Sacred Heart in Highland Falls until 1926 when it became a separate parish.[27]

Cornwall was a mission of St. Patrick's Church in Newburgh as far back as 1856. The Catholics in that community built two small mission chapels even before Cornwall became a parish in 1870. Father John Ambrose Keogh, the first pastor, built a third Catholic church in Cornwall in 1872 and named it in honor of St. Thomas of Canterbury, the eleventh-century English martyr. The construction of the present church was begun on July 2, 1967, and was completed the following year.

Newburgh joined the ranks of upstate cities with more than one Catholic Church in 1875 when Cardinal McCloskey sent Father Michael J. Phelan to establish St. Mary's Church (St. Mary of the Assumption) for the Catholics in the northern and poorer part of the city. He soon erected a small frame church and replaced it with a larger brick church that was dedicated by Cardinal McCloskey in October 1880. The new church had no pews, but the resourceful Father Phelan discovered a Protestant church in New York City that was disposing of its old pews. To transport them to Newburgh, he got a local brick company to load them onto one of their barges which usually returned empty to Newburgh after delivering a consignment of bricks in New York City. Finally, to get the pews from the riverfront in Newburgh to St. Mary's, he asked all the men at Mass one Sunday to return home, change their clothes and meet him at the dock. [28]

The first Church of St. Thomas of Canterbury, Cornwall.

The Church of St. Thomas of Canterbury, Cornwall, built in 1968.

St. Mary's Church, Newburgh, dedicated by Cardinal McCloskey in 1880.

---

27 - AANY, Unpublished history of Most Holy Trinity Church, West Point. When Father O'Keefe died in 1918 after twenty-seven years of service in Highland Falls and West Point, he was buried in the West Point cemetery with the permission of the War Department.

28 - *St. Mary's 100th Anniversary* (Newburgh: St. Mary's Church, 1975), unpaginated.

Farther north along the Hudson, Port Ewen was already past its prime when the Church of the Presentation of the Blessed Virgin Mary was opened in 1874. The little village on the south side of Rondout Creek across from Kingston, was founded in 1851 by the Pennsylvania Coal Company, which shipped its anthracite coal to Port Ewen by means of the Delaware and Hudson Canal. At Port Ewen (named after the president of the Pennsylvania Coal Company), the coal was unloaded from the canal barges to larger river craft. In 1875 the company moved its operations to Newburgh, inaugurating a long period of decline for the waterfront village. The Redemptorists, located ten miles south at their seminary in Esopus, were given charge of the parish in 1913. The first Redemptorist pastor, Father Michael Geary, found $3.91 in the parish treasury.[29]

Irish Catholics began to arrive in Marlboro in the 1850s. For Sunday Mass some went south to St. Patrick's Church in Newburgh while others went north to Milton where they took a horse-powered (treadmill) ferry across the Hudson to Poughkeepsie or Wappingers Falls. In 1867 Marlboro became a mission of Port Ewen and later of Milton. It became a parish in 1900. Father James Hanley, who was the pastor from 1913 to 1958, blessed the cornerstone of the present church in 1922. It replaced a former Methodist church dating back to 1867.

The Catholic community in Milton was served from St. Peter's Church in Rosendale until February 1874 when Father James Mee was appointed the first resident pastor. He built a church two years later. Few rural pastors had the luxury of only caring for one church, and the pastors of Milton were no exception. They also had out-missions in Marlboro, Ireland Corners, Highland, New Paltz and Roseton.[30]

Small country mission churches were still relatively inexpensive to build. St. Augustine's Church in Highland cost less than $4,000 in 1899, $350 for the property and $3,600 for the building, which included everything except the vestment cases, confessional and an organ. At another mission of Milton, Our Lady of the Rosary in Roseton, the church that was erected in 1887 cost the parish nothing. It was the gift of Mr. and Mrs. Juan Jova, who owned the local brickyard.[31]

In the northern reaches of Ulster County several out-missions were established for the quarrymen and their families who found it too difficult to travel to the Church of St. Mary of the Snow in Saugerties for Sunday Mass. In 1848 a small mission church, St. John the Evangelist, was built in Fish Creek, also known as Clow Quarries. In 1875 another small mission church, St. Patrick, was founded in Quarryville by the pastor of the Church of Our Lady of the Snow, Father Michael Power. In 1886 St. Patrick's in Quarryville became an independent parish with the appointment of Father Michael Haran as the first resident pastor, and St. John the Evangelist in Clove Quarries became an out-mission. In the twentieth century the parish acquired two additional out-missions, St. Thomas the Apostle in Veteran in 1908, and Our Lady of the Mountains in West Saugerties in 1939. Finally in 1969 all of these churches and missions were consolidated into the new Church of St. John the Evangelist in Centerville.[32]

29 - John McGuire, C.Ss.R., in *100th Anniversary Presentation Parish, 1874-1974* (Port Ewen: Church of the Presentation, 1974), 7-13.

30 - *St. James R.C. Catholic Church, 1874-1999* (Milton: Church of St. James, 1999), unpaginated.

31 - AANY, Edward J.A. Kenny to Joseph Connolly, April 11, 1900.

32 - I am indebted to Msgr. William E. Williams, the pastor of the Church of St. John the Evangelist, Centreville, and the Regional Vicar of Ulster County, for explaining to me the complicated history of his parish. See also *St. John the Evangelist, Saugerties, New York* (Custombook, 1973), 6-29.

The Church of the Sacred Heart, Esopus,
a mission of the Presentation of
the Blessed Virgin Mary, Port Ewen.

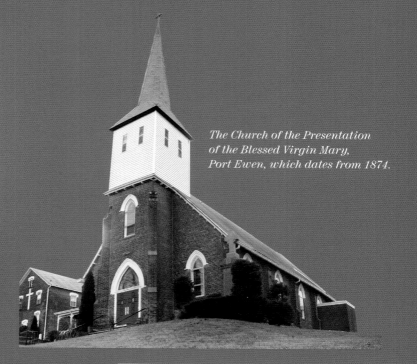

The Church of the Presentation
of the Blessed Virgin Mary,
Port Ewen, which dates from 1874.

St. James Church, Milton,
as it appeared in the 1920s.
Credit: St. James Church

St. James
Church,
Milton,
which dates
from 1876.

Father James
Mee, the
first pastor
of St. James
Church, Milton.
Credit: St. James
Church

St. Mary's Church, Malboro, which was built in 1922.

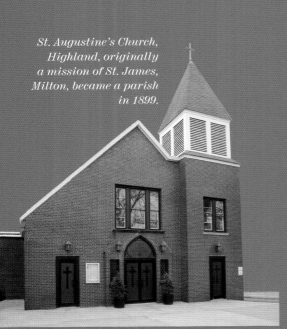

St. Augustine's Church, Highland, originally a mission of St. James, Milton, became a parish in 1899.

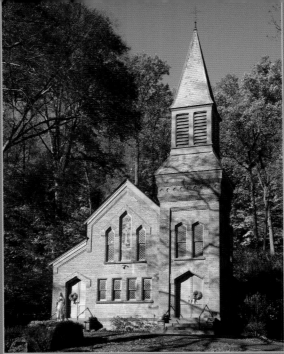

Our Lady of Mercy Church, Roseton, a mission first of St. James Church, Milton and now of St. Mary's Church, Marlboro.

St. Patrick's Chapel, Quarryville, erected in 1875.
Credit: St. John the Evangelist Church.

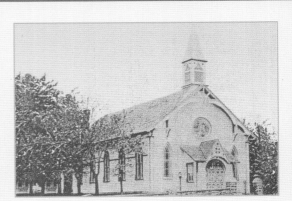

The Church of St. John the Evangelist in the Clove Quarries, dedicated by Archbishop Corrigan on November 2, 1884. The cost was $5,805.99. Credit: St. John the Evangelist Church

Father Michael Power, the pastor of St. Mary of the Snow, Saugerties, 1852-1878. He announced in 1877 that the parish church and the two out-missions were debt free.
Credit: St. John the Evangelist Church.

The modern Church of St. John the Evangelist, Saugerties, which dates from the consolidation of four smaller churches and out-missions in 1969.

Between the Hudson and
the Shawangonk Mountains

Farther inland in Orange County the village of Montgomery got its own parish in 1872 when the Church of the Holy Name of Mary, a mission of St. John's Church in Goshen since 1868, became a parish. The new parish had its own out-missions in Bullville and Walden. St. Paul 's in Bullville remained a mission of Montgomery until 1901 when it was given to the Carmelites in Middletown. In 2007 it was scheduled to become a parish.

In Walden a group of Catholic families tried to transform their mission into a separate parish in 1887. Six years later Archbishop Corrigan sent them a resident pastor, Father Charles A. Meredith. He arrived in Walden on July 1, 1893, the feast of the Most Precious Blood. Hence the name of the parish. In August of the following year, however, the pastor of Montgomery died, and Father Meredith was sent to replace him. Walden's first experience as an independent parish had lasted thirteen months, and it once again became a mission of Montgomery.

Nevertheless, the Catholics in Walden continued their efforts to have their own church. They broke ground for the church on October 28, 1894, and had it ready for Bishop John Farley to dedicate it on July 5, 1896. However, the Catholics of Walden had to wait another sixteen years before they again had a resident pastor.[33]

The Catholics in Gardiner, a small hamlet in the foothills of the Shawangonk Mountains, were mostly Irish immigrants. It was also known as Ireland Corners after two brothers, John and Charles Geirigan, who opened a store at the intersection of two country roads. The Catholics

in Gardiner had an even more protracted struggle than the Catholics of Walden to get their own parish with a resident pastor. Their Church of St. Charles Borromeo in Gardiner was founded as an out- mission St. James in Milton in 1874 and made a parish in 1883. However, in subsequent years St. Charles Borromeo twice reverted to the status of a mission, first in 1884 and again in 1929, before it finally became a parish in 1976. The present church, renovated and redecorated over the years, is essentially the same church that was built by the men of the parish in 1883 with lumber from a former barn. It was dedicated by Msgr. William Quinn, the Vicar General, on October 14, 1883.[34]

The first Catholic church in New Paltz was a mission of St. Charles Borromeo in Gardiner, established by Father Bernard F. Duffy sometime after 1892. It remained an out-mission of Gardiner until 1929 when Father William C. Humphrey moved his residence to New Paltz because it was the site of the State Normal School and the more populous of the two locations. Father Humphrey's decision was New Paltz's gain, but Gardiner's loss. The present church in New Paltz was dedicated by Cardinal Spellman on June 6, 1966.

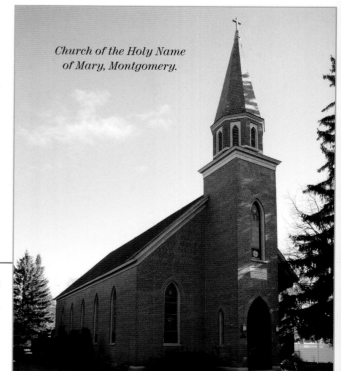

Church of the Holy Name of Mary, Montgomery.

33 - *Church of the Most Precious Blood* (Walden: Church of the Most Precious Blood, 1953), 10-18.

34 - *100 Years: St. Charles Borromeo Church* (Gardiner: St. Charles Borromeo Church, 1983), 8-22.

*St. Paul's Church, Bullville, a mission first of the Church
of the Holy Name of Mary, Montgomery, and later of the Church
of Our Lady of Mount Carmel, Middletown.
It was scheduled to become a parish in 2007.*

The Church of the Most Precious Blood, Walden, in 1900.

IRELAND CORNERS CHURCH.

Report of Receipts and Expenditures from January 1st, 1880. to
January 1st, 1881 :

RECEIPTS.

Balance on hand from January 1st, 1880	$71.73
Collection for poor of Ireland	24.50
Collections for repairing Church, Coal and Sexton	132.25
Total Receipts,	$228.48

EXPENSES.

Collection for poor of Ireland	$24.50
Pic Nic expenses	12.00
For Livery	12.00
To Sexton	10.00
To Carpenter for repairing Church	89.25
Coal	6.00
Memorial to D. Fallon, in Church	8.00
	$161.75

Total Receipts	$228.48
Total Expenses	161.75
Balance in Treasury January 1st, 1881	$66.73

Insurance..............$1,400.00
Mortgage..................None.

JAMES F. MEE, Pastor.

*In 1880 it did not take long
to count the Sunday collection
in St. Charles Borromeo
Church in Ireland Corners
as Gardiner was then called.*

*The Church of the Most Precious Blood, Walden,
dedicated by Cardinal Spellman on July 5, 1953.*

*The Church of St. Benedict,
Wallkill, a mission of the
Church of the Most Precious
Blood, Walden, built
between 1915 and 1917.*

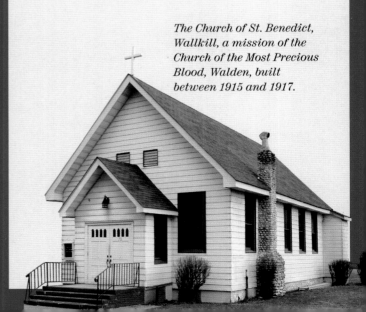

*The Church of
St. Charles Borromeo,
Gardiner, which dates
from 1883.*

Our Lady Help of Christians, High Falls, a mission of St. Peter's Church, Rosendale.

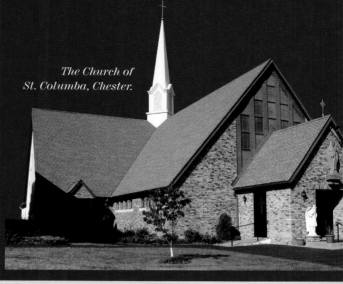

The Church of St. Columba, Chester.

The first St. Joseph's Church, New Paltz, as it appeared around 1907.

St. Joseph's Church, New Paltz, dedicated by Cardinal Spellman on June 6, 1966.

Along the Erie Track

Five of the new parishes in Rockland, Orange and Sullivan counties were located along the tracks of the Erie Railroad, St. Columba in Chester, Holy Cross in Calicoon, St. Joseph in Spring Valley, Our Lady of Mt. Carmel in Tuxedo, and St. Mary in Arden.

In Orange County St. Columba's Church in Chester traces its origins to 1875 as an out-mission of the Church of St. John the Evangelist in Goshen. The following year the Catholics in Chester began work on a church that they did not complete until 1884. It was heavily damaged in a fire in February 1946, but was rebuilt on the same foundation with the addition of a side chapel.[35]

Tuxedo Park was one of the first planned and gated communities in the United States. It was founded by Pierre Lorillard IV, the tobacco magnate, in 1886 as a luxury resort with spacious homes located on winding roads in a parkland setting surrounded by an eight-foot high barbed wire fence. Few if any of the original homeowners in Tuxedo Park were Catholics, but Lorillard imported some 1,800 Italian and Slovak workmen to build the resort. They were housed in separate villages. The Church of Our Lady of Mount Carmel was established in 1895 to care for them. It is clear which ethnic group won the contest to name the church.

Four years later, Father Patrick F. MacAran was sent to Arden to transform St. Mary's mission

---

35 - *Centennial Journal* (Chester: St. Columba's Church, 1981).13-30.

into a parish. He quickly decided that the best place to locate the parish was not in the declining village of Arden, but a few miles farther north in Turners (today's Harriman). Shortly after his arrival he began the construction of St. Anastasia's Church, which was dedicated by Archbishop Farley in 1902. That same year Father MacAran started an out-mission in Highland Mills where he erected St. Patrick's Church in 1907. By the 1970s the church in Harriman was inadequate for the size of the congregation. A multi-purpose building was erected that could seat 500 people for Sunday Mass while the original church was used for weekday Mass. The new building was dedicated by Cardinal Cooke on April 8, 1978.[36]

In Calicoon along the Delaware River in Sullivan County, Father Gerard Huntmann founded Holy Cross parish in 1876 in a former Methodist church that he bought for $2,000. In 1895 Calicoon and its out-missions were given to the Franciscans of Holy Name Province, who have staffed it to the present day. When the Franciscans opened their new seminary in Calicoon in 1910, they closed the church and used the seminary chapel as the parish church. The sale of the seminary in the 1970s required the construction of a new parish church, which was dedicated on July 20, 1980. In 1904 the Franciscans in Calicoon established St. Patrick's mission in Long Eddy. A second out-mission, Sacred Heart in Hankins, which was started in 1919, has since been closed.[37]

St. Anastasia's Church, Harriman, dedicated by Cardinal Cooke on April 8, 1978.

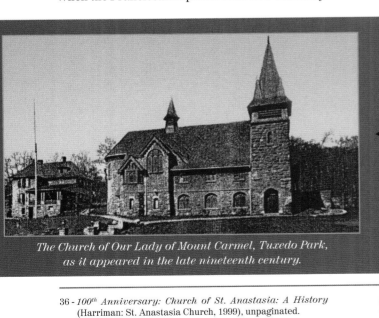

The Church of Our Lady of Mount Carmel, Tuxedo Park, as it appeared in the late nineteenth century.

The Church of Our Lady of Mount Carmel, Tuxedo Park.

36 - *100th Anniversary: Church of St. Anastasia: A History* (Harriman: St. Anastasia Church, 1999), unpaginated.

37 - "Holy Cross Parish: The Long Search for a Permanent Home," *Dedication of Holy Cross Church* (Calicoon: Holy Cross Church, 1980), 10-15.

St. Patrick's Church, Long Eddy, a mission of the Church of the Holy Cross, Calicoon.

The Church of the Holy Cross, Calicoon, dedicated on July 20, 1980.

In Rockland County St. Joseph's Church in Spring Valley began as an out-mission Piermont, and later of Suffern, and for a time was served by the chaplains at St. Agatha's Home for Children in Nanuet. A small mission church was built around 1870, and in 1893 Father John J. Hughes was appointed the first pastor. In September of that year he broke ground for a church on Main Street that was dedicated by Archbishop Corrigan on August 11, 1895. The Church of St. Margaret of Antioch in Pearl River, located farther south on the same branch line of the Erie, originated as a mission of Spring Valley. The cornerstone of the church was blessed on May 19, 1901.

In Congers it was not the Erie but the West Shore Railroad that was the connecting link with the outside world. In fact the village of Congers owes it name to the West Shore Railroad. It was known as Waldberg until 1883 when one A.B. Conger donated land for a depot and the railroad compensated him by naming it Congers. The local Catholics were Irish, Italian and Slovak immigrants who worked in the quarries or made a living during the winter by "ice-farming," cutting blocks of ice in Rockland Lake and shipping it to New York City. St. Paul's Church began as a

mission of St. Peter's in Haverstraw in 1891. Three years later the local Catholics erected a church and in 1896 they got their own parish when Father Michael J. Mulhern was appointed the first resident pastor.

In 1898 he was replaced by Father John Nageleisen, who played a major role in the development of the Catholic Church in Rockland County. He inherited an out-mission in Bardonia for a mostly German-speaking congregation for whom he built St. Anthony's Church in 1899. Four years later it became a parish with its own mission church of St. Augustine in New City. The first pastor was Father Martin Grasser, Father Nageleisen's curate in Congers.

Meanwhile in 1901 Father Nageleisen opened St. Michael's mission in a former Protestant church in the hamlet of Rockland Lake. It became a separate parish in 1901. Congers started still another mission in 1927, the Church of St. Thérèse in Valley Cottage. Both St. Michael's and St. Thérèse were closed in 1963. In Congers itself the original church was replaced with the present St. Paul's Church in 1968. [38]

---

38 - Muriel Rokos, *History of St. Paul's Parish, Congers, New York,* 1891-1958 (Congers: St. Paul's Church, 1958), -22.

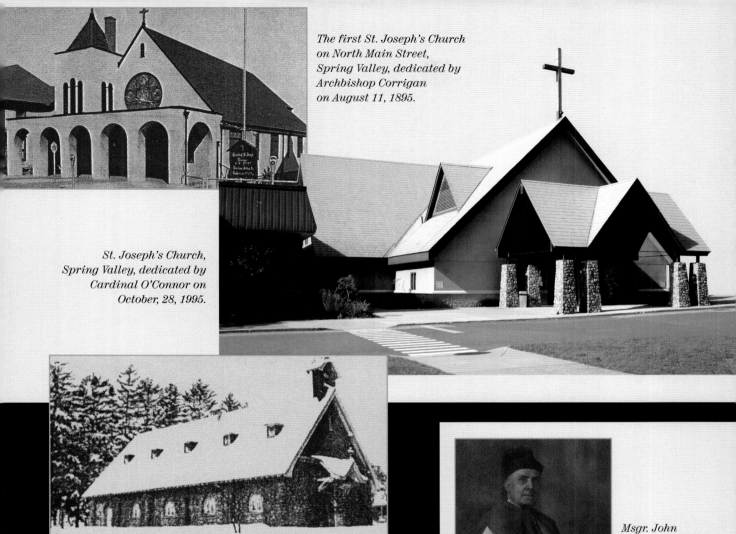

The first St. Joseph's Church on North Main Street, Spring Valley, dedicated by Archbishop Corrigan on August 11, 1895.

St. Joseph's Church, Spring Valley, dedicated by Cardinal O'Connor on October, 28, 1995.

The St. Vincent de Paul Chapel on the grounds of St. Joseph's Church, Spring Valley.

Msgr. John A. Nageleisen, second pastor of St. Paul's Church, Congers.

St. Paul's Church, Congers, erected in 1968.

St. Anthony 's Church in Bardonia burned to the ground on August 21, 1912. The pastor, Father Anthony Strube, replaced it with a new stone church on donated property in the neighboring village of Nanuet. Completed in 1923 by Father Nicholas Hans, it became popular as a shrine church, although not quite one of "the better known shrines in America" as was claimed by the parish history published in 1948. Although St. Anthony's never became a German national parish, the first pastors were all German and some became pastors of German national parishes in Manhattan. Like many suburban parishes after World War II, St. Anthony's experienced a population explosion which led to the erection of a new and larger parish church in 1971.[39]

The first St. Anthony's Church in Bardonia.

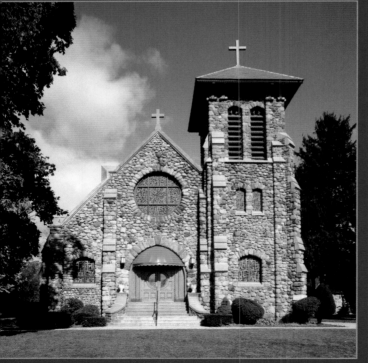

St. Anthony's Shrine Church, Nanuet, completed in 1923.

St. Augustine's Mission Church in New City.

The Last Frontier: The Catskills

Sullivan County was the most remote of the seven upstate counties of the archdiocese except for the area of the county along the Delaware River. However, the interior of Sullivan county experienced the impact of the railway age in 1884 with the construction of the New York, Ontario and Western Railway from Cornwall through the Catskills to its ill-chosen terminus in Oswego. The railroad's passengers called it the "Old and Weary," and noted that it took almost as long to get from New York City to Oswego on the O & W as it did to get from New York to Chicago on the New York Central. Despite its shortcomings, the railroad spurred the development of parishes in Monticello, Wurtsboro, Liberty, Livingston Manor, and Forestburg .

39 - *Golden Jubilee: St. Anthony's Parish* (Nanuet: St. Anthony's Church, 1948), 13-21.

Beginning in the 1920s the scenery and cool mountain air made the Catskills a popular vacation resort for many New Yorkers.
Credit: John A. Boehning

St. Peter's Church in Monticello antedates the coming of the railroad. Like all of the parishes in the interior of Sullivan County, it began as an out-mission of Ellenville in 1864. A mission church was built in Monticello in 1867. It became the parish church in 1874 when Father Edward McKenna was appointed the first resident pastor of St. Peter's. A new greystone church was dedicated in 1899, the same year that St. Peter's opened St. Joseph's mission in Mongaup Valley. A second out-mission, St. Anne in White Lake, was established in 1913. On December 14, 1975 an arsonist set fire to St. Peter's Church, causing heavy damage to the building, but it was restored and rededicated by Cardinal Cooke on May 15, 1977.

Wurtsboro was originally called Rome and was renamed in honor of the Wurts brothers who built the Delaware and Hudson Canal through the village in 1825. In 1849 Catholics bought an unused Dutch Reformed Church and renamed it St. Joseph's Church. It served as a mission church for priests from Ellenville until St. Joseph's became an independent parish in 1880.

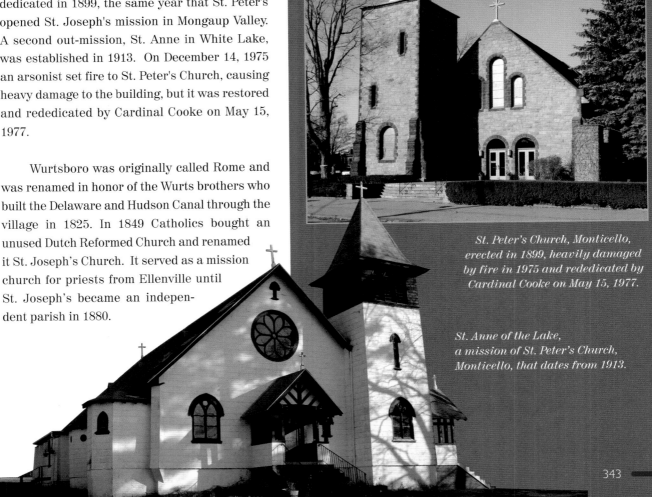

St. Peter's Church, Monticello, erected in 1899, heavily damaged by fire in 1975 and rededicated by Cardinal Cooke on May 15, 1977.

St. Anne of the Lake, a mission of St. Peter's Church, Monticello, that dates from 1913.

*St. Joseph's Church, Mongaup Valley,
a mission of St. Peter's Church, Monticello.*

St. Joseph's Church, Wurtsboro.

*The first
St. Peter's Church,
Liberty, built
in 1872 at a cost
$5,000 could
accommodate
400 people
for Mass.*

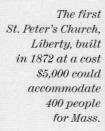

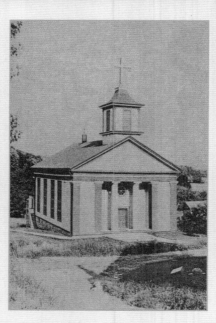

*St. Peter's Church, Liberty, built in 1926 at a cost of over $100,000,
is one of the largest churches in Liberty.*

Autumn scene of the Catskill.
Credit: *John A. Boehning*

Liberty was a thirty-mile hike from Ellenville by horse-and-buggy over unpaved roads in the nineteenth century, but one pastor in Ellenville begged Archbishop Corrigan not to deprive him of the out-mission in Liberty because he needed it to support his parish. There was a mission church in Liberty as far back as 1872, and in 1897 St. Peter's Church severed the ties with Ellenville when it became an independent parish. Liberty and other Sullivan County towns prospered as summer resorts in the 1920s as vacationers traveled to the Catskills first on the trains of the O & W and later in their own cars on traffic-clogged Route 17. The present church in Liberty was dedicated by Cardinal Hayes on May 20, 1926. Damaged by arson by 1956, it was restored with much of the work done by volunteers from the parish.[40]

Livingston Manor began as an out-mission of St. Peter's Church in Liberty in 1896. Archbishop Corrigan blessed the cornerstone of St. Aloysius Church that same spring. In 1899 it became a parish with the appointment of Father John T. Powers as the first resident pastor.

A year later Father John J. McEvoy told Archbishop Corrigan that, despite the isolation, the lack of a rectory and the bigotry of some of the local Protestants, his first Christmas in Livingston Manor in 1900 was the happiest Christmas of his life. He preached in German as well as English and assured the archbishop that "everything was almost cathedral-like in grandeur."[41]

A parish that comprised some 336 square miles, St. Aloysius was the westernmost church in the archdiocese. In 1901 an out-mission was established in Roscoe, Gate of Heaven, only a few miles from the border of Delaware County and the diocese of Albany. The popularity of the Catskills as a summer vacation area led to the founding of two additional seasonal out-missions, the Church of the Sacred Heart in DeBruce in 1906, and All Souls Church in Shandalee in 1917. The pastors of Livingston Manor may have suffered from lack of financial resources and creature comforts, but they showed considerable originality in naming their mission churches. To this day Livingston Manor contains the only two mission churches in the archdiocese called All Souls and Gate of Heaven.

40 -AANY, J.H. Hayes to Charles McDonnell, March 16, 1889. *St. Peter's Church Centennial Celebration* (Liberty: St. Peter's Church, 1972), unpaginated.

41 - AANY, McEvoy to Corrigan, Decembe r 29, 1900.

St. Aloysius Church, Livingston Manor

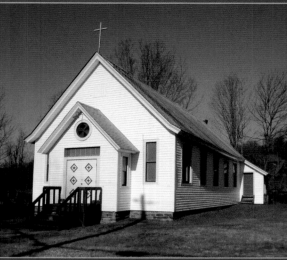

The Church of the Sacred Heart, DeBruce,
a mission of St. Aloysius Church,
Livingston Manor

Gate of Heaven Church in Roscoe,
a mission of St. Aloysius Church, Livingston Manor

The Church of St. Thomas Aquinas,
Forestburg, built by Father Vincent Arcese
who became the pastor in 1900.

The number of Sullivan County parishes was rounded off that year with the establishment of the Church of St. Thomas Aquinas in Forestburg. The first pastor was Father Vincent Arcese, who had been the chaplain at the academy in Forestburg run by the Dominican Sisters of Amityville. Father Arcese began his parish with sixteen families and built a little wooden church on an acre of land donated by Thomas Woods, an Irish immigrant. Although he was offered a parish in Manhattan (St. Lucy's), Arcese remained as pastor until his death forty-six years later.

After the establishment of St. Thomas Aquinas in Forestburg, fifty-seven years elapsed before another parish was founded in the county, the Church of the Immaculate Conception in Woodbourne.[42]

Pastors and Their Discontents

Country pastors often led a lonely existence. When the pastor of St. Peter's Church in Monticello, Father Thomas McGare, complained of boredom, Archbishop Corrigan suggested that he write articles for periodicals. He pleaded lack of talent and asked for a parish closer to the city where he could teach the catechism to school children. Whether he believed him or not, the archbishop sent him to Haverstraw. Perhaps anticipating a similar request from Father John McEvoy in even more distant Livingston Manor, Archbishop Corrigan sent him five volumes of the works of Francis Parkman.

In the archdiocese of New York in the later nineteenth century the archbishop as well as the clergy drew a sharp line between a country parish and a city parish. A "city" parish meant a parish in Manhattan. It was a coveted assignment for diocesan priests as Archbishop Corrigan reminded Father William O'Neil, the pastor of St. Ann's Church on East 12th Street, in 1901 when he requested a change of assignment because of the financial difficulties of his church and school. "If I consider the labor of priests," said the archbishop, "surely those who have been years in the country districts, attending poor and distant missions without any of the material comforts of city rectories, ought to have first claim upon me."[43]

Father Denis Paul O'Flynn, the pastor of the Church of St. Mary of the Snow, Saugerties, 1878-1892.
Credit: *St. John the Evangelist Church*

Father Denis Paul O'Flynn, an Irish-born cleric who was educated in Paris and Louvain, and then spent the better part of fourteen years in Saugerties, commented caustically about "that numerous class of priests who think that any place outside of the city is not a fit appointment for them." One cleric in this category was Father John B. McGrath. After five years as pastor in Gardiner, he informed Archbishop Corrigan's secretary that "country life does not at all agree with me." "I have had to endure innumerable hardships," he said, "such as long drives in all kinds of weather, fasting Sunday after Sunday until two p.m., and a score of other difficulties." Father McGrath wanted a city parish because, as he admitted candidly, "I know that I could do more good where I would be well and happy." Archbishop Corrigan gave him St. Mary Star of the Sea in City Island.[44]

42 - AANY, Arcese to Joseph Connolly, December 1, 1899, January 9, 1900.

43 - AANY, Corrigan to O'Neill, April 23, 1901.

44 - AANY, C-11, O'Flynn to Corrigan, February 4, 1886; AANY, McGrath to James Connolly, April 12, 1899.

A city parish offered the advantages of a larger congregation in a more compact area without the burden of mission churches, fewer financial worries and the inestimable blessing of curates to share the pastoral responsibilities. The prospect of being rewarded with a large and solvent city parish was a powerful inducement for country pastors to do a good job in what was usually their first assignment as a pastor. Under Cardinal Farley in the early twentieth century it became the norm to assign priests to an apprenticeship in a country parish before giving them a city parish.[45]

Even in the city, however, not all parishes were equal as Father Charles F.X. Walsh, the pastor in Croton-on-Hudson, discovered when he requested a city parish and was given the Church of St. Martin of Tours in the Bronx. He complained about the lack of creature comforts in his new assignment, especially the inconvenience of having to share one bathroom with two other priests. The vicar general, Bishop John Dunn, who lived in regal splendor in Annunciation rectory, was not sympathetic. "I washed out of a pitcher and basin and enjoyed the comfort of a tin tub for twenty-five years and never found any hardship in so doing," he informed Cardinal Hayes.[46]

As far back as the 1890s the diocesan consultors noted that the new uptown parishes in New York City did not contain as many people as the older downtown parishes. An earlier generation of city pastors was quick to request

Father Joseph Roesch, the Austrian-born pastor of St. Mary's Church, Obernburg, from 1854 to 1879. He was too poor to afford either a horse or a housekeeper and was responsible for out-missions in Jeffersonville, French Woods and Narrowsburg.
Credit: *St. Mary's Church*

the division of their parish when it became too big for them to handle. Sometimes they even offered to give up their own established parish to start a new one in the same neighborhood. Now Manhattan pastors were more likely to resist the creation of new parishes and even to demand larger boundaries for their parish. They were also quick to accuse neighboring pastors of poaching on their domain.

The pastor of St. Jean Baptiste Church, Father Arthur Letellier, S.S.S, complained about the paucity of parishioners. He asked Bishop Farley to make his national parish a territorial parish with boundaries taking in a wide swath of the Upper East Side. His request touched off howls of protest from the Jesuits at St. Ignatius Loyola and the Dominicans at St. Vincent Ferrer. Once he became the archbishop, Farley sent Letellier a blessing instead and St. Jean Baptiste had to wait another seventy years to get territorial boundaries.[47]

One reason for the prickliness of pastors was financial, precipitated by the decline in the number of parishioners as they were divided among more parishes. As the system of pew rents gradually disappeared, the bulk of the income in most parishes came from the Sunday collection. Most parishioners were likely to be poor people, who could ill afford to give much in the collection. At St. Michael's Church in 1862 the average contribution at Mass on Sunday varied between five cents and twenty-five cents.[48] That was better than in many other parishes. The decrees of the

45 - Michael J. Lavelle, "John Cardinal Farley, Archbishop of New York," *The Ecclesiastical Review 60* (1918): 120-121.

46 - AANY, Dunn to Hayes, November 6, 1931.

47 - AANY, Arthur Letellier, S.S.S., to Farley, February 6, 1901; Farley to Letellier, June 5, 1903.

48 - AANY, A-11. Arthur Donnelly to Hughes, September 22. 1862.

Fourth Provincial Council of New York in 1886 referred to the offertory collection as the "penny collection."[49] It took many pennies, nickels, dimes and quarters in the collection basket to pay the bills. Pastors tried to compensate for the loss of pew rents and the meager collections by imposing a five or ten-cent "seat money" charge at the entrance to the church.

In many parishes there was a sliding scale for seat money with a higher fee at the more popular later Masses on Sunday morning. Father James Galligan at Holy Name Church in Manhattan charged five cents at 6:00 a.m., 10 cents at 7:00 and 8:00 a.m., and fifteen cents at 9:00, 10:00 and 11:00 a.m. He salved his conscience by announcing once a year from the pulpit that the fees were voluntary. He claimed that this sliding scale had the incidental advantage of combating indolence among his parishioners. At least his parishioners were better treated than those at St. Michael's Church. Those who failed to pay the ten-cent seat charge were confined behind a grill in the rear of the church like steerage passengers on a trans-Atlantic liner.[50]

The practice of seat money became almost universal through the archdiocese and resulted in an embarrassingly brisk business of money changing at the door of the temple to accommodate parishioners who wished to break a dollar bill. Seat money was outlawed at the synod of 1950, which decreed that admittance to church for divine services must be *omnino gratuitus* ("completely free").[51] However, many pastors ignored the legislation by using their seminary training in casuistry to argue that it was a "free will" offering. St. Peter's Church on Barclay Street

was jammed on holydays with workers from the nearby office buildings. The ushers collected seat money from those standing outside the front doors.

Another reason for the turf war among the clergy was more personal. In theory all diocesan priests received the same annual salary, $600 for pastors and $400 for curates. In fact, however, their real income varied widely depending on the "perquisites," the amount of supplementary income that they received from baptisms, weddings and funerals. Some priests made three or four times as much money as others. At Sacred Heart Church in Barrytown the perquisites for the year 1899 amounted to a grand total of $17.00.[52]

In 1867 several priests sent a petition to Archbishop McCloskey, asking him to equalize the income of the diocesan clergy by establishing a reasonable salary for all and then requiring them to surrender any additional income to the parish. They predicted that as a result "the pastors will not be dissatisfied with the division of their parishes, as their labors, and not their income, will be diminished." Nothing came of the proposal and the diocesan clergy continued to argue about equality of income for the next century-and-a-half without coming to any agreement.[53]

49 - *Acta et Decreta Concilii Provincialis Neo-Eboracensis IV* (New York, 1886), 78.

50 - AANY, Galligan to Corrigan, September 4, 1894; Browne, *Parish of St. Michael*, 26.

51 - *Acta et Statuta Synodi Neo-Eboracensis Decimae Septimae*, 1950, p. 114.

52 - AANY, G-17, Annual Report of Sacred Heart Church, Barrytown, New York, 1899.

53 - AANY, A-30. James McMahon, Charles McCready and Michael McAleer to McCloskey, October 7, 1867.

12

The Impact of the Religious Communities

The shrine of St. Elizabeth Ann Seton, St. Patrick's Cathedral.

As late as 1840 there was only one religious community in the whole state of New York, the Sisters of Charity, founded by Mother Elizabeth Ann Seton at Emmitsburg, Maryland, in 1809. Over the next two decades the number of religious grew slowly and then took off in an unprecedented fashion in the later nineteenth century. By 1864 there were five communities of men and six communities of women in the archdiocese of New York alone. By 1900 the comparable figures were eighteen communities of men and thirty-one communities of women. Their collective achievement was to create a vast network of educational and charitable institutions that characterized the archdiocese by the end of the nineteenth century.

The Sisters of Charity

The Sisters of Charity, who had come to Manhattan in 1817 to open the Catholic Orphan Asylum on Prince Street, made the largest contribution to the diocese. However, in 1845 their services nearly came to an abrupt end when their superiors announced intention of recalling the sisters from New York to the motherhouse in Emmitsburg. They had come to blows with Bishop Hughes over two issues. First, they announced that their rule forbade them from continuing to care for boys and well as girls in their orphanages. Secondly they refused to submit to Bishop Hughes' demand that they should consult him about the appointment and transfer of local religious superiors.

The decision to withdraw from the orphanages came at a particularly bad tine for the bishop because he was negotiating with the city for property on Fifth Avenue for a new and bigger orphan asylum. He knew that he would get no

The plaque outside the parochial school of St. Patrick's Old Cathedral commemorates the arrival of the first Sisters of Charity in New York from Emmitsburg in August 1817. The school was formerly the Roman Catholic Orphan Asylum

financial support from New York's Catholic community if the Sisters of Charity were not in charge of the new orphanage. He thought their scruples about caring for little boys was a ridiculously pedantic interpretation of their rule occasioned by their desire to affiliate with the French Daughters of Charity. Hughes accused the superiors of threatening to destroy with a dash of the pen thirty years of charitable work by their sisters in his diocese. "This business has gone far enough," he told their Sister Visitor in New York.

The first Motherhouse of the Sisters of the Charity of St. Vincent de Paul at McGowan's Pass in what is now Central Park

Be assured that I mean no personal disrespect when I communicate to you a message addressed to a Christian and religious lady, viz., that I wish, and request, and require that you shall leave the diocese of New York with as little delay as possible. I shall tolerate no officer of a religious community, male or female, exercising without my previous advisement and consent, powers of disturbance and embarrassment, such as have been exercised, conscientiously no doubt, in my diocese of late.

He added as a postscript, "If for this the sisters are to be recalled, let them go; I shall look for others to take their place."[1] They were brave or foolhardy words from a bishop who knew there were no other sisters available to take their place. The same day that Bishop Hughes dispatched this letter, he summoned all the priests in Manhattan and Brooklyn to meet with him two days later in Transfiguration Church. There, in a rare instance of consulting with his clergy, he read them the correspondence between himself and the religious superiors in Emmitsburg. The priests gave him virtually unanimous backing for his plan to allow the Sisters of Charity in New York the choice of returning to Maryland or remaining in New York to form a new religious community under his jurisdiction.

After strenuously resisting Bishop's Hughes' plan, the superiors capitulated in 1846 and allowed the sisters in New York to make their own decision. Nineteen returned to the motherhouse in Emmitsburg, while thirty-one chose to remain in New York. They were incorporated as a diocesan community, the Sisters of Charity of St. Vincent de Paul, three years later, on January 23, 1849. The first superior of the new community was Mother Elizabeth Boyle, a convert like Mother Seton and one of the original Sisters of Charity. After successfully guiding the new community for the first three years, Hughes did not want her to stand for reelection. "What shall I do, Your Grace?" she asked. Shall I return to the orphans?" With one of those caustic remarks for which he was notorious, Hughes belittled her in

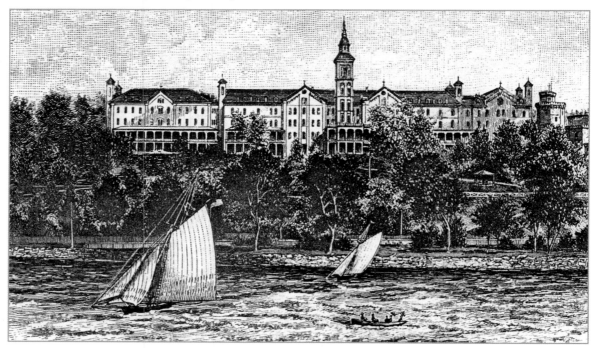

Academy of Mount St. Vincent, Riverdale, and second motherhouse of the Sisters of Charity of St. Vincent de Paul

---

1 - Hughes to Sister Rosalia, August 24, 1846, in Hassard, *Hughes,* 299-300.

public and replied: "You will now take the last place in the community, Mother, and read the lives of the saints."[2] Gratitude was not one of John Hughes' more notable virtues.

The growth of the new community was phenomenal. Twenty-five years after their separation from Emmitsburg, the community grew from 31 sisters to 420 sisters. By 1871 they were operating thirty free parochial schools, fourteen academies, three orphan asylums, two shelters and St. Vincent's Hospital. Their first mother house was located at McGowan's Pass around 107th Street in what later became the upper reaches of Central Park and was later moved to a picturesque location in Riverdale overlooking the Hudson River. During the Civil War, at the request of the War Department, they operated a military hospital adjacent to their original motherhouse.[3]

Unlike every other religious community of women in the United States (including the Sisters of Charity of Emmitsburg after they affiliated with the French Daughters of Charity in 1852), the Sisters of Charity in New York did not adopt a European-style religious habit. Instead, they continued to wear the same simple black dress with cape and bonnet that Mother Seton had introduced for the first American Sisters of Charity. As a result they looked little different from a widow or a Quaker woman and were less threatening to a Protestant public that was unaccustomed to the presence of Catholic sisters. By contrast, when the first Sisters of the Good Shepherd arrived in New York in 1842 on their way to Kentucky, their religious habit caused so much hostile comment that they traveled the rest of the way in civilian clothes. In Kansas City a Sister of St. Joseph said that when a group of

Mother Elizabeth Boyle, S.C., the first Mother General of the Sisters of Charity of St Vincent de Paul, seated with the children from the Roman Catholic Orphan Asylum.
Credit: *Sisters of Charity of St. Vincent de Paul*

them traveled across town, "the people thought we were the circus."[4]

Throughout the nineteenth and twentieth centuries the Sisters of Charity remained by far the largest community of women religious in the archdiocese. By 1900 they numbered 1,145 professed sisters, almost twice as many as all the other women religious combined. Their Mother General, Mother Mary Rose Dolan, probably had more authority and responsibility than any other

2 - Sr. Mary de Lourdes Walsh, S.C., *The Sisters of Charity of New York, 1809-1959* (New York: Fordham University Press, 1960), I, 142, 149.

3 - *New York Freeman's Journal and Catholic Register,* February 18, 1871.

4 - [Mary Garvey], *Mary Aloysia Hardey* (New York: America Press, 1910), 91. Carol K. Coburn and Martha Smith, *Spirited Lives: How Nuns Shaped Catholic Culture and American Life, 1836-1920* (Chapel Hill: University of North Carolina Press, 1999), 102.

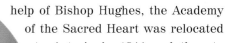

woman in New York City, since she was ultimately responsible for the seventy-seven schools, hospitals orphanages, and other institutions that her sisters staffed. Two-thirds of these "missions," as the sisters called them, had been established by Mother Mary Jerome Ely, their Mother General for almost a quarter century. With good reason she has been called the real founder of the Catholic school system in the archdiocese of New York.

Mother Mary Jerome Ely, S.C., the Mother General of the Sisters of the Charity of St. Vincent de Paul in the late nineteenth century.
Credit: *Sisters of Charity of St. Vincent de Paul*

The Religious of the Sacred Heart

The second community of women religious to make a permanent foundation in New York was the Religious of the Sacred Heart. Founded in France in 1800 by St. Madeleine Sophie Barat, they modeled themselves after the Jesuits and specialized in running schools for the daughters of the French aristocracy, who rediscovered the consolations of religion en masse as a result of their travails during the French Revolution. In 1841 Mother Barat decided to open a house in New York at the urging of Bishop Hughes, who wanted to offer wealthier Catholics an alternative to the private schools that many of them favored for their daughters.

The key figure in the establishment of the Religious of the Sacred Heart not only in New York but in the whole eastern United States was Mother Aloysia Hardey, the descendant of an old Maryland Catholic family, who opened an academy at Houston and Mulberry Streets in 1841. Thirty-one years old at the time, Mother Hardey quickly won the confidence of both Bishop Hughes and Mother Barat. With the

help of Bishop Hughes, the Academy of the Sacred Heart was relocated to Astoria in 1844 and then to the spacious grounds of the former Lorillard estate in Manhattanville in 1847. As the superior in New York for thirty years and then as the American provincial, Mother Hardey opened twenty-five new houses in the United States, Canada and Cuba.

By 1864 the enrollment of the two Academies of the Sacred Heart in New York was 364 students, an indication that there was a sizeable Catholic middle class population who could afford the steep tuition of $250 per year for their daughters. Some of the students came from Latin America and from local Protestant families who valued the social cachet of an academy "for young ladies of the higher class." To their credit, like other congregations of women religious in New York, the Ladies or Madames, as they called themselves, used the revenue from their academy to support a free school for poor children.[5] By 1900 there were 165 Religious of the Sacred Heart in New York City operating three academies.

The Sisters of Mercy

Bishop Hughes' favorite community of women religious was the Sisters of Mercy, founded in Dublin by Catherine McAuley in 1832. On a visit to Dublin in 1845, he personally asked them to open a house in New York City. The following year seven sisters arrived in the city. Their superior was Mother Agnes O'Connor, who was thirty-one years old, the same age as Aloysia Hardey when she came to New York.

---

5 - *The Metropolitan Catholic Almanac,* 1842, 154.

The Academy of the Sacred Heart, Manhanttanville

In 1848 the Sisters of Mercy moved into the former convent of the Religious of the Sacred Heart on Houston Street which they renamed St. Catherine of Mercy Convent. There they opened the House of Mercy, which offered temporary lodging and vocational training for young women, especially single Irish immigrant girls. In the first six years of its existence the House of Mercy provided shelter for 2,323 women and found jobs for 8,650 women. During those same years the community itself tripled in size.[6]

The Sisters of Mercy visited the poor in their homes, hospitals and prisons, even ministering to condemned convicts on death row in the Tombs prison. In June 1862, at the request of Secretary of War Edwin Stanton, the Sisters of Mercy in New York took charge of a military hospital in New Berne, North Carolina. During the course of the Civil War twenty-seven sisters from New York served in the hospital, caring for the wounded and dying soldiers.[7] One of their duties was to write to the families of dead soldiers, informing them of the loss of their loved ones. In keeping with a spirituality that discouraged them from calling attention to themselves, they never identified themselves by name, but simply as a Sister of Mercy.

In March 1863 one sister informed a father of the death of his son, Pvt. William Anthony of the 3rd New York Light Artillery, and sent him his son's ring and a lock of his hair. She wrote, "You will wonder who your correspondent is. She is one of a band of Sisters of Mercy from New York City." Another sister told the mother of the same soldier that they never tried to proselytize the patients. "We never speak to the patients about religious matters much," she explained, "for as we are Roman Catholic Sisters of Mercy, our faith is different from theirs, and they might not like us to interfere." Nevertheless, she assured the mother that her son had been visited by "the minister's lady and several other persons of the Protestant religion."[8]

Mother Mary Agnes O'Connor, R.S.M., the first superior of the Sisters of Mercy in New York City.
Credit: *Sisters of Mercy*

6 - *Leaves from the Annals of the Sisters of Mercy* (New York: Catholic Publication Society, 1889), III, 156.

7 - Bernadette McCauley, *Who Shall Take Care of Our Sick?* (Baltimore: The Johns Hopkins University Press, 2005), 23.

8 - Archives of the U.S. Pension Office, A Sister of Mercy to My Dear Sir, A Sister of Mercy to Mrs. Anthony, March 24, 1863. I am indebted to the Rev. Thomas A. Lynch for a copy of this letter.

The Sisters of the Good Shepherd

The most specialized community of women in New York was the Religious of Our Lady of the Good Shepherd, popularly known as the Sisters of the Good Shepherd. Founded in France in 1641 by St. John Eudes, and re-founded after the Revolution, they devoted themselves to the care of "wayward girls" and "fallen women." The Sisters of the Good Shepherd came to the diocese in 1857 at the invitation of Catholic and Protestant lay women who were concerned about the number of Catholic prostitutes in the Tombs and in the institutions on Blackwell's Island.

The sisters received a chilly reception from Archbishop Hughes, who even blocked their coming to New York for several years, because he could not bring himself to admit that prostitution was a problem among Irish Catholic immigrant women. Mrs. George Ripley, a convert, befriended the sisters and rented a house for them on East 14th Street. Another convert, Henry Anderson, gave them property at the foot of 90th Street and the East River where they built the House of the Good Shepherd. Some of the residents were court

The House of the Good Shepherd at 90th Street and the East River

referrals, but most came voluntarily to receive shelter and vocational training. A few even remained for their whole life, taking vows similar to those of the sisters.[9] In 1900 there were seventy-nine sisters at the House of the Good Shepherd caring for 782 women. Unfortunately, it was difficult to provide jobs or shelter for them after they left the House of the Good Shepherd because of the stigma attached to the institution.

Other Communities of Women Religious

Two other communities of women made foundations in New York during the episcopate of John Hughes. The School Sisters of Notre Dame, founded in Bavaria in 1833, spread rapidly in Germany, and the sisters followed the German immigrants to the United States. They came to the diocese of New York in 1854 at the request of the Redemptorists to take charge of the

St. Joseph's German Catholic Orphan Asylum at the corner of 89th Street and Avenue A (York Avenue), founded by the School Sisters of Notre Dame

parochial schools in their parishes. They quickly established the same reputation among German-speaking Catholics in New York that the Sisters of Charity and the Sisters of Mercy enjoyed among the Irish Catholics.

The Ursulines, founded by St. Angela Merici in northern Italy in 1535, are one of the oldest teaching orders of nuns in the Catholic Church. They were also among the first women religious to come to the New World, establishing a convent in New Orleans in 1727. In 1812 a group of Irish Ursulines came to New York City at the invitation of Father Anthony Kohlmann to open a school, but they returned to Ireland three years later because of the scarcity of students and vocations to their community. The first permanent foundation of the Ursulines in New York dates from 1855 when several Ursulines came from Missouri to establish an academy in Morrisania.

The Redemptorists

The first community of men to make a permanent foundation in New York City was the Congregation of the Most Holy Redeemer, better known as the Redemptorists, who came to the diocese in 1842 to care for the German-speaking Catholics. As a result of their difficulties with the lay trustees at St. Nicholas Church, they established the Church of the Most Holy Redeemer a few blocks away. The Redemptorists also established St. Alphonsus Church on the Lower West side of Manhattan in 1847 and took charge of Immaculate Conception Church in Melrose in 1886. That same year the Redemptorists were asked to care for the Bohemian or Czech Catholics in New York City and founded the Church of Our Lady of Perpetual Help for them on East 61st Street.

---

9 - Maureen Fitzgerald, "Irish-Catholic Nuns and the Development of New York City's Welfare System, 1840-1900." Ph.D. diss., University of Wisconsin at Madison, 1992, 363-372.

The institutions on Ward's Island in 1860

In addition to their pastoral care for the German and Czech Catholics in New York, the Redemptorists became famous for their parish missions, which consisted of several weeks of intense preaching and religious devotions that were the Catholic equivalent of a Protestant revival service. They specialized in fire-and-brimstone sermons with vivid descriptions of hell. One veteran preacher, Henri Giesen, was said to have perfected the technique to such an extent that one summer day, when he was preaching in a church with the doors and windows open, a frightened passerby summoned the fire department to put out the blaze.[10]

Still another contribution was their service as chaplains in the public institutions on Blackwell's Island (now Roosevelt Island), Randall's Island and Ward's Island where they ministered to the patients in spite of the danger of contagious diseases and the bigoted attitude of some of the hospital administrators. Two of the chaplains died from typhoid fever that they contracted in the Emigrant Hospital on Ward's Island. During the cholera epidemic of 1849 two Redemptorists visited the penitentiary, almshouse and insane aslyum on Blackwell's Island everyday. The officials in these institutions were so impressed that they appointed Father Robert Kleineidam the first regular Catholic chaplain. The Redemptorists continued this ministry in the institutions on the East River islands until 1854 when they were replaced by the Jesuits.[11]

The Alms House Buildings on Blackwell's Island (today Roosevelt Island) where the Redemptorists and later the Jesuits served as chaplains

---

10 - Dolan, *Immigrant Church,* 155.

11 - Byrne, *Redemptorist Centenaries,* 154-157.

The Third Coming
of the Jesuits

The Jesuits were no strangers to New York. They made a brief initial appearance in the colonial period during the governorship of Thomas Dongan until they were forced to flee as a consequence of the Glorious Revolution in England in 1688. They returned in 1808 when Bishop John Carroll sent Father Anthony Kohlmann to administer the new diocese in the

St. John's College, Rose Hill, 1846, the year that the Jesuits assumed control of the college from the diocesan clergy.
Credit: *Fordham University Archives*

absence of its first bishop. They withdrew again shortly after the arrival of Bishop Connolly in 1815. They came for the third time in 1846 when Bishop Hughes extended an invitation a group of exiled French Jesuits who were struggling to maintain a college in Kentucky. He turned to them to realize his dream of giving New York a seminary and a Catholic college.

John Hughes' dream went back to April 29, 1839, when he had purchased 106 acres at Rose Hill in Fordham for $29,750 through a third party, Andrew Carrigan, a Catholic layman. "I had not,"

he said, "when I purchased the site of this new college... so much as a penny wherewith to commence the payment for it."[12] Nonetheless, he opened the seminary in the fall of 1840 and the following year he started St. John's College (with an enrollment of six students). Both institutions were staffed by diocesan priests, except for a brief period when Italian Vincentians took charge of the seminary. The two institutions were a heavy burden on the diocesan clergy and in 1846 Hughes was delighted to hand over his college to a community of professional educators. He retained the ownership of the seminary but placed the Jesuits in charge of the administration and teaching until 1855 when he ousted them.

Despite John Hughes' later carping that St. John's College "retrograded" under Jesuit management, it made steady progress. However, it was soon overshadowed by a second Jesuit college in New York City. The year after the Jesuits came to Rose Hill, they dispatched one of their most gifted educators, Father John Larkin, to establish the College of St. Francis Xavier in the heart of Manhattan. According to Larkin's own account, his superiors sent him on his mission with fifty cents. He claimed that he spent twenty cents on carfare, spent another twenty-five cents on transporting his trunk, and arrived in Manhattan with five cents in his pocket. It is said that, upon considering his slender resources, "he gave himself to earnest prayer for the success of his plans."[13]

---

12 - Hughes, *Memoir,* 144.

13 - Charles G. Herbermann, J.E. Cahalan, and J.J. Wynne, eds., *The College of St. Francis Xavier, A Memorial and a Restrospect, 1847-1897* (New York: The Meany Printing Company, 1897), 9.

Father Larkin's prayers were answered. The College of St. Francis Xavier quickly overshadowed its rival institution at Rose Hill. By 1900, it had 500 students and was the largest of the twenty-one Jesuit colleges in the United States and Canada.[14] The College of St. Francis Xavier was also an illuminating example of how the Society of Jesus adapted its educational apostolate to meet the needs of the local community. The lower middle-class Catholics who were just beginning to climb the ladder of success could not afford to send their sons to St. John's College at Rose Hill where the tuition was $200 per year.

Father John Larkin, S.J., the first Jesuit dean of St. John's College, Rose Hill, and the founder of the College of St. Francis Xavier, New York City.
Credit: *Fordham University Archives*

indispensable contribution to the local Catholic community and to the city at large. For several generations it produced the Catholic elite of New York City, hundreds of priests, lawyers, doctors and businessmen.[15]

Perhaps the best index of the importance of the College of St. Francis Xavier was the prestige of its alumni association, the Xavier Union, founded in 1871 by Father Patrick Dealy, later the president of St. John's College at Rose Hill. The Xavier Union became so popular in the Catholic community, and there were so many requests for membership from non-alumni, that in 1888 the Xavier Union reconstituted itself as the Catholic Club of New York. The members built an imposing five-story Club House at 120 Central Park South that was the center of Catholic social life in New York City for several decades.[16]

Although the Jesuits made their most noticeable contribution to the Catholic Church in New York in the field of education, they were also active in the pastoral ministry, first at St. Francis Xavier Church on West 16th Street and later at the Church of St. Lawrence O'Toole in Yorkville, which they renamed in honor of St. Ignatius Loyola in 1898 at the time of the dedication of the present church. They were also instrumental in founding St. Joseph's Church in Yorkville in 1873, which replaced the Church of the Most Holy Redeemer as the principal German parish in the diocese. They continued to staff the parish until 1888, when they were replaced by diocesan priests.

The College of St. Francis Xavier on East 15th Street

However, they could afford to send them to the College of St. Francis Xavier, which was primarily a day school where the tuition was a mere $60 per year. The college lasted only sixty-five years, but, during that brief time span, it made an

14 - Raymond A. Schroth, S.J., *Fordham, A History and Memoir* (Chicago: Loyola University Press, 2002), 89.

15 - Herbermann, *College of St. Francis Xavier,* 153-154.

16 - On the history of the Catholic Club of New York, see David Edward Nolan, "The Catholic Club of the City of New York: A Study of Lay Involvement in the Archdiocese of New York, 1888-1960," M.A. thesis, St. Joseph's Seminary, Dunwoodie, 1995

Finally, as their numbers increased, in 1854 the Jesuits took over from the Redemptorists the responsibility for the institutions on the East River islands, where five resident chaplains often endured severe privations. One of them told his provincial that the two most important requirements for the job were good health and a knowledge of several languages. He began his day at 5:00 a.m. and made his last tour of the wards at 7:00 p.m. "Once on duty means always on duty," he explained. He also listed the languages that he needed in his ministry, "first English, then German, Italian, Polish, Bohemian, Hungarian, Slavonic and Russian." He was not complaining about his difficulties, only hoping that young Jesuits would prepare themselves to follow in his footsteps.[17]

The Christian Brothers at St. Patrick's School in Newburgh in the 1950s.
Credit: *Jubilee*

The Fathers of Mercy and the Christian Brothers

The Fathers of Mercy came to New York in November 1842, only three months after the Redemptorists, when Father Annet Lafont became the pastor of the French parish of St. Vincent de Paul on Canal Street, which had been founded the previous year. In 1848 he was instrumental in bringing to New York the Brothers of the Christian Schools, better known as the De la Salle Brothers, after their founder, St. John Baptist de la Salle, the French diocesan priest who founded the institute in Rouen in 1680.

Four Christian Brothers arrived in New York City on July 26, 1848, only three years after they had made their first permanent foundation in the United States in Baltimore. The first thing that Father Lafont did was to introduce the brothers to Bishop Hughes and then to take them to a tailor who outfitted them in long frock coats so that they could appear in public without creating a sensation in their religious habits. Within a

The De La Salle Institute, the academy opened by the Christian Brothers on East 2nd Street.

month the brothers got their first novice, Francis Barat, a parishioner of St. Vincent de Paul, who became a legendary figure among the Christian Brothers in New York as Brother John Chrysostom. On September 4, 1848, the five Christian Brothers (four of them speaking imperfect English) opened their first parochial school in the diocese in St. Vincent de Paul Church with ninety-six students squeezed into makeshift quarters in the basement of the church and the attic of the rectory.

17 - "Requisites for Missionary Work on Blackwell's Island," *Woodstock Letters 26* (1897): 382-386.

When one New York priest complained to John Hughes that the Christian Brothers were too French to become successful American educators, he replied, "Don't be afraid. It is true that most of the Brothers that we have just now are French, but soon there will be many American young men coming to join them and the order in this country will become just as American as we are." Hughes proved to be a good prophet.[18]

By 1900 the Christian Brothers were probably the largest community of male religious in the archdiocese. In addition to Manhattan College and three academies, they operated the boys' department in some two dozen parochial schools. Together with the Sisters of Charity, they jointly administered the largest Catholic child-caring facility in the archdiocese, the Catholic Protectory, with eighty brothers caring for over 2,400 boys.

The Paulist Fathers

The last of the religious communities of men to be established in New York before the Civil War was the Missionary Society of St. Paul the Apostle, better known as the Paulist Fathers. The first community of priests to be founded in the United States, it was the work of Isaac Hecker, Francis Baker, George Deshon, Augustine Hewitt and Clarence Walworth, all of whom were converts to the Catholic Church. All five had become Redemptorist priests, but they encountered difficulties with their superiors when they wished to concentrate their efforts on evangelizing American Protestants.

When Hecker made a trip to Rome in August 1857 to present his case to the Redemptorist superior general, he was abruptly dismissed from the order for disobedience. While awaiting a

Manhattan College at its first location near Broadway in Manhattanville.

18 - Brother Angelus Gabriel, F.S.C., *The Christian Brothers in the United States, 1848-1948* (New York: The Declan McMullen Company, 1948), 105-106, 117, 630-633.

clarification of his status, Hecker described Rome as "a crucible in which one's faith either becomes wholly supernatural or disappears entirely." Ultimately Hecker received support from Pus IX himself and from several American bishops. Upon his return to the United States the following year, he and three of his associates, Hewitt, Baker and Deshon, founded their new religious community. (Walworth withdrew and became a diocesan priest.). Archbishop Hughes formally approved their rule on July 10, 1858.

Brother Patrick, F.S.C., (John J. Murphy), who was instrumental in transforming the Christian Brothers Academy in Manhattanville into Manhattan College.
Credit: *Archives of the Christian Brothers*

Isaac Hecker was a born optimist who was convinced that there was a natural compatibility between Catholicism and America. One of the main objectives of the Paulists was to erase mutual misunderstandings and prejudices between Catholics and Protestants in the United States. Hecker was also quick to appreciate the value of the press as a means of evangelization. In April 1865 he began a monthly magazine, the *Catholic World,* and the following year started the Catholic Publication Society to produce a wide variety of religious pamphlets. It flourishes today as the Paulist Press.

The Parochial School System

In 1839 the only Catholic schools in the whole state of New York were two academies for girls, conducted by the Sisters of Charity, and eight free schools for poor children. A few years later, when John Hughes locked horns with the Public School Society, he estimated that in New York City alone there were 4,000 or 5,000 Catholic children crowded into the two academies and eight free schools in Manhattan. Only St. Peter's

Father Isaac Hecker (1819-1888), the founder of the Paulist Fathers

Free School had a school building. All the other free schools were located in the basement of the parish churches.[20]

The problem was not only the inadequate physical facilities (800 to 1,000 children squeezed into the basement of the old cathedral), but also the poor quality of the teaching staff. Although the Sisters of Charity provided instruction for the girls in some of the free schools, for the most part the teachers were laymen who had little educational background themselves. As John Talbot Smith observed, "Such teachers as had the necessary qualities and virtues ran their own [private] schools, in which they made money, enjoyed a fine patronage, and lived on the surface of the earth, not under it."[21]

After John Hughes lost his battle to secure the reinstatement of state subsidies for religious schools in 1842, he decided to build his own network of Catholic schools. Hard as he tried, however, he was never able to achieve his goal of providing a place in a Catholic school for every Catholic child. Although two-thirds of the churches had parochial schools by 1870, and the number of students in Catholic schools increased from 5,000 in 1840 to 22,215 in 1870, the percentage of Catholic children enrolled in Catholic schools actually declined from twenty percent in 1840 to nineteen percent in 1870.

19 - David J. O'Brien, *Isaac Hecker, An American Catholic* (New York: Paulist Press, 1992), 155.
20 - *The Metropolitan Catholic Almanac and Laity's Directory for the Year of Our Lord 1839* (Baltimore: Fielding Lucas, Jr., 1839), 111-113.
21 - Smith, *Catholic Church in New York*, I, 186.

The children from a class at St. Francis Xavier school in 1865.

The archdiocese simply did not have the resources in money or personnel to keep pace with the rapidly increasing Catholic population.[22]

By 1900 there were 121 parochial schools and 45 fee-charging academies with an enrollment of 52,184 students. The parochial schools varied in size and quality. In Amenia there was a one-room schoolhouse with forty-five students taught by one lay teacher. The pastor wanted to close it because most parents preferred the public schools, but he was told to keep it open.[23] At the other end of the spectrum was the parochial school at St. Patrick's Old Cathedral, which had 2,018 students in 1900 with only twenty-seven teachers, which meant an average class size of about seventy-five students. It was not uncommon in large city parishes to have schools with well over 1,000 children. A small school was one with fewer than 600 students.

Teachers' salaries were not a major concern for pastors when most of the teachers were sisters and brothers assisted by a few poorly paid lay teachers, who numbered about 300 in 1900. Archbishop Corrigan thought that many of the lay teachers were happy to work for "pin money" (his phrase). The situation in Yonkers illustrated the cost effectiveness of Catholic education. In 1900 there were three parochial schools in the city with a total of 2, 171 students. There were only thirty-one teachers. The total cost for salaries that year was $10,556.96 or $4.86 per pupil. Nonetheless, in Manhattan, Father Henry Brann, the pastor of St. Agnes Church, wanted to reduce the salaries of the nine Sisters of Charities who staffed his school even though they received only $300 per year or less than one dollar a day. The board of diocesan consultors unanimously rejected the request, pointing out that the sisters were already underpaid.[24]

---

22 - Dolan, *Immigrant Church,* 105-106.

23 - AANY, G-17, Dennis F. Coyle to Corrigan, September 4, 1899; Minutes of the Meetings of the Board of Archdiocesan Consultors, September 6 1899,

24 - AANY, Annual Financial Reports of St. Mary's, St. Joseph's and Sacred Heart Church, 1900; AANY, G-16, Corrigan to Brann, November 9, 1899.

The contrast between St. Gabriel's school, erected in 1859 by Father William Clowry, and the second St. Gabriel's school, erected in 1910 by Father William Livingston, illustrates the progress of Catholic education in New York City

Catholic Charitable Institutions

The growth of Catholic charitable institutions lagged far behind that of the schools. As late as 1839 there were no more than five charitable institutions in the whole state, two orphanages in Manhattan, one in Brooklyn and two upstate, all operated by the Sisters of Charity. The sum total of the additions made in the archdiocese during Hughes' twenty-five years was one hospital, one orphanage and one reformatory.

New York City's got its first Catholic hospital in November 1849, when four Sisters of Charity opened St. Vincent's Hospital in a rented building on East 13th Street between Third and Fourth

Avenues. It was only the third hospital in the city and took its place alongside Bellevue Hospital and New York Hospital. The building had no running water; the only light came from oil lamps and the only heat from a small stove in the basement. The sisters slept on mattresses placed on the floor of the community room that they used during the day. It was adjacent to the porch that served as the hospital morgue for the first four years.

The first administrator of St. Vincent's Hospital was Sister Angela Hughes, the sister of Bishop Hughes. In 1856 the hospital was moved to its present location in Greenwich Village at 195 West 11th Street, the former premises of St. Joseph's Half-Orphan Asylum, a four-story building where the sisters and patients enjoyed such unaccustomed luxuries as running water on every floor, steam heat and gas lighting.[25]

St. Vincent's Hospital at 11th Street and Seventh Avenue in the late 1850s.

25 - Sr. Marie de Lourdes Walsh, S.C., *With a Great Heart: The Story of St. Vincent's Hospital and Medical Center of New York, 1849-1964* (New York: St. Vincent's Hospital and Medical Center, 1965), 9-12, 21-23, 40..

The oldest charitable institution in the archdiocese was the Roman Catholic Orphan Asylum, which dated from 1817. By the 1840s, however, the building on Prince Street, which had been erected in 1826, was badly overcrowded as was St. Joseph's Half-Orphan Asylum on West 11th Street. In 1845 John Hughes appealed to the city for land on which to build a new and larger facility. Surprisingly the Common Council, which had been quick to rebuff him over the monopoly of the Public School Society only a few years earlier, offered him a whole city block. The deed, signed on August 1, 1846, made available to the Roman Catholic Orphan Asylum the square block between Fifth and Madison Avenues from 51st to 52nd Streets, just north of the site where John Hughes would later build his new cathedral. The rent was the nominal sum of one dollar a year as long as the property was used for an orphanage.[26]

The boys were moved into the new asylum in 1851, but it was not until 1886 that the last of the girls were moved from Prince Street and the old orphanage was converted into a parish school. By that time, however, the development of midtown Manhattan made the new site increasingly unsuitable for an orphanage and too lucrative to be used for that purpose. With the permission of the city and the state, Archbishop Corrigan sold most of the property to private developers in 1900 for $2,100,000, retaining only the Boland Trade School on Madison Avenue for the use as his projected minor seminary, Cathedral College. The profit from the sale of the midtown property enabled him to build a new orphanage at Kingsbridge Road and Sedgwick Avenue in the Bronx and to set aside one million dollars as an endowment for the orphanage.[27]

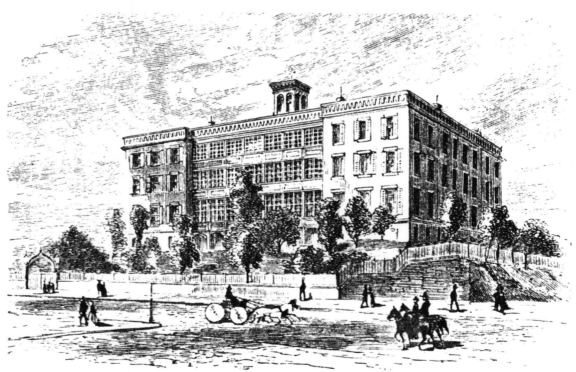

The Roman Catholic Orphan Asylum on Fifth Avenue between 51st and 52nd Streets.

---

26 - George Paul Jacoby, *Catholic Child Care in Nineteenth Century New York* (Washington, D.C.: The Catholic University of America Press, 1941), 97-98.

27 - AANY, G-21, Corrigan to Rev. Dear Sir, April 5, December 18, 1900. In 1921 the archdiocese sold the Kingsbridge property to the U.S. government for a veterans' hospital and the few remaining children were either sent to foster homes or to other Catholic institutions.

The last of the institutions founded under John Hughes was the Catholic Protectory, a reformatory that dates from 1863 when Hughes was already terminally ill. The initiative did not come from him, but from the members of the St. Vincent de Paul Society, who had firsthand experience of the need for such an institution. The first two directors were both converts and leading Vincentians, Dr. Levi Silliman Ives, the former Protestant Episcopal bishop of North Carolina, and Dr. Henry J. Anderson, a professor at Columbia University. The Protectory began its existence in rented quarters on East 36th Street in Manhattan in 1863, but was moved two years later to a 114-acre site in the Parkchester area of the Bronx where a complex of dormitories and school buildings was erected. The Christian Brothers and the Sisters of Charity took charge of the boys' and the girls' division respectively.

The Catholic Protectory in the Bronx in the late nineteenth century.

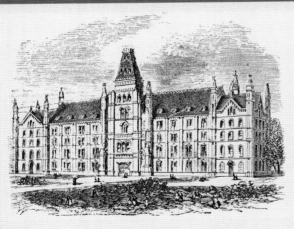

The Boys' Division of the Catholic Protectory, administerd by the Christian Brothers

The House of the Holy Angels, the Girls' Division of the Catholic Protectory, administerd by the Sisters of Charity

After the closing of the Catholic Protectory, the Christian Brothers continued their ministry to troubled boys at Lincoln hall in Lincolndale. Above the community at Lincoln Hall in the 1960s.
Credit: *Archives of the Christian Brothers*

Catholics vs. the Protestant "Child-Savers"

The establishment of the Catholic Protectory in 1863 was the opening skirmish in a major battle between Catholics and Protestants in late nineteenth-century New York over the care of orphans, and homeless and delinquent children, most of whom were Catholic. The battle dragged on for three decades and was reminiscent of the Great School Controversy waged earlier in the century between Catholics and Protestants over public education. Like the educational battles of the 1840s, it pitted the immigrant Catholic community against powerful Protestant institutions and organizations that claimed to be non-sectarian because they were non-denominational. It also involved deep cultural divisions between Catholics and Protestant reformers about the causes and treatment of poverty and the rights of parents with regard to their own children.

The principal custodial institutions for children in New York City were the Juvenile Asylum and the House of Refuge on Randall's Island. The former was a government-subsidized private institution for orphans and homeless children operated by the Association for Improving the Condition of the Poor; the latter was a state institution for juvenile delinquents. Most of the children in both institutions were Catholics, but they were required to attend Protestant church services. Catholic priests were barred from visiting them until the state legislature passed the Freedom of Worship Bill in April 1891.

The House of Refuge on Randall's Island in 1860

The *New York Times* expressed deep regret at the passage of the Freedom of Worship Bill. "What these priests really ask for in reality," said the *Times*, "is the destruction of the essential principle of freedom of worship, a principle which is abhorrent to the Roman Catholic Church on its own avowal."[28]

Catholics regarded the Children's Aid Society as an even bigger threat to their children than the two institutions on Randall's Island. It was founded in 1853 by Charles Loring Brace, a Methodist minister and graduate of Yale with impeccable Yankee credentials. Working closely with the Children's Aid Society after 1872 was the State Charities Aid Association, an organization composed mainly of upper class Protestant women. One of the founding members was Josephine Shaw Lowell, who was to become the first woman appointed to the State Board of Charities and one of the most prominent social reformers in the state.

Charles Loring Brace and like-minded Protestant "child-savers" were motivated by a sincere desire to rescue the large number of homeless and delinquent children on the streets of New York from a life of vice and crime. Their solution was to separate the children permanently from the pernicious influence of their dysfunctional families and to place them in good "Christian" (i.e., Protestant) households. They favored the same placement policy for orphans. "To keep such families together," said Robert Hartley, the head of the Association for Improving the Condition of the Poor, "is to encourage their depravity. These nurseries of debauchery and intemperance are moral pests on society and should be broken up." In practice this meant the removal of children (many of them Catholic) from their families and their placement with Protestant families, usually in rural areas of the Midwest.

The draft riots of 1863 intensified Protestant fears of the growth of a dangerous underclass of Catholics immigrants and their children who were held responsible for much of the crime and vice in New York City. The leadership of the Association for Improving the Condition of the Poor referred to these children as "accumulated refuse." The Children's Aid Society embarked upon a program of child-removal on a large scale. In 1872 Brace claimed that he could easily "locate" 5,000 children a year in good homes in the West at "an average net cost of fifteen dollars per head."[29]

Street crime in nineteenth-century New York City.
Credit: Charles Loring Brace, *Dangerous Classes*

THE

DANGEROUS CLASSES OF NEW YORK,

AND

TWENTY YEARS' WORK AMONG THEM.

BY

CHARLES LORING BRACE,

AUTHOR OF

" HUNGARY IN 1851," " HOME LIFE IN GERMANY," " THE RACES OF THE OLD WORLD," ETC., ETC.

" Améliorer l'homme par la terre et la terre par l'homme."— *Demetz.*

NEW YORK:
WYNKOOP & HALLENBECK, PUBLISHERS,
113 FULTON STREET.
1872.

The title page of Charles Loring Brace's influential call to arms

---

28 - *New York Times,* April 14, 1891.

29 - Charles Loring Brace, *The Dangerous Classes of New York* (New York: Wynkoop and Hallenbeck, 1872), 266. By the 1930s, when the Orphan Trains to the Midwest were discontinued, about 105,000 children had been resettled in the West. Stephen O'Connor, *Orphan Train* (New York: Hougthon Mifflin Company, 2001), 149.

"Street Arabs"-- the common name for New York's wild and homeless youth who lived by their wits on the city streets.
Credit: Charles Loring Brace, *Dangerous Classes*

An idealized sketch of a New York City newsboy faithfully hawking his papers in the middle of a snowstorm.
Credit: Charles Loring Brace, *Dangerous Classes*

earlier. First, after 1870 the Irish-Catholic politicians who controlled Tammany Hall were sympathetic to Catholic demands for government subsidies for Catholic child-caring institutions to combat the child-removal polices of the Children's Aid Society. Secondly the steady growth in the number of men and women religious meant that the Catholic community possessed a large and dedicated labor force to staff their child-caring institutions.

Protestant reformers attempted to offset Catholic control of the city government by using their considerable influence in Albany. They were instrumental in passing the so-called Children's Law of 1875, which was intended to facilitate the placing-out system. It also mandated government support of children in orphanages and other institutions until permanent placement could be found for them. However, the legislation backfired when the Catholics attached an amendment to the bill, requiring the placement of children in institutions of the same religious faith as that of their parents.

Much to the chagrin of its sponsors, the Children's Law of 1875 became the *magna carta* of Catholic child-caring institutions in New York due especially to the women religious who interpreted it in their own fashion. They accepted thousands of children into their institutions, knowing the state was now legally obliged to subsidize them. However, instead of placing them out, as the law envisioned, they kept the children until the age of eighteen, if only because there were few Catholic families who were able and willing to accept these children. As a result of this perfectly legal maneuver, says Maureen Fitzgerald, "within ten years, the city's Catholic nuns were able to invert the entire state- and city-supported child caring system from that intended by Protestant reformers."

By 1875 over 40,000 poor children in New York City, most of them Catholics, had been resettled with Protestant families in the Midwest. As Maureen Fitzgerald has demonstrated,

Anti-Catholicism was not a superficial or cosmetic fault of the individuals involved in these reform movements; it was inherent in the very basis of Protestant and secular child-saving efforts. Despite decades of protests from the Catholic community, the Children's Aid Society and [most other Protestant organizations] would not agree to place children within even a wealthy Catholic home until the turn of the twentieth century.[30]

In the battle over child care in the late nineteenth century, Catholics in New York had two advantages that they did not possess at the time of the Great School Controversy several decades

---

30 - Maureen Fitzgerald, "Irish-Catholic Nuns and the Development of New York City's Welfare System, 1840-1900," Ph.D. dissertation, University of Wisconsin at Madison, 1992, 406-420, 448, 482-486. See also Dorothy M. Brown and Elizabeth McKeon, *The Poor Belong to Us: Catholic Charities and American Welfare* (Cambridge: Harvard University Press, 1997), 2.

THE AMERICAN RIVER GANGES.

If one turns this famous Thomas Nast cartoon on the left side, the alligators appear as bishops in their miters. The prelates are attacking public school children who are defended by an intrepid teacher with a Bible in his jacket. The sad looking figure on the bluff is Boss Tweed next to a ruined public school while in the background St. Peter's Basilica features a sign that says "Tammany Hall." This cartoon was immensely effective in touching all the bases of the Anti-Catholic bigotry of the later nineteenth century.
Credit: *Library of Congress*

The Constitutional Convention of 1894

The success of Catholics in using the Law of 1875 to their own advantage over the following two decades led Protestant and secularist reformers to redouble their efforts to deprive Catholic institutions of state funding. Their opportunity came at the New York State Constitutional Convention in 1894 when they tried to amend the state constitution to outlaw this aid. Their efforts coincided with one of those cyclical outbursts of anti-Catholic sentiment that has characterized American history from the founding of the Republic. Hugh J. Grant, New York City's second Catholic mayor, said in 1892, that "it is within the recollection of many, when to proclaim oneself a Catholic in this city meant a sacrifice of interest, which might be great or small, but was at all times appreciable."[31]

31 - AANY, C-29, Grant to Corrigan, December 29, 1892.

In the 1890s the principal promoter of anti-Catholic bigotry was the American Protective Association, founded in Clinton, Iowa, in 1887. Members of the APA promised not to vote for a Catholic, not to employ a Catholic, and not to join a strike with a Catholic. The APA claimed a membership of two-and-a-half million.

The APA was never as powerful in New York as it was in some of the rural areas of the Midwest. However, that was small solace to the Catholics of New York because of the presence in their state of another and even more formidable anti-Catholic organization, the National League for the Protection of American Interests. The xenophobia of the NLPAI recalled that of the Know Nothings. From its headquarters in New York City it waged a national campaign to amend the federal constitution to outlaw government assistance to religious schools and charitable institutions.

The first president of NLPAI was John Jay, as anti-Catholic as his more famous ancestor. An ardent supporter was the Reverend R.S. McArthur, the pastor of Calvary Baptist Church in New York City, whose weekly harangues against popery attracted a steady audience. What made the organization especially formidable that its members included J. Pierpont Morgan, John D. Rockefeller, Cornelius Vanderbilt, Russell Sage, Henry C. Potter, the Episcopal bishop of New York, and virtually the entire Wasp establishment.

As the leading Catholic prelate in the state, Archbishop Corrigan took the initiative in organizing resistance to what he called "this impending calamity." First he formed a Committee on Catholic Interests. It was composed of seventeen laymen, most of them members of the

Judge Morgan J. O'Brien of the New York State Court of Appeals who headed the Committee on Catholic Interests at the State Constitutional Convention in 1894.

Catholic Club of New York, headed by Justice Morgan O'Brien of the State Court of Appeals. Then the committee, acting closely with Archbishop Corrigan and Bishop McQuaid, executed what one historian called "a brilliant tactical maneuver."[32] They decided that it was useless to fight for state aid for Catholic schools, since public opinion was overwhelmingly opposed to it. Instead they concentrated their efforts on preserving state aid for children in religiously-sponsored charitable institutions. The stakes were high: $1,684,946 in annual aid to 20,500 children in fifty-eight Catholic institutions. In an revealing replay of the struggle with the Public School Society fifty years earlier, the proposed amendment would have deprived only Catholic and Jewish institutions of state aid, since nondenominational Protestant institutions were classified as non-sectarian.[33]

It was a long and bitter struggle with the outcome in doubt all summer, despite able presentations of the Catholic position by Frederic Coudert, a Democrat, and Colonel George Bliss, a Republican and a convert to the Catholic Church. The Catholics received strong support from Elbridge Gerry, the founder of the Society for the Prevention of Cruelty to Children, and Edward Lauterbach, a Jewish delegate to the convention who headed a key committee. Opposition came not only from the NLPAI, but also from the State Charities Aid Association under Homer Folks. Only at the very close of the convention, on September 16, 1894, did the delegates agree to continue government funding to private charities, thanks to a last-minute switch by two of the most influential Republicans in the convention, Joseph Choate and Elihu Root.

32 - Samuel T. McSeveny, *The Politics of Depression" Political Behavior in the Northeast, 1893-1896* (New York: Oxford University Press, 1972), 69-79.

33 - New York *Sun*, June 21, 1894; John T. McDonough, "Catholic Schools and Charities under the New Constitution," *Catholic World 62* (1896): 682-694.

The most eloquent defense of the Catholic institutions came from Elbridge Gerry the head of the Society for the Prevention of Cruelty to Children. Not only at the convention, but throughout the long struggle over child care in the late nineteenth century, this powerful Protestant organization consistently sided with the Catholic position. Elbridge Gerry believed that the placing-out system as practiced by the Children's Aid Society was itself a form of cruelty to children.

The Catholic victory at the state convention in 1894 assured the continuation of the "New York System" which provided for the direct distribution of public funds to Catholic and Jewish charities. This in turn led to a substantial increase in the number of children in Catholic child-caring institutions like those operated by the Dominican Sisters and the Sisters of Charity in Blauvelt, Sparkill and Nanuet in Rockland County. The expansion was particularly evident at the Catholic Protectory in the Bronx. By the end of the century it was the largest reformatory in the United States with over 2,400 boys and 700 girls. The increase in the number and size of these Catholic institutions spelled the death knell of the placing-out system. Destitute Catholic parents now had the option of placing their children in Catholic institutions on a temporary basis under the care of Christian Brothers or the sisters rather than surrendering them permanently to the Protestant "Child-Savers."[34]

Mission of the Immaculate Virgin

The Law of 1875 also benefited New York's second largest Catholic child-caring institution, the Mission of the Immaculate Virgin. It was the creation of one person, Father John C. Drumgoole, an Irish immigrant who was ordained in 1869 at the advanced age of fifty-three. As a curate in a parish in Lower Manhattan, he interested himself in the plight of the city's homeless youth, especially the "newsboys," who often slept in the same streets where they hawked their news-papers. Two years later, with the permission of Archbishop McCloskey, he took over the direction of a faltering home for newsboys from the St. Vincent de Paul Society and reorganized it to provide shelter for 5,000 boys over the next six years. In 1874 he started St. Joseph's Union to support the institution with membership dues of twenty-five cents a year. By the end of the century the dues and voluntary contributions brought in twice as much money as the state subsidy.

In 1881 Father Drumgoole replaced the Newsboys' Home with the Mission of the Immaculate Virgin located in a new ten-story building with dormitory accommodations for 400 boys at the corner of Great Jones Street and Lafayette Place. The following year he purchased 250 acres on Staten Island at a site in Pleasant Plains that he called Mount Loretto where he built

Father John C. Drumgoole, 1816-1888

a large complex of buildings. That same year, with the help of Bishop Ryan of Buffalo, he enlisted the services of Franciscan Sisters who came to New York and formed their own diocesan community, the Sisters of St. Francis of the Mission of the Immaculate Virgin, with their motherhouse in Hastings. Eventually there were eighty sisters at the City House and Mount Loretto caring for 1,180 children. Although Drumgoole was often critical of Charles Loring Brace because of its anti-Catholic bias, he readily adopted many of the educational programs of the Children's Aid Society. Father Drumgoole died only six years after founding Mount Loretto, on March 28, 1888, a victim of the Great Blizzard of that year.[35]

34 - Ibid., 494-495.

35 - Jacoby, *Catholic Child Care,* 158-168.

The City House of the Mission of the Immaculate Virgin, at Great Jones Street and Lafayette Place, built by Father Drumgoole in 1881.

A dormitory at the Mission of the Immaculate Virgin on Staten Island.

Father Drumgoole, the Franciscan Sisters of Hastings and the children celebrates the jubilee of Pope Leo XIII in 1888.

The first site of the New York Foundling Hospital on East 12th Street in 1869.

A posed photo at the famous creche in the vestibule of the New York Foundling Hospital. Until the practice was abandoned in 1918, it is estimated that 66,000 infants had been left here.

The New York Foundling Hospital

The counterpart to Father Drumgoole among the Sisters of Charity was Sister Irene Fitzgibbon, who established one of the city's most famous institutions, the Foundling Asylum. When Archbishop McCloskey asked the Sisters of Charity to establish a home for abandoned infants in 1869, Mother Jerome assigned Sister Irene to the task and gave her $5.00 to get it started. Sister Irene and her assistant, Sister Teresa Vincent McCrystal, organized a women's auxiliary and raised enough money to rent a house on East 12th Street. Sister Irene had forty-five infants in her care within one month. She moved to larger quarters the following year and moved again in 1876 to a site on the Upper East Side that occupied the entire city block between Third and Lexington Avenues from 68th Street to 69th Street. There she erected buildings to house 2,000 infants as well as a maternity hospital and a children's hospital.

Sr. Irene Fitzgibbon, S.C., 1823-1896, the founder and first director of the New York Foundling Hospital.
Credit: *Sisters of Charity*

She also founded Seton Hospital in Riverdale for tuberculosis patients.

Even Josephine Russell Shaw had nothing but praise for the Foundling Asylum after a visit in 1886. She noted especially that "the personal influence of the devoted Sisters is apparent everywhere." In most nineteenth-century hospitals and orphanages the infant mortality rate ran between 60 and 80 percent; at the Foundling Asylum it was less than 26 percent, lower than in the city at large. At the time of Sister Irene's death in 1896 the New York Foundling Hospital, as it was then called, had given shelter to 28,000 infants. The *New York Times* hailed her as "the most remarkable woman of her age in her sphere of philanthropy." Two years earlier Elbridge Gerry told the State Constitutional Convention that "child murder has been practically stamped out in the City of New York from the time that [Sister Irene's] institution commenced."

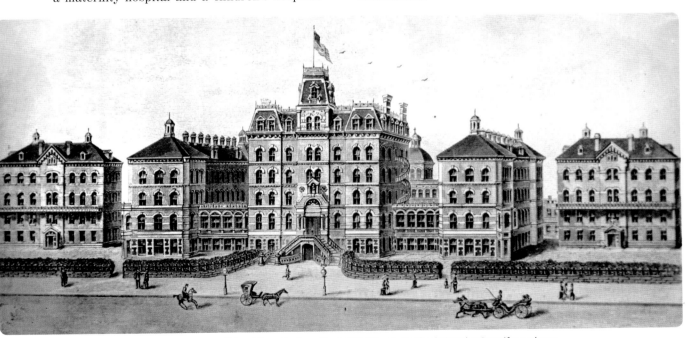

The New York Foundling Hospital on East 68th Street in the late nineteenth century.

Like the Children's Aid Society, the Foundling Hospital began its own program of Orphan Trains, in 1873, placing children with families in the West. Unlike the Children's Aid Society, however, the Foundling Hospital relied upon the local clergy to make sure the children were placed only with Catholic families. The children were also visited at least once a year by an agent of the Foundling Hospital to be sure that they received proper care. Sister Irene's successor at the Foundling was Sister Teresa Vincent McCrystal, who had been her collaborator from the beginning of the institution. She remained in charge until her death in 1917, assuring almost a half-century of continuity in leadership.[36]

Moving Day at the New York Foundling Hospital in September 1958 when the staff and infants moved to new larger facilities across the street on Third Avenue.

The new Foundling Hospital in 1958. It has since been relocated to smaller facilities on Sixth Avenue.

Sister Teresa Vincent McCrystal, S.C., the longtime assistant to Sr. Irene Fitzgibbon and her successor as the director of the New York Foundling hospital.
Credit:
Sisters of Charity

36 - Walsh, *Sisters of Charity*, II, 64-88; O'Connor, *Orphan Trains*. 172-174. See also Willaim Joseph Damroth III, "The New York Foundling Hospital," M.A. thesis, St. Joseph's Seminary, Dunwoodie, 1993.

Thomas Mulry and the St. Vincent de Paul Society

Thomas Mulry, 1855-1916, the president of the Emigrant Industrial Savings Bank and the leading figure in the St. Vincent de Paul Society.

Throughout the nineteenth century the single most important Catholic charitable organization in New York was the St. Vincent de Paul Society. It was a lay organization, restricted to men, whose membership ran the gamut from working-class men on the margin of poverty themselves to some of the wealthiest Catholic New Yorkers. Mention has already been made of the work of Levi Silliman Ives and Henry Anderson in connection with the founding of the Catholic Protectory. For many years the heart and soul of the St. Vincent de Paul Society in New York was Thomas Maurice Mulry. One of fourteen children of Irish immigrants, he became a successful businessman and President of the Emigrant Savings Bank despite a limited education. He joined the St. Vincent de Paul Society at the age of seventeen in his home parish of St. Bernard on West 14th Street and remained an active member until his death forty-four years later. Cardinal Hayes praised him as "one who had done more in the interests of Christian charity than any other American layman of his generation."

The St. Vincent de Paul Society was organized on the parish level with a priest chaplain. The Vincentians, as they called themselves, visited the poor in their homes every week, distributing funds to needy families. "We encourage them by our kind words," Mulry explained, "give them 'the alms of good advice,' [and] they in return teach us patience under trials and gratitude to God for favors received." In 1892 the Vincentians aided needy families with 11,000 children. Mulry estimated that almost half of the children would have been sent to institutions without the assistance provided by the Vincentians to keep these families together.[37]

The charitable work of Mulry and the Vincentians won praise even from Charles Loring Brace and Josephine Shaw Lowell, who recommended Mulry for the new position of Commissioner of Charities of Manhattan and the Bronx in 1898. Lowell said: "The ten thousand helpless and suffering men, women and children in our public institutions need the protection and care of a man of his character and capacity." Mulry was one of the first Catholics to play an active role in Protestant and secular charitable organizations and was appointed to the State Board of Charities in 1907.[38]

The opposition of Lowell and other Protestant and secular reformers to large child-caring institutions was not based solely on anti-Catholic bias. It was also due to their recognition that even the best institutions were no substitute for the experience of family life for a child or adolescent. Mulry was one of the first leaders of the Catholic community to come to the same conclusion although he cautioned against "institution-phobia." He was a Catholic pioneer in advocating foster care for dependent children provided that their religious interests were safeguarded. Largely as a result of his efforts the Catholic Home Bureau for Dependent Children was opened on March 1, 1899, under the sponsorship of the St. Vincent de Paul Society. Mulry served as the President of the Board of Managers for the first eight years.[39]

37 - AANY, G-2, Mulry to Sirs and Dear Brothers, August 29, 1893; Mulry to Corrigan, November 18, 1893.

38 - AANY, G-14, Brace to Robert A. Van Wyck, November 23, 1897, copy; Lowell to Corrigan, November 10, 1897.

39 - McColgan, *A Century of Charity*, 376-379; Brown and McKeon, *The Poor Belong to Us*, 39.

In 1905 Mulry turned down the opportunity to receive the Democratic nomination for mayor of New York City. "I detest political life and dread political office," he explained to one of his daughters. "The work of the Society of St. Vincent de Paul gives me plenty of work, and I have always determined to allow nothing to interfere with that work."[40]

New Religious Communities

The influx of the new religious communities in the later nineteenth century reflected the growing ethnic diversity of the archdiocese. Many of the new communities came to New York to care for the members of their ethnic groups, like the Capuchins and the Benedictines who staffed a number of German parishes. The Franciscans were to be found in both German and Italian parishes. The Carmelites remained prominent in Irish-American affairs and became famous for their service as chaplains at Bellevue Hospital. In the case of both the Dominicans and the Augustinians, they were renewing their presence in New York after an absence of many years. The Pallotines, Salesians and Scalabrinians all came to the archdiocese in response to Archbishop Corrigan's plea for Italian-speaking priests.

Two small French communities found refuge in New York from an anticlerical regime at home. The LaSalette Fathers came to Ulster County in 1902, the same year that the Augustinians of the Assumption opened New York's first Spanish parish, Our Lady of Guadalupe in Manhattan. Still another French community with a long history in the United States came to New York in 1896 when Archbishop Corrigan invited the Society of St. Sulpice to provide the core faculty for his new seminary at Dunwoodie. Rounding off the list were two communities of teaching brothers, French-speaking Marists from Quebec, and German-speaking Marianists from Alsace,

who came to the archdiocese by way of Dayton, Ohio.

The increase in the number of religious communities of women was even more extraordinary than that of the men's communities. By 1900 there were four communities of Franciscan Sisters and seven communities of Dominican Sisters. The Dominicans included the first community of contemplative women religious in New York State, the Dominican Nuns of Perpetual Adoration, at Corpus Christi monastery in Hunts Point, which was founded in 1889.

The ethnic dimension was particularly noticeable among the women religious. No fewer than eight of the new communities were either French or French-Canadian in origin, the Little Sisters of the Assumption, the Sisters of Bon Secours, the Marianite Sisters of the Holy Cross, the Little Sisters of the Poor, the Sisters of Misericorde (all of whom specialized in nursing), the Helpers of the Holy Souls, the Ladies of the Cenacle and the Sisters of the Congregation of Notre Dame. The Sisters of St. Agnes, the Dominican Sisters of Amityville, the Sisters of Christian Charity, and the Sisters of Divine Providence were either of German or German-American origin. The Felician Sisters were Polish, the Presentation Sisters were Irish and Mother Cabrini's Missionary Sisters of the Sacred Heart were of course Italian.

Several of the new communities were of local origin, including the Dominican Sisters of Sparkill, founded by Alice Mary Thorpe, an English-born convert, and the Dominican Sisters of Blauvelt, founded by Sister Mary Ann Sammon. Both were active in child care and teaching. Another new community of local origin was the Religious of the Divine Compassion, which was founded in New York City in 1886 by Mother Veronica Starr, assisted by Monsignor

40 - Mulry to Sister Parthenia, October 13, 1905, Thomas F. Meehan, *Thomas Maurice Mulry* (New York: The Encyclopedia Press, 1917, 59-60.

Thomas Preston, another convert. Established during the height of the conflict with the Protestant "Child-Savers," the Religious of the Divine compassion devoted themselves to child care and social work and later to teaching.[41]

Still another new local community was founded by Rose Hawthorne Lathrop, the daughter of Nathaniel Hawthorne. As a lay woman in 1899 she established a hospice on the Lower East Side of Manhattan, St. Rose's Free Home for Incurable Cancer. The following year she and two coworkers received Archbishop Corrigan's approval for a new religious community, the Dominican Sisters of the Congregation of St. Rose of Lima, better known as the Servants of Relief for Incurable Cancer. She took the name of Mother Mary Alphonsa and in 1901 opened a second hospice, which came to be called Rosary Hill Home in Hawthorne, New York.

Alice Mary Thorpe, a convert to the Catholic Church, who founded the Dominican Sisters of Sparkill in 1876 and took the name of Mother Catherine Mary Antoninus.
Credit: *Dominican Sisters of Sparkill*

Sister Mary Ann Sammon, O.P., founder of the Dominican Sisters of Blauvelt

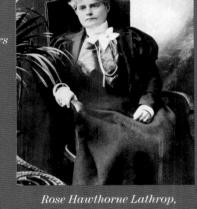

Rose Hawthorne Lathrop, who founded the Servants of Relief for Incurable Cancer.

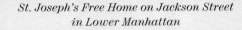

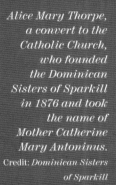

Mother Mary Veronica Starr, the founder of the Sisters of the Divine Compassion.
Credit: *Religious of the Divine Compassion*

The House of the Holy Family and the Convent of the Sisters of the Divine Compassion.

St. Joseph's Free Home on Jackson Street in Lower Manhattan

41 - On the origins and history of the the Religious of the Divine Compassion, see Anthony D. Andreassi, "Begun in Faith and Grit and God: The Sisters of the Divine Compassion, 1869-1954," Ph.D. diss., Georgetown University, 2004.

As a religious superior Mother Alphonsa lived an extremely acetical life. A strong-willed woman, she engaged in protracted disagreements with the Dominican friars who were sent to advise her with the result that the constitution of her congregation was not approved until after her death. She insisted that her sisters accept no money from either the patients in their hospices or from their families, or even from the government, a tradition that the community has faithfully observed to the present day. In the early years Mother Alphonsa supported the community financially from personal appeals to her friends, but, as the reputation of the community grew, voluntary contributions more than met their needs.

Oddly enough Archbishop Corrigan initially hesitated to approve of the work of Rose Hawthorne Lathrop because in 1890 a group of widows known as the Women of Calvary had begun a similar institution for women on Perry Street. Founded by Annie Blount Storrs, it was originally called the House of Calvary and later was relocated to the Bronx where it developed into Calvary Hospital. Far from being a rival to the work of Rose Hawthorne's Dominican Sisters, the House of Calvary complemented their work at a time when cancer was widely regarded as a shameful and contagious disease. Like Mother Teresa in Calcutta a century later, both Mother Alphonsa and the Women of Calvary gave poor people in New York City a place to die in peace and dignity.[42]

Women Religious in a Man's World

Women religious made such a vital contribution to Catholic life in New York that one would think that any pastor would jump at the opportunity to have a community of sisters in his parish. However, in 1873, when Father Arthur Donnelly invited the Presentation Sisters to come to New York City from Ireland to staff the girls' division of St. Michael's school, he included a list of stiff demands. He told the sisters that they were to pay their own traveling expenses to New York, furnish their convent, support themselves financially, and promise not to open a fee-paying school in the neighborhood. Donnelly wanted no fewer than fourteen sisters, each competent to teach her respective grade. When the sisters balked at these terms, Donnelly made a hurried visit to Ireland and dropped most of his demands. As a result six Presentation Sisters came to St. Michael's parish in the summer of 1874 to start their first establishment in the eastern United States.[43] Ten years later the sisters also agreed to staff St. Michael's Home, the parish orphanage that Donnelly started on Staten Island.

Mother Mary Joseph Hickey, P.B.V.M.,
the first superior of the Presentation Sisters
who came to New York in 1874 with a pupil
at St. Michael's school.
Credit: *Presentation Sisters of Newburgh*

---

42 - AANY, G-16, Corrigan to Mother Alphonsa, January 25, 1900; New York *Catholic News,* April 28, 1900.

43 - AANY, A-20, Arthur J. Donnelly, Ultimatum proposed by the Pastor of the Church of St. Michael to the Nuns of the Presentation,. n.d. ; Mary Agatha Cullen to McCloskey, September 24, 1873. Browne, *Parish of St. Michael,* 12-15.

Sister Benedict Rahelly, P.B.V.M.,
with a child at St. Michael's Home
on Staten Island.
Credit: *Presentation Sisters of Newburgh*

The women religious in New York did not limit their services to the Catholic community. Shortly after the Sisters of Charity opened St. Vincent's Hospital in 1849, they published their admission policy. "The doors of the institution are always open to suffering humanity of whatever denomination," they announced, "regarding it as but a poor exemplification of the Divine virtue of charity to turn from the door any of God's creatures simply because they may have worshipped Him at a different altar or prayed in a different form."

In the summer of 1866 an outbreak of cholera in New York City led to near panic among large segments of the population. One place that was especially hard hit by the disease was the Emigrant Hospital on Ward's Island. At the beginning of August, the superintendent of the hospital sent an urgent plea for help to Archbishop McCloskey. "Your Grace," he wrote,

you have, I am certain, seen by the newspaper reports how bad we have the cholera in this institution. It has been and is now exceedingly fatal. A panic set in among the inmates, and all or nearly all the able-bodied portion of them fled the island, leaving us with only the enfeebled, the sick and helpless. Some of the more heroic women volunteered to nurse the cholera patients. The numbers of sick are increasing and those women are being worn out, and we have none to take their places, and the thought has often struck me that, when all other sources failed, to make an appeal to those noble bands of women, the Sisters of Charity or of Mercy, and I hope that this appeal will not be made in vain."[44]

That same day, August 3, 1866, Archbishop McCloskey went to Mount St. Vincent, where the Sisters of Charity were on retreat, to ask for volunteers. A large number of the sisters responded to the archbishop's appeal. Mother Mary Jerome Ely, the Mother General, selected five of them. They spent the next three weeks working with the cholera patients on Ward's Island and did not leave until the epidemic had subsided. A few weeks later a grateful Board of Commissioners of Emigration sent the Sisters of Charity a donation of $500 as a "slight recognition" of their services. In their enclosed letter of thanks, the commissioners mentioned "the courage and devotion exhibited [by the sisters] in nursing the cholera patients at the State Emigrant Hospital, Ward's Island, at a time when extraordinary difficulty was experienced in procuring the assistance of paid nurses."[45]

Two years after this, in 1868, another community of women religious gave a remarkable example of the sisters' commitment to all the people of New York City. This was a community of sisters who had recently arrived from Germany, the Sisters of the Poor of St. Francis, founded by Blessed Frances Shervier. They established

44 - AANY, A-27, James P. Fagan to McCloskey, August 3, 1866.
45 - Walsh, *Sisters of Charity,* II, 206-207.

St. Francis Hospital on Fifth Street near Avenue B, founded by the Sisters of the Poor of St. Francis with the assistance of the Redemptorists at the Church of the Most Holy Redeemer. In addition to caring for the sick, the sisters provided one hot meal a day from October to May to all who called at the hospital. The hospital was later relocated in the South Bronx.

Blessed Frances Shervier, 1819-1876,
the founder of the Sisters of the Poor of St. Francis.
Credit: *Franciscan Sisters of the Poor*

St. Joseph's Hospital
for Tuberculosis Patients in the
South Bronx, founded by the Sisters
of the Poor of St. Francis in 1882.
Credit: *Franciscan Sisters of the Poor*

St. Francis Hospital on East 5th Street in 1865 with the assistance of the Redemptorists at the Church of the Most Holy Redeemer. The Redemptorists told the sisters to restrict admission to the hospital exclusively to Catholic patients. Mother Shervier happened to be visiting New York at the time from the motherhouse in Aachen. The Redemptorists had failed to reckon with the determination of this diminutive German religious superior. She told them that she would pull her sisters out of the hospital rather than obey this order.

In explaining her decision to Archbishop McCloskey, she and the local superior told him that "it is their vocation, according to their holy rule, to take care of the sick and the poor, either in hospitals or in their own houses, without any distinction of creed or denomination." "For this purpose," the sisters went on to say, "[they] beg and collect alms from all, from Jews and Christians. And as they receive these charitable gifts from all, without any distinction, so they have likewise to extend their mercy and charity towards all without any distinction." As a clincher, the sisters added, "This is strictly according to the spirit and doctrine of their great Father, St. Francis of Assisi."[46] The sisters won their tug-of-war with the Redemptorists, and St. Francis Hospital continued to care for poor people of all religions and of none.

Friction between different religious communities sometimes took an amusing turn. In 1888 a Sister of Mercy protested to Archbishop Corrigan that the Sisters of Charity were interfering with their ministry at the Tombs prison where they had worked for thirty-seven years with the convicts, especially those on death row. "They have no experience and we cannot work together," she said, "and we do not feel that we should be the ones to withdraw." The author of this complaint about the alleged shortcomings of Mother Seton's spiritual children was none other than Sister Catherine Seton, R.S.M., Mother Seton's own daughter.[47]

The increase in the number of parishes and the number of diocesan priests is often used as a gauge to indicate the vitality of Catholic life in the archdiocese of New York in the nineteenth century. Another important gauge was the growth of the religious communities of men and women, and the educational and charitable institutions that they founded and operated. The sisters, brothers and religious order priests became so deeply embedded in every aspect of organized Catholic life in New York that it became impossible to conceive of the archdiocese without them.

Mother Catherine Seton, R.S.M., the daughter of Elizabeth Ann Seton, who devoted many years to prison ministry at the Tombs. Credit: *Sisters of Mercy.*

46 - AANY, A-20, Mother Francis and Sister Paul to McCloskey, August 14, 1868.

47 - AANY, C-21, Catherine Seton, R.S.M. to Corrigan, June 8, 1888.

13

Leadership and Laity

New York Harbor in the 1890s.

John Joseph McCloskey and Michael Augustine Corrigan presided over the fortunes of New York Catholicism for almost equal periods during the four decades after the death of John Hughes, McCloskey from 1864 to 1885 and Corrigan from 1885 to 1902. Neither had the vision, imagination or assertive personality of New York's first archbishop nor did either of them relish the limelight as he did. Nonetheless, both were indebted to him for the political clout and social recognition that Hughes had acquired for Catholics in New York. They were also the beneficiaries of the demographic changes that had already made Catholics the largest religious community in the city, state and nation. Building upon these advantages, both Cardinal McCloskey and Archbishop Corrigan made their own distinctive contributions to the Catholic Church in New York.

During the Gilded Age not only were New York Catholics becoming more numerous, but some were becoming more wealthy. No Catholic in New York could rival the Rockefellers or the Vanderbilts or the Morgans, but a few did achieve substantial wealth on a more modest scale such as the banker Eugene Kelly, the shipping magnate William R. Grace, the entrepreneur Thomas Fortune Ryan and the contractor John Crimmins. Many more climbed into the ranks of the middle class while others found the road to advancement through politics. Among the latter was the shameless rascal George Washington Plunkett, the boss of Hell's Kitchen and a pewholder in Sacred Heart Church on West 51st Street, who held down three municipal jobs simultaneously while announcing that "the Irish was [sic] born to rule, and they're the honestest [sic] people in the world."

William G. Grace, the first Catholic Mayor of New York City.

John D. Crimmins, wealthy contractor and benefactor of Catholic causes.

John D. Rockfeller, Sr., the wealthiest man in the United States in the 1890s.

"Honest John" Kelly, the first Catholic leader of Tammany Hall

In the early 1870s, after the ouster of Boss Tweed, the Irish took control of Tammany Hall, the local Democratic organization, and dominated it for most of the next century. As early as 1871 James Raymond, the editor of the *New York Times,* complained that "there is an established church and a ruling class in New York, but the church is not Protestant and the ruling class is not American."[1] Tweed's successor at Tammany Hall was "Honest" John Kelly, who was married to John McCloskey's niece. The son of Irish immigrants, Kelly had a genius for organization. It was said of him that "he found Tammany a horde and left it an army." In 1880 New York's Catholics demonstrated their political clout by electing the first Catholic mayor, William Grace, who quickly demonstrated his own political independence by breaking with Tammany Hall. Before the end of the century two other Catholics were elected mayor, Hugh J. Grant in 1888 and Thomas F. Gilroy in 1892.

John Talbot Smith thought that New York was a predominantly Catholic city for about a dozen years, from about 1885 to the creation of Greater New York in 1898 when Catholics again became a minority. Nevertheless, even during the brief period of Catholic demographic hegemony,

he complained about the timidity of the Tammany leaders in protecting and promoting Catholic interests. A good case in point was the composition of the Board of Education, which never numbered more than two or three Catholics among its twenty-two members.[2]

Annie Leary, a wealthy heiress and benefactor of many Catholic causes.

1 - *New York Times,* January 7, 1871.

2 - Smith, *Catholic Church,* II, 446

John Joseph McCloskey

John McCloskey was the first native-born New Yorker to be ordained to the diocesan priesthood. It was the beginning of a long line of "firsts" in his life that was to culminate in his selection as the first American cardinal in 1875. He was born in Brooklyn on March 10, 1810, the son of Patrick McCloskey and Elizabeth Harron McCloskey, who had emigrated from Dungiven in County Derry two years earlier. Following the death of McCloskey's father in 1820, the philanthropist Cornelius Heeney became his guardian. After completing his college and seminary education at Mount St. Mary's College in Emmitsburg, McCloskey was ordained by Bishop Dubois in St. Patrick's Old Cathedral on January 12, 1834.

Archbishop John McCloskey

After a year as a professor at Dubois' ill-fated seminary in Upper Nyack, McCloskey left for Europe to restore his never robust health. He spent the next three years studying in Rome, the first New York diocesan priest to have this opportunity. He failed to meet the not-too-demanding requirements to earn his doctorate because, as he admitted candidly in his old age, "I did not want to take the trouble."[3]

Upon his return to New York he served as pastor of St. Joseph's Church in Greenwich Village where his kindness and forbearance overcame the opposition of the trustees. In 1841 he became the first president of St. John's College at Fordham, a post that he held for only one year while remaining the pastor of St. Joseph's Church. In 1844 John Hughes selected him as New York's first coadjutor with the right of succession and ordained him the titular bishop of Axiere on March 10, 1844. Hughes' choice of McCloskey remains a puzzle. It must have been the attraction of opposites, since it would be difficult to imagine two people more dissimilar in personality and temperament than John Hughes and John McCloskey.

John McCloskey's service as coadjutor lasted only three years. On May 27, 1847, Pope Pus IX appointed him the bishop of the new diocese of Albany, which then comprised more than two-thirds of New York State. He remained in Albany for the next seventeen years, a period when the Catholic population increased from about 60,000 to 290,000 and the number of churches more than doubled from 47 to 120. After the death of John Hughes, McCloskey was a leading contender to be his successor, but he made clear to the Roman authorities that he did not want the position. "I possess neither the learning nor prudence nor energy nor firmness nor bodily health and strength which are requisite for such an arduous and highly responsible office," he informed one of the curial cardinals three weeks after the death of Archbishop Hughes.[4] It was not entirely a conventional expression of humility.

3 - John Cardinal Farley, *The Life of John Cardinal McCloskey.* (New York: Longmans, Green and Company, 1918), 120.

4 - Farley, *John Cardinal McCloskey,* 205-206

Skating Pond in Central Park in the 1860s. Credit: *Archdiocese of New York*

Second Archbishop of New York

Despite McCloskey's protestations, he was appointed the second archbishop of New York on May 6, 1864, and installed in the Old Cathedral on August 21, 1864. The more creative period of his life may have been the years that he spent in Albany. In New York he reacted to events rather than shaped them, and admitted modestly that it was his good fortune to reap what others had sown. He was slow to recognize the need for more churches in Manhattan, resisted the establishment of St. Benedict the Moor Church for African Americans, and remained impervious to complaints about the dire living conditions in the provincial seminary in Troy.

In his funeral homily for Cardinal McCloskey in 1885, Archbishop Gibbons pointed to St. Patrick's Cathedral and the Catholic Protectory as the deceased cardinal's two outstanding monuments. In fact the initiative for the first came from John Hughes and for the second from the St. Vincent de Paul Society. Nonetheless,

McCloskey completed the cathedral and donated the money for the girls' building at the Protectory. He also deserves credit for initiating the establishment of the Foundling Hospital and for supporting Father Drumgoole's efforts to organize the Mission of the Immaculate Virgin.

A gentleman who loathed confrontation, McCloskey selected as his vicar general in 1873 someone who was his polar opposite, Father William Quinn. A hard-edged Ulsterman with a flair for finances and fundraising, Quinn was also a bully with the social graces of a drill sergeant. "For the conventions he had not the slightest regard,' observed one contemporary. "[He] walked his own path through custom and etiquette with perfect unconsciousness of their demands." Even the eulogist at his funeral admitted that he was "rough and possibly rude." The shy and self-effacing McCloskey was happy to have Quinn serve as his enforcer for fourteen years and made him one of New York's first two domestic prelates in 1881. The other monsignor was Thomas Preston.[5]

---

6 - Smith, *Church in New York*, II, 302-303; *New York Catholic News*, May 22, 1887

Monsignor Thomas Preston

Monsignor William Quinn, Vicar General 1873-1887

One of the most painful moments in John McCloskey's life occurred during the Second Plenary Council of Baltimore in 1866. He was about to address the council when he was handed a telegram informing him that his cathedral had just burned to the ground. He showed no reaction, placed the telegram his pocket and proceeded to deliver his address. Thereafter he had the double task of rebuilding the old cathedral while completing the construction of the new cathedral, which was dedicated on May 25, 1879, in the presence of six archbishops, twenty-five bishops, several hundred priests and 7,000 lay people. The ceremony lasted a full five hours, including a sermon by Patrick Ryan, the coadjutor of St. Louis, who droned on for an unmerciful one hour-and-forty minutes.

The building (without the twin spires and the Lady Chapel that were added later) cost the enormous sum of almost $2,000,000. Although the initial funding came from the eighty-three people who each contributed $1,000, most of the rest of the money came from the contributions of countless poor people. "Where in this great city," asked Bishop Ryan

The burning of the St. Patrick's Old Cathedral, October 6, 1866.
Credit: *Archdiocese of New York*

in one of his better flourishes, "have thousands of bondholders erected a temple like this temple, built up and adorned by the pennies of the poor?"[6]

In an age of galloping ultra-montanism, the Roman-trained McCloskey remained a theological moderate of an older school. At the First Vatican Council in 1869-1870,

Archbishop Patrick Ryan, Coadjutor of St. Louis and future Archbishop of Philadelphia

he was an "inopportunist" on the question of a papal infallibility, like most of the American hierarchy, believing that such a definition was unnecessary and likely to inflame anti-Catholic feeling both in Europe and the United States. As late as five days before the final vote on papal infallibility, McCloskey wanted changes made in the wording of the text, but he accepted the definition without enthusiasm as the will of the majority of the bishops and voted for it on the final ballot.[7]

Upon his return to the United States he assured his flock that the Council had created no new doctrine but merely confirmed traditional Catholic teaching. He was equally moderate on the question of the temporal power of the pope, which John Hughes had elevated to a dogma of the faith. Having lived for three years in papal Rome, McCloskey was under no illusions why many Italians regarded the Papal States as a painful anachronism.

A constant thorn in McCloskey's side was the presence in New York of James McMaster, the editor of the *New York Freeman's Journal and Catholic Register*. A convert twice over, first from the Presbyterians and then from the Episcopalians, he became more Catholic than the pope and fancied himself the authentic voice of Catholic orthodoxy in New York City. A facile writer with a vitriolic pen, he consciously modeled

himself after the inflammatory French Catholic journalist Louis Veuillot. McMaster heaped abuse upon any Catholics who disagreed with him with an arrogance and self-righteousness that suggested a lack of connection with reality.

James A. McMaster, the editor of the New York Freeman's Journal and Catholic Register

St. Patrick's Cathedral as it looked at the dedication on May 25, 1879

6 - Cit. in Charles R. Morris, *American Catholic* (New York: Times Books, 1997), 21, which contains a detailed description of the dedication of the cathedral.

7 - James Hennesey, *The First Council of the Vatican; The American Experience* (New York: Herder and Herder, 1963), 275-282.

McMaster taunted McCloskey for lack of loyalty to the Holy Father not only over papal infallibility but also over the loss of the Papal States. When the Italian army seized Rome on September 20, 1870, McCloskey issued a statement of sympathy for the pope. McMaster asked: "Is this *all* that is to be done in New York?" What he wanted was a monster rally in Central Park that he claimed would turn out 100,000 Catholic men and the mayor of New York. Not content with this, he called upon the Catholic youth of America to launch a Grand Crusade to recover the Papal States by force. "It is the glory of youth to die young," the fifty-year old McMaster announced, "when they die in a good cause."[8]

Such wild and irresponsible statements were the last thing that McCloskey wanted to see printed in a Catholic newspaper published in New York, but it was not in his nature to confront McMaster publicly as John Hughes would have done and did do with far less justification in the case of Orestes Brownson. Instead McCloskey followed the advice that he gave Archbishop Martin Spalding of Baltimore about dealing with McMaster over another issue. "Let McMaster alone," McCloskey said. "His insolence and intemperance simply disgust the laity."[9]

The First American Cardinal

McCloskey's selection as the first American cardinal on March 15, 1875, was the climax of his ecclesiastical career, but it may have been due more to the prominence of the archdiocese than its archbishop. He attributed it to the influence of Cardinal Cullen, the archbishop of Dublin. With a nice sense of history, he was given as his titular church in Rome the Dominican church of Santa Maria Sopra Minerva because of its associations with New York's first two bishops, Richard Luke Concanen and John Connolly. He arrived in Rome

Cardinal John McCloskey,
Archbishop of New York, 1864-1885

too late to participate in the conclave that elected Pope Leo XIII in 1878, but he was present at the coronation of the new pope and received the cardinal's red hat from him on March 28, 1878.

During his last years Cardinal McCloskey grew increasingly feeble and received a coadjutor in 1880 in the person of Michael Augustine Corrigan, the bishop of Newark, who was not McCloskey's first choice. He died at Mount St. Vincent on October 10, 1885, and was immediately succeeded by his coadjutor, who once remarked that it was Cardinal McCloskey's privilege "to grow up with Catholicity" in New York. He was born into a Catholic community that numbered no more than 15,000 in the whole state and at his death there were 600,000 Catholics in the archdiocese of New York alone.

---

8 - *New York Freeman's Journal and Catholic Register,* October 1, November 5, 1870; January 21, February 18, 1871.
9 - AAB, 36A-N11, McCloskey to Spalding, March 3, 1869.

Archbishop Michael Augustine Corrigan

*The young Michael Augustine Corrigan,
Coadjutor to Cardinal McCloskey, 1880-1885.
Archbishop of New York, 1885-1902*

Michael Corrigan's succession as the third archbishop of New York at the age of forty-six capped a brilliant ecclesiastical career. He was born in Newark, New Jersey, on August 13, 1839, the son of Thomas and Mary English Corrigan. His father was an Irish immigrant who became a wealthy businessman. Raised in Madison, New Jersey, young Michael Corrigan struck up a friendship with the pastor, Father Bernard McQuaid who was to be his lifelong admirer and mentor. Delicate in health, highly intelligent and pious, Michael Corrigan graduated first in his class from Mount St. Mary's College, and was sent to Rome for his seminary education where he was a member of the first class of the North American College. Ordained in Rome on September 19, 1863, he returned home a year later with a doctorate to become the rector of the diocesan

seminary at Seton Hall College and in 1869 he became the president of the college. In 1873 he succeeded Bishop James Roosevelt Bayley as the bishop of Newark. His efficient administration of the diocese of Newark led to his appointment as coadjutor to Cardinal McCloskey in 1880. Both as coadjutor and as archbishop after 1885, he presided over the period of the greatest expansion in the history of the archdiocese.

*Bernard J. McQuaid,
First Bishop of Rochester
(1868-1909)*

Young Michael Corrigan was something of a *wunderkind* in the American Catholic Church. At the tender age of thirty-four he was the youngest bishop in the United States. However, Marvin O'Connell, that perceptive historian of the diocesan clergy, suggested that Corrigan's meteoric rise to high office was a mixed blessing for him. "To a degree," said O'Connell, "Corrigan's rapid rise up the greasy pole of ecclesiastical preferment had done him a disservice: he had never spent a day as a parish priest, and the common touch, that indefinable sense of the aspirations of others, was entirely foreign to him." O'Connell also noted that he displayed a weakness "not unique to him by any means, for surrounding himself with second-rate functionaries who could pose no threat to him."[10]

The archbishop was most comfortable when he was at his desk. "He had a genius and love for administrative detail," said John Talbot Smith. "His chief work was the effective and minute organization of the diocese. He worked at its perfection to the last minute, and the calamities of his career never interrupted or disturbed its progress... [He] built up an almost perfect diocese by steady and faithful labor."

---

10 - Marvin R. O'Connell, *John Ireland and the American Catholic Church* (St. Paul: Minnesota Historical Society Press, 1988), 175.

However, Archbishop Corrigan did not confine his activities to his desk. During his first fifteen years in New York Corrigan performed all of the episcopal functions in the largest archdiocese in the United States without the help of a single auxiliary bishop. During a three-month period in 1894 he attended eighteen meetings, presided at six college commencement exercises and visited forty-five parishes and institutions in six counties. It is estimated that he confirmed 194,000 people. In a pastoral letter that he issued in April 1900 he said that during the previous decade he had opened a new church, school, chapel, convent, rectory or institution every two weeks---a total of over 250 buildings. He founded ninety-nine new parishes, a record unmatched by any other archbishop of New York. He officiated at the dedication of so many churches that he must have known the words of the ritual by heart.[11]

Unlike Cardinal McCloskey, Archbishop Corrigan was a national figure as a leader of the conservative wing of the American hierarchy along with his mentor Bishop Bernard McQuaid of Rochester. He was a fervent believer in the value of Catholic schools and won the gratitude of German-American Catholics by supporting their efforts to preserve their language and cultural heritage when "Americanist" prelates like Archbishop John Ireland of St. Paul were urging them to assimilate as quickly as possible.

Unfortunately, however, Corrigan's comfortable upper middle class background and lack of pastoral experience left him with little appreciation of the economic and social problems of most of his flock. He would have welcomed a papal condemnation of the Knights of Labor, the first large labor union in American history, which would have alienated millions of working-class Catholics from the Church. The condemnation was averted in 1887 by Cardinal Gibbons with the help of Bishops John Ireland and John Keane.

Diocesan Visitation.

1883.

Day	Date	Church	Location
Sunday,	Aug. 12.	Immaculate Conception, St. Joseph's Church,	Yonkers. "
Monday,	" 13.	Immaculate Conception, St. Teresa's,	Irvington. Tarrytown.
Tuesday,	" 14.	Our Lady of Loretto,	Cold Spring.
Wednesday,	" 15.	St. Francis of Assisi, St. Joseph's,	Mount Kisco. Croton Falls.
Thursday,	" 16.	St. Lawrence's,	Brewsters.
Friday,	" 17.	Immaculate Conception,	Amenia.
Saturday,	" 18.	St. Jacob's,	Mount Vernon.
Sunday,	" 19.	St. Mary's, Blessing Corner Stone.	Port Richmond:
Monday,	" 20.	St. Peter's, St. Joseph's,	New Brighton. Rossville.
Wednesday,	" 22.	St. Joseph's, Immaculate Conception,	Tremont. Melrose.
Thursday,	" 23.	St. Joachim's,	Matteawan.
Friday,	" 24.	St. James', Milton, and Ireland Corners.	
Saturday,	" 25.	Church of the Nativity,	Poughkeepsie.
Sunday,	" 26.	Regina Coeli,	Hyde Park.
Sunday,	Sept. 2.	Blessing Chapel, Mount Loretto, Staten Island.	
Monday,	" 3.	St. John's, St. Catherine's,	Piermont. Blauveltsville.
Tuesday,	" 4.	St. Rose of Lima,	Suffern.
Wednesday,	" 5.	Holy Cross,	Calliooon.
Thursday,	" 6.	St. Mary's,	Obernburg.
Friday,	" 7.	Immaculate Conception,	Port Jervis.
Saturday,	" 8.	St. Peter's	Monticello.
Sunday,	" 9.	St. Joseph's,	Middletown.
Monday,	" 10.	Holy Name of Mary,	Montgomery.
Friday,	" 14.	St. Stanislaus', Polish Church. Sts. Cyril and Methodius, Bohemian Church.	
Saturday,	" 15.	Sacred Heart,	High Bridge.
Sunday,	" 16.	Dedication Church,	Dobb's Ferry.

The schedule of a busy Coadjutor Archbishop. In the space of six weeks in August and September 1883, Archbishop Corrigan visited every county in the archdiocese.

11 - Smith, *Catholic Church*, II, 418; *New York Catholic News*, April 28, 1900

Controversy swirled around Corrigan not only because of his rigidly conservative views, but also because of his devious manner of promoting them. When plans got under way in 1887 for the establishment of the Catholic University of America, Corrigan was dismayed for fear that the institution, located in Cardinal Gibbon's diocese, would become a hotbed of liberalism. However, rather than express his misgivings openly, he came down on both sides of the issue. In America he publicly supported the establishment of the university but privately he tried to undermine it through backstairs intrigue in Rome. When Bishops Keane and Ireland encountered evidence in Rome of this duplicity, they alerted their fellow bishops that "somebody has whispered" against us. Their well chosen words illustrate perfectly Florence Cohalan's comment about Corrigan's "love of indirect methods [that] infuriated his opponents and bewildered his friends." Robert Emmett Curran put it more bluntly when he observed that Corrigan "seemed unable to translate private piety into public probity."[12]

John Ireland,
Archbishop of St. Paul, 1888-1918

James Cardinal Gibbons, Archbishop of Baltimore, 1877-1921

Terence Powderly, the Catholic President of the Knights of Labor

Bishop John J. Keane, the first Rector of the Catholic University of America

Caldwell Hall, The Catholic University of America, Washington, D.C.

12 - AANY, C-16, Ireland and Keane to U.S. bishops, December 14, 1886; Cohalan, *Popular History*, 108; Robert Emmett Curran, *Michael Augustine Corrigan and the Shaping of Conservative Catholicism in America, 1878-1902* (New York: Arno Press, 1978), vi.

The McGlynn Affair

Within year of his installation as the third archbishop of New York, Corrigan came into conflict with one of his priests, Dr. Edward McGlynn. McGlynn had been a controversial figure in New York for over a decade, but remained a priest in good standing under the easy-going

Dr. Edward McGlynn

September 27, 1837, he was sent to Rome for his seminary education at the age of thirteen, was ordained there on March 24, 1860, and returned to New York later that year with a doctorate from the Urban College of the Propaganda. Forever afterwards he was known as Dr. McGlynn. In 1866, at the age of twenty-nine, he succeeded Jeremiah Cummings as the pastor of St. Stephen's Church, which was the largest parish in the archdiocese. A product of the New York City public schools, McGlynn first attracted public notice in 1870 when he publicly questioned the value of parochial schools. He was especially critical of the relationship between the archdiocese and Tammany Hall, which provided an annual subsidy of eight dollars a year for each child in the parochial schools. There was no parochial school in St. Stephen's parish, although McGlynn did establish a parish orphanage.

Father John Talbot Smith, the pastor of Sacred Heart Church, Dobbs Ferry, and the historian of the Archdiocese of New York

McCloskey. Corrigan's confrontation with McGlynn was to polarize the clergy of the archdiocese and to have national and international repercussions, since it sharpened the ideological divisions in the American hierarchy and intensified Roman suspicions of a leftward drift in American Catholicism. "With the best intentions in the world," said John Talbot Smith, "[Corrigan] caused more controversy [in New York] in a decade than the Catholic body had known in its history."[13]

Like Corrigan, McGlynn came from middle class Irish parents. Born in Manhattan on

McGlynn was the most outspoken priest in New York, but he was not an isolated figure. He was part of an informal group of priests known as the Accademia who met regularly in St. Joseph's rectory in Greenwich Village under the auspices of the pastor, Father Thomas Farrell. They included young priests like Richard Burtsell, James Nilan, Patrick McSweeny, Thomas McLoughlin and Sylvester Malone of Brooklyn, who were to emerge as the leading "Americanists" in the local presbyterate in the 1890s. Politically progressive, they were sympathetic to the Radical Republicans at home, and to the Fenians and later the Land League in Ireland. At their monthly meetings they debated such sensitive theological topics as biblical inspiration, the temporal power of the pope, papal infallibility, clerical celibacy, vernacular liturgy, and the relevance of religious orders.[14]

---

13 - Smith, *Catholic Church,* II, 426.

14 - On the Accademia, see Robert Emmett Curran, "Prelude to 'Americanism': The New York Accademia and Clerical Radicalism in the Late Nineteenth Century," *CH* 47 (1978): 48-65. For a more critical view of the Accademia, see Cohalan, *Popular History,* 119-124.

Dr. Richard Burtsell, the first pastor of Epiphany Church, and close friend and adviser to Dr. McGlynn

Dr. Patrick F. Mc Sweeny, the pastor of St. Brigid's Church.

Father Thomas Farrell, the pastor of St. Joseph's Church, Greenwich Village, 1857-1880, and the organizer of the New York Accademia.

After McGlynn, the best-known member of the Academia was Richard Burtsell, who like McGlynn was a native-born New Yorker and an alumnus of the Propaganda College in Rome. He was a self-taught canon lawyer, "the one species of cleric so dreaded by Cardinal McCloskey," according to John Talbot Smith. Burtsell furnished legal advice to many priests in their difficulties with their bishop, including his close friend Dr. McGlynn. Because of Burtsell's canonical expertise Bishop Patrick Ludden of Syracuse regarded him as more dangerous than McGlynn.[15]

The Irish-born Patrick McSweeny was another Roman-educated member of the Accademia and the author of the famous Poughkeepsie Plan. As the pastor of St. Peter's Church in Poughkeepsie, McSweeny leased his parochial school to the Board of Education in 1873 for one dollar a year. It functioned as a public school from 9:00 a.m. to 3:00 p.m with all the expenses paid by the Poughkeepsie Board of Education, including the salaries of the sisters, who taught religion before and after regular school hours. The so-called Poughkeepsie Plan remained in effect for twenty-five years and only came to an end over a controversy about the sisters wearing their religious habits in a "public" school.[16] When McSweeny applied for St. Brigid's Church in New York City in 1877, Cardinal McCloskey asked if he could pay debts. "I can stop leaks," was his tart reply.[17]

Monsignor Cornelius O'Keefe, the pastor of Sacred Heart Church, Highland Falls

Another friend of Mc Glynn, although not a member of the Accademia, was Cornelius O'Keefe, Irish-born and Roman-educated, who remained his staunch supporter throughout his troubles. In 1886 O'Keefe founded the mission in Nassau in the Bahamas when the islands were placed under the jurisdiction of the archdiocese of New York. Later, as pastor in Highland Falls, O'Keefe played a key role in establishing the Catholic parish on the grounds of the U.S. Military Academy at West Point.

The major clash between Corrigan and McGlynn occurred during the mayoralty election of 1886, which has been described as the greatest challenge to the existing order in New York City since colonial days because of the third party candidate, the economist and social reformer Henry George. As the candidate of the United Labor Party, Henry George headed a motley coalition of labor leaders, Irish nationalists, radicals and socialists who ran the gamut from Samuel Gompers to Karl Marx's son-in-law. Defying an order from Archbishop Corrigan to refrain from politics, McGlynn gave the nominating speech for Henry George, which resulted in his temporary suspension from the priesthood. Further clashes with Corrigan and a refusal to obey an order from the pope to come to Rome led to McGlynn's permanent suspension, his removal as pastor of St. Stephen's and finally his excommunication on July 3, 1887.[18]

---

15 - AANY, G-3, Ludden to Corrigan, August 31, 1893. On Burtsell, see Anthony D. Andreassi, ""The Cunning Leader of a Dangerous Clique?': The Burtsell Affair and Archbishop Michael Augustine Corrigan," *CHR* 86 (1999): 620-639.

16 - Edward M. Connors, *Church-State Relationships in Education in the State of New York* (Washington: The Catholic University of America Press, 1951), 109-123.

17 - "Edward McSweeny, "A New York Pastor in the Latter Half of the Nineteenth Century," *RACHSP* 19 (1908): 45.

18 - The most recent study of McGlynn is Alfred Isacsson, O. Carm., *The Determined Doctor: The Story of Edward McGlynn* (Tarrytown: Vestigium Press, 1997).

Even after his excommunication McGlynn remained a larger than life figure, reviled by many as a clerical demagogue but admired by others as a rare Catholic proponent of the Social Gospel. As the president of the Anti-Poverty Society, which he founded in March 1887, he continued to expound Henry George's single tax theory as the panacea for the social injustices of the Gilded Age. On a typical hot and humid Sunday evening in July 1888, before a capacity crowd in Cooper Union, McGlynn made his entrance as the choir sang "Sweet Peace Descending." Minutes later he shattered the peace and brought the audience to their feet by bellowing from the center of the stage: "I am a free man and have essential inalienable rights and liberties... and no state, no town, no city, no country, no federal government, no power in the world can ever take them from me."[19]

*Richard Croker,
the successor to
John Kelly
as the leader
of Tammany Hall*

If McGlynn was an embarrassment to Corrigan, he was also a threat to Tammany Hall. The Irish politicians who ran Tammany were more concerned about reassuring the business interests of the city of their fiscal conservatism than they were about inaugurating meaningful social reform for the working class and the poor. For Richard Croker, who succeeded John Kelly at the helm of Tammany in 1886, it was a nightmare to have a popular Irish-American priest like McGlynn rallying Catholic support for a new political party dedicated to social reform. Shortly before the election of 1886, Monsignor Thomas Preston, the vicar general, obligingly issued a statement that "the great majority of the clergy of this city are opposed to the candidacy of Mr. George." It was distributed by Tammany operatives outside Catholic churches after Sunday Mass.[20]

Monsignor Preston was undoubtedly correct that most of the New York clergy were opposed to Henry George's economic theories. Even Dr. Burtsell voted for Abram Hewitt, the Democratic candidate in the mayoralty election of 1886. However, that did not mean that the New York presbyterate approved of their archbishop's inept handling of the McGlynn Affair. For one thing, Corrigan committed a major tactical blunder when he removed McGlynn as the pastor of St. Stephen's without first giving him a hearing. Both McSweeny and Farley, who were diocesan consultors, opposed the move as unwise and unfair. Archbishop Corrigan's response to McSweeny was : *Fiat justitia, ruat coelum* ("Let justice be done and the heavens roar").[21]

The New Crusade,
the text of Dr. McGlynn's most famous speech

---

19 - Edward McGlynn, *Equal Taxation* (New York: The Anti-Poverty Society, 1888), 2.

20 - Burrows and Wallace, *Gotham*, 1106.

21 - Curran, *Corrigan*, 210-213.

The view from the Battery in 1892

Then, as support for McGlynn began to wane among the laity, Corrigan needlessly escalated the conflict by making membership in the Anti-Poverty Society or even attendance at its meetings a reserved case, which meant that only the archbishop or his delegate could give absolution in confession. "Are we in Russia or America?" asked Sylvester Malone. When a member of the Anti-Poverty Society died in October 1889, the archdiocese refused her Christian burial. She happened to be a parishioner of Burtsell at Epiphany Church. For his efforts on her behalf and on behalf of his friend Edward McGlynn, Corrigan transferred Burtsell to Rondout, New York.

An attempt was made to demonstrate the clergy's support for the archbishop by circulating several addresses of loyalty. The maneuver backfired when about one-fifth of the priests (83 out of 440) refused to sign the address from the diocesan clergy. The recalcitrants included Burtsell, Patrick McSweeny and most of the New York alumni of the Propaganda College. John Farley initially refused to sign but then gave in to pressure and penned his name to the printed list at the very last minute, earning the scorn of both sides. One of Dr. Burtsell's curates, who found the housekeeper at Epiphany rectory unbearable, declined to sign in the hope that the vindictive diocesan officials would transfer him to another parish. They unwittingly obliged. Like that curate, any priest who refused to sign the petition for whatever reason was regarded thereafter as a personal enemy of the archbishop and was treated accordingly. More than anything else, the loyalty address poisoned Archbishop Corrigan's relationship with his priests. He never recovered from it.[22]

The McGlynn Affair was a public scandal that the secular press was happy to keep alive. Since Corrigan seemed unable to end it, Rome decided to intervene. An opportunity occurred in November 1892 when Archbishop Francesco Satolli came to the United States as the papal ablegate to the Columbian Exposition in Chicago. He brought with him instructions to try to reconcile McGlynn. Through the intervention of Richard Burtsell and Cornelius O'Keefe, McGlynn agreed to submit his economic and political theories to the faculty of the Catholic University of America, which pronounced them unobjectionable. Thereupon, on December 23, 1892, without consulting Corrigan or even informing him, Satolli lifted the excommunication and reinstated McGlynn as a priest in good standing. Archbishop Corrigan learned of it in the newspaper the next day.

22 - Ibid., 241.

He was devastated by the news. "We are in a reign of terror," he told Bernard McQuaid. He reported to him that the laity in New York City were terribly worked up, "particularly the better classes," and that many said that they would not go to church anymore. Richard Croker, who had as much to fear from a rehabilitation of McGlynn as Corrigan himself, told him that it was "the greatest blow that the Church in this country has ever received."[23] Corrigan vowed that he would never give McGlynn a parish in New York, but he relented after two years and sent him to St. Mary's Church in Newburgh, where he died on January 7, 1900. With Burtsell already in Rondout, and James Nilan in Poughkeepsie and Cornelius O'Keefe in Highland Falls, one priest commented, "The brains of the diocese is up the Hudson."

Corrigan's fear of a reign of terror at the hands of Archbishop Satolli was understandable, if a bit hysterical. Initially Satolli was strongly prejudiced against Corrigan because of his close association with the leaders of the "Americanist" wing of the American hierarchy who attempted to manipulate Satolli and use his authority to their own advantage. When Satolli arrived in New York in 1892, he was accompanied by Msgr. Denis O'Connell, the rector of the North American College and a close confidant of Cardinal Gibbons. The cardinal arranged for a revenue cutter to take Satolli from his ship in the harbor so that Corrigan would not know the time or place of his arrival. Unaware of this maneuver, Satolli thought that Corrigan's failure to welcome him at the pier was a deliberate snub.

From New York Satolli was whisked off to St. Paul where he spent several months with Archbishop John Ireland in what was undoubtedly a series of one-sided conversations, since Satolli spoke no English and Ireland rarely had an unspoken thought in any language. He then proceeded to Washington where he took up residence at the Catholic University of America as a guest of the rector, Bishop John Keane. In the course of the next few years, however, as Satolli became increasingly disenchanted with the liberal views of these new friends, he turned against them and allied himself with Corrigan and the conservative wing of the American hierarchy. Bishop McQuaid was ecstatic with the unexpected turn of events. "What collapses on every side!" he exclaimed, "Gibbons, Ireland and Keane!!! They were cock of the walk for a while and dictated to the country and thought to run our dioceses for us."[24]

Locally the friction between Archbishop Corrigan and the McGlynnites lessened not only with the reinstatement of McGlynn, but even earlier with the death of Arthur Donnelly in 1890 and Thomas Preston the following year. Both were inveterate foes of McGlynn, and Corrigan replaced them as vicars general with John Farley and Joseph Mooney, who were eager to play the role of peacemakers between the archbishop and the disaffected clergy. The appointment of Charles McDonnell, Corrigan's secretary, as the bishop of Brooklyn in 1892 removed another irritant from the local scene.

The statue of Dr. McGlynn in Woodlawn Cemetery.
Credit: *John T. Monaghan*

23 - ADR, Corrigan to McQuaid, December 28, 1892.
24 - AANY, G-15, McQuaid to Corrigan, October 3, 1896.

The Day of the Blockade

The McGlynn Affair was not Archbishop Corrigan's only preoccupation. At the diocesan synod of 1886, in the middle of his difficulties with Dr. McGlynn, the archbishop announced his intention of giving his archdiocese a modern seminary. The existing seminary, St. Joseph's Provincial Seminary in Troy, New York, which dated from 1864, and trained over 700 priests in its thirty-two year history, had long been regarded as inadequate. It was a notoriously unhealthy place with a high mortality rate among both seminarians and alumni, especially from tuberculosis. In 1868 one seminary official informed Archbishop McCloskey's secretary that "many are hopelessly gone from consumption or some other equally fatal malady." When Bishop Henry Gabriels, the rector from 1871 to 1892, compiled his history of the seminary, he identified fifty-nine students who died before ordination, adding at the bottom of the list: "And many others not recorded."[25]

The Troy seminary also left much to be desired academically even though the core faculty was composed of Belgian diocesan priests who were graduates of the Catholic University of Louvain. The formational program at Troy was based on seclusion from the world rather than preparation for leadership in it. The students were forbidden to read newspapers, the library was open for less than two hours a day, and the seminarians were warned that "they should not accumulate books in their room lest they be confused by a variety of opinions." The intellectual vitality that characterized Louvain obviously did not survive the trip across the Atlantic.[26]

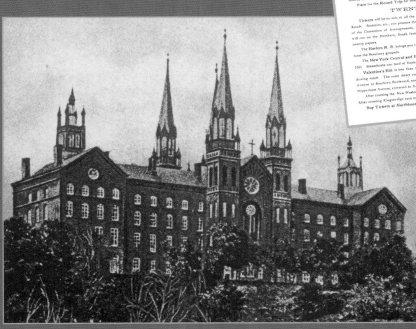

Advertising the new seminary. The circular urging parishioners to attend the laying of the cornerstone. AANY, G-63

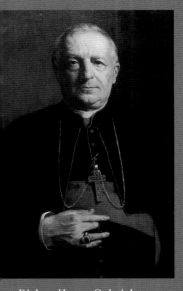

Bishop Henry Gabriels of Ogdensburg, the rector of St. Joseph's Provincial Seminary, 1871-1892

St. Joseph's Provincial Seminary, Troy, New York

---

25 - AANY, I-1, Alexander Sherwood Healy to Farley, May 4, 1868.

26 - *Regula Seminarii*, caput IV, no. 4; caput IX, no. 1-6. On the Troy seminary, see Thomas J. Shelley, " 'Good Work in its Day': St. Joseph's Provincial Seminary, Troy, New York," *RHE* 88:2 (1993): 416-438.

Once Archbishop Corrigan announced his intention of building a new seminary, it took him four years to find a suitable location at Valentine Hill in the Dunwoodie section of Yonkers where the archbishop purchased fifty-acres for $70,694.06 on March 6, 1890. The cornerstone was blessed on Pentecost Sunday, May 17, 1891. The event had been promoted in every parish of the archdiocese for months. The result was that some 60,000 people descended upon Yonkers, almost twice the population of the city.

That morning over 7,000 people arrived by steamboats at the Yonkers Public Dock. Others came on the trains of the Hudson Division of the New York Central Railroad. Together they proceeded to march from downtown Yonkers to the seminary. Father Charles Corley, the pastor of St. Mary's, provided a carriage for the mayor of Yonkers while Father Lings arrived in Getty Square on horseback at the head of two brass bands.

The most convenient route to Dunwoodie from New York City was the New York and Northern Railroad (later the Putnam Division of the New York Central) whose right of way paralleled the seminary grounds. However, so many New Yorkers tried to get to Yonkers that morning that they overwhelmed the facilities of the railroad. Trains left the 155th Street terminal jammed to capacity with men and boys riding on the roof of the coaches. The normal running time to Dunwoodie was fifteen minutes, but on that Sunday morning some trains took three hours to travel the seven miles.

The problem was the single track between Van Cortland Park and Dunwoodie. As each crowded train arrived at the Dunwoodie station and discharged its passengers, it had to be backed down the line using a series of sidings. Meanwhile more and more northbound trains came to a dead halt. The newspaper reporters referred to the impasse as a "blockade," and the name stuck. May 17, 1891, became the Day of the Blockade.

The blockade was no respecter of persons.

Among those trapped on the stalled trains were the banker Eugene Kelly, the contractor John Crimmins, the newspaper publisher Herman Ridder, the historian John Gilmary Shea and William Schickel, the architect of the seminary building. Archbishop Corrigan fared no better than the others. After spending thee hours as his train inched its way north, he got out and walked the last two miles to Dunwoodie. Mayor Hugh Grant did the same. It was nearly five o'clock when the archbishop and his party reached the seminary grounds.

The main speaker, Archbishop Patrick J. Ryan of Philadelphia, had preached for almost two hours at the dedication of the cathedral in 1879. On this occasion he was shorter, saying, "Let this seminary go up and let God's blessing descend upon it." After he finished, Archbishop Corrigan blessed two cornerstones, one for the main building and the other for the chapel.

As soon as the clergy retired from the field, there was a mad scramble for the main cornerstone. Men wanted to stand on it; some women tried to kiss it; and still others attempted to chop off pieces for souvenirs. When the granite proved too hard to dent, they began to scratch away at the fresh cement, much to the alarm of the contractor, who dispatched one of his workman to stand guard over the stone.

Then came the finale, when a huge avalanche of humanity, 20,000 strong, ran down Valentine Hill for a return encounter with the New York and Northern Railroad. True to form, the railroad was unready for its passengers. A half-hour elapsed before the first train for the city pulled into the Dunwoodie station. The waiting passengers stormed aboard the ten coaches and the engine. "When the train pulled out of the station," one reporter wrote, "the natives of Dunwoodie were treated to a novel spectacle of a locomotive literally covered with human beings. Men sat on the cowcatcher, in the cab, beside the boiler and all over the tender." Two months later

Archbishop Corrigan received a letter from a laborer named Timothy Quinn, who explained his crucial role on the day of the blockade:

> Mr. Stewart [the contractor] sent me to watch the cornerstone and gave me orders to stay day and night until I was informed to leave. This I did, and on the 9th of June, I was finished, this making 21 days and 21 nights at the cornerstone…

According to Quinn, the contractor had promised to pay him $76.50 for his services, but he had given him only $48.00. "If you can prevail upon Mr. Stewart to settle with me," he explained, "you will confer a very great favor on your very obedient servant."[27] The archbishop's answer is not recorded, but he kept the letter.

The Dunwoodie Station of the New York Central's Putnam Division as it looked some years after the Day of the Blockade.

The Grandest Seminary Building in Christendom

Bishop McQuaid began construction of St. Bernard's Seminary in Rochester at the same time that Archbishop Corrigan was starting work at Dunwoodie. "We shall have a friendly race in putting up the two seminaries," he said. "I propose, *Deo volente*, to open mine in September 1893."[28] He finished it precisely on schedule. At Dunwoodie it required five years to erect the massive stone building with blocks of granite that were quarried on the site. Money was a constant problem. The architect, William Schickel, estimated the cost at $400,000, but his final bill came to $857,627.38. Corrigan himself contributed $50,000 for the chapel, but he received no contribution larger than $10,000 from the laity. Richard Croker, who had just invested $400,000 in race horses, gave $5,000.

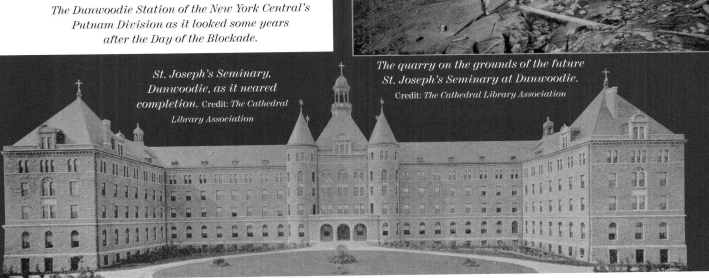

The quarry on the grounds of the future St. Joseph's Seminary at Dunwoodie. Credit: *The Cathedral Library Association*

St. Joseph's Seminary, Dunwoodie, as it neared completion. Credit: *The Cathedral Library Association*

27 - AANY, G-63, Timothy Quinn to Corrigan, July 18, 1891.
28 - AANY, C-16, McQuaid to Corrigan, January 13, 1891.

Most of the money came in the form of small donations collected in the parish churches. The Franciscan pastor of St. Mary's in Obernburg collected $6.00 and added another $4.00 from his own pocket. Dr. Burtsell gave nothing, claiming that his predecessor in Rondout had stolen the money he got in the seminary collection. One curate said that the pastor owned him three months' salary and asked the vicar general how to collect it. The German-born pastor of Our Lady of Sorrows begged off completely. "To [sic] much is to [much]," he protested. "We are full in depths [sic]." Father Joseph Dworzak explained the situation at St. Valentine's in lapidary Latin: "*Expensae cotidianae magnae, parochiani vero pauci*" ("Daily expenses are great, but the parishioners are few."[29]

Archbishop Corrigan wanted Dunwoodie to be run by priests of the Society of Saint Sulpice, a small French religious community that specialized in seminary education. He met determined opposition from most of the diocesan consultors as well as from the two vicars general, Joseph Mooney and John Farley. Farley, now New York's first auxiliary bishop well as the senior vicar general, wanted the diocesan clergy to run the seminary. "I don't see why," he told Corrigan, "if we could build a million dollar seminary, we could not provide a staff of professors." Corrigan cut short the discussion with an unanswerable argument. "I have had a great many prayers said, day and night," he revealed, "and I feel clear in mind as an answer to prayer that it is better to have the Sulpicians."[30]

Corrigan wanted the Sulpicians to run Dunwoodie because he thought that they would provide "a higher grade of piety." Farley wanted diocesan priests because he thought that they would provide "a higher grade of intellectuality." Both misjudged the Sulpicians and failed to realize that they were undergoing a major transformation in the United States. A new breed of American-born Sulpicians like Charles Rex, Edward Dyer and James Driscoll were as eager as Farley to encourage intellectual development as well spiritual formation in their seminaries. Rex, Dyer and Driscoll were to be the first three rectors of Dunwoodie.[31] A good indication of their enlightened approach to seminary education was the arrangement that Dyer worked out with Columbia University so that Dunwoodie seminarians could take courses in the university, although none of them ever availed themselves of the opportunity.

On August 12, 1896, the new St. Joseph's Seminary was formally dedicated by the departing Apostolic Delegate, Cardinal Francesco Satolli, now a fast friend of Corrigan, in a private ceremony attended by 300 invited guests. There was still a mortgage of $250,000 on the seminary, but it was paid off by 1898 as a present to Corrigan on the occasion of his episcopal silver jubilee. Even Dr. Burtsell was impressed with Dunwoodie, describing it as "a splendid building with every comfort and convenience."

Bishop McQuaid pronounced Dunwoodie "the grandest seminary building in Christendom." However, in his usual blunt manner, he declared: "It takes more than bricks and mortar to make a seminary. You must have men to teach, and you must have methods that are up to date." Perhaps the tribute that meant the most to Archbishop Corrigan was the one that he received from Cardinal Gibbons, who told him that "this is your grand crowning work and the one that will bring you the greatest consolation." Over the next century Dunwoodie would train over 2,200 priests for the archdiocese of New York, amply repaying Archbishop Corrigan for the time and effort that he had expended on it.[32]

29 - Thomas J. Shelley, *Dunwoodie: The History of St. Joseph's Seminary* (Westminster, Md.: Christian Classics, 1993), 57-58, 84-85.

30 - AANY, Minutes of the Meetings of the Diocesan Consultors, February 5, March 4, April 1, 1896.

31 - Technically Father Charles Rex, S.S., was the rector of Dunwoodie from 1894 until 1896 while he continued to teach at St. Charles College, Ellicott City, Maryland. He worked closely with Archbishop Corrigan on the final preparations and selected the original faculty. He died of tuberculosis in 1897 at the age of forty-one. Christopher Kauffman, *Tradition and Transformation in Catholic Culture: The Priests of Saint Sulpice in the United States from 1791 to the Present* (New York: Macmillan, 1988), 199-201.

32 - *The History of St. Joseph's Seminary* (New York: The Cathedral Library Association, 1896), 98-99. AANY, G-15, Gibbons to Corrigan, December 26, 1896.

St. Joseph's Seminary, Dunwoodie

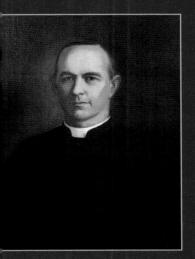

The Reverend Edward Dyer, S.S., the rector of St. Joseph's Seminary, Dunwoodie, 1896-1902

The Dedication of St. Joseph's Seminary, Dunwoodie, August 12, 1896. Front row center: Cardinal Satolli, Archbishop Corrigan, Bishop McQuaid (in white socks)
Credit: *The Cathedral Library Association*

Early aerial view of St. Joseph's Seminary, Dunwoodie.
Credit: *Archdiocese of New York*

Archbishop Corrigan's other major building project was the completion of St. Patrick's Cathedral. The twin spires were added between 1885 and 1888 at a cost of $200,000. The Lady Chapel, was a gift of Mrs. Eugene Kelly, who left a bequest for that purpose in 1899. When the expenses proved greater than expected, her two sons contributed an additional $165,000 and Mass was celebrated in the chapel for the first time on Christmas Day in 1906.

Meanwhile, while inspecting the progress of the construction on February 25, 1902, Archbishop Corrigan slipped and fell into an unguarded excavation, sustaining a painful injury to his leg. During convalescence he developed pneumonia and died unexpectedly on the evening of May 5, 1902. He left behind the largest and reputedly the wealthiest diocese in the nation. At Dunwoodie the rector, Father Edward Dyer, S.S.,

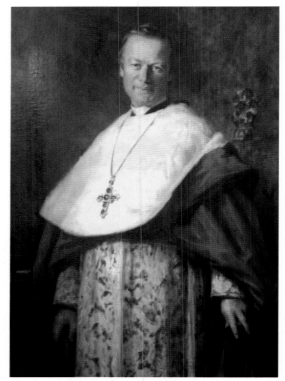

Michael Augustine Corrigan,
Archbishop of New York, 1885-1902.
Credit: *Archdiocese of New York*

told the assembled seminarians that everyone agreed that the seminary was the work nearest his heart. He reminded them that the chapel was his personal gift. "The lesson he wished above all to convey," said Dyer, "was the dignity and richness of all that refers to divine worship."[33]

Michael Augustine Corrigan remains the master builder among the archbishops of New York, not only because of Dunwoodie, but also because of the unprecedented number of parishes that he started. He was also a fearless advocate for parochial schools even when it put him on a collision course with the Apostolic Delegate and the pope himself. He waged a fierce and successful battle to protect Catholic charitable institutions in the state. Unlike many Irish-American bishops, Archbishop Corrigan showed consistent sensitivity to the ethnic minorities among his flock. No American bishop did more than he did for the Italian immigrants. Even more remarkable was his enlightened attitude to the Greek Catholics. He assured the Metropolitan of Lviv through Dean Lings that he would respect all the rights and privileges accorded to the Greek Catholics by the Holy See.

Unfortunately his sensitivity to the ethnic diversity among his flock was not matched by a comparable awareness of their social and economic plight. His vision of political reform did not extend beyond the confines of Tammany Hall. His maladroit handling of the rambunctious Dr. McGlynn left him with a divided presbyterate and cost him the support of some of his most talented priests. On occasion Corrigan could adopt a paternal approach to his priests that was quite different from his public image.

When Father Thomas McGare, the pastor of St. Peter's Church in Haverstraw, incurred the wrath of his parishioners, Corrigan gave him wise and affectionate advice. "Do not scold the people

33 - AANY, Dyer, House Diary, May 6, 1902.

in your sermons, " he told him. "There is a large debt on the church and it must be paid by patient endeavor. To succeed in this you must acquire the good will of the parishioners, and this cannot be done by recriminations." He added: "I have no doubt that with a little tact and gentleness every thing can be nicely arranged in Haverstraw." The advice worked. McGare remained in Haverstraw for another eighteen years. However, it was the kind of gentle advice that the priests did not often hear from their archbishop.[34]

The Modern New York Parish

According to John Talbot Smith, the most important achievement of the New York presbyterate in the later nineteenth century was the creation of the modern parish. Before the Civil War, when priests were scarce, the typical New York parish offered its parishioners little more than a bare minimum of services like two or three Masses on Sunday, a sermon at the high Mass, a rudimentary catechetical program for the children, confessions on Saturday, sometimes a parish library and a few devotional societies. By the end of the century, however, virtually every parish in Manhattan could boast of two or even three curates in addition to the pastor. The abundance of clerical manpower made possible a consierable expansion in parish services.

Two parishes set the standard for the rest of the archdiocese, the new cathedral and the Paulist Church of St. Paul the Apostle. The cathedral had six priests to care for about 12,000 parishioners, which was roughly the equivalent of the total number of people and priests that Bishop Connolly found in the whole diocese on his arrival in 1815. There were six Masses on Sunday with a sermon at each Mass, and a solemn Mass at 11:00 a.m. accompanied by two male choirs, one in the sanctuary and the other in the choir loft. Confessions were heard on Fridays,

Saturdays and the eve of holydays. Two priests were always on duty in the rectory, one to receive visitors and the other to go on sick calls.

The priests were expected to make regular visits to the parochial school (which had 1,600 students), especially to supervise the preparation of the children for their first confession, first Communion and Confirmation. They were also responsible for the management of the parish library and reading room and served as spiritual directors of one or more parish societies or sodalities like the Holy Name Society for the men or the Rosary and Altar Society for the women.

Even more than the cathedral parish, the Church of St. Paul the Apostle was the model for the rest of the diocese because of the solemn celebration of the liturgy and the multiplicity of parish programs. The Paulists were pioneers in introducing New York Catholics to the beauty of Gregorian chant and even more remarkably to congregational singing. As one might expect from a society of priests founded by Isaac Hecker, the Paulists were famous for the quality of their preaching. Their catechetical program was the best in the city, and the Paulists expanded it by establishing their own printing press to publish their monthy magazine, *The Catholic World,* as well as numerous pamphlets intended for non-Catholics as well as Catholics.

The Celebration of the Eucharist

The celebration of the Eucharist remained the heart and soul of Catholic spiritual life, but few New York Catholics had the opportunity to experience the solemn celebration of the liturgy at the high Mass in St. Patrick's Cathedral or St. Paul the Apostle. More common was the experience of a friendly Protestant observer who traveled through the deserted streets of the city one cold winter morning in 1868 to attend the

34 - AANY, Corrigan to McGare, October 9, 1891

6:00 a.m. Mass in St. Stephen's Church. The church gradually filled up with about 1,100 worshippers, ninety percent of them women. The visitor surmised that most of the women were servants and most of the men were coachmen, but all were respectably dressed. He noticed that hardly anyone gave more than a penny in the collection, but that every single person gave at least a penny, no matter how poor they might have been.

The people were more punctual than the priest, who started Mass sixteen minutes late, attended by two well-trained altar boys. The Protestant visitor strained to hear the priest's voice, but, he said, "not a sound came from his lips. He rose, he knelt, he ascended the steps of the altar, he came down again, he turned his back to the people, he turned his face to them, he changed from one side of the altar to another, he made various gestures with his hands, but he uttered not an audible word."

The silence was broken again only by the sound of a gong-like bell announcing the consecration and communion when the intense muffled prayers of many worshippers could be overheard. No more than two dozen people approached the communion rail to receive the Eucharist. There was neither a homily nor a hymn nor music of any kind. The only words that the priest spoke in English were the announcements and a request for prayers for the dead.[35]

Sunday Mass began as early as 5:30 in some parishes because many parishioners had to work on Sunday. The last Mass in New York parishes was at 11:00 a.m., but Dr. McGlynn defied convention in the 1880s by introducing a noon Mass at St. Stephen's that drew 2,500 worshippers to his church every Sunday. "Churches are for the people, and not the people for the churches," McGlynn informed Archbishop Corrigan, explaining that the noonday Mass had brought back

The interior of St. Stephen's Church in 1870.
Credit: *Archdiocese of New York*

to the practice of the faith many Catholics who had ceased to attend Sunday Mass.

McGlynn had to defend himself from the complaints of other pastors who called the noonday Mass "the Mass of the Weak" and accused him of encouraging sloth among his parishioners. Such accusations, McGlynn said, "come with poor grace from any who have so much leisure every day of the week and are so generously supported by our hard-working people." Even Sunday was not full day of rest for many of Dr. McGlynn's parishioners. "Very many have to work all night or from 3 or 4 o'clock in the morning of Sundays as well as other days," he said.[36]

35 - James Parton, "Our Roman Catholic Brethren," *Atlantic Monthly,* April 21, 1868, 432-435, in Joseph P. Chinnici, O.F.M., and Angelyn Dries, O.S.F.,eds., *Prayer and Practice in the American Catholic Community* (Maryknoll: Orbis Books, 2000), 65-68.

36 - AANY, C-10, McGlynn to Corrigan, March 11, 1886.

Devotional Services

The thin ranks at the communion rail in St. Stephen's Church would have surprised no one. Before the liturgical reforms of Pope Pius X in the early twentieth century even devout lay people rarely received Holy Communion more than once or twice a year. It was a lingering vestige of the Jansenist spirituality that discouraged frequent reception of the sacrament from a misguided sense of reverence for the Eucharist. As an antidote to the fear-driven spirituality of the Jansenists, which was widespread among Irish-Americans, a major effort was made to promote devotion to the Sacred Heart of Jesus with its emphasis on the humanity of Jesus and his love for sinners expressed through the symbolism of his heart.

The Jesuits had been encouraging this devotion for several centuries, but it got a new lease on life from Pope Pius IX who established the feast of the Sacred Heart in 1876. Ten years later, at the Fourth Provincial Council of New York in 1886, the bishops of the state strongly recommended devotion to the Sacred Heart especially through the reception of Holy Communion on the first Friday of each month. It proved to be extremely popular, especially the practice of receiving Holy Communion on nine consecutive First Fridays, which came to be considered practically a guarantee of eternal salvation.

A further development of devotion to the Sacred Heart was the day-long exposition of the Blessed Sacrament in the parish churches on the first Friday of each month. This particular type of Eucharistic piety was associated with a theology of reparation or expiation. Catholics were encouraged to spend some time in silent prayer and adoration before the Blessed Sacrament as a way of making reparation for sins of impiety and sacrilege. When Father Joseph McMahon asked to introduce this practice at St. Patrick's Cathedral in 1897, he told Archbishop Corrigan that "this act of reparation… already is very generally practiced throughout the diocese and in other dioceses." In many parishes First Friday devotions concluded with an evening service consisting of a sermon and Benediction of the Blessed Sacrament.[37]

Although many Catholics came to church only at Christmas and Easter, and perhaps on Ash Wednesday and Palm Sunday as well, the more devout parishioners not only attended Mass every Sunday morning but returned in the afternoon for vespers, the official evening prayer of the Church. Like the Mass, vespers was sung entirely in Latin. It gradually gave way to an afternoon service in the vernacular that consisted of the rosary, the litany of the Blessed Virgin, a sermon and Benediction of the Blessed Sacrament.

During May and October there were evening devotions to Mary and in June evening devotions to the Sacred Heart. There were also "perpetual novenas" throughout the year to Our Lady of Perpetual Help, St. Anthony and other popular saints. During Holy Week parishes vied with one another to erect ornate shrines (repositories) for the Blessed Sacrament on Holy Thursday, since the faithful were encouraged to visit seven churches on that evening. First Communion Day and Confirmation Day were special occasions in every parish when the boys were outfitted in blue suits and the girls in white dresses. In a poor West Side parish like Sacred Heart there were special evening classes to prepare working children for Confirmation.[38]

---

37 - AANY, G-2. McMahon to Corrigan, December 12, 1897.

38 - Browne, *One Stop Above Hell's Kitchen*, 40.

First Communion procession in St. Margaret Mary Church, Bronx, in the 1950s under the watchful gaze of the Sisters of Mercy.
Credit: *Sisters of Mercy*

Many Protestant churches increasingly limited their liturgical services to Sunday. By contrast Catholic churches had two or three scheduled Masses every weekday morning between 6:00 a.m. and 9:00 a.m., which were attended by both men and women on their way to work. The churches remained open all day for private prayer and meditation. One Protestant social worker in Greenwich Village called attention to the different atmosphere in the Catholic and Protestant churches. "Go to any prayer meeting or weekday service in a local Protestant church," she said, "and then drop in at Benediction at Our Lady of Pompei's and see the difference in attendance and interest."[39]

Sacramental Practice

Sacramental practice placed great emphasis on confession. Saturday was the traditional day for Catholics to go to confession in preparation for Sunday Mass. Parish priests could expect to hear confessions on Saturday from 4:00 p.m. until late in the evening with a brief break for supper. The same was true on the eve of holydays and the eve of the First Friday of the month. The dairy of Richard Burtsell is filled with references to numerous occasions when he heard confessions for four or five hours at a stretch or even longer. Many Catholics would never have dared to receive

Holy Communion without first going to confession, although there was no church law that obliged them to do so.

At St. Alphonsus Church the Redemptorists attracted large numbers of people for confession. "We lived in the confessional," said one pastor,

spending every week from thirty-five to forty hours hearing confessions. Many a Saturday and many an eve of feasts we spent twelve out of the twenty-four hours in hearing confessions, People came to us from every part of the city and from miles outside of the city.

At that time, 1868-1870, there were not half enough churches and priests for the numerous Catholics in New York living below Thirtieth Street. Hence immense crowds came to our church to hear Mass and especially to go to confession. The church was always filled to overflowing at all the Masses and at the evening services. Our sermons and instructions were all very simple and practical, partaking of the nature of mission-preaching; and as after every sermon or instruction we went to the confessional, we could at once reap the fruit of our preaching.[40]

In striking contrast to the meticulous attention given to confession, baptism and marriage were treated in an almost nonchalant fashion. There was no pre-baptismal catechesis or even an interview with the parents. Parents were simply advised to present their child for

39 - Mary Kingsbury Simkhovitch, *Neighborhood: My Story of Greenwich House* (New York: Norton, 1938), 117.
40 - John F. Byrne, C.Ss.R., *The Redemptorist Centenaries* (Philadelphia: The Dolphin Press, 1932), 152.

Rules and Regulations
of St. Joseph's Church in 1896

wedding ceremony itself was extremely simple, consisting of little more than the exchange of vows by the bride and groom and a blessing by the priest. In busy parishes weddings were scheduled at fifteen-minute intervals on a weekend.

The visitation of the sick was a major pastoral responsibility in an era where many people avoided hospitals and died at home. At St. Joseph's Church in Greenwich Village the parishioners were urged to inform the rectory by 10:00 a.m. if they wished a priest to visit a sick person in their home on that day. Many Catholics deferred asking for the Sacrament of the Sick until the last minute, since even the contemporary name, Extreme Unction, implied that it was a sacrament only for the dying rather than for the aged and ill. To combat this mentality, at St. Joseph's Church the printed instructions for sick calls pointedly called attention to the fact that "one effect of the Sacrament of Extreme Unction is to heal."[41]

baptism on Sunday afternoon. It was presumed that any parent requesting baptism would raise the child as a Catholic. Only under the most exceptional circumstances was the mother present at the baptism, since no Catholic parents risked deferring the ceremony for more than one or two days after the child's birth

In the case of weddings, there was a three-week waiting period, but only to allow sufficient time for the reading of the banns at Mass on three successive Sundays, a relic from a rural society where such announcements were used to forestall bigamous unions. There was no spiritual preparation for the sacrament other than an exhortation to the bride and groom to receive Holy Communion on their wedding day. The

---

41 - AANY, Rules and Regulations of St. Joseph's Church, 1896.

Rules and Regulations of St. Peter's Church, Rondout, New York c. 1900

Parish Missions

Parish missions---the Catholic equivalent of a Protestant revival---were an integral feature of the parish life of that era. They served a vital purpose at a time when it was estimated that only half of the Catholics in New York City were regular churchgoers. Parishes were expected to have a mission at least every three or four years. The Redemptorists, the Jesuits and the Paulists were especially active in this work, and the Redemptorists were well known for their fire-and-brimstone sermons which were designed to bring their listeners to confession.[42]

John Talbot Smith described how the Redemptorists conducted their parish missions. "[They] take possession of a parish for a period of a week, or of two, three and four weeks, according to the need," he said.

Their preaching is of the simple and vivid order on the chief doctrines and duties of a Catholic; it would be thought coarse by the more cultured people, and even extravagant; the pictures of hell and purgatory are medieval in color; the consequences of sin, the judgment deserved by faithless parents and ungrateful children, the woe of drunkards and fornicators and thieves, are described with vigor; but the result justifies the method, for the people flock to the confessional, their good resolutions are strengthened by the vivid impressions made upon them, and the revival of faith and religious life is sincere and enduring."[43]

Copyright 1900 by P. J. KENEDY, New York.

Order of Exercises

And Souvenir of the

MISSION

Conducted by the

Carmelite Fathers

IN THE

Church of St. John the Evangelist

AT

CLOVE,

ULSTER CO., NEW YORK.

March 8th to March 15th, 1908.

MORNING

6 o'clock.—Mass and Instruction
9 o'clock.—Mass and Instruction.
CONFESSIONS—Hours announced from the altar.

EVENING

7.30 o'clock.—Rosary, Instruction, Sermon and Benediction of the Most Blessed Sacrament

Even small country churches sponsored parish missions at least every three years. An advertisement for parish mission conducted by the Carmelite Friars in the Church of St. John the Evangelist, Clove, New York, in 1908.

Credit: *Archdiocese of New York*

At first the Redemptorists in the United States conducted parish missions only in German, but in 1851 they gave their first English-language mission in St. Joseph's Church in Greenwich Village from April 6 to April 20. They estimated that there were about 10,000 Catholics in the parish. They described the people who attended the mission as mostly Irish, "servants, laborers and other persons of the poorer class," although some Catholics "of a higher class" also attended out of curiosity. St. Joseph's Church was so crowded that the priests could hardly make their way to the sanctuary. People knelt to kiss their habits as they walked down the aisle. News of the mission spread throughout Greenwich Village, attracting Catholics who had not been to confession in thirty or forty years. Some were so poor that they had to borrow clothes to come to church. Before the mission was over, the Redemptorists said that they had heard 6,000 confessions and prepared sixty adults to make their first Communion. On the last evening of the mission emotions ran so high that the preacher could hardly be heard above the weeping of the congregation.[44]

Like contemporary Protestant evangelists, Catholic mission preachers advertised a forthcoming parish mission well in advance of their arrival. They plastered the neighborhood with handbills and placed advertisements in the newspapers. In preparation for a parish mission

---

42 - Jay P. Dolan, *Catholic Revivalism* (Notre Dame: University of Notre Dame Press, 1978), 42-44.

43 - Smith, *Catholic Church,* I, 202.

44 - Archives of the Paulist Fathers, Chronicle of Missions of the English Missions Given by the Redemptorist Fathers in the United States of North America, 1851, Mission at St. Joseph's Church, New York City.

at St. Paul the Apostle in January 1895 the Paulists took advantage of their proximity to the Ninth Avenue El to stretch an eye-catching banner across the front of the church announcing "A Great Mission."

On that same occasion the Paulists distributed a four-page pamphlet explaining the purpose of the mission as

> a time when God calls with a more earnest voice than at other times all persons, but sinners especially, to work out their salvation with fear and trembling. It is an extraordinary time to make your friendship with God. It is a time when the greatest truths of religion--- heaven, hell, the evil of mortal sin, the justice of God, His tender mercy---are preached to you. It is a time when priests from early morning till night wait in the confessionals for you, to absolve you from your sins, and restore you to God's favor. It is a time for you to remember that you have a soul to save, and to try and save it.[45]

Parish missions were such an effective way of revitalizing a parish that many American dioceses, including the archdiocese of New York,

organized their own Mission Band composed of diocesan priests who specialized in this work. In 1897 the Diocesan Mission Band conducted a four-week mission at St. Joseph's Church in Greenwich Village. Three diocesan priests were assisted by Father Walter Elliott, a well-known Paulist mission preacher. As was customary, each week was set aside for a specific group of parishioners.

The first week was reserved for married women because they were the ones who were most likely to attend in large numbers and set the tone for the subsequent three weeks, which were targeted at young women, married men and young men. The technique worked at St. Joseph's where almost 1,700 married women filled the church to capacity for the morning Mass and evening sermon, and flocked to the confessionals throughout the day. One newspaper reporter was especially impressed with the congregational singing at the services. Another unusual aspect of this parish mission, due perhaps to Father Walter Elliott, was that it concluded with a series of lectures on the Catholic Church for prospective converts.[46]

The members of the Holy Name Society of St. Stephen's Church, Warwick, New York in 1922.
Credit: *Archdiocese of New York*

---

45 - Dolan, *Catholic Revivalism*, 57-58.

46 - *New York Catholic News*, December 5, 1897.

The annual Communion Breakfast of the Holy Name Society of St. Joseph's Church, Tremont, in 1938
Credit: *Archdiocese of New York*

Parish Societies

In the heyday of big city Catholicism in the United States parish churches were not only religious centers, but also educational, cultural and social centers for their parishioners. A dense network of sodalities, confraternities and parish societies created strong bonds between the parishioners and the parish, and among the parishioners themselves. These organizations served different age groups, but they all had their own officers and a priest moderator. They held regularly scheduled meetings and performed specific functions in the parish, many of which would be described today as lay ministries.

One of the smallest but most valuable organizations in any parish was the local conference (chapter) of the St. Vincent de Paul Society, which was the principal means of bringing material assistance to the needy of the parish. Unlike some of the bigger parish societies, it was a highly structured, no-nonsense organization. Members were required to attend a weekly meeting and to visit the poor in their homes at least once a week. The guiding force behind the St. Vincent de Paul Society in New York City in the 1890s was Thomas Mulry, the secretary of the Supreme Council of New York. "There is no room in our society for drones," he warned the members in 1893. "The man who does not earnestly enter into this work had better retire at once." That same year Mulry proudly pointed out to Archbishop Corrigan that, in the previous year, the Society had aided needy families with 11,000 children, 5,000 of whom would probably have been sent to institutions without the help provided by the Vincentians on their home visits.[47]

In most parishes the two largest organizations were the Holy Name Society for the men and the Rosary Society for the women, each of which held a monthly meeting. For the younger parishioners there was the Sodality of the Children of Mary and the Sodality of the Holy Angels. Many parishes also had a branch of the League of the Sacred Heart, a national organization sponsored by the Jesuits to promote devotion to the Sacred Heart and the Eucharist especially in connection with the First Friday of the month.

In many Italian parishes there were lay-led mutual aid societies that were often responsible for the founding of the parish and remained active in fund raising and organizing the annual festa in

---

47 - AANY, G-2, Mulry to Sirs and Dear Brothers, August 29, 1893; Mulry to Corrigan, November 18, 1893.

honor of the patron saint of the parish. In Polish and Slovak parishes there were usually local branches of one or more national fraternal societies like the Polish Roman Catholic Union of America or the First Catholic Slovak Union. Although these societies were intimately linked with the life of the parish, the elected lay officers who ran them carefully guarded their autonomy especially with regard to financial matters.

Last but not least was the Altar Boys' Society, which provided trained servers for Mass and was often a fruitful source of vocations to the priesthood. The altar boys had their own jealously guarded internal hierarchy. Beginners were relegated to the role of torchbearers who paraded across the sanctuary with lighted candles at the consecration of the Mass and at Benediction. They might advance to the rank of acolytes who mumbled memorized Latin phrases at Mass that were a vestigial relic of the participation of the faithful in the public worship of the Church.

A more coveted position was that of thurifer, which enabled altar boys to display their dexterity in producing the maximum amount of fragrant smoke from a pot full of burning charcoal and incense in the sanctuary by twirling it a full 360 degrees at high speed in the sacristy. Finally there was the lordly position of the master of ceremonies who was responsible for guiding the clergy through the intricate rubrics of the Solemn High Mass by his knowledge of such arcane matters as how many times they were supposed to doff their biretta during the singing of the Gloria.

Dr. Patrick McSweeny was an ardent promoter of the temperance movement among his parishioners at St. Brigid's Church. His Christmas card to his parishioners in 1887
Credit: *Archdiocese of New York*

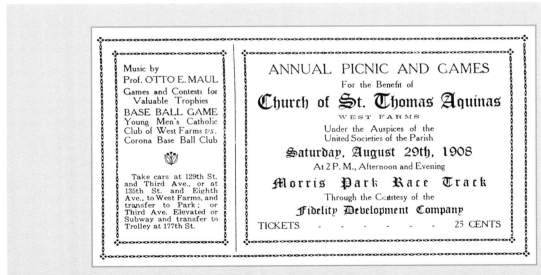

Social events were a means of promoting parish unity. An advertisement for the annual picnic at Thomas Aquinas Church, Bronx, in 1908
Credit: *St. Thomas Aquinas Church*

The Altar Boys at Incarnation Church, Manhattan, in 1955.
Credit: *Archdiocese of New York*

A Place for Everyone

Protestant evangelists liked to publicize their revival meetings with the slogan that there was a place for everyone under the big tent. Likewise there was a place for everyone in the modern parish that emerged in New York and in many of the big cities of the Northeast and Midwest during the late nineteenth century. While the Eucharist remained the central act of Catholic worship in every parish, there was also a wide variety of devotional practices and parish societies whose appeal cut across ethnic and generational barriers. Such parishes gave Catholic immigrants and their children a secure spiritual home, helped them to preserve their cultural heritage in an alien environment and enabled them to assimilate into American society from a position of strength.

14

On Top of the World

*The Ancient Order of Hibernians march up Fifth Avenue in the parade on May 2, 1908,
to commemorate the centennial of the diocese.*

The first half of the twentieth century was a golden age for American Catholics, an era of tremendous institutional growth and increasing self-confidence. As Jay Dolan observed, Catholics in the United States felt that they were "on top of the world." They had good reason for their optimism. The Catholic population almost doubled from twelve million in 1900 to twenty-one million in 1940 despite a series of restrictive immigration laws in the 1920s and the Depression of the 1930s. Bishops across the country struggled to keep up with the demand from the laity for more churches, schools, hospitals and other institutions. Remarkably they were able to satisfy most of these demands because vocations to the priesthood and religious life had never been more abundant.

Not only were Catholics more numerous than ever before, but they were no longer exclusively a community of poor immigrants. More and more of them found their way into the middle class as businessmen and managers, lawyers, teachers and doctors. Although anti-Catholicism was far from dead and surfaced in an ugly way in the 1920s with the Ku Klux Klan and the bigotry manifested during the presidential campaign of 1928, Catholics enjoyed more acceptance in American society than ever before. In fact they sometimes found themselves in the unusual position of being "insiders" instead of "outsiders." Millions of Catholics volunteered to serve in the armed forces during World War I and World War II, a demonstration of Catholic patriotism did much to convince other Americans of their loyalty.

The heartland of American Catholicism in that era remained the big industrial cities of the Northeast and Midwest with their large blue collar ethnic population. In cities like Boston and Philadelphia, Chicago and Cleveland, many working class neighborhoods were heavily Catholic. The local Catholic parish church was such a dominant institution that even Protestants and Jews sometimes referred to the neighborhood where they lived by the name of the nearest Catholic church. Living off the legacy of the Immigrant Church of the nineteenth century, American Catholics managed to create their own self-contained subculture. Charles Morris said that "an alien anthropologist landing in a working-class Philadelphia parish in the 1930s or 1940s would know instantly the centrality of religion to the lives of the inhabitants."[1] His comment about Philadelphia could easily be applied to New York.

It was certainly a golden age for the pastors of big city parishes. Once appointed to their position, they enjoyed lifetime tenure and functioned like feudal barons or Afghan warlords within a decentralized diocese with only minimum oversight from the bishop and even less accountability to the laity. They could usually rely upon the services of three or four docile curates to discharge their pastoral responsibilities, and they could leave the administration of the parochial school in the hands of a community of sisters who sometimes taught classes of sixty or more students.

The pastor's own area of expertise was expected to be the financial management of the parish. The distinguishing mark of the successful pastor of that era was not personal sanctity or eloquence as a homilist, but acumen as a businessman and a fund raiser. Both bishops and laity often measured the ability of their pastors by those criteria. In Depression-era New York Bishop John Dunn, the vicar general, sang the praises of a Bronx pastor who increased his parish revenue three-fold in seven years because he was "gifted with the genius of forcing the people to give until it hurt."[2]

For the laity in big-city parishes, the parish plant, which included the church, school, rectory, convent and sometimes a parish hall and gymnasium, was often the center of their social world as well as their religious life. A variety of parish-sponsored events such as plays, musicals, outings, and card parties provided relief from the monotony of working-class life that was later to be supplied by the movies and television. An array of athletic programs and inter-parish sports competition, and later the diocesan-wide Catholic Youth Organization (founded in Chicago in 1930), served a similar purpose by involving young people in the life of the parish. An integral feature of parish life was the proliferation of parish societies such as the Holy Name Society for the

---

1 - Morris, *American Catholic*, 174.

2 - AANY, St. Martin of Tours parish file, Dunn to Hayes, November 6, 1931.

men, and the Rosary Altar Society for the women, sometimes numbering hundreds of members, each with its own elected lay officers and a priest as spiritual director.

Other factors also served to reinforce a sense of Catholic identity and convince Catholics that they were a people set apart. Among the most powerful of these factors was the influence of the parochial schools, although they never enrolled a majority of Catholic children. There were also rigid rules governing contacts between Catholics and non-Catholics in any religious context. Attendance at non-Catholic religious services was frowned upon, except at weddings and funerals, and even then there was a stern warning to avoid active participation in the ceremonies. When the *New York Times* reported in February 1941 that Father George Barry Ford, the pastor of Corpus Christi Church on Morningside Heights, had sent a bouquet of Easter lilies to Riverside Church as an anniversary present, he was scolded like a naughty schoolboy by Msgr. J. Francis McIntyre, the chancellor. "Is not this a manifestation of brotherhood that borders on *communicatio [in sacris?]*" McIntyre asked.[3]

Many Catholics were eager to assert their religious identity in their workplace as well as in their neighborhood. Policemen, firemen, mailmen, telephone operators, department store clerks, and employees of other companies with a high percentage of Catholics, organized their own religious associations like the Police Department Holy Name Society. These societies typically sponsored an annual Mass and Communion Breakfast with a prominent speaker at a fancy downtown hotel. They attracted such large numbers of participants that local politicians vied with one another for a place on the dais. In New York in May 1950, 2,300 women employees of

AT&T (they called themselves the "Telephone Ladies") turned out to hear former Postmaster General James A. Farley speak at their Communion Breakfast at the old Astor Hotel. That same month 1,200 longshoremen attended Mass on the United States Line pier on the North River and then marched in military procession across midtown Manhattan to the Waldorf Astoria for their Communion Breakfast.[4]

While many men and women carried their Catholic identity with them from their neighborhood to school or workplace, the neighborhoods themselves proved to be amazingly resilient to outside influences, such as the movies, the most popular form of mass entertainment in the 1930s and 1940s. By that date Hollywood had blanketed urban neighborhoods with theatres that posed a potential threat to the local clergy as the arbiter of moral standards. However, the hierarchy defused the looming crisis by opting for a mutually beneficial alliance with Hollywood. The movie studios avoided the threat of government censorship by adopting a Production Code that followed closely the standards of the Legion of Decency, an agency created the U.S. bishops in 1934 to police the movies.

Moreover, the Church had little reason to complain about the way that Hollywood depicted the Catholic priesthood. The image of the Catholic priest that movie-goers saw in their neighborhood theatres in 1944 in Leo McCarey's *Going My Way* was that of the "superpadre," a dynamic spiritual leader who was played by a handsome young Bing Crosby. Gary Wills noted wryly that "the film celebrated all of the church's faults as if they were virtues." Despite that fact, or perhaps because if it, *Going My Way* won seven Oscars.[5]

3 - AANY, McIntyre to Ford, February 11, 1941.

4 - *New York Times*, May 8, 22, 1950.

5 - Garry Wills, *Bare Ruined Choirs* (Garden City: Doubleday, 1971), 23. Morris, *American Catholic*, 196-197.

When Catholics wished to marry outside the faith, they could only obtain ecclesiastical permission to do so, if the non-Catholic spouse promised in writing to raise the children as Catholics. Even then the couple had to forgo a church wedding and suffer the indignity of exchanging their vows at a private ceremony in the rectory. Catholic identity even persisted beyond death to the grave. Unless the deceased were to be buried in a Catholic cemetery, they were denied a funeral Mass in their parish church. Few protested a rule that seemed to be the logical culmination of womb-to-tomb Catholicism.

Indian Summer in New York

In New York this Golden Age of big-city Catholicism coincided with the administrations of John Cardinal Farley (1902-1918) and Patrick Cardinal Hayes (1919-1938), and petered out under Francis Cardinal Spellman (1939-1967). In some respects it was not so much a Golden Age in New York as an Indian summer, the last hurrah of the traditional Irish parishes that had defined Catholicism in New York City for over a century. While the Catholic population of the country continued to grow, in the archdiocese of New York it declined for the first time in history from 1,350,000 in 1902 to 1.000,000 in 1938. By that date New York had ceased to be the most populous diocese in the country, supplanted first by Chicago in 1936 and then by Boston a year later. The population of the archdiocese only began to increase again in the late 1940s with the great Puerto Rican migration.

In 1938 there were already 372 parishes in the archdiocese, compared to 405 parishes seventy years later, so that the bulk of the parish infrastructure was already in place, at least in New York City, seventy years ago. However,

during the last seventy years more than twice as many new parishes were founded in the seven upstate counties (42) as in New York City (18), reflecting the shift of the Catholic population to the suburbs. During that same period some 30 parishes were closed or consolidated. All but five of them were located in Manhattan and most were national parishes, another indication of the changing demographics of the Catholic population.

Archbishop John Murphy Farley

The appointment of auxilary Bishop John Farley as the fourth archbishop of New York on September 15, 1902, was significant for several reasons. He was the last foreign-born archbishop of New York, born in Newtown Hamilton, Armagh, on April 20, 1842. Orphaned at an early age, he emigrated to the United States where he was raised by his uncle, John Murphy, a prosperous businessman. After studies at St. John's College, Rose Hill, and one year at St. Joseph's Provincial Seminary in Troy, he was sent to the North American College in Rome where he was ordained a priest of the archdiocese of New York on June 11, 1870.

His star rose early in his career. Two years after his ordination he was appointed the secretary to Cardinal McCloskey, who made him the pastor of St. Gabriel's Church in 1884. Under Archbishop Corrigan he became one of the two vicars general in 1891, succeeding Monsignor Preston. On December 21, 1895, he was appointed the titular bishop of Zeugma and New York's first auxiliary bishop. The initial letter from Rome appointed Farley the coadjutor with the right of succession, much to the consternation of Archbishop Corrigan, who feared that it would be interpreted as a vote of non-confidence. He moved quickly to have Rome rectify the mistake.[6]

---

6 - AANY, G-34, Satolli to Corrigan, December 16, 1895

*John Murphy Farley, the pastor of
St. Gabriel's Church and New York's first
auxiliary bishop in 1895.*

Monsignor Joseph F. Mooney

Archbishop Farley's appointment was also significant because it was the only time that the local presbyterate played a role in the selection of a new archbishop. According to the rules adopted at the Third Plenary Council of Baltimore in 1884 at the insistence of Rome, every bishop was required to have a board of consultors and to make ten percent of the pastors in his diocese "permanent rectors." At the death of the bishop the diocesan consultors and the permanent rectors were to meet and draw up a *terna* (a list of three nominees) for the vacant see. The bishops of the province were to do likewise. The Holy Father was free to accept any of the names on the *ternae* or to reject them and choose someone else.

The process was abandoned shortly before the promulgation of the Code of Canon Law in 1917 so that the only time that it was ever used in New York was to decide the successor to Archbishop Corrigan in 1902. Bishop Farley was

the favored candidate on both *ternae*. The two other nominees on the *terna* of the priests were Monsignor Joseph Mooney and Dr. Patrick McSweeny. Notably absent was the name of Bishop Charles McDonnell of Brooklyn, Corrigan's former secretary, who was closely identified with the policies of that administration. McDonnell blamed Mooney for keeping his name off the *terna*. Even the senior suffragan bishop, Bernard McQuaid of Rochester, a close friend of Corrigan, threw his weight behind the nomination of Bishop Farley, not McDonnell. He told Farley that his letter of recommendation was the strongest letter that he ever sent to Rome.[7]

Still another significant aspect of Farley's appointment was that, after the turmoil of the Corrigan years, it represented a return to the less abrasive kind of episcopal leadership that had characterized the administration of Cardinal McCloskey. One of the new archbishop's first priorities was to unify the clergy after the polarizing tactics of his predecessor. He appointed eight monsignors, including Dr. Burtsell and

---

7 - AANY, I-5, McQuaid to Farley, September 8, 1902.

Dr. Patrick McSweeny, two of the leaders of the loyal opposition under Corrigan. Such a lavish distribution of Roman honors was unprecedented in New York, which led John Talbot Smith (who was not one of the recipients) to observe impishly that Archbishop Farley had made half the clergy purple and the other half blue. Monsignor Michael J. Lavelle, Farley's first vicar general and the longtime rector of St. Patrick's Cathedral, thought that one of Farley's greatest achievements was the elimination of cliques and factions among the clergy after "the troubles of 1886 and thereafter."[8]

Monsignor Michael J. Lavelle, vicar general, 1902-1918, 1934-1939, and rector of St. Patrick's Cathedral, 1887-1939

Another major priority for Archbishop Farley was the expansion of the Catholic school system. By 1918 fifty new elementary schools had been started and the enrollment had almost doubled from 49,772 to 91,139. On the secondary school level the Jesuits, the Christian Brothers and the Marists operated several academies for boys while the Sisters of Charity operated ten academies for girls. After the turn of the century

they were joined by the Augustinian Fathers (1903), the Sisters of the Holy Child (1904), the Christian Brothers of Ireland (1906), French Ursulines (1913), and the Religious of the Sacred Heart of Mary (1915).

Several other religious communities came to the archdiocese during the first decade of the twentieth century. The Friars and Sisters of the Atonement were Anglican Franciscans who were founded in Graymoor, New York, by Father Paul Wattson and Mother Lurana White in 1898. They were received into the Church on October 30, 1909, and preserved their own distinctive Franciscan identity as Catholics as well as their special apostolate to promote the unity of all Christians. In 1912, at Cardinal Farley's invitation, the Holy Ghost Fathers came to St. Mark's Church in Harlem to initiate the apostolate to African Americans, and Mother Katherine Drexel's Blessed Sacrament Sisters joined them two years later.

The first Catholic women's colleges in the archdiocese date from the early years of the twentieth century, the College of New Rochelle in 1904, the College of Mount St. Vincent in 1910 and Manhattanville College of the Sacred Heart in 1917. New York got its first Catholic university in 1904 when St. John's College became Fordham University.[9]

Another indication of a growing Catholic intellectual life in New York was the founding of the United States Catholic Historical Society in New York City on December 9, 1884. The inspiration came from the encouragement of church history by the bishops at the Third Plenary Council of Baltimore (which had concluded two days earlier). Between 1889 and 1984 the society published numerous works on New York Catholic history through the thirty-eight volumes of its

8 - Michael J. Lavelle, "John Cardinal Farley, Archbishop of New York," *The Ecclesiastical Review 60* (1919): 118.
9 - Cohalan, *Popular History*, 184-185.

The College of New Rochelle

Keating Hall, Fordham University

monograph series and the fifty volumes of the annual *Historical Records and Studies.* In 1981 it began the publication of a quarterly journal, the *U.S. Catholic Historian,* under the editorship of Christopher Kauffman. Archbishop Corrigan served as the first honorary president of the society and every archbishop of New York since then has continued the tradition.

New York City was also the scene of another promising initiative when Father John J. Wynne, S.J., launched *America* magazine on April 17, 1909. An experienced journalist and energetic organizer, Father Wynne correctly surmised that there were enough educated Catholics to support a weekly magazine. Although *America* is a national Catholic magazine sponsored by the Jesuits throughout the United States, the editorial offices have always been located in New York City.

Father Wynne served as the editor of *America* for only a brief period, but he was deeply involved in another important venture, the publication of *The Catholic Encyclopedia,* which appeared in sixteen volumes between 1907 and 1914. It was a monumental achievement for a Catholic community with limited scholarly resources to produce a reference work of this scope and quality, and Father Wynne saw it through to completion. Cardinal Farley also provided indispensable financial assistance.

Father John Wynne, S.J., was a versatile man who wore many hats. On July 1, 1934, he was made an honorary Iroquois chief for his efforts to promote the beatification of Kateri Tekakwitha.
Credit: *Archdiocese of New York*

The editorial board of *The Catholic Encyclopedia: left to right, Father Edward Pace, Father Thomas Shahan, Dr. Charles C. Herbermann, Father John Wynne, S.J., Dr. Condé Pallen.*
Credit: *New York Province of the Society of Jesus*

Maryknoll

The establishment of the Catholic Foreign Mission Society of America (popularly known as Maryknoll) was a milestone in the coming of age of American Catholicism. Maryknoll was different from all the other religious communities that had been established in the United States to that date. The sole purpose of Maryknoll was to send men and women to the foreign missions. It was a declaration that, after years of dependence on European missionaries, the American Catholic Church was now ready to repay the debt by dispatching American missionaries to the far corners of the globe.

Two of the founders of Maryknoll were diocesan priests, Father James Anthony Walsh of Massachusetts, and Father Thomas Frederick Price of North Carolina. They met in 1910 and agreed to establish an American foreign missionary society. Father Price pointed out in 1911 that, although there were 17,000 priests in the United States, only about sixteen of them were serving in the foreign missions. After receiving approval from Rome for their new society of priests and brothers on June 29, 1911, Father Walsh and Father Price established their headquarters first in Hawthorne, New York, and shortly thereafter near Ossining on a hilltop or knoll dedicated to the Virgin Mary (Maryknoll).

Father Walsh became the first superior of the Maryknoll priests and brothers and directed the society for the next twenty-five years. In 1933 he was made a bishop in recognition of his service to the foreign missions and died at Maryknoll on April 14, 1936. Tragically Father Price had a much shorter life as a Maryknoller. In 1918 he headed the first contingent of Maryknoll missionaries to go to China and died there a year later, in a hospital in Hong Kong, on September 12, 1919.

In subsequent years Maryknoll extended its missionary work to Korea, Japan, the Philippines, Latin America and Africa. Maryknoll missionaries continued to work in China until the 1950s when the Communist regime expelled them. In 1982 Maryknoll was allowed to return to China, although only to conduct educational and cultural ministries.

The third founder of Maryknoll was Mary Josephine Rogers, who was born in Boston on October 27, 1882. She was one of six young lay women who came to Maryknoll in 1912 to assist with the work of the society, especially with the publication of the monthly periodical *The Field Afar*, which dates from 1907 and is older than the society itself. These lay women called themselves the Teresians after St. Teresa of Avila and wanted to be foreign missionaries themselves. In 1920 they received permission to form a religious community, the Foreign Mission Sisters of St. Dominic, and elected as their superior Mary Josephine Rogers, who took the religious name of Mother Mary Joseph. The next year they dispatched their first missionaries to China. Mother Mary Joseph remained their superior until her retirement in 1947. At her death on October 27, 1955, there were 1,127 Maryknoll Sisters in nineteen countries.

The first young man to apply for admission to the Maryknoll seminary was Francis Xavier Ford, a native of Brooklyn and a graduate of Cathedral College in Manhattan. He was one of the first three missionaries to accompany Father Price to China in 1918. In 1935 he was appointed a bishop, taking as his episcopal motto *condolere* ("to have compassion"). As a bishop Francis Ford tried hard to make the Catholic Church in his diocese thoroughly Chinese by encouraging native vocations to the priesthood and to the religious life as well as by promoting a well-educated laity. He also gave women religious

Bishop James A. Walsh, M.M.
Credit: *Maryknoll Archives*

Father Thomas F. Price, M.M.
Credit: *Maryknoll Archives*

Bishop Francis Xavier Ford, M.M.,
1892-1952.
Credit: *Maryknoll Archives*

Mother Mary Joseph Rogers,
M.M., 1882-1955.
Credit: *Maryknoll Archives*

important leadership roles in missionary work. Despite his long record of faithful service to the Chinese people, Bishop Ford was arrested by the Chinese Communists in December 1950 and accused of being an American spy. He was sentenced to prison where he died of mistreatment in February 1952. He is considered a martyr by those who knew him and witnessed his work in China.

Cathedral College

In September 1903 the archdiocese got is first minor seminary with the establishment of Cathedral College. Although Archbishop Farley founded the institution and appointed Father Patrick J. Hayes the first president, it was Archbishop Corrigan who conceived and planned Cathedral College to complement the new seminary at Dunwoodie. The need for a minor seminary became especially acute after 1899 when Manhattan College ceased to be a feeder for Dunwoodie because the Christian Brothers were forbidden by their European superiors from teaching Latin in their schools.

An ideal site became available in 1900 when the trustees of the Roman Catholic Orphan Asylum, which occupied the whole square block north of the cathedral between Madison and Fifth Avenues, announced plans to move the institution to Kingsbridge. Archbishop Corrigan bought the property fronting Madison Avenue where the Boland Trade School was located, and converted the four-story red brick building into Cathedral College. It represented a daring innovation in clerical education because it was a six-year day school rather than a boarding school, comprising four years of high school and the first two years of college. Archbishop Corrigan justified the innovation on two grounds, economy of operation and his desire to have the students "grow up under the influences of home virtues and parental supervision."[10]

Cathedral College on Madison Avenue between 51st and 52nd Streets.
Credit: *Archdiocese of New York*

10 - Corrigan, Pastoral Letter of March 30, 1901, in *Silver Jubilee of Cathedral College* (New York, 1928), 7-8. After the success of Cathedral College, several other dioceses adopted the concept of a non-residential minor seminary, including Brooklyn, Hartford, Chicago, St. Louis, St. Paul, and San Francisco, ibid., 12. On the history of Cathedral College, see [Florence D. Cohalan], *The Golden Jubilee Book of Cathedral College* (New York, 1953), 11-23. In 1942 Cathedral College was relocated to a former Episcopal girls' school at West End Avenue and 87th Street.

The Chapel of St. Joseph's Seminary, Dunwoodie.
Credit: *Yvon Meyer*

At the first graduation of Cathedral College in 1907 Archbishop Farley startled the guests by announcing that it had been necessary to build Cathedral College because the training in the local Catholic colleges was "rather promiscuous." He explained that the students in those institutions were being prepared for various professions while preparation for the priesthood was the sole purpose of Cathedral College. Farley was the first archbishop of New York who did not have to worry about a shortage of vocations. In June 1907 all sixty graduates of Cathedral College announced their intention of entering Dunwoodie. By 1916 there were 486 students in Cathedral College, fulfilling Bishop McQuaid's prediction that "whenever Dunwoodie is filled up with graduates from Cathedral College, the future of Dunwoodie will be secure.[11]

The End of Saint Sulpice in New York

There were two major crises at Dunwoodie early in the administration of Archbishop Farley. Although they were related, the first crisis was really of his own making while the second was part of a worldwide phenomenon in the Catholic Church known as the Modernist Crisis. The first crisis involved Farley's decision to replace the Sulpicians with his own diocesan priests. He had never been happy with Archbishop Corrigan's decision to entrust the seminary to the Society of St. Sulpice, and they were well aware of it. An opportunity occurred for him to get rid of them when tension developed between the Dunwoodie Sulpicians and their major religious superiors in France.

The root of the tension was the attempt of the Sulpicians at Dunwoodie to make the seminary a center of serious theological studies. It was a role that Dunwoodie was well equipped to play because of the high quality of the faculty. In addition to the rector, James Driscoll, a distinguished Scripture scholar in his own right, two of the French Sulpicians were also well-regarded Scripture scholars, Joseph Bruneau and Francis Gigot. The majority of the faculty always consisted of "auxiliary professors," the Sulpicians' cute phrase for New York diocesan priests. Several of them brought their own special strengths to Dunwoodie. Father John F. Brady had earned a medical degree before entering the priesthood; Father Gabriel Oussani, a Chaldean Catholic born in Baghdad, had spent three years studying Semitic languages and biblical archaeology at the Johns Hopkins University; Father Francis P. Duffy, a native of Canada, was the best pedagogue and spiritual director on the faculty, as the Sulpician rector admitted.

Thanks to the presence of these scholars Dunwoodie possessed the strongest seminary faculty in the United States. In the opinion of Monsignor John Tracy Ellis it was second only to the Catholic University of America as a center of American Catholic intellectual life. Michael V. Gannon, the pioneer historian of Modernism in the United States, said that "more than any other

---

11 - *Catholic News*, June 29, 1907; AANY,)-5, Hughes to Farley, January 15, 1918; AANY, O-1, McQuaid to Hayes, February 20, 1908.

[seminary], it was preparing American Catholicism for what a later age would call *aggiornamento*.[12]

As part of the effort to promote American Catholic intellectual life, on May 15, 1905, Driscoll, Duffy and Brady launched the *New York Review,* a bimonthly periodical which quickly made its mark as the best Catholic theological journal in the United States. The editors indicated the purpose of the *Review* with the motto that appeared on the front page of every issue: "A Journal of the Ancient Faith and Modern Thought." Scott Appley called its appearance "unprecedented in the history of American Catholic publications" because the editors realized that they were "the heralds of, and would-be contributors to, a twentieth-century synthesis of traditional Catholic belief and modern thought." [13]

About half of the articles were written by Dunwoodie professors. Gigot was especially prolific in explaining the new developments in Biblical exegesis. Duffy wrote a particularly helpful column called "Notes" where he summarized the most recent books and periodical articles by European Catholic scholars. In addition to the Dunwoodie faculty the contributors included American, British and European Catholic writers such as George Tyrrell, S.J., Vincent McNabb, O.P., Wilfrid Ward, Henri Brémond, Ernesto Buonaiuti and Joseph Turmel.

THE
NEW YORK
REVIEW.

A Journal
of
The Ancient Faith and Modern Thought.

ST. JOSEPH'S SEMINARY
DUNWOODIE, N. Y.

June-July, 1905.

St. Joseph's Seminary, Yonkers,
NEW YORK.

Copyright, 1905, by John F. Brady.

The title page of the first issue of the New York Review

Archbishop Farley gave the new journal his enthusiastic blessing, but the Sulpician superiors in France were increasingly apprehensive about the *New York Review* and tried to censor the contents. They also tried to prevent Gigot from publishing the second volume of his *Special Introduction to the Study of the Old Testament.* The reason for their concern was the signals that were coming from Rome of an imminent crackdown on Catholic scholarship that was soon to be known as the Modernist Crisis. On this side of the Atlantic the Dunwoodie Sulpicians became increasingly restive about the prohibitions emanating from Paris. One of them, Richard Wakeman, complained about their "ultra-conservative, ultra-fossilized or ultra-dyspeptic" brand of leadership.[14]

Edward Dyer, the rector of Dunwoodie from its opening to 1902, had become the first American vicar general of the Sulpicians when he left Dunwoodie. He tried to mediate between the Sulpicians at Dunwoodie and the superiors in Paris. He did his best to defend Gigot. "He does have advanced opinions," he told Pierre Garriguet, the superior-general, "but he expresses them with great prudence and true moderation."[15]

On the other hand, Dyer was decidedly unenthusiastic about the *New York Review* and warned James Driscoll that he was playing with

12 - John Tracy Ellis, interview, Washington, D.C., August 5, 1989. Michael V. Gannon, "Before and After Modernism: The Intellectual Isolation of the American Priest," in John Tracy Ellis, ed., *The Catholic Priest in the United States: Historical Investigations* (Collegeville: St. John's University Press, 1971), 335.

13 - R. Scott Appleby, *"Church and Age Unite!": The Modernist Impulse in American Catholicism* (Notre Dame: University of Notre Dame Press, 1992), 117-118. See also Michael J. DeVito, *The New York Review,* 1905-1908 (New York; U.S. Catholic Historical Society, 1977).

14 - Wakeman to Dyer, February 5, 1905, in Dyer, *Dunwoodie Letter,* 22-25. The *Dunwoodie Letter* was a 160-page white paper published by Dyer in 1906 to give the Sulpician version of the events that led to their dismissal from Dunwoodie.

15 - SAP, Dyer to Garriguet, August 2, 1905.

Father James F. Driscoll, rector of St. Joseph's Seminary, Dunwoodie, 1902-1909.
Credit: *Archdiocese of New York*

fire. He told Garriguet that Archbishop Farley "is no more aware than a child about the topics to be treated in the new review." "He would like to be a cardinal," Dyer added, "and if a word of disapproval should come from Rome, he would abandon the review completely and pounce upon the editors."[16]

Dyer was caught in a dilemma. As Driscoll's religious superior, he could have removed him as the rector of Dunwoodie and replaced him with someone else. He did not dare to do so because Driscoll had won Farley's confidence. At the same time Driscoll and his friends at Dunwoodie were less than candid with Farley. They did not make clear to him how radical their views were in the context of the time. Moreover, if Walter Sullivan--the Paulist priest who left the Church because of the Modernist crisis, is to believed---they made fun of Farley's intellectual limitations even as they sought the protection of his authority. Appleby's accusation of manipulation on the part of Driscoll and Gigot seems justified.[17]

The simmering crisis came to a head in January 1906 when Gigot asked Farley to give him a diocesan assignment. Farley replied that he could stay at Dunwoodie whether he remained a Sulpician or became a New York diocesan priest. He extended the same invitation to the other Sulpicians on the faculty. Five of the six accepted the offer. Only Joseph Bruneau turned down the offer and left Dunwoodie. Since the Sulpicians were now unable to supply the requisite number of professors for the faculty, Farley used this as the justification to terminate the contract with them. It was the end of the Sulpician era at Dunwoodie less than ten years after it had begun.

Dyer was furious at both the Dunwoodie Sulpicians, whom he accused of treason, and at Farley for accepting them into New York. He believed that the five would never have left the Sulpicians, if Farley had not previously offered them a place in his diocese. Farley pleaded that the five had threatened to return to their home dioceses and that he had no alternative except to offer them a place in New York in order to keep Dunwoodie open. Dyer did not believe Farley's claim about the Sulpicians threatening to return to their home dioceses. He told Farley that that he could have kept Dunwoodie open simply by preserving the status quo at the seminary. If he had done so, Dyer told him scathingly, "there would have been the advantage that the young levites trained there would not have had before them the example of a premium received upon the betrayal of a sacred trust."[18]

The Modernist Crisis in New York

Whether Farley or the Sulpicians themselves initiated their incardination into New York, it is clear that they did so because they hoped that the archbishop would protect them from the kind of harassment they had been receiving from their religious superiors. Their hopes were soon dashed. On July 3, 1907, the Holy Office issued *Lamentabili Sane Exitu,* a list of sixty-five condemned propositions said to be found in the

16 - SAP, Dyer to Garriguet, n.d. [January or February 1905].

17 - Appleby, *"Church and Age Unite!,"* 105.

18 - SAB, RG 8, Box 1, Dyer to Farley, February 5, 1906, copy. Both Dyer and Driscoll published *pièces justificatives.* After Dyer issued the Dunwoodie Letter, Driscoll wrote *A Statement of the Facts and Circumstances that Led to the Withdrawal of Five of the Professors of Dunwoodie Seminary from the Society of Saint Sulpice* (Yonkers, 1906).

writings of unnamed Modernist writers. Two months later, on September 8, 1907, Pope Pius X issued the encyclical *Pascendi Dominici Gregis,* denouncing a new heresy called Modernism, which he described as "the synthesis of all heresies." The objective of the Modernists, said the Holy Father, was to leave "nothing stable, nothing immutable in the Church."

The background to this papal condemnation of Modernism was the revival of Catholic intellectual life in Europe during the previous quarter-century as Catholic scholars tried to use such secular disciplines as history, archaeology, philology, psychology, and ancient literature to enhance their own understanding and pre- sentation of the Catholic faith. The results of their efforts were mixed, leading to what Roger Aubert identified as three kinds of Modernism. Some developments, said Aubert, were completely unobjectionable and caused no controversy. Other developments were basically sound, but they frightened conservatives because of their novelty. Still other developments ceased to have any Christian content and were incompatible with orthodox Catholicism.[19]

The encyclical *Pascendi* did not make these distinctions about varieties of Modernism but lumped them together as undermining belief in divine revelation, the divinity of Christ, and the definitive character of the Church's most solemn doctrinal pronouncements. The Integralist Reaction, as the campaign against Modernism was called, quickly degenerated into a witch hunt as "Modernist" became a term of abuse, used by ideologues as recklessly as the names "fascist" and "communist" were used at the height of the Cold War. Devout Catholics like the French Dominican exegete Marie-Joseph Lagrange, and even the young Angelo Roncalli, the future Pope John XXIII, were treated with the same

suspicion as the excommunicated French priest, Alfred Loisy, one the few genuinely heterodox Modernists.

Another aspect of the Modernist crisis, which helps to explain the panic in Rome, was the belief that Modernism was an organized movement rather than an orientation or methodology shared by many scholars. There was also widespread fear in Rome that the faculties of Catholic universities and seminaries were honeycombed with scholars who had lost their faith and were intent on destroying the Church from within under the guise of modernizing it.

Dunwoodie was prime target for integralist *zelanti* especially since the *New York Review* had published articles by writers like George Tyrrell and Joseph Turmel, who were subsequently accused of Modernism. In 1903 Driscoll himself had offered to translate two of the most controversial works of Alfred Loisy. Driscoll made clear to Loisy that he had reservations about his views, but he wanted to make the two books available in English so that readers in America could form their own judgment.[20]

At first Driscoll minimized the impact of *Pascendi,* warning the readers of the *New York Review* not to extend the papal condemnations to include "everybody who has studied biology or Hebrew." As the campaign against Modernism gathered strength, however, Driscoll confided to his friend Charles Augustus Briggs, the Protestant Scripture scholar, that "nothing so violent and drastic as the recent curial documents has appeared on the part of the Vatican authorities since the days of the Inquisition." He added: "I can compare the crisis to nothing but a cyclone, during which people must simply make for the cellar…"[21]

19 - Roger Aubert, *The Church in a Secularized Society* (New York: Paulist Press, 1978), 186-187.

20 - BN, Fr. Nouv. Acq. 15652, Driscoll to Loisy, December 11, 1903. The two books were *L'Evangile et l'Eglise and Autour d'un Petit Livre.*

21 - *New York Review 3* (November-December 1907): 342-349. AUTS, Briggs Papers, Driscoll to Briggs, December 8, 1907.

As Dyer had predicted, Archbishop Farley was anxious to reassure the Roman authorities of the orthodoxy of his seminary. After complaints from the Apostolic Delegate in Washington that the *New York Review* had carried advertisements for two books of George Tyrrell, the *Review* ceased publication in June 1908. The editors denied that the review "has ever been made the object of official condemnation." They came closer to revealing the real reason for its demise, however, when they declared: "At its inception three years ago its editors promised to present the best work of Catholic scholars at home and abroad on theological and other problems of the day. It is the keeping of that promise, not the breaking of it, that is the cause of the suspension of the *Review*."[22]

The following summer Farley made a long-planned trip to Rome where he had a conversation with Cardinal Satolli and decided to remove Driscoll, Gigot and Duffy from the faculty of the seminary. Farley was worried what the reaction might be back in New York. Then he changed his mind and decided just to dismiss Driscoll, which he did upon his return to New York in September. Driscoll had offered to resign a year earlier. It not seem to matter to Farley whether or not the allegations against Driscoll were true. "An important seminary like ours suffers more than others would from unfavorable reports about its teaching," Farley told Driscoll, "and only a change of some kind can remove the outside impression, whether well-founded or not."[23]

Farley replaced Driscoll as rector with Father John Chidwick, the first hero of the Spanish-American War and the chaplain to the New York City Police Department. Dunwoodie's Golden Age was over. Father Joseph H. McMahon,

the pastor of Our Lady of Lourdes Church, feared that, as a result of what he considered a mistaken interpretation of *Pascendi,* many Catholics "would become become fearful of all progress… and indeed become obscurantists."[24] That is what happened at Dunwoodie. Like seminaries throughout the United States and throughout the world, the students settled into a mind-numbing routine of studying theology in the form of desiccated neo-scholasticism from Latin manuals. The church historian Peter Guilday described his own experience of this kind of education at St. Charles Borromeo Seminary in Philadelphia as "an intellectual coma."

The Centennial of the Diocese

In the spring of 1908 the interest of most New York Catholics was not focused on some nebulous heresy called Modernism, but on the celebration of the centennial of the diocese. For one whole week, from Sunday, April 26 until Saturday, May 2, a series of religious and civic events commemorated the founding of the diocese in 1808. The celebrations conveyed two unmistakable messages to even the most casual observer. They were a vivid demonstration of Catholic political power in New York, and of the Irish domination of the local church, both of which would begin to erode in the following decades.

The week began with the arrival in New York of Michael Cardinal Logue, the Archbishop of Armagh, the Primate of All Ireland, and (as he was invariably identified) the 114th successor of St. Patrick. The tone was set by the reception that was arranged for the diminutive Irish cardinal when he arrived in New York on April 27 on the R.M.S. *Lucania*. He was greeted by a brass band from the Catholic Protectory that struck up a rousing rendition of *The Wearing of*

---

22 - *New York Review* 3 (May-June 1908), cover. See Thomas J. Shelley, "John Cardinal Farley and Modernism in New York," *CH* 61 (1992): 350-361.

23 - AANY, St. Ambrose Parish File, Farley to Driscoll, June 29, 1909.

24 - AANY, I-4, McMahon to the editor of the *New York Press,* July 14, 1908.

the Green, probably the first and last time a Cunard liner received such a greeting. As he stepped ashore in that pre-skyscraper era, one of the first sights he saw in the distance from the pier on the North River at West 50th Street was a huge American flag suspended between the twin spires of St. Patrick's Cathedral. Reporters asked the Irish cardinal about Modernism in his homeland. "There is none of that in Ireland," he replied emphatically.

Cardinal Logue arrives in New York for the celebration of the centennial of the diocese on April 27, 1908. Credit: *Archdiocese of New York*

That same day, April 27, two events epitomized how far the Catholics of New York had come since the days when John Hughes had tangled with the Public School Society. In every parish church that day there was a special Mass for the school children of the archdiocese. The superintendent of public education declared a holiday for the Catholic children in the public schools so that they could attend Mass "without loss of marks or credit."

That evening, in Fifth Avenue mansions only two doors apart, Catholic socialites held rival *soirées* for the two cardinals in town, Cardinal Logue and Cardinal Gibbons. Among those in attendance were not only prominent Catholics, but much of New York's high society, including John Jacob Astor, Mr. and Mrs. Andrew Carnegie, Mr. and Mrs. Stuyvesant Fish, Mrs. Cornelius Vanderbilt, Nicholas Murray Butler and Mayor George McClellan.

Three years earlier Mayor McClellan, a reform Democrat who was not a Catholic, gave a graphic illustration of Catholic political power in New York when he called at the archbishop's residence shortly after his election to inquire if Archbishop Farley had any recommendations for city commissioners. Farley surprised him when he replied that he would prefer to see fair-minded non-Catholics in those positions rather than Catholics who would bend over backwards for fear of being accused of favoritism to their own Church. Said the delighted mayor: "A very broad-minded, liberal, fine old gentleman was the cardinal."[25]

The highlight of the religious observances was a solemn pontifical Mass in the cathedral celebrated by Cardinal Logue in the presence of fifty archbishops and bishops, 800 priests and 6,500 lay people who filled the streets around the cathedral. The final event of the centennial celebrations was a parade of 40,000 men and boys up Fifth Avenue from Washington Square to 57th Street while a half-million people lined the avenue to watch them. "I never saw such an impressive gathering in all my life," said Cardinal Logue. "You real [sic] young men might live to see another centennial in New York," the Irish cardinal said with obvious exaggeration. "If you do," he predicted, "you will live to see the Church in New York and in America the most flourishing in Christendom."

25 - George B. McClellan, Jr., *The Gentleman and the Tiger,* ed. Harold C. Syrett (Philadelphia: J.B. Lippincott Co., 1956), 237-238.

Also in attendance at most of the festivities was the sole American cardinal, James Gibbons of Baltimore, who delivered the most memorable address of the week when he extolled the unique American heritage of religious freedom in a pluralistic society. Only nine years earlier, in a famous public letter addressed to him, Pope Leo XIII had warned American Catholics of possible dangers to their faith because of the American system of separation of church and state. At that time Cardinal Gibbons had reassured the pope that, on the contrary, Catholicism flourished in the free soil of America.

He repeated that message before a packed house in Carnegie Hall on May 1. "Let us never forget, my dear friends, he said, "to whom we are indebted under God for the blessings that we enjoy. We owe it to our country, we owe it to the freedom we possess to think." Turning to Cardinal Logue, he repeated a phrase that he had first used in Rome twenty years earlier when he took possession of his titular church as a cardinal, "Here, I say, we enjoy liberty without license, Your Eminence, and authority without despotism." The *New York Times* commented: "We have long believed that there was no better American than Cardinal Gibbons." Some years later, on the occasion of Gibbons' eighty-second birthday, former President Theodore Roosevelt told him: "Taking your life as a whole, I think you now occupy the position of the most respected and venerated and useful citizen of our country."[26]

Cardinal Gibbons and President Theodore Roosevelt.
Credit: *Library of Congress*

Cardinal Logue and Archbishop Farley review the parade celebrating the centennial of the diocese on May 2, 1908, from the front steps of St. Patrick's Cathedral.
Credit: *Archdiocese of New York*

---

26 - John Tracy Ellis, *The Life of James Cardinal Gibbons* (Milwaukee: Bruce Publishing Company, 1952), II, 500.

15

Full Steam Ahead

John Cardinal Farley, Archbishop of New York, 1902-1918.
Credit: *Archdiocese of New York*

Archbishop Farley became the second archbishop of New York to receive the Red Hat, which he got on November 27, 1911. He was also the last cardinal archbishop of New York to have as his titular church in Rome Santa Maria sopra Minerva, the Dominican church where both of New York's first two bishops resided at some point in their life. Upon his return from Rome Cardinal Farley received a hero's welcome, riding in an open carriage from the Battery up Broadway and Fifth Avenue to St. Patrick's Cathedral where the exterior of cathedral was illuminated with 50,000 light bulbs for a week.

*Archbishop Farley
at the consecration of the cathedral
on October 5, 1910.*

*Cardinals Logue, Gibbons,
and Vincenzo Vannutelli enter
St. Patrick's Cathedral for the
consecration on October 5, 1910.*
Credit: *Archdiocese of New York*

World War I

Farley's last four years as archbishop coincided with World War I. The attitude of New York Catholics to the conflict, like that of most American Catholics, was shaped to a considerable degree by their ethnic heritage. Most German-Americans and Irish-Americans favored American neutrality. In the case of Irish-Americans, they had an added reason for their stand after the ruthless British suppression of the abortive Easter Rising of 1916 in Dublin. On the other hand, Polish, Slovak and Czech Catholics saw the conflict as an opportunity to gain independence for their homelands if Germany and Austria-Hungary went down to defeat. Some Irish-American leaders like Judge Daniel F. Cohalan harbored the same thoughts about the positive consequences of a British defeat for Ireland and were not shy about expressing them.

However, once the United States entered the conflict in April 1917, American Catholics bishops were caught up in the same frenzy of emotional patriotism that swept across the rest of the nation. They outdid one another in bombastic protestations of support for the war effort. William Cardinal O'Connell of Boston announced solemnly that "the spirit of God is working through Woodrow Wilson." In New York Farley was more restrained, pledging full Catholic support and noting that "we have never been wanting in any crisis in our history." Millions of Catholics served in the Armed Forces, helping to eliminate the fears that some Americans still entertained about the loyalty of their Catholic fellow citizens.

The American Catholic bishops faced a major dilemma in trying to translate their patriotic rhetoric into action because of the lack of a national organization to coordinate their efforts and to act as a liaison between them and the government. The Knights of Columbus tried to fill to void and did invaluable work in organizing Catholic recreation centers at army camps and in supplying assistance to Catholic chaplains. However, the scope of the Knights' activities was limited because they were a lay organization, and some of the bishops thought that the Knights were usurping their authority.

Finally a Paulist priest came to the rescue, Father John J. Burke, a native New Yorker, who took the initiative in giving the American hierarchy and the American Catholic Church their first national organization. With the approval of the three American cardinals (Gibbons, Farley and O'Connell), he organized the National Catholic War Council beginning with a meeting in Washington of representatives from 68 dioceses and 27 societies in August 1917.

By January 1918 the NCWC had become the official organ of the American hierarchy with an administrative committee of four bishops, selected by Cardinal Gibbons. One of the four bishops was Patrick J. Hayes, the auxiliary bishop of New York. The NCWC proved to be so valuable that the American bishops continued it after the end of the war as the National Catholic Welfare Council (later changed to Conference), giving the United States the equivalent of a national episcopal conference forty years before Vatican Council II. Father Burke served as the first general secretary of the NCWC from its inception in 1919 until his death in 1936.

A few months before Bishop Hayes' appointment to the administrative board of the NCWC, he had been appointed to another national post. The rapid expansion in the size of the armed forces created an urgent demand for

Father John J. Burke, C.S.P., the founder of the National Catholic War Council and the General Secretary of the National Catholic Welfare Conference 1919-1936.
Credit: *Archives of the Paulist Fathers*

Catholic chaplains. Their numbers swelled from 28 in 1917 to 1,525 at the war's end. The Holy See moved quickly to provide for the needs of Catholic servicemen and their families by creating a non-territorial diocese for them called the Military Ordinariate with its headquarters in New York City. Hayes was appointed the Bishop Ordinary of the U.S. Army and Navy Chaplains on November 24, 1917, after Bishop William Russell of Charleston had declined the post when it was offered to him by Cardinal Gibbons in July. The Military Ordinariate remained in New York under the supervision of the archbishop of New York until March 1985 when it was reorganized as the Archdiocese for the Military Services and its headquarters were transferred to Washington, D.C.[1]

Father Duffy and the Fighting Sixty-Ninth

Eighty-seven New York diocesan priests served as chaplains during World War I. The most famous was Father Francis P. Duffy, who had been eased out of Dunwoodie in 1912 on suspicion of Modernism and sent to found Our Savior Church in the Bronx. Duffy was already on active duty with the New York 69th Regiment when the United States entered the war. By the time that the war was over, he would be a national hero and one of the best-known priests in the country. From the camp in Texas near the Mexican border where the regiment was on patrol duty, Duffy described for Farley how he spent Christmas 1916. "We had a Solemn High Midnight Mass on the fine drill field of the 69th Regiment," he told Farley, "probably the first event of the kind in the country at least since the Civil War, perhaps the very first in our church history in the United States."

1 - Douglas J. Slawson, *The Foundation and First Decade of the National Catholic Welfare Council* (Washington: The Catholic University of America Press, 1992), 32.

Duffy and the other chaplains spent all of Christmas Eve hearing confessions. "They came and they came," he said, "men who were never known to be Catholics." At midnight Monsignor James N. Connolly, a New York priest who was the senior Catholic chaplain, began Mass for 3,000 or 4,000 troops assembled on the field. Duffy wished that Farley could have witnessed the scene himself. The Mass was offered, said Duffy,

Father Francis P. Duffy as chaplain to the New York 69th Regiment in World War I.
Credit: *Our Saviour Church*

on the outposts of the nation, under the open sky of midnight. The vast crowd picked out by the light of carried lanterns, vanishing away in the gloom, intent on the solemn ceremonies of the Mass, and the old Christian hymns rolling out from the breasts of thousands of hearty rugged soldiers, and, best of all, the continuous surge of manly forms towards the place where four priests were giving Communion. It was something that stirred the blood when looked upon, and that will remain as an inspiring memory until life is over.[2]

Duffy was enormously proud of the men of the 69th Regiment. On the way to Europe their troopship stopped in Halifax. A Canadian priest came aboard and was astonished to find a large number of men assembled below deck reciting the rosary under the direction of a sergeant. In France the local clergy were equally astounded at the faith of the Catholic soldiers. "When Sunday came," said Duffy, "and the churches were so full that a cat could go from door to altar from head to head without touching the floor, you may imagine the joy of the *curés*. And after payday and the collection: 'Ah, how good! How generous your brave soldiers!'"

One Sunday Duffy preached in French for twenty minutes. He was so proud of his performance that he said: "I really ought to make it a matter of confession." Seriously, however, his major concern was the difficulty of coping with the huge number of confessions that he was asked to hear. "I could keep ten priests busy for the next four days," he told Farley. At one point he planned to bring priests from Paris at his own expense, but the constant movement of the regiment made that impractical. Instead he distributed copies of a bilingual card that the soldiers could use to make their confession to the local French priests.

The vestiges of Jansenism died hard among these young Irish-American servicemen. "Most of the men have done so little wrong," Duffy mentioned to Farley, "that they could receive Communion without confession, but you know the respect of our people. I have most of them trained at any rate to go to confession standing or walking any place or time they can get hold of me…. The method is open to objection, I know, on the score of sacramental dignity, but the main thing in the dangerous career that they have chosen is to help them have the life of grace."

Father Francis P. Duffy and Cardinal Hayes

2 - AANY, I-22, Duffy to Farley, December 27, 1916.

Waving the Flag: Monsignor Lavelle on the steps of the cathedral reviewing a parade of the 69th New York Regiment, flanked by (left to right) Father Francis P. Duffy, Father John M.J. Byrne, Father Joseph Dineen, and Father Bernard McQuade.
Credit: *Archdiocese of New York*

Despite the physical and psychological strain of his responsibilities, Duffy said that he never regretted his decision to volunteer as a chaplain. "After all," he said, "a priest's home is the parish he is assigned to, and the old Sixty-Ninth is a mighty comforting parish." One of his proudest moments occurred one day when he was standing next to some French army officers as a detachment of American troops marched past them. "But you know them all," the French officers exclaimed, "and they all know you, and they seem so pleased to see you." As Duffy told the story later, he admitted"

> I am afraid that I did not disclaim knowing them all individually, but I did explain that the smiles that wreathed their countenances were a tribute to my priesthood rather than my person. They did not quite see it, but I know that if it were not for my priesthood, I would not count for much with them. And that's the way I like it best.[3]

The New York Catholic War Fund

One of the best indications of Catholic patriotism was the series of fund-raising drives conducted by the National Catholic War Council in the spring of 1918. Nowhere were the results more successful than in New York. Cardinal Farley hoped to collect $2.5 million. Instead, he got twice as much, $4,962,424.85, with a fifth of the total coming from non-Catholic contributors. In the 1890s it had taken Archbishop Corrigan seven years to raise one million dollars to pay for the cost of the Dunwoodie seminary. In 1918 Cardinal Farley raised almost five times as much in one week. Even the organizers of the campaign were surprised at their success. The lay chairman of the drive, John C. Agar, said: "No campaign waged in New York has gone so far over the top as the New York Catholic War Fund."[4]

One reason for the success was the fact that this was the first really professional fund-raising drive conducted by the archdiocese based on a comprehensive index-card list of parishioners provided by each pastor. The whole archdiocese was divided into thirteen zones and 297 parish committees, which coordinated the work of 5,000 ten-man teams of volunteers. At least 37,610 workers were engaged in the campaign, almost five percent of the total Catholic population of the archdiocese. The final sum collected was the equivalent of a $6.50 contribution from every Catholic.[5]

3 - AANY, U-4, Duffy to Farley, November 11, 1917; I-22, Duffy to Farley, December 21, 1917, I-24, Duffy to Farley, February 24, 1918,

4 - ACUA, NCWC, CSWA, Report of John C. Agar, April 2, 1918,

5 - ACUA, NCWC, CSWA, Report to Cardinal Farley, May 1918.

The success of the fund-raising drive was also due to the wave of wartime patriotism that swept across the country. Father Henry O'Carroll, the pastor of St. Patrick's Church in Newburgh, gave the credit for the successful collection in his parish to a layman who spoke at all the Masses on the Sunday that the drive began. "I shall never forget the opening remarks with which he addressed the congregation," said O'Carroll. "He said that the world was divided into two classes, the good people and the Prussians. That Sunday we took over the Communion rail over $857." In one parish a wealthy woman told the pastor that she would write a check for the entire parish assessment before he could even tell her the amount. The Church of St. Ignatius Loyola was assessed $50,000 and collected $144,000.

Well-timed press releases also helped to heighten interest in the campaign, and to pry open wallets and purses. Father Peter Spellman, the pastor of St. John's Church in West Hurley, was said to be "living on chickens" in order to devote more of his income to the war effort. Father John M.J. Quinn ("God Almighty Quinn," as he was called by his clerical confreres), a curate at St. Patrick's Cathedral, told a story that would have melted hearts left unmoved by the death of Little Nell. One Saturday night after confessions, one little lad asked how close they were to their goal of $150,000. When informed that they had raised only $144,000, he handed Quinn a nickel "to help reach the mark."[6]

"Orphans and Pigs Fed from the Same Bowl"

For the better part of 1916 and 1917 New York Catholics were caught up in a bitter and highly publicized controversy over the quality of the care provided by the city's private child-caring institutions. It began in 1914 when Mayor John Purroy Mitchel appointed an advisory committee headed by John A. Kingsbury, the Commissioner of Public Charities, to investigate the city's private charitable institutions. The Kingsbury Committee criticized conditions in twenty-six of the thirty-eight institutions and also criticized the State Board of Charities for lax supervision of the institutions. As a result of these allegations Governor Charles S. Whitman set up a state investigative commission headed by Charles A. Strong.

The Strong Commission conducted public hearings in New York City from January 23 to April 24, 1916. A parade of witnesses told horror stories about unsafe and inhumane conditions in the private institutions that were sensationalized by the press. One of the most famous stories (which was later demonstrated to be untrue) was that at the Mission of the Immaculate Virgin on Staten Island the pigs at the farm were fed from the same pails as the children. "Orphans and Pigs Fed from the Same Bowl," was the inevitable headline in the newspapers the next day.

The hearings of the Strong Commission were welcomed by many secular social reformers and organizations like the State Charities Aid Association, which had long been opposed to state subsidies for religious institutions. Catholics suspected that the purpose of Mayor Mitchel, Commissioner Kingsbury, and the Strong Commission was to discredit the Catholic charitable institutions and pave the way for the end of state subsidies to them. Child care was a sensitive issue for Catholics in New York. They had long memories of the "placing-out" system of the Children's Aid Society and the effort to prohibit state funds for religious charitable institutions at the state Constitutional Convention in 1894. Some of the proponents of that proposal were the most ardent supporters of the Strong Commission.

6 - ACUA, NCWC, CSWA, Report of Zone Directors, April; 2, 1918.

The controversy escalated in February 1916 when a priest of the diocese of Brooklyn, Father William B. Farrell, publicly accused the Strong Commission of anti-Catholic bias in an open letter to the governor. The State Charities Aid Association came to the defense of the Strong Commission with an anonymous pamphlet that was a compilation of the more lurid newspaper stories. Farrell responded in March with three strongly worded pamphlets repeating his accusations of anti-Catholic bias on the part of the Strong Commission. Monsignor John J. Dunn, the chancellor of the archdiocese of New York, printed 750,000 copies of Farrell's first pamphlet, *A Public Scandal,* and distributed them outside every Catholic church in Manhattan on Sunday, March 5, 1916. They had a major impact in mobilizing Catholic public opinion. However, the tone of the pamphlets was so caustic and vituperative that Father Joseph McMahon thought they actually hurt the Catholic cause.[7]

In April the controversy took another unexpected twist when Alfred J. Talley, Monsignor Dunn's lawyer, accused the New York Police Department of tapping the phones of Dunn, Farrell and several other people. The wiretapping issue now became the focus of the controversy, especially in the press, because it was a relatively new law enforcement technique, and the Police Department appeared to have been done it illegally to feed information to the Strong Commission. On May 23, 1916, a King's County grand jury indicted Commissioner Kingsbury and his legal counsel, William Hotchkiss, for breaking the wiretapping law. According to Talley, the grand jury came within one vote of indicting Mayor Mitchel as well.

That same day Mitchell caused a sensation when he appeared before the Thompson Com-

A cartoonist's dim view of the wiretapping activities of Mayor Mitchel.
Credit: *New York American, May 23, 1916*

mittee, a committee established by the state legislature to investigate the wiretapping issue. In a wild tirade the mayor accused the Catholic Church of organizing a conspiracy against him and his administration. "We hold that the government shall not lay its hands on the sacred altar of the Church and that conversely the Church must not lay its hands on the sacred altar of the government," he declared. "And, gentlemen," he added, "as long as I am mayor of this city, it never shall..."[8]

In July Dunn, Farrell and two laymen, Daniel C. Potter and Robert H. Hebberd, were indicted for trying to prevent witnesses from appearing before the Strong Commission. Their trial provided hilarious copy for the newspapers

7 - AANY, 0-3, McMahon to Hayes, April 14, 1916, cit. in Neil A. Kelly, " 'Orphans and Pigs Fed from the Same Bowl': Catholics and the New York Charities Controversy of 1916," M.A. thesis, St. Joseph's Seminary, Dunwoodie, 1991, 42-43. I have relied heavily on Father Kelly's thesis for his lucid, balanced and well-documented account of the controversy.

8 - The next day Mitchel modified his outburst by saying: "It is not the Catholic Church that has so conspired to pervert justice and obstruct or control government, but a small group within the Church cooperating with a few non-Catholic laymen." Kelly, "Pigs and Orphans," 65-66.

because the evidence against them was based largely on the mangled transcripts of the wiretaps made by the police. One transcript had someone saying, "He is out with his ambulance" instead of "He is out with His Eminence." The counsel for Thompson Committee said that "on such evidence no sane person would condemn a yellow dog." One distraught police wiretapper attempted to commit suicide. On the witness stand Monsignor Dunn claimed that he suspected that the police were tapping his telephone and deliberately made provocative statements to induce them to reveal their illegal activities.

The Protestant and secular press generally supported Mitchel and faulted Catholics for raising the religious issue as a red herring to distract attention from the criticism of their institutions. A Citizens' Committee of 100 issued a statement strongly supporting the mayor and insinuating that Farrell and Dunn did not represent the views of most Catholics. They were answered by William D. Guthrie, a prominent lawyer, acting on behalf of a Committee of Catholic Laymen. In a written statement, Guthrie said: "We are not living in an age when Catholics or members of any other church may not freely challenge and refute slanders calculated to destroy all trust and confidence in the management, integrity, decency and humanity of their charitable institutions."[9]

All of the defendants in the case were acquitted, Kingsbury and Hotchkiss as well as Dunn, Farrell, Hebberd, and Potter (who died during the course of the trial). Dunn actually emerged as a winner. Patrick Hayes, the auxiliary bishop who handled the controversy for the ailing Cardinal Farley, was so impressed with Dunn's verbal dexterity in dodging accusations of perjury on the witness stand that he made him a key figure and an auxiliary bishop in his own administration.

The big loser was Mayor Mitchel. When he ran for reelection in 1917, he went down to defeat at the hands of angry Catholic voters who thought that he had tried to sabotage their child-caring institutions. Mitchel then volunteered for service as a pilot in World War I. While in training, however, he suffered a fatal mishap on July 6, 1918, when he fell out of his biplane and became the first New Yorker to die for neglecting to fasten his seatbelt.

The conclusion that Bishop Hayes drew from the controversy was the need for Catholics in New York to coordinate their charitable activities and to have their institutions and agencies adopt modern professional standards of accountability. He would make that task his first and highest priority as the archbishop of New York, earning for himself the title of the Cardinal of Charities.

Patrick Cardinal Hayes

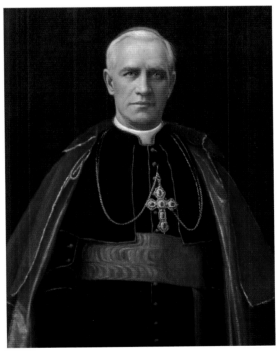

Patrick Cardinal Hayes,
Archbishop of New York, 1919-1938.
Credit: *Archdiocese of New York*

9 - *New York Catholic News,* July 29, 1916, cit. in Kelly, "Pigs and Orphans," 81.

Patrick Hayes was the first native of Manhattan to become the archbishop of New York. He was born on the Lower East Side on November 20, 1867, to Daniel and Mary Gleason Hayes, both of whom were immigrants from Killarney. St. Andrew's Church now occupies the site of the house where he was born. His mother died was he was four and he was raised by a maternal aunt and her husband, Ellen and James Egan. He was a "Brothers' Boy," educated by the Christian Brothers at De La Salle Institute and Manhattan College where one of his contemporaries was George Mundelein, the future cardinal archbishop of Chicago.

He entered the seminary at Troy in 1888 and was sent to the Catholic University of America for further studies before he finished his seminary coursework. Ordained ahead of his class by Archbishop Corrigan on September 8, 1892, he spent two additional years at the Catholic University before returning to New York as a curate at St. Gabriel's Church on East 37th Street. At St. Gabriel's he won the confidence of the pastor, Monsignor John Murphy Farley, who was responsible for Hayes' rapid ascent up the ladder of ecclesiastical preferment. He became Farley's secretary when Farley was made an auxiliary bishop in 1895, and moved with him to the cathedral after Farley became the archbishop in 1902.

During the Farley administration Hayes served as both the chancellor and the president of Cathedral College. On October 28, 1914, he was ordained titular bishop of Tagaste and auxiliary to Cardinal Farley. The following July he became the pastor of St. Stephen's Church, ending twenty-one years of living under the same roof as Farley. During Farley's last years, as he grew increasingly feeble, he relied heavily upon Hayes, especially during the charities controversy of 1916-1917. As was mentioned already, during World War I Hayes was given national responsibilities as the military vicar for the armed forces and as one of the four bishops on the administrative board of the National Catholic War Council.

When Cardinal Farley died of pneumonia on September 17, 1918, Hayes' long involvement in the administration of the diocese made him the logical choice as Farley's successor. He was appointed the archbishop of New York on March 10, 1919, and was made a cardinal five years later, on March 24, 1924.

Patrick Joseph Hayes was born and raised in more humble circumstances than any other American-born archbishop of New York. Even more than John Hughes, he never forgot his origins. His personal experience of poverty as a youth gave him an appreciation for the plight of the poor that was totally different from that of Archbishop Corrigan who was raised in middle-class comfort. Hayes' attitude to the poor was also shaped by his father and uncle, who were both active members of the St. Vincent de Paul Society. He himself served as the archdiocesan spiritual director of the Society when he was the pastor of St. Stephen's Church.

Hayes had an opportunity to demonstrate his commitment not only to poor relief, but also to social reform shortly after becoming the archbishop of New York. As one of the four members of the administrative board of the National Catholic War Council, he signed the famous *Bishops' Program of Social Reconstruction*, written by Father John A. Ryan and issued in the name of the American hierarchy. It was a remarkably progressive document calling for such innovations as a federal minimum wage, social security, subsidized housing, equal pay for women and a host of other social reforms that were to be enacted fifteen years later as part of the New Deal.

The recommendations of the *Bishops' Program* scared many conservative American businessmen who thought that they reeked of socialism. One of them was Nicholas Brady, a Wall Street banker and generous benefactor of the archdiocese and the Society of Jesus, who protested to Hayes that the bishops were undermining the "sane individualism" that was the basis of American democracy. Hayes did not attempt to rebut Brady's objections, but neither did he repudiate any of the bishops' proposals. Instead he defended the document as "a masterly bit of strategy." He pointed out to Brady that "we now are able to talk to our own people as we were not able [to do] before we manifested an interest in their problems."[10]

Hayes was a distinguished-looking man of less than medium height whose paternal visage, snow-white hair and mellifluous voice (which was rarely heard from the pulpit of St. Patrick's Cathedral) fulfilled American expectations of a Catholic prelate as did his flawless celebration of the intricate Tridentine pontifical liturgy. He was a shy and kindly person who avoided the limelight and turned down most invitations to civic functions. However, Henry Browne noted that "observers

Monsignor John A. Ryan, the author of the Bishops' Program for Social Reconstruction

sometimes missed the angle of his jutting jaw which betrayed another aspect of his personality."

Although he carefully abstained from involvement in American politics, especially during the presidential campaign of 1928, Hayes made no secret of his preferences in Irish politics. When one New York priest expressed fear that Hayes was waffling in his support Eamon DeValera, the President of the Irish Free State, because of the influence of Judge Cohalan, Hayes assured him that the opposite was true. "I became the friend and supporter of Mr. DeValera the first hour that I spoke to him on his arrival in America," he said. "Nothing has happened to change my opinion or confidence in him since that day. Nobody will ever be able to change me except Mr. DeValera himself."[11]

Cardinal Mercier, the Archbishop of Malines, Belgium, and World War I hero, with Archbishop Hayes in New York City on September 18, 1919.
Credit: *Archdiocese of New York*

---

10 - AANY, O-5, Brady to Hayes, March 29, 1919; Hayes to Brady, April 4, 1919.

11 - AANY, Q-6, Hayes to James Power, November 9, 1931.

The Formation of Catholic Charities

Stung by the charities controversy of 1916-1917 Hayes was determined to rationalize and modernize Catholic charitable work in the archdiocese. The underlying difficulty was the lack of uniform standards of accountability in an age when poor relief was undergoing a major transformation from volunteer charitable work to professional social service. Hayes recognized the need for the archdiocese to adopt rigorous professional standards for its own charitable activities if it hoped to continue to receive government funding for them. The stakes were high, since New York had the highest concentration of poor and needy Catholics in the United States.

Hayes set his own example of professionalism by turning to the Catholic University of America and the National Catholic War Council for help. He enlisted the services of Dr. John H. Lapp of the N.C.W.C. to conduct a survey of the 175 Catholic charitable activities in the archdiocese, including 26 hospitals, 20 child-caring institutions, 24 day nurseries and 5 homes for the aged. Lapp had at his disposal a team of 42 paid professional workers to conduct the survey. He was also assisted by two young priests, Father Robert F. Keegan and Father Bryan J. McEntegart. Both had studied at the Catholic Unviersity under the direction of Father William J. Kerby and at the New York School of Social Service.

Monsignor Robert F. Keegan, the Executive Director of Catholic Charities, 1920-1947

The reception for Archbishop Daniel Mannix of Melbourne, Australia, when he was granted the Freedom of the City on July 19, 1920. Left to right: Father Francis P. Duffy, Archbishop Patrick J. Hayes, Mayor John F. Hylan, and Archbishop Mannix.
Credit: *Archdiocese of New York*

The survey produced by Dr. Lapp in February 1920 revealed numerous instances of underfunding of institutions as well as overlapping and duplication of services by various agencies. It also revealed that Catholics were far more generous in supporting their charities than anyone had suspected. They contributed $4.4 million annually, almost twice as much as the government subsidies.

The Catholic Charities of the Archdiocese of New York was incorporated on June 12, 1920, to act as a central coordinating and supervising agency for the Catholic charitable network in the archdiocese. Another innovation introduced by Archbishop Hayes was a fund-raising drive conducted in every parish on the model of the New York Catholic War Fund campaign of 1918. Originally intended to last only three years, the first Catholic Charities collections were so successful that they became an annual event.

To head the new Catholic Charities organization, Archbishop Hayes selected Father Robert F. Keegan, whom he had known as a student in Cathedral College. Keegan was ordained only three years when he was placed in charge of this vast operation in 1920 and continued to operate it until his death in 1947. He made it a model for other dioceses and earned the respect of social welfare administrators throughout the nation. He himself was elected the president of the prestigious National Conference of Social Work in 1936. At the time of Keegan's death, one official of that organization said: "Under the auspices of his diocese, [Keegan] developed the social work program of Catholic Charities until its standards were second to none in that city."

In the 1930s Monsignor Keegan was an outspoken supporter of the New Deal. He also a notably imperious and irascible character whose rages were legendary. One of his assistants,

President Franklin D. Roosevelt at the Catholic University of America in 1933 on the occasion of receiving an honorary doctorate. Left to right: President Roosevelt, Mrs Eleanor Roosevelt, Cardinal Hayes, Archbishop Michael Curley of Baltimore, Archbishop Ameleto Cicognani, the Apostolic Delegate, and Monsignor James Hugh Ryan, the president of the University..
Credit: *Archdiocese of New York*

Father E. Roberts Moore, said that when Keegan lost his temper, which was a daily if not hourly occurrence, "all the neighbors and the neighbors' children took to the bomb shelters." Each morning when Keegan left Blessed Sacrament rectory on west 71st Street (where he was the pastor) for the Catholic Charities Office on East 22nd Street, the sole elevator in the office building was held at the ground floor until his arrival.[12]

Hard Times on Valentine Hill

Although Hayes did a splendid job of organizing Catholic Charities, his penny-pinching economies at Dunwoodie brought the seminary to the one of the lowest points in its history. The chancellor, Monsignor Dunn, convinced Hayes that the seminary budget had to be cut. "If the bills continue this way," he told Hayes in 1919, "we will go broke."

Hayes' solution was to appoint a new procurator to oversee the finances, Father John J. Donovan, a close friend of both Dunn and himself. Hayes assured the rector, Monsignor John D. Chidwick, that Donovan's appointment was only temporary, but Donovan remained at Dunwoodie for the next twenty-one years, overshadowing three rectors and exercising greater influence than any of them because he enjoyed the confidence of Hayes. From the day of his arrival at Dunwoodie, Donovan came into conflict with Chidwick.[13]

Fifty-six years old in 1919, Chidwick was almost twice Donovan's age and already had an eventful career behind him. Twenty-one years earlier, as the chaplain on the U.S.S. *Maine,* when it exploded in Havana harbor, Chidwick had become the first hero of the Spanish-American War because of his care for the dead and wounded. "You have set an example for the emulation of every chaplain in the navy," John D. Long, the Secretary of the Navy, told him.[14]

Chidwick was extremely diffident and deferential to his ecclesiastical superiors, but he was neither fawning nor subservient (as Hayes soon discovered). Nor was he a man to back away from a fight when he believed that a matter of principle was at stake. On one occasion when Chidwick was the chaplain aboard the U.S.S. *Newark,* an enlisted man made an insulting remark to him in the presence of a large number of sailors. He told the man to see him after breakfast, then appeared with two pairs of boxing gloves and handed him one pair, whereupon the man backed down and apologized. One tough old chief petty officer said of Chidwick: "He was one of the gamest little men I ever met. He was always getting someone out of the brig. He would come along on Sunday morning and wake the men to go to Mass. They would fight to a man for him."[15]

For ten years as the rector of Dunwoodie under Farley, Chidwick had obediently presided over the intellectual emasculation of the institution because he believed that it was his duty to do so. However, when Donovan embarked upon a draconian cost-cutting program, Chidwick reacted altogether differently. He protested strongly and repeatedly to Hayes because he saw Donovan's actions as both a challenge to his own authority as rector and also as a threat to the health and welfare of the students for whom he was responsible.

The rancid food and the lack of heat led to serious health problems among the students during the winter of 1921. "The habitable condition of the seminary has been for the majority of the seminarians unbearable,"

12 - There is no biography of Keegan, but see *DHGE,* 18: 1134-1135.

13 - AANY, O-5, Dunn to Hayes, June 27, October 31, 1919.

14 - AANY, I-43, Long to Chidwick, April 9, 1898,

15 - AANY, Chief Petty Office William Degnan to Hayes, January 15, 1935.

The most photogenic of the archbishops of New York, Cardinal Hayes waits to disembark upon his return from the consistory of 1924.

Credit: *Archdiocese of New York*

Cardinal Mundelein with Cardinal Hayes, probably leaving for the consistory of 1924 at which they received the Red Hat. In the rear is Bishop John J. Dunn, the vicar general.

Credit: *Archdiocese of New York*

Cardinal Hayes walking up Fifth Avenue after his return from the consistory of 1924.

Credit: *Archdiocese of New York*

Full Steam Ahead

Chidwick reported to the vicar general. He went to the boiler room himself one day, picked up a handful of coal and discovered that it was mostly dirt and dust. "It is rotten," the fireman told him, "and no heat can be obtained from it." "Does not one assume a tremendous responsibility when he experiments with the health of young men, especially those who are studying for the priesthood?' Chidwick asked Hayes.[16]

On New Year's Day in 1922 Chidwick resigned in disgust after his repeated complaints to Hayes went unanswered. Hayes accepted the resignation at the end of the academic year and made him the pastor of St. Agnes Church on East 43rd Street. Donovan remained at Dunwoodie for another eighteen years, fine tuning his spartan regime with the full approval of Hayes.

Despite the deplorable living conditions, the enrollment at Dunwoodie hit an all-time high of 303 students in September 1932. The rector, Msgr. Arthur J. Scanlan (who had been appointed in 1930 despite the unanimous opposition of the diocesan consultors), devoted one section of his annual report to "The Present Problem of Increased Vocations." Thereupon a deliberate decision was made to reduce the numbers for two reasons.

First, Dunwoodie was not physically equipped to accommodate 300 students. "Dunwoodie might well be compared to sardines in a rush-hour subway," said Scanlan. Secondly, said Scanlan, "It is felt that the number of vocations is far in excess of the ability of the diocese to absorb them." He recommended accepting no more than forty new applicants each year instead of the customary sixty. Hayes accepted Scanlan's proposal with the result that by 1939 the enrollment had been reduced by almost one-third to 209 students.[17]

Rear Admiral Sigsbee, U.S.N., former captain of the U.S.S. Maine, *and Monsignor John Chidwick at the annual* Maine *Memorial ceremony in New York City on May 30, 1919.*
Credit: *Archdiocese of New York*

The Tribal Twenties

After World War I the United States retreated from the world scene, refusing to join the League of Nations. Isolationism in foreign policy was matched by nostalgia at home for "normalcy," a hankering for a simpler past that had never really existed, a mythical, self-reliant America of small towns and family farms untroubled by class or racial conflict. This romanticized vision of the past had an ugly side to it, however, for its model was a white Protestant America with little room for Catholics, Jews or African Americans. In fact all members of religious or racial minorities were likely to be lumped together with the anarchists who exploded a bomb in Wall Street or the alleged Bolsheviks whom Attorney General A. Mitchell Palmer dispatched to Russia with much fanfare in the fall of 1919.

16 - AANY, AANY, P-17, Chidwick to Lavelle, February 29, 1921; Chidwick to Hayes, n.d.
17 - ASJSD, Scanlan, Annual Reports, 1933-1939.

446

In short the Roaring Twenties were not only the decade of the flapper and the flivver, but also the occasion for one of America's periodic outbursts of xenophobia. John Higham, the historian of American nativism, called it the Tribal Twenties. One manifestation was the restrictive immigration laws of 1921 and 1924, which imposed a quota on immigration from southern and eastern Europe to keep out Italians, Greeks, Poles, Russian Jews, and other "undesirables." "Refuse the refuse" was a popular redneck slogan. In New York the impact of the immigration laws was noticeable by the end of the decade in the declining number of new parishioners in the Italian national parishes of the archdiocese.

Another manifestation of the neo-Nativism of the 1920s was the Oregon School Law of 1922, which required parents to send their children to public schools. It was the result of a well-orchestrated campaign by the Masons and reflected neo-Nativist fears that only the public schools could make good citizens of the children of immigrants. The implications were obvious for the future of Catholic schools throughout the country, and the National Catholic Welfare Conference under the leadership of Father John J. Burke and Father James Hugh Ryan challenged the constitutionality of the law all the way to the U.S. Supreme Court.

The chief counsel for the NCWC before the Supreme Court was William D. Guthrie, a prominent New York lawyer, an outstanding Catholic layman, and a Horatio Alger hero if there ever was one. Born in San Francisco in 1859, Guthrie came to New York as a teenager where he worked as a messenger in a law firm for $5.00 a week. In 1879 he enrolled in Columbia Law School (although he had never attended college), graduated in one year, and four years later became a partner in the law firm where he had been a messenger boy. From 1902 to 1922 he was professor of constitutional law at Columbia University.

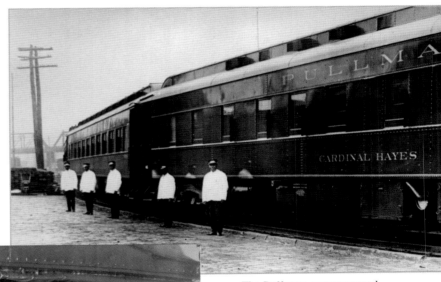

The Pullman car renamed for Cardinal Hayes on the "Red Train".
Credit: *Archdiocese of New York*

The European cardinals and bishops on the "Red Train" that took them from New York to the International Eucharistic Congress in Chicago in 1926.
Credit: *Archdiocese of New York*

Cardinal Hayes seems a bit overdressed on a visit to Mangrove Island in the Bahamas c. 1937. From 1886 until 1929 the Bahamas were under the jurisdiction of the Archdiocese of New York.
Credit: *Archdiocese of New York*

The Supreme Court decided the case on June 1, 1925. In a unanimous decision the justices upheld the earlier decision of a federal district court declaring the Oregon Compulsory School Law unconstitutional. Justice McReynolds in delivering the decision of the court, declared: "The child is not the mere creature of the state." Louis Marshall, a New York attorney who had written the amicus curiae brief for the American Jewish Commmittee, told John Burke: "I do not think that the importance of this decision can be exaggerated. It will prove a landmark in our constitutional history." He was correct. Never again has there been a serious legal challenge to the existence of private or parochial schools in the United States.[18]

Still another example of the temper of the times was the Eighteenth Amendment, prohibiting the manufacture or sale of alcoholic beverages. It became the law of the land on January 16, 1920, with the passage of the Volstead Act over the veto of President Wilson. While the temperance movement had deep roots in American history among both Protestants and Catholics, in the 1920s the focus shifted to a crusade of rural Protestant America against the vices of the alien populations in the big cities. Sydney Ahlstrom called it "the great Protestant crusade of the twentieth century." The Baptist and Methodist churches were especially active in promoting Prohibition through the efforts of the Women's Christian Temperance Union and the Anti-Saloon League.

It was the misfortune of Yonkers "wets" that their city happened to be the home of William H. ("Pussyfoot") Anderson, the state superintendent of the Anti-Saloon League and a fanatical enemy of Demon Rum. In the spring of 1920 Anderson declared that the "officiary [sic] of the Roman Catholic Church in this state are indignant over what they consider to be a Protestant victory for Prohibition... and are in sympathy with the Tammany efforts to destroy that victory and bring back the saloon for purposes respecting which your guess is as good as mine." Cardinal Hayes rarely issued any statement on public affairs,

18 - Thomas J. Shelley, "The Oregon School Case and the National Catholic Welfare Conference," *CHR* 75 (1989): 439-457.

but he made an exception in the case of Anderson. He denounced him with uncharacteristic vehemence and perhaps unintended humor as "a sinister figure in American politics, a sower of strife [and] a brewer of bigotry."[19]

Unfortunately Hayes' criticism gave Anderson the publicity that he craved. He thereupon attacked both Archbishop Hayes and the venerable Cardinal Gibbons, vowing to keep up the fight until "it is finished in terms that are in harmony with Americanism." One amused observer was Archbishop George J. Mundelein of Chicago, an old friend of Hayes from Manhattan College, who assured him that Anderson "has certainly not dimmed your popularity and is more likely to make you a national hero than to rally straying Protestants about him as he hoped." "One thing you can be sure of," Mundelein told Hayes, "my money is placed on you."[20] It was a prudent wager. In January 1924 Anderson was indicted on charges of grand larceny, fraud and extortion and sentenced to one-to-two years in Sing Sing. He claimed that he had been framed by a "wet" jury.[21]

A few years later employees of the Yonkers Public Works Department discovered a mysterious four-inch wide hose that ran for a distance of a mile through the city's sewers from an old brewery to a garage. The brewery was licensed to produce "near beer," but perhaps for as long as three years it had been sending a steady stream of real beer through the hose line in the sewer to the garage where it was distributed to retailers. The beer hose made the second city of the archdiocese nationally famous or notorious, depending on one's point of view. The city officials all expressed shock and chagrin. A professor of physics at New York University pronounced the

hose line "the outstanding engineering feat" in the history of Prohibition. Neither the reaction of "Pussyfoot" Anderson nor that of Cardinal Hayes has been preserved for posterity.

While the efforts to enforce the Volstead Act had its humorous moments, there was nothing humorous about the prominence of the Ku Klux Klan in many parts of the country by the mid-1920s. Hooded Klansmen even paraded through the streets of the nation's capital. Although the Klan was anti-black and anti-Jewish, its venom was especially directed against Catholics. The Klan had little influence in New York City, but in some upstate villages like Livingston Manor there were instances of cross burnings intended to intimidate local Catholics. Even in New York City, at the Democratic convention in Madison Square Garden in 1924, the delegates refused to pass a resolution condemning the Klan.

A Catholic Runs for President

The anti-Catholic bigotry of the Tribal Twenties culminated in the presidential election of 1928 when the Democrats nominated Governor Alfred E. Smith for the White House. A year earlier, when it became likely that Smith would be the Democratic candidate, an open letter appeared in the *Atlantic Monthly* that threatened to derail his bid for the presidency before it ever got started. The author was Charles C. Marshall, a constitutional lawyer and Episcopalian layman, who claimed that no conscientious Catholic could discharge the duties of the President of the United States because his Church required him to place church teaching above the constitution of the United States. He based this claim primarily on certain encyclicals of Pius IX and Leo XIII.[22]

---

19 - Yonkers *Statesman,* January 16, 1920; *New York Times,* March 6, 9, 1920.

20 - AANY, U-25, Mundelein to Hayes,. March 6, 1920.

21 - *New York Times,* January 31, 1924.

22 - Charles C. Marshall, "An Open Letter to the Honorable Alfred E. Smith," *Atlantic Monthly* 139 (April 1927): 540-549.

When the article was first brought to the attention of Smith, he is supposed to have said: "What the hell is an encyclical?" Although he was a highly intelligent man who had taught himself the intricacies of the legislative process in Albany, he had no background in theology. Therefore, he asked a trusted aide, Judge Joseph M. Proskauer, to reply to Marshall's open letter. "Well," replied Proskauer, "that would make it perfect. A Protestant lawyer challenges a Catholic candidate on his religion, and the challenger is answered by a Jewish judge."

On the Boardwalk in Atlantic City in 1916: Alfred E. Smith and Tammany Leader Charles F. Murphy.

Smith finally agreed to write a response, but he asked Proskauer to help him compose it. "But I need help too," Proskauer said. "I need the help of a Catholic priest, and it isn't just any Catholic priest who will do. I want one with a record of Americanism and patriotism that no person in the world can possibly question." At this point Smith and Proskauer agreed to enlist the services of the Father Francis P. Duffy.[23]

Duffy was now the pastor of Holy Cross Church on West 42nd Street. Because of his record in World War I, he was the best known Catholic priest in New York City, almost as popular with Protestants and Jews as with Catholics. His parish included both the theatre district and a swath of Hell's Kitchen. Duffy was at home in both worlds, moving effortlessly between the literati and the longshoremen. Alexander Wolcott, who first met Duffy as a war correspondent in France, said that when Duffy "walked down the street---any street---he was a *curé* striding through his own village. Father Duffy was of such dimensions that he made New York into a small town."

Al Smith and Judge Proskauer knew that in Duffy they were getting a proven patriot and a popular hero. They may not have realized, however, that they were also getting a theologian who welcomed the opportunity not only to respond to critics like Charles Marshall, but also to those Catholics who anachronistic theological opinions gave credibility to Marshall's accusations of Catholic intolerance. Duffy and Proskauer worked together on the draft of Smith's reply and then Smith revised it in his own inimitable way. The ideas were Duffy's, but the words were Smith's.

Proskauer then suggested that they should submit the text to Cardinal Hayes for his approval. Proskauer was impressed with Hayes' reaction. "I would give almost anything to see Al Smith President of the United States," Hayes said, "but I can take no part in a political campaign." He made clear that the only question he would answer was whether Smith's statement contained anything contrary to Catholic teaching. Proskauer agreed. The cardinal read it carefully and pronounced it "good Catholicism and good Americanism."[24]

23 - Emily Smith Warner with Hawthorne Daniel, *The Happy Warrior: The Story of My Father, Alfred E. Smith* (Garden City: Doubleday, 1956), 182.

24 - Joseph Proskauer, *A Segment of My Times* (New York: Farrar, Straus and Company, 1950), 56.

The birthplace of Al Smith at 174 South Street beneath the Brooklyn Bridge.

Smith's response to Marshall appeared in the next issue of the *Atlantic Monthly,* and it was an instant success. Marshall had adopted the tone of a prosecuting attorney. Smith wrote with the ingenuousness of a decent man whose most cherished beliefs had been unfairly assailed. He also knew how to turn his personal limitations into assets. "So little are these matters of the essence of my faith," he told Marshall, "that I, a devout Catholic since childhood, never heard of them until I read your letter." He also mentioned that he had turned to Father Duffy for advice on theological matters.[25]

As to Marshall's contention that Catholics were committed to the union of church and state, Smith could hardly deny that this was the ideal enshrined in papal encyclicals, but he claimed that it applied only to purely Catholic states and that such states no longer existed anywhere in the world. He quoted Archbishop Austin Dowling of St. Paul who had said a short time earlier that this traditional Catholic church-state theory "may well be relegated to the limbo of defunct controversies." "I think that you have taken your

thesis from this limbo of defunct controversies," Smith told Marshall.

Marshall also contended that Catholics must always side with the Church in the case of church-state conflict. Smith replied that the teaching of the Catholic Church was no different from that of Marshall's own Episcopal Church which stated in the Thirty-Nine Articles that Christians "must render unto Caesar the things that are Caesar's and unto God the things that are God's." He quoted Archbishop John Ireland who once said that, if the pope should interfere in civil or political matters, American Catholics would respond by telling him: "Back to your sphere of rights and duties, back to the things of God."

The *pièce de résistance* was Smith's penultimate paragraph. In nine short crisp sentences Smith summarized his creed as an American Catholic. Unlike John F. Kennedy thirty years later, who tried to privatize his religion and minimize the influence that it would have in shaping his political decisions, Al Smith gloried in his religion and boldly asserted his belief in "the faith and practices of the Roman Catholic Church." At the same time he declared his commitment to "absolute freedom of conscience for all men" and "the absolute separation of Church and State."

Al Smith's response to Marshall was an unqualified triumph for Smith (and for Duffy). Throughout the country editorial opinion was overwhelmingly favorable to Smith, even in the Deep South where suspicion of his religion was the strongest. One Episcopalian clergyman told Marshall: "I am quite sure that you are going to go down in history as the man who elected Al." There was so much speculation that Marshall had written his open letter in collusion with Smith that he got the *Atlantic Monthly* to publish a one-paragraph disclaimer from him.[26]

25 - "Catholic and Patriot" Governor Smith Replies," *Atlantic Monthly* 139 (May 1927): 721-728.

26 - LC, Manuscript Division, Marshall Papers, Joseph Barry to Marshall, April 20, 1927..

Photos like this scared millions of Protestants all across America in the 1920s. Left to right: Papal Marquis George MacDonald, Cardinal Hayes, Governor Alfred E. Smith, and Judge Alfred Tally.
Credit: *Archdiocese of New York*

Duffy minimized his own contribution to Smith's reply, but he obviously furnished the theological arguments as Smith himself admitted. Duffy used essentially the same approach that Father John Courtney Murray, S.J., would take thirty years later when he claimed that there had been a development of doctrine in papal teaching on church-state relations. "It seems to me," Duffy told Frederic R. Coudert, "that Mr. Marshall's trouble lies in the fact that he is himself a thirteenth-century theologian, and cannot conceive that a twentieth-century theologian can possibly be right." Duffy denied any intention of soft-pedaling Catholic teaching, but he revealed his own personal involvement in the issue when he said, "I have held very ardent convictions on these matters since I was nineteen years of age, and it was a matter of keen joy to me to take advantage of Governor Smith's prestige to win a victory over the opposing Catholic school of thought."

Duffy faulted Marshall for failing to recognize what a later age would call theological pluralism. "Mr. Marshall cannot be made to see," Duffy complained, "that there can be in the Catholic Church various schools of thought. He cannot deny that the hierarchy of America is opposed to the union of Church and State, and with an intolerance greater than he could attribute to a pope, he would read them all out of the Church. But he cannot. We are Catholics and we are Americans, and to both loyalties we stick."[27]

Unknown to Marshall, and perhaps even to Smith and Duffy, Cardinal Hayes sent a copy of Governor Smith's response to Cardinal John Bonzano, the former apostolic delegate to the United States, now a curial cardinal in Rome. Bonzano told Hayes that Smith's response was a *capo lavoro* ("a masterpiece"), and that it was judged such by everybody here who knows conditions in America."[28]

---

27 - LC, Marshall Papers, Duffy to Coudert, June 3, 1927, copy.
28 - AANY, Q-17, Bonzano to Hayes, July 4, 1927.

Even if Charles Marshall had seen Cardinal Bonzano's letter to Hayes, it is unlikely that it would have satisfied him. He insisted that Al Smith and Father Duffy were only speaking for themselves, not for the Catholic Church. He stoutly maintained that he would not believe that the Catholic Church had come to accept the principle of religious liberty unless the Vatican Council of 1869-1870 was reconvened and issued such a declaration. Marshall did not live to see it, but that is what happened when Vatican Council II issued the Declaration on Religious Liberty.

Al Smith won the debate with Charles Marshall in 1927, but he lost the election to Herbert Hoover the following year. The campaign produced a wave of anti-Catholic bigotry that deeply distressed Smith, who did not have a bigoted bone in his body. In rural Georgia photographs were distributed of Smith at the dedication of the Holland Tunnel the year before with the explanation that it was a tunnel to Rome that the pope would use to come to America after Smith was safely installed in the White House.[29]

Religion was not the only factor, perhaps not even the decisive factor, in Al Smith's defeat, but the venom of the anti-Catholic bigotry left many American Catholics disappointed that they had still had not achieved full acceptance from many of their fellow citizens. Nonetheless, they still preserved their sense of humor and enjoyed the story that Al Smith had sent a one-word telegram to the pope on election night. It said: "Unpack."

The Great Depression

The Great Depression had a devastating impact on New York City. By 1932 a third of the city's factories had closed, a quarter of the population was unemployed, and the municipal debt amounted to almost two billion dollars. The magnitude of the crisis exhausted the resources of private charity, necessitating unprecedented government assistance. Cardinal Hayes never publicly endorsed the New Deal legislation of President Franklin D. Roosevelt, but neither did he join the chorus of the President's conservative critics. As far back as 1919, he had signaled his support for social reform when he had signed the *Bishops' Program for Social Reconstruction*.

During the 1930s Hayes remained as cautiously aloof from partisan politics as he had been during the presidential campaign of 1928. Nonetheless, he gave his full support to Monsignor Robert Keegan, an admirer of Roosevelt, who declared in 1933 that "economic forces must be subjected to the law of social justice and industrial life so directed as to promote the welfare of all the people." At the same time Hayes indicated his disapproval of Father Charles Coughlin, the demagogic radio priest, through an article that appeared in a prominent clerical periodical, *The Ecclesiastical Review*. The author, Father Edward Dargin, a New York priest, accused Coughlin of violating canon law by his political activities.

It was in the midst of the Great Depression that the liturgical renewal movement made its first hesitant appearance in the less than welcoming atmosphere of the archdiocese of New York. At Corpus Christi Church in Morningside Heights, the pastor, Father George Barry Ford, introduced an embryonic form of popular participation with the "dialogue Mass." In its early formative years the liturgical renewal movement often went hand in hand with a concern for social justice.

The New York priest who best epitomized that tradition was Father John Monaghan a feisty, Irish-born, Roman-educated cleric who combined a weekend ministry at Corpus Christi Church with a fulltime assignment as a teacher and librarian

---

29 - Alfred E. Smith, *Up to Now* (New York: Viking Press, 1929), 413-414.

at Cathedral College. There, from 1922 until 1939, he introduced a whole generation of New York's future priests to the social teaching of the Church and instilled in many of them his own love of learning. Florence Cohalan said that, when he went to Dunwoodie in the early 1930s, any seminarian who admitted to reading a book attributed it to the influence of "Doc" Monaghan, as he was invariably called. In 1937 Monaghan was also instrumental in founding the Association of Catholic Trade Unionists and served for many years as the chaplain to the organization.[30]

A year earlier, at the suggestion of Father John LaFarge, S.J., the Jesuits had started the first of their "labor colleges" in New York City, the Xavier Labor School, which quickly became famous under the direction of Father Philip Carey, S.J., and John Corridan, S.J. The latter was the model for the courageous labor priest in Bud Schulberg's movie *On the Waterfront*. In the 1940s both ACTU and the Xavier Labor School played important roles in eliminating Communist influence in the Transport Workers Union and in combating racketeers in the International Longshoremen's Association.

The versatile Father LaFarge, together with George K. Hunton, a layman, founded the Catholic Interracial Council of New York on May 20. 1934, to promote racial justice and harmony between blacks and whites. Hunton, a graduate of Fordham Law School, served as the executive secretary of the organization for more than thirty years and also edited its magazine, *Interracial Justice*.

Perhaps the most famous of all efforts made by New York Catholics to alleviate the sufferings of the poor during the Great Depression came to light on May 1, 1933, when passersby in Union Square, then a gathering place for local radicals,

noticed a new newspaper on sale for one penny a copy. It was called *The Catholic Worker*. Edited by Dorothy Day, a journalist who had become a Catholic in 1927, the eight-page newspaper was only the most visible aspect of the Catholic Worker Movement, which provided shelters, or "houses of hospitality" as Dorothy Day preferred to call them, for the homeless and the unemployed during the depths of the Depression. The Catholic Worker Movement also called attention to unjust working conditions and offered support to struggling labor unions.

Paradoxically the Catholic Worker Movement proved to be both radical and reactionary at the same time. It was radical in the sense that it was a lay movement independent of hierarchical control, and, as one follower put it, "as far left as one could go within the Catholic Church." Jay Dolan once observed that its radicalism was so nebulous that to define it was "like trying to bottle a morning fog." The reactionary or romantic dimension was evident in the distaste for modern industrial society and the social welfare state, so much so that the Catholic labor activist John Court complained once that the movement had a tendency to identify Christianity with "handicrafts and subsistence farming."

The heart and soul of the Catholic Worker Movement was Dorothy Day herself, who attracted to her houses of hospitality young idealistic volunteers like Thomas Merton, Michael Harrington and Daniel Berrigan, who were eager to experience her own commitment to voluntary poverty and pacifism. Her personal devotion to the poor was a sharp contrast to the ever-growing army of well-paid government bureaucrats. When a fussy social worker with a clipboard asked Dorothy Day how long she allowed "clients" to remain in her houses of hospitality, Jim Forrest relates that "she answered with a fierce look in

---

30 - On Monaghan, see Thomas A. Lynch, "Above All Things the Truth: John P. Monaghan and the Catholic Church in the Archdiocese of New York," M.A. thesis, St. Joseph's Seminary, Dunwoodie, 1992.

her eye" and said, "We let them stay forever. They live with us, they die with us, and we give them a Christian burial. We pray for them after they are dead. Once they are taken in, they become members of the family.[31]

Even many American Catholics who did not share her doctrinaire pacifism or her fuzzy economic theories

Mrs. Coretta Scott King and Dorothy Day in March 1973.
Credit: *Archdiocese of New York*

admired Dorothy Day personally for her integrity and witness to the Gospel. In 1973, at the age of seventy-three, she was jailed for the last time for picketing on behalf of striking farm workers. Recognized by many as a saint in her own lifetime, Dorothy Day turned away such compliments by saying, "I don't want to be dismissed so easily." "If I have achieved anything in my life, she once remarked, "it is because I have not been embarrassed to talk about God." She died in New York City on November 28, 1980. In 2005 Edward Cardinal Egan took the first steps to introduce the cause of her canonization in Rome.

Catherine de Hueck Doherty was another original figure in New York Catholicism. Born in Russia in 1896, she became a convert to the Catholic Church in England in 1919. She came to New York City in 1938 to open Friendship House in Harlem. Like her friend Dorothy Day, Catherine de Hueck was an advocate for social and racial justice who had credibility because she practiced what she preached. She left New York in 1947 for Canada where she founded a community known as Madonna House. She is also remembered as an influential spiritual writer who introduced many Americans and Canadians

to the spiritual legacy of her native Russia. She died in Canada on December 14, 1985.

Two of the most famous and effective communicators of the Gospel message in mid-twentieth century America established a New York connection in the 1930s, Monsignor Fulton J. Sheen and Thomas Merton. Monsignor Sheen, a professor at the Catholic University of America, built his reputation as America's foremost Catholic preacher first at the Church of St. Paul the Apostle and after 1930 at St. Patrick's Cathedral where he was the Lenten preacher every year from 1930 until 1952. In 1930 he also began a weekly broadcast over NBC radio that made him a household name among American Catholics. In 1952 he made the difficult transition from radio to television with a half-hour show, "Life Is Worth Living," that was a huge success.

Catherine de Hueck Doherty

31 - Jim Forest, "Dorothy Day," *EACH,* 413-417.

Thomas Merton's connection with New York was more tangential. While a student at Columbia University, he was baptized at Corpus Christi Church on November 16, 1938. Three years later he entered the Trappist monastery at Gethsemani, Kentucky, and spent the second half of his life as a monk, influencing millions of people with a steady stream of books, beginning with *The Seven Storey Mountain.*

The New York Apostolate to Harlem

In the late 1920s central Harlem rapidly became an overwhelmingly African American community. In 1926 at St. Charles Borromeo school there was one black girl in the all-white eighth grade and one white child in the all-black first grade. Sister Mary Robert, a Blessed Sacrament sister who taught in the school, remembered how "Harlem had turned Black over night."

Many white residents came to us in tears saying they were ordered out of their homes. It was of interest to the tenement owners to put the whites out and rent the places to colored people at exactly double the rental. It meant a terrible overcrowding for families who had to double up in order to pay the rental.[32]

A decade earlier, in 1912, the Church of St. Mark the Evangelist on West 138th Street had become Harlem's first black Catholic parish with the arrival Holy Ghost Fathers. Two years later Mother Katherine Drexel's Blessed Sacrament Sisters opened a parochial school. However, as far back as 1923 Cardinal Hayes realized that the Catholic Church needed to adopt new pastoral initiatives and he considered organizing a group of diocesan priests to begin an apostolate to the African American population in Harlem.

He got an opportunity to do so in July 1933 when he appointed Father William H. McCann the pastor of St. Charles Borromeo Church. McCann accepted the assignment to the all-black parish on two conditions. He insisted of the right to choose his own assistant priests and the assurance of financial support from the archdiocese. Hayes agreed to both conditions, and thus was born the New York Apostolate to Harlem. It eventually included six other priests, Father McCann's brother Walter, Owen J. Scanlon, Bernard F. Russell, Lawrence J. Cahill, Joseph M. Walsh and Frank J. Dohman. Hayes also placed McCann in charge of St. Aloysius Church and St. Benedict the Moor, although he refused McCann's request to place him in charge of all of the Harlem parishes.

The evangelization of African Americans was the primary objective of the Harlem Apostolate, and the technique that they employed was adult convert classes. Actually the classes had been started earlier at St. Charles by Sister Mary Barbara S.B.S., but now they got into high gear. There were three sessions every year, each lasting three months and culminating in a solemn baptismal ceremony attended by dozens of priest and hundreds of parishioners. Cardinal Hayes himself presided at the first baptism in January 1934.

At first the priests advertised convert classes with processions through the streets of Harlem like the Salvation Army. Later it was the converts themselves who recruited their relatives and friends for the classes. By 1962 over 6,500

ADULT BAPTISMS (17 years of age or older) At St. Charles Borromeo		
1926 – 14	1934 – 203	1950 – 320
1927 – 75	1935 – 220	1951 – 259
1928 – 20	1936 – 208	1952 – 263
1929 – 26	1937 – 170	1953 – 290
1930 – 33	1938 – 174	1954 – 273
1931 – 44	1939 – 250	1955 – 179
1932 – 50	1940 – 431	1956 – 160
1933 – 46	1941 – 305	1957 – 185
	1942 – 233	1958 – 146
	1943 – 205	1959 – 120
	1944 – 267	1960 – 108
	1945 – 255	1961 – 65
	1946 – 230	1962 – 75
	1947 – 339	
	1948 – 288	2,443
	1949 – 317	
	4,095	
Total	1934-1949 – 4,095	
	1950-1962 – 2,443	

In addition St. Aloysius in the years 1935 to 1947 when it was served by the priests of St. Charles registered over 1,700 adult baptisms.

Adult Baptisms at the Church of St. Charles Borromeo, 1926-1962.
Source: *Hugh F. Corrigan, St. Charles Borromeo*

---

32 - This whole section on the Apostolate to Harlem is based on the excellent account in Hugh F. Corrigan, "A History of the Catholic Church in Harlem," *St. Charles Borromeo* (Custombooks, 1973), 22-31.

adult baptisms had taken place at St. Charles Borromeo and St. Aloysius.

The Apostolate to Harlem was not without its critics. Father John LaFarge, S.J., the Holy Ghost Fathers at St. Mark's, and Catherine de Hueck at Friendship House all faulted Father McCann and his associates for their failure to become involved in the economic and social problems facing the residents of Harlem during the Depression. Father McCann insisted on a purely sacramental ministry. That changed under Father McCann's successor at St. Charles, Monsignor Cornelius Drew, who took an active and much-appreciated interest in community affairs.

A decade before the formation of the New York Apostolate to Harlem, a community of African American sisters came to Harlem, the Franciscan Handmaids of Mary. One of only three communities of black sisters in the United States,

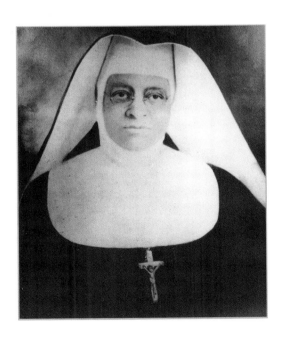

Mother Mary Theodore, F.H.M., the founder of the Franciscan Handmaids of Mary.
Credit: *Archives of the Franciscan Handmaids of Mary*

the Handmaids were founded in Savannah, Georgia, by Father Ignatius Lissner, a French priest, and Miss Elizabeth Williams, who took her religious vows as Mother Mary Theodore on October 15, 1916. The Handmaids came to New York in 1923 at the invitation of Cardinal Hayes. Their early days were not easy. They were so poor that they had to beg for food and take in laundry to pay their bills. Nonetheless they persevered, staffing St. Benedict's Day Nursery and teaching in two parochial schools in Harlem.

The End of an Era

The last half of the Hayes administration unfolded under the shadow of the Depression. He added 65 new parishes, but 60 of them were founded before 1929. He himself suffered a serious heart attack in 1932 and was a semi-invalid thereafter. He died in his sleep at St. Joseph's Camp in Monticello, New York, on September 4, 1938.

The title of "Cardinal of Charities" was well deserved not only because of his role in organizing the Catholic Charities of the Archdiocese of New York, but also because of his genuine concern for the poor and the downtrodden. Like his friend Al Smith, Cardinal Hayes was a quintessential New Yorker with all of the strengths and weaknesses that this implies. American-educated without any close ties to Roman officials and thoroughly familiar with the local presbyterate, he was completely at home in New York's Irish Catholic subculture during its waning years and had no ambitions beyond the confines of his own archdiocese. His successor was to be a person of an altogether different stamp.

16

Topping Off the Brick and Mortar

The sanctuary of Corpus Christi Church on West 121st Street. Credit: *Yvon Meyer*

Manhattan

As far as the Catholic Church was concerned, the churching of Manhattan was largely completed by the end of World War I. There were thirty-one new parishes established in Manhattan between 1902 and 1918 during Cardinal Farley's administration, but only seven more under Cardinal Hayes, and only six others since the death of Hayes in 1938. However, the statistics for the period 1902-1938 are misleading because two-thirds of the new parishes (23) were national parishes, and almost half of them were Italian (9) or Polish (2) national parishes. As was mentioned in Chapter Nine, in the early twentieth century Manhattan witnessed the founding of the first Lithuanian, Slovenian, Croatian, Magyar, and Spanish parishes. New York also got a short-lived Belgian parish, St. Albert, and in 1936 Father Andrew Rogosh, an archpriest of the Byzantine-Russian Rite, established a Russian chapel on Mulberry Street adjacent to St. Patrick's Old Cathedral on Mulberry Street.

*St. Michael's Russian Chapel in Mulberry Street
on the grounds of the Old Cathedral*

The Hispanic Presence

In view of the demographic changes that were to occur in the archdiocese in the second half of the twentieth century, perhaps the most significant development in these years was the establishment of the first four Spanish parishes in the archdiocese. The first was Our Lady of Guadalupe, which was founded in 1902 on West 14th Street to care for the Spanish colony in the West Village, most of them seamen from Galicia and their families. For the next forty years the Augustinians of the Assumption, who founded the parish, advertised it as the parish for all Spanish and Portuguese-speaking Catholics in New York even as the parish bulletin carried advertisements every week for trips to Ireland.

In 1912 New York got a second Spanish church, Our Lady of Esperanza in Washington Heights, thanks to a non-Catholic benefactor, Archer M. Huntington, the son of the railroad magnate Collis P. Huntington. The younger Huntington was a devotee of Spanish culture and the founder of the Hispanic Society of America as well as the Spanish Museum in Washington Heights. The wife of the Spanish consul-general in New York, Manuela de Laverrerie de Barril, suggested to Huntington that he should also build a Spanish church next to the museum, since Catholicism was such an integral part of Spanish culture. Huntington accepted the suggestion and donated $100,000 in land and cash for the church.

*The Church of Our Lady of
Esperanza as it looked before the
addition of the present façade*

*The Church of Our Lady of Esperanza
on West 156th Street, dedicated by
Cardinal Farley on July 21, 1912*

*Mr. Archer M. Huntington,
the principal benefactor
of the Church of
Our Lady of Esperanza*

*Maria de Baril,
the daughter of the
Spanish consul-general in
New York and another
benefactor of the Church of
Our Lady of Esperanza*

Archbishop Farley gave his blessing to the project and placed the Augustinians of the Assumption in charge of the church. Manuela de Barril did not live to see the finished church, but her daughter, Maria de Barril, and the Augustinians raised the rest of the money to build the church, which was dedicated by the now Cardinal Farley on July 21, 1912. The King of Spain donated the sanctuary lamp and a painting. Less than a year later, the church was debt-free and consecrated. Farley himself suggested the name of Our Lady of Hope.

In concluding remarks at the dedication of Our Lady of Esperanza, Farley said : "In this church let there be no North or South among you. Let South Americans, Cubans, Mexicans, Spaniards all come here without the thought of racial distinction and kneel together as Catholics." The first pastor was Father Adrian Buisson, A.A., who had been the pastor of Our Lady of Guadalupe. He may have remembered Farley's advice to the first pastor of Our Lady of Guadalupe, Thomas Darboy, A.A., when Darboy expressed doubts whether the Spanish community would support the new church in 14th Street. Farley told him not to worry because the Irish would gravitate to the church and support it.[1]

Apparently that is what happened at Our Lady of Esperanza within a decade. By the mid-1920s most of the parishioners were Irish, not Spanish, which resulted in a sharp rebuke from Cardinal Hayes through his chancellor, Monsignor Thomas Carroll. "The Church of Our Lady of Esperanza, as you well know," Carroll told Father Buisson, "was established for the Spanish-speaking people, and de facto it does not serve the Spanish-speaking people. The majority of these still come from English-speaking people and the Cardinal is trying to pin you down to the persons for whose service you exist."[2]

The following year Cardinal Hayes received a report from his own Catholic Charities office warning him of the "most alarming deficiencies in the spiritual care of the various Spanish-speaking nationals in New York City." This report was the background to his complaints about the Augustinians of the Assumption at Our Lady of Esperanza. That same year the Cardinal asked the Spanish Vincentians to open a church in New York City.[3]

A year later the Vincentians had acquired a former synagogue at Seventh Avenue and 114th Street and converted it into the Church of Nuestra Señora de la Medalla Milagrosa (Our Lady of the Miraculous Medal), which was popularly known as La Milagrosa. By 1928 the Vincentian community numbered seven priests including the pastor, Father Gabriel Ginard, C.M., who had been a professor at St. John's University in Brooklyn. During the course of the next thirty years or more La Milagrosa was the most important Hispanic church in New York. Between 1927 and 1952 the Vincentians recorded 31,746 baptisms and 5,841 marriages. One of the Vincentians, Father Leandro Mayoral, C.M., taught Spanish language courses in Cathedral College, giving many future New York priests their first acquaintance with the language they would later find invaluable in their pastoral ministry.[4]

In addition to their work at La Milagrosa, the Spanish Vincentians established two missions. One was the mission chapel of Saint Teresa of Jesus in Washington Heights at 187th Street and Broadway. Founded in 1932, it was destroyed by fire in 1935. The mission chapel of the Holy Agony

1 - *Our Lady of Esperanza, New York, Fiftieth Anniversary* (New York: Our Lady of Esperanza Church, 1962), unpaginated. AANY, Zachary Saint-Martin, A.A., to John J. Dunn, February 28, 1926.

2 - AANY, Carroll to Buisson, December 12, 1925.

3 - AANY, Carroll to John B. Coleman, June 10, 1926.

4 - Leandro Mayoral, C.M., "Algo sobre Nuestra Iglesia 'La Milagrosa,'" *Album Conmemorativo* (New York: Parroquia La Milagrosa, 1952), 11-19.

Interior of La Milagrosa.
Credit: *Parroquia La Milagrosa*

Father Leandro Mayoral, C.M.
Credit: *Parroquia La Milagrosa*

The Church of the Holy Agony, originally a mission of La Milagrosa.

had a happier history. It was the first Hispanic church in El Barrio, founded in 1930 in a former synagogue on East 98th Street between Second and Third Avenues. The initiative came not only from the Vincentians, but also from the Helpers of the Holy Souls, a community of women religious who were engaged in catechetical work among the Hispanic immigrants. The little mission chapel developed into the Church of the Holy Agony at 3rd Avenue and 101st Street. La Milagrosa is long gone, but the Vincentians continue to staff the Church of the Holy Agony.[5]

The West Side

Nine of the twelve new territorial parishes established under Cardinal Farley were located on the West Side of Manhattan, stretching from midtown to the northern tip of the island. Both St. Matthew's Church and St. Malachy's Church were founded in 1902. St. Malachy's proved to be the more durable of the two parishes. While St. Matthew's succumbed to the wrecker's ball in 1959 to make way for Lincoln Center, the clergy at St. Malachy's cultivated its location in the heart of the theatre district where it became known as the Actors' Chapel.

St. Malachy's Church, the Actor's Chapel, on West 49th Street.

5 - *Bodas de Plata* (New York: Parroquia de la Santa Agonia, 1978), unpaginated.

A third West Side parish, St. Gregory the Great, was established in 1907 on West 90th Street midway between Holy Name of Jesus on 96th Street and Holy Trinity on 82nd Street. Since Father James Fitzsimmons, the first pastor, did not have enough money for both a church and a school, he built a four-story school with a large hall on the ground floor that could be used as a temporary church. The building was blessed by Cardinal Farley on October 19, 1913. As in the case of many other New York parishes that were started in that era, the temporary church became the permanent church.[6]

Morningside Heights

Farther north on Morningside Heights where Columbia University was creating its new campus and the Episcopalians were erecting the Cathedral of St. John the Divine, two Catholic parishes were established, Corpus Christi in 1906 and Notre Dame in 1910. Notre Dame was the second parish in the archdiocese to be founded by

The Church of St. Gregory the Great on West 90th Street, dedicated by Cardinal Farley on October 19, 1913.

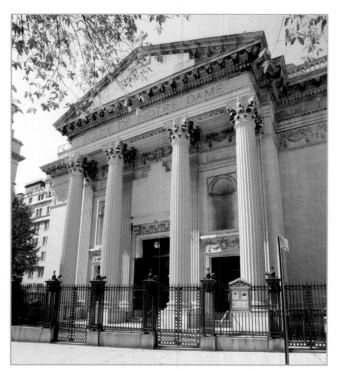

Notre Dame Church on Morningside Heights, founded by the Fathers of Mercy in 1910 and now staffed by Polish Dominicans.

the Fathers of Mercy. For many years they had complained about the poverty of their Church of St. Vincent de Paul on West 23rd Street and had asked permission to relocate it farther north. The compromise was to keep St. Vincent de Paul on West 23rd Street, but to allow the Fathers of Mercy to build Notre Dame Church. Unlike St. Vincent de Paul, it never functioned as a French national parish, but it helped the Fathers of Mercy to pay their bills by attracting Catholics from all over the city to its shrine of Our Lady of Lourdes.

Corpus Christi was a diocesan parish that was founded by Father John H. Dooley in 1906. The following year he built a church, school and rectory that were dedicated by Archbishop Farley on June 30, 1907. His successor in 1934 was Father George Barry Ford who had lived at Corpus Christi rectory for the previous six years as the chaplain to the Catholic students at Columbia University. Ford was acutely aware of his unique responsibilities in the archdiocese as the pastor of a parish that included within its boundaries not only Columbia University, but also Teachers College, Union Theological Seminary and Jewish Theological Seminary.

5 - *Bodas de Plata* (New York: Parroquia de la Santa Agonia, 1978), unpaginated.

The Holy Family:
Corpus Christi Church.
Credit: *Yvon Meyer*

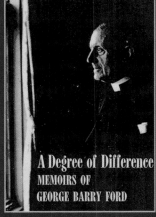

Father George Barry Ford,
the pastor of Corpus Christi
Church, 1934-1958

Detail from window
in Corpus Christi Church.
Credit: *Yvon Meyer*

Corpus Christi Church
on West 121st Street, dedicated
by Cardinal Hayes on October 25, 1936

Father Ford moved quickly to establish a Catholic presence in the academic community on Morningside Heights. Although it was in the depths of the Depression, he persuaded Cardinal Hayes to allow him to build a combination church, school and convent on West 121st Street between Broadway and Amsterdam Avenue. The cardinal presided at the dedication on October 25, 1936. Unlike many combination church-and-schools, Corpus Christi Church really looked like a church with splendid stained glass widows and tasteful interior appointments.

Once he had completed the new church, Father Ford made Corpus Christi as famous as the Church of St. Paul the Apostle had been a half-century earlier for the celebration of the liturgy. There was a vested choir at the High Mass on Sunday, and at the Low Masses New Yorkers were introduced to the "dialogue" Mass. During these Masses a priest other than the celebrant led the congregation in the recitation in English of all the prayers except the canon (the Eucharistic prayer) and the final blessing. Father Ford was also a pioneer in originating a parish bulletin in order to eliminate the lengthy pulpit announcements. He also inaugurated a monthly newsletter, the *Corpus Christi Chronicle,* which made available to its readers short essays by some of the best European and American writers. Ford also recognized that the parish school, located across the street from Teachers College, had to meet the highest educational standards. For that reason in 1936 he dismissed the Sisters of Charity and entrusted the school to the Dominican Sisters of Sinsanawa, Wisconsin, who had established a reputation as progressive educators.

The press often referred to Ford as a "maverick" priest because of his interest in ecumenism and his advocacy of liberal political causes that caused heartburn in the New York Chancery Office and sometimes led to sharp reprimands from the chancellor or the vicar general. Ford often had the better of the exchange. When the vicar general ordered Ford not to speak at a meeting of the New York Teachers Guild in 1954, he obeyed. However, he told Monsignor John Maguire that he had "instant respect for the historic and important office you hold," but he warned him that, "when it becomes a police station where suspects report, it no longer enjoys esteem."[7]

Perhaps in compensation for his failure to get the recognition that he expected (and deserved) from his fellow Catholics, Ford sometimes displayed a tendency to pander to critics of his own church, like Methodist Bishop G. Bromley Oxnam, a neo-Nativist bigot of a bygone era. At the Mass celebrating the fiftieth anniversary of Corpus Christi Church, Ford fawned over Eleanor Roosevelt as "the first lady of the world… who brings the distinction of her presence to us this morning." Ford invited Cardinal Spellman to the Mass, but he declined to appear alongside the "first lady of the world" and sent as his representative auxiliary Bishop Joseph Donahue, who was so deaf that he probably did not hear a word of what Ford said.[8]

Washington Heights and Inwood

A mile north of Morningside Heights on West 142nd Street in the Hamilton Grange section of Washington Heights Father Joseph McMahon gave the archdiocese an unusual architectural heritage when he built the Church of Our Lady of Lourdes between 1902 and 1903. A curate at

6 - *The Parish of St. Gregory: A Profile and a History, 1907-1996* (New York: St. Gregory's Church, 1996), unpaginated.

7 - AANY, Ford to Maguire, March 1, 1954.

8 - *New York Times,* November 15, 1947; E. Harold Smith, *The History of Corpus Christi Parish, 1906-1956* (New York: Corpus Christi Church, 1956), 2-24.

St. Patrick's Cathedral for fifteen years, McMahon was appointed to start the new parish in 1901. He acquired building materials at bargain prices from the recently demolished A.T. Stewart mansion and the National Academy of Design, and from the east wall of St. Patrick's Cathedral, which was being replaced by the Lady Chapel. Our Lady of Lourdes remains unique among New York's Catholic churches because, like the National Academy of Design, it was built in the Venetian Gothic style and was designated a New York City landmark in 1975. After the building of the parochial school in 1913, the parish had a debt of $380,000, which McMahon completely paid off six years later.[9]

Like Father Ford, Monsignor McMahon (he did became a monsignor) was a liturgist, but of a safer and more traditionalist variety. He was also an ardent Anglophile who was appalled at the failure of New York's Irish Catholics to rally to England's side during World War I. Whenever possible McMahon liked to feature English preachers for the annual Lenten sermons at Our Lady of Lourdes Church. On one occasion Father Bede Jarrett, O.P., is alleged to have begun a sermon with the disclaimer that he was "prescinding from the Aristotelian notion of time."

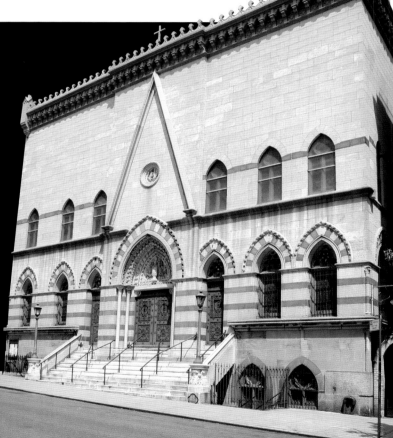

Monsignor Joseph H. McMahon, the pastor of the Church of Our Lady of Lourdes, 1901-1939

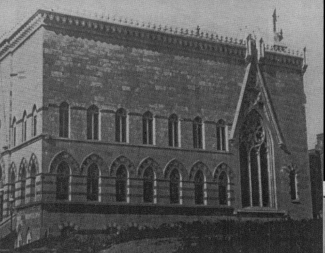

The Church of Our Lady of Lourdes as it looked shortly after its completion in 1903

The Church of Our Lady of Lourdes on West 142nd Street, built between 1901 and 1903

9 - *The History of Our Lady of Lourdes* (Custombook, 1976), 4-8.

One can follow the course of empire, or at least the progress of the West Side IRT subway, through Washington Heights and Inwood, by noting the dates of the founding of the next two parishes in northern Manhattan, the Church of the Incarnation in 1908 and the Paulist Church of the Good Shepherd in 1911. The first pastor of Incarnation Church, Father Patrick J. Mahoney, followed the time-honored New York tradition of building a school first, which was opened in 1910. The auditorium served as the church until the second pastor, Monsignor Joseph F. Delaney, built the present church, which was dedicated by Cardinal Hayes on June 1, 1930. A handsome Gothic building constructed of Dunwoodie granite, it is modeled after the Church of St. Maclou in Rouen.[10]

The Church of the Good Shepherd was the first Catholic church in Inwood and the second Paulist parish in the archdiocese. In 1914, three years after the parish was founded, the first Church of the Good Shepherd was dedicated at the corner of Broadway and Isham Street. By the 1930s the original frame church was inadequate for the growing number of parishioners. It was moved on rollers to a nearby site and replaced by a Romanesque church seating 1,100 people that was dedicated by Cardinal Hayes on December 5, 1937.[11]

Inwood got its second parish in 1927 with the establishment of the Church of Lady Queen of Martyrs. If the area was not exactly rural, it was known as "the woods" and the new Catholic parish antedated the coming of the IND subway, the construction of the Henry Hudson Bridge and the creation of Fort Tryon Park. The first pastor, Father William C. Ryder, built a church that was dedicated by Cardinal Hayes in May 1929. It was replaced by the present church when the new school was opened in 1950.

The original Church of the Good Shepherd as it looked c. 1914.
Credit: *Church of the Good Shepherd*

The Church of the Good Shepherd at Broadway and 211th Street, dedicated by Cardinal Hayes on December 5, 1937

10 - *Challenge and Achievement: A Record of Fifty Years, 1908-1958* (New York: Church of the Incarnation, 1958), unpaginated.
11 - *Good Shepherd Parish* (New York: Church of the Good Shepherd, n.d.), 18-25.

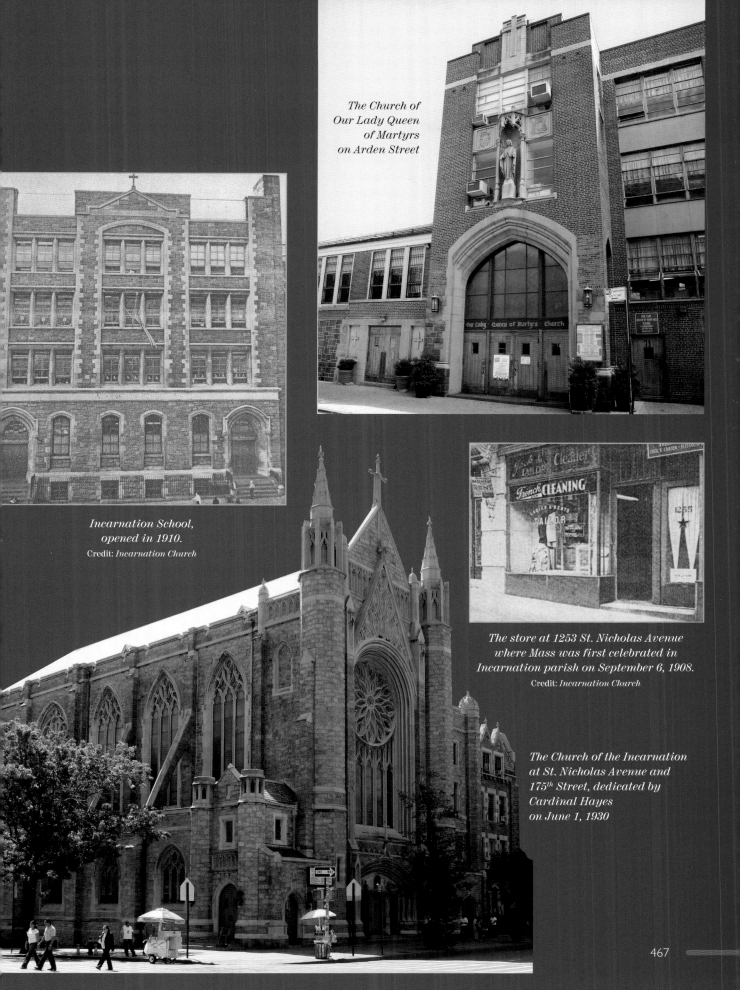

The Church of Our Lady Queen of Martyrs on Arden Street

Incarnation School, opened in 1910.
Credit: *Incarnation Church*

The store at 1253 St. Nicholas Avenue where Mass was first celebrated in Incarnation parish on September 6, 1908.
Credit: *Incarnation Church*

The Church of the Incarnation at St. Nicholas Avenue and 175th Street, dedicated by Cardinal Hayes on June 1, 1930

The last of Inwood's Catholic churches, the Church of St. Jude, dates from 1949, when the construction of the Dyckman Houses, a middle-income housing project for almost 1,400 families, led Cardinal Spellman to establish this new parish. St. Jude's and St. Joan of Arc, founded the same year in the Bronx, were the first two parishes in the archdiocese established to provide pastoral care for the residents of city housing projects. In 1953 the first pastor of St. Jude's, Father Francis J. Kett, gave the parish a permanent place for Mass with the combined school and church-auditorium that was dedicated by Cardinal Spellman on May 17, 1953.[12]

Completing the Picture

Three new territorial parishes were established in Harlem before World War I. St. Lucy's on East 104th Street in East Harlem, founded in 1900, quickly became a de facto Italian parish as the Italians became the dominant ethnic group in East Harlem. The other two parishes were in Central Harlem, both founded in 1907 when the area was still predominantly white, the Church of the Resurrection on West 151st Street,

The Church of St. Jude, dedicated by Cardinal Spellman on May 17, 1953.

and the Church of St. Mark the Evangelist on West 138th Street. In 1912 the Holy Ghost Fathers took charge of St. Mark's Church and began an outreach to the rapidly growing African American population. The also assumed the responsibility of serving as chaplains at Harlem Hospital.

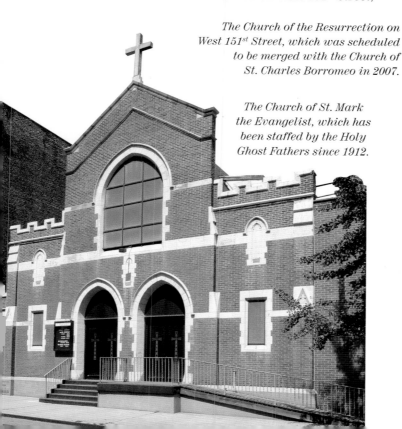

The Church of the Resurrection on West 151st Street, which was scheduled to be merged with the Church of St. Charles Borromeo in 2007.

The Church of St. Mark the Evangelist, which has been staffed by the Holy Ghost Fathers since 1912.

---

12 - *Church of St. Jude* (Custombook, 1975), 5-17.

Three Eastern-rite churches rounded off the list of new Catholic churches in pre-World War I Manhattan, the Church of the Exaltation of the Holy Cross, St. George's Ukrainian Catholic Church on East 7th Street (1905), and St. Mary's Ruthenian Catholic Church on East 15th Street (1912).

In addition to St. Jude's Church in Inwood, Cardinal Spellman added four other Catholic churches to the roster in Manhattan. On the Lower East side St. Emeric's parish was started in 1949 to replace the German Church of St. Mary Magdalen on East 17th Street, which was demolished to make way for the construction of Stuyvesant Town. Spellman chose the name of the Hungarian saint to call attention to the Communist persecution of the Chruch in Hungary, particularly the show trial of the Hungarian primate, Cardinal Mindszenty.

The other three parishes started by Spellman were all located on prime Manhattan real estate. He purchased the site of Our Lady of Victory Church in the heart of the financial district at Pine and William Street with $120,000 left from the $2,000,000 that Mayor Bowes, the radio personality, bequeathed to the archdiocese. Spellman said that he had a two-fold purpose in building the church, which he dedicated on June 23, 1947. He wanted to provide a "business" parish for the workers in the financial district and he also wanted to commemorate the U.S. victory in World War II. The first pastor was Monsignor Richard J. Pigott.[13]

In 1950 Spellman added a new parish in the Carnegie Hill area of the Upper East Side when he purchased a former Dutch Reformed Church on 89 Street between Park and Madison Avenues and named it in honor of St. Thomas More. The church had been built by the Episcopalians and sold to the Dutch Reformed congregation when they built a new church at Fifth Avenue and 90th Street. The first pastor was Monsignor Philip J. Furlong, who later became an auxiliary bishop.

Five years later Spellman established the Church of Our Savior on Park Avenue at 38th Street in Murray Hill and appointed Monsignor Thomas J. McMahon the first pastor. It was projected to cost over $3 million and was dedicated by Spellman on September 27, 1959. Monsignor McMahon did not live to see it completed and was succeeded by Monsignor John M. Fleming. In 1960 the Fifth Avenue Association cited it as one of the three outstanding institutions built during the previous year within the Fifth Avenue Area. The two others were the new Presbyterian Church House on West 12th Street and the Guggenheim Museum.[14]

The construction of the headquarters of the United Nations led to the loss of one Manhattan church and the transformation of another. The old German Church of St. Boniface was closed in 1951 and demolished, but the Church of the Holy Family on 47th Street, which had been founded as an Italian national parish in 1924, was rebuilt on its original foundations and designated as the UN Parish. Cardinal Spellman dedicated the modernized church on March 14, 1964, at a Mass attended by U Thant, the Secretary General of the UN. The following year Pope Paul VI met non-Catholic religious leaders at the church when he visited the UN.[15]

From 1958 until 1986 St. Patrick's Cathedral had a Chapel of Saints Faith, Hope and Charity, named after three individuals whom Cardinal Spellman revealed were child martyrs under the Emperor Hadrian. Originally located on the ground floor of the building at 487 Park Avenue at 59th Street, it was twice plagued by bad luck. In 1978 the archdiocese sold the Park Avenue

---

13 - AANY, Spellman, Remarks at the Blessing of the Cornerstone of the Church of Our Lady of Victory, September 17, 1946.

14 - AANY, Andrew Goodman to Fleming, May 9, 1960.

15 - AANY, Anthony Andreassi, unpublished History of Holy Family Church, 28-35.

*The Church of Our Savior
on Park Avenue at 38th Street,
dedicated by Cardinal Spellman
on September 27, 1959.*

*The Church of St. Thomas More on East 89th Street,
which was acquired from
a Dutch Reformed Congregation in 1950.*

*The Church of Our Lady of Victory
at Pine and William Streets,
dedicated by
Cardinal Spellman
on June 23, 1947*

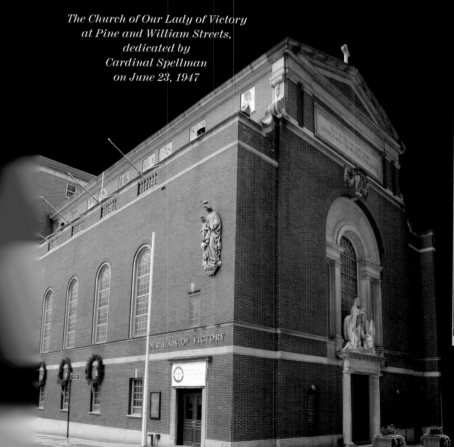

*The Church of St. Emeric
which was built in 1962.*

*The plaque commemorating
the visit of Pope Paul VI to
the Church of the Holy Family
on October 4, 1965.*

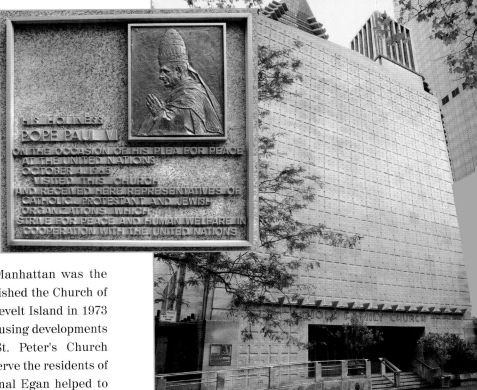

building because of the prohibitive cost of repairs and moved the chapel around the corner to the former Fine Arts Theatre on 58th Street. Eight years later the new location had to be abandoned for the same reasons.

The last parish founded in Manhattan was the work of Cardinal Cooke who established the Church of St. Francis Xavier Cabrini on Roosevelt Island in 1973 to serve the residents of the new housing developments on the island. More recently St. Peter's Church established St. Joseph's Chapel to serve the residents of Battery Park City. In 2005, Cardinal Egan helped to continue the never-ending variations in the saga of the Immigrant Church in New York when he designated the former Italian Church of the Most Holy Crucifix on Broome Street the Filipino Chapel of San Lorenzo Ruiz.

*The Church of the Holy Family on East 47th Street,
rebuilt and dedicated as the United Nations parish
by Cardinal Spellman on March 14, 1964.*

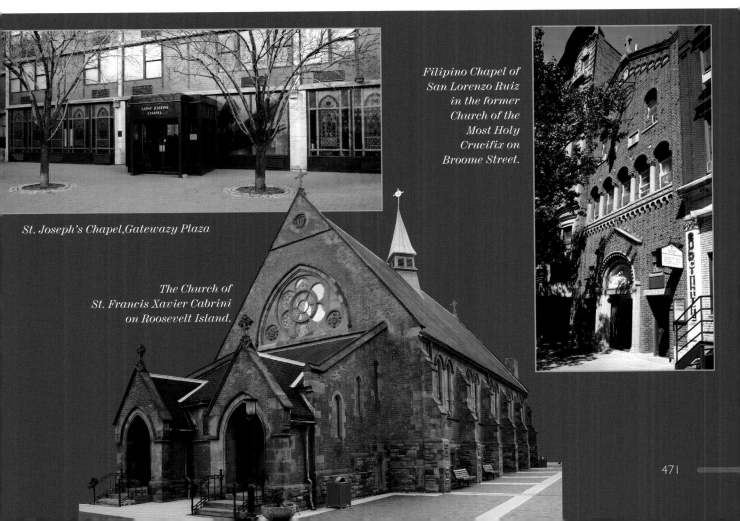

St. Joseph's Chapel, Gatewazy Plaza

*Filipino Chapel of
San Lorenzo Ruiz
in the former
Church of the
Most Holy
Crucifix on
Broome Street.*

*The Church of
St. Francis Xavier Cabrini
on Roosevelt Island.*

471

The Urbanization of the Bronx

In the Bronx the great age of Catholic church building peaked slightly later than in Manhattan. Between 1901 and the Stock Market crash in 1929, thirty-five new parishes were founded in the Bronx, twelve of them before World War I and the other twenty-three between 1919 and 1929, no fewer than seven of them in 1923 and 1924 alone. Only eight new parishes were added during the last eighty years, and one of them has since been consolidated with an older parish.

In Manhattan Catholics were long accustomed to being the dominant religious group in the immigrant population. In many parts of the Bronx, however, the Catholics found themselves outnumbered by Jewish immigrants and their descendants, especially in the central Bronx along the length of the Grand Concourse, and in Tremont and along Southern Boulevard and some areas of the South and East Bronx. The sparsity and relative poverty of the Catholic population in these neighborhoods was reflected in the difficulties they experienced in trying to build churches and schools. In many instances, a temporary basement church or a school auditorium became the permanent church.

Central Bronx

The Grand Concourse was intended to be the Champs Elysée of the Bronx, a wide tree-lined boulevard with six-story elevator apartment buildings, many of them built in the Art Deco style. There were numerous synagogues on the Grand Concourse and the adjacent streets, but only one Catholic church was built on the five-mile stretch of the Grand Concourse between 161st Street and Fordham Road, the basement Church of Christ the King, dedicated by Cardinal Hayes on September 15, 1929. East of the Concourse the Carmelite Church of St. Simon Stock, which was founded in

1919, was also a basement church, and west of the Concourse the Church of St. Margaret Mary, which dates from 1923, was housed in a plain one-story brick building.

In Fordham the new Church of Our Lady of Mercy on Marion Avenue was dedicated in 1908. Two years earlier Father Daniel Burke of St. Philip Neri Church established the Church of Our Lady of Mount Carmel for the Italians in the Belmont area of the Bronx. The first "church" was a converted store on East 187th Street. The following year Burke bought property where the present church now stands. A basement church was ready for Mass on December 23, 1907, celebrated by Father Joseph Caffuzzi, Monsignor Burke's curate. The upper church was dedicated by Archbishop John Bonzano, the Apostolic Delegate, on October 14, 1917. Four years later Father Caffuzzi succeeded Burke as the pastor.

Bishop Joseph M. Pernicone

In subsequent years Our Lady of Mount Carmel would become the largest and most important Italian parish in the Bronx, and quite likely the largest parish in the archdiocese. At the time of the golden jubilee of the parish in 1956, the pastor was a bishop (auxiliary Bishop Joseph M. Pernicone), who had nine fulltime curates. There was an eighteen-classroom school staffed by nine Holy Cross Brothers and twenty-three Sisters of the Catholic Apostolate and there were four Sisters of Our Lady of Lourdes.[16]

In 1909 the Church of Our Lady of Victory was established on Webster Avenue near Claremont Parkway. In 1912 Father Francis P. Duffy was sent to establish the new parish of Our Savior in the area east of Our Lady of Mercy. The scholarly Father Duffy found that there was not a single

---

16 - Joseph L.J.Borgatti, *Our Lady of Mount Carmel Parish Golden Jubilee* (Bronx: Our Lady of Mount Carmel Church, 1956), unpaginated.

The Church of Christ the King, Grand Concourse.
The basement church was dedicated
by Cardinal Hayes on September 15, 1929.

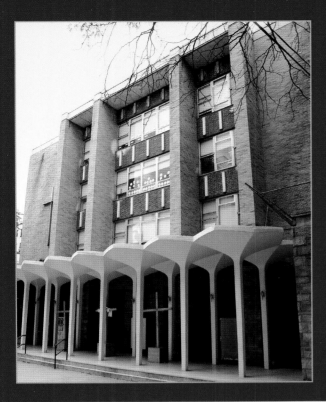

The Church of St. Margaret Mary which dates from 1923.

The first church and priory of the Church of St. Simon Stock.
Credit: St. Simon Stock Church

The Carmelite Church
of St. Simon Stock
on East 182nd Street.

The church and school of St. Simon Stock.
Credit: St. Simon Stock Church

*The Church of
St. Francis of Assisi on
Shakespeare Avenue,
scheduled to be merged
with the Church of the
Sacred Heart in 2007.*

*The Church of
Our Lady of Victory
on Webster Avenue
erected in 1911.*

*Our Lady
of Victory.*

*The Church of Our Lady of Mount Carmel
on 187th Street, dedicated by Archbishop
John Bonzano on October 14, 1917.*

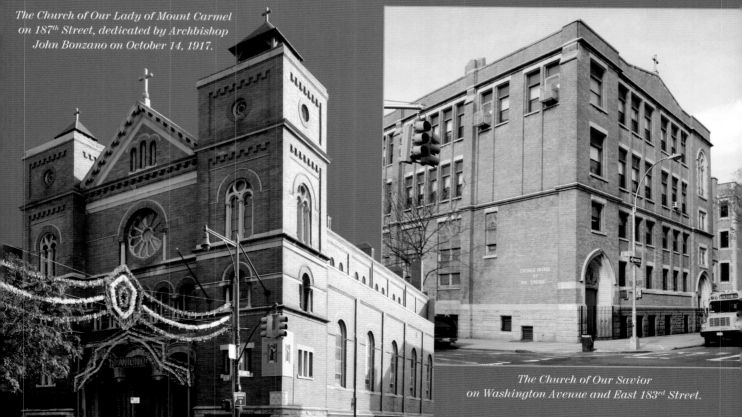

*The Church of Our Savior
on Washington Avenue and East 183rd Street.*

college-educated person in the parish. He made the comment not to complain, but to persuade Cardinal Farley to give his parish more extensive boundaries because of the poverty of his parishioners.

At both Our Lady of Victory and Our Savior straightened financial situations led to the building of a combination school-and-church, in 1911 and 1914 respectively. The same solution was also employed at the Church of the Holy Spirit on University Avenue, which was founded in 1901. As the West Bronx filled up with new apartment buildings following the completion of the Jerome Avenue IRT subway line, the Church of St. Francis of Assisi was founded in 1928 to relieve some of the pressure on Holy Spirit Church and Sacred Heart Church in Highbridge.

Although Bronx Catholics could not boast of any impressive church to make their presence known on the Grand Concourse, they got an imposing cathedral-like church at the intersection of Fordham Road and University Avenue when the new Church of St. Nicholas of Tolentine was built in 1928. It replaced the original church which dated from 1907.

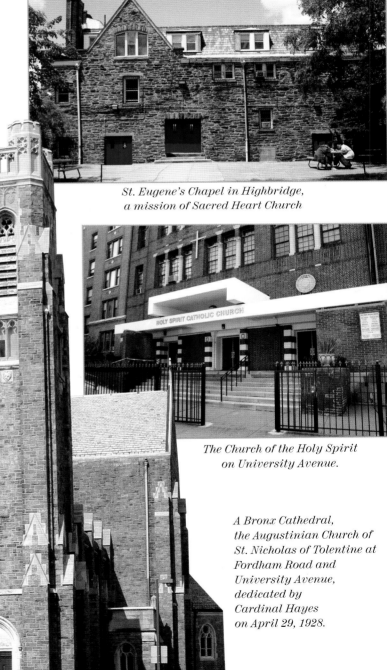

St. Eugene's Chapel in Highbridge,
a mission of Sacred Heart Church

The Church of the Holy Spirit
on University Avenue.

A Bronx Cathedral,
the Augustinian Church of
St. Nicholas of Tolentine at
Fordham Road and
University Avenue,
dedicated by
Cardinal Hayes
on April 29, 1928.

475

In the heavily Irish South Bronx the parish of St. Pius V was founded in 1906 by Father Francis M. Fagan, who had spent the previous eight years as a pastor in Phoenicia and Whiteport. He built a church on East 145th Street in 1908 and a parochial school in 1912, paid off the debt on the church in 1928 and opened a commercial high school in 1930. On his visits to parishioners in St. Francis Hospital, he was usually accompanied by his formidable pet dog to the consternation of the health-conscious German Franciscan Sisters. Father Fagan's curates also suffered from his obsessive concern for the safety of the Blessed Sacrament because he frequently failed to turn off the tabernacle alarm that rang throughout the rectory while he was distributing Holy Communion at the early morning Mass.[17]

A few blocks north of St. Pius V Church on East 151st Street the Franciscans established the first Italian parish in Melrose, Our Lady of Pity (Madonna del Suffragio), and built a church that was dedicated the following year.

In Hunts Point Father William Doherty began St. Anthansius Church in 1907 by using the chapel of the cloistered Dominican Sisters at Corpus Christi monastery for two Masses on Sunday that drew about 160 people. That same year he bought property on Fox Street and announced plans to build a basement church. Instead he threw caution to the winds and built the present church, only twenty feet high but preferable to an underground church. Cardinal Logue, the archbishop of Armagh, blessed the cornerstone of the church on May 31, 1908, during his visit to New York for the centennial of the diocese.

After World War I the parish was nearly closed when the neighborhood became predominantly Jewish. The new pastor, Father Henry Xavier, persuaded Cardinal Hayes to keep it open, and an influx of Irish and German Catholics brought stability and solvency. In the 1950s St. Athanasius became a model for all the parishes in the archdiocese because of its dynamic and successful response to the challenge of the massive Hispanic presence within the parish boundaries.[18]

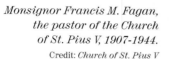

Monsignor Francis M. Fagan,
the pastor of the Church
of St. Pius V, 1907-1944.
Credit: *Church of St. Pius V*

The Church of St. Pius V
on East 145th Street erected in 1908.

---

17 - *Church of Saint Pius V: Diamond Jubilee* (New York: Church of St. Pius V, 1982), unpaginated.
18 - *The 75th Anniversary of St. Athanasius* (New York: St. Athanasius Church, n,d.), ujnpaginated.

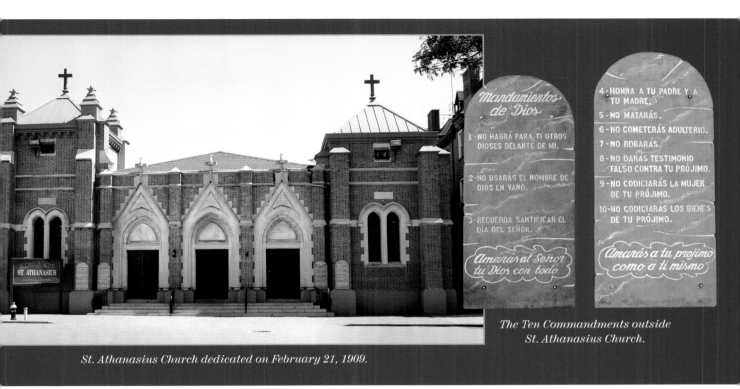

St. Athanasius Church dedicated on February 21, 1909.

The Ten Commandments outside
St. Athanasius Church.

The Italian Church of Our Lady of Pity
on East 151st Street in Melrose, now closed

North of Fordham Road

Fordham Road would become the dividing line between the South Bronx and the rest of the borough in the 1960s when the South Bronx endured its ordeal by fire and became synonymous with crime, arson and urban decay. In the 1920s, however, Fordham Road had no such sinister connotation. It was a popular shopping center for much of the borough and the dividing line between the endless rows of apartment buildings to the south and the one-family homes to the north. Even in the 1920s, however, the apartment buildings were winning the battle with the private dwellings north of Fordham Road. With the increase in population density came the need for more Catholic churches and schools.

St. Brendan's Church was founded in 1908 when Norwood was still semi-suburban. The founding pastor, Father Denis O'Donovan, began the construction of a Gothic church the following year. It was replaced in 1967 with a strikingly modern church with a maritime motif that evoked the memory of St. Brendan the Navigator. Meanwhile two other parishes were founded nearby, both on Bainbridge Avenue a few miles apart, Our Lady of Refuge in 1923 and St. Ann's 1927.

In both parishes the pastor opted for a combination school-and-church, which were opened in 1930 and 1928 respectively. At St. Ann's Shrine Church, the founding pastor, Father Martin Cavanaugh, received permission from Montefiore Hospital, a Jewish institution, to use the hospital auditorium for Sunday Mass for eighteen months until the church was finished just in time for Christmas Mass in 1928.[19]

Farther north, in Wakefield, the Italian parish of St. Anthony was founded in 1919 by Father Alexander Indelli, who used a converted store for a church. In 1925 he was able to purchase a former Lutheran church which he enlarged and used for Mass for the first time on February 8, 1925. The new St. Anthony's Church on Richardson Avenue was built in 1976 by Monsignor John L. Guido.[20] Another Italian parish, Our Lady of Grace, was started by Father Victor Bassi in May 1924 in two rented stores on White Plains Road near 227th Street. A year later he broke ground for a church where he celebrated the first Mass on October 11, 1925. A new church was planned by Monsignor Bonaventure Fillitti in the 1960s, but he died before he could build it, and it was erected by his successor, Monsignor John Rettagliata, and dedicated by Cardinal Cooke on May 26, 1968.

In Woodlawn St. Barnabas Church began in a store on McLean Avenue in 1910. As the parish developed into one of the largest in the archdiocese, the church erected in 1911 proved to be too small, necessitating the use of several locations for over a dozen Masses on Sunday morning. In Kingsbridge the Church of Our Lady of the Angels dates from 1924 when Father Francis A. Kiniry began celebrating Mass in the Passionist monastery located on the former Claflin estate. The first Mass was celebrated in the new parish church on June 29, 1925.[21] It was replaced with the present colonial-style church in 1958. In the Van Cortland Park area of the West Bronx the Church of the Visitation was founded in 1928 by Father Joseph V. Stanford, who erected the familiar church-school building two years later. It was sold to the state in 1950 for $354,000 for the construction of the Major Deegan Expressway. A new church, school and rectory were built and dedicated by Cardinal Spellman in 1953.

The Church of Our Lady of Refuge built in 1930.

The contemporary Church of St. Brendan erected in 1967

---

19 - *Shrine Church of St. Ann: 75th Anniversary* (Bronx: St. Ann's Church 2002), unpaginated.

20 - *The Story of St. Anthony's Church* (Custombook, 1977), 4-11.

21 - See Kevin J. O'Reilly, *Our Lady of Angels Parish* (Bronx: Our Lady of Angels Church, 1999).

The Shrine Church of St. Ann, built in 1928.

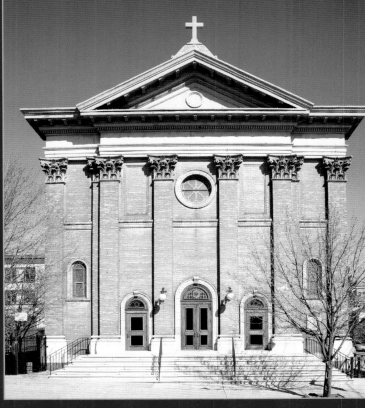

*St. Barnabas Church
in Woodlawn built in 1911.*

*The Church of
Our Lady of Grace
dedicated by
Cardinal Cooke
on May 26, 1968.*

*The Church of St. Anthony,
Richardson Avenue,
dedicated in 1976 and
scheduled to be merged
with the Church of
St. Frances of Rome
in 2007.*

The first Church of Our Lady of Angels built in 1925.

*The Church of the Visitation dedicated
by Cardinal Spellman in 1953.*

*The Church of Our Lady of the Angels dedicated
by Bishop Philip J. Furlong on October 26, 1958.*

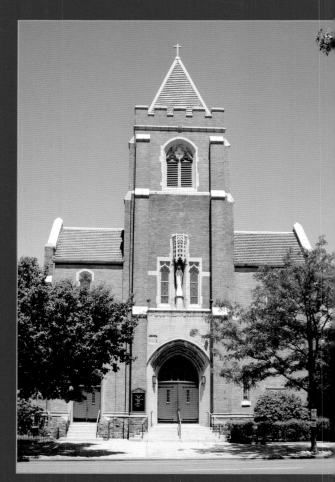

*The Church of Our Lady of Solace dedicated
by Bishop Daniel J. Curley on June 16, 1929.*

The East Bronx

The opening of the IRT Pelham Bay subway line spurred real estate development in the East Bronx, although, as late as the 1950s, a ride on the two-car Dyre Avenue shuttle resembled a trip on the Toonerville trolley through miles of vacant lots. Proportionately it was the part of the borough that experienced the largest increase in new parishes, thirteen between 1919 and 1929. Almost half were Italian parishes, reflecting the movement of many Italians to the Bronx from the crowded Little Italies of Manhattan.

The first of the new parishes in the East Bronx went back to 1903 when the Church of Our Lady of Solace was founded in the Van Nest area by Father Daniel J. Curley, who built a frame church that same year on White Plains Road. In 1923 Curley was appointed the bishop of Syracuse, but he returned to the Bronx to dedicate the new Romanesque Church of Our Lady of Solace on June 16, 1929.

The first Italian Church in the East Bronx was St. Anthony's in the Van Nest area, founded by the Italian-born Father Henry DeVivo in 1908, who built a church that was dedicated in November of the following year. Like the Church of St Philip Neri in Bedford Park, however, St. Anthony's became a predominantly Irish parish by the 1930s. In April 1931 a school was opened on Commonwealth Avenue and in 1938 the school auditorium replaced the original church.

Several of the largest parishes in the Bronx today date from the mid-1920s. The Church of Our Lady of the Assumption was started in Pelham Bay in 1923. Ground was broken for a church on May 25, 1924, and it was dedicated by Cardinal Hayes on October 19 of the same year. It was replaced with the present cavernous church that was dedicated by Cardinal Spellman

The Church of St. Anthony on Commonwealth Avenue.

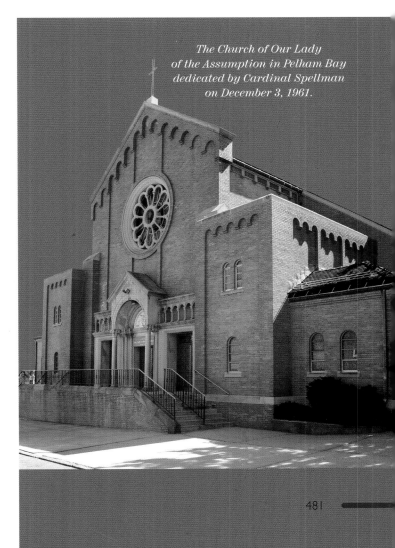

The Church of Our Lady of the Assumption in Pelham Bay dedicated by Cardinal Spellman on December 3, 1961.

481

on December 3, 1961. St. Benedict's Church in Unionport was the second parish founded by the Benedictine monks from St. John's Abbey in Collegeville, Minnesota. Many Catholic churches in New York began in stables, rented stores or even tents. St. Benedict's was unique because the first pastor, Father Louis Treufler, O.S.B., bought two old barracks that had been used during World War I in the naval training base in Pelham Bay Park. The present church was dedicated on May 15, 1960.

St. Frances de Chantal Church in Throgs Neck began in 1922 as a mission first of Holy Family Church and then of St. Benedict's Church. It became a parish in 1926 with the appointment of Father William J. Jordan as the first resident pastor. Father Jordan built the original church in

1930. It was replaced by the present church which was dedicated by Cardinal Cooke on October 25, 1970.

St. Dominic's Church was founded as an Italian parish in the Van Nest section of the Bronx in 1924, and the church was erected in 1927. That same year St. Theresa's Church was established as a national parish for the Italians in the Pelham Bay area. Father Bonventure Fillitti built the first church in 1928. It was destroyed by fire in February 1965 and replaced with the present church, which was dedicated by Cardinal Cooke on May 17, 1970. St. Lucy's Church was also established as an Italian parish in 1927 and a church was built the following year. It became a popular shrine church because of its replica of the grotto at Lourdes.

The first St. Benedict's Church: two former U.S. Navy barracks.

St. Benedict's Church dedicated on May 15, 1960. Since 1976 the diocesan clergy have administered the parish

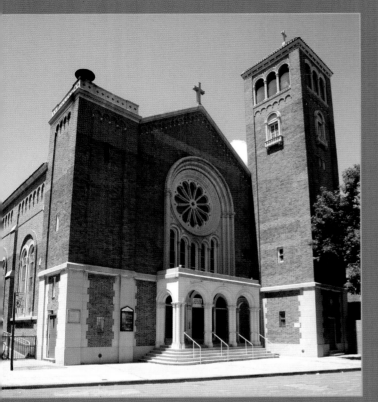

The Church of St. Dominic dedicated in 1927.

The Church of St. Frances de Chantal dedicated by Cardinal Cooke on October 25, 1970.

The first St. Teresa's Church, built in 1928 and destroyed by fire in 1965.

The Church of St. Teresa of the Infant Jesus dedicated by Cardinal Cooke on May 17, 1970.

The Church of St. Clare of Assisi was still another East Bronx Italian parish, founded in July 1929 by Father Francis Canigna, who had been a curate of Father Daniel Burke at St. Philip Neri for eighteen years. Father Canigna broke ground for a church on October 20, 1929, one week before the Stock Market Crash on Black Friday. Despite the Depression, he completed the church, which was dedicated by Cardinal Hayes on May 7, 1931. Santa Maria, founded in Tremont in 1926, was one of the smaller Italian national parishes in the East Bronx.

The Franciscan Church of the Holy Cross, founded in 1921, was the first parish in Clason Point. Likewise the Church of the Nativity of the Blessed Virgin Mary, which dates from 1924, was the first Catholic church in the extreme northeastern section of the Bronx. The Church of the Holy Rosary was started by Father James Winters in a prefabricated building in 1925. The

present church at the intersection of Eastchester Road and Gun Hill Road, was dedicated by Cardinal Cooke on April 6, 1970. Blessed Sacrament Church, founded in 1927, took in much of the southern part of Holy Family parish. It was still another combination church-and-school.

In the Morris Park area the Church of St. Francis Xavier was founded in July 1928 by Father James E. Kearney with territory taken from the Church of Our Lady of Solace. By December Father Kearney had built a frame church at Lurting and Van Nest Avenues for $11,100. Father Kearney was appointed the bishop of Salt Lake City in 1932. His successor, Father John Quinn, had to cope with the challenge of building a new church after the original church was destroyed by fire on February 7, 1948. The new church was dedicated by Cardinal Spellman on July 22, 1951.[21]

The Shrine Church of St. Lucy founded in 1927.

The Church of St. Clare of Assisi dedicated by Cardinal Hayes on May 7, 1931.

21 - Arthur T. Welton, Batholomew Daly, M.H.M., et al, *Church of St. Francis Xavier, 1928-2003* (Bronx: Church of St. Francis Xavier, 2003), unpaginated.

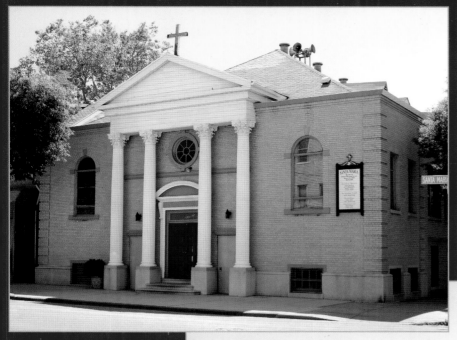

The Church of Santa Maria built in 1926 and remodeled in 1936.

Holy Cross Church, Soundview Avenue.

The Church of the Nativity of the Blessed Virgin Mary.

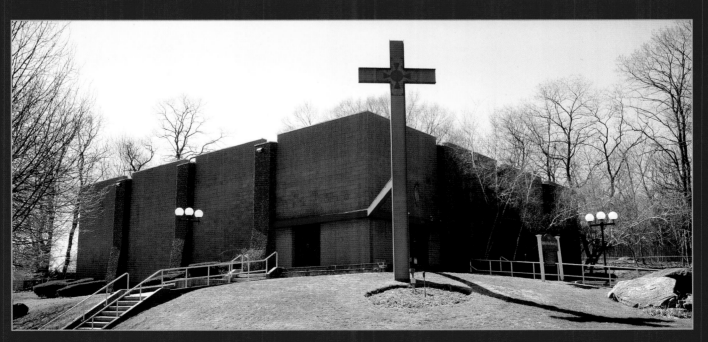

The Church of the Holy Rosary dedicated by Cardinal Cooke on April 6, 1970.

The first St. Francis Xavier Church.
Credit: *St. Francis Xavier Church.*

*St. Francis Xavier Church dedicated
by Cardinal Spellman on July 22, 1951.*

*Blessed Sacrament Church
built in 1929.*

Up to the Present

Cardinal Spellman added seven new parishes in the Bronx. The first was St. Gabriel's in Riverdale, named after the East Side parish that was demolished in 1939 to make way for the Queens Midtown Tunnel. Father Francis W. Walsh was appointed the first pastor on December 8, 1939. He used the Manhattan College chapel as a temporary church until the auditorium of the school was completed in October 1941.

St. Helena's Church (named after Spellman's mother) was begun in 1940 to provide a parish for the thousands of Catholics who had moved into Parkchester, the huge housing complex built by the Metropolitan Life Insurance Company on the site of the old Catholic Protectory. Ground was broken for the church on June 8, 1941, by Monsignor Arthur J. Scanlan, the former rector of Dunwoodie, and the first Mass was celebrated in the church that Christmas. Many of the Catholic residents of Parkchester were young couples with children. St. Helena's school opened with 800 students and the number soon swelled to 3,000. Each year there were 600 youngsters in the First Communion and Confirmation classes.

St. Gabriel's Church, Riverdale, built in 1941.

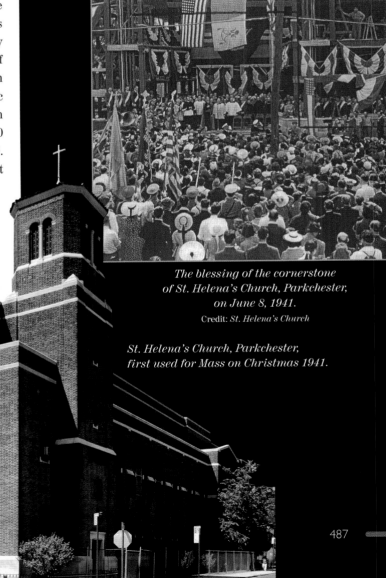

The blessing of the cornerstone of St. Helena's Church, Parkchester, on June 8, 1941.
Credit: *St. Helena's Church*

St. Helena's Church, Parkchester, first used for Mass on Christmas 1941.

The store on Elder Avenue that served as the first Church of St. Joan of Arc.
Credit: *St. John of Arc Church*

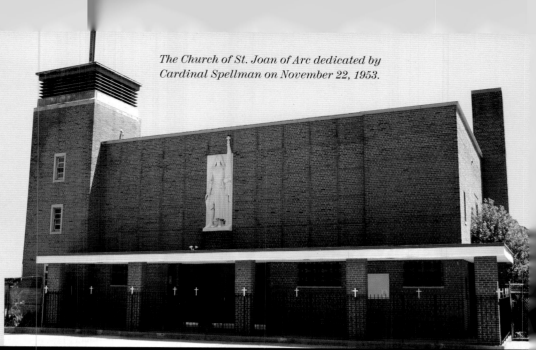

The Church of St. Joan of Arc dedicated by Cardinal Spellman on November 22, 1953.

The Korean Church of St. John Nam, founded in 1989 and housed in the former St. Mary's Church on White Plains Road.

The Church of St. Francis of Assisi on Baychester Avenue. It was merged with the Church of St. Frances of Rome in 2007.

The Church of Sts. Philip and James founded in 1949.

Cardinal Spellman established three Bronx parishes in 1949, St. Joan of Arc in the Longwood area, Saints Philip and James on Boston Post Road between Gun Hill Road and Eastchester Road, and St. Francis of Assisi in the Wakefield area. St. Francis of Assisi had originated as

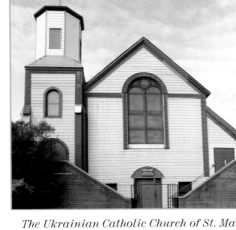

The Ukrainian Catholic Church of St. Mary Protectress on Washington Avenue.

a mission of the Italian Church of Our Lady of Mt. Carmel in Mount Vernon. In 2007 it was consolidated with the Church of St. Frances of Rome. The Bronx got is first Ukrainan Catholic Church with the founding of the Church of St. Mary Protectoress on Washington Avenue in 1945.

The establishment of the parish of St Joan of Arc was a milestone in the evolution of the Church in the Bronx because it was the first time that a parish had been founded in the borough specifically to care for the residents of a public housing project. (St. Jude's Church was established in Inwood that same year for the same reason.) St. Joan of Arc was carved out of the parish of St. John Chrysostom for the sake of the Catholics in the Bronx River Houses. The original plans for a church, school, convent and rectory had to be scaled back for financial reasons, but the Church of St. Joan of Arc on 174th Street between Stratford and Morrison Avenues was dedicated by Cardinal Spellman on November 22, 1953.[22] Spellman repeated the performance in 1960, when he established the Church of St. John Vianney on Castle Hill Avenue, to provide a parish for the thousands of Catholics in the new public housing projects in the neighborhood.

St. Michael's Church in Co-Op City founded by Cardinal Cooke in 1969.

In 1969 Cardinal Cooke did something similar when he established St. Michael's Church for the Catholics in Co-op City, the mammoth private middle-income housing complex in the Baychester area. The Bronx got its last new parish in 1989, the Korean Church of St John Nam, which was housed in St. Mary's Church on White Plains Road. More recently the Bronx got its first Syro-Malabar Church when Indian Catholics of that rite took over the former Polish Church of St. Valentine.

The Church of St. John Vianney founded in 1949.

22 - William J. Delaney, *St. Joan of Arc, Bronx, New York* (New York: Church of St. Joan of Arc, 1978), 13-15.

Staten Island Parishes and Missions

Parishes

1839 - 1902

1. St. Peter, New Brighton, 1839
2. St. Mary, Clifton (Rosebank), 1852
3. St. Joseph, Rossville, 1855
    Mission of St. Peter, New Brighton, 1848-1852
    Mission of St. Mary, Clifton (Rosebank), 1852-1855
    42. St. Thomas, Pleasant Plains, added 1938
4. St. Mary of the Assumption, Port Richmond, 1877
    Mission of St. Peter 1853-1855
    Mission of St. Joseph, Rossville, 1855-1877
5. St. Patrick, Richmond, 1884
    Mission of St. Joseph, Rossville 1862-1884
6. Sacred Heart, West Brighton, 1875
    Mission (St. Rose of Lima) of St. Peter, New Brighton, 1864
7. Immaculate Conception, Stapleton, 1887
    Mission of St. Mary, Clifton (Rosebank), 1882-1887
8. Our Lady Help of Christians, Tottenville, 1898
    Mission of St. Joseph, Rossville, 1890-1898
9. Our Lady of Good Counsel, 1899
10. St. John Baptist de la Salle (German), Stapleton, 1901
    Closed 2007
11. St. Adalbert (Polish), Port Richmond, 1901
12. St. Joseph (Italian), Rosebank, 1902

1902-1918

13. St. Anthony of Padua (Polish), Linoleumville (Travis), 1908
14. St. Clement, Mariners Harbor, 1910
    Merged with St. Michael, Mariners Harbor, 1945
15. Blessed Sacrament, West Brighton, 1910
16. Our Lady of Mount Carmel (Italian), West Brighton, 1913
17. St. Ann, Dongan Hills, 1914

1918-1928

18. St. Rita (Italian), Meiers Corners, 1921
19. Assumption (Italian), New Brighton, 1921
20. St. Sylvester, Concord, 1921
    Mission of St. Ann, Dongan Hills, 1917-1921
21. St. Michael (Italian), Northfield (Mariners Harbor), 1922
    Mission of Our Lady of Mt. Carmel, 1913-1922
    Merged with St. Clement, Mariners Harbor, 1945
22. St. Roch (Italian) Elm Park, Port Richmond, 1922
23. Our Lady Queen of Peace, New Dorp, 1922
    Mission (Our Lady of Lourdes) of St. Patrick, Richmond, 1918-1922

24. Our Lady of Pity, Graniteville (Bull's Head), 1923
    Mission of Our Lady of Mount Carmel, West Brighton, 1919-1923
25. St. Stanislaus Kostka (Polish), New Brighton, 1923
26. St. Clare, Great Kills, 1925
    Mission of St. Patrick, Richmond, 1918-1925
27. St. Benedicta (Italian), West Brighton, 1927
    Mission of Our Lady of Mt. Carmel, West Brighton, 1922-1927
    Merged with Our Lady of Mt. Carmel 1957
28. St. Theresa, Castleton Corners, 1926
29. St. Christopher, Grant City, 1926
    Mission of St. Ann, Dongan Hills
30. St. Paul, New Brighton, 1926
    Mission of St. Peter, New Brighton, 1924-1926
    To be merged with Assumption, New Brighton, 2007
31. St. Margaret Mary, Midland Beach, 1926
    Mission of St. Patrick, Richmond, 1914-1917
    Mission of St. Ann, Dongan Hills, 1917-1926
32. Holy Rosary (Italian), South Beach, 1927
    Mission of St. Joseph, Rosebank, 1914-1927

1928-2007

33. Our Lady Star of the Sea, Huguenot, 1935
    Mission of Our Lady Help of Christians, Tottenville, 1916-1935
34. Holy Trinity Ukrainian Catholic Church 1949
35. St. Charles, Oakwood Heights, 1960
    Mission of St. Patrick, Richmond, 1922-1960
36. Holy Child, Eltingville, 1966
37. Holy Family, Westerleigh, 1966
38. St. John Neumann, Greenridge, 1982

Missions

39. Christ the King, Port Richmond 1928
    Mission of Our Lady of Mt. Carmel, 1928-1930
    Mission of St. Mary of the Assumption, Port Richmond, 1930
40. Our Lady of Lourdes, New Dorp Beach, 1918
    Mission of St. Patrick, Richmond, 1918-1922
    Mission of Our Lady Queen of Peace, New Dorp, 1922
41. St. Nicholas, 1923, Clove Lake
    Mission of Our Lady of Mt. Carmel 1923
    Mission of St. Teresa, Castleton Corners, 1926

STATEN ISLAND
parishes in 1902

St. PETER
NEW BRIGHTON
1839

St. JOHN BAPTIST
DE LA SALLE
STAPLETON
1901

St. MARY OF
THE ASSUMPTION
PORT RICHMOND
1877

SACRED HEART
WEST BRIGHTON
1875

IMMACULATE CONCEPTION
STAPLETON 1887

St. ADALBERT 1901

VICTORY BLVD

St. MARY
CLIFTON 1850

St. JOSEPH
ROSE BANK
1902

St. PATRICK
RICHMOND
1884

ARTHUR KILL RD

RICHMOND RD

OUR LADY OF
GOOD COUNSEL
1899

St. JOSEPH ROSSVILLE 1855

AMBOY RD

R LADY HELP
F CHRISTIANS
TOTTENVILLE
1898

STATEN ISLAND PARISHES
& missions 2007

14+21

30

1

39

6

25

4

16+27

19

10

15

7

11

28

34

37

41

9

22

VICTORY BLVD

2

STATEN ISLAND EXPRESS WAY

20

24

18

12

13

17

29

32

23

RICHMOND RD

5

ARTHUR KILL RD

38

31

26

20

3

35

40

33

36

42 AMBOY RD

8

Cardinal Hayes' Other Island

At the death of Archbishop Corrigan in 1902 there were only a dozen parishes on Staten Island, and three of them were national parishes for the Poles, Germans and Italians. During the following sixteen years Cardinal Farley added only five additional parishes. The real expansion came in the 1920s under Cardinal Hayes when no fewer than fifteen new parishes were established. In one decade he practically doubled the number of parishes created during the previous one hundred years. By contrast, since 1935 only six new parishes (including one Ukrainian Catholic church) have been opened on the island, although many parishes have built bigger churches especially since the completion of the Verrazano-Narrows Bridge in 1964.

Two of the new parishes that were opened just before the First Word War were national parishes. St. Anthony of Padua was founded in 1908 for the Poles in Travis (then called Linoleumville). Our Lady of Mount Carmel was established for the Italians in West Brighton in 1913. The moving spirit behind the latter church, as he never ceased to remind the world, was Father Louis Riccio. The other three pre-war parishes were St. Clement in Mariners Harbor in 1910, Blessed Sacrament in West Brighton in 1910 and St. Ann in Dongan Hills in 1914.

St. Ann's Church, Dongan Hills.

St. Clement's Church, Mariners Harbor, founded in 1910, now the Church of St. Clement and St. Michael.

Blessed Sacrament Church, Manor Road, West Brighton.

Just as St. Peter's Church, New Brighton, was the mother church of many of the new parishes established in the nineteenth century, no fewer than six of the new parishes or missions established in the 1920s originated as out-missions of either St. Patrick's, Richmond, or St. Ann's, Dongan Hills. Both parishes had far-sighted pastors who recognized the need to build more churches as the population of Staten Island grew at an unprecedented rate from 85,969 in 1916 to 116,531 in 1920 and 158,346 in 1930. In that era Staten Island also became more accessible to the outside world following the opening of the Goethals Bridge and the Outerbridge Crossing in 1928 and the Bayonne Bridge in 1931.

The pastor of St. Patrick's, Richmond, from 1917 to 1922 was Father Charles J. Parks, a native of Tompkinsville and a graduate of St. Peter's Academy in New Brighton. During his brief pastorate he established three out-missions. The year after his arrival at St. Patrick's Father Parks built Our Lady of Lourdes Mission chapel in New Dorp Beach at a cost of $3,000. Occasionally the priests from St. Patrick's also celebrated Mass at the Black Horse Tavern in New Dorp. In 1922 New Dorp became a separate parish, Our Lady Queen of Peace, under Father John Hopkins, who built the present church in 1928. In 1918 Father Parks established a second mission in Great Kills where Mass was celebrated in a frame building until the construction of the first St. Clare's Church in 1921. Shortly before his death in October 1922 Father Parks established a third mission, St. Charles in Oakwood Heights, which became a parish in 1960.

The pastor of St. Ann's in Dongan Hills from 1917 to 1926 was Father Joseph A. Farrell, who was to spend all of his sixty years as a priest on Staten Island, half of them as the dean. At St. Ann's Father Farrell was responsible for the establishment of three new parishes. The first was St. Sylvester's in Concord, which originated as a mission of St. Ann's in 1917. For the first four years the congregation met for Sunday Mass in a rented hall and used the discarded seats from old trolley cars for pews. Before the seats could be used, the parishioners had to paint over the signs on the back of each seat: "Smoking in the Last Four Seats Only." In January 1921 Father Farrell purchased the Wandell Memorial Methodist Church for $25,000. Six months later it became St. Sylvester's Church following the appointment of Father Michael Donnelly as the first resident pastor in June 1921. The interior of the church was so small that Father Donnelly was alleged to have said: "I could stand before the altar and almost shake hands with the people in the last row."[23]

In 1926 two other missions of St. Ann's became parishes, St. Christopher in Grant City, and St. Margaret Mary in Midland Beach. In Grant City the first pastor, Father Alexander Cahill, was no stranger to rural life. A native of Kingston, he had been the pastor in Sawkill before coming to Staten Island. For his new parish in Grant City, he bought a prefabricated building from Sears Roebuck which became the first St. Christopher's Church. When it proved to be too small for the congregation, he purchased a second prefabricated building and attached it to the first. It served as the parish church for sixty-five years until it was replaced by the present church in June 1991.[24]

Midland Beach had become a popular summer resort by the First World War. Father William J. Donovan, the pastor of St. Patrick's in Richmond, began celebrating Mass in Midland Beach in 1914 on Sundays during the summer at a casino for upwards of a thousand people. In 1917 the Midland Beach mission was transferred to St. Ann's, Dongan Hills, just as Father Farrell was appointed the pastor. He built a mission church in Midland Beach in 1922 dedicated to St. Margaret Mary. It became a parish in 1926 with the appointment of Father Martin F. Drury as the first resident pastor.

23 - *St. Sylvester's Church, Staten Island, New York* (Custombnook, 1972), unpaginated.

24 - *St. Christopher Church, 50th Anniversary* (St. Christopher's Church, 1976), 4-6.

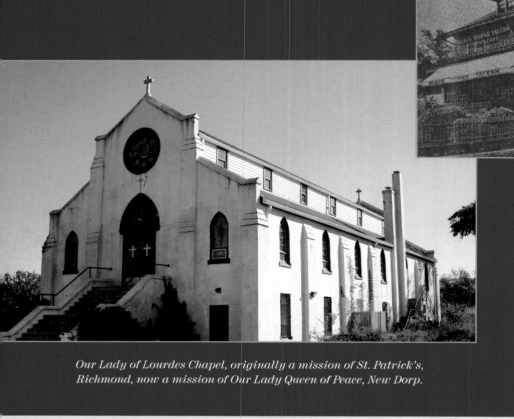

Black Horse Tavern, New Dorp, where priests from St. Patrick's, Richmond, occasionally celebrated Mass.
Credit: *Church of Our Lady Queen of Peace.*

Our Lady of Lourdes Chapel, originally a mission of St. Patrick's, Richmond, now a mission of Our Lady Queen of Peace, New Dorp.

St. Sylvester's Church, Concord, a former Protestant church acquired as a mission of St. Ann's Church, Dongan Hills, in 1917.

The celebration of the incorporation of St. Sylvester's Church on June 30, 1921.
Credit: *St. Sylvester's Church*

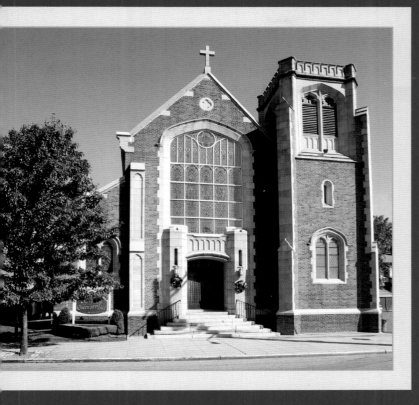

The Church of Our Lady Queen of Peace, New Dorp, built in 1928.

St. Christopher's Church, Grant City, dedicated by Cardinal O'Connor on June 11, 1991.

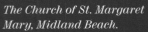

The Church of St. Margaret Mary, Midland Beach.

As a later episcopal vicar of Staten Island, Monsignor Andrew Quinn, once remarked, the parish in Midland Beach "never quite got into orbit." The impact of the Depression was especially severe in Midland Beach where many of the year-round residents lived in winterized bungalows. As late as 1939 sixty percent of the men in the parish were unemployed. When Father John P. Monaghan arrived that year as the new pastor, he told the parishioners, "We are a poor parish and we are going to do great things as a poor people."

Father Monaghan was true to his word. He had instructed a whole generation of New York priests in the social teaching of the Church as a professor at Cathedral College, and now he had the opportunity to put that teaching into practice. He remodeled the church, introduced the dialogue Mass to his parishioners, encouraged an innovative curriculum in the school, provided night classes to prepare adults to take civil service exams, and formed a credit union that helped many parishioners to save their home from foreclosure by the banks. More than anything else, "Doc" Monaghan instilled a sense of pride and self-respect in his parishioners.[25]

St. Theresa's Church dates from 1926 when Father Philip Conran was assigned to start the parish. He used the mission chapel of St. Nicholas as the base from which to build his new parish. The first parish church was a converted children's home that was purchased from the Volunteers of America. Father Conran replaced it with the present church, which was dedicated by Cardinal Spellman on May 4, 1952.[26]

St. Paul's Church in New Brighton began as an out-mission of St. Peter's in 1922. The following year a small chapel was erected and it became a parish in 1924. In 1963 the chapel was replaced with a large all-purpose hall attached to the school. In 2007 St. Paul's was slated to be merged with the Church of the Assumption.

Father Stephen Kelleher,
Father John P. Monaghan,
and Father John Riordan.
Credit: *St. Margaret Mary Church*

The dialogue Mass at St. Margaret Mary Church.
Credit: *St. Margaret Mary Church*

---

25 - *St. Margaret Mary Church, 1926-1976* (New York: Park Publishing Company, 1976), 4-16.
26 - *Church of St. Teresa of the Infant Jesus* (Staten Island: Church of St. Teresa, 1976), 7-8.

*Monsignor Philip Conran,
the pastor of St. Theresa's Church,
1926-1957.*
Credit: *St. Theresa's Church.*

*The first St. Theresa's
Church.*
Credit: *St. Theresa's Church.*

*St. Theresa's Church,
Castleton Corners,
dedicated by
Cardinal Spellman
on May 4, 1952.*

*St. Paul's Church, New Brighton, erected in 1963.
In 2007 the parish was slated to be merged with the Church of the Assumption.*

The Italian Parishes

Almost half of the new parishes established on Staten Island during the 1920s were Italian national parishes, bringing the total number of Italian parishes to nine. The first Italian parish to be established on the island was St. Joseph's in Rosebank. It was founded by Father Paolo Iacomino, a native of Italy, who came to Rosebank in 1901, built a small wooden church the following year and died in 1905 at the age of thirty-eight. His successor, Father Anthony Catoggio, was another native of Italy, who was pastor from 1905 to 1959 and built the present St. Joseph's Church in 1957. He was a familiar figure riding his bicycle in his cassock as he made his round of sick calls. His parish included South Beach where he established Holy Rosary mission chapel in 1914. It became a separate parish in 1927 when Father Dominic Epifanio was appointed the first resident pastor. The present church was built by Monsignor Richard Guastella and dedicated by Cardinal O'Connor on April 20, 1991.[27]

On the north shore the first Italian parish was Our Lady of Mount Carmel in West Brighton, founded in 1913 by Father Louis Riccio, who also was instrumental in founding at least five out-missions of Our Lady of Mount Carmel, St. Michael's in Mariners Harbor in 1913, Our Lady of Pity in Graniteville in 1919, Assumption in West Brighton in 1921, St. Benedicta in West Brighton in 1922, and St. Nicholas in Clove Lakes the following year. In his more theatrical moments, which were a frequent occurrence, Father Riccio claimed credit for establishing virtually all of the new Italian parishes in the 1920s. An energetic but volatile individual, he combined shameless flattery of Cardinal Hayes with disdain for the administrative abilities of every Italian priest on Staten Island except himself. Frustrated at what he considered lack of recognition for his work on Staten Island by both his superiors and his confreres, he threatened to join a Trappist monastery but calmed down and settled for a new assignment in New Rochelle in 1929.[28]

Father Riccio's chronic complaints had a basis in the poverty of his parishioners. On one Sunday in November 1924 the total collection from Our Lady of Mount Carmel and two mission churches amounted to $88.59. Like many Staten Island parishes, Our Lady of Mount Carmel was hard hit by the Depression and became a mission of Blessed Sacrament Church from 1936 to 1949. Meanwhile, St. Benedicta, became a separate parish in 1927 with the appointment of Father Bonaventure J. Fillitti as the first resident pastor. In 1957 St. Benedicta was merged with Our Lady of Mount Carmel. The following year ground was broken for a new Mt. Carmel- St. Benedicta School and Hall. In 1960 St. Benedicta's Church was demolished to make way for the construction of the West Brighton Housing Project.

Two Italian parishes were founded in 1921, the Church of the Assumption in New Brighton and St. Rita's Church in Meiers Corners. In New Brighton a group of lay people established a chapel that served as a mission of Our Lady of Mount Carmel until Archbishop Hayes appointed Father Carmelo Crisci the first permanent pastor in 1921. That same year Father Crisci broke ground for a permanent church, which was dedicated by Bishop John Dunn on the feast of the Assumption in 1922. The building of the church and rectory left the parish with a debt of $200,000. It was a huge burden to shoulder after the onset of the Depression, when many parishioners were unemployed. After 1929 Father Crisci returned his salary to the church every year as a donation.

27 - Diane Lore Palladino, *Holy Rosary Church: A History of 'Dedication'* (Staten Island: Holy Rosary Church, 1991), unpaginated.
28 - AANY, Riccio to Hayes, January 9, 1928.

Monsignor Anthony Catoggio,
the pastor of St. Joseph's Church,
Rosebank, 1905-1959.
Credit: *St: Joseph's Church*

The first St. Joseph's Church, Rosebank,
as it appeared in 1940.
Credit: *St: Joseph's Church*

St. Joseph's Church in Rosebank
dedicated in 1957.

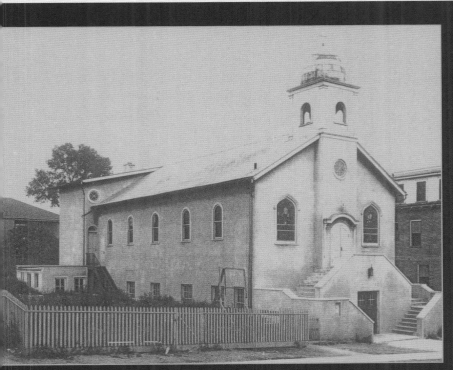

Father Dominic Epifanio,
the pastor of Holy Rosary Church, 1927-1947.
Credit: *Holy Rosary Church*

The mission church of the Holy Rosary in South Beach in 1927.
Credit: *Holy Rosary Church*

The Church of
the Assumption,
New Brighton, dedicated
by Bishop John J. Dunn
on August 15, 1922.

Father Carmelo Crisci, the first pastor
of the Church of the Assumption,
New Brighton. Credit: Church of the Assumption

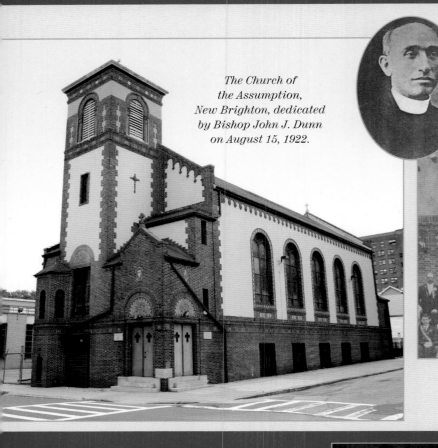

The Assumption Society at the dedication
of the church on August 15, 1922.
Credit: Church of the Assumption

Monsignor Louis Riccio, pastor
of the Church of Our Lady of
Mount Carmel. Credit: Church of
Our Lady of Mount Carmel

The Chruch of Our Lady of
Mount Carmel-St. Benedicta,
West New Brighton.

Church of Our Lady of Mt. Carmel
West New Brighton, N. Y.

SUNDAY, NOVEMBER 16, 1924

Collections and Seats at Mt. Carmel	$64
" " " St. Benedicta's	18
" (no seats) St. Nicholas	5
Total Collections plus Seats	88
Candles	5
Baptisms	6
Grand Total of Receipts	100
Debt on Three Churches	$80,000
Interest at 5%—$4,000 yearly—$11.04 a day—$99.10 weekly	
Weekly Balance	1

TOTAL DEBT

American Trust Co.	$33,000
Yorkville Bank	28,000
Emigrant Savings Bank	15,000
Staten Island Building Loan Association	2,600
	$78,600
Note for Balance on Contract of St. Benedicta's Church	1,400
Total	$80,000

The weekly collection at
the Church of Our Lady of
Mount Carmel and two
missions in September 1924.
Credit: Church of Our Lady
of Mount Carmel

OUR LADY OF MT. CARMEL ✝ SAINT BENEDICTA

The problem was not only the Depression, but also what he called the superfluity of Catholic churches. "We have here six Catholic churches in less than a square mile," he informed the chancellor in 1934. He had already brought that to the attention of the vicar general several times without getting a response.[29]

St. Rita's was another Italian parish that experienced severe financial problems in its early years. The first pastor, Father Emmanuel Taverna, said that most of the men were construction workers who were employed only eight months of the year. Work was so hard to find that sometimes they left home at 4:00 a.m. and did not return until 8:30 p.m. From 1936 to 1948 the parish could not support a resident pastor, but it experienced a remarkable renaissance under Monsignor Paul Andrews, who became the administrator in 1950 and served as pastor from 1953 to 1985. He built a new school in 1957 and a new church in 1975, and was the episcopal vicar of Staten Island from 1975 to 1981.[30]

Two more Italian parishes were founded in 1922, St. Roch's Church in Elm Park, Port Richmond, and St. Michael's Church in Mariners Harbor. St. Roch's was an offshoot, if not technically an out-mission, of the Church of the Assumption. The first pastor, Father Catello Terrone, built a small wooden church that was used until 1928 when the present church was built. Parishioners sold individual bricks from door to door at a dollar each so that every family literally owed a piece of the the church.[31]

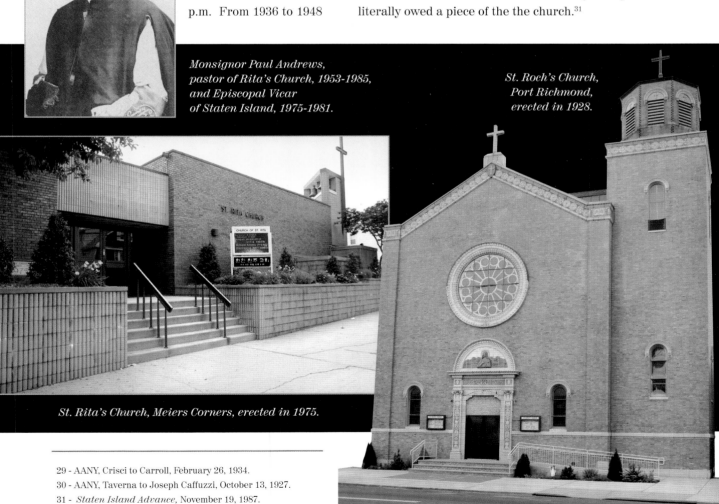

Monsignor Paul Andrews,
pastor of Rita's Church, 1953-1985,
and Episcopal Vicar
of Staten Island, 1975-1981.

St. Roch's Church,
Port Richmond,
erected in 1928.

St. Rita's Church, Meiers Corners, erected in 1975.

29 - AANY, Crisci to Carroll, February 26, 1934.
30 - AANY, Taverna to Joseph Caffuzzi, October 13, 1927.
31 - *Staten Island Advance,* November 19, 1987.

St. Michael's originated in 1913 as an out-mission of Our Lady of Mount Carmel. The original mission church was located only 300 feet away from the St. Clement's Church on the same street. In 1922 St. Michael's became a parish with the appointment of Father Emil Molinelli as the first resident pastor. Born in Italy, but raised in Lower Manhattan, Father Molinelli was one of a new generation of Italian priests in New York who were born abroad but educated at St. Joseph's Seminary, Dunwoodie.

St. Michael's Church, Mariners Harbor, dedicated by Cardinal Hayes on April 16, 1928, today the Church of St. Clement-St. Michael.

Although he was a native of Genoa, he quickly won the confidence of his Southern Italian parishioners whom he described as mostly "hard-boiled" Sicilians, Calabrians and Neapolitans. While the Irish in Mariners Harbor were still worshipping in the little wooden church they erected in 1910, Father Molinelli built an impressive Romanesque church on Harbor Road at a cost of $120,000 that was dedicated by Cardinal Hayes on April 16, 1928. Even before he erected the new church, however, Father Molinelli questioned the wisdom of maintaining two Catholic churches in Mariners Harbor.[32]

In 1932 during the Depression he repeated his recommendation that the two churches should be merged. Since he had twice as many parishioners as St. Clement and a bigger church, he suggested the consolidation of the two parishes at St. Michael's with an Italian pastor and an "English-speaking" (i.e., Irish) assistant. The chancellor, Monsignor Thomas G. Carroll, thought that Molinelli was being excessively nationalistic in wanting an Italian pastor. Thirteen years later, when the archdiocese finally heeded Father Molinelli's suggestion and combined the two parishes, Cardinal Spellman appointed as pastor Father John J. McEvoy, an Irish-American who was fluent in Italian. However, the part swallowed the whole, since McEvoy was appointed the pastor of St. Clement's but the administrator of St. Michael's.[33]

The Church of Our Lady of Pity was still another parish that originated as an out-mission of Our Lady of Mount Carmel in New Brighton. In 1919 a small prefabricated building was erected as a chapel, and it became a parish in 1923 with the appointment of Father John Gallo as the first resident pastor. Even before the crash of the Stock Market in 1929, the parish had difficulty in paying its bills and needed to be rescued by the archdiocese to keep the creditors away from the front door. However, Monsignor Thomas Carroll proved to be a good prophet when he predicted that year that the parish was ideally located to be the center of a real estate boom.[34]

32 - AANY, Molinelli to Carroll, April 10, 1926.
33 - AANY, Carroll to Hayes, October 20, 1932.
34 - AANY, Carroll to Hayes, January 6, 1929

The construction of the Staten Island Expressway led to the demolition of the original church in 1955, but it also spurred the real estate boom that Monsignor Carroll had predicted in 1929. As late as the 1960s, according to Monsignor Robert Mazziotta, much of the area consisted of empty lots and some of it was still farmland. Twenty years later, when Monsignor Mazziotta returned to Staten Island as the pastor of Our Lady of Pity, he found the real estate development in full bloom. At the urging of Cardinal Cooke, he began the building of the present church, which was dedicated by Cardinal O'Connor on December 10, 1988.[35]

The last two Italian national parishes on Staten Island were both established in 1927, St. Benedicta and Our Lady of the Rosary. The Depression precluded the building of additional Italian parishes, but even earlier, Monsignor Carroll noted that the restrictive immigration laws of the 1920s were having a paralyzing effect on the Italian national parishes throughout the archdiocese and he questioned the wisdom of establishing additional ones. For example, at Father Molinelli's parish in Mariners Harbor, there were few parishioners who did not know English by the 1920s.

In the 1950s the process was reversed. Instead of founding new Italian parishes, three Italian parishes, St. Rita's, St. Roch's and Our Lady of Pity, were made territorial parishes. In the petition that Cardinal Spellman sent to Rome requesting the change, he stated that "each parish has lost its distinctive Italian character."[36] The Italians remained the dominant ethnic group in the Catholic community on Staten Island, although by 2007 the great majority were second and third-generation Italian-Americans. The only church on the island that still had a regularly scheduled Italian Mass on Sunday was the Church of the Holy Rosary in South Beach.

The South Shore

Only one new parish was opened on Staten Island during the 1930s. In fact only one new parish was opened between 1927 and 1960, Our Lady Star of the Sea in Huguenot. It originated in 1916 as an out-mission of Our Lady Help of Christians in Tottenville and became a parish in 1935 with the appointment of Father Joseph V. Hyland as the first resident pastor. In the 1950s, as the population began to increase on the South Shore, Monsignor James O'Meara purchased some fifteen acres for $36,500, and built a school

35 - *Staten Island Advance,* December 17, 1987.
36 - AANY, Spellman to Pietro Cardinal Ciriaci, June 7, 1954.

and auditorium in 1959 which served as the parish church until the erection of the present church in 1982.

St. Clare's parish in Great Kills was another South Shore parish that experienced large-scale growth in the 1950s. The original church, which dated from 1921, was replaced by Monsignor John Flanagan with a much larger colonial-style church that was built between 1958 and 1960. In 1979 Monsignor John Keogh added the Cardinal Cooke Center, which contained a parish hall and gym. By the 1980s it was the largest parish on the island with over 5,000 registered families.[37]

St. Charles in Oakwood Heights was also caught up in the population explosion on the South Shore. From 1922 until 1960 it was an out-mission of St. Patrick's Church, and the small frame mission chapel sufficed for the needs of the parishioners and summer visitors until after World War II. The pastor of St. Patrick, Monsignor Patrick Gallagher, drew up plans for a combination chapel and auditorium shortly before St. Charles became a separate parish in May 1960

with the appointment of Father John J. Manning as the first resident pastor. The second pastor of St. Charles, Monsignor John McGowan, shelved plans for a church until he could build a school, which was opened in September 1964. The church was completed by Monsignor Robert Kelly and dedicated by Cardinal Cooke on June 9, 1973.[38]

The opening of the Verrazano Narrows Bridge in 1964 accelerated real estate development all over Staten Island, but especially on the South Shore. Two years after the completion of the bridge, new parishes were established in Westerleigh and Eltingville. On May 17, 1966, Father Francis J. Glynn was appointed the pastor of the Church of the Holy Family in Westerleigh. Real estate prices and construction costs had changed considerably since the 1920s when Father Charles Parks built Our Lady of Lourdes chapel in New Dorp Beach for $3.000. The new Holy Family Church that was planned by Father Glynn and completed by Father Thomas Marinak cost $3.5 million. It was dedicated by Cardinal O'Connor on January 13, 1990.

The first St. Clare's Church, Great Kills, erected in 1921. Credit: *St. Clare's Church*

St. Clare's Church, Great Kills, dedicated by Cardinal Spellman on May 22, 1960.

---

37 - *Staten Island Advance,* September 24, 1987.

38 - *St. Charles Parish, Oakwood, Staten Island* (Custombook, n.d.), 4-13.

The Chapel of St. Charles Borromeo, Mill Road, built as a mission church of St. Patrick's in the 1920s.
Credit: *St. Charles Church*

The Church of St. Charles Borromeo, Oakwood Heights, dedicated by Cardinal Cooke on June 9, 1973.

Holy Rosary Church, South Beach, dedicated by Cardinal O'Connor on April 20, 1991.

The Church of the Holy Family, Westerleigh, dedicated by Cardinal O'Connor on January 13, 1990.

The Church of Our Lady Star of the Sea, Huguenot, erected in 1982.

The new parish in Eltingville, Holy Child, got its start when the first pastor, Father Francis M. Brennan, celebrated the first Mass outdoors on the porch of the Elks Club in Greenridge on July 10, 1966, in the presence of 800 people. The Church of the Holy Child, which was built by Monsignor John J. Burke, was dedicated by Cardinal O'Connor on May 28, 1994.

The last parish to be established on Staten Island was St. John Neumann in Greenridge in 1982, located on the grounds of the former St. Michael's Home. When the home was closed in 1978, the archdiocese sold most of the seventy-three acre property, but retained six acres as a site for the new parish. The first pastor, Father John Sheehan, had earlier spent twenty years as an assistant in three Staten Island parishes before taking an assignment in Putnam County. Upon his return to Staten Island to take the reins at St. John Neumann, Father Sheehan remarked, "I am happy to be back on Staten Island to take on this pleasant challenge. It seems to have gotten more crowded, but I guess that is why St. John Neumann is here."[39]

It is not quite accurate to say that only one new parish, Our Lady Star of the Sea, was established on Staten Island between 1927 and 1960. In 1949 a new parish was added to the roster in a most unusual way when the lay leaders of the Ukrainian Orthodox Church of the Holy Trinity in Stapleton severed their ties with the Eastern Orthodox Church and joined the Catholic Church. Today it is a parish in the Ukrainian Catholic eparchy (diocese) of Stamford.

The Church of the Holy Child, Eltingville, dedicated by Cardinal O'Connor on May 28, 1994.

39 - *Staten Island Advance,* August 7, 1982.

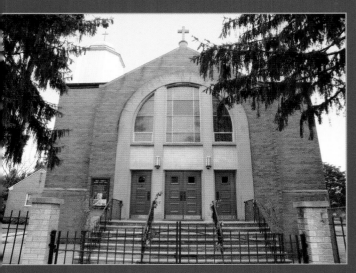

Holy Trinity Ukrainian Catholic Church.

The Chapel of Christ the King,
a mission of the Church of St. Mary of the Assumption,
Port Richmond.

The Church of St. John Neumann, Greenridge, founded in 1982.

The Chapel of St. Nicholas, Clove Lake,
a mission of St. Theresa's Church, Castleton Corners.

Catholic Education and Monsignor Joseph Farrell

For at least the past century a notable feature of Staten Island Catholicism has been the encouragement of Catholic education on the part of both the laity and the clergy. By 2004 thirty-four of the thirty-seven Latin-rite parishes had parochial schools, and there were seven Catholic high schools. Some of the schools were started and maintained at great sacrifice. In 1922, when St. Rita's parish could barely support a church, Father Emmanuel Taverna started a school because he considered it essential to the survival of the parish. Forty years later at St. Charles parish Monsignor John McGowan opted to build a school rather than a badly-needed new church.

One of the foremost promoters of Catholic education on Staten Island, especially Catholic secondary education, was Monsignor Joseph Farrell. He came to the island immediately after ordination in June 1900 as a curate at St. Peter's Church. In 1917 he became the pastor of St. Ann's in Dongan Hills and in 1926 he was appointed the first pastor of St. Paul's in West Brighton. Four years later he returned to St. Peter's as the pastor where he died on June 13, 1960. When Cardinal Hayes appointed Father Farrell the dean of Staten Island in November 1931, he specifically mentioned to him that he was the unanimous choice of the diocesan consultors for the post.

Father Farrell's response to Cardinal Hayes must have been one of the most unusual and transparently honest letters that any archbishop of New York ever received from one of his priests. "I am well aware of my unfitness for the appointment," Farrell told Hayes. "My long service on the island is my only asset. There is in me a dislike of for publicity and a decided uneasiness for public

Monsignor Joseph A. Farrell.

talking and participation in public affairs. A most unsociable person am I, not drinking or smoking nor possessing wit or humor." He added: " You must have noticed these defects or impediments or whatever you choose to call them, and, if in spite of them, you have appointed me, then all I can say is but to accept and obey."[40]

In 1941 Monsignor Farrell was erroneously listed in the *Catholic News* as one of the bene-factors who had contributed $5,000 to the new St. Peter's High School. Embarrassed by the publicity, he told the vicar general, "I never had that much money and never expect to have it." However, he added, "Would I give it? Certainly if I had it." He also revealed that he had contributed $1,000 per year for the previous forty years to support Catholic high school education on Staten Island. Nineteen years later Cardinal Spellman came to Staten Island to inform him on his death-bed that the new diocesan high school on the island was to be named in his honor.[41]

40 - AANY, Hayes to Farrell, November 15, 1931; Farrell to Hayes, December 11, 1931.

41 - AANY, Farrell to McIntyre, n.d. [February 1941].

17

The Changing of the Guard

The Changing of the Guard: the arrival of Archbishop Spellman in New York on May 5, 1939,
flanked by Bishop Stephen J. Donahue and Monsignor Michael J. Lavelle.
Credit: *Archdiocese of New York*

For a century every archbishop of New York spent some time in the entourage of his predecessor ever since John Hughes moved into the residence of John Dubois on Mulberry Street in 1838. It was not always a cordial relationship as in the case of Hughes and Dubois, and to a lesser extent with Farley and Corrigan, who was shocked when Farley was initially appointed his coadjutor rather than his auxiliary in 1895. However, the relationship was especially warm between Farley and Hayes who lived under the same roof for twenty-one years, first at St. Gabriel's rectory and then at the Cardinal's residence at 452 Madison Avenue.

The person who was the obvious candidate to continue this tradition after the death of Cardinal Hayes on September 4, 1938, was Stephen J. Donahue, the sole auxiliary bishop and former secretary to Hayes. Donahue would probably have been the first choice of the senior clergy as well, if they had the opportunity to suggest a candidate as they had been able to do in 1902. Seven months elapsed between the death of Cardinal Hayes and the appointment of the new archbishop, a delay due largely to the illness of Pope Pius XI.

The front-runner for New York was believed to be Archbishop John T. McNicholas, the Dominican archbishop of Cincinnati. Speculation also centered around Francis J. Spellman, the auxiliary bishop of Boston. At first Spellman was not optimistic about his own chances. "With all the opposition," he confided to his diary, "I believe it is impossible." His chief Roman confidant, Count Enrico Galeazzi, confirmed his own bleak assessment of his prospects and told him bluntly, "No chance." After Pius XI rallied from a heart attack in November, Spellman noted wryly in his diary, "Archbishop McNicholas is clearing his desk preparing to go to New York."[1]

However, the death of Pius XI on February 10, 1939, created an entirely new situation. "There are certainly lots of possibilities opened up by this conclave," said Spellman. After the election of Eugenio Pacelli as Pius XII on March 2, he commented, "I suppose that I am back 'on the list again.'"[2] Six weeks later, on April 15, 1939, Pius XII named Bishop Francis J. Spellman the new archbishop of New York.

Francis J. Spellman

Francis Spellman was born in Whitman, Massachusetts, on May 4, 1889, the oldest of five children of William and Ellen Conway Spellman. His father was a prosperous grocer who was able to give his children a college education. The two youngest sons became doctors. Francis (he was always called Frank) attended Fordham College from which he graduated in 1908. After deciding to study for the priesthood, he was sent to the North American College in Rome as a candidate for the archdiocese of Boston.

Students at the North American College attended classes at the Urban College of the Propaganda Fide. The professors were diocesan priests who frequently moved on to fill important positions in the Roman Curia where they were instrumental in advancing the careers of their favorite students. As a seminarian Spellman attracted the attention of Father Francesco Borgongini-Duca, a future nuncio to Italy and curial cardinal, who was to play a key role in his rise to power. Spellman's career nearly came to an abrupt end in 1914 when he was hospitalized for six months with "a weakness of the lungs." The rector of the North American College wanted to send him home to die in Boston. However, he recovered and was ordained a priest in Rome on May 14, 1916.

Back in Boston young Father Spellman incurred the displeasure of William Cardinal O'Connell, the autocratic archbishop of Boston, for reasons that have never been satisfactorily explained. Perhaps O'Connell saw in the ambitious young priest a mirror image of himself. He assigned Spellman to a series of unglamorous jobs such as the circulation editor of the diocesan newspaper and diocesan archivist. O'Connell had become the archbishop of Boston in 1906 by cultivating the favor of important Roman officials, especially Cardinal Merry del Val, the secretary of state under Pope Pius X. Spellman now used the same means to escape from Cardinal O'Connell's control. Through his friendship with Archbishop Borgongini-Duca, he secured a job in Rome in 1925 as the director of the Knights of Columbus playgrounds. The real significance of the

1 - AANY, Spellman, Diary, September 4, 22, 1938.
2 - AANY, Spellman, Diary, March 8, 1939.

appointment was that it made Spellman an attaché at the Vatican secretariat of state.

Spellman's second Roman sojourn lasted from 1925 until 1932. He honed his talent for ingratiating himself with important people, including Nicholas Brady, the American millionaire, and his wife, Genevieve, and Enrico Galeazzi, the Vatican architect. Through another former professor, Monsignor Giuseppe Pizzardo, Spellman met Archbishop Eugenio Pacelli, the nuncio to Weimar Germany and papal secretary of state from 1930 to 1939. As far back as 1927 Spellman told his mother, "All the time I was with him in Berlin, I kept thinking of the great possibilities he has of becoming the next pope."[3]

In 1931 Spellman won the gratitude of Pius XI when he arranged for the publication in Paris of *Non Abbiamo Bisogno,* his encyclical criticizing Mussolini's treatment of the Catholic Church in Italy. The following year the pope made him an auxiliary bishop of Boston. He was ordained the titular bishop of Sila by Archbishop Pacelli in St. Peter's Basilica on September 8, 1932. The co-consecrators were Borgongini-Duca and Pizzardo.

Back in Boston Spellman was still persona non grata to O'Connell, now perhaps more than ever, since O'Connell suspected that he might be his successor. O'Connell showed his displeasure by making his new auxiliary bishop the pastor of a debt-ridden parish in Newton Center. At a clergy conference in September 1935, O'Connell scolded the Boston priests for attending the funerals of people whom they barely knew. Spellman noted in his diary that "the

Mrs. Nicholas F. Brady.
Credit: *Archdiocese of New York*

priests naturally thought that the Cardinal was referring to [my] mother's funeral," which had taken place only five weeks earlier. Despite such petty humiliations, Spellman carefully observed the ecclesiastical proprieties, never criticizing O'Connell in public.

Meanwhile, he continued to cultivate his Roman connections and solidified his friendship with Joseph P. Kennedy through whom he acquired access to the White House. In 1936 Bishop Spellman gained national prominence when he escorted Cardinal Pacelli on his tour of the United States and arranged for a meeting between Pacelli and President Franklin D. Roseevelt at Hyde Park on November 5, 1936. On March 2, 1939, Pacelli was elected pope. On April 12 Spellman was privately informed that he was to be the new archbishop of New York. The first person (outside his family) to whom he told the news was President Roosevelt. On May 23, 1939, Francis J. Spellman was installed as the sixth archbishop of New York in St. Patrick's Cathedral by the Apostolic Delegate, Archbishop Amleto Cicognani. It was to be the longest administration in the history of the archdiocese.

Monsignor Lavelle leads Cardinal Pacelli into St. Patrick's Cathedral in 1936.

3 - AANY, Spellman to Ellen Conway Spellman, September 13, 1927.

The Past, the Present and the Future: Cardinal Pacelli in Boston in 1936 with Cardinal William O'Connell and Bishop Francis J. Spellman.
Credit: *Archdiocese of New York*

Archbishop of New York

A young priest, Father Florence Cohalan, who witnessed Spellman's arrival in New York thought that "only a very superficial observer could miss his intense awareness of his own authority and his determination that it be recognized and accepted by his subordinates on every level." Spellman was well aware that during the interregnum Bishop Stephen Donahue had appointed eighteen administrators in various parishes, one on the day of the new archbishop's appointment. "This seems a strange procedure" was Spellman's laconic comment. Throughout his long administration, Spellman kept his distance from his priests. Although he made them monsignors in unprecedented numbers, Florence Cohalan also noted that "he never tried, and presumably never wanted, to put them at ease in his presence."[4]

Cohalan was not the only New Yorker to size up Spellman as a determined if not exactly a dynamic leader. He made the same impression on Robert Moses, the scion of a wealthy German Jewish family and the quintessential New York power broker of that era. Moses recognized a kindred soul in the shopkeeper's son from Whitman, Massachusetts. At the dedication of every new bridge and tunnel that Moses built, and he built many of them, there in the first limousine with Moses and the mayor was the diminutive figure of Francis J. Spellman. Spellman was soon on a first-name basis with Moses, but Moses always addressed him as Your Eminence.[5]

The first issue that Spellman had to face was the dire financial condition of the archdiocese. On the day of his installation as archbishop, he received a patronizing letter from Robert Louis Hoguet, the president of the Emigrant Industrial

---

4 - Cohalan, *Popular History*, 276-277. AANY, Spellman, Dairy, April May 2, 1939.

5 - Robert Caro, *The Power Broker: Robert Moses and the Fall of New York* (New York: Vintage Books, 1975), 738-741.

Savings Bank, informing him that "mortgages in the New York Archdiocese aggregate in the vicinity of $28,000,000." That night, said Spellman's authorized biographer, Father Robert I. Gannon, S.J., "he found himself smouldering and could not sleep until he had planned his first steps in the refinancing of the archdiocese."[6]

Spellman informed the board of diocesan consultors, his principal advisory body, that the financial situation in New York was "entirely different from conditions existing in the diocese from which [I come]." With the help of Monsignor James Francis McIntyre, the chancellor, Spellman immediately set to work negotiating better terms from bankers in New York and Boston. On July 19 he had an interview with Hoguet, which, he said, "was very satisfactory to me." Two days later he calculated that he had already saved the archdiocese $500,000 a year in interest payments.[7]

Immediately after his installation Spellman embarked on a series of administrative changes and buildings projects. He had been advised by both Cardinal O'Connell and the Apostolic Delegate to get rid of the chancellor, Monsignor McIntyre. However, he said, "I am satisfied, so why make changes." However, he did follow the advice of Archbishop Cicognani to make changes at Dunwoodie, replacing both the rector and the procurator.[8]

Under Hayes the archdiocese functioned like a feudal kingdom with pastors enjoying the same autonomy as medieval barons. When Robert Brown was ordained in 1934 and assigned to St. Peter's Church in Haverstraw, the chancellor informed him that the pastor might refuse to accept a new curate. In that case, Brown was told to come back to the Chancery Office where he would get another assignment.

Spellman transformed the pastors from feudal barons into agents of a centralized monarchy as Cardinal Mundelein had already done in Chicago by introducing modern management techniques such as a diocesan bank, insurance office, building commission and central purchasing agency. Annual parish reports and financial statements got closer scrutiny at headquarters than they had received in the past.

Like the European nobility in the age of absolutism, the pastors lost real power but were compensated with a carefully calibrated hierarchy of honorific titles and uniforms, ranging from entry level papal chamberlains through domestic prelates and protonotaries apostolic to auxiliary bishops. Hayes had made do with one auxiliary bishop; Corrigan had none for ten years. At one point Spellman had an even dozen, their numbers reflecting his ability to create them.

Despite the precarious financial condition of the archdiocese in 1939, Spellman began a number of ambitious building projects. When he established his first parish, St. Gabriel's Church in Riverdale in 1939, he personally selected the site and bought it at a bargain price before the real estate agents got wind of his plans. Likewise, when he began one of his most innovative contributions, the organization of a diocesan high school system, he personally selected the site of the first school, which he named in honor of his predecessor.

On an unpromising piece of real estate overlooking a railroad yard in the South Bronx, which he purchased for the bargain price of $165,000, he erected an architecturally stunning school, Cardinal Hayes High School, which opened its doors in 1941. He assigned twenty-one diocesan priests to the school. In addition to three communities of brothers, there were

---

6 - AANY, Hoguet to Spellman, May 23, 1939. Robert I. Gannon, S.J., *The Cardinal Spellman Story* (Garden City: Doubleday, 1962), 141.

7 - AANY, Minutes of the Meetings of the Diocesan Consultors, June 6, 1939; Spellman, Diary, July 21, 1939.

8 - AANY, Spellman, Diary, June 29, 1939.

eventually forty-three priests on the faculty, more than the total number of priests in some dioceses. Thanks to the contributed services of the priests and brothers, the annual cost per pupil was $80 and the tuition was $5.00 per month. The forty-three priests on the Hayes faculty did not seem to be missed in the parishes, despite the large number of priests who volunteered as military chaplains during World War II, confirming the opinion of Monsignor Arthur Scanlan that New York was oversupplied with priests.

In 1941 Spellman added a new wing to St. Vincent's Hospital (named after himself) and in 1942 he moved Cathedral College to new quarters at West End Avenue and 87th Street. He sold the old building on Madison Avenue for a whooping $2,800,000. A more delicate building project was the renovation of the sanctuary of the cathedral. Monsignor Lavelle, the rector since 1887, was strongly opposed to the plan and reportedly said that it would only be done "over my dead body." Spellman obliged by waiting until Lavelle's death and then interring him in the crypt under the new altar. Further building projects had to wait until after World War II.

The interior of St. Patrick's Cathedral before it was remodeled by Cardinal Spellman in the early 1940s.
Credit: *Archdiocese of New York*

Cardinal Hayes High School in 1941.
Credit: *Archdiocese of New York*

Archbishop Spellman
as a National Figure

Like Cardinal Hayes, Archbishop Spellman was also the Military Vicar for the Armed Forces, an appointment that he received on December 11, 1939. It gave him a high profile during World War II. However, even before the entry of the United States into the conflict after Pearl Harbor, Spellman was already playing an important role on both the national and international levels. He elbowed aside the Apostolic Delegate and took charge of the negotiations between the Holy See and the White House that led to the announcement by President Roosevelt on December 24, 1939, that he would send a "personal representative," Myron Taylor, to represent the U.S. at the Vatican. At one point in the negotiations Spellman rewrote a letter from Cicognani to him, giving himself the credit for initiating the process.[9]

Pope Pius XII and Cardinal Spellman in Rome.
Credit: *Archdiocese of New York*

During World War II, as the number of Catholic servicemen and servicewomen swelled to several million, Spellman's role as the Military Vicar became increasingly important and prominent. He chose Father John F. O'Hara, C.S.C., the president of the University of Notre Dame, to run the day-to-day business of the Military Ordinariate as the auxiliary bishop while he concentrated on such activities as visits to American troops throughout the world. From 1942 to 1966 Spellman never missed a Christmas visit to troops overseas. A mystery-shrouded visit to Rome in 1943 through neutral Spain aroused intense speculation in the American press that he was on a diplomatic mission to persuade Italy to change sides. Thanks to such well-publicized trips, Spellman came to personify the patriotism of American Catholics.

As Edward Kantowicz remarked, Spellman and other American bishops of his generation managed to achieve in a non-ideological way the synthesis of loyalty to both Church and country that had eluded the "Americanist" bishops of the late nineteenth century. Gerald P. Fogarty, S.J., went even further and described Spellman as "the personification of Americanization and Romanization." Not since John Hughes had any archbishop of New York achieved such fame. Spellman was the most prominent American Catholic prelate since the death of Cardinal Gibbons. Not even Gibbons had the same close connection with both the pope and the President of the United States that Spellman enjoyed during World War II.

During World War II at least 147 alumni of Dunwoodie (most but not all of them priests of the archdiocese of New York) served as military chaplains. Three never returned home. Father Joseph Gilmore, U.S.A., was killed in action at Anzio. Father John Robinson, U.S.N.,

---

9 - Gerald P. Fogsrty, S.J, *The Vatican and the American Hierarchy from 1870 to 1965* (Wilmington: Michael Glazier, 1985), 261-262.

Cardinal Spellman celebrating a field Mass in Belgium during World War II.
Credit: *Archdiocese of New York*

and Father Lawrence Gough, U.S. Air Corps, died in plane crashes. Fathers George Zentgraf and Lafayette Yarwood served in both World Wars. Father Herman Heide received the Silver Star for gallantry in the Battle of the Bulge and spent three months in a German prisoner-of-war camp. In the Pacific Father Joseph N. Moody was the chaplain on the U.S.S. *Yorktown* and flew over Tokyo the day after the Japanese surrender.

In North Africa Father Edward R. Martin, who spoke fluent German, served as the interpreter at the surrender of the Afrika Corps. Not all of his war experiences were so gratifying. On one occasion a German bomb scored a direct hit on a jeep seventy-five feet from Martin's tent. "We picked up fragments of the men in a circle of 300 yards from the spot," he said. "The biggest part was three right hands and one left, which I had to fingerprint---six times each hand. A soldier watching me work said, 'Gee, you're hard.' I looked up at him, and I am not ashamed, tears ran down my cheek. What could I say? Nothing. The soldier put his hand on my shoulder and said, 'Gee, I'm sorry, Sir.' "[10]

Postwar America

At the first post-war consistory on February 18, 1946, Spellman recived the Red Hat from Pius XII. As America moved to a peacetime economy, Cardinal Spellman began a major building campaign that was to be the last such effort in the history of the archdiocese. Relatively few new parishes were established, except in the suburbs, but there was a massive expansion in the number and size of Catholic schools. In a memorandum prepared in the spring of 1952, Monsignor John J. Voight, the superintendent of schools, listed 134 elementary and secondary schools that had either been built or expanded between 1939 and 1952 including some still in the planning stage. They ranged from three additional classrooms at St. Mary of the Assumption School in Port Richmond to the huge Cardinal Hayes High School in the Bronx.[11]

Spellman's building campaign intensified in the late 1950s. Between 1953 and 1959 the Archdiocese of New York erected or expanded 15 churches, 94 schools, 22 rectories, 60 convents

---

10 - ASJSD, Martin to Christopher O'Hara, November 7, 1943.

11 - AANY, Voight, memorandum, April 3, 1952.

and 30 other institutions at a cost of $139,700,000. One of the principal recipients of Spellman's generosity was the seminary at Dunwoodie. He spent over $4,000,000 on renovations in addition to building a new library at a cost $1,500,000. Later he would add a gymnasium and recreation center.[12]

The press release issued by the Chancery Office in 1964 to commemorate the twenty-fifth anniversary of Spellman's administration required twenty-four pages to list his accomplishments. While he added thirty-six new parishes (all but eleven of them in the suburbs), the growth of the Catholic school system and social services was the really impressive statistic. He practically doubled the enrollment in the elementary and secondary schools from 117,907 in 1939 to 222,232 in 1964. According to one calculation, by the mid-1960s the archdiocese of New York and the diocese of Brooklyn together had more students in their schools than any public school system in the United States outside of New York City and Chicago.

Francis Cardinal Spellman,
Archbishop of New York, 1939-1967.
Credit: *Archdiocese of New York*

A familiar scene in the 1950s: Cardinal Spellman blesses the new school of Our Lady Star of the Sea on Staten Island in November 1959. To the right, Monsignor Gustav Schultheiss, the dean of Staten Island, and to the right, Monsignor Patrick V. Ahern, the cardinal's secretary.
Credit: *Church of Our Lady Star of the Sea*

---

12 - AANY, Eugene Hult to Leonard Hunt, April 30, 1959.

Between 1939 and 1964 the archdiocese spent $54,788,905 on the expansion of Catholic hospitals. The showcase was St. Vincent's Medical Center which had just completed a twenty-three year building and modernization program that included the addition of five new buildings. During that same period the arch-diocese invested $34.600,500 on the improvement of child-caring facilities, including a new eleven-story New York Foundling Hospital.[13]

Spellman's influence waned at the White House after Harry Truman replaced Roosevelt as president in 1945, but he still commanded national attention as an outspoken foe of Communism at home and abroad. To call attention to the Communist persecution of the Church in Eastern Europe, he named a new diocesan high school in White Plains after Archbishop Aloysius Stepinac, the victim of a show trial by the Yugoslav government.

The Calvary Cemetery Strike

Spellman's suspicions of communism led him to make one of the most ill-considered decisions of his career when the cemetery workers went on strike at Calvary Cemetery and Gate of Heaven Cemetery in January 1949. By March there were 1,000 unburied bodies in the two cemeteries. Persuaded by his advisers that a Communist-controlled labor union was responsible for the crisis, the cardinal decided to break the strike by sending seminarians from Dunwoodie to work as substitute gravediggers. He described his decision as "the most important work of my ten years in New York."

When the seminarians arrived at Calvary Cemetery, the strikers made no effort to block the buses. Instead the pickets at the gate doffed their caps in deference to the cardinal. It only added to the discomfiture of one seminarian, who said, "We felt the full weight of the unpleasant incident and only wished it could have been avoided. Strange to say, we were school boys, who would rather have been in school."[14]

Many Catholics applauded his action, including over one hundred priests who offered their services at the cemeteries. However, many other Catholics were appalled at Spellman's action. One of them was John Cort, a founder of the Association of Catholic Trade Unionists, who complained that "rightly or wrongly [it] puts the Church in the role of strikebreaker and union-buster." Spellman, however, was not the least bit apologetic. "I admit to the accusation of strikebreaker," he said, "and I am proud of it."[15]

Dunwoodie seminarians digging graves in Calvary Cemetery as Cardinal Spellman watched during the 1949 strike.
Credit: *Archdiocese of New York*

---

13 - AANY, S/C 57, Growth of the Archdiocese of New York, 1939-1964.

14 - AANY, Regulator's Book, March 2, 3, 1949.

15 - *New York Times,* March 4, 5, 1949; *Commonweal,* February 18, 1949, 471.

The cemetery strike posed an especially painful dilemma for the priest-chaplains of ACTU. Spellman expected them to disavow the organization and to side with him. Those who refused to do so on grounds of conscience, such as John P. Monaghan, John E. Byrne, and George A. Kelly, incurred Spellman's bitter enmity. For Spellman the Calvary cemetery strike became what the McGlynn Affair had been for Archbishop Corrigan, the litmus test of loyalty to the archbishop.

After the strike was over, in an act of petty vindictiveness, Spellman forbade pastors from selling the *Labor Leader,* the official newspaper of ACTU, in their parish churches. The ban brought an angry protest from Father John Monaghan, who told Spellman, "You have been counseled by advice that is as hateful to the work of ACTU as if it had come from a Communist, as belittling to the ACTU chaplains as if they were guttersnipes." Spellman replied with icy formality, telling Monaghan that the attitude of "his priest associates and disciples" had been "disedifying" to both the clergy and the laity.[16]

Two months later at the annual clergy retreat at Dunwoodie Spellman excoriated the priests who had been "disloyal" to him. Father George Kelly noticed that Spellman failed to receive the applause from the priests that was customary on such occasions and he thought that he was "a pathetic figure" as he left the seminary that evening.[17]

Kelly himself was one of the few priests who ever achieved rehabilitation to some semblance of official favor. Spellman could not ignore his contributions to the Catholic family movement in the archdiocese in the 1950s. In the space of a few years Kelly produced several books and enlisted scores of priests in the formation of an extensive

network of Cana and Pre-Cana Conferences. Spellman recognized the value of Kelly's work and gave it his strong endorsement.

Cardinal Spellman at the annual Christmas Party at the New York Foundling Hospital.
Credit: *Archdiocese of New York*

The Cardinal and the Former First Lady

The same year as the cemetery strike Spellman became involved in an ugly public dispute with Mrs. Eleanor Roosevelt over the issue of federal aid to private and parochial schools. The background to the quarrel was the Barden Bill, a bill introduced in the House of Representatives on May 11, 1949, by Representative Graham Barden of North Carolina to provide federal aid for education. The bill not only excluded private and parochial schools from the benefits of federal assistance, but it also prohibited states like New York from using federal aid to provide "auxiliary services" such as transportation and health care to non-public schools.

16 - AANY, Monaghan to Spellman, March 29, 1949; Spellman to Monaghan, April 11, 1949.

17 - George A, Kelly, *Inside My Father's House* (New York: Doubleday, 1989), 57-59, 69-73.

After Eleanor Roosevelt voiced support for the Barden Bill several times in her syndicated newspaper column, the cardinal took issue with her in an open letter to the press. "Your record of anti-Catholicism stands for all to see," he told her, "a record which you yourself wrote on the pages of American history which cannot be recalled, documents of discrimination unworthy of an American mother." Mrs. Roosevelt had the better of the exchange when she denied the cardinal's allegations of anti-Catholic bias and replied, "The final judgment, my dear Cardinal Spellman, of the unworthiness of all human beings is in the hands of God."

The confrontation between the cardinal and the former First Lady placed many New York politicians in the uncomfortable position of having to choose between the two of them. Some solved the problem by supporting both sides. Mayor William O'Dwyer of New York City said: "I have great respect for the Cardinal and equally great respect for Mrs. Roosevelt."

A few weeks later Mrs. Roosevelt told reporters that she had no objection to meeting with Spellman to settle their differences, but she expected him to take the initiative. The night before Spellman had read to her over the telephone a clarifying statement in which he said he was only advocating federal aid to parochial schools for auxiliary services like school buses and health care. Shortly thereafter Spellman called upon Mrs. Roosevelt at Hyde Park. "We had a pleasant chat," she reported in her newspaper column, "and I hope the country proved as much of a tonic for him as it always is for me." Tactically she outmaneuvered Spellman, but the Barden Bill did not become law.[18]

The Great Puerto Rican Migration

The greatest pastoral challenge facing the archdiocese of New York in the post-war years was the influx of several hundred thousand Puerto Ricans, who transformed many of the old ethnic parishes in Manhattan and the Bronx into solidly Hispanic neighborhoods. Spellman's response to this challenge was one of his most impressive pastoral achievements. In this instance he sought and accepted good advice, from his chancellor, Monsignor John A. Maguire, and from two young priest sociologists, George A. Kelly and Joseph P. Fitzpatrick, S.J., of Fordham University.

In a scientific study begun in 1952, Kelly estimated that the Puerto Rican population of the archdiocese was already 300,000 and that it would reach 880,000 by 1960. Kelly predicted that within ten years the Puerto Ricans might constitute one-half of the Catholic population of the archdiocese. He said: "There is little doubt that the archdiocese has on its hands a pastoral and missionary problem of such magnitude as to tax its resources, ingenuity and manpower for years to come." He called particular attention to the need for more Spanish-speaking priests. "It would almost seem imperative, he warned, "that every priest being ordained speak Spanish and that his training in this language be compulsory."[19]

In 1952 Father Fitzpatrick caught Spellman's attention when he publicly criticized the inertia of the archdiocese in responding to this situation at a World Sodality Day ceremony on the campus of Fordham University. Cardinal Spellman, who presided at the ceremony, turned to the president of the university, Father Robert I. Gannon, S.J., and said: "I thought I solved that problem." Gannon replied: "Well, evidently Joe Fitzpatrick does not think that you did." To his credit, Spellman reacted, not by calling for Fitzpatrick's head, but by calling a meeting of a dozen or so priests who were already engaged in the Hispanic ministry. Fitzpatrick was present at the meeting, and he said that it was one of the finest examples of efficient leadership that he ever witnessed.

Spellman sat at the head of the table, whipped out a small notebook, and said to those present,

---

18 - Gannon, *Cardinal Spellman Story*, 312-322.

19 - AANY, George A. Kelly, Catholic Survey of the Catholic Population in New York City, 1955.

"Now I intend to go around this table, and I want each of you to tell me two things. What am I doing that I should not be doing, and what am I not doing that I should be doing?" He listened to each person, jotted down a few notes, and then said, "All right, I have come to three conclusions. First, we do not have enough Spanish-speaking priests. Beginning this June, half of the priests ordained each year will be sent to study Spanish. Secondly, we need some annual celebration for the Puerto Ricans comparable to the St. Patrick's Day parade for the Irish. Hereafter we will have an annual San Juan Fiesta on the feast of St. John the Baptist, the patron saint of Puerto Rico. Thirdly, we need someone in charge of Hispanic ministry." At that point, he turned to Monsignor Joseph Connolly, who had been sitting next to him, and said, "Monsignor Connolly, you are in charge of the Spanish Apostolate." Then he got up and left the room.[20]

Spellman made two major policy decisions with regard to the pastoral care of the Puerto Rican immigrants. First, he abandoned the hallowed tradition of national parishes, which had been the standard way of meeting the needs of immigrants for over a century. Instead he opted for all-inclusive integrated parishes for the Puerto Ricans. In recent years this decision has drawn criticism from Hispanic leaders who have complained that it deprived Puerto Ricans and other Hispanic immigrants of the benefits of a national parish where they could best preserve their own distinctive religious heritage. However, the main reason for the cardinal's decision was the lack of Puerto Rican priests. The Puerto Ricans were the only Catholic ethnic group to come to America without their own priests. In Puerto Rico itself there were only 310 priests for 2,250,000 Catholics, and less than a quarter of them were native Puerto Ricans.[21]

ST. JOHN CHRYSOSTOM CHURCH

1952   1974

St. John Chrysostom Holy Name Society
Join in Celebrating Our Diamond Jubilee
✝
La Sociedad del Santo Nombre
Se Une en Conmemora el 75.o Anniversario de Nuestra Iglesia

Diamond Jubilee • 75th Year

The Changing Face of the Catholic Bronx:
Father William Smith and the Holy Name Society
of St. John Chrysostom Church in 1974.
Credit: *St. John Chrysostom Church*

Spellman's second major policy decision was his determination that the diocesan clergy rather than religious communities should assume responsibility for the pastoral care of the Puerto Rican immigrants. According to Ana Maria Diaz-Stevens, "Spellman's great contribution to the Puerto Ricans was to recognize the need for the archdiocese to adopt a missionary character to the apostolate."[22]

---

20 - Joseph P. Fitzpatrick, S.J., Lecture to seminarians at St. Joseph's Seminary, March 3, 1989.

21 - Robert L. Stern, "Evolution of Hispanic Ministry in the New York Archdiocese," *Hispanics in New York: Religious, Cultural and Social Experiences,* ed. Ruth T. Doyle and Olga Scarpetta (New York: Archdiocese of New York, 1989), 2nd edn.,328.

22 - Ana Maria Diaz-Stevens, *Oxcart Catholicism on Fifth Avenue: The Impact of the Puerto Rican Migration upon the Archdiocese of New York* (Notre Dame: University of Notre Dame Press, 1993), 99.

In the course of 1953 the cardinal gave several clear indications of his commitment to the new apostolate. On March 24 he formally appointed Monsignor Connolly the first Coordinator of Spanish Catholic Action. On June 24 of that year the first San Juan Fiesta took place with a Mass in St. Patrick's Cathedral attended by 4,500 people. In 1956 the Fiesta was moved to the Rose Hill Campus of Fordham University for a field Mass and cultural celebration attended by 30,000 people. The following year it was moved to the stadium on Randall's Island to accommodate even larger crowds.

In June 1953 two of the newly ordained diocesan priests were sent to Puerto Rico to study Spanish. As the requirements of the Puerto Rican apostolate became clearer, the cardinal increased the archdiocese's involvement. In 1956 he sent half of the Dunwoodie ordination class to Georgetown University to study Spanish. The following year half of the newly ordained priests went to the Catholic University of Puerto Rico in Ponce for firsthand experience of the language and culture. Spellman continued the practice in subsequent years, although not with the same number of priests. In 1959 the various programs

in New York and Puerto Rico to train priests and religious for the Hispanic ministry were organized into the Institute of Inter-Cultural Communication.[23]

Two years earlier Spellman informed the apostolic delegate that the population of Manhattan was now one-third Puerto Rican. "I do not know whether this information is important to the Holy See," he said, "but it is certainly significant to us." By that date there were 150 Spanish-speaking priests in the archdiocese and almost one-quarter of the parishes were providing religious services in Spanish. By 1964 there 217 Spanish-speaking priests working in 67 parishes in Manhattan, 26 parishes in the Bronx and 22 parishes upstate.[24]

The leadership of the Spanish Apostolate remained firmly in the hands of the diocesan clergy. All three of Joseph Connolly's successors as coordinators---James Wilson, Robert Fox and Robert Stern---were New York diocesan priests and fluent Spanish speakers. Hovering over the whole operation was the vice-rector of the Catholic Unversity of Ponce, the charismatic Monsignor Ivan Illich, a Yugoslav-born priest

The San Juan Fiesta in the 1960s: left to right: Father Joseph Fitzpatrick, S.J., Auxiliary Bishop Terence Cooke, Father Gerald Ryan, Cardinal Spellman, and Monsignor Thomas O'Brien, the pastor of St. Athanasius Church.
Credit: *Archdiocese of New York*

23 - Stern, "Evolution of Hispanic Ministry," 333.

24 - AANY, Spellman to Cicognani, October 3, 1957; AANY, Growth of the Archdiocese of New York, 1939-1964.

whom Spellman accepted into the archdiocese in 1952. Father Fitzpatrick considered it a minor miracle that the avant-garde Illich and Spellman worked together so harmoniously.

Optimism and enthusiasm pervaded the Spanish apostolate as more and more young Spanish-speaking diocesan priests appeared in the Puerto Rican parishes of Manhattan and the Bronx where they were joined by many sisters and brothers. Religious communities such as the Vincentians, Augustinian Recollects, Augustinians of the Assumption, Franciscans, Canons Regular of the Lateran, Jesuits, and Redemptorists were also active in the Hispanic apostolate in their own parishes as were a number of diocesan priests from Spain. Reviewing the results of a sociological survey published by the archdiocese in 1982, Joseph Fitzpatrick was impressed by the overwhelmingly favorable attitude to the Catholic Church manifested by most Hispanics in New York. He attributed it largely to the work of the diocesan clergy and the men and women religious during the previous thirty years.[25]

Winds of Change

On September 7, 1957, Cardinal Spellman celebrated the silver jubilee of his episcopal ordination with a Mass at Yankee Stadium. The ballpark had been transformed into a reasonable facsimile of an outdoor cathedral with an imposing gold-and-white sanctuary a dozen feet above the ground surmounted by a large wooden cross suspended from a forty-eight foot-high platform. In attendance were all four North American cardinals (McIntyre of Los Angeles, Stritch of Chicago, Mooney of Detroit, and McGuigan of Toronto) as well as eighteen archbishops and eighty-five bishops. The large phalanx of New York monsignors made a colorful display in their choir robes. Clearly visible from home plate as he lumbered across the infield was the dreadnought silhouette of Monsignor Aloysius Dineen, his awesome girth wrapped in yards and yards of Roman purple.

Lining the perimeter of the stadium were 1,000 uniformed New York City policemen, firemen and sanitation workers from the Holy

The celebration of the 25th anniversary of the episcopal ordination of Cardinal Spellman at Yankee Stadium on September 7, 1957.
Credit: *Archdiocese of New York*

25 - Joseph Fitzpatrick, S.J, "Hispanics in New York: An Archdiocesan Survey" *America* 148 (March 12, 1983): 185-188.

Name Societies of their respective departments. The Knights of Malta and the Knights of the Holy Sepulchre were segregated from the more plebian elements. There was an honor guard of one hundred Fourth Degree Knights of Columbus resplendent in capes, swords and mock Lord Nelson hats. One whole section of the grandstand was filled with nuns and sisters, all still dressed in ankle-length habits, their headgear a forest of veils and bonnets and the distinctive cornettes of the Daughters of Charity.

Guests like Governor W. Averell Harriman must have thought that they had stepped inside an ecclesiastical Noah's Ark, for the special grab of virtually every religious community of men and women was on display that afternoon. As expected, Cardinal McIntyre extolled the virtues of the guest of honor. Cardinal Spellman responded by speaking about the dignity of the priesthood. Choosing his words carefully, he said that his mother "never imagined or wished for me any greater honor or glory than to be a good priest."

All afternoon, as the trains rattled by on the adjacent tracks of the IRT elevated line, the Irish motormen tooted their horns in salute. One retired New York City policeman, possibly of the same ethnic background, summed up his impressions of the day in one word, "Power." "Next thing you know," he said, "the bigots will be crying 'Break up the Church' just as some are crying 'Break up the Yankees.'"

However, many of the clergy came away from the event with a different impression. They noticed one disquieting detail. The grandstand was only half-filled. The laity did not turn out in the expected numbers, nothing like the crowds that had once lined Fifth Avenue to welcome Cardinal Farley and Cardinal Hayes home from Rome after receiving the Red Hat. Whether they realized it or not, the crowd in Yankee Stadium

was witnessing a far more historic event than another one of Cardinal Spellman's numerous personal jubilees. It was the sunset of a whole era in New York Catholic history.

The Presidential Election of 1960

Rightly or wrongly Spellman was thought to favor Richard Nixon in the 1960 race because of Kennedy's opposition to two of Spellman's long-cherished goals, federal aid to Catholic schools and American diplomatic relations with the Holy See. At the annual Al Smith dinner in New York in October 1960, at which both Nixon and Kennedy were present, Kennedy teased Spellman about his alleged Republican sympathies. He hailed the cardinal as "the only man so widely respected in American politics that he could bring together amicably at the same banquet... two men who have disagreed so strongly both publicly and privately---Vice President Nixon and Governor Rockefeller."

Nevertheless, whatever Spellman's personal political preferences were, he was too shrewd ever to tip his hand. Moreover, he did Kennedy a great service by minimizing the potential political embarrassment to him caused by the bishops of Puerto Rico two weeks before the election.

In a pastoral letter read at Mass on Sunday, October 23, the three bishops (only one of whom was a native Puerto Rican) announced that it was their obligation "to prohibit Catholics from giving their votes" to the Popular Democratic Party of Governor Luis Muñoz Marin. The pastoral letter caused an uproar throughout Puerto Rico, especially after it became known that the devoutly Catholic Mayor of San Juan, Felisa Rincon de Gauthier, was told that she would be refused Holy Communion if she attended Sunday Mass in the cathedral. The action of the Puerto Rican bishops was widely reported in the United States, creating

Governor Nelson Rockefeller and Senator John F. Kennedy with Cardinal Spellman at the Al Smith dinner on October 31, 1957.
Credit: *Archdiocese of New York*

a nightmare for Kennedy, for it resurrected all the ghosts that he had tried to lay to rest about the control that the hierarchy would exercise over a Catholic President.

Richard Cardinal Cushing of Boston and Archbishop Egidio Vagnozzi, the apostolic delegate to the United States, both issued statements obliquely disavowing the statement of the Puerto Rican bishops. An anonymous ecclesiastical spokesman in Boston was quoted as saying that Catholics would incur no penalty if they failed to comply with the bishops' directive. When Spellman was queried about this statement by reporters, he replied, "That's right. I agree with it."[26]

Spellman had actually been alerted to the pastoral letter the day before it appeared by Muñoz Marin himself. The governor sent Spellman a telegram urging him to intervene with Domenico Cardinal Tardini, the papal secretary of state, "for the good of both church and state in Puerto Rico and in the United States." Spellman not only wrote to Tardini, but he wrote directly to Pope John XXIII. He called the bishops' action both "foolish" and "disgraceful."[27]

Spellman told Tardini that he had received a tremendous amount of mail concerning the pastoral letter of the Puerto Rican bishops. One of the samples that Spellman passed on to Tardini was an excerpt from a letter of the newly-elected President of the United States. "While I do not know all the facts on the situation in Puerto Rico," President-elect Kennedy told Spellman, "it seems to me that recent matters have been handled very poorly. It is American territory, and the recent action in regard to the Mayor of San Juan seems injudicious. The big fight in Latin America in the new decade will be against the Communists, and I believe an important influence is being diminished by lack of judgment and prudence."[28]

Spellman kept up the pressure on Tardini, telling him, "Great damage has already been done and the situation still needs to be corrected." Tardini finally intervened with Archbishop James Davis of San Juan after reading the excerpt of Kennedy's letter to Spellman.[29]

26 - *New York Times,* October 24, 1960.

27 - AANY, S/C 42, Muñoz Marin to Spellman, October 22, 1960; Spellman to Tardini, November 7, 1960, copy; Spellman to Pope John XXIII, November 23, 1960, copy.

28 - AANY, S/C 42, Spellman to Tardini, December 7, 1960, copy.

29 - AANY, S/C 42, Spellman to Tardini, February 11, 1961.

The American Pope?

One of Spellman's least satisfactory bio-graphers called him the American Pope. It was a gross exaggeration, but he did wield extra-ordinary influence in the American Church especially during the pontificate of Pope Pius XII. He was a kingmaker, engineering the appoint-ment of James Francis Mc Intyre as archbishop of Los Angeles and Patrick O'Boyle as archbishop of Washington, D.C. Both were New York priests and Dunwoodie classmates. He also was respon-sible for the appointment of John O'Hara, C.S.C., his auxiliary bishop in the Military Ordinariate, as archbishop of Philadelphia. All three became cardinals, as did Archbishop Richard Cushing of Boston, another friend of Spellman. When the diocese of Brooklyn was split in 1957 and the new diocese of Rockville Center was created for Long Island, both of the new bishops were New Yorkers, Bryan McEntegart and Walter Kellenberg.

However, Spellman's control of the American Church was never total. He was foiled in his attempt to dominate the central administrative organ of the American Church, the National Catholic Welfare Conference, by three determined Midwestern bishops, Samuel Stritch of Chicago, Edward Mooney of Detroit and John McNicholas, O.P., of Cincinnati. They established what they called the "Hindenburg Line," a *cordon sanitaire* to keep Spellman from appointing bishops west of the Appalachians. With the exception of McIntyre's appointment to Los Angeles, they were successful.[30]

On more than one occasion Spellman used his considerable clout in Rome to protect the interests of his own archdiocese. In the fall of 1948 Spellman read a news dispatch that St. John's Seminary in Brighton, the major seminary of the archdiocese of Boston, had

Because It Was There. On January 2, 1964, Cardinal Spellman becomes the first (and last) cardinal to visit the South Pole.
Credit: *Archdiocese of New York*

received authorization to issue pontifical degrees. He sent a stiff protest to his friend, Cardinal Giuseppe Pizzardo, the prefect of the Congre-gation of Seminaries and Universities, saying that this authorization would be injurious to his own seminary at Dunwoodie, and to the Catholic University of America, "which is a bona fide institution of post-graduate level."

Spellman told Pizzardo that Archbishop Cushing should never have made such a request, "and, if he did make such a request, it should have been categorically denied." An embarrassed Pizzardo pointed out to Spellman that the matter had already become public, but another vehement protest from Spellman forced him to reverse himself, and---thanks to native-son Francis J. Spellman---Boston's seminary never issued a pontifical degree.[31]

---

30 - Fogarty, *Vatican and American Hierarchy*, 311-314.

31 - AANY, Spellman to Pizzardo, September 13, 1948, copy; Pizzardo to Spellman, September 23, 1948; Spellman to Pizzardo, October 2, 1948.

Spellman was not only loyal to his seminary, but he was also loyal to his priests and seminarians when they came under hostile fire from ecclesiastical authorities. Henry J. Browne, a New York priest on the faculty of the Catholic University of America, stirred up a hornet's nest, when he invited Father John Courtney Murray, S.J., to deliver a lecture at the university on the topic of church-state relations in the spring of 1954. Father Francis J. Connell, C.Ss.R., the conservative dean of the theology faculty, protested that "Murray's ideas do not represent the approved teaching of the Church." Cardinal Alfredo Ottaviani, the powerful secretary of the Holy Office, also complained that "Father Murray affirmed many things that were not true." He reported to Spellman that "you[r] diocesan priest, after the lecture, spoke thanking for the lecture Fr. Murray and approving all that was said." Despite pressure from both Connell and Ottaviani, Spellman refused to remove Henry Browne from the faculty of the Catholic University.[32]

Closer to home, in April 1960, Father Myles Bourke, the professor of Scripture at Dunwoodie, came under fire from Ottaviani because of an article that he wrote on the Matthean infancy narratives in the *Catholic Biblical Quarterly*. Ottaviani was equally critical of a similar article by Richard Dillon, a seminarian, which appeared in the first issue of the *Dunwoodie Review,* a scholarly student journal fostered by Bourke and edited by Dillon.

Ottaviani complained to Spellman about the two articles and urged him to dismiss Bourke from his teaching position at Dunwoodie. Instead Spellman asked Bourke for a reply to Ottaviani's criticism and his answer convinced Spellman of Bourke's orthodoxy. He refused to remove him from Dunwoodie. Instead he told him in writing: "I have complete confidence in you and consider you a great asset to St. Joseph's Seminary." Spellman gave the same kind of support to another New York priest, Monsignor Patrick J. Skehan, professor of Semitic Languages at the Catholic University of America, when he tangled with one of Ottaviani's leading American protégés at the university, Monsignor Joseph C. Fenton.[33]

The Second Vatican Council

At Vatican II Spellman was the senior American cardinal and the titular leader of the American hierarchy. He was also generally regarded as one of the leading conservatives at the Council, especially on matters of liturgical reform. He was especially opposed to the introduction of the vernacular in the liturgy. Back in 1955, when Pope Pius XII restored the ancient Rite of Holy Week, he was so upset that he stopped in Rome on his annual Christmas visit to the troops to plead with the pope to delay or mitigate the implementation of the decree.

When Spellman got no satisfaction from his private audience with the pope, he sent him an extraordinarily candid letter in which he insisted that "the bishops and priests of my own region are appalled at the confusion that will be caused by the application of such a revolutionary decree." Moreover, he made no secret that he was furious at the unilateral way that the decision had been made. "Not one of the bishops of this country claims to have been consulted," he complained. He even challenged the accuracy of the pope's claim that most of the bishops favored the decree. "It is my certain knowledge," he retorted, "that those who applauded this decree are in the very definite minority." He assured his old friend that he would obey the decree, but he said that he would do it "despite the feelings of reluctance, annoyance and confusion."[34]

---

32 - ASJSD, Connell to McEntegart, April 1, 1954; McEntegart to Spellman, April 13, 1954; Ottaviani to Spellman, April 1, 1954.

33 - Bourke: interview, New York City, October 14, 1990. AANY, Spellman to Bourke, March 27, 1961; ASJSD, Spellman to Patrick O'Boyle, October 2, 1961, copy; Spellman to Egidio Vagnozzi, October 2, 1961.

34 - AANY, S/C 63, Spellman to Pius XII, January 28, 1956, copy.

By the time of the Council Spellman had mellowed to the point that he was willing to accept the use of the vernacular in the administration of the sacraments. As far as the Mass was concerned, however, the most that he would agree to was that a lector might read the Epistle and Gospel in the vernacular while the priest read it in Latin at the altar. At the same time he advocated permission for clerics to recite the breviary in English, leading one bemused Italian prelate to exclaim: "*Ah! Questi Americani!* Now they want the priest to pray in English and the people to pray in Latin!"

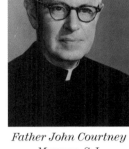

Father John Courtney Murray, S.J.
Credit: *New York Province of the Society of Jesus*

Most of the American bishops at Vatican II parted company with Spellman on the question of liturgical reform, which was the first topic that the Council Fathers debated in detail. Two days after Spellman pleaded for restricting the use of the vernacular, Archbishop Paul Hallinan of Atlanta called for the widespread use of it. "The liturgy of the Church must be public," said Hallinan, "but this can have real meaning for our people only if they understand enough of it to be part of it." It was widely interpreted as a declaration of independence from Spellman on the part of the American bishops on the issue of liturgical reform.

If Spellman found himself out of step with the majority over the liturgy, he enjoyed widespread support for his advocacy of the Council's *Declaration on Religious Freedom.* As the debate on the topic became more heated and the opposition resorted to procedural maneuvers to block the passage of the declaration, Spellman played a crucial role in assuring its success. Even earlier he made an indispensable contribution when he insisted on the appointment of Father John Courtney Murray,

S.J., as a *peritus* at the second session. Murray was to be one of the principal architects of the document. "My Eminent friend of New York," Murray called Spellman. When Murray encountered opposition from Archbishop Egidio Vagnozzi, the Apostolic Delegate to the United States, he told his provincial not to worry. "I am sure that His Eminence of New York will stand behind me," he said. "He is one of the few American bishops who can be counted on to speak back to the Delegate. And he has--bless his heart---elected to be my patron."[35]

The Pope in New York

Even before the end of the Council Spellman found it difficult to come to terms with the changing conditions in the Church, particularly the liturgical changes. "In my opinion the [liturgical] changes are too many and too fast," he told Galeazzi in Rome. Moreover, the changes in the Church coincided with a whole series of domestic crises in the United States such as the Civil Rights movement, the escalation of the Vietnam war and a wave of student protests. In the spring of 1965, he admitted to Galeazzi, "I am having a difficult time," and he added, "I do not think that things in Rome could be any more 'dizzy' than they are in the United States."[36]

The visit of Pope Paul VI to New York in the fall of 1965 was a welcome respite from a mounting list of cares and worries. It was the first visit ever of a pope to the New World. The formal occasion was the twentieth anniversary of the United Nations. Papal visits anywhere outside of Rome were still rare and unusual events, and Pope Paul had decided to limit his trip to a one-day whirlwind visit. From the moment that the

35 - Murray to John J. McGinty, S.J., May 16, 1964, cit. in Fogarty, *Vatican and the American Hierarchy,* 395.
36 - AANY, Spellman to Galeazzi, March 30, 1965; April 9, 1965.

*Pope Paul VI and Cardinal Spellman
at the Mass closing the second session
of Vatican II on December 4, 1963.*
Credit: *Archdiocese of New York*

*Pope Paul VI and Cardinal Spellman
outside St. Patrick's Cathedral on October 4, 1965.*
Credit: *Archdiocese of New York*

pontiff landed at Idlewild airport (as JFK was still called) on October 4 until his departure that evening, Spellman never left his side.

A fast-moving motorcade whisked the pope on a twenty-five mile tour through Queens and upper Manhattan to St. Patrick's Cathedral where the formal liturgical reception took place in the presence of 5,000 guests with another 50,000 people gathered in the streets outside the cathedral. That afternoon the pope made a courtesy call on President Lyndon Johnson at the Waldorf-Astoria and then addressed the General Assembly of the United Nations where he made an impassioned plea for peace. Afterwards the pontiff attended an ecumenical service at the Church of the Holy Family on East 47th Street. That evening he celebrated Mass at Yankee Stadium before 92,000 worshippers and stopped to visit the Vatican Pavilion at the World's Fair before boarding his plane for Rome.

The Civil Rights Movement

Like most American Catholic priests and bishops of his era, Spellman had little firsthand experience of African Americans, or of their political, economic and social plight. On the other hand, Spellman was no bigot either. The first parishes where he administered Confirmation after coming to New York in 1939 were in Harlem. At the dedication of a new parochial school in Harlem in 1941, Spellman declared that all the schools of the archdiocese were open to both black and white students. In 1952, at the dedication of another new parochial school in Harlem, Spellman took note of "the sins of segregation and discrimination" but praised African Americans for their loyalty because they did not let the Communists exploit their grievances against American society.[37]

---

37 - Gannon, *Cardinal Spellman Story,* 270.

With that background, it is not surprising that Spellman was bewildered by the emergence of the civil rights movement in the 1960s. In the spring of 1965 he told his old Roman friend, Count Enrico Galeazzi, "The situation with the Negroes is fraught with great tension... The situation is very serious."[38] However, despite his own conservative instincts, Spellman began to take a more sympathetic and assertive position on civil rights. Much of the credit for that change was due to his vicar general, Archbishop John J. Maguire. For example, when Spellman hesitated to join the National Association for the Advancement of Colored People, Archbishop Maguire took out a life membership for him. Shortly thereafter, at a public appearance in Harlem, Spellman shamelessly boasted about the fact that he was a life member of the NAACP. Of course, he did not mention how recent his membership was or how he had acquired it.[39]

At the same speech in Harlem in which he boasted of his life membership in the NAACP, Spellman also said: "Doors cannot continue to close in the face of Negroes as they search for jobs, as they strive for membership in some unions, as they seek the chance for specialized job training." These remarks came on the eve of the March on Washington for Jobs and Freedom organized by Dr. Martin Luther King, Jr. in 1963. Some 1,000 Catholics from New York, both blacks and whites, took part in that march. Spellman still hesitated to get too closely involved. He did not directly endorse Catholic participation in the

John J. Maguire, Vicar General, 1953-1967, Coadjutor Archbishop, 1965-1967.

march, but he allowed Archbishop Maguire to endorse it in the form of a pastoral letter.[40]

Two years later, on the occasion of the more famous march from Selma to Montgomery, Alabama, a defining moment in the Civil Rights movement, Spellman himself publicly approved participation in that march by priests and religious from New York. A sympathy march through Harlem at the same time brought out hundreds of priests and religious, and received extensive favorable coverage in the diocesan newspaper. Matthew Ahmann, the executive director of the National Catholic Conference for Interracial Justice, thanked Spellman personally for the Catholic presence in both of those marches. When a white Unitarian minister was slain in Selma, Spellman donated $10,000 to a Selma hospital in his memory. This time, rather than leave the task to Archbishop Maguire, Spellman himself issued a pastoral letter in which he described "racial and civil injustice [as] a cancer attacking the very life of our nation and society."[41]

Shortly after that pastoral letter appeared, Spellman received a hand-written note from a black woman in his diocese. She said: "Once about five years ago I wrote a formal letter asking you to please intervene in your archdiocese in the affairs of Negroes. The answer came loud and clear when the Charity order and other orders marched for freedom in Harlem. It has come out loud and clear in Selma where the priests have

38 - AANY, Spellman to Galeazzi, March 8, April 9, 1965, copies.

39 - New York *Catholic News*, July 18, 1963. AANY, Maguire Papers, George A. Kelly, Cardinal Spellman and His Coadjutor Archbishops: The Second---John J. Maguire,: A Memoir, 16-17.

40 - New York *Catholic News*, August 15, 1963.

41 - AANY, Matthew Ahmann to Spellman, April 8, 1965; New York *Catholic News*, March 18, 1965.

gone to be God's witnesses." This woman went on to explain why these developments meant so much to her personally. "I have been a Catholic all my life," she told Spellman, "a Negro Catholic, a loner, a shadow in the Church. But now I am beginning to feel that I belong. I was able to show my four boys pictures of our Catholics taking part in the movement to make them first class citizens. I felt proud to be a Catholic, Your Excellency. Please continue to heed the pleas of your concerned Catholics. Continue to allow and even urge further participation in America's greatest struggle."[42]

Spellman saved that letter, and it may well have made a deep impression on him. A week after he received it, he spoke at a dinner in his honor in New York City. Alluding to the civil rights struggle, Spellman declared that "no price is too great to pay, no sacrifice too painful, no labor too demanding." Shortly thereafter Archbishop Egidio Vagnozzi, the Apostolic Delgate, consulted Spellman about the participation of priests and religious in Civil Rights demonstrations. Vagnozzi did not like it, and Spellman told him that he did not like it either. However, Spellman added, "I have taken no public position in the matter because I prefer to leave the decision to the religious superiors and in fact to the individuals themselves." "If participation were denied," Spellman warned Vagnozzi, "the reaction would be strong and serious." Moreover, Spellman added, "The participation of priests, religious and sisters in this diocese has for the most part evoked widespread approval as indicating sympathetic involvement of congregations and communities in favor of human and civil rights."[43]

The Sisters of Charity march through Harlem in a Civil Rights and anti-war demonstration.
Credit: *Sisters of Charity*

42 - AANY, S/C, Phyllis Brown to Spellman, March 19, [1965].
43 - *New York Times,* March 28, 1965. AANY, S/D 2, Vagnozzi to Spellman, n.d.; Spellman to Vagnozzi, June 29, 1965, copy.

Even the most enthusiastic revisionist historian would have a difficult time trying to reinvent Spellman as a Catholic Martin Luther King. Jr. However, the record shows that he was a person who was at least open to change at a time in his life when most people are inclined to dig in their heels. By no stretch of the imagination could Spellman be considered a leader of the Civil Rights movement, but, at the very least, he did not stand in the way of those who wanted to support it. His position, tentative and cautious as it was, stands in marked contrast to that of Bishop Thomas J. Toolen of Mobile-Birmingham, the ranking Catholic prelate in Alabama at the time of the Selma March. Toolen called the priests and religious who took part in the Selma march "eager-beavers who feel that this is a holy cause" and said that "their place is at home doing God's work."[44] If Spellman did not exactly mount the barricades on behalf of the civil rights movement, at least he did not try to prevent others from doing do so.

The Vietnam War

Nothing has hurt Spellman's reputation more than his endorsement of the American military involvement in the Vietnam War, particularly his unguarded comment at a Christmas Mass in Saigon in 1966, when he said that anything "less than victory is incomprehensible." Among other things, it seemed to put Spellman in direct opposition to Pope Paul VI, who was calling for an extension of the Christmas truce and a negotiated settlement of the war. The *New York Times* compared Spellman's statement to President Lyndon Johnson's recent admonition to the troops to "be sure to come home with the coonskin cap on the wall." In New York City members of the Catholic Peace Fellowship picketed the Cardinal's residence, and, on January 22, 1967, anti-war demonstrators staged a protest at the high Mass in St. Patrick's Cathedral.[45]

Spellman was not quite the redneck that he seemed to be on the Vietnam War. Essentially he justified the war as a legitimate form of self-defense. "It is my view," Spellman said in a speech in August 1966, "that every individual and every nation has a God-given right to protect and defend itself and others against unjust aggression." Directing his attention to conscientious objectors to the war, Spellman asserted that "conscientious objection is not a right to heap ridicule upon the choice of others who, with the same freedom of conscience, elect to defend with arms the freedoms they enjoy."

The weakness in Spellman's position was that he confined himself to abstract moral principles and did not apply them to the context of the Vietnam War. He admitted in theory that "the means used in such defense must, of course, be themselves just and no more and no other than are necessary to overcome the unjust attack." However, he failed to apply this standard to the Vietnam War. As casualties mounted and the hope of military victory faded, the damage inflicted on the civilian population seemed to be out of proportion to the possible good to be achieved, not just to pacifists, but to many other Americans as well.

In the mid-1960s the media had an easy time depicting Spellman, the Military Vicar for the Armed Forces, as the leading Catholic hawk. Such labels left him unmoved. "I think this business of hawks and doves is a lot of nonsense," he said. "Presumably a hawk is a man who wants war and a dove is one who wants peace. If that definition is correct, I don't know of a single

44 - N.C.W.C. News Service, March 19. 1965.

45 - *New York Times,* December 27, 28, 29, 1966; January 18, 23, 1967.

General Westmoreland welcomes Cardinal Spellman to Saigon, December 23, 1965.
Credit: *Archdiocese of New York*

responsible person in this nation who is a hawk. We all want peace." Then Spellman added a sentence which revealed the perspective from which he viewed the Vietnam War. "I do not remember a day in my life," he said, "that I have not prayed for peace. We prayed for it during the dark and terrible days of two World Wars, and we rejoiced when at last it came." Like many Americans of his generation, Spellman equated the Vietnam War with World War II, and he could not comprehend why many other Americans, particularly young Americans, saw a profound difference between the two conflicts.[46]

Ten months after his celebrated comments in Saigon, Spellman saw no reason to modify them. In October 1967 he said: "I find no substantial reason to withdraw or weaken those statements. I still believe that [we] are fighting on the side of freedom and against aggression, and I do not, for one moment, think that a lasting peace will be secured simply through the withdrawal of the United States Forces from Vietnam." Spellman took those convictions with him to the grave two months later.[47]

Shortly before Spellman's death anti-war protestors (including some sisters) were arrested for disrupting Mass in St. Patrick's Cathedral. Spellman was not present to witness the scene, but it must have been an incomprehensible development for someone like himself who belonged to an earlier age when faith and patriotism were unquestioning allies. A notably ambitious man, it can at least be said that Spellman wedded his ambition to the service of both his church and his country and made notable contributions to both. He died in New York City on December 2, 1967.

46 - AANY, S/A 14, Spellman, Address to the Veterans of Foreign Wars, New York City, August 21, 1966.

47 - AANY, S/A 14, Spellman, Remarks at the 47th Annual Convention of the Military Order of the World Wars, San Diego, California, October 20, 1967.

18

The Crabgrass Frontier

Blessed Kateri Tekakwitha Church, LaGrangeville, established as a parish on July 1, 2002.
Credit: *Catholic New York:* Chris Sheridan

No sooner did America become a predominantly urban nation in the early twentieth century than the reverse process began of movement from the cities to the suburbs. In New York City this demographic shift had a long history. As early as the mid-nineteenth century Horace Greeley abandoned the dirt and noise of Manhattan for a daily ride on the New York and Harlem Railroad to his rural retreat in Westchester County. By the end of the century Monsignor James McGean, the pastor of St. Peter's Church on Barclay Street, was complaining of the exodus of his better-off parishioners to Brooklyn and New Jersey. The move to suburbia picked up steam between 1900 and 1929, then slowed to a snail's pace as the result of the Depression and World War II only to become a flood after the end of the war.

As Monsignor McGean noted, many Catholics who left the crowded neighborhoods of Manhattan moved outside the archdiocese. This flight to Brooklyn and New Jersey, together with the restrictive immigration laws of the 1920s, resulted in the decline of the Catholic population of the archdiocese from 1,350,000 in 1900 to about 1,000,000 in 1940. For those Catholics who remained within the archdiocese, the favorite destination was Westchester. The new suburbanites in the county were not all new-comers from New York City. Many of the cities in Westchester itself like Yonkers, Mount Vernon, New Rochelle and White Plains experienced the same phenomenon of movement from downtown to their own leafy streetcar suburbs.

Yonkers

Yonkers had two parishes in 1890, nine in 1900 (five of them national parishes for as many ethnic groups) and twenty parishes by 1931. Several of the new parishes were located in the old city, Our Lady of the Rosary on Warburton Avenue, Holy Eucharist at the foot of Nodine Hill, St. Denis in South Yonkers, and a second Italian church, Our Lady of Mt. Carmel, located a half-block from St. Anthony's Church on Willow Street, founded in 1901 by Father Michael Sarubbi.

The Church of Our Lady of the Rosary was started in 1907 and the permanent church, a combination church-and-school, was dedicated by Cardinal Farley on May 23, 1915. John Talbot Smith, who deplored the proliferation of combi-nation church-and-schools, because he thought that most of them were so ugly, made an exception

for Holy Rosary, as the church was usually called. "A handsome hall is in the basement," he wrote, "the church proper is next, and the school is on the top floor. The front view of the triple structure is amazing: only the church stands revealed; the towers right and left of the façade contain the doors, stairways and other conveniences for the school hall; they seem to be part of the church, but really these towers are the means by which the cunning architect shut off the church from the other sections and concealed them from the observer. It is a very striking and handsome building."[1]

The first pastor of Our Lady of Mount Carmel, Father Ercole J. Rossi, claimed that Cardinal Farley told him personally that he was responsible for the pastoral care of "all the Italians in Yonkers." Within two years of his arrival in Yonkers, Father Rossi erected the present Church of Our Lady of Mount Carmel on Park Hill Avenue. It was dedicated by Arch-bishop John Bonzano, the Apostolic Delegate to the United States, on July 16, 1916.[2]

At St. Denis the English Gothic church, constructed of local Mile Square granite, was the gift of one person, Mrs. Elizabeth Horgan, who defrayed the construction costs in return for the right for her and her family to be buried in the church. Since it was debt-free at completion, it was consecrated by auxiliary Bishop Thomas F. Cusack on May 29, 1912. By the 1920s the pastor of St. Mary's Church was complaining that there were too many Catholic churches in downtown Yonkers.[3]

---

1 - The two other combination church-and--schools that John Talbot Smith admired were Our Lady of Victory in the Bronx and St. Ambrose in Manhattan. The architect of all three buildings was John V. Van Pelt. John Talbot Smitj, *New York Freeman's Journal,* November 6, 1915.

2 - AANY, Rossi to Carroll, May 6, 1919. "History of Our Lady of Mt. Carmel Church," *Golden Jubilee* (Yonkers: Church of Our Lady of Mt. Carmel, 1965), unpaginated.

3 - *Church of St. Denis: Diamond Jubilee* (Yonkers: Church of St. Denis, 1985), unpaginated.. AANY, Charles T. Murphy to Carroll, August 16, 1929.

Holy Rosary Church, Yonkers,
as it appeared in 1915.

The Church of Our Lady of the Rosary
in Yonkers, now closed.

St. Anthony's Church and rectory,
Willow Street, the first Italian church
in Yonlkers, founded in 1900 and closed
in 1968. Credit: St. Anthony's Church

The Church of Our Lady of Mount Carmel,
Yonkers, dedicated by Archbishop John
Bonzano on July 16, 1916.

One of the new parishes was a national parish, St. Margaret of Hungary, founded in 1928 a few blocks north of St. Joseph's Church on Ashburton Avenue for the Magyars who no longer felt comfortable worshipping at the Slovak Church of the Most Holy Trinity after World War I. All of the other new churches were located north or east of downtown Yonkers.

The first was the Church of St. John the Baptist on Yonkers Avenue, which owed its origin to the real estate boom in the Dunwoodie area after the building of St. Joseph's Seminary. In 1891 lots across the street from the seminary were selling for as low as $275. In 1903 Archbishop Farley established the Church of St. John the Baptist as a mission of the seminary. It only got a resident pastor in 1919, and the church was dedicated by Cardinal Hayes on October 24, 1926. A local newspaper reporter who was present at the ceremony wrote: "Those who approach the church are inspired by its Gothic majesty and its massive beauty."[4]

The Church of St. John the Baptist was followed in 1910 by St. Bartholomew's Church on Palmer Road just north of the sprawling Alexander Smith carpet shops. The strikingly modern present church was dedicated by Cardinal Cooke on November 18, 1973. The completion of the IRT subway to Woodlawn spurred real estate development in the Lincoln Park area, leading to the establishment of still another new church in Yonkers, St. Paul's Church on McLean Avenue in 1923.

That same year St. Anthony's mission church in Nepera Park became a parish with the appointment of Father John W. Murphy as the pastor. Shortly thereafter he bought a small Protestant church on North Broadway and converted it into a mission church. "Father Murphy has opened a Protestant church on North Broadway," Bishop Dunn told the board of consultors. Presumably they knew what he meant. Speculating that the mission had a brighter future than the parish church in Nepera Park, Murphy moved to a new rectory on North Broadway and became the first pastor of the Church of Christ the King when it was made a separate parish in 1927.[5] The new St. Anthony's Church was dedicated by Cardinal Spellman on September 12, 1954, after Father Murphy's old church was destroyed by fire on March 21, 1951.

4 - *Yonkers Herald,* May 18, 1891; October 25, 1926.

5 - AANY, Minutes of the Meetings of the Board of Diocesan Consultors, April 6, 1927.

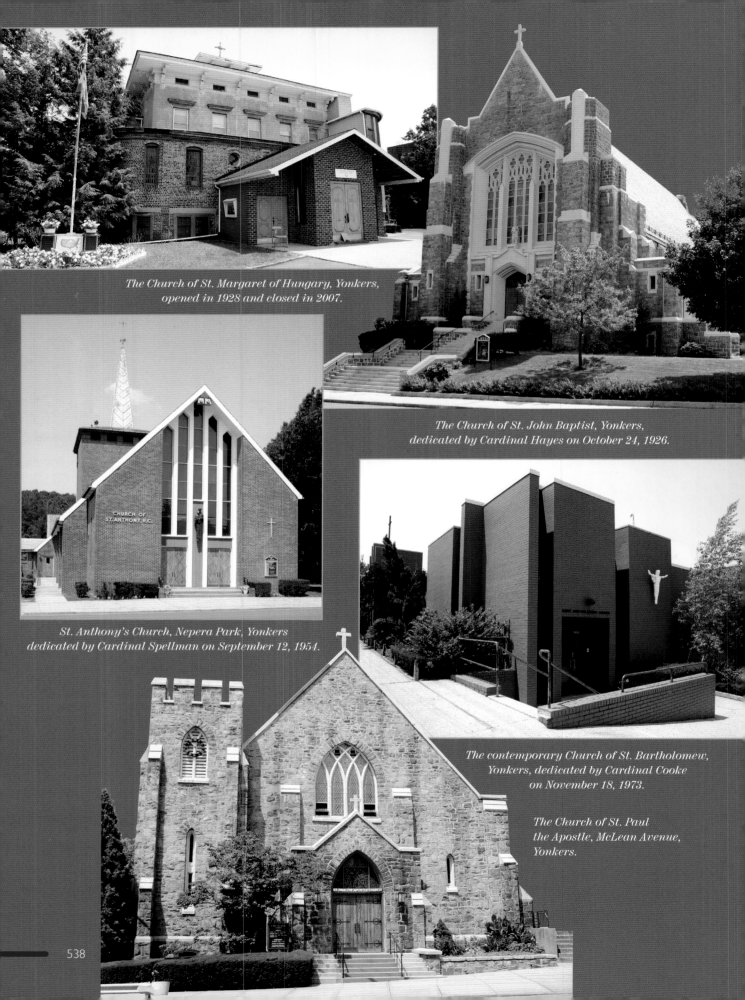

The Church of St. Margaret of Hungary, Yonkers,
opened in 1928 and closed in 2007.

The Church of St. John Baptist, Yonkers,
dedicated by Cardinal Hayes on October 24, 1926.

St. Anthony's Church, Nepera Park, Yonkers
dedicated by Cardinal Spellman on September 12, 1954.

The contemporary Church of St. Bartholomew,
Yonkers, dedicated by Cardinal Cooke
on November 18, 1973.

The Church of St. Paul
the Apostle, McLean Avenue,
Yonkers.

*The Protestant Church that
Father John Murphy was said
to have opened on North Broadway:
the Church of Christ the King
as it appeared in 1927.*
Credit: *Church of Christ the King*

*The Church of Christ the King,
North Broadway, Yonkers.*

*Father Timothy J. Dugan,
the founding pastor of the Church
of the Annunciation, Crestwood.*
Credit: *Church of the Annunciation*

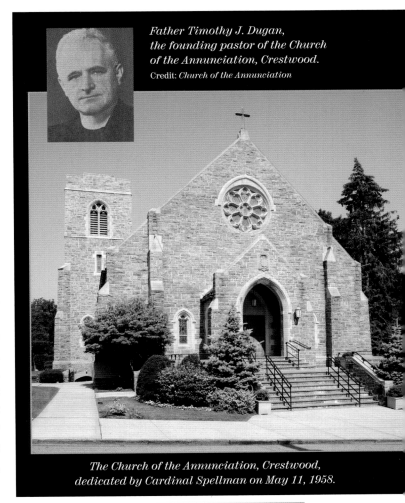

*The Church of the Annunciation, Crestwood,
dedicated by Cardinal Spellman on May 11, 1958.*

The roots of Church of the Annunciation in Crestwood, the last Yonkers parish to be established before World War II, were not in Yonkers, but in Tuckahoe. In 1927 Father Edward J. Beary, the pastor of Immaculate Conception Church in Tuckahoe, set up a mission church called St. Patrick's Chapel, in a prefabricated Sears Roebuck building on the grounds of St. Eleanora's Home (today St. Vladimir's Seminary). A year earlier Monsignor Cornelius Crowley, the local dean, had advised against starting a parish in Crestwood because he calculated that there were no more than forty Catholic families in the area.[6]

Nonetheless, in 1931 Crestwood got its own parish with the appointment of Father Timothy J. Dugan as the first resident pastor. At that time the name of the church was changed from St. Patrick to the Church of the Annunciation. In May 1936 Dugan broke ground for the present church. The lower church was dedicated six months later, on November 22, 1936, but the upper church was not finished until 1958. It was dedicated by Cardinal Spellman on May 11, 1958, a year after the death of Father Dugan.[7]

6 - AANY, Crowley to Dunn, October 30, 1926.

7 - "A History of the Founding of Annunciation Parish, Crestwood, N.Y.," *Golden Jubilee of Annunciation Parish* (Crestwood: Annunciation Church , 1918), unpaginated.

Mount Vernon, New Rochelle and White Plains

Mount Vernon, New Rochelle and White Plains produced their own mini-suburbs with new more-or-less suburban parishes. In Mount Vernon St. Ursula's Church dates from 1908 and the Church of Saints Peter and Paul in the Fleetwood section of the city from 1929. Cardinal Hayes assigned Father John V. Delaney to start the new parish in Fleetwood in June 1929, four months before the Stock Market crash. Despite the Depression he was able to build an English Gothic church that Cardinal Hayes dedicated on May 20, 1934.[8]

New Rochelle got two new parishes, the Church of the Holy Family and the Church of the Holy Name of Jesus. When Father Andrew T. Roche arrived in 1913 to start Holy Family Church, the suburban era was just beginning in northern New Rochelle. Real estate developers were busy buying up farms and subdividing them into housing tracts. After three years of celebrating Mass in a former

butcher shop, Father Roche built the present church, which was dedicated by auxiliary Bishop Patrick Hayes on October 14, 1917. The second pastor, Monsignor Thomas G. Carroll, the former chancellor, added a school above the church. The third pastor, Father William B. Martin, had more ambitious plans. He defied the Depression by launching a major building campaign in 1929 that gave the parish a larger church and school as well as a palatial rectory and for a brief period even a high school. However, at his death in 1939, he left his successor a debt of $350,000.[9]

The Church of the Holy Name of Jesus dates from the summer of 1929 when Father James J. Halligan was assigned to start a new parish in northeast New Rochelle. He celebrated Sunday Mass in the chapel of the Salesian School on Boston Post Road until a basement church was ready for use in September 1930. The present church was built above the basement church in 1962.[10]

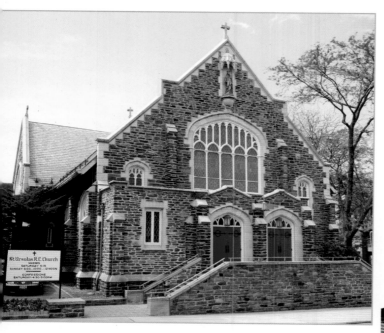

St. Ursula's Church, Mount Vernon.

The Church of the Holy Name of Jesus, New Rochelle.

8 - *The Golden Jubilee of Saints Peter and Paul Parish* (Mount Vernon: Saints Peter and Paul Church, 1979), unpaginated.

9 - *Fiftieth Anniversary of the Founding of Holy Family Parish* (New Rochelle: Holy Family Church, 1963), 9-30.

10 - *Holy Name of Jesus Church: 75th Anniversary* (New Rochelle: Holy Name Church, 2004), 7-9.

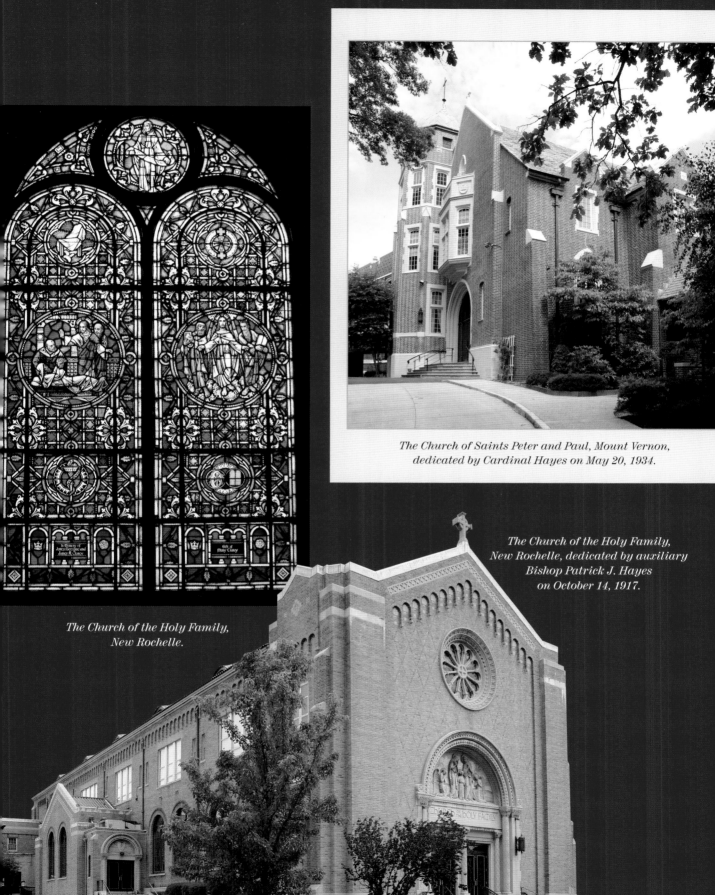

The Church of Saints Peter and Paul, Mount Vernon,
dedicated by Cardinal Hayes on May 20, 1934.

The Church of the Holy Family,
New Rochelle, dedicated by auxiliary
Bishop Patrick J. Hayes
on October 14, 1917.

The Church of the Holy Family,
New Rochelle.

In White Plains, the suburban sprawl took place south of the downtown business district in the Highlands and Gedney Farms sections of the city. In 1926 Cardinal Hayes appointed Father John B. Murphy to begin St. Bernard's Church. A private residence on Mamaroneck Avenue served as a mission church until a frame building was erected at the corner of Prospect Street and South Lexington Avenue. It was first used for Christmas Mass in 1926. Construction of the present church-school building was begun in 1931, and it was officially dedicated by Cardinal Hayes on November 4, 1933.[11]

The Church of Our Lady of Sorrows in Gedney Farms began in 1929 in the original mission church of St. Bernard. The first pastor was Father Patrick F. Mackin, who built a rustic wooden church that was dedicated on May 25, 1930. Expanded and renovated several times, it still serves as the parish church in 2007."[12]

As was true in the Bronx and Staten Island, a number of the new parishes in Westchester County were national parishes. As was mentioned in Chapter Nine, two were Polish parishes, St. Stanislaus in Hastings-on-Hudson (1912) and Sacred Heart of Jesus Church in Port Chester (1917), and one Slovak parish, the Church of the Holy Cross in Sleepy Hollow (1922). Eight of the national parishes were Italian, but many other parishes throughout the county had a high percentage of Italian parishioners.

Westchester's Italian Parishes

The Church of Our Lady of Mount Carmel in White Plains is the second oldest Catholic church in that city. It traces its origin to 1902 when Father Joseph Marinaro, a diocesan priest, became the pastor of a small wooden church just west of the New York Central Railroad. The construction of the Bronx River Parkway in 1917 led to the loss of the original property and the relocation of the church to the other side of the tracks closer to the business district. In 1922 the church was entrusted to the Stigmatine Fathers, a small Italian religious congregation. The first Stigmatine pastor, Father Leo Sella, C.S.S., began the construction of the present church with its signature 200-foot campanile visible to every rider on Metro North. The façade is a reproduction of the Church of Santa Maria della Pietà in Venice, and the interior is modeled after the Basilica of Santa Maria Maggiore in Rome.[13]

In 1911 Westchester got two more Italian churches. The Church of the Assumption in Tuckahoe was started for the Italian community that had been worshipping in the Church of the Immaculate Conception. In Mamaroneck St. Vito's Church actually dates from May 1910 when the vicar general, Monsignor Michael J. Lavelle, blessed the small wooden church on Madison Street built by the first pastor, Father Cocozza. The second pastor, Father Biago del Negro, replaced it with a larger church at Underhill Avenue and New Street. It was officially opened for Mass on Christmas Day in 1930.[14]

By the mid-1920s Port Chester could boast of two Italian churches, both staffed by the Salesians of Don Bosco. The first, Holy Rosary Church, dates from 1903 when Archbishop Farley sent Father Pasquale Maltese, a diocesan priest, to start a parish for the Italian community in Port Chester. Within a year he built the present church which Archbishop Farley blessed on May 15, 1904. In 1912 the Salesians took charge of the parish. Two years later they established a mission church, Corpus Christi, in the Washington Park area of the city, which became a parish in 1925. The present church was completed in October 1927.

11 - *St. Bernard's Church: 75th Anniversary* (White Plains; St. Bernard's Church, 2001), unpaginated,

12 - *The First Fifty Years* (White Plains: Our Lady of Sorrows Church, 1979), 6-8.

13 - Celebrating 100 Years (White Plains: Church of Our Lady of Mt. Carmel, 2002), unpaginated.

14 - *Church of St. Vito: Golden Jubilee* (Mamaroneck: Church of St. Vito, 1961), 3-6.

The first St. Bernard's Church, White Plains, built in 1926.
Credit: *St. Bernard's Church*

St. Bernard's Church, White Plains, dedicated by Cardinal Hayes on November 4, 1933.

The Church of Our Lady of Sorrows, White Plains, dedicated on May 25, 1930.

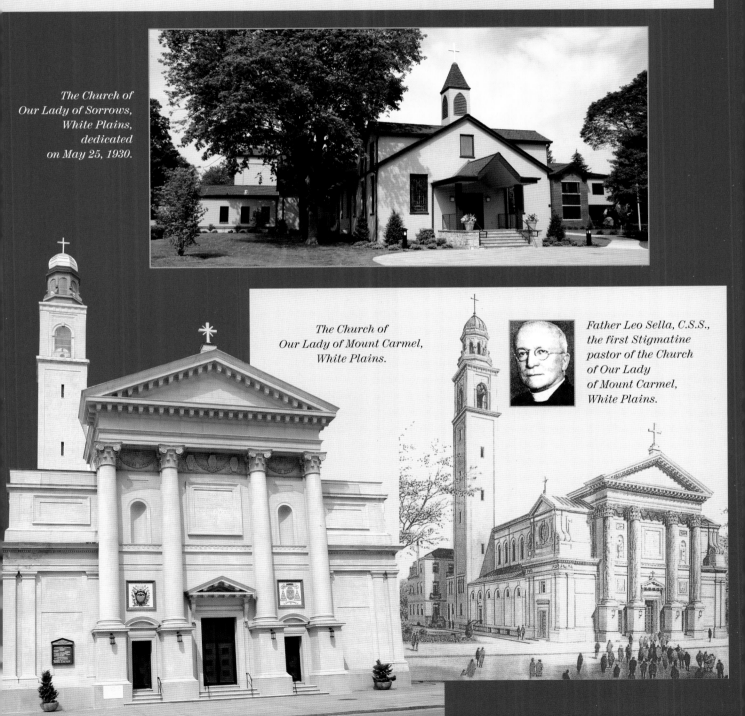

The Church of Our Lady of Mount Carmel, White Plains.

Father Leo Sella, C.S.S., the first Stigmatine pastor of the Church of Our Lady of Mount Carmel, White Plains.

The Church of the Assumption, Tuckahoe.

St. Vito's Church, Mamaroneck.

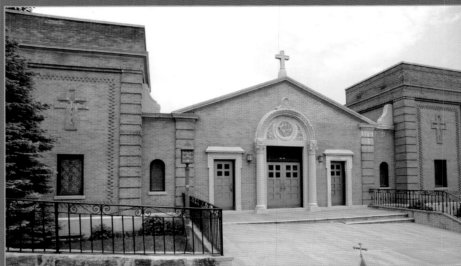

Holy Rosary Church, Port Chester, dedicated by Archbishop Farley on May 15, 1904.

Corpus Christi Church, Port Chester, completed in October 1927.

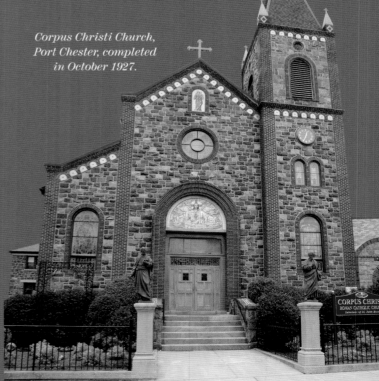

As part of their ministry in Port Chester the Salesians also brought Polish-speaking Salesian priests to Port Chester to care for the Polish immigrants in the Brooksville area. Their labors led to the establishment of the Polish Church of the Sacred Heart of Jesus in 1917. Holy Rosary Church suffered a major disaster in December 1985, when it was heavily damaged by fire. It was rebuilt and rededicated by Cardinal O'Connor on October 3, 1989.[15]

At the other side of the county the Church of Our Lady of Pompei was founded in Dobbs Ferry in 1923. The first three pastors were diocesan priests. Cardinal Hayes asked both the Jesuits and the Scalabrinians to take over the parish, but they refused. Finally in 1931 the Augustinians agreed to take charge of Our Lady of Pompei and ran it for more than fifty years. It has recently been merged with Sacred Heart Church in Dobbs Ferry.

In Sleepy Hollow the pioneer Italian priest was Father Domenico M. Coda whom Cardinal Farley sent to North Tarrytown in 1917, as the village was

The Church of Our Lady of Pompei, Dobbs Ferry, now merged with the Church of the Sacred Heart, Dobbs Ferry.

then called, to organize a parish for the local Italians. After operating out of two storefront churches, Father Coda purchased a former German Lutheran church in 1920 and renamed it the Church of the Immaculate Conception. Five years later he began construction of a larger brick church. Like Monsignor Arthur Donnelly at St. Michael's Church in New York City eighty years earlier, Father Coda literally built his new church around the old one so that there was no interruption in church services. It was completed on December 23, 1926, and dedicated by Cardinal Hayes on May 1, 1927.

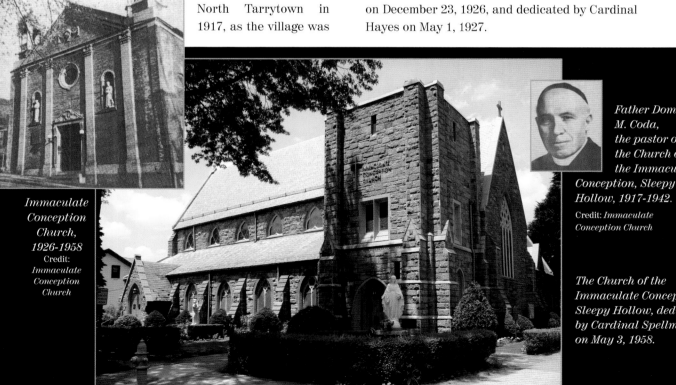

Immaculate Conception Church, 1926-1958
Credit: *Immaculate Conception Church*

Father Domenico M. Coda, the pastor of the Church of the Immaculate Conception, Sleepy Hollow, 1917-1942.
Credit: *Immaculate Conception Church*

The Church of the Immaculate Conception; Sleepy Hollow, dedicated by Cardinal Spellman on May 3, 1958.

---

15 - *Celebrating 100 Years* (Port Chester: Holy Rosary Church, 2004), unpaginated. *Corpus Christi Church* (Custombook, 1975), 10-11.

By the 1950s the congregation was too large for Father Coda's church. In 1956 the third pastor of Immaculate Conception, Monsignor Nicasio Viso, bought the former St. Mark's Episcopal Church on Broadway and renovated it at a cost of over $400,000. It was dedicated by Cardinal Spellman on May 3, 1958.[16]

In Ossining a committee of lay people headed by Giuolo Tuono took the initiative in giving the Italian community their own church. In response to a petition from them in 1927, Cardinal Hayes sent them Father John B. Eula, a sixty-two year old native of Italy, to organize St. Ann's parish. He celebrated Mass in temporary quarters until the basement of St. Ann's Church was finished in January 1929. The second pastor, Father Arthur Tommaso, completed the decoration of the upper church, added the stained glass windows and an organ.[17]

A Catholic Presence throughout Westchester

Elsewhere in the county the Church of St. Gregory the Great in Harrison originated in 1900 as an out-mission of the Church of the Resurrection in Rye. Two years later a small mission church was erected at the corner of Halstead Avenue and Featherbed Lane. It became the parish church on April 30, 1911, with the appointment of Father O'Sullivan as the first resident pastor.

On June 26, 1915, the church was severely damaged by fire, but was repaired and renovated by Father William S. Prunty, who became the pastor in 1918. Prunty was fluent in Italian, an advantage in a parish with many Italian-speaking parishioners. He was also less than subtle as a fund-raiser, telling his parishioners that he could create a traffic jam on Halstead Avenue by bringing to life all the Indians and buffalo on the pennies and nickels that he got in the collection. In 1934 Prunty demolished the original church and had the basement of the new church in operation the following year. Bishop Edward Dargin completed the upper church which was dedicated in 1961.[18]

Father John B. Eula, the founder of St. Ann's Church, Ossining, in 1927.

St. Ann's Church, Ossining.

---

16 - E.V. Zegarelli, "A Fifty Year History of the Church of the Immaculate Conception," *Golden Jubilee* (North Tarrytown: Church of the Immaculate Conception, 1967), unpaginated.

17 - *Church of St.Ann, Golden Anniversary* (White Plains: Monarch Publications, 1978), unpaginated.

18 - A Brief History of St. Gregory the Great Parish, unpublished paper.

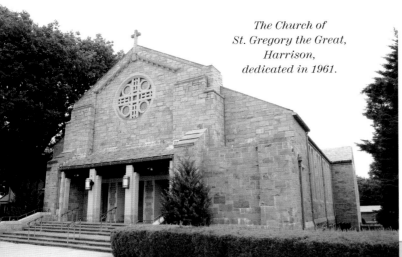

The Church of St. Gregory the Great, Harrison, dedicated in 1961.

Our Lady of Mount Carmel Church and rectory, Elmsford, 1925.

The Church of Our Lady of Mount Carmel, Elmsford, completed in September 1929.

In Elmsford, a one-square mile village, the Church of Our Lady of Mount Carmel began in 1904 as a mission of the Carmelite Church of the Transfiguration in Tarrytown. Both Carmelite pride and ethnic considerations may have combined to suggest the title of the church, since many of the first parishioners were Italians. Before the end of the year a small wooden church was constructed on the site of the present church. In 1913 Elmsford became a parish with the appointment of Father Arthur Kennedy, a diocesan priest, as the first resident pastor. In 1928 Father James Hackett began the construction of the combined church-and-school building that serves the parish to this day. It was completed in September 1929.[19]

Father north in Hawthorne, Holy Rosary Church owes its origins to a community of exiled French Dominicans who settled in the area, then known as Sherman Park, and opened a house of studies called Rosary Hill in 1894. It eventually led to the founding not only of Holy Rosary Church, but also of two other Dominican parishes, Holy Innocents in Pleasantville and Holy Name of Jesus in Valhalla.

In 1901 the Dominicans sold Rosary Hill to Mother Alphonsa (Rose Hawthorne Lathrop) for her hospice for cancer patients and built a new house of study. They also did pastoral work in the neighboring parishes. In 1911 they offered hospitality to Father Thomas Price and Father James Walsh, the founders of Maryknoll, who moved to their permanent home the following year.

In 1915 Holy Rosary Church was officially made a parish. From 1916 until 1950 two Dominican scholars, Father Charles Callan and Father James McHugh, staffed the parish,

19 - History of Our Lady of Mount Carmel Church, unpublished paper.

Holy Rosary Church, Hawthorne, dedicated on March 13, 1988.

alternating every three years as pastor and religious superior in accordance with the Dominican rule. Meanwhile they were fulltime professors at the Maryknoll seminary and authors of numerous theological books and periodical articles, using their salaries and royalties to support the struggling parish. In 1956 a school was built with a hall that served as the church until the present church was completed and dedicated on March 13, 1988.[20]

Like many parishes in the lower Harlem Valley, the Church of Our Lady of the Assumption in Katonah began as an out-mission of St. Joseph's Church in Croton Falls in 1867. It later became a mission of St. Francis of Assisi in Mount Kisco, and in 1883 once again reverted to the status of a mission of Croton Falls until it was made a parish in 1908. A mission church was built in Katonah 1890, which became the parish church in 1908 with the appointment of Father Cornelius Crowley as the first pastor. At the same time the out-mission in Bedford Hills was detached from Mount Kisco and assigned to Katonah.[21]

Like Katonah, Bedford was once an out-mission of St. Francis of Assisi in Mount Kisco. Mass was originally celebrated every other

Sunday in the Bedford Village Court house until a small wooden chapel dedicated to St. Patrick was built in 1883. In 1928 a parishioner, Thomas O'Brien, donated land east of the Village Green where a fieldstone church was erected that year. Designed in the colonial style, it successfully blended with the other buildings on the Village Green. The following year St. Patrick's became a parish when Cardinal Hayes appointed Father Thomas P. Gavin the first pastor.[22]

St. Joseph's Church in Bronxville began as an out-mission of the Church of the Immaculate Conception in Tuckahoe when priests from that parish began celebrating Mass in 1905 in the Gramatan Hotel and after 1907 in St. Joseph's mission church. In 1922 Cardinal Hayes made St. Joseph's a parish and assigned Father Joseph McCann as the first pastor. In 1924, when Father McCann purchased the property for a new church on Kraft Avenue, he had 260 parishioners. Two years later, when he began the construction of the present St. Joseph's Church, he had 1,000 parishioners, the vast majority of them blue-collar workers. The church was first used for Mass on April 1, 1928, and dedicated by Cardinal Hayes on September 16, 1928.[23]

20 - *Rosary Hill and Holy Rosary: A Short History, 1901-1981* (Hawthorne: Holy Rosary Church, 1918), 33-57.

21 - *St. Mary's Parish Golden Jubilee* (Katonah: Church of St. Mary of the Assumption, 1958), unpaginated.

22 - Rob Ryser, *St. Patrick's Church: Diamond Jubilee* (Bedford: St. Patrick's Church, 2004), unpaginated.

23 - *The Church of St. Joseph* (Bronxville: St. Joseph's Church, 1986), unpaginated.

The Church of Our Lady of the Assumption, Katonah, which dates from 1890.

St. Matthias mission chapel, Bedford Hills.

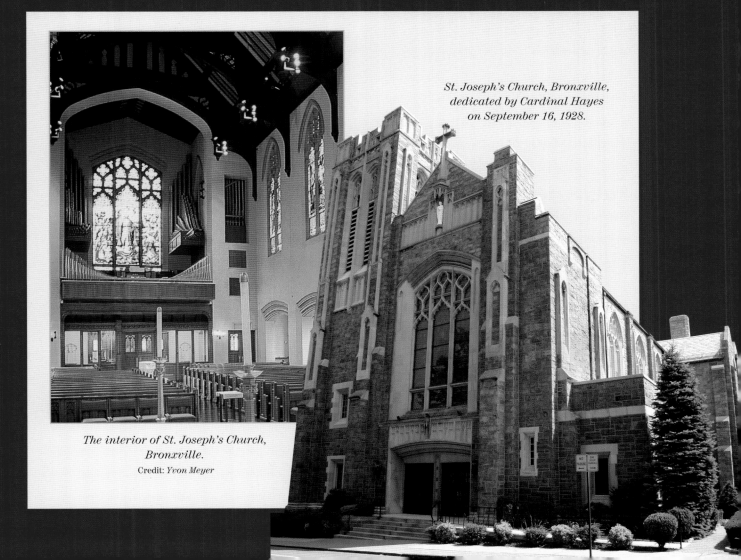

St. Joseph's Church, Bronxville, dedicated by Cardinal Hayes on September 16, 1928.

The interior of St. Joseph's Church, Bronxville.
Credit: *Yvon Meyer*

St. Patrick's Church, Bedford, erected in 1928.

Like the Catholics in Bedford, the Catholics in Chappaqua had a handsome church before they had a parish. In 1922 Mrs. Catherine Manning McKeon built a small stone church in Chappaqua as a memorial to her parents, John and Mary Manning. At her request Archbishop Hayes established the parish of St. John and St. Mary and dedicated the church on June 3, 1923. Like Scarsdale a decade earlier, Chappaqua had only a few dozen Catholics families who had traveled to Holy Innocents Church in Pleasantville prior to the building of Mrs. McKeon little church. The first pastor was Father Martin F. Cavanaugh, who started out-missions in Armonk, Millwood and Purchase between 1923 and 1926. By the 1970s the Catholic community in Chappaqua was far too large for the church and used the school auditorium for Sunday Mass. In 1997 Monsignor Timothy McDonnell (now the bishop of Springfield, Massachusetts), converted it into a permanent Upper Church to complement the Little Church.[25]

In the early twentieth century the easiest way for Catholics in Scarsdale to get to Sunday Mass was to take the trolley car St. John's Church in White Plains. In 1912 a committee representing thirty-nine families asked Cardinal Farley to establish a parish for them. He responded by sending them Father William C. Rourke, who broke ground for the Church of the Immaculate Heart of Mary the following year and had it ready to be dedicated by auxiliary Bishop Thomas Cusack on July 12, 1914. The church was enlarged and remodeled between 1948 and 1951. Despite the creation of new parishes in Scarsdale in 1948 and 1954, the parish numbered 1,800 families in the 1960s.[24]

Both the Church of the Sacred Heart in Hartsdale and St. Theresa's Church in Briarcliff Manor date from 1926. The first pastor of St. Theresa's Church was the Irish-born Father James Kelly, who asked Cardinal Hayes to name the church in honor of the recently canonized St. Theresa of the Child Jesus. Father Kelly celebrated Mass on Sunday in the laundry room of the Briarcliff Lodge, a local resort hotel, until he was able to build a church, which was dedicated by Cardinal Hayes in September 1928. He also took over responsibility from the Church of St. John and St. Mary in Chappaqua for the mission church of Our Lady of the Wayside in Millwood, which Cardinal Hayes named in honor of his own titular church in Rome, Sancta Maria in Via.[26]

24 - "History of the Immaculate Heart of Mary Church," *Diamond Jubilee* (Scarsdale: Immaculate Heart of Mary Church , 1987), 4-11.

25 - *The Catholic Church of Saint John and Saint Mary* (Chappaqua: Church of St. John and St. Mary, n.d.), 5-16.

26 - *Church of St. Theresa, Briarcliff Manor* (White Plains: Monarch Publications, 1976), 7-14.

Window of Our Lady, Immaculate Heart of Mary, Scarsdale.
Credit: *Yvon Meyer*

Father William C. Rourke, the founder of the Church of the Immaculate Heart of Mary, Scarsdale.
Credit: *Immaculate Heart of Mary Church*

The Church of the Immaculate Heart of Mary, Scarsdale, dedicated by auxiliary Bishop Thomas Cusack on July 12, 1914.

Father Martin F. Cavanaugh, the founder of the Church of St. John and St. Mary,

Father James F. Kelly, the first pastor of St. Theresa's Church, Briarcliff Manor, as a chaplain in the U.S. Army.
Credit: *St. Theresa's Church.*

The Church of the Sacred Heart, Hartsdale.

St. Theresa's Church, Briarcliff Manor.

The mission Church of Our Lady of the Wayside, Millwood.

St. Christopher's Church, Buchanan, dedicated by Cardinal Spellman on July 13, 1965.

The year 1929 began as a banner year for Catholics in Westchester. In addition to new parishes in Mount Vernon, New Rochelle and White Plains, St. Christopher's Church was established in Buchanan and the Church of Our Lady of Perpetual Help in Ardsley. St. Christopher's began in 1926 as an out-mission of the oldest parish in Westchester County, St. Patrick's Church in Verplanck, which dates from 1843. For the next three years Catholics in Buchanan met for Sunday Mass in a tavern until the mission was made a parish with the appointment of Father Christopher Dunleavy as the first resident pastor.

Father Dumleavy relieved the immediate problem of finding a more suitable place for Sunday Mass by purchasing a large boarding house which he renovated into a church and rectory. Following a long-standing New York tradition, he named the church after his patron saint. Following another New York tradition, he later expanded the church by building a larger structure around it and then dismantling the original building. By the 1960s even the enlarged church was inadequate for the needs of the growing congregation. Monsignor Leo G. Farley solved the problem by building the present church, which was dedicated by Cardinal Spellman on July 13, 1965.[27]

The general affluence of Westchester County was not always reflected in its Catholic parishes, especially during the Depression. The Church of Our Lady of Perpetual Help in Ardsley is a good case in point. Founded in 1929 with territory taken largely from Sacred Heart Church in Dobbs Ferry, the first two pastors had a difficult time trying to make ends meet. In 1934 Father John A. Dougherty had over $1,000 in unpaid bills and $12.00 in the bank He appealed to the Society for

The Church of Our Lady of Perpetual Help, Ardsley.

the Propagation of the Faith for help, saying, "I feel my parish is a home mission." For the next six years the parish was without a resident pastor and was administered by Monsignor Arthur J. Scanlan, the rector of St. Joseph's Seminary.[28]

Upstate

In Dutchess County Poughkeepsie experienced the same growing pains as the Westchester cities, leading to the establishment of two new parishes, Our Lady of Mount Carmel in 1910 and Holy Trinity Church in 1921. The Italian community in Poughkeepsie first worshipped in the basement of St. Peter's Church where the pastor, Father William Livingston, provided an Italian priest to celebrate Mass for them. A census in 1906 revealed that there were approximately 500 Italians in Poughkeepsie by that date. Father Pavone, the Italian-born curate at St. Peter's, worked with a committee of laymen to establish their own Italian parish. Early in 1910 the cornerstone of the Church of Our Lady of Mount Carmel was blessed and the church was

---

27 - *St. Christopher's Church, 1929-1979* (Buchanan: St. Christopher's Church, 1979), unpaginated.

28 - AANY, Dougherty to Thomas J. McDonnell, March 13, 1934.

dedicated that same year on October 12, the feast of Our Lady of Mount Carmel.[29] In 1965, the wheel came full circle when St. Peter's Church was relocated to Hyde Park and Mount Carmel took over the former St. Peter's Church.

A decade after the founding of Our Lady of Mount Carmel Church, in June 1921, Archbishop Hayes appointed the Irish-born Father Peter P. Conaty to organize Holy Trinity parish in suburban Arlington. He used the local firehouse for Mass until a frame church was erected the following June. That same month the cornerstone was blessed for the permanent church where the first parish Mass was celebrated on March 11, 1923. A Tudor Gothic structure built with local blue and gray stone, it was designed by a Poughkeepsie architect, John Draney, and constructed at the bargain price of $150,000.[30]

Northeast of Poughkeepsie on State Route 44 St. Stanislaus Church was established as far back as 1903 in rural Pleasant Valley. It may be the only church of that name in the United States that did not originate as a Polish national parish. This St. Stanislaus Church began as a mission cared for by the Jesuits at St. Andrew's novitiate in Hyde Park. They named it in honor of the Polish Jesuit, St. Stanislaus Kostka. In 1922 the Jesuit mission became a diocesan parish and the present church was erected in 1956. Rural Dutchess County got another parish in 1919 when Father Robert A. Ross was appointed the pastor of the Church of the Immaculate Conception in Bangall.

West of the Hudson, two new parishes were founded in Ulster County, St. Colman in East Kingston in 1904 and St. Joseph's in Glasco in 1919. St. Joseph's originated as an out-mission of the Church of St Mary of the Snow in Saugerties.

Fifty years later St. Joseph's was a barely self-sustaining rural parish with 150 families, a small century-old church and a rectory that was described as in deplorable condition.[31]

Newburgh got an Italian parish with the establishment of the Church of the Sacred Heart in 1912. It was intended not only for the Italian community in Newburgh, but also for the scattered pockets of Italians between Highland and Haverstraw. Father John B. Gallo, the founding pastor, celebrated the first Mass in the parish on September 8, 1912, in a vacant store on Washington Street. Five months earlier he had begun work on a permanent church, and on December 8, 1913, he celebrated the first Mass in the new church. The church was damaged by a fire in 1944 and restored, but by the 1960s it was far too small for the congregation. Monsignor Salvatore Celauro replaced it with a modern circular Church of the Sacred Heart that was first used for Midnight Mass in 1964.[32]

Elsewhere in Orange County St. Mary's Church in Washingtonville began in 1872 as an out-mission first of St. Thomas of Canterbury in Cornwall and then of St. Columba in Chester. In 1902 it became a parish with the appointment of Father John Tetreau, a native of Canada, as the first resident pastor. In 1914 he decided to move the church to a more central location. The movers ran into a snag when they encountered an historic elm tree in their path. For several weeks the church sat on pulleys in the middle of the town while the movers and the environmentalists debated the relative merits of the church and the elm tree. The church won. Meanwhile, in 1908, Father Tetreau built a mission church in Maybrook, Our Lady of the Assumption, which became a parish in 1923.[33]

---

29 - *Golden Jubilee* (Poughkeepsie: Our Lady of Mount Carmel Church, 1960), unpaginated.

30 - *A Thriving, Growing Congregation* (Poughkeepsie: Holy Trinity Church, 1997), 7-13.

31 - AANY, parish file, profile 1968.

32 - *75th Anniversary Souvenir Edition* (Newburgh: Sacred Heart Church, 1987), 11-16.

33 - *St. Mary's Church, Washingtonville* (Washingtonville: St. Mary's Church, n.d.), unpaginated.

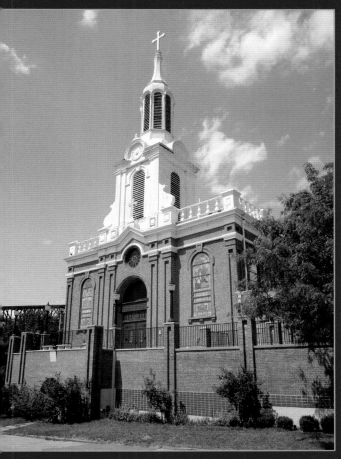

The Church of Our Lady of Mount Carmel,
Poughkeepsie, the former St. Peter's Church.

*Father Peter P. Conaty,
the founder of Holy Trinity
Church, Poughkeepsie, in 1921.*
Credit: *Holy Trinity Church.*

Holy Trinity Church, Poughkeepsie, completed in 1923.

The store on Washington Street
that was the first Church
of the Sacred Heart
in Newburgh in 1912.
Credit: *Sacred Heart Church*

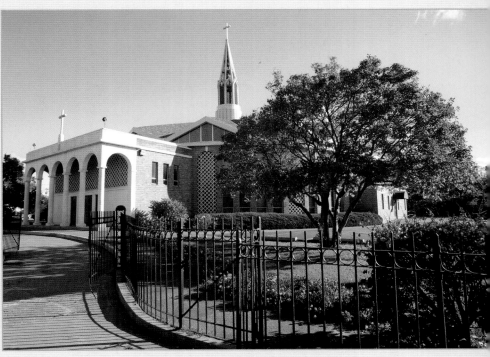

The Church of the Sacred Heart, Newburgh, built in 1964.

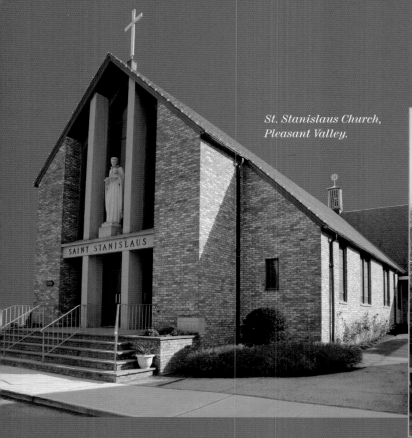

*St. Stanislaus Church,
Pleasant Valley.*

The Church of the Immaculate Conception, Bangall.

St. Joseph's Church, Glasco.

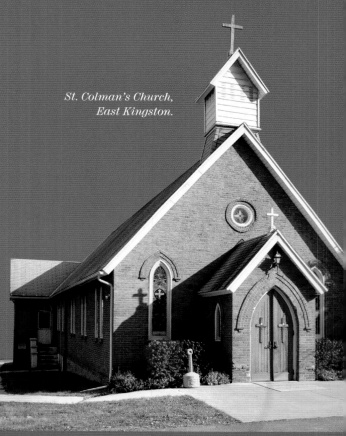

*St. Colman's Church,
East Kingston.*

Father John Tetreau, the pastor of St. Mary's Church, Washingtonville, 1902-1929.

St. Mary's Church, Washingtonville.

The Church of Our Lady of the Assumption, Maybrook.

In Rockland County, the Church of St. Margaret of Antioch in Pearl River, founded as a mission of St. Joseph's Church in Spring Valley, became a separate parish in 1923.

The Carmelites established their third parish in the archdiocese, Our Lady of Mount Carmel in Middletown, in 1912. Located in the south end of the town, it was Middletown's second parish. The first Mass was celebrated on Christmas Day in a former barn, which must have provided a point of reference for the homilist. The construction of the church began in 1923, and the first Mass was celebrated on the following Christmas Eve. A new church was built in the early 1990s and dedicated in June 1991. From their church in Middletown the Carmelite friars began five out-missions in Bullville, Otisville, Unionville, South Centerville and Bloomingburg in Sullivan County.[34]

34 - *Our Lady of Mount Carmel, Middletown, New York* (Custombook, 1976), 3-7.

The Church of St. Margaret of Antioch, Pearl River.

The Church of Our Lady of Mount Carmel, Middletown, dedicated in June 1991.

The Flight to the Suburbs
after World War II

The suburbanization of America accelerated in the decades following the end of World War II. The GI Bill of Rights of 1944 enabled millions of veterans---many of them Catholics---to become the first people in their families to get a college education and buy their own home. As middle class whites left the old ethnic neighborhoods that had been the stronghold of American Catholicism, their places were taken by poor blacks and Hispanics. The transition was often marred by racial tension and resentment of the newcomers on the part of the older generation of white ethnics.

In the New York metropolitan area the clearest example of this social change was the transformation of Nassau and Suffolk Counties where the population more than tripled from 604,103 in 1940 to 1,996,995 in 1950. The Diocese of Rockville Centre, established in 1957, quickly became one of the largest in the United States. In the former potato farms of central Nassau County Levitt houses were selling for $7,990 with monthly carrying charges of only $58. Robert Moses, who never learned to drive a car, was busy building bridges, parkways and expressways to provide east access to them by automobile.

In New York City the process was visible even within the city limits as the white middle class left Manhattan, the Bronx and Brooklyn for Queens and Staten Island. In St. Jerome's Church in the South Bronx, Mass attendance dropped from 6,100 in 1950 to 795 in 1975.[35] The census returns of 1950 were a blow to the pride of city officials who had predicted a substantial increase in the population. "Lost: 400,000 New Yorkers," cried the *New York Times,* which lamented that New York city could not compete with "the beckoning fingers of the Palisades, the soft Connecticut countryside, or the broad flat reaches of Long Island."

A similar phenomenon occurred in Yonkers and many of the cities in the upstate counties of the archdiocese. As was mentioned already, in Yonkers the downtown area around Getty Square became predominantly black, Hispanic and poor, while the northern and eastern parts of the city resembled the typical white suburban villages of Westchester County. In 1950 new colonial-style houses were selling for as low as $11,500 in northern Yonkers without the stigma of a Yonkers address. The builder advertised the area as "rural." Sociologists began to speak of the "balkanization" of Yonkers as residents increasingly identified themselves with their neighborhood rather than with the city as a whole.

The division between the old and new Yonkers became more pronounced in the 1950s. "Yonkers is a city with a split personality," wrote Harrison Salisbury in 1955. "There are actually two Yonkers," he explained, "one, the old river town; the other, the new suburban community 'beyond the Alps.' " By "the Alps" he meant the hills bordering the Saw Mill River Parkway. He found that "the old nesters" east of the Alps had little in common with the new suburbanites whom they called "carpetbaggers." Many did not know where Getty Square was and preferred to have Scarsdale, Crestwood or Bronxville addresses.[36]

In the 1980s Father Bernard Donachie, the pastor of Holy Rosary Church, said that his church had become two parishes. One parish was the parish of some 350 Irish, German, Italian and Slavic churchgoers who came to Mass on Sunday even though many had moved out of the neighborhood. The other parish was the parish school with 300 children most of whom were African American and Baptist. He was only able to maintain both parishes with an annual subsidy of $45,000 from the archdiocese.[37]

---

35 - AANY, Annual Cura Animarum Reports of St. Jerome's Church, 1950, 1975.

36 - New York Times, April 20, 1955. See Thomas J. Shelley, *Slovaks on the Hudson: Most Holy Trinity Church, Yonkers and the Slovak Catholics in the Archdiocese of New York, 1894-2000* (Washington, D.C.: The Catholic University of America Press, 2002), 211-233.

37 - Yonkers *Herald-Statesman,* November 13, 1980.

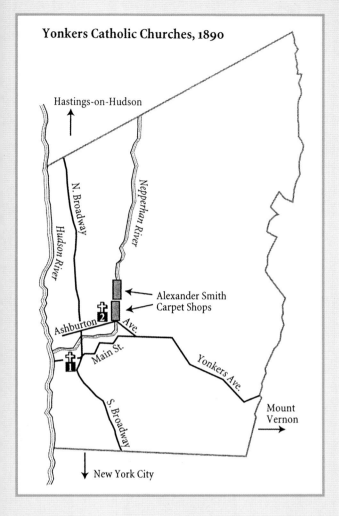

Yonkers Catholic Churches, 1890

Hastings-on-Hudson

Hudson River

N. Broadway

Nepperhan River

Alexander Smith
Carpet Shops

Ashburton Ave.

Main St.

Yonkers Ave.

S. Broadway

Mount
Vernon

New York City

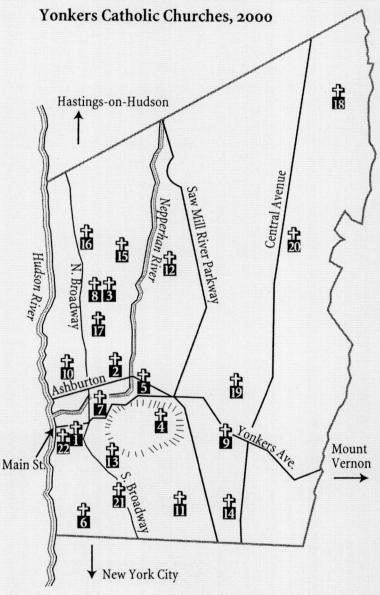

Yonkers Catholic Churches, 2000

Hastings-on-Hudson

Hudson River

N. Broadway

Nepperhan River

Saw Mill River Parkway

Central Avenue

Ashburton

Main St.

Yonkers Ave.

S. Broadway

Mount
Vernon

New York City

1. Immaculate Conception (St. Mary's),
   1848
2. St. Joseph, 1871
3. Sacred Heart, 1891
4. St. Nicholas of Myra (Ruthenian), 1892
5. Most Holy Trinity (Slovak) 1894
6. St. Peter, 1894
7. St. Casimir (Polish), 1899
8. St. Michael (Ukrainian), 1899
9. St. John the Baptist, 1903
10. Our Lady of the Rosary, 1907
11. St. Denis, 1910
12. St. Bartholomew, 1910
13. Our Lady of Mount Carmel (Italian),
    1913
14. St. Paul, 1923
15. St. Anthony, Nepera Park, 1923
16. Christ the King, 1927
17. St. Margaret of Hungary (Hungarian),
    1928
18. Annunciation, 1931
19. St. Ann (Italian), 1947
20. St. Eugene, 1949
21. Our Lady of Fatima (Portuguese), 1977
22. Christ the Savior (Melkite), 1978

Credit: Thomas J. Shelley, *Slovaks on the Hudson:
Most Holy Trinity Church, Yonkers, and the Slovak
Catholics of the Archdiocese of New York*,
(Washington, D.C.: The Catholic University
of America Press, 2002), 25, 237.

Between 1947 and 2007 four new parishes were established in Yonkers, two in the old river town west of "the Alps" and two in suburbs east of "the Alps". The two parishes in the old city were both national parishes. In 1977 the Portuguese community organized the Church of Our Lady of Fatima. For a number of years they worshipped in a former bank building on South Broadway, which they renovated into a church that was dedicated by auxiliary Bishop Robert A. Brucato on March 30, 2003. Christ the Savior Melkite Catholic Church was organized in 1978 by Arab Catholics from the Middle East. Like many other ethnic groups before them in Yonkers, they worshipped at first in the chapel of St. Mary's Church until they were able to build their own church.

During the last fifty years four parishes in the old city were closed, Holy Eucharist in 1960, the Italian Church of St. Anthony in 1968, and Our Lady of the Rosary and the Hungarian Church of St. Margaret of Hungary, both in 2007.

Meanwhile, the Polish Church of St. Casimir and the Slovak Church of the Most Holy Trinity suffered a steady decline in the number of active parishioners. Both St. Joseph's Church on Ashburton Avenue and St. Peter's Church in South Yonkers became predominantly Hispanic parishes, reflecting the continued role of Yonkers as a magnet for immigrants. One city official described Getty Square in 1991 as "the Ellis Island of Westchester County." The 1990 census revealed that one-third of the population of Yonkers was African American, Hispanic and Asian, but northeast Yonkers was 92 percent white and southeast Yonkers was 95 percent white.

The two new parishes in east Yonkers were St. Ann's in Dunwoodie and St. Eugene's on Tuckahoe Road. St. Ann's, founded in 1947, was formerly a mission of Our Lady of Mount Carmel in downtown Yonkers and the last Italian national parish to be established in the archdiocese. The first pastor, Father Francis P. Ferme, was a short stocky man with an ebullient personality and boundless energy, who built the new parish into a thriving operation. His habit of making un-complimentary remarks about diocesan officials from the pulpit did not seem to disturb his parishioners, but it did not win him any friends in the Chancery Office.

The Church of Our Lady of Fatima, Yonkers.

Christ the Savior Melkite Catholic Church, Yonkers.

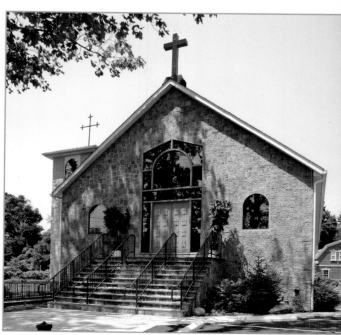

St. Ann's Church, Yonkers.

Nativity Scene, St. Ann's Church, Yonkers. Credit: *Yvon Meyer.*

The Church of Saints John and Paul, Larchmont.

Father John C. Dougherty, who founded St. Eugene's parish in 1949, had little of Father Ferme's charm, but, after two years of celebrating Mass in the basement of an apartment building, he rallied his parishioners to support the building of the present church at Tuckahoe Road and Central Avenue. It was dedicated by Cardinal Spellman on October 21, 1951.[38] The same year that St. Eugene's was founded, Larchmont got a second parish with the establishment of the Church of Sts. John and Paul. Father John J. Flynn built the church on Weaver Street in 1952.

Scarsdale got two additional parishes in the space of six years. The first was Our Lady of Fatima, which was founded in 1948 and included parts of Eastchester, Greenburgh and Yonkers. Father Leo Madden celebrated Mass for two years in the Scarsdale Theatre until he built the present church on Strathmore Road, which was dedicated by Cardinal Spellman on December 2, 1950. The second parish was St. Pius X in the northeast area of Scarsdale, which was founded on May 29, 1954. It was the date of the canonization of Pope Pius X. Cardinal Spellman sent a cable from Rome to Father Clement J. Rieger, a curate at St. Jerome's Church in the Bronx, appointing him the pastor of the new parish. He broke ground for a school and church-auditorium the following year. [39]

The Catholics of Pelham Manor owed their new parish to the generosity of a Protestant millionaire, W.T. Grant, the founder of Grant's Five-and-Ten Cent Stores, and Monsignor Henry F. Hammer, the pastor of St. Catherine's Church in Pelham. Grant donated almost six acres for a Catholic church in Pelham Manor, and Monsignor Hammer managed the tedious legal process that enabled him to open an out-mission of St. Catherine's Church in Grant's Manor House in December 1939. It remained a mission of St. Catherine's Church until July 1954 when Cardinal Spellman appointed Monsignor Robert E. McCormick to establish the Church of Our Lady of Perpetual Help in Pelham Manor. Monsignor Vincent Jeffers built the present church, which was dedicated by Cardinal Cooke on April 21, 1968.[40]

St. Anthony's Church in West Harrison or Silver Lake began in 1923 as an out-mission of the Church of Our Lady of Mount Carmel in White Plains. The first church was a frame building that had been a public school. It was made a parish in 1952 with the appointment of Father Francis J. Boyle as the first resident pastor. The present church was built in 1967.

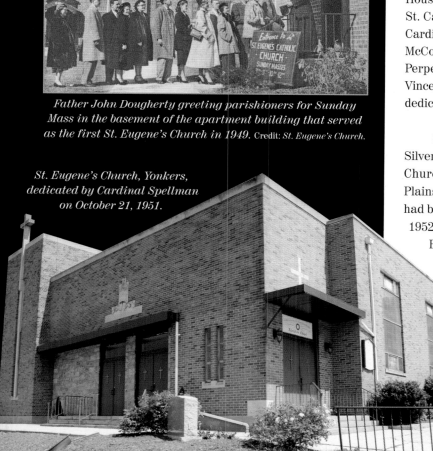

Father John Dougherty greeting parishioners for Sunday Mass in the basement of the apartment building that served as the first St. Eugene's Church in 1949. Credit: *St. Eugene's Church.*

St. Eugene's Church, Yonkers, dedicated by Cardinal Spellman on October 21, 1951.

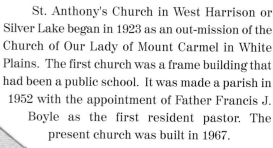

38 - *The Church of Saint Eugene* (Yonkers: Church of St. Eugene, 1974), unpaginated.

39 - *Thirtieth Anniversary* (Scarsdale: Church of Our Lady of Fatima, 1978), unpaginated; *Silver Jubilee* (Scarsdale: Church of St. Pius X, 1979), unpaginated.

40 - *Our Lady of Perpetual Help Church* (Pelham Manor: Our Lady of Perpetual Help Church, 1968), 6-13.

The Church of Our Lady of Fatima, Scarsdale, dedicated by Cardinal Spellman on December 2, 1950.

The Church of St. Pius X, Scarsdale.

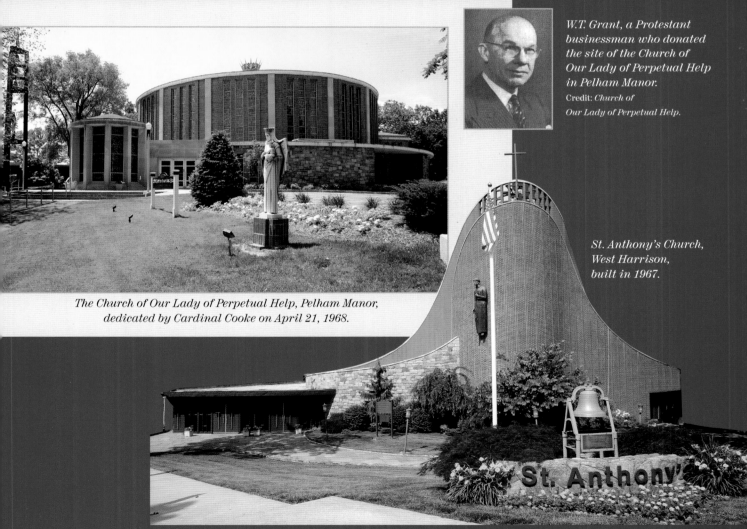

W.T. Grant, a Protestant businessman who donated the site of the Church of Our Lady of Perpetual Help in Pelham Manor.
Credit: *Church of Our Lady of Perpetual Help.*

The Church of Our Lady of Perpetual Help, Pelham Manor, dedicated by Cardinal Cooke on April 21, 1968.

St. Anthony's Church, West Harrison, built in 1967.

The Crabgrass Frontier

St. Patrick's Church in Armonk was an out-mission of the Church of St. John and St. Mary in Chappaqua for fifty years until it as made a parish in June 1966. The first pastor, Father John J. Wallace, built the present church, which was dedicated by Cardinal Cooke on June 15, 1970.

The last Catholic Church to be established in southern Westchester County, the Albanian Church of Our Lady of Shkodra, was an illustration of the ongoing character of the Catholic Church in the archdiocese of New York as the Immigrant Church. Albanian Catholics first came to New York City in the early 1960s. By the end of the decade they had organized the Church of Our Lady of Good Counsel in the Tremont section of the Bronx with Monsignor Joseph J. Oroshi as the pastor. Shortly thereafter a second Albanian Catholic community was formed in the Bronx at Holy Rosary Church. The two groups combined to organize the Church of Our Lady of Shkodra in Hartsdale, which was dedicated by Cardinal O'Connor on April 25, 1999. Parishioners contributed almost $5 million for the acquisition of the property and the construction of the church.[41]

As real estate prices and taxes grew ever stepper in southern Westchester County in the 1960s, young families moved farther north in search of affordable housing. St. Patrick's Church in Yorktown built a new church to accommodate its rapidly growing congregation. In 1963 the Church of Blessed Ann Seton was established in Shrub Oak. For the first three years the congregation used St. George's Chapel in Mohegan Lake, a link with the earlier history of the Church in Shrub Oak going back to the Church of St. John the Evangelist sixty years earlier. Monsignor Arthur Nugent, the founding pastor, built the present church and rectory, which were dedicated by Cardinal Cooke on January 4, 1981.

The Peekskill area also experienced the impact of suburban sprawl, leading to the establishment of two new parishes. The first was the Church of the Holy Spirit, which was founded in 1966 when Father Edward G. Finnerty was appointed the first pastor. He used the chapel of the Sisters of the Good Shepherd and later a local theatre for Sunday Mass. In 1972 he was succeeded by Monsignor John J. Gillen, who built an all-purpose center. The second new parish in Peekskill was St. Columbanus, north of the city in Cortland Manor, established in June 1950 with the appointment of Father James J. Weber as the first pastor. He built a chapel that was dedicated by Cardinal Spellman on October 27, 1951. It was replaced by the present church, which was dedicated by Cardinal Spellman on October 30, 1966.

Suburban development was no respecter of county boundaries and pushed north of the Westchester County line into Putnam County where the growth of the Catholic population led to the founding of two new parishes. The first was the Church of St. James the Apostle in Carmel, which began in 1909 as an out-mission of the Church of St. John the Evangelist in Mahopac. In January 1947 it became parish with the appointment of Father Edward R. McQuade as the first pastor. In 1954 he built a school and an auditorium which was used for Sunday Mass until the completion of the present church, which was dedicated ten years later on June 14, 1964. The parish also includes Our Lady of the Lake Mission at Lake Carmel, which was opened in 1938.[42]

The second new parish in Putnam County was the Church of the Sacred Heart in Patterson. It was founded in the 1930s in what was then called Putnam Lake as an out-mission of the Church of St. Lawrence O'Toole in Brewster. In Garrison, St. Joseph's Chapel remained a mission of Putnam County's oldest Catholic parish, Our Lady of Loretto in Cold Spring.

41 - *Catholic New York,* April 29, 1999.

42 - *Church of St. James the Apostle* (Carmel: Church of St. James the Apostle, 1964), unpaginated.

The Church of Our Lady of Shkodra,
Hartsdale, which was dedicated
by Cardinal O'Connor
on April 25, 1999.

St. Patrick's Church, Armonk,
dedicated by Cardinal Cooke on June 15, 1970.

The Church of St. Elizabeth Ann Seton, Shrub Oak,
dedicated by Cardinal Cooke on January 4, 1981.

The Church of the Holy Spirit,
Peekskill.

The original mission chapel of St. James the Apostle Church, Carmel, opened in 1909.

Credit: *St. James tue Apostle Church.*

St. Columbanus Church, Cortland Manor, dedicated by Cardinal Spellman on October 30, 1966.

The Church of St. James the Apostle, Carmel, dedicated on June 14, 1964.

St. Joseph's mission chapel, Garrison.

Our Lady of the Lake mission chapel, Lake Carmel.

The Church of the Sacred Heart, Patterson.

A Tale of Two Bridges

Unlike Westchester County, where the railroads played a key role in the development of commuter communities, the automobile was responsible for development of Rockland and Orange Counties. The opening of the George Washington Bridge in 1931 and the construction of the Palisades Interstate Parkway between 1947 and 1958 first brought Rockland County within easy commuting distance of New York City. However, the Depression and World War II delayed large-scale growth until the late 1940s and the early 1950s.

The first of the post-war parishes to be established in Rockland County was the Church of Our Lady of the Sacred Heart in Tappan close to the border with New Jersey. It originated as an out-mission of St. Catherine's Church in Blauvelt in 1929 and became a parish in 1952. The remodeled stable that had served as a mission chapel was too small for Sunday Mass, necessitating the building of a hall that was completed in 1954. A school followed ten years later and finally a new church where Father John F. Dwyer celebrated Mass for the first time on December 12, 1999.[43]

Even more than the George Washington Bridge and the Palisades Interstate Parkway, the opening the Tappan Zee Bridge in 1955, together with the completion of the New York State Thruway the following year, spurred the development of commuter communities in Rockland County and later in Orange County as well. In 1956 there were thirteen parishes in Rockland County, including the Ukrainian Catholic Church of Sts. Peter and Paul in Spring Valley. Six new parishes were opened during the following ten years. Several others built new and bigger churches.

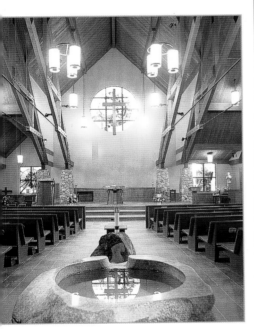

The interior of St. Joseph's Church, Spring Valley.
Credit: *Yvon Meyer*

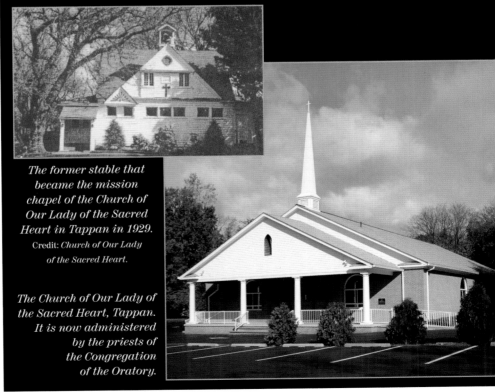

The former stable that became the mission chapel of the Church of Our Lady of the Sacred Heart in Tappan in 1929.
Credit: *Church of Our Lady of the Sacred Heart.*

The Church of Our Lady of the Sacred Heart, Tappan. It is now administered by the priests of the Congregation of the Oratory.

43 - John F. Dwyer, *A History of the Parish* (Tappan: Our Lady of the Sacred Heart, 1999), 8-24.

The first of the new parishes in Rockland County, St. Augustine's in New City, began in 1907 as an out-mission of St. Anthony's Church in Nanuet and became a parish in 1957. The old mission church and the school hall were used for Sunday Mass until Monsignor William J. Foley built the new church, which was dedicated by Cardinal Egan on November 25, 2001. It was the second stage of a $5 million project that also included the construction of a new parish center. The Church of St. Gregory Barbarigo was founded in June 1961 with territory taken from St. Peter's Church in Haverstraw and the Church of the Immaculate Conception in Stony Point. By Christmas of that year an all-purpose building had been constructed. It was completely re-modeled as a church by Father John J. Backes in 1996-1997 and rededicated by Cardinal O'Connor on November 30, 1998.

In West Nyack the Church of St. Francis of Assisi was founded in 1964 by Father Charles W. Rader, who had been a curate at St. Anthony's Church in Nanuet for the previous twenty-one years. His new parish consisted of territory taken from St. Anthony's Church and St. Augustine's Church in New City. Father Rader celebrated Sunday Mass in the auditorium of Albert Magnus High School until the following year when a parish hall was completed. It was used for Mass until the new church was built by Father Dennis S. Fernandes and dedicated in December 1989.

In 1966 Rockland County got three additional parishes, in Sloatsburg, Pearl River and Wesley Hills. St. Joan of Arc Church in Sloatsburg began in 1924 as an out-mission of the Church of Our Lady of Mount Carmel in Tuxedo. St. Aedan's Church in Pearl River began as an out-mission of St. Margaret's Church in 1965. The mission chapel built by Monsignor Michael J. Toner of St. Margaret's became the first parish church a month after its dedication when Father Joseph Devlin was appointed the pastor of St. Adean's on July 25, 1966. Twenty years later the present church was built by Father Edward J. Quirk.

St. Boniface's parish was carved out of the northern portion of St. Joseph's parish in Spring Valley, where the population was predominantly Jewish. Father John P. Keogh inherited a tiny unused Chapel of St. Rita on Route 306, but a church was built in seven months and completed in time for the celebration of Mass on Christmas Eve. It was replaced with the present church in 1980, which, like its predecessor, was first used for Mass on Christmas Eve of that year.[44]

St. Augustine's Church, New City, dedicated by Cardinal Egan on November 25, 2001.

---

44 - *Dedication Journal* (Wesley Hills: Church of St. Boniface, 1918), unpaginated.

Forester's Hall, the first site of the Church of St. Gregory Barbarigo in 1961.
Credit: *St. Gregory Barbarigo Church.*

The Church of St. Gregory Barbarigo, rededicated by Cardinal O'Connor on November 30, 1998.

The interior of St. Francis of Assisi in West Nyack.
Credit: *Yvon Meyer.*

The Church of St. Francis of Assisi in West Nyack, completed in December 1989.

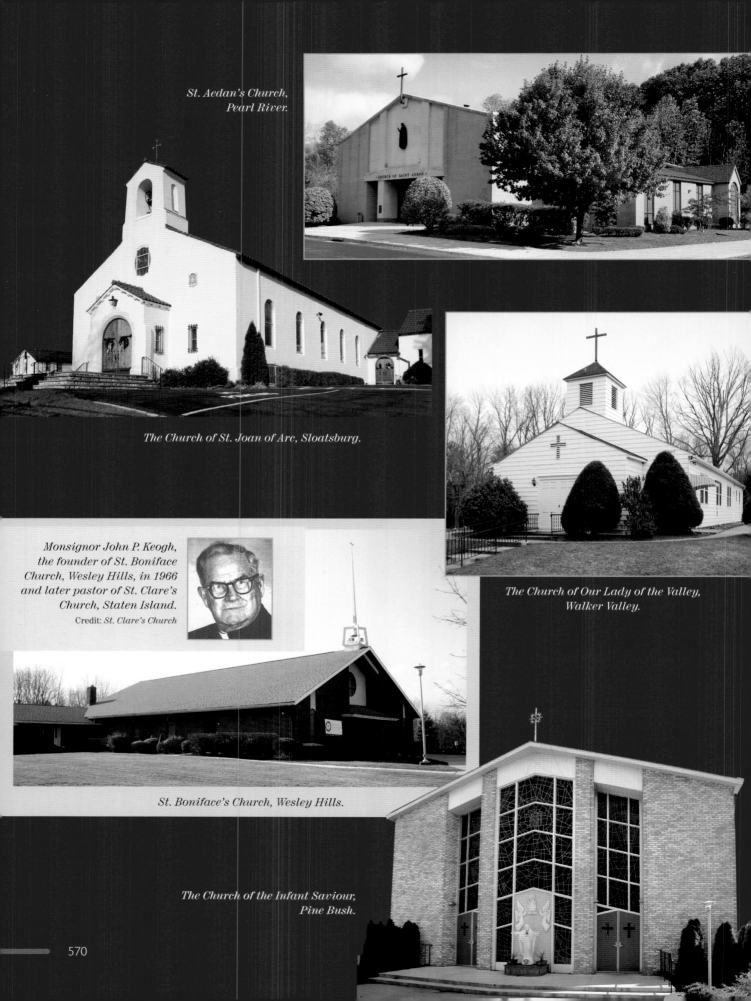

St. Aedan's Church,
Pearl River.

The Church of St. Joan of Arc, Sloatsburg.

Monsignor John P. Keogh,
the founder of St. Boniface
Church, Wesley Hills, in 1966
and later pastor of St. Clare's
Church, Staten Island.
Credit: *St. Clare's Church*

The Church of Our Lady of the Valley,
Walker Valley.

St. Boniface's Church, Wesley Hills.

The Church of the Infant Saviour,
Pine Bush.

In Orange County the Church of the Infant Saviour in Pine Bush became a parish in 1951. It originated as an out-mission of the Church of the Most Precious Blood in Walden and was formed from territory taken from seven neighboring parishes. It had its own out-mission, the Church of Our Lady of the Valley in Walker Valley in Ulster County.

Three years later, in 1954, in Greenwood Lake, at the other end of Orange County, the Church of the Holy Rosary became a parish. Greenwood Lake was a popular summer resort in the 1920s, and Holy Rosary was started as an out-mission of St. Stephen's Church in Warwick by Father Matthew Duggan in 1925. He built a stone church in the late 1920s that was used for Mass only during the summer months. Beginning in 1938 Sunday Mass was celebrated in Greenwood Lake the year round. One Sunday the weather was so cold and the congregation was so small that they gathered in the boiler room for Mass. The growth of the Catholic population led to its establishment as a parish in 1954 with the appointment of the first resident pastor, Father Joseph Kennedy, who had been the pastor in Warwick for the previous two years.[45]

Two additional parishes were established in Orange County in 1957, St. Patrick's Church in Highland Mills and Sacred Heart Church in Monroe. Both were located close to the New York State Thruway and attracted many commuters who found themselves priced out of the real estate market in Rockland County. St. Patrick's originated as an out-mission of St. Anastasia in Harriman in 1907.

The Church of the Holy Rosary, Greenwood Lake.

St. Patrick's Church, Highland Mills.

The first Church of the Sacred Heart in Monroe, dedicated by Archbishop Corrigan on October 11, 1896.
Credit: *Sacred Heart Church.*

The Church of the Sacred Heart, Monroe, dedicated by Cardinal O'Connor on November 4, 1994.

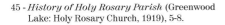

45 - *History of Holy Rosary Parish* (Greenwood Lake: Holy Rosary Church, 1919), 5-8.

Sacred Heart began as an out-mission of St. Columba's Church in Chester as far back as 1881. A mission church was built in Monroe and was dedicated by Archbishop Corrigan on October 1l, 1896. It is still in use today. Sacred Heart became a parish in 1957 with the appointment of Father John J. McCallen as the first resident pastor. He built a school and auditorium in 1964 that was used for Sunday Mass until the completion of the present church, which was dedicated by Cardinal O'Connor on November 4, 1994.[46]

The establishment of St. Joseph's Church in New Windsor in 1962 gave Orange County a new parish on Route 9W between Newburgh and Cornwall-on-Hudson. In the northwest corner of the country the founding of the Church of the Holy Name in Otisville in 1969 provided a new parish between Port Jervis and Middletown. More recently Holy Cross Church in South Centreville, which had been an out-mission of the Carmelite Church of Our Lady of Mount Carmel in Middletown, was made a separate parish with the

appointment of Father Robert Porpora as the first resident pastor. The new parish relieved the Carmelites of responsibility for the mission of Our Lady of the Scapular in Unionville, but they continued to administer the mission of Our Lady of the Assumption in Sullivan County.

As part of Cardinal Egan's general reorganization of the parishes in 2007, it was announced that the mission of Our Lady of the Assumption would become a parish. Two mission churches in Orange County were also slated to become parishes, St. Paul's Church in Bullville, and the Church of Our Lady of the Lake in Orange Lake. The latter was an out-mission of St. Patrick's Church in Newburgh. Monsignor Henry J. O'Carroll, the pastor of St. Patrick's, built the present church in Orange Lake in 1937 when it was a popular resort area, but it was not until the 1950s that Mass was celebrated there all year round.[47] One church in Orange County was closed, Most Sacred Heart in Port Jervis, which had already been merged with the Church of the Immaculate Conception in Port Jervis.

St. Joseph's Church, New Windsor.

The Church of the Holy Name of Jesus, Otisville.

46 - Angelo Cosaro, *Chapel of the Sacred Heart of Jesus* (Monroe: Sacred Heart Church, 1996), unpaginated.

47 - St. Patrick's Church, *Our Lady of the Lake Mission* (Newburgh: St. Patrick's Church, 1986), unpaginated.

Holy Cross Church,
South Centerville.

The Chapel of Our Lady of the Scapular,
Unionville, a mission of Holy Cross Church,
South Centerville.

The Chapel of Our Lady of Assumption,
Bloomingburg, a mission
of the Church of Our Lady of Mount Carmel,
Middletown.

The Church of the Most Sacred Heart of Jesus,
Port Jervis, now closed.

The Church of Our Lady
of the Lake, Orange Lake.

Ulster and Sullivan Counties

After World War II two new parishes were established in Ulster County and two in Sullivan County. In Ulster County the first was the Church of St. Philomena, which was founded in 1957 in Lake Katrine north of Kingston on Route 9W, to provide for the influx of Catholics who worked in the new IBM plant in Kingston. It was also intended to be the successor to St. Ann's Church in Sawkill. The church was built in 1959 with an adjacent school that closed in 1972. In 1962 the name of the new parish was hurriedly changed to that of St. Catherine Labouré after the non-existent St. Philomena was dropped from the Church's official list of saints.

The other new Ulster County parish, Our Lady of Fatima in Plattekill, began as an out-mission of St. Joseph's Church in New Paltz in the late 1940s, when the pastor, Father George B. Fagan, began to celebrate Mass in the homes of local Catholic families. They raised $10,000 to convert an old barn into a mission church where Father John M. Mahoney celebrated the first Mass in 1950. In 1960 the parish was entrusted to the Theatine Fathers, a small but famous Italian religious community that dates from the sixteenth century. The first Theatine pastor, Father Anthony Sagrera, C.R., expanded and remodeled the church, which was rededicated by auxiliary Bishop Joseph M. Pernicone on April 10, 1961.

The first new parish in Sullivan County in over fifty years was the Church of the Immaculate Conception in Woodbourne. It originated as an out-mission of the German Church of St. Andrew in Ellenville as least as far back as 1898, perhaps even earlier. It became a parish in 1957 with the appointment of Father William J. Guinon as the first resident pastor. He built a new church that was dedicated by Cardinal Spellman on May 25, 1960. St. Anthony of Padua in Yulan became a parish in 1970. In 1981 St. George's Church in Jeffersonville became St. George-St. Francis when St. Francis mission in Youngsville was made a parish.

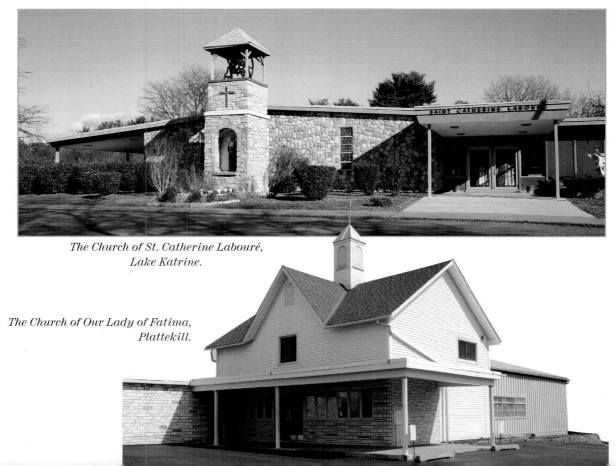

*The Church of St. Catherine Labouré,
Lake Katrine.*

*The Church of Our Lady of Fatima,
Plattekill.*

The dedication of the Chapel
of Our Lady of the Lake,
Lake Huntington,
on August 15, 1920.
Credit: *Church of Our Lady of the Lake.*

*The chapel of
Our Lady of the Lake,
Lake Huntington,
a mission of
the Church of
St. Francis Xavier,
Narrowsburg.*

*The Church of the Immaculate
Conception, Woodbourne,
dedicated by Cardinal
Spellman on May 25, 1960.*

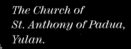

*The Church of
St. Anthony of Padua,
Yulan.*

*The chapel of
the Sacred Heart
in Pond Eddy,
a mission of
the Church of
St. Anthony of
Padua in Yulan.*

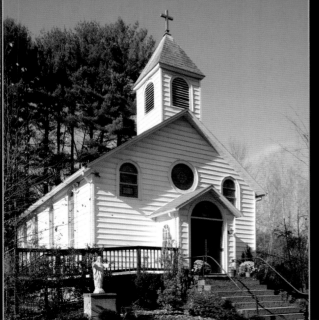

Dutchess County

In Dutchess County St. Mary's Church in Fishkill became a parish in 1953 after ninety-two years as an out-mission of St. Joachim's Church in Matteawan (present-day Beacon). The first resident pastor was Father Francis J. McKeon, who renovated the old mission church and built a school. The present church was dedicated by Cardinal Cooke on November 17, 1968. The name of the church has since been changed to that of St. Mary, Mother of the Church.[48]

In northern Dutchess County a new parish was established in Pine Plains in 1958 when St. Anthony's mission was made a parish with Father Joseph McCambley as the first resident pastor. St. Anthony's history went back to 1913 when Father Francis Lavelle, the pastor of Immaculate Conception in Amenia, established it as an out-mission of his church. The parish boundaries included territory taken not only from Amenia, but also from Barrytown and Rhinecliff.

In Poughkeepsie the flight to the suburbs and the opening of another IBM plant led to the founding of the parish of St. Martin de Porres in Red Oak Mills in 1962. The name of the parish was chosen by Cardinal Spellman because he happened to be in Rome for the Second Vatican Council at the time of the saint's canonization. A new neo-Gothic church was built by Father Brian McWeeney and dedicated by Cardinal O'Connor on May 24, 1998.

Southern Dutchess County experienced an economic boom in the 1990s. As was mentioned already, the Church of St. Denis in Sylvan Lake was divided in 1992 when St. Columba's mission in Hopewell Junction became a separate parish. Reflecting on the change nine years later, Monsignor Dominic Lagonegro, the pastor of St. Columba's Church and the vicar of Dutchess County, said: "When we split in 1992, St. Columba's had 3,000 families and St. Denis had 1,500 families. The numbers are now more than 5,000 for St. Columba's and 2,000 for St. Denis. There is standing room only at most of our Masses." The pastor of St. Mary's in Fishkill, Monsignor Joseph A. Martin, had the same experience. "The weekly collection has doubled since 1994," he said.[49]

Six years after becoming a parish, in 1998, St. Columba established its own mission church of Blessed Kateri Tekakwitha in LaGrangeville. Only four years later, on July 1, 2002, it became the newest parish in Dutchess County with the appointment of Monsignor William Belford as the first resident pastor.

The first St. Mary's Church, Fishkill, built as a mission chapel in 1861.
Credit: *Church of St. Mary, Mother of the Church.*

The Church of St. Mary, the Mother of the Church, Fishkill, dedicated by Cardinal Cooke, on November 17, 1968.

48 - *Church of St. Mary, Fishkill,* New York (Cusotmbook, 1969), 4-15.
49 - *Catholic New York,* January 4, 2001.

St. Anthony's Church,
Pine Plains.

The Church of St. Martin de Porres, Poughkeepsie,
dedicated by Cardinal O'Connor on May 24, 1998.

Cardinal Egan with
Monsignor William Belford
at the Church of Blessed Kateri
Tekakwitha, Lagrangeville,
on October 20, 2003.
Credit: *Catholic New York:*
Chris Sheridan.

One of the newest parishes in
the archdiocese, the Church
of Blessed Kateri Tekakwitha,
established by Cardinal Egan
on July 1, 2002.

19

After the Council

*Pope John XXIII presides at the opening of the Second Vatican Council
in St. Peter's Basilica on October 11, 1962.*
Credit: *Elledici.*

The last three archbishops of New York---Terence Cardinal Cooke, John Cardinal O'Connor and Edward Cardinal Egan---have all had the common task of guiding the Catholic Church in New York through a world very different from that experienced by any of their predecessors. Changes in both American society and in the Universal Church have profoundly altered the landscape, creating new problems as well as new opportunities.

The secularization of American society, although modest by European standards, has been most noticeable in cities like New York. Abortion was not an issue that John Kennedy had to confront in the 1960 presidential campaign because of the common moral consensus that still existed among most Americans. On Monday morning the *New York Times* published summaries of the Sunday sermons in the city's principal churches because religion was still a powerful influence in shaping public opinion. By the 1970s such public recognition of religion had pretty well disappeared among the city's movers and shakers. The days when New Yorkers referred to the Cardinal's residence at 452 Madison Avenue as the Powerhouse were now a distant memory.

At the same time that American society was becoming more secularized, the Catholic Church experienced a series of changes, in some instances convulsions, in the wake of the Second Vatican Council. Some of the changes introduced by the Council won widespread acceptance such as a vernacular liturgy and a more open and friendly attitude to Protestants and Jews. Other changes that followed in the wake of the Council were disquieting such as the abrupt decline in Mass attendance and the catastrophic falling off in vocations to the priesthood and religious life. Some blamed the Council for these developments. Others pointed to long-term changes in society and claimed that the Church would have been even less prepared to confront them without the Council.

Terence Cardinal Cooke

Terence Cardinal Cooke, Archbishop of New York, 1968-1983. Credit: *Archdiocese of New York.*

Terence James Cooke was appointed the seventh archbishop of New York on March 2, 1968, replacing Cardinal Spellman after the shortest vacancy in the history of the see to that point. His appointment caused general surprise, if not astonishment, especially among those who expected Archbishop John Maguire, the coadjutor archbishop *without* the right of succession, to be Spellman's successor. Only forty-seven years old and an auxiliary bishop for less than three years, Cooke hardly seemed a serious contender for the post, especially since he lacked the Roman credentials and connections deemed essential for the appointment. Pundits attributed his selection to Spellman's influence *d'outre tombe*. As expected, the new archbishop quickly received two additional offices. He was appointed the Military Vicar for the Armed Forces on the day of his installation, April 4, 1968, and he was made a cardinal one year later, on April 28, 1969.

Terence Cooke was a native New Yorker, born in Manhattan on March 1, 1921, the youngest of three children of Michael and Margaret Gannon Cooke, who were both natives of County Galway. The family moved to the Bronx when he was five years old. After the death of his mother in 1930, her sister, Marry Gannon, came to live with the family. He followed the traditional path to the diocesan priesthood in New York, education at Cathedral College and St. Joseph's Seminary, Dunwoodie, followed by ordination at St. Patrick's Cathedral by Archbishop Spellman on December 1, 1945.[1]

After brief stints in pastoral work, Father Cooke earned a M.S.W. degree from the Catholic University of America and spent the following four years in the Catholic Youth Organization. In 1954 he was made the procurator of St. Joseph's Seminary where his talents came to the attention of Cardinal Spellman. Thereafter Cooke's start ascended rapidly in the ecclesiastical firmament, as he moved up the ranks from Spellman's secretary to vice-chancellor, chancellor, vicar general, and in 1965 auxiliary bishop.

Cooke was a warm and friendly man with a prodigious memory and an extraordinary capacity for hard work. As his close friend, Bishop Patrick V. Ahern put it, "He was just, in his own words, 'a boy from the Bronx,' with an accent to prove it." Terence Cooke was not in any sense a visionary. He dreamed no big dreams and expressed no passionately held opinions about what new kind of Catholic Church might emerge from Vatican Council II. If anything, he seems to have hoped that the post-Vatican II Church would look very much like the pre-Vatican II Church. "Let us improve the institutions that have served us so well," he said at his installation. "Let us avoid that iconoclasm which would tear down the past before moving ahead in the present to build a future."

Cardinal Cooke in October 1982 with the first-grade children in St. Athanasius school, the parish where he served briefly as a young curate shortly after his ordination. Credit: *Archdiocese of New York.*

As the leader of what was commonly called "the world's wealthiest archdiocese," Cardinal Cooke was automatically an important figure, but he never exerted the same influence as Spellman on either the national or the international scene. No one recognized the difference more clearly than he did himself. He told an interviewer in 1973: "I don't think my key role is to be a leader in national or international affairs."

His fellow bishops elected him the chairman of the U.S. Bishop's Pro-Life Activities Committee. In that capacity Cooke worked vigorously to stem the rising tide of abortions in the United States, especially after the Roe v. Wade decision of the U.S. Supreme Court in 1973 eliminated most of the legal barriers to abortion. Cooke also served as the spokesman for the U.S. bishops on the question of tax credits for the parents of parochial school children. In addition he chaired a committee to devise a system of uniform accounting for U.S. dioceses.

However, Cooke made his main contribution to the American Church in his own native city,

---

1 - See Benedict J.Groeschel, C.F.R., and Terrence L.Webber, *Thy Will Be Done: A Spiritual Portrait of Terence Cardinal Cooke* (New York: Alba House, 1990).

bringing to the task of archbishop of New York two qualities vitally needed at that time, managerial skills and pastoral sensitivity. A long apprenticeship under Spellman left Cooke thoroughly familiar with the operations of the archdiocese when he assumed the reins in 1968. "When I take on a job," he said, "I try to do my homework." "He loves annual reports," said one of his advisers. "He can sit with a seventy-page memo on how to rescue the hospitals and master it." That facet of his personality surfaced at the 200 board meetings that he attended each year, when he often surprised the bankers and businessmen in attendance with his detailed knowledge of the financial condition of each institution. He excelled not only at saving money, but also at raising it. One pastor commented that "he's the kind of guy who can pat you on the back until the change falls out of your pockets."

As much as Cooke excelled as the CEO of the archdiocese, he regarded himself primarily as a pastor. "I don't want to be a politician," he said on one occasion. "I have enough problems already." "My job, first and foremost," he explained, "is to be a shepherd and servant of God's people. I have no other purpose or desire in life." While critics complained of his lack of vision ("He has no message," complained one unhappy Chancery official), Cooke's pastoral sensitivity led him to prefer consensus to confrontation at a time of growing polarization in the Church among both clergy and laity. "He managed to provide a context within which a lot of viewpoints could be at home," said Monsignor Philip Murnion, the director of the National Pastoral Life Center. "People could pursue a variety of interests." "He allows many flowers to grow even though he may not like them all," observed Monsignor James Connolly, the Director of Priest Personnel.[2]

Church and Country After Vatican II

Archbishop Cooke's baptism of fire began on the day of his installation as archbishop of New York, April 4, 1968, which was the same day that Dr. Martin Luther King, Jr., was assassinated in Memphis. By nightfalll riots had erupted in many cities across the country, including New York City. That evening the new archbishop traveled to Harlem where he pleaded for peace and calm. Two months after Cooke's installation, St. Patrick's Cathedral was again packed with worshippers, including the President of the United States, this time for the funeral Mass of Senator Robert F. Kennedy, the victim of another assassin.

Senator Robert F. Kennedy with Bishop Terence J. Cooke on St. Patrick's Day 1965.
Credit: *Archdiocese of New York.*

The unfinished agenda of the Civil Rights movement, the unpopularity of the Vietnam War, and then the Watergate scandal all combined to produce one of the most tumultuous periods in American history. In New York City a severe financial crisis that had a devastating impact on city services, further aggravated the situation. Public discontent reached such proportions that

---

2 - *New York Times,* March 17, 1983.

the President of the United States could not appear in public without provoking widespread protest demonstrations, especially from young Americans. In this climate, all forms of authority, religious as well as civil, were called into question, often to be subjected to searing criticism, sometimes to be rejected with cynical derision.

At the same time that the nation was experiencing this crisis of confidence, the Catholic Church was contending with equally serious problems. The effort to implement the conciliar reforms often produced jarring dislocations in a Church that had no living tradition of candid criticism or devolution of authority, illustrating once again Alexis de Tocqueville's famous dictum that the most dangerous period for an antiquated government is when it begins to make reforms. The self-described Boy from the Bronx treaded his way gingerly through this minefield, taking his cue from Pope Paul VI, and like the pope, trying to find a middle path between the impatient reformers and the die-hard reactionaries.

Even those two nebulous political labels became more fluid and more difficult to apply to factions in the Church. Some of the more progressive figures at the time of Vatican II now drew back in consternation at unexpected developments such as the decline in Mass attendance, the falling off in vocations, and the unprecedented number of resignations from the

priesthood and religious life. In the background were demands for a married clergy and the first murmurs of the women's ordination movement. The hostile reception given to *Humanae Vitae,* Pope Paul VI's reaffirmation of the prohibition against contraception, only increased fears that the Church's authority was in the process of disintegration.

"Unless we are blind," said Louis Bouyer, the French Catholic scholar, in a book published the same year as *Humanae Vitae*, "we must state bluntly that what we see looks less like the hoped-for regeneration of Catholicism than its accelerated decomposition." Jean Cardinal Daniélou gave voice to these same apprehensions in the fall of 1969 at the Synod of Bishops, when he declared: "The state of the Church today is no longer that existing during Vatican II... We are witnesses today... of a very grave crisis."

However, at the same synod, Cardinal Suenens, the Belgian primate, warned against a panic-driven return to a nineteenth-century concept of papal authority that would leave no room for the collegial leadership of pope and bishops envisioned by the Council. It is significant that the expression of such views by Suenens only four years after the end of the Council had already become so suspect in certain quarters that he had to assure a group of journalists that "there are no heretics here."

*Cardinal Cooke
with Jimmy Carter outside
452 Madison Avenue in 1976.*
Credit: *Catholic New York,*
Chris Sheridan

John Cardinal Wright, the former bishop of Pittsburgh and once the darling of *Commonweal* Catholics, fully shared Daniélou's fears. He was now a curial cardinal. On his way to the synod after a visit to the United States, he left a note for Cooke at 452 Madison Avenue. "Your Eminence," the message read, "I stopped by today to say 'Hi' on the way from the worries at home to the worries in Rome. They are about the same, so I might as well go back to the office." Earlier that year Wright had been one of the architects of a pastoral letter of the U.S. bishops that gave a grim assessment of the state of the American Church.

President Ronald Reagan with Cardinal Cooke.
Credit: *Archdiocese of New York.*

The optimism that had been pervasive among the American bishops during the Council had now given way to alarm that they had lost the ability to direct the shape and pace of reform. "Many of us think that we see an unfortunate eclipse of the clear and separate status of the ordained priesthood," the bishops warned. Stunned by the unprecedented umber of resignations from the active ministry, they lashed out at such priests as "derelict" and a source of scandal to the laity. However, the bishops reserved their heaviest thunder for what they called "a new Pelagianism [that] seeks salvation in the correction of structures rather than in conversion to God."

One of the signers of the pastoral letter was Archbishop Cooke, who was faced with a demand for new structures in his own archdiocese. Even before his appointment had been announced, 563 priests had signed a petition asking the pope for some role in the selection of their new archbishop. They had couched their request in deferential language. "With sentiments of profound respect and filial obedience," they told Pope Paul VI, "we make bold to address to Your Holiness these words concerning our bishop and our diocese." However respectful the rhetoric, the fact that the priests even dared to make such a request was an indication that the forelock touching days were over. "We wanted to express our opinion and be consulted," said Father Neil Connolly. In fact what the priests were requesting was not all that different from the procedures that Rome had instituted in the American Church in 1884 as an antidote to episcopal cronyism in the selection of bishops.

Once it became clear that Cooke was to be the new archbishop, he was presented with a Memorandum of Priorities by the Priests' Interim Advisory Committee, which was the name adopted by the Senate of Priests when their mandate lapsed during the interregnum between the death of Spellman and the appointment of Cooke. Among the recommendations of the Advisory Committee was that Cooke should disclose the financial condition of the archdiocese, consult the priests on the appointment of diocesan officials, appoint an Archdiocesan Pastoral Council, and establish a diocesan department of urban affairs.

Cooke eyed the Advisory Committee with the same wariness that Louis XVI had once displayed before the Estates General especially after a spokesman for the priests declared that the archdiocese of New York "displayed some of the classic signs of revolution." A master of the soft answer that turns away wrath but concedes nothing, Cooke cheerfully described the report as "just suggestions" from a "really terrific group of priests."

Cooke displayed the same finesse at a potentially embarrassing situation in 1971 during the ordination of Jesuit seminarians to the priesthood at Fordham University. Two of the newly ordained Jesuits refused to exchange the traditional sign of peace with Cooke as a protest against his role as Military Vicar of the Armed Forces. Unfazed, Cooke explained that he worked for peace everyday in his role as Military Vicar and invited the two protestors to reconsider their snub. One of them did and came forward to shake Cooke's hand. The other still refused, and to him Cooke said softly, "Peace to you, especially, my friend."

"A Traveling Curse"

One area of the archdiocese that received massive media attention in the 1970s was the South Bronx, which became a symbol of the problems of America's inner cities. The *New York Times* declared that a visit to the South Bronx was "as crucial to the understanding of American urban life as a visit to Auschwitz is to understanding Nazism." The South Bronx included the poorest Congressional district in the nation, a police station that was known as Fort Apache, and Charlotte Street, a burnt-out stretch of rubble and decay that became a mandatory photo stop for Presidential candidates.

A visitor to Charlotte Street in 1968, Adele Chatfield Taylor, called it "a place beyond description [where] wild dogs roamed the streets, tearing in and out of buildings, and through the trash that covered the sidewalks and the buildings. People scarcely recognizable as human were prey and predator to one another. Fires burned everywhere."[3]

"The 60s were a troubled time," said Father Paul LeBlanc, the pastor of St. Pius V Church on East 145th Street. "A parish like St. Pius, at the pressure point of society, was profoundly affected. The decade ended in flames. Literally. More than half the parish was burned out. Those who had to, and those who could, moved. Whether they were Spanish, black or white, they moved. Those who had no choice stayed, whether they were Spanish, black or white."[4]

Abandoned apartment buildings, a familar scene in the South Bronx in the 1970s.
Credit: *Archdiocese of New York.*

3 - Jill Jonnes, *We're Still Here: The Rise, Fall and Resurrection of the South Bronx* (Boston: Atlantic Monthly Press, 1986), xxi.
4 - Paul LeBlanc, *Church of St. Pius V* (Bronx: St. Pius V Church, 1982), unpaginated.

As Jill Jonnes the historian of the South Bronx has pointed out, the designation "South Bronx" became a "traveling curse" in the 1970s as crime, arson, and the abandonment of apartment buildings spread from the original South Bronx, a one-square mile section of Mott Haven, to Melrose, Morrisania, Hunts Point, West Farms, Tremont, Highbridge and Morris Heights, until the plague engulfed twenty square miles of the borough south of Fordham Road. In 1960 there were 11, 185 fires in the Bronx; in 1974, 33,465 fires.[5]

During the worst period of the Bronx's ordeal by fire, Jonnes also noted, "The Catholic Church quietly emerged as the institution most committed to preserving and resurrecting the benighted South Bronx. Not one Catholic church [or] school was closed." A former parishioner of Sacred Heart Church in Highbridge was appalled at what he saw on his return to his old neighborhood. "Apartment houses on Woodycrest Avenue that used to sing with the life of bustling families had become burnt-out tombs," he discovered. The one bright spot he found was Sacred Heart School, as spotless and well-organized as it was forty years earlier. "The smiling alert faces I saw that day at Sacred Heart School," he said, " belong to children who have had hope instilled in them."[6]

Some years earlier, when Father Peter O'Donnell was made the pastor of Sacred Heart Church, he said that the neighborhood resembled Dresden after the firebombing of World War II. "There were gutted buildings on every street and sheet metal boarding up the windows with painted flowerpots on them. It was like living in a movie set," he recalled. "It is a place that should have died, but it didn't." Minimizing his own contribution, he added, "There is no explanation for it except the immense love and creativity of so many people and the grace of God"

Catholics in Highbridge in the 1970s: Sister Mary Alfred, R.S.M., prepares young scouts for the procession at the 100th anniversary of Sacred Heart Church.
Credit: *Archdiocese of New York.*

New housing on Tiffany Street in St. Athanasius parish built by SEBCO, South East Bronx Community Organization.
Credit: *Archdiocese of New York.*

5 - Jonnes, *We're Still Here*, 8.
6 - Michael Scanlon, "Return to Highbridge," *Catholic New York*, October 7, 1993.

Edward J. Logue, the head of New York City's South Bronx Development Corporation and a professional builder, thought that the Catholic clergy played an indispensable role in saving the South Bronx. He was especially warm in his praise of Father Louis Gigante's efforts to rebuild the devastated Hunts Point area in St. Athanasius parish. Logue gave Gigante's South East Bronx Community Organization credit for completing "the most successful critical mass of neighborhood rebuilding in the whole city."

Father Neil Connolly, the vicar of the South Bronx, led a coalition that pressured the district attorney to institute a special Bronx Task Force in 1975 to combat arson. Father John Grange, the pastor of St. Jerome's Church, was instrumental later in the founding of South Bronx Churches, a coalition of Protestant and Catholics churches that taught poor people how to use their political muscle to obtain better housing and city services to stem the decline of their neighborhoods. In St. Pius parish Father LeBlanc said: "We were decimated ten times over, but we are still alive. We have no money in the bank, and are supported by the diocese, but we are still a community of faith. Crime is still high; drugs and fires are still common, but saints still walk the streets of St. Pius. Only the names, faces and circumstances have changed."

In the mid-1970s Paul Brandt, a Jesuit scholastic at Fordham, and Monsignor John McCarthy, the pastor of Holy Spirit Church in Morris Heights, organized the Northwest Bronx Community and Clergy Coalition, which included sixteen parishes. They used their influence to form tenant associations in order to prevent panic flight and the spread of arson and the abandonment of buildings to the rest of the Bronx. They also enlisted the services of Bishop Patrick V. Ahern, the vicar of the Northwest Bronx, who visited every parish in the area, speaking at the Sunday Masses and telling the people, "If the Bronx dies, then the hopes of a million-and-a-half people for justice and a decent life will die with it. We're trying to stop that from happening."[7]

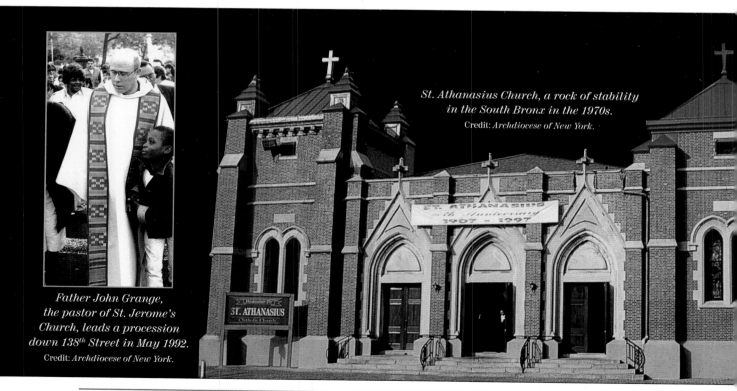

Father John Grange, the pastor of St. Jerome's Church, leads a procession down 138th Street in May 1992.
Credit: *Archdiocese of New York.*

St. Athanasius Church, a rock of stability in the South Bronx in the 1970s.
Credit: *Archdiocese of New York.*

7 - Ibid, 345-350.

Catholic education in the South Bronx:
Sister Patricia Quinn, S.C.,
with Gina Rosales, a student in
Saints Peter and Paul school,
in September 1989.
Credit: *Archdiocese of New York.*

Father Patrick McNamara addresses a rally on behalf
of South Bronx Churches on the steps of the Bronx County
Courthouse in July 1987. Credit: *Archdiocese of New York.*

By the 1980s the worst of the arson was over, if only because there was little left to burn. Fort Apache, standing alone amid the rubble, was renamed the Little House on the Prairie. Slowly but surely the Bronx began to recover and rebuild. Commenting on the situation in 1985, Senator Daniel Patrick Moynihan said, "After much travail, and much failure, and much avoidance of the obvious, the people of the South Bronx and the Catholic Church got together and have set to work. And the Lord's work it is." One example of that effort was South Bronx People for Change, organized by Father Neil Connolly when he was the vicar of the South Bronx. He told the people of the South Bronx, "The greatest temptation we have to face is that we don't believe enough to bring a new world into existence with the help of God."[8]

A major reason for the Church's credibility in the South Bronx was the fact that the priests and religious who staffed the churches, schools and social agencies not only worked in the area but lived there. Many of them were natives of the Bronx or Manhattan who grew up in solidly middle-class white neighborhoods and returned to those same neighborhoods to minister to a largely African American or Hispanic population. Monsignor Gerald Ryan, the pastor of St. Luke's Church, had spent a total of sixty-two years in two

Karol Cardinal Wojtyla, Archbishop of Krakow,
with Monsignor Arthur Rojek and Cardinal Cooke
at the Polish Center in Yonkers on the occasion of his first visit
to New York in September 1976. Credit: *Archdiocese of New York.*

South Bronx parishes in 2007. He said modestly: "I really feel that the South Bronx has done more for me than I have done for the South Bronx."

Calmer Waters

In the course of Cardinal Cooke's first few years as archbishop, many of the recommendations of the Priests" Advisory Council were adopted in one form or another, but with few of the results that had either been anticipated or feared. Other changes followed as well. One of the most far-sighted innovations that Cooke made was to establish the Commission for Inter-Parish Financing in 1970. This commission, admi-

8 - *Catholic New York*, May 1, 1986.

nistered by the priests of the archdiocese, levied a tax of six or seven percent on the annual income of all parishes and used the proceeds to assist financially ailing parishes. During the first year of its operation, the commission distributed $2,900,000 to fifty-three needy parishes. By 1979 the total funds disbursed reached $26 million and the amount has continued to increase.

Cardinal Cooke with Pope John II at a youth rally in Madison Square Garden on the occasion of John Paul's first visit to New York as pope in October 1979.
Credit: *Archdiocese of New York.*

Cardinal Cooke also created the Inner-City Scholarship Fund, which was soon providing subsidies of over one million dollars a year to minority students (two-thirds of them non-Catholic) in parochial schools. The fund has attracted generous contributions from corporations and non-Catholic benefactors who appreciate the contribution of the Catholic schools to the economy of New York City. Thanks to such innovative financial strategies, only 20 of the 294 Catholic elementary schools were closed during the Cooke administration despite a massive decline in enrollment (from 157,435 in 1968 to 88,753 in 1983) and the departure from the classrooms of three-quarters of the 4,000 teaching sisters.

Not all of the changes were financial. Priests had long complained that they had to wait as long as thirty years to become a pastor. That began to change in 1971, when pastors were appointed for a six-year term with the possibility of renewal for another six-year term. By that date parish councils were functioning in most parishes, and an Archdiocesan Parish Council was also established. In 1972 the archdiocese issued its long-awaited financial report, listing a net worth of $643 million, a deceptively inflated figure because nine-tenths of the archdiocesan assets consisted of real estate of questionable market value. By 1975 much of the post-conciliar turmoil had subsided and Cooke could breathe a sigh of relief. Commenting on the condition of the archdiocese in that year, he said, "Though it runs a temperature once in a while, it is basically very healthy."

In 1979 Pope John Paul II made a week-long visit to the United States. He spent two days in New York, addressing the United Nations where he repeated Pope Paul's plea for world peace. At a prayer service for priests and nuns in St. Patrick's Cathedral, the pontiff said: "I consider it a special grace to come back to New York City," which he had visited as the archbishop of Krakow in 1976. A rally for school children in Madison Square Garden drew a capacity crowd of 19,000.

The pope's itinerary included a visit to Harlem. Monsignor Emerson Moore, the pastor of St. Charles Borromeo Church, welcomed him by saying: "We see in your visit here your support and encouragement for our continuing struggle for justice and human rights, not just in our own community, but in all the Harlems in America." The pope also made a brief stop in the South Bronx where he spoke in both Spanish and English. Father Neil Connolly told him: "Your presence here tonight means that we count. One grateful woman said: "If the politicians don't care about us, at least God loves us."

The highlight of the pope's visit was a Mass at Yankee Stadium before 80,000 people. The crowd was smaller than the one that had turned out for Pope Paul fourteen years earlier, but so attentive that one could hear the sound of the elevated trains rattling by on River Avenue behind center field. The changes in the liturgy since the first papal visit were especially noticeable. The scriptural readings were in Spanish and English, the intercessory petitions were offered in nine languages, and it would now have been unthinkable not to give everyone an opportunity to receive Holy Communion.

Major demographic changes took place in New York City during the Cooke years. Between 1970 and 1980 the city lost 1,750,000 residents, mostly middle class whites who fled in droves from areas like the South Bronx. They were replaced by African Americans, Hispanics, and immigrants from Asia. By 1980 there were two million African Americans and two million Hispanics in New York City, in addition to growing numbers of immigrants from Japan, China, Korea, India, Pakistan and the Philippines. "The city has always been a city of newcomers," said Father Joseph Fitzpatrick, an expert on immigration, "but never did it have such a variety in such numbers crowding into it in such a short time."

In the archdiocese, between 1968 and 1983, the overall Catholic population fell by about 30,000 to 1,839,000. The decline in the Catholic population would have been much greater except for the large-scale influx of Hispanics and other Catholic immigrants. However, many of the newcomers were not regular churchgoers. During that same period the number of baptisms fell from 53,102 to 33,050, and the number of marriages fell from 16,065 to 10,235.

On March 1, 1983, Cardinal Cooke celebrated his sixty-second birthday. His outward demeanor was as cheerful and effervescent as ever. "He is the most ebullient man you'd meet," said Monsignor Florence Cohahan. "He doesn't like to admit the existence of problems." Less than six months later, on August 27, the archdiocese shocked usually unflappable New Yorkers with the announcement that the cardinal was terminally ill with cancer, a disease that he had been secretly battling for twenty years. He died at his residence forty-one days later, on October 6, 1983. One of the first things that his successor did was to introduce the cause of his canonization.

For someone who was essentially a local rather than a national figure, the outpouring of mourners was exceptionally large. Huge crowds filed past his bier in St. Patrick's Cathedral and over 900 priests attended his funeral. The New York *Daily News* commented: "On Cardinal Cooke's final day, a line from Shakespeare seems uniquely appropriate. 'Nothing in this life became him like his leaving of it.' This was a man who showed us all how to pass from time to eternity with courage and grace."

John Cardinal O'Connor

The death of Cardinal Cooke, three weeks after the death of Humberto Cardinal Medeiros of Boston, gave Pope John Paul II the opportunity to fill two of the most important American sees. In both instances he picked men who reflected his own vision of the Church, Bernard Law for Boston and John O'Connor for New York.

John O'Connor was born in Philadelphia on January 15, 1920, the son of Thomas and Genevieve Gomble O'Connor. He attended the minor and major seminaries of the archdiocese of Philadelphia and was ordained a priest of that archdiocese on December 15, 1945. After several diocesan assignments, he spent twenty-seven years in the U.S. Navy, rising to position of the Chief of Naval Chaplains with rank of rear admiral. He also earned a doctorate in political science from Georgetown University. He was no stranger to New York, having lived in the city from 1979 to 1983

while serving as an auxiliary bishop in the Military Ordinariate. Appointed the bishop of Scranton, Pennsylvania on May 10, 1983, he was promoted to New York only eight months later on January 31, 1984.

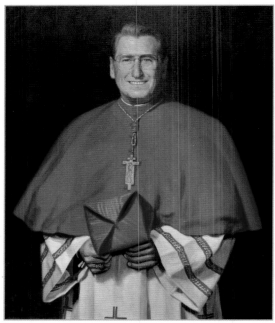

John Cardinal O'Connor; Archbishop of New York, 1984-2000. Credit: *Archdiocese of New York.*

Much had changed in New York since the appointment of Francis Sepllman almost a half-century earlier. Religion had since been reduced to a peripheral role in public life by an aggressively secularistic culture, which promoted among other objectives a value-free acceptance of abortion and homosexuality. "In New York's liberal media, abortion is a religion," said William Reel, a veteran Catholic journalist. During his twenty-eight years as archbishop Cardinal Spellman appeared in the pulpit of St. Patrick's Cathedral fewer than a dozen times, but he was able to wield enormous influence indirectly through the courtship paid to him by the city's power brokers.

Mother Theresa and Cardinal O'Connor.
Credit: *Archdiocese of New York.*

By 1983, however, this cozy relationship of church and state had disappeared in New York with the erosion of Irish political power. Jimmy Breslin, the pugnacious columnist for the New York *Daily News,* taunted the new archbishop as "Yesterday O'Connor" in the belief that he would try to resurrect Spellman's *modus operandi.* As O'Connor later admitted, he had decided to move in a different direction from Cooke, but that decision did not mean that he would attempt to return to the halcyon days of Spellman. In the Secular City of the 1980s there were no halcyon days for religious leaders, who had to fight for a hearing amid the clamor of many other competing voices in the public marketplace of ideas.

John O'Connor signaled his awareness of the situation even before taking up his duties as the archbishop of New York. In a television interview a week before his installation, he drew an analogy between the legalization of abortion in the United States and the Holocaust in Nazi Germany. The *New York Times,* one of the prime arbiters of America's secular culture, pounced upon the interview to fire a warning shot across the bow of

Admiral O'Connor's ship before it even reached home port. In an editorial the *Times* skewered O'Connor's incautious reference to Hitler's "Jewish problem" to imply that he was anti-Semitic and suggested condescendingly that, "if he means to instruct the community at large, a change of tone would be welcome."

O'Connor's indignant rebuttal produced a half-hearted apology from the *Times* under the guise of a clarification and a grudging welcome to New York. Far more significant, however, was the letter that appeared a week later from Arthur J. Goldberg, former U.S. Supreme Court justice and chairman of the American Jewish Commission on the Holocaust. Goldberg recounted how O'Connor, when chief of Navy chaplains, had arranged a visit to Dachau for the chief chaplains of the NATO forces. Any imputation of anti-Semitism, said Goldberg, "constitutes an unwarranted aspersion on Bishop O'Connor's total dedication to human rights and his abhorrence of anti-Semitism in any form."

John O'Connor was installed as the eighth archbishop of New York on March 19, 1984. A little over a year later, on May 25, 1985, he was made a Cardinal. During that first year he established a style of leadership that he would continue throughout his administration. It resembled closely the leadership style of Pope John Paul II, with heavy emphasis on preaching and public appearances, the use of both the press and television, pastoral visits to parishes and institutions, and the staging of special events like the annual Mass for the disabled in St. Patrick's Cathedral and a youth rally in Yankee Stadium in the spring of 1985 that attracted 40,000 people.

A major theme in O'Connor's public pro-nouncements was the threat to the sanctity of life posed by widespread acceptance of abortion and euthanasia. His fellow bishops recognized

His Honor and His Eminence:
Mayor Ed Koch and Cardinal O'Connor in August 1987.
Credit: *Archdiocese of New York.*

his contribution to the pro-life movement by electing him the chairman of the U.S.Bishops' Pro-Life Activities Committee in 1989. Another contentious public issue that tested O'Connor's mettle shortly after his arrival in New York was the effort of the city's large and powerful gay community to gain public acceptance of their lifestyle. The new archbishop challenged a recently issued executive order from Mayor Ed Koch, regulating the hiring practices of private charitable institutions. The regulations were so broadly framed that O'Connor feared they could require Catholic child-caring institutions to hire even militant homosexual activists. "We would rather close our child-caring institutions than violate church teaching," said O'Connor. He won the court case on appeal, and the dispute did not damage his burgeoning friendship with Mayor Koch. "New York," said the Cardinal, "is the only place in the world where good friends sue one another."[9]

The ongoing dispute with the gay community did not prevent the archdiocese from expanding its hospital and hospice services for the victims of

9 - *Catholic New York,* January 17, July 4, 1985.

AIDS. "The health care institutions operated by the archdiocese were the very first to respond to the state's call for dedicated units to care for AID's patients," said Governor Mario Cuomo in January 1990. "They were the first and they do the most. It's an inspiration to the community and it has shown leadership."[10]

O'Connor also provided leadership on a number of other social issues, condemning racism, opposing Medicaid cuts in the state budget, offering support to labor unions, most notably the hospital workers union, which represented some of the poorest paid workers in the city. In testimony before a Congressional subcommittee in 1985, he said that it was wrong to increase defense spending, but not housing allocations. At the time of the immensely popular Persian Gulf War in 1991, the former admiral tried to temper the emotional euphoria by saying, "No war is good. Every war is at best the lesser of evils."[11]

One area in which O'Connor achieved spectacular success was in establishing a close working relationship with the New York Jewish community. In February 1988 Ronald B. Sobel, the senior rabbi of Temple Emanu-El, said, "From the very moment that Cardinal John J. O'Connor was consecrated the archbishop of New York, it was clear that the Jewish people had found a new and powerful friend... I know of no member of the American Catholic hierarchy who has been more consistently sensitive to the interests of the Jewish people." In 1992 the bishops signaled their agreement by choosing O'Connor to head Catholic-Jewish Relations Committee of the National Conference of Catholic Bishops. He was widely credited in the Jewish community with paving the way for the establishment of diplomatic relations between the Holy See and Israel.

Five years after O'Connor's arrival in New York two perceptive observers of American

Cardinal O'Connor speaking at the Park Avenue Synagogue on Catholic-Jewish relations on March 28, 1988.
Credit: *Archdiocese of New York.*

10 - *Catholic New York,* January 11, 1980.
11 - *Catholic New York,* January 31, 1991.

*Cardinal O'Connor
with President Ronald Reagan
and J. Peter Grace
on January 13, 1989.*
Credit: *Archdiocese of New York.*

Catholicism gave him high marks for his performance. Monsignor George Higgins, the heir of John A. Ryan and the Grand Old Man of Catholic social teaching in America, remarked that "the cardinal's record in support of social justice, if only because of his willingness to stand up and be counted on controversial issues, regardless of the cost, has relatively few parallels in the recent history of the American hierarchy." Monsignor John Tracy Ellis, the church historian, characterized him as "a classic example of an oft-recurring type among modern churchmen who simultaneously portray a progressive attitude toward social questions and a conservative stand on theological matters."

On his fifth anniversary in New York, O'Connor wondered if he had devoted too much of his time to the media and regretted his inability to have more impact on the city's moral standards and social problems. However, that same year, a friendly non-Catholic critic, Joseph Berger, described the Cardinal as "a man of contra-dictions," but identified his deft use of the media as the source of his strength as a public figure. "Many local politicians believe that the Cardinal has already heightened the archdiocese's political impact---its ability to move the city's bureaucracy on behalf of its extensive social programs and its ability to get city policy makers to respect

Catholic doctrine," said Berger. Moreover, added Berger, he has done this not so much through influential friends in business and politics, as Cardinal Spellman did... but more through his assets as a communicator."

Eventually O'Conor himself seemed to realize that he had spread himself too thin. In 1990 he discontinued the weekly press conference after the 10:15 a.m. Mass in the cathedral. He explained to an interviewer that the press corps "would come swooping in at the end and ask me about everything under the sun. Well, what do I know about everything under the sun? But I would dutifully give them answers and I said some dumb things."

Nevertheless, in 1997, Father Thomas Reese, the Jesuit scholar and astute observer of the American hierarchy, described O'Connor as "the highest profile bishop in the country." "Part of that is because he is in New York where all the media are located," explained Reese, "and part is due to his own personality and talents." The following year, when O'Connor tangled with Mayor Rudolph Giuliani over legislation to give domestic partners the same legal rights as married couples, his old nemesis, the *New York Times,* admitted that O'Connor was "perhaps the one person in New York with a platform to rival that of the mayor."

Plus Ça Change...

The variety and complexity of the arch-diocese continued to be amazing, ranging from prosperous suburban villages to desperately poor inner-city neighborhoods. In the wealthy Dutchess County hamlet of Millbrook a major community concern was preserving 50,000 acres of private land for fox hunting. In the Bronx parish of Our Savior, 58 percent of the families lived below the poverty line in the mid-1980s, and any foxes were likely to be of the two-legged kind. The pastor, Father Jesus Iriondo, C.R.L., said, "When I came to this country from the Basque region of Spain, I didn't expect to have to deal with basic problems of food, clothing and shelter." Poverty was not an exclusively urban phenomenon. In rural Sullivan County, an area of great natural beauty, the median annual income of one-fifth of the families was less than $7,500. "You have to get up here to see the poverty," Cardinal O'Connor said on a visit in the summer of 1991.

Pope John Paul II and Cardinal O'Connor in Rome in the summer of 1989.
Credit: *Archdiocese of New York.*

The Church of New York remained the Immigrant Church as it had been since its inception as a diocese in 1808 and even earlier with the first parish in 1785. The single biggest group of Catholic immigrants continued to be the Hispanics. Immigrants from the Dominican Republic now outstripped those from Puerto Rico, and they were augmented by growing numbers of immigrants from Mexico and Central and South America. They were joined by a growing number of immigrants from Haiti who formed a community of at least 25,000 in Rockland County by the mid-1980s.

The ethnic character of New York City's neighborhoods was constantly in flux. St. Ann's parish in East Harlem was once a thriving Italian parish. By 1990 it was 60% African American, 30% Hispanic and 10% Italian. In 1995, in the neighboring parish of Our Lady of Mount Carmel, the annual procession, made famous by Robert Orsi's *Madonna of 115th Street,* was now preceded by Masses in Spanish, Italian, French Creole and Latin. The Redemptorist Church of the Most Holy Redeemer on the Lower East Side, once New York's unofficial German cathedral, where almost 10,000 people attended Mass every Sunday, was now home to 250 families, half English-speaking, half-Spanish speaking who came, said the pastor, "from a great many nations."

On the Upper West Side the Church of the Holy Name of Jesus nearly perished from urban blight in the 1960s, but experienced a renaissance as the neighborhood made a comeback in the 1990s. "It was really like a phoenix," said the pastor, "it rose from the ashes." Every Sunday 7,000 people were attending Mass in three languages. By contrast, when St. George's parish in Jeffersonville celebrated its 150th anniversary in 1994, little had changed in a century-and-a-half. The parish contained 370 families spread over 324 square miles. The same Franciscan friars of Holy Name province who administered both parishes also staffed New York's most famous midtown business parish, St. Francis of Assisi, where they celebrated thirteen Masses everyday, and heard confessions from 6:45 a.m. to 7:00 p.m.

Window in St. Francis of Assisi Church, New York City.
Credit: *Archdiocese of New York.*

The Church's presence was also evident in the construction and renovation of affordable housing in Highbridge, East Harlem, the Lower East Side of Manhattan and other devastated neighborhoods. One of the most promising developments was the formation in 1987 of South Bronx Churches, a non-partisan, ecumenical organization spearheaded by priests in the South Bronx. Explaining the purpose of the organization, Father Peter Gavigan said: "We have to help the people become agents of change." At a rally and "accountability session" that drew 1,000 people to the steps of the Bronx County Courthouse that year, Rudolph Giuliani, then the U.S. Attorney for the Southern District of New York, told the crowd: "This gathering is the most appropriate way I know to celebrate 200 years of the Constitution. You are making that promise of 'We the People' a reality."

The Pope in the Secular City

In October 1995 Pope John Paul II returned to New York City sixteen years after his first visit. The seventy-five year old pontiff had visibly aged in the interval, but he had already traveled to three other continents that year. The visit had been scheduled for 1994, but was postponed for a year after the pope fractured his leg. To a reporter's question about the state of his health, John Paul II replied, "As you can see, the pope is still alive."

The pope's visit was a huge success, attracting large crowds to every public event and receiving extraordinarily favorable coverage in the usually skeptical media. "Almost universally for a handful of days," said Cardinal O'Connor, "the media became magnificent instrumentalities for millions for a message of hope." One observer suggested that the respectful attention he commanded was due to the fact that he was advocating causes and values that few American

leaders any longer dared to mention, such as compassion for the poor, the homeless, refugees, and immigrants.

The pope's itinerary included Vespers in Sacred Heart Cathedral in Newark, an outdoor Mass (in drenching rain) in Giants Stadium, an address to the General Assembly of the United Nations, another outdoor Mass at Aqueduct Race Track, and a visit to St. Joseph's Seminary in Dunwoodie. For most New Yorkers, however, the highlight of the pope's trip was a Mass on October 7 on the Great Lawn in Central Park before 125,000 people, many of whom had arrived in the pre-dawn darkness because of stringent security measures.

Speaking alternately in Spanish and English at the Central Park Mass, the pope made an impassioned plea for the sanctity of life and for social justice. "You are called to respect and

defend the mystery of life always and every-where," the pope said, "including the lives of unborn babies." He also called upon his listeners to "stand up" for the life of the aged and the handicapped, the poor, homeless and hungry, and for "those who are alone or are ill, for example those suffering from AIDS."

Later that afternoon the pope presided at a rosary service in St. Patrick's Cathedral attended by 3,000 people. After the service, he delighted the onlookers outside by walking along 50th Street to the Cardinal's Residence. Still later that evening he met informally with non-Catholic religious leaders. When he departed for Baltimore the next day, he left behind a Secular City a little less secular than he found it.

Dagger John Redux

In January 1995, when he reached the mandatory retirement age of seventy-five, Cardinal O'Connor submitted his resignation to the pope, who allowed him to remain in office for another five years. Late in 1999 he developed a brain tumor, but continued to function as archbishop almost to the end, which came on May 3, 2000. Although he admitted that he had never heard of John Hughes until he became the archbishop of New York, John O'Connor came to admire him and resemble him in many ways, both positive and negative. Not the least of the similarities was John O'Connor's confronta-tional style of leadership, a description that he acknowledged and embraced. Another may have been his inability to handle a checkbook. His good friend Ed Koch said that he was a wonderful person but that he had as little understanding of how to save money as the Pentagon. Historians will have as busy a time assessing John O'Connor as they have had in dealing with John Hughes, but none will be able to ignore him

Cardinal O'Connor, Cardinal Joseph Ratzinger, Cardinal Agostino Casaroli and Pope John Paul II at the meeting of the American metropolitans with the pope in March 1989.
Credit: *Archdiocese of New York.*

20

Preparing for the Future

The interior of the restored St. Jerome's Church in the South Bronx.

O nly one week after the death of Cardinal O'Connor, on May 11, 2000, Pope John Paul II appointed his successor, Bishop Edward Egan of Bridgeport, Connecticut. It was the shortest vacancy in the history of the archdiocese. Edward Egan was born in Oak Park, Illinois, a suburb of Chicago, on April 2, 1932, the son of Thomas J. and Genevieve Costello Egan. As a young man he attended Quigley Preparatory Seminary in Chicago, St. Mary's Seminary in Mundelein, Illinois, and the North American College in Rome where he was ordained a priest of the archdiocese of Chicago on December 15, 1957.

Returning to Chicago the following year with his Licentiate in Sacred Theology, Father Egan served briefly as a curate in Holy Name Cathedral and then as an assistant chancellor and secretary to Cardinal Albert Meyer. From 1960 to 1965 he was again in Rome, earning a doctorate in canon law while serving on the faculty of the North American College. Back home once more in his native Chicago, he served as the secretary to Cardinal John Cody and as chairman of the Archdiocesan Commission on Ecumenism and Human Relations and later as co-chancellor. He returned to Rome for the third time in 1971 when he was appointed the only American judge of the Sacred Roman Rota, the supreme judicial body of the Catholic Church. In 1982 he was one of six canonical experts who briefed Pope John Paul II on the new Code of Canon Law.

Archbishop Edward Egan at his installation in St. Patrick's Cathedral on June 19, 2000.

On May 22, 1985, Monsignor Egan was ordained the titular bishop of Allegheny to serve as the auxiliary bishop of New York where he remained for the next three-and-a-half years, serving as the Vicar for Education under Cardinal O'Connor. On November 8, 1988, he was appointed the bishop of Bridgeport, a post he would continue to hold until his appointment to New York eleven-and-a-half years later. His installation in St. Patrick's Cathedral on June 11, 2000, began with a forty-five minute procession that included six cardinals, more than one hundred archbishops and bishops and nearly one thousand priests. Four thousand guests packed the cathedral. On June 29 the new archbishop flew to Rome to receive the pallium from Pope John Paul II on the feast of Sts. Peter and Paul.

Two Cardinals for New York

Less than a year later, on February 21, 2001, Archbishop Egan was made a cardinal and assigned the titular church of Sts. John and Paul, the same church as his three predecessors in New York. At that same consistory Pope John Paul II gave New York a second cardinal for the first time in history when he also appointed to the Sacred College Father Avery Dulles, the distinguished Jesuit theologian and professor at Fordham University.

Cardinal O'Connor had made the High Mass each Sunday morning in St. Patrick's Cathedral the focal point of his pastoral ministry. Cardinal Egan alternated between celebrating Sunday Mass in the cathedral and in one of the parishes in the archdiocese. His pastoral visits took him as far north as Sullivan County to the old German Catholic farming community at St. Mary's Church in Obernberg and as far south as the Church of Mary Help of

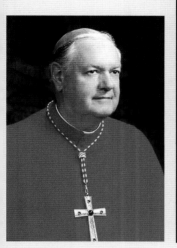

Edward Cardinal Egan,
Archbishop of New York.
Credit: *Archdiocese of New York*

Avery Cardinal Dulles, S.J..
Credit: *Fordham University*

Pope John Paul II and Edward Cardinal Egan
at the Consistory of February 21, 2001
Credit: *Fotographia Felici*

Christians in Tottenville on Staten Island where Dorothy Day was baptized. At many of the city parishes he visited he had the opportunity to celebrate Mass and preach in Spanish or Italian or sometimes in both languages as he did at St. Lucy's Church in East Harlem.

In addition to his Sunday visits to parishes for Mass, the new archbishop undertook a get-acquainted visit to each of the nineteen vicariates during which he met privately with the priests and deacons and had dinner with them. In the evening he conducted a prayer service for lay representatives from each parish, followed by an informal meeting and a question-and-answer period. One recurring theme in the Cardinal's comments at these meetings was his plea for patience as he grappled with the financial condition of the archdiocese and struggled to balance the books. Drawing upon his previous experience in New York as the Vicar for Education, he pledged his best efforts to preserve Catholic schools insofar as it was financially feasible.

One of the more pleasant tasks that falls to every archbishop of New York is the tradition of celebrating Mass in St. Patrick's Cathedral throughout the year for the various ethnic groups that call the archdiocese home and then standing on the steps of the cathedral to review their parade up Fifth Avenue.

On his first Labor Day in New York Archbishop Egan pledged the continued support of the archdiocese for economic justice in his homily at the Labor Day Mass. He repeated that message the following spring at a memorial service sponsored by UNITE, a union of textile workers, commemorating the ninetieth anniversary of the fire at the Triangle Shirtwaist Factory in 1911 that claimed 147 lives. "I stand proudly with you," Cardinal Egan told a thousand people gathered on the sidewalk outside the site of the former factory in Lower Manhattan, "to witness to New York and to the world the dignity of every human being and the dignity of labor."[1]

In his remarks at the anniversary of the Triangle Shirtwaist Factory fire, Cardinal Egan noted that many of the women who were killed were immigrants. Two months earlier, he had sponsored a special service in St. Patrick's Cathedral in conjunction with National Migration Week. On that occasion he spoke about the rights and human dignity of immigrants and the responsibility of Americans to treat them with justice and compassion.[2]

Archbishop Egan's first appearance before a Jewish audience took place in November 2000 when he was invited to address 400 delegates at the national convention of the Anti-Defamation League. He mentioned that he had been involved in inter-faith affairs since the 1960s when he served for six years as a vice chairman of the Chicago Conference on Religion and Race. While voicing strong support for continued cooperation between Catholics and Jews, he also went beyond the usual niceties on such occasions by noting the areas of disagreement between Catholics and Jews over such issues as abortion and parental choice in education.

Laying aside the customary euphemisms, he said that he would address such issues "Chicago style, clear and open." "I could say this diplo-

Edward Cardinal Egan.
Credit: *Archdiocese of New York*

matically," he explained, "but no, we're friends." He actually got chuckles, if not agreement, from a tough audience when he took exception to the remarks of Howard Berkowitz, the chairman of the ADL, that the Jewish community was opposed to the use of public money for religious schools. "Public money?" Archbishop Egan asked in mock disbelief. "That's not public money," he said. "That's the public's money. It's the parents' money, and they're the first educators. They should decide how their children should be educated."[3]

Six years later, on May 30, 2006, Cardinal Egan delivered a major address on Catholic-Jewish relations at the Jewish Center in Manhattan, to mark the fortieth anniversary of *Nostra Aetate,* Vatican II's declaration on the Jews. He began on a personal note by revealing that the first time he ever visited St. Patrick's Cathedral was when he stopped in the city as a seminarian on his way to Rome. He was taken to the cathedral by a Jewish couple who were friends of his father. "I have a proposal," he told the audience. "Why don't we get together, figure out what it is that all of us believe needs our religious attention and get to it. Nothing in my estimation is more important than to see to it that we never again need another *Nostra Aetate*." In an interview afterwards Abraham Foxman, the national director of the Anti-Defamation League, commented that "the fact that he was comfortable enough in this audience to put out a challenge to come together, and was sensitive enough not to set the agenda, was very welcome."[4]

1 - *CNY,* March 29, 2001.
2 - *CNY,* January 11, 2001.
3 - *CNY,* November 9, 2000.
4 - *CNY,* June 8, 2006

In an interview with *Catholic New York* a year after his installation Cardinal Egan expressed gratitude to the people of the archdiocese for the warm welcome that they had given him. He also voiced his admiration for the spiritual vitality that he had found in so many of the parishes he visited. "Never in my forty-three years as a priest have I witnessed dedication to parish life as we are blessed to have it here," he said.

He raised the issue of the realignment of parishes as a necessity in view of the changing demographics of the Catholic population. Virtually every large archdiocese in the country has had to face a similar situation, and in New York he mentioned that priests had brought it to his attention even fifteen years earlier when he was the Vicar for Education. In fact the diocesan consultors had first discussed it over a century earlier in the 1890s without coming to any decision. Of immediate concern to the new archbishop was the appointment of a commission to explore the needs of the archdiocese, the overhauling of the diocesan seminary system and the construction of a retirement home for priests. The last two items were related. When Cardinal Egan moved the St. John Neumann Residence to the campus of Dunwoodie, he converted the former Neumann Residence in Riverdale into a new state-of-the-art retirement home for priests which he named in honor of Cardinal O'Connor. He also renovated an older retirement home for priests in Riverdale, Our Lady of Consolation Residence.[5]

5 - *CNY,* June 21, 2001.

Dome of St. John Neumann Residence and Hall.

St. John Neumann Residence and Hall at Dunwoodie.

The John Cardinal O'Connor Clergy Residence in Riverdale.
Credit: *John T. Monaghan*

9/11: The Terrorist Attack on America

Less than three months after that, on the morning of September 11, 2001, an event occurred in New York City that changed the course of world history. On that bright cloudless Tuesday morning terrorists seized control of four commercial airplanes filled with highly inflammable jet fuel. They crashed two planes into the twin towers of the World Trade Center in New York and a third plane into the Pentagon. The fourth plane was apparently destined for the White House or the Capitol in Washington, but heroic passengers on board the plane overpowered the high-jackers and thwarted their plans by forcing the plane to crash in southwestern Pennsylvania.

It was the worst terrorist attack in American history. Most of the casualties were in New York City, in the collapsed twin towers of the World Trade Center. Only nineteen people on the floors above the point of impact managed to escape.

The Twin Towers on fire on the morning of September 11, 2001. A photo taken from the roof of St. Joseph's Church, Greenwich Village, by the pastor, Father Aldo Tos.
Credit: *Aldo Tos*

Some 2,819 innocent people either died in the flames or leapt to their death. One of the most poignant comments on 9/11 came from a little child at a nearby school who witnessed the scene from the window of her classroom. She wrote that the "birds were on fire," unaware that she was witnessing the victims jumping to their death. Among the casualties were 343 New York City firefighters who had rushed to the scene of the attack and rescued many people before losing their own life. One city official said: "New York City took a hit for America on September 11."

The hero of the hour was Mayor Rudy Giuliani who was nearly killed himself. The mayor seemed to be everywhere on September 11 and in the following days, rallying New Yorkers and encouraging them not to lose heart. "We're going to get through this," he told the mourners at a funeral Mass for a firefighter three days later.

"I hate to say this in a church," the mayor added. "I probably shouldn't say it, but we're not going to let these miserable, horrible cowards who attacked our city, attacked our nation, kill our people. They're not going to kill us."

One of the first bodies to be pulled from the wreckage of the Twin Towers on the morning of September 11 was that of Father Mychal Judge, a sixty-eight year old Franciscan friar who was a chaplain to the F.D.N.Y. He was killed by falling debris as he tried to minister to the dead and injured. Some 3,000 thousand mourners, including former President Bill Clinton, crowded into St. Francis of Assisi Church for Father Judge's funeral, at which Cardinal Egan presided. Father John M. Felice, O.F.M., provincial minister, said, "Mychal died doing what he loved, among the people he loved, his firefighters, He would not want this any other way."[6]

Father Mychal Judge, O.F.M., the Fire Department chaplain who was killed in the line of duty at the World Trade Center on September 11, 2001.

On the morning of September 11 Cardinal Egan was directed by the Office of the Mayor to go the Chelsea Piers where the bodies were expected to be brought from Ground Zero. On his way there in a police car he was redirected to St. Vincent's Hospital where he anointed the victims of the attack. During the days immediately following the tragedy, Cardinal Egan and his priest secretary, Monsignor Gregory Mustaciuolo, joined the police officer and firefighters searching for bodies at Ground Zero. During this time the Cardinal blessed body bags and on one more occasion watched as two fire-fighters were pulled alive from under what seemed to be tons of rubble. Later the Cardinal and his secretary worked at a school near Ground Zero consoling and counseling the loved ones of persons lost in the attack. At the first reports of the terrorist attack on September 11, priests from nearby parishes rushed to the scene. Among them were Fathers Kevin V. Madigan and Donald Fusser from St. Peter's Church, only a block away, and Monsignor Marc J. Filacchione, the pastor of Our Lady of Victory Church and a Fire Department chaplain.

Father James Hayes, a Blessed Sacrament priest who was the pastor of St. Andrew's Church, saw a group of firefighters from Rescue Five preparing to enter the South Tower and said a prayer with them while he searched the stores on the ground floor looking for victims. Not one of the firefighters in Rescue Five survived. Father Hayes emerged from the Tower as it began to collapse and dived under a parked car to escape the falling rubble. For the next three or four weeks he returned everyday to the on-site morgue to bless the remains of the bodies that were recovered. "I'm not a hero," he said, "I was in the company of many heroes." Like Father Hayes, many other priests also volunteered their services at the morgue in Ground Zero for weeks after September 11. They commented on the reverence with which they rescuers treated the remains of the victims that they found.

In the weeks after September 11, there were many funeral Masses in churches throughout the metropolitan area for the victims of the terrorist attack. Cardinal Egan celebrated a special evening Mass in St. Patrick's Cathedral on Sunday, September 16, for all of the victims, and another Mass the following day for the police, firefighters and other rescue workers who lost their lives.

Throughout the following weeks, he celebrated or presided at numerous funerals in St. Patrick's Cathedral, often two a day. On September 23 he delivered the opening prayer at an interfaith service at Yankee Stadium before flying to Rome five days later for a Synod of Bishops that Pope John Paul II had appointed him to lead shortly after he was named a cardinal. Upon his arrival in Rome, he asked to return to New York but was told to remain until October 11, when he returned for a "Month's Mind Mass" in St. Patrick's Cathedral.

In the meantime, burying the dead was a long drawn-out process as families gradually abandoned hope that the bodies of their loved ones would ever be recovered. Staten Island was especially hard hit by the tragedy. At St. Clare's Church in Great Kills, which lost twenty-nine parishioners, the parish organized a World Trade Center Outreach Committee to aid and support the families of the victims. At one of the many funeral Masses that he offered, the pastor, Monsignor Joseph P. Murphy, also baptized the baby of a deceased parishioner who perished in the terrorist attack.[7]

Pope John Paul II sent his condolences to the American people on September 12. "Yesterday was a dark day in the history of humanity, a terrible affront to human dignity," said the pope. "Today my heartfelt sympathy is with the American people, subjected yesterday to inhuman terrorist attacks which have taken the lives of thousands of innocent human beings and caused unspeakable sorrow in the hearts of all men and women of good will."

The inscription at the base of the Cross from the World Trade Center. Credit: *John T. Monaghan*

The Cross that was found in the wreckage of the World Trade Center and temporarily relocated to Church Street outside St. Peter's Church. Credit: *John T. Monaghan*

7 - *CNY,* September, 2003.

The Sexual Abuse Crisis

Just as the city and the nation began to recover slowly and painfully from the shock of September 11, American Catholics had to face one of the worst crises in the history of their church. Early in 2002 stories began to appear in the press and on television with increasing frequency about the sexual abuse of children by Catholic priests and even bishops. Some of the reports were recycled news, involving incidents that had already been made public, but many of the revelations were new. As the trickle of stories from across the country became a flood, exposing the full dimensions of the scandal, the cumulative effect was devastating. It became headline news for weeks. Although only a small fraction of the clergy was implicated, a cloud of suspicion descended upon all American Catholic priests, who suddenly found themselves the butt of jokes on late-night television talk shows.

The scandal horrified both liberal and conservative Catholics, who offered different explanations for it, but were united in their indignation over the crimes committed against children. Their anger was directed especially at those bishops who had reassigned priests who were serial sexual offenders from one parish to another where they continued to prey on vulnerable young people. The firestorm, fueled by the media but not created by it, began to abate only after the meeting of the U.S. bishops in Dallas in June 2002, when they voted to remove from ministry any deacon or priest who had been guilty of the abuse of a minor.

Despite their hurt and indignation, very few American Catholics left the Church. Even in Boston, one the major centers of the scandal, where dissatisfaction with Cardinal Bernard Law was so intense that he was forced to resign as archbishop, the laity made discerning distinctions in assigning responsibility. They remained remarkably supportive of their own parish priests as long as those priests offered them honest and caring leadership.

The U.S. bishops commissioned the John Jay College of Criminal Justice in Manhattan to conduct a survey of the incidence of sexual abuse of minors by the Catholic clergy. Their survey concluded that, in the fifty-two years between 1950 and 2002, four percent of the U.S. Catholic clergy were accused of sexual abuse of minors. The comparable figure for the archdiocese of New York during that same period was less than one percent for the diocesan and extern clergy.

Despite the relatively "favorable" local statistics, the archdiocese did not seek to minimize the seriousness of the situation. "Any case of sexual abuse of a minor by a member of the clergy is a tragedy," said a spokesman for the archdiocese. The archdiocese spent $8.2 million for settlements and legal costs, and mostly for psychological counseling for victims of sexual abuse, all of which occurred before Cardinal Egan's tenure. More than half of the money came from the Archdiocesan Self-Insurance Fund and the rest from operating funds and investments. By contrast, when the archdiocese of Los Angeles settled some 500 cases of clerical abuse in 2007, the total payments came to $660 million.

In keeping with the national policy of the U.S. bishops, Cardinal Egan established a Safe Environment Office to prevent future acts of abuse. Before the meeting of the bishops in Dallas, he had had all the files of priests reviewed for the previous fifty-two years to be sure that he was aware of any who had been accused before his coming to New York. He also established a review board made up primarily of lay people to advise him about accusations and formulated a Code of Conduct for Clergy. "The Church has been suffering greatly over recent years" Cardinal Egan said in the summer of 2002, "because of sexual misconduct on the part of a small number of priest and bishops. Happily the faithful know that the vast majority of our clergymen are good, holy, dedicated servants of their people who have been deeply hurt because of the misconduct of a few."[8]

8 - *CNY*, August 2002, March 2004.

Realignment of Parishes

One Sunday in the fall of 2002 Cardinal Egan celebrated Mass in Dutchess County in the newest parish of the archdiocese, Blessed Kateri Tekakwitha in LaGrangeville, and then headed back to the city for a Mass that afternoon in St. Patrick's Cathedral for some 2,000 Peruvian Catholics on their patronal feast. He mused on the complexity and variety of a diocese 180 miles long whose boundaries had not changed in a century-and-a-half but whose Catholic population was constantly in flux. The Peruvain Mass was one of the dozen and more that he celebrates or presides at each year on Sunday afternoon in the Cathedral for immigrants from various nations in Latin America and the Caribbean.

In Lower Manhattan St. Peter's Church and Our Lady of Victory Church had been exclusively weekday "business" parishes for decades, but in 2007 both had a growing residential population and Sunday Mass attendance was increasing. The once moribund St. Bernard's Church on West 14th Street snapped back to life as Our Lady of Guadalupe at St. Bernard's. The Italian national Church of the Most Holy Crucifix on Broome Street got a new lease on life as the Filipino Chapel of San Lorenzo Ruiz.

In the Bronx the German parishes of the Immaculate Conception and St. Anselm in Melrose and St. Anthony of Padua in Morrisania were now Hispanic parishes. The century-old Church of St. Jerome in Mott Haven received a multi-million dollar restoration thanks to a grant from the Homeland Foundation arranged by Cardinal Egan with the enthusiastic support of the pastor, Father John Grange. St. Mary's Church in Williamsbridge became the Korean Church of St. John Nam while the nearby Polish Church of St. Valentine became St. Thomas Syro-Malabar Church for Indian Catholics. Catholics from Ghana organized their own community at St. Margaret Mary Church in Tremont and Igbo-speaking Catholics from Nigeria did the same at St. Angela Merici in Melrose. In Port Chester in the former Polish Church of the Sacred Heart Mass was no longer celebrated in Polish, but in four other languages every Sunday.

The Annunciation in a window
of St. Jerome's Church.

In view of these constantly shifting population patterns there had been pleas for over a century for a more rational organization of parishes. In the 1890s the pastor of St. Peter's Church on Barclay Street complained that Brooklyn and New Jersey were stealing his middle-class parishioners and Bishop Farley suggested closing some downtown parishes to pay for the new seminary at Dunwoodie. In fact some thirty parishes were closed on a piecemeal basis over the past century. In 2007 Cardinal Egan announced the first comprehensive realignment of parishes in the history of the archdiocese. The planning went back several years to a committee headed first by Bishop Timothy McDonnell and then by Bishop Dennis Sullivan assisted by Monsignor Douglas Mathers.

The realignment plan called for the closure of ten parishes (seven of them founded decades ago as national parishes for Germans, Italians, Poles and Slovaks) as well as three rural mission churches (two in Ulster County and one in Orange County). The fate of five other parishes was left undecided pending further review. Eleven other parishes were to be merged or become the site of new chapels. In addition five new parishes were to be established and nine new churches were to be erected in existing parishes. Some parishioners were bitterly disappointed at the loss of their parish churches, and in one instance the police had to be called in to eject sit-in demonstrators who occupied the church. Nonetheless, the fallout was much less severe than the reaction to similar closings a decade earlier in Chicago and Detroit. The realignment won general acceptance as a recognition of the changing needs of an archdiocese with an increasing number of people and a diminishing number of priests.

Reflecting on the condition of the archdiocese in an interview with a newspaper reporter in the spring of 2007, Cardinal Egan noted that an annual operating deficit of over $20 million had been eliminated within two years after his being named archbishop. Moreover, in the summer of 2007, a spokesman for the archdiocese announced that the last of an internal debt of $40 million would be eliminated that year. However, in the aforementioned interview Cardinal Egan insisted: "[Pope John Paul II] didn't send me here for financial reasons."[8] The Cardinal admitted that he had to deal with difficult fiscal matters, the sexual abuse scandal, and the realignment of parishes and schools. Still, though not mentioned in the newspaper article, he told the reporter that his primary duties were to preach the Gospel, join the people in prayer, and lead them in the areas of justice and charity.

He further observed that the school system of the archdiocese was the largest private school system, religious or otherwise, in the nation with an enrollment in 2006 of 106,000; that almost 10,000 women and men teach the faith every week in parish catechetical programs; that the archdiocesan newspaper, Catholic New York, was the largest Catholic newspaper in the nation with a circulation of over 140,000; that the annual budget of Catholic Charities hovered around a half billion dollars; and that the archdiocese had been given a channel on Sirius Satellite Radio at no cost to itself to carry Catholic programming throughout the United States and Canada, seven days a week, twenty-four hours a day. Little of this made the newspaper article, but it was all regularly repeated by the Cardinal in writings and addresses over the months that followed.

Continuity and Discontinuity

At the time of the centennial of the archdiocese in 1908 the Irish Cardinal Logue predicted that a century hence the Catholic Church in New York and in the United States would be "the most flourishing in Christendom." Only six years earlier Pope Leo XIII contrasted the youthful vigor of the

American Church with the sad state of the Church in many of the traditionally Catholic countries of Europe. John Henry Newman had said the same thing as far back as 1872. "While religion goes down in Europe," he told a New York priest, Monsignor Thomas Preston, "you will by divine mercy succeed in making it rise and flourish in America." Today few would be so bold as to make such a prediction. American Catholics are now more likely to identify with the problems of European Catholics and to look to the young churches of Asia and Africa for the signs of spiritual vitality that European Catholics once observed in American Catholicism.[9]

In the course of the past two hundred years, the Catholic Church in New York has often been a microcosm of the strengths and weaknesses of American Catholicism. On both the national and local level there has been a fascinating interplay of continuity and discontinuity. The most obvious change has been the astonishing growth in the size of the Catholic community. The 25,000 American Catholics of 1784 have become the largest religious community in the nation. In New York a diocese that began in 1808 with 12,000 Catholics, three churches and six priests now comprises two archdioceses and nine dioceses, with 2,000 churches, 6,000 priests, and eleven million people. Not even the wildest optimist could have foreseen such a development two centuries ago. Even though the archdiocese of New York ceased to be the largest archdiocese in the nation seventy years ago (the archdiocese of Los Angeles is now larger), it still commands a leading position because of its location in the capital city of the world, as Pope John Paul II once called New York City.

Despite the fact that most American Catholics have long since achieved middle-class status, in New York at least the continuity with the Immigrant Church of the nineteenth century is continually being renewed with the arrival of new immigrants from Latin America and the Caribbean, and more recently

from Asia and Africa. In the bicentennial year the Catholic Church in New York was more catholic than it had ever been in its history. The first pastor of St. Peter's Church, Father Charles Whelan, said in 1785 that the pastor should be fluent in six languages, English, French, German, Spanish, Portuguese and Irish. In 2008 Mass was celebrated in the archdiocese every Sunday in thirty-three languages, including Akan, Arabic, Igbo and Tagalog.

A less happy statistic was the fact that in recent decades the growth of the Catholic population in the archdiocese of New York had not been matched by a comparable increase in religious practice. In fact there had been a precipitous decline accross the nation. Even nominal Catholics used to intersect with the institutional Church at least three times in their life, at birth, marriage and death. That was happening with decreasing frequency. In 1965 in the archdiocese of New York there were 55,908 infant baptisms; in 2006, there were less than half as many, 25,059, for a Catholic population that had increased by almost three-quarters of a million people, from 1,807,880 in 1965 to 2,554,454 in 2006. The same was true of funerals: there were 29,814 in 1965, but only 13,850 in 2006. The statistics for weddings showed an even steeper decline, from 20,216 in 1965 to 5,225 in 2006.

It was a disturbing development, but not an altogether new phenomenon. At St. Peter's Church in 1785 Father Whelan complained that only about twenty of his 200 parishioners were regular churchgoers. Many of the Irish immigrants in the early nineteenth century were not regular church goers either. Dr. Richard Burtsell said that many were only Catholic in the sense that Catholicism was the predominant religion in the land of the their birth. The same complaint was made later in the century about many of the Italian immigrants. As Jay Dolan pointed out, the task and the achievement of the clergy and religious in New York was not only to minister to immigrants from traditionally Catholic countries, but in many instances to turn nominal

9 - Leo XIII to Cardinal Gibbons, April 15, 1902, DACH, II, 547-549; ARDC, Newman to Preston, January 8, 1872. I am indebted to Father R. Kent Wilson for bringing this letter to my attention.

Catholics into practicing Catholics. The clergy and religious of the twenty-first century face the same challenge in New York as their nineteenth-century counterparts.

The primary means of handing on the faith in New York was the Catholic school system whose enrollment increased from 22,215 in 1870 to 53,059 in 1902 to 228,058 in 1965. By 2006 its enrollment stood at 106,000, which left it the largest private school system—religious or secular—in the nation, but approximately the same that it was ninety years earlier in 1918. One of the major changes in the schools was the shift from a predominantly religious faculty to a predominantly lay faculty. In 1965 there were 4,184 sisters, 643 brothers and 491 priests teaching in the elementary and high schools of the archdiocese. In 2007 the comparable figures were 295 sisters, 84 brothers and 79 priests as well as 4,035 lay teachers. It is worth noting that in 1965 there were already 3,496 lay teachers in Catholics schools.

The shift from a religious to a lay faculty represented a sharp break with the immediate past, but it also represented a return to the earliest years of Catholic primary education in New York. Parochial schools began in the basement of parish churches with poorly-paid lay teachers. John Talbot Smith observed that the more capable teachers opened their own private schools so that they could live on the surface of the earth rather than under it.

The great expansion of the Catholic school system would never have taken place without the corresponding increase in the number of teaching brothers and especially teaching sisters. In 1850 there were only about 1,500 women religious on the United Stares. By 1965 there were over 160,000 women religious. American Catholics came to regard this abundance of sisters as the normal state of affairs in the Church rather than the result of an unprecedented growth in the size and number of communities of women religious in the nineteenth century. Although there were still 3,000 sisters in New York in 2007, many were well past retirement age and there were few recruits to take their place. New York Catholics faced the prospect of a Catholic community virtually without women religious in education and health care for the first time since 1817.

The Catholic school system not only experienced a change in personnel, but the nature of the system itself was changing. Thirty-four percent of the students in inner-city schools in 2006 were non-Catholics whose parents greatly valued Catholic schools, where ninety-five percent graduate from high school in four years and ninety-eight percent of them go on to college. The Inner-City Scholarship Fund, the Inner-City Endowment, the Student-Sponsor Scholars, "Be a Student's Friend," "Young Executives Serving Schools," and the Cardinal's Scholarships all raise tens of millions of dollars each year for the schools, much of it from corporate donors and non-Catholics who recognize the contribution of the Catholic school system to the economy and future of Greater New York.

All the same, pastors often find themselves in the unenviable position of trying to pay lay teachers a decent salary while keeping tuition within the reach of parents. In many parishes parochial schools were no longer parish schools, but attracted youngsters from beyond the parish boundaries. In 2006 Cardinal Egan started several pilot projects to organize regional schools as a way of addressing this new situation.

Neither John Hughes nor any other archbishop of New York had been able to provide a place in a Catholic school for every Catholic child, although in 1965 almost twice as many Catholic children were in Catholics schools as in the catechetical programs for public school children. Today, with a majority of Catholic school children

in public schools, the archdiocese has made a major effort to expand and enhance the religious instruction programs for public school children, increasing class hours each week and requiring parental involvement in the catechetical process.

In the past few decades several new religious orders came to the archdiocese. One was Mother Teresa's Missionaries of Charity who arrived in 1971 and established their first convent in the Bronx the following year. Two new communities were founded in the archdiocese. One of them was the Congregation of the Franciscan Friars of the Renewal, who began on April 28, 1978, when Father Benedict Groeschel

and seven Capuchin friars received permission from their superiors to begin a new religious community. By 2007 they had grown to ninety friars with five houses in New York and two abroad, and they had been joined by a religious community of women, the Sisters of the Renewal.[10] In 1991, Cardinal O'Connor founded the Sisters of Life when eight women responded to his public appeal for a community of women religious with the special purpose of defending the sacredness of human life. By 2004, when they were formally accorded the status of a religious congregation, they numbered thirty-three professed sisters. Both communities drew their members from far beyond the borders of the archdiocese.

In 2002 Cardinal Egan presided at a liturgy in St. Patrick's Cathedral at which the Sisters Oblates to the Blessed Trinity, a teaching order, became a religious congregation of "diocesan right," that is under the guidance of the archbishop of New York. The sisters teach in archdiocesan schools and assist at St. Patrick's Cathedral. Finally, new communities of religious priests have over the past decade accepted leadership in several parishes in the archdiocese. Among them are the Institute of the Incarnate Word, the Apostles of Jesus, the Idente Missionaries, and the Congregation of the Oratory in the archdiocese of New York.

The Chapel of Corpus Christi Monastery in the South Bronx.
Credit: *Yvon Meyer.*

---

10 - *A Drama of Reform: Fr. Benedict Groeschel, C.F.R., and the Franciscans of the Renewal* (San Francisco: Ignatius Press, 2005).

In 2007 the Catholic Charities of the Archdiocese of New York remained the largest private provider of social services in New York state. Many of most famous nineteenth-century institutions, such as Father Drumgoole's Mission of the Immaculate Virgin, Sister Irene's Foundling Hospital, and Thomas Mulry's Catholic Home Bureau, St. Agatha's Home in Nanuet and St. Dominic's Home in Blauvelt continued their work of child care by adapting their services to the changing needs of their apostolate. In 2007 the 137-year old New York Foundling Hospital was the second-largest foster home provider and the third largest child welfare agency in the city.[11]

At Rosary Hill in Hawthorne and St. Rose's Home in Manhattan the Dominican Sisters of St. Rose of Lima continued the hospice work of Rose Hawthorne Lathrop. The modern Calvary Hospital in the Bronx was the successor to the House of Calvary founded by a group of widows in 1890. The Carmelite Sisters of the Aged and Infirm, founded in New York in 1929 by Mother Angelina Teresa, continued to operate their nursing homes as did Mother Cabrini's Missionary Sisters of the Sacred Heart. On an altogether different level the Dominican Sisters of Perpetual Adoration continued their century-old tradition of prayer at Corpus Christi Monastery in the South Bronx.

New forms of service continued to take their place alongside older ones. To mention just a few, Father Bruce Ritter's Covenant House, founded in 1979, made a major contribution to the care of homeless and exploited young people in Manhattan. Thanks to the intervention of Cardinal O'Connor and the dedication of its staff, it survived the crisis that forced Ritter to sever his ties with Covenant House in 1989 because of allegations of personal misconduct.[12] The three

St. Francis Residences, founded by Father John Felice, a Franciscan friar of the Holy Name Province, provided housing for 300 men and women suffering from mental illness. Abraham House in the South Bronx, was the work of the Little Sisters of the Gospel of Charles de Foucauld, who devoted themselves to the care of prisoners and their families.

Of all the challenges facing Cardinal Egan and every American bishop, none proved more intractable than that of vocations to the priesthood. In 2007 Cardinal Egan had at his disposal 493 active diocesan priests, less than half the 1,126 priests that Cardinal Spellman had in 1965 and fewer even than the 518 priests that Archbishop Corrigan had in 1902 when the population of the archdiocese was half as large as in 2007. One bright spot was the number of permanent deacons. There were none prior to 1967. There were 377 in 2007 and they have become indispensable in many parishes.

As for the priesthood the wheel seemed to come full circle. The first resident bishop of New York, John Connolly, complained in 1816 that "American Catholics have absolutely no inclination to become ecclesiastics." Down to the 1880s John Talbot Smith said that New Yorkers presumed that any priest they met would be either a native of Ireland or Germany. Therefore "international priests" were not as new a phenomenon in New York as they might appear to be. All that changed was their country of origin. Nor did the "international priests" of the nineteenth century escape the criticism that they were not American. Bishop Dubois could testify to that. Archbishop Ireland complained that many of them "remained in heart and mind and mode of action as alien to America as if they had never been removed from the Shannon, the Loire or the Rhine."[13] Like the permanent deacons the "inter-

11 - *New York Times,* September 3, 2007.

12 - See Peter J. Wosh, *Covenant House: Journey of a Faith-Based Charity* (Philadelphia: University of Pennsylvania Press, 2005).

13 - Walter Elliott, C.S.P., *The Life of Father Hecker,* (New York: Columbus, 1891), ix.

national priests" of the late twentieth century became indispensable in many parishes.

As an interesting footnote to all of this, it might be observed that there are no less than six priests, religious and laity whose causes for canonization are being considered in Rome. They are Pierre Toussaint, Terence Cardinal Cooke, Father Felix Varela, Dorothy Day, Mother Rose Hawthorne Lathrop and Father Isaac Hecker.

Envoi

Writing in the nineteenth century about the fourth century, Cardinal Newman remarked that "this is a world of conflict and of vicissitude amid the conflict. The Church is ever militant," said Newman, "sometimes she gains, sometimes she loses, and more often she is at once gaining and losing in different parts of her territory." "What is ecclesiastical history," he asked, "but a record of the ever-doubtful fortune of the battle, though its issue is not doubtful? Scarcely are we singing *Te Deum* than we have to turn to our *Misereres;* scarcely are we in peace, when we are in persecution; scarcely have we gained a triumph, when we are visited by a scandal. Nay we make progress by means of reverses; our griefs are our consolations; we lose Stephen to gain Paul, and Matthias replaces the traitor Judas."[14]

"It is so in every age," said Newman. "It is so in the nineteenth century; it was so in the fourth century." So it has been in the two-hundred year history of the archdiocese of New York. It is a story of continuity and discontinuity, loss and gain, progress and reverses. If there is one invariable factor that holds the story together and explains how the Catholics of New York have survived to celebrate the bicentennial of their archdiocese, it is the faith of the people, priests and prelates who have populated this part of the Lord's vineyard for the past two hundred years.

---

14 - John Henry Newman, *Historical Sketches* (London: Longmans, Green and Company, 1903), II, 1,

A Select Bibliography

- Albion, Robert. *The Rise of New York Port, 1815-1860.* New York: Scribner's, 1939.

- Anbinder, Tyler. *Five Points.* New York: A Plume Book, 2001.

- Andreassi, Anthony. "Begun in Faith and Grit and God: The Sisters of the Divine Compassion, 1869-1954." Ph.D. diss., Georgetown University, 2004.

- _____. " 'The Cunning Leader of a Dangerous Clique?': The Burtsell Affair and Archbishop Michael Augustine Corrigan." *Catholic Historical Review* 86 (1999): 620-639.

- Appleby, R. Scott. *"Church and Age Unite!":The Modernist Impulse in American Catholicism.* Notre Dame: University of Notre Dame Press, 1992.

- Arlotta, Jack M. "Before Harlem: Black Catholics in the Archdiocese of New York and the Church of St. Benedict the Moor." *Dunwoodie Review* 16 (1992-1993): 69-108.

- Bayley, *A Brief Sketch of the Early History of the Catholic Church on the Island of New York.* New York: The Catholic Publication Society. 1870.

- Bennett, William Harper. *Catholic Footsteps in Old New York.* New York: U.S., Catholic Historical Society, 1909.

- Brown, Mary Elizabeth. *Churches , Communities and Children: Italian Immigrants in the Archdiocese of New York, 1880-1945.* New York: Center for Migration Studies, 1995.

- _____. *From Italian Villages to Greenwich Village: Our Lady of Pompei.* New York: Center for Migration Studies, 1992.

- Browne, Henry. *One Stop Above Hell's Kitchen: Sacred Heart Parish in Clinton.* New York: Sacred Heart Church, 1977.

- _____. *St. Ann's on East Twelfth Street, New York City, 1880-1945.* New York: St. Ann's Church, 1952.

- _____. *The Parish of St. Michael, 1857-1967.* New York: The Church of St. Michael, 1957.

- Burrows, Edwin G, and Mike Wallce. *Gotham: A History of New York City to 1898.* New York: Oxford University Press, 1999.

- Carey, Patrick W. *People, Priest and Prelates: Ecclesiastical Democracy and the Tensions of Trusteeism.* Notre Dame: University of Notre Dame Press, 1987.

- Cohalan, Florence D. *A Popular History of the Archdiocese of New York.* Yonkers: U.S. Catholic Historical Society, 1983. 2nd edn., 1999.

- Connors, Edward M. *Church-State Relationships in Education in the State of New York.* Washington, D.C.: The Catholic University of America Press, 1951.

- Curran, Robert Emmett. *Michael Augustine Corrigan and the Shaping of Conservative American Catholicism, 1878-1902.* New York: Arno Press, 1977.

- _____. "Prelude to 'Americanism': The New York Accademia and Clerical Radicalism In the Late Nineteenth Century." *Church History* 47 (1978): 48-65.

- Curran, Francis X., S.J. *The Return of the Jesuits.* Chicago: Loyola University Press, 1966.

- Damroth, William J. "The New York Foundling Hospital." M.A. thesis, St. Joseph's Seminary, Dunwoodie, 1993.

- DeLora, John P. "Corrigan, Cabrini and Columbus: The Foundation of Cabrini Medical Center in New York City." M.A. thesis, St. Joseph's Seminary, Dunwoodie, 1994.

- DeVito, Michael J. *The New York Review (1905-1908).* New York: U.S. Catholic Historical Society, 1977.

- Diaz-Stevens, Ana Maria. *Oxcart Catholicism on Fifth Avenue: The Impact of the Puerto Rican Migration upon the Archdiocese of New York.* Notre Dame: University of Notre Dame Press, 1993.

- DiGiovanni, Stephen M. *Archbishop Corrigan and the Italian Immigrants.* Huntington, In.: Our Sunday Visitor Press, 1994.

- Dolan, Jay P. *Catholic Revivalism: The American Experience, 1830-1900.* Notre Dame: University of Notre Dame Press, 1978.

- _____. *In Search of an American Catholicism.* New York: Oxford, 2002.

- _____. *The Immigrant Church: New York's Irish and German Catholics, 1815-1865.* Baltimore: The Johns Hopkins University Press, 1975.

- Ellis, John Tracy. *The Life of James Cardinal Gibbons.* 2 vols. Milwaukee: Bruce Publishing Company, 1952.

- Ernst, Robert. *Immigrant Life in New York City, 1825-1863.* Syracuse: Syracuse University Press, 1994.

- Farley, John Cardinal. *The Life of John Cardinal McCloskey.* New York: Longmans, Green and Company, 1918.

- Fitzgerald, Maureen. *Habits of Compassion: Irish Catholic Nuns and the Origins of New York's Welfare System, 1830-1920.* Urbana and Chicago: University of Illinois Press, 2006.

- Fogarty, Gerald, P., S.J., *The Vatican and the American Hierarchy from 1870 to 1965.* Wilmington: Michael Glazier, 1985.

- Gannon, Robert I., S.J. *The Cardinal Spellman Story.* Garden City: Doubleday and Company, 1962.

- Greer, Allan. *Mohawk Saint: Catherine Tekakwitha and the Jesuits.* New York: Oxford University Press, 2005.

- Guilday, Peter. *The Life and Times of John Carroll.* One-volume reprint. Westminster, Md.: The Newman Press, 1954.

- _____.. *The Life and Times of John England.* 2 vols. New York: America Press, 1922.

- _____. "Lay Trusteeism in New York." *Historical Records and Studies* 18 (1928): 7-73.

- Hassard, John R. *Life of the Most Reverend John Hughes: First Archbishop of New York.* New York: D. Appleton, 1866.

- Hennessy, Thomas C., S.J. *Fordham: The Early Years.* New York: Something More Publications, 1998.

- Hoehmann, George A. " 'My Eminent Friend of New York': Francis Cardinal Spellman and the Second Vatican Council." M.A. thesis, St. Joseph's Seminary, Dunwoodie, 1992.

- Isacsson, Alfred, O. Carm., *The Determined Doctor: The Story of Edward McGlynn.* Tarrytown: Vestigium Press, 1997.

- Jonnes, Jill. *We're Still Here: The Rise, Fall and Resurrection of the South Bronx.* Boston: The Atlantic Monthly Press, 1986.

- Kelly, George A. *The Parish as seen from the Church of St. John the Evangelist, New York City, 1840-1973.* New York: St. John's University, 1973.

- Kelly, Neil A. " 'Orphans and Pigs Fed from the Same Bowl': Catholics and the New York Charities Controversy." M.A. thesis, St. Joseph's Seminary, Dunwoodie, 1991.

- Lynch, Thomas A. " 'Above All Things the Truth': John P. Monaghan and the Church In New York." *Dunwoodie Review 16* (1992-1993): 109-165.

- _____. "Dorothy Day and Cardinal McIntyre: Not Poles Apart." *Church* 8 (summer 1992): 10-15.

- Mahoney, Martin J. Catholic Evangelization in Black Harlem: The Harlem Apostolate, 1933-1949. M.A. thesis, St. Joseph's Seminary, Dunwoodie, 1994.

- McCauley, Bernadette. *Who Shall Take Care of Our Sick? Roman Catholic Sisters and The Development of Catholic Hospitals in New York City.* Baltimore: The Johns Hopkins University Press, 2005.

- Nolan, David. "The Catholic Club of New York." M.A. thesis, St. Joseph's Seminary, Dunwoodie, 1995.

- Orsi, Robert A. *The Madonna of 115th Street: Faith and Community in Italian Harlem, 1880-1950.* New Haven: Yale University Press, 1985.

- Ryan, Leo R. *Old St. Peter's: The Mother Church of Catholic New York.* New York: U.S. Catholic Historical Society, 1935.

- Shaw, Richard. *Dagger John: The Unquiet Life and Times of Archbishop John Hughes of New York.* New York: Paulist, 1977.

- _____. *John Dubois: Founding Father.* Yonkers: U.S. Catholic Historical Society, 1983.

- Shea, John Gilmary, ed. *The Catholic Churches of New York.* New York: Lawrence C. Goulding and Company, 1878,

- Shelley, Thomas J. *Dunwoodie: The History of St. Joseph's Seminary.* Westminster, Md.: Christian Classics, 1993.

- _____. *Greenwich Village Catholics: St. Joseph's Church and the Evolution of an Urban Faith Community, 1829-2002.* Washington, D.C.: The Catholic University of America Press, 2003.

- _____. *Slovaks on the Hudson: Most Holy Trinity Church, Yonkers, and the Slovak Catholics of the Archdiocese of New York.* Washington, D.C.: The Catholic University of America Press, 2002.

- _____. "Black and Catholic in Nineteenth-Century New York: The Case of Pierre Toussaint." *Records of the*

American Catholic Historical Society of Philadelphia 102 (1991): 1-19.

• _____. "John Cardinal Farley and Modernism in New York." *Church History* 61 (1992): 350-361.

• _____. " 'Good Work in Its Day': St. Joseph's Provincial Seminary, Troy, New York." *Revue d'Histoire Ecclésiastique* 88 (1993): 416-438.

• _____. "Cardinal Spellman and his Seminary at Dunwoodie." *Catholic Historical Review* 80 (1994): 282-298.

• _____. *Neither Poles nor Bohemians nor Magyars: The Catholic Slovaks of Yonkers, New York. Records of the American Catholic Historical Society of Philadelphia* 105. (Spring-Summer 1994): 16-31.

• _____. "Dean Lings' Church: The Success of Ethnic Catholicism in Yonkers, New York, in the 1890s." *Church History* 65 (1996): 28-41.

• _____. " 'What the Hell Is an Encyclical?' Governor Alfred E. Smith, Charles C. Marshall, Esq., and Father Francis P. Duffy." *U.S. Catholic Historian* 15:2 (Spring 1997): 87-105.

• _____. " "Slouching toward the Center: Francis Cardinal Spellman, Archbishop Paul J. Hallinan and American Catholicism in the 1960s." *U.S. Catholic Historian* 17:2 (1999): 23-49.

• _____. " 'Only One Class of People to Draw Upon for Support:' Irish-Americans and the Archdiocese of New York." *American Catholic Studies* 112:1-4 (Spring-Winter 2001): 1-22.

• _____. " 'A Good Man but Crazy on Some Points': Father Thomas Farrell and Liberal Catholicism in Nineteenth-Century New York." *Revue d'Histoire Ecclésiastique* 97:1 (2002): 110-132.

• _____. "Catholic Greenwich Village: Ethnic Geography and Religious Identity in New York City, 1880-1930." *Catholic Historical Review* 89:1 (January 2003): 60-84.

• Smith, John Talbot. *The Catholic Church in New York.* 2 vols. New York: Hall and Locke, 1908.

• Spann, Edward K. *The New Metropolis: New York City, 1840-1857.* New York: Columbia University Press, 1981.

• Young, Thomas G. *A New World Rising: The Story of St. Patrick's Cathedral.* New York: Something More Publications, 2006.

• Walsh, Sister Marie de Lourdes, S.C. *The Sisters of Charity of New York, 1809-1959.* 3 vols. New York: Fordham University Press, 1960.

• Wilson, R. Kent. "The Oxford Movement and the Church of New York." M.A. thesis, St. Joseph's Seminary, Dunwoodie, 1990.

• Wróblewski, John J. *"Non Recuso Laborem:* The Life And Times of Monsignor Joseph C. Dworshak." M.A. thesis: St. Joseph's Seminary, Dunwoodie, 1992.

Index